D1860569

Highlander's Plainspeak
An Administrative Rede

Highlander's Plainspeak
An Administrative Rede

Dr. Taradatt

GYAN

© **Author**

All rights reserved. No part of this work may be reproduced, stored, adapted, or transmitted in any form or by any means, electronic, mechanical, photocopying, micro-filming, recording or otherwise, or translated in any language, without the prior written permission of the copyright owner and the publisher. The book is sold subject to the condition that it shall not, by way of trade or otherwise, be lent, resold, hired out, or otherwise circulated without the prior publisher's written consent in any form of binding or cover other than that in which it is published.

The views and opinions expressed in this book are author's own and the facts reported by him have been verified to the extent possible, and the publisher is not in any way liable for the same.

Published, 2020

Published by

Gyan Publishing House
5, Ansari Road
Daryaganj, New Delhi-110002
Phone: 011-47034999, 9811692060
www.gyanbooks.com
E-mail: books@gyanbooks.com

Printed at: G. Print Process, Delhi.

Cataloging in Publication Data—DK
Courtesy: D.K. Agencies (P) Ltd. <docinfo@dkagencies.com>

Taradatt, 1956- **author.**
Highlander's plainspeak an administrative rede / Dr. Taradatt.
pages cm
ISBN 9788121219686 (HB)

1. Taradatt, 1956- 2. India—Officials and employees—Biography. 3. Odisha (India)—Officials and employees—Biography. 4. Civil service—India—Biography. 5. Civil service—India—Odisha—Biography. 6. Public administration—India. 7. Public administration—India—Odisha. I. Title.

LCC JQ612.T37 2020 | DDC 352.63092 23

दत्त्वा सुदुर्लभमिदं भुवि जीवनं यैः
सम्बर्धितः प्रतिपदं प्रतिबोधितश्च।
यैः शिक्षितोऽहमिह नैकगुणैरुदारैः
तेभ्यः समर्प्यत इयं रचना मदीया॥

This book is dedicated to

My parents who after giving me a rare life in this world brought me up every step with care and sound values,

and to

My teachers who enriched me in multiple ways with liberal thoughts and quality education

मौनान्मूकः प्रबचनपटुर्वातुलो जल्पको वा
धृष्टः पार्श्वे च वसति सदा दूरतश्चाप्रगल्भः।
क्षांत्या भीरुः यदि न सहते प्रायशो चाभिमानी
सेवाधर्मः परमगहनो योगिनामप्यगम्यः॥

नीतिशतकम्, 58. भर्तृहरि
(Fifth Century, AD)

Silence is taken for dumbness; competent articulation for garrulousness or nonsense.

Proximity to the boss is taken for temerity; distance as a sign of stupidity.

Tolerance is misunderstood as timidity; lack of tolerance is deemed as arrogance.

The dharma of service is the most serious equilibrium to be realised even by great Yogis.

Contents

Foreword

Writing the foreword for a book that chronicles the professional career of an 'uncommon' albeit extraordinary civil servant, who has been a dear friend and colleague for over three decades, is both a privilege as well as a challenge. It is a privilege because Dr. Taradatt has an awesome reputation, both at the State and Centre, as a fearless, upright and 'no-nonsense' officer with a formidable capacity to complete tasks, implement projects and deliver results 'on time' even in most adverse and constrained circumstances, defying all odds. At the same time it is also a challenge since a foreword is ordinarily expected to honestly and dispassionately assess the contents of the book in order to bring out succinctly and in a persuasive manner what makes it relevant and interesting, what makes it worth reading and how it might enrich the domain knowledge of the readers.

Though I have read a few memoirs of distinguished civil servants – starting notably with Mr. Noronha's 'A Tale Told by an Idiot' right at the inception of my own career in Lal Bahadur Shastri National Academy of Administration (LBSNAA) and Sivaraman's 'Bitter Sweet' among others – I have all along been fairly skeptical about the audience these books actually address. I believe these books are mostly read by serving and retired civil servants and attract the attention of few others outside these charmed circles. Hence, it is my presumption, though rebuttable, that this book too will have the same target audience. In a manner of speaking, having a rich audience like this is a distinct advantage, both for the author as also the readers. For the author since he is well aware of what might engage and hold the interest of the prospective readers. For the readers since they would not find the extensive and exhaustive narratives and details, which many of those memoirs contain, uninteresting or irrelevant. It is in this spirit I urge the readers to appreciate Tara's painstaking efforts manifested in this book.

Let me begin with the title of this book. When Tara requested me to go through the first draft of the manuscript and to suggest a suitable title, my first thought was to explore an appropriate description of his 'personality type'. It struck me that in the colloquial parlance of 'Sambalpuri-Koshali' – the local language spoken by the people of Western Odisha, which includes my own home town – a 'highlander' typifies and evokes the image of a person who is absolutely honest, diligent, transparent, simple, totally trustworthy and uncomplicated by nature, may be even naïve at times. To the best of my judgment, Tara essentially possesses all those traits in ample measure, which is why I suggested that his memoir could be best described as the tales of a highlander.

This book traces and tracks, in depth, the author's eventful journey from the idyllic, pristine hills of Uttarakhand to the arguably most well-known poverty geography of India – the infamous KBK region – and subsequently, to capital regions of New Delhi and Bhubaneswar. The story begins with childhood years spent in a remote village high up in the hills. Economic deprivation compelled him to trek miles to a State-funded, unfancied vernacular school. Subsequently, he had to substantially depend on private charity, philanthropy and scholarships for graduate and post-graduate studies, including a doctoral degree, in Banaras Hindu University. The abysmal conditions in which he had to live during this period is so touching and poignant that I had actually suggested to him to make the first chapter a little more elaborate and anecdotal. However, as he has indicated in the preface he chose not to do so. That said, one can quite clearly discern his passion as well as commitment to promote equity and to strive to offer equality of opportunities to the socially and economically-deprived and marginalised sections of the society throughout his career in civil services spanning over thirty years. Having personally experienced how education can be a powerful and transformative instrument to ensure social and economic mobility and pull people out of the morass of abject poverty and deprivation, it is hardly surprising that he fought all odds to set up a thousand hostels within an incredible record time of one year for tribal girls though the State Government had hardly provided any financial allocation for the project.

I do not consider it either necessary or feasible to comment on each of the chapters. However, some facets of his managerial leadership style and orientation, which comes out strongly in his narratives, merit a brief discussion in this foreword. First of all, he has taken up each and every assignment, howsoever 'marginal' it might be generally considered in the civil service fraternity, as a substantive opportunity to bring about perceptible changes, through reforms which are cost-effective and not resource- intensive, to make a visible difference – be it in his stint as a Charge Officer of the Survey and Settlement organization, as a Collector, as a Joint Secretary in Ministry of AYUSH or even as Secretary in charge of Cooperation Department in the State Government.

Secondly, he is quintessentially a field-officer *par excellence*, reminiscent of some of the legendary ICS officers for whom spending as much time as possible in the field and among the people was a key element of good governance and effective delivery of public services. Very often we hear trenchant criticism of senior civil servants crafting public polices in their secluded chambers, blissfully unaware of the field realities. Although this charge is not universally true, one cannot brush it aside altogether. For Tara, however, this was never an issue. He would undertake sustained field-tours even as a Secretary, often sacrificing his holidays, to oversee projects and policy implementation on the ground and to get un-filtered feedback from the citizens. I do sincerely hope that those who are still in service would emulate Tara in this respect and switch from monitoring governance solely through the virtual mode of video-conferencing and similar technological fixes and spend some quality time in the field in the old-fashioned way.

Third notable feature of Tara's career in civil services is his extraordinary capacity to deliver projects on a mission mode which necessarily calls for meticulous planning, bold and decisive approach whenever the situation demands, immense ability to co-ordinate and bear risks and above all, a 'never give-up' mindset. All these elements come out clearly in the pivotal role he played in his 'unsung rescue act' of salvaging the Commonwealth Games from a nearly hopeless and disastrous situation in 2010. It is for these reasons that I had also assigned him the task of monitoring timely evacuation of a million people from the vulnerable areas before the extraordinarily severe cyclone 'Phailin' struck the Odisha coast on 12th October, 2013. Finally, Tara's propensity to take the righteous stance and stick to the well-established norms and principles, regardless of the adverse consequences it might entail for his own career, deserves special mention. I wonder how many officers would dare to act in a manner he did to challenge the attempt to upgrade a senior functionary of the PMO in the 'order of precedence'! Though, he had to pay a heavy price for this, he remained stoic about this episode. To me, Tara is a rare 'Karma Yogi' who truly believes in *nishkama karma.*

Before concluding I wish to share with the readers two important assignments which I would have entrusted to him, if I had the requisite liberty and authority. The first job would have been Chief Administrator of the Sri Jagannath Temple in Puri. Carrying out radical and transformative reforms in the temple administration requires a person like Tara who is erudite, well versed in scriptures, whose devotion is unquestionable and whose reputation for boldness, fairness and integrity is beyond reproach. Unfortunately for me, my tenure as the Chief Secretary was too short to push for this. The second job for which I personally think Tara was possibly most suitable is the project leader of Mission for Ganga cleaning and rejuvenation. I strongly believe that with his phenomenal project management skills and experience, emotional connect with Ganga, the mission would have gained substantial traction and momentum and quite possibly the World would have seen the difference during the Kumbha Mela in 2018-19. Lamentably this too remained as my wishful thinking.

To conclude, this memoir would serve as a valuable guide to the current generation of civil servants who have joined the profession, not for the trappings of power and privileges, but to serve the society with empathy, compassion, fairness and unflinching commitment to equity. I profusely thank Tara for giving me the opportunity to scramble my thoughts about his painstakingly compiled memoirs.

Jugal Kishore Mohapatra
Former Chief Secretary
Government of Odisha
&
Former Secretary
Department of Rural Development
Government of India

* * * *

Preface

I joined the Indian Administrative Service for necessary livelihood after having lost all hope of a secure job in academia and having no sustainable alternative. Once in Service I tried to serve with sincerity in whichever wing of administration I was posted. My experiences were largely exciting, spurring me to innovate in order to squeeze more into every professional minute and grab every possible public service opportunity. Occasional pinpricks and difficulties dotted the decades of service which required bluntness or implacability on my part. These took an emotional toll, but strengthened me in many visible and invisible ways. After 33 years of active service, I was liberated on 30 June 2016.

I wanted to spend my time after retirement in quiet study of ancient, oriental philosophical literature, which has inspired and sustained me since my very formative days. I bought a flat in a village close to my native place in Uttarakhand to fulfil my desire. I had no pending familial or personal financial liabilities to be discharged and the pension was more than enough to keep body and soul quite well together. A few well-wishers, however, persisted for months that I should write an account of my eventful administrative life. The **Highlander's Plainspeak: An Administrative Rede** is born from their implacability. Definitely this book need not be viewed as my autobiography as that would necessarily involve deeper self-examination to present introspective perspectives. At best it is a limited narrative containing some events which I feel were important in my administrative career.

The book provides glimpses of my early life, tracking my education and skills grounding from childhood onwards. My background differed markedly from those who had joined the civil service with me, but came handy in manifold and unusual ways in public service. Those who saw the first draft asked me to elaborate on my early life. However, I have not listened to their voices to maintain the administrative strength of this book. Thus, it quite swiftly goes on to recount how an accidental administrator learnt on the job, while persistently endeavouring to deliver timely and outcome-oriented public service at every professional rung, with reform, systematisation and simplification as the bulwarks. Notably, it seeks to bring out with factual experiences that if the administrator's eye is unblinkingly fixed on public interest, a natural corollary is gaining the public's voluntary recognition and appreciation in abundance.

This strengthens and firewalls the intrepid public servant against vested interests, malafide and hierarchical pressures, all of which could otherwise derail a budding career and cast a dark shadow on family life as well.

The book contains experiences in the important posts held by me. Notably, it looks into the genesis and philosophy of development interventions that have taken place in various fields of administration after India gained its Independence. Efforts are also to show how the system rewards and motivates but also punishes and bruises, sometimes without rhyme or reason. Misunderstandings with seniors, contemporaries and friends can be common, and at times vicious. Without any defamatory intent, the narratives thus focus squarely on facts while drawing out some unusual experiences involving vested interests, land grabbers, industrialists, colleagues in bureaucracy, those in the political arena and the public at large.

I held a number of significant assignments in the State and Central Governments. The descriptions of desk jobs and field-level hands-on experiences provide insights with a wide angle in dealing with a spectrum of opportunities and challenges in delivering public service. Some of these may find resonance even with those who have joined IAS or other civil services in a very different or recent milieu. The narratives span across the nitty-gritty of survey and settlement, general and revenue (land) administration, to how I got exposed to the vast fields of rural development, Panchayat Raj and decentralized planning. I worked to transform agriculture and allied sectors in Odisha with missionary zeal. Indian systems of medicine, and education particularly of deprived ST&SC communities, were also taken up with vigour that brooked no compromises. Communally-charged ST&SC development, OBC and Minority Welfare at State level, and quite sensitive matters in the highest office, the Cabinet Secretariat, at Central level, factually bring out the shades of views seen and approaches to tackle them. I learnt that taking some risks in enforcement of law and policy is productive. My hallmark right through was experimentation and innovation.

I have narrated experiences serving at different levels of hierarchy in a vertical, drawing out the different forces at play and nuances in governance of the same subject matter and themes when duties were handled from entirely different perspectives and requirements. Thus, while the most exciting job of an administrator, viz. the Collector & District Magistrate, is a uniquely decisive one at the cutting-edge of field-level governance for a young officer, as Additional Chief Secretary for Revenue and Disaster Management I got the chance to institute far-sighted and long-pending reforms in land administration and effect recovery of large chunks of government land. I found that internalising revenue administration into every pore of my being in my first posting, greatly helped me right through till my superannuation. Similarly, after having supervised the upscaling of disaster management preparedness of State Governments at Central Government level, I coined the objective of 'saving precious lives' and went on to supervise its successful achievement when the very severe cyclone 'Phailin' struck the coastal districts of Odisha in October 2013. I usefully drew upon my early administrative experiences in handling unprecedented rains and flash floods as District Collector of Ganjam. I served as Chief Administrator, KBK Districts for little more than two years. It is a story of how a post considered peripheral in administrative perception could be the springboard for the head of these eight districts to contribute significantly in effectively addressing issues of under-development. In a nutshell, the book is about how I started my professional journey and its satisfying end.

My last post, Director General,Gopabandhu Academy of Administration, albeit held for a short 14 months, enabled me to sign-off from IAS in a manner consistent with and befitting a public service of 33 years. In a die-hard spirit of an emotionally-detached administrator, I tried to turn this assignment into a most productive one, planning and executing the development of 30 District Gazetteers, one for each district of Odisha, and each of around 400 pages. It was a gargantuan task of documenting in complete detail the state-of-play in each of Odisha's districts across its economy, society, institutions, natural resources, environment, forest and natural resources, topography, literary and fine arts. These Gazetteers were drafted, involving domain experts of eminence, and each of them went through at least two rounds of painstaking editing by me. Once the task was done, ironically, I encountered administrative hindrances which obstructed the final printing and publication of these Gazetteers.

I am not sure whether my administrative experiences would be of relevance to the new breed of administrators in Odisha or elsewhere in India. Rapid changes are taking place in all walks of life, including administration – in value systems, societal norms, personal preferences, information flows via social media, artificial intelligence and technological advancements. Anonymity is hardly regarded as a virtue by civil servants. The State is only one among many providers of services. Although I belong to the first generation in my family to have worked in the organized sector, I was fortunate enough to have handled important positions in the State and Union Governments. I believed in disciplined anonymity and opted to remain far removed from the glitter and glory of administrative life. Yet, I earned the sobriquet of 'Terror Datt' which despite it not having a negative context, pained me at times.

There is also no question of hurting or exposing anyone by describing events and situations even though some might sound critical. Nothing prejudicial, let alone pejorative, is intended. The book contains my perception of the truth which for others may be anecdotal or puerile. I do not claim that my perception of the administrative reality is the only accurate one as it is quite possible that either I did not understand and analyse the issue critically, dispassionately and comprehensively, or that my memory has failed me somewhere. The truth or reality as we notice it in the practical world is like a mountain standing vertically and climbers situated at different levels describing their positions differently and relatively.

I owe a debt of gratitude to my senior colleague and dear friend J.K. Mohapatra under whose leadership as Chief Secretary I felt privileged to work. He has been kind and concerned enough to go through the first draft of this book and provided numerous invaluable inputs including title of the book. I am also thankful to Anupam Bose (former Deputy Director, Agriculture), Sahadeb Sahu (former Additional Commissioner, Commercial Taxes), Dr. A.B. Hota (Director, ST&SCRTI), Dhirendra Kumar Das (former Senior Consultant, Special Cell, R&DM Department), Kamal Lochan Mishra (former General Manager, OSDMA), Dr. R.B. Singh (former Special Secretary, Planning & Coordination Department) and C.R. Satpathy (former District Planning Officer, Ganjam; all of whom not only supported me when I held charge of the office concerned, but also took the pain to go through the relevant parts of this book and offered factual and observational comments. I have no words that could measure the affection and regard I feel for my family. My siblings, who have lived a life quite like mine in fundamentals albeit in different professional walks, have stood shoulder-to-shoulder with me at every turn and stage. Finally, I thank Amit Garg of Gyan Publishing, New Delhi for the book to get published.

Errors, likely to be plenty, remain singularly mine. I apologize for my failure to those who wanted me to recount my administrative experiences if they do not now find me as having been equal to this task.

Dr. Taradatt

08.10.2019

* * * *

Acronyms and Abbreviations

AAO : Assistant Agriculture Officer
ACCT : Assistant Commissioner Commercial Taxes
ACO : Assistant Consolidation Officer
ACS : Additional Chief Secretary
ACTO : Assistant Commercial Tax Officer
ADGM : Air Defence & Guided Missile
ADM : Additional District Magistrate
AMC : Annual Maintenance Contract
APICOL : Agriculture Promotion and Investment Corporation
ARI : Assistant Revenue Inspector
ASHA : Accredited Social Health Activist
ASO : Assistant Settlement Officer
AYUSH : Ayurveda, Yoga & Naturopathy, Unani, Siddha and Homeopathy
BDA : Bhubaneswar Development Authority
BDO : Block Development Officer
BFDA : Brackish Water Development Agency
BHU : Banaras Hindu University
BRGF : Backward Region Grant Fund
BRO : Border Roads Organization
C&AG : Comptroller & Auditor General
CAT : Central Administrative Tribunal
CBI : Central Bureau of Investigation
CCIM : Central Council of Indian Medicine
CCS : Cabinet Committee on Security
CCT : Commissioner of Commercial Taxes
CD&RR : Community Development & Rural Reconstruction
CDA : Cuttack Development Authority
CEO : Chief Executive Officer
CMD : Chairman & Managing Director
CMRF : Chief Minister's Relief Fund
Cr.P.C. : Code of Criminal Procedure
CRRI : Central Rice Research Institute
CSIR : Council of Scientific & Industrial Research
CSR : Corporate Social Responsibility
CST : Central Sales Tax
CTO : Commercial Tax Officer
CVC : Chief Vigilance Commissioner
CWG : Commonwealth Games
DA&FP : Directorate, Agriculture & Food Production
DAO : District Agriculture Officer
DAP : Di-ammonium Phosphate
DCCB : District Central Cooperative Bank
DCP : Deputy Commissioner of Police
DCSO : District Civil Supply Officer
DDA : Delhi Development Authority
DFO : Divisional Forest Officer
DG : Director General
DGP : Director General of Police
DIC : District Industries Centre

DIG	:	Deputy Inspector General
DM	:	District Magistrate
DoPT	:	Department of Personnel & Training
DPAP	:	Drought Prone Area Programme
DPC	:	Departmental Promotion Committee
DPR	:	Detailed Project Report
DRDA	:	District Rural Development Agency
DSP	:	Deputy Superintendent of Police
DWO	:	District Welfare Officer
EAS	:	Employment Assurance Scheme
EMRS	:	Ekalavya Model Residential School
ERRP	:	Economic Rehabilitation of Rural Poor
FARD	:	Fisheries & Animal Resource Development
FCI	:	Food Corporation of India
FIR	:	First Information Report
FWP	:	Food-for-Work Programme
GA	:	General Administration
GAA	:	Gopabandhu Academy of Administration
GMP	:	Good Manufacturing Practice
GOM	:	Group of Ministers
GPS	:	Global Positioning System
GRIDCO	:	Grid Corporation of Odisha
H&FW	:	Health & Family Welfare
H&TW	:	Harijan & Tribal Welfare
H&UD	:	Housing & Urban Development
HAL	:	Hindustan Aeronautics Limited
HRD	:	Human Resource Development
H&UD	:	Housing & Urban Development
HYV	:	High Yielding Variety
IAP	:	Integrated Action Plan
IAS	:	Indian Administrative Service
IAY	:	Indira Awas Yojana
ICAR	:	Indian Council of Agriculture Research
IDCO	:	Industrial Infrastructure Development Corporation
IFAD	:	International Fund for Agriculture Development
IG	:	Inspector General
IIM	:	Indian Institute of Management
IIT	:	Indian Institute of Technology
IMD	:	India Metrology Department
IMFL	:	Indian Made Foreign Liquor
IOA	:	Indian Olympics Association
IPICL	:	Industrial Promotion and Investment Corporation Limited
IPS	:	Indian Police Service
IRDP	:	Integrated Rural Development Programme
ISM&H	:	Indian System of Medicine & Homeopathy
ISRO	:	Indian Space Research Organization
IT	:	Information Technology
ITDA	:	Integrated Tribal Development Agency
ITDP	:	Integrated Tribal Development Project
JAO	:	Junior Agriculture Worker
JRY	:	Jawahar Rozgar Yojana
KBK	:	Kalahandi Balangir Koraput
LAD	:	Local Area Development
LAMPS	:	Large Scale Agriculture Multipurpose Society
LBSNAA	:	Lal Bahadur Shastri National Academy of Administration
LRS&C	:	Land Records Settlement & Consolidation
MADA	:	Modified Area Development Approach
MCD	:	Municipal Corporation of Delhi

MCS	:	Multipurpose Cyclone Centre
MD	:	Managing Director
MGNREGS	:	Mahatma Gandhi National Rural Employment Guarantee Scheme
MHA	:	Ministry of Home Affairs
MLA	:	Member, Legislative Assembly
MOP	:	Muriate of Potash
MoU	:	Memorandum of Understanding
MP	:	Member of Parliament
MHRD	:	Ministry of Human Resource Development
MSP	:	Minimum Support Price
MT	:	Metric Tonnes
NABARD	:	National Bank for Agriculture and Rural Development
NALCO	:	National Aluminium Company
NCRMP	:	Nation Cyclone Risk Mitigation Project
NDMA	:	National Disaster Management Authority
NDMC	:	New Delhi Municipal Corporation
NDRF	:	National Disaster Response Force
NGO	:	Non-Governmental Organisation
NIC	:	National Informatics Centre
NLRMP	:	National Land Record Modernization Programme
NPK	:	Nitrogen, Phosphorous, Potash
NREP	:	National Rural Employment Programme
NRSC	:	National Remote Sensing Centre
OAIC	:	Odisha Agro Industries Corporation
OAS	:	Odisha Administrative Service
OBC	:	Other Backward Classes
OCAC	:	Odisha Computer Application Centre
OCC	:	Odisha Construction Corporation
ODRAF	:	Odisha Disaster Rapid Action Force
ODRP	:	Odisha Disaster Recovery Project
OEA	:	Odisha Estate Abolition
OFS	:	Odisha Finance Service
OMTES	:	Odisha Model Tribal Education Society
OPEPA	:	Odisha Primary Education Promotion Agency
OPLE Act	:	Odisha Prevention of Land Encroachment Act
OPPE Act	:	Odisha Public Premises Eviction Act
ORS	:	Odisha Revenue Service
ORSAC	:	Odisha Remote Sensing Application Centre
OSAMB	:	Odisha State Agriculture Marketing Board
OSBC	:	Odisha State Beverage Corporation
OSCB	:	Odisha State Cooperative Bank
OSCSC	:	Odisha State Civil Supplies Corporation
OSDMA	:	Odisha State Disaster Management Authority
OSFC	:	Odisha State Finance Corporation
OSHB	:	Odisha State Housing Board
OSSC	:	Odisha State Seeds Corporation
OSWAS	:	Odisha Secretariat Workflow Automation System
OTDP	:	Odisha Tribal Development Project
OUAT	:	Odisha University of Agriculture & Technology
PACS	:	Primary Agriculture Cooperative Society
PBMSA	:	Prevention of Black Marketing & Maintenance of Supplies (Essential Commodities) Act
PDS	:	Public Distribution System
PHC	:	Primary Health Centre
PIL	:	Public Interest Litigation
PMGSY	:	Prime Minister's Gram Sadak Yojana
PMO	:	Prime Minister's Office
PSU	:	Public Sector Undertaking

PVTG	:	Particularly Vulnerable Tribal Group
R&DM	:	Revenue and Disaster Management
R&R	:	Rehabilitation and Resettlement
RBI	:	Reserve Bank of India
RD	:	Rural Development
RDC	:	Revenue Divisional Commissioner
RI	:	Revenue Inspector
RIDF	:	Rural Infrastructure Development Fund
RKM	:	Rama Krishna Mission
RLEGP	:	Rural Landless Employment Guarantee Programme
RLTAP	:	Revised Long Term Action Plan
RMC	:	Regulated Market Committee
RoR	:	Record of Right
RSP	:	Rourkela Steel Plant
RWSS	:	Rural Water Supply and Sanitation
S&ME	:	School and Mass Education
SAG	:	South Asian Games
SAI	:	Sports Authority of India
SAIL	:	Steel Authority of India Limited
SAT	:	State Administrative Tribunal
SC	:	Scheduled Caste
SCA	:	Special Central Assistance
SCP/SCCP	:	Scheduled Caste Component Plan
SDMP	:	State Disaster Management Plan
SEBC	:	Socially and Educationally Backward Classes
SFDA	:	Small Farmers' Development Agency
SJ&E	:	Social Justice & Empowerment
SMFP	:	Small and Marginal Farmers' Programme
SOP	:	Standard Operating Procedure
SP	:	Superintendent of Police
SRC	:	Special Relief Commissioner
SSA	:	Sarva Shiksha Abhiyan
SSI	:	Small Scale Industries
SSP	:	Senior Superintendent of Police
ST	:	Scheduled Tribe
ST&SC	:	Scheduled Tribe & Scheduled Caste
STSCRTI	:	Scheduled Tribe & Scheduled Caste Research-cum-Training Institute
TDCC	:	Tribal Development Cooperative Corporation
THRTI	:	Tribal & Harijan Training-cum-Research Institute
TISCO	:	Tata Iron & Steel Company
TKDL	:	Traditional Knowledge Digital Library
TLC	:	Total Literacy Campaign
TRYSEM	:	Training of Rural Youth for Self-Employment
TSP	:	Tribal Sub-Plan
UNDP	:	United Nations Development Programme
UNICEF	:	United Nations International Children's Emergency Fund
UPSC	:	Union Public Service Commission
USA	:	United States of America
VAT	:	Value Added Tax
VAW	:	Village Agriculture Worker
VCL	:	Village Committee Leader
VIP	:	Very Important Person
VHP	:	Vishwa Hindu Parishad
WR	:	Water Resources
YTM	:	Yield to Maturity

* * * *

1

Firmly Grounded Early Life, Education and Training

FAMILY AND EDUCATION

I was born in the Himalayan highlands on 15 June 1956, as recorded in my school certificates, in a small hamlet called Kaphalet under Dashauli village. The hamlet, which comprised just a few families, subsequently came under Pankhusera village of Pithoragarh district in what is now the State of Uttarakhand. Pithoragarh, bordered by Tibet and Nepal, became a separate district after reorganization of Almora in 1962. A most backward district of undivided Uttar Pradesh, posting of a public servant to it was viewed as a punishment. Road communication improved slowly, perhaps for strategic reasons after the 1962 debacle with China. Though not quite the worst, the closest access from my native village to an all-weather motorable road was 15 km away. The nearest school that provided formal education up to higher secondary levels was 32 km away at the time of my passing Class VIII. Only a fortunate few could afford the expensive formal education beyond Class VIII by moving out of the village.

I stand fourth among five brothers and four sisters. Our family of twelve, well-knit and respected in the village for their open-door to all, included my father's aunt. Widowed at the young age of twelve; she had brought up my father after he had lost his mother in infancy. Coincidentally, my mother too had lost her parents in an epidemic when she was two years old. She was brought up by her maternal uncle. Once I moved to the city, I remember facing incredulity even ridicule about having numerous siblings, which after repeated instances forced a reticence on me about sharing details about my family.

My father received elementary education up to Class IV but had a passion for the Scriptures and discipline in work. My mother displayed a rare brilliance and acute memory right till her passing away, but had no formal education due to the circumstances of her childhood. Our family was no exception among those inhabiting the Kumaoni Himalayan snowline. The small parcels of our agricultural holdings on which we practiced terraced cultivation were scattered over a radius of about five km around the village. Land for settled agriculture, the source of our livelihood, being scanty and prone to the vagaries of weather, was grossly insufficient to sustain our family of twelve. As children we learnt early to become productive assets to support the meagre earnings and struggles of our parents. Priestly services rendered by my father for families in the environs supplemented the slim agricultural earnings of the family-combine. Prevailing societal biases against girls and compulsions of poverty precluded three of my sisters, including two who were my elder, from trekking to the school which provided formal education up to Class VIII to their five brothers. The fourth sister and youngest among all siblings was luckier, as when her time came my elder brother and I were gainfully employed and the family's financial condition had improved. Like her relatively more privileged brothers, she managed to get educated and could eventually use her intellectual acumen in a government school.

My elder brother after completing Class VIII from the Junior High School at Pankhu wanted to study Sanskrit. The nearest school was about 25 km away. Established decades prior by a great Saint, the late Narayana Swami, the Headmaster of the Narayana Sanskrit Pathshala at Kamedi Devi turned out to be a distant relative. On being approached, he agreed to extend support for his education, but for the next 2 years deployed my brother virtually as a domestic help in the name of Sanskrit teaching! After long perseverance, in frustration, he revealed his intention to our mother to run away to Haridwar or Kashi (Varanasi) finding no scope for study at this Pathshala. He again left the village in sheer desperation, this time armed with two old, faded references. One was of a Sanskrit scholar in Varanasi, who had left his home more than 40 years ago by accompanying an unknown Sanyasi, but who had made no contact with his family in our neighbourhood for over 30 years. The other bow in his quiver was a sliver of information about another person, who too had left his village accidently and was believed to be teaching at the Faculty of Oriental Learning and Theology, Banaras Hindu University (BHU). My brother had managed to reach Varanasi soon enough, but could locate these two references only after many wanderings. Perforce he spent the intervening nights at the Railway Station or temple compounds, with the Ghats of the River Ganges also offering refuge when all else failed. The scholar once somehow located was found teaching Buddhism at Sampoornanand Sanskrit University. Eventually, my brother got admitted at the "Marwari Seva Sangh Sanskrit Pathshala" for poor and destitute Brahmin students located at Assi Ghat. The school, funded by a group of Marwari businessmen admitted no more than 25 students, but thankfully provided dormitory accommodation. Sanskrit was taught from Prathama to Uttar Madhyama, equivalent of Classes VIII to XII. Inmates were expected to participate in religious rituals occasionally which also gave them some income by way of "dakshina" to meet their other essential needs. This was in the year 1971.

I will never forget that day when as usual I had gone to a distant forest to collect green grass and fresh oak leaves to feed our household animals. On my return in the afternoon, I heard that my Secondary Board Examination was scheduled to commence from the next day at an examination centre at Pithoragarh. Without eating food and wearing torn and dirty clothes, I ran about 15 km to catch the last bus for Pithoragarh. After reaching there, with a lot of difficulty I managed to locate a distant relative whom I had never met before, but who generously gave me shelter during the examinations. I thus passed the Secondary Board Examination as a private candidate in Third Division with grace marks in mathematics. Yet, I enjoyed a very happy feeling and pride in my achievement, not unlike a frog ruling in the well might feel. I remain forever grateful to the traditional head of a neighbouring village who had accompanied me to Pithoragarh for registering to appear for these examinations earlier. In fact, he had made it his métier to help all local lads and invariably accompanied them for their respective registration as private candidates. He was also instrumental in the opening of a private High School at Pankhu which was later taken over by State Government.

But there was no possibility of my continuing with studies. My father made it clear that the family's finances could not be stretched further and he would be only too happy if he could provide similar level of matriculate education to my three younger brothers. I was now expected to help him more actively by finding a job elsewhere. This was in the year 1972. I was then 15 years old.

My elder brother had come home after his first year in Varanasi for his summer vacation. I insisted to join him, fully confident about finding a job to improve the economic condition of our family now that I was a Matriculate. After all, young illiterates and semi-literates from our neighbourhood had found employment in the Army and elsewhere. A neighbour and a distant uncle, working as a Process Server in the Income Tax Department in Dhanbad had come home on his annual vacation. He offered to assist in finding suitable employment for me in Varanasi as he happened to know an income tax payee entrepreneur who according to him, had an industrial unit in Varanasi. With pride I carried my Matriculation Certificate and accompanied my elder brother to Varanasi in search of this employment. However, I ran from pillar to post only to suffer humiliating job rejections wherever I went by myself or was taken to by others. The businessman cited by the distant uncle was eventually located. He ran a bakery, and the job he offered me involved making door-delivery of his bakery products at a monthly remuneration of ₹ 100. To my chagrin, I was unable to grab this offer as I did not know cycling. I stayed for nearly two months in a small cow-shed of the astrology teacher at BHU referred to earlier, while utilising every ounce of my energy running around and begging for employment. The shed was without electricity. Away from the cool Himalayan climes, I felt the full blast of summer heat and also got my first exposure to mosquitoes! But it was my inability to supplement the family income during these trying times that haunted me every day.

I was not fluent in Hindi when I came to Varanasi, since the local dialect had been the medium of communication in my village school. Whatever sense of pride in being I had, got demolished to dust by now. Finally, help came from another teacher-friend of the astrology teacher at BHU who had served as head of the same Marwari Sanskrit School some years earlier in which my elder brother had enrolled the previous year. I too got admission and dormitory accommodation there after a couple of months. I passed the entrance test by reciting the Gayatri Mantra from memory, which incidentally I had learnt from my father's recitations. I could finally find a place to study due to the kindness and help of these two teachers during the most critical yet almost stranded phase of my formative life.

Unlike my brother who had come to Varanasi with the clear objective of studying Sanskrit in a traditional way and had assimilated well, I took some time to adjust to the new social and educational environment. After feeding an equal number of Sanyasis, students were offered simple food, mostly cooked rice and watered-down dal or khichdi during lunch, and chapatis with mixed vegetables for dinner. In the early days I went hungry, because these meagre watery offerings on leaf-plates would quickly flow off on to the floor unless consumed with deftness. At times, small dead insects could be found clearly visible in the cooked food. Like my brother and other fellow students, I too put on the sacred thread (the Janeu), learnt how to wear a white dhoti, and got used to reciting some Vedic hymns as a matter of routine. I began communicating in Hindi.

After attending Sanskrit classes in the morning, I pursued study of modern subjects aiming to appear privately in the Higher Secondary Board Examination to be conducted by Uttar Pradesh Board. It was not difficult to self-study subjects like Hindi, Sanskrit, Civics and Economics, but learning English language which I had opted to take as a subject was proving challenging. I was fortunate to find a very generous elderly person who had stopped practicing law since long, who volunteered to teach me English for an hour every afternoon. I thus passed the Intermediate Board Examination in 1974 in Second Division with marks that could enable me to pursue the Bachelor's course in BHU, something I had not imagined even in my wildest dreams till now.

After taking admission in the Faculty of Arts, BHU, my life as a regular student was not without challenges. Lectures held in the morning clashed with my classes at the Sanskrit Pathshala, which I did not wish to leave mid-way. Also, if I left the Pathshala I would be deprived of food and dormitory accommodation. I decided to pursue both educational streams – traditional and modern – made possible by the understanding and benevolence of Shri

Suryakant Shashtri, the then Principal of Sanskrit Pathshala and an eminent Sanskrit scholar. He had no family and considered the students as his own. He was generous beyond compare towards all, but especially so towards my brother whom he had learnt to value for his straight-forwardness and lack of guile. I surrendered and prayed before him to allow me to simultaneously pursue the modern education system at BHU. As I had expected, he granted permission informally with firm instructions that the matter would not be disclosed to fellow students and school's management till I passed out from the Pathshala. He was kind enough to teach me during extra hours, as I missed his regular classes in order to attend BA classes at BHU. Punctuality at BHU was being insisted upon with stricter monitoring due to the national internal 'Emergency'. I somehow managed to meet the minimum percentage of class attendance by missing some sessions at both these institutes.

The next two years were quite hectic and hard for me. Apart from study-related difficulties, I had to invariably skip lunch which was served at the Marwari school at 1.00 p.m. when I would be attending lectures at BHU about 2 km away. Varanasi being a religious place, there were many outlets around the Ganges' banks and a few other common places, run by individuals and charitable trusts that offered sprouted horse-gram with a piece of jaggery free of cost along with drinking water to beggars and homeless. I had no option and sustained myself on such charities during these years. I won a small cash prize in my first year at University along with another small scholarship after securing second position in the written test on the philosophy of the Gita and Hinduism. These enabled me to buy the cheapest brand of an HMT wrist-watch and a pair of terrycot trousers, my very first pair in life. Occasional participation in religious rituals with my brother which included reciting the Gita for the elderly and the dying, or even at death rituals, for the liberation of their soul at the Marwari Seva Sangh also brought some income which met my education-related expenditures at the University. After passing out from the Pathshala, my brother joined the nearby Sanskrit College for higher education with scholarship and moved into its hostel facilities.

After I passed out from the Sanskrit Pathshala, one after the other my three younger brothers also joined us in Varanasi. The younger two had done their schooling up to secondary level from the same poorly-managed High School at Pankhu, which had by now been taken over by the State Government. For accommodation, a small cow-shed lying unoccupied and hardly habitable near Ass Ghat was offered to us by its owner in return for priestly services to be offered to his family deity every morning and evening at his larger house which was a km away. We carried out the necessary repairs to the cow-shed and also added a small temporary thatched shed in the adjoining area which could be used for cooking, except during rains. Nights were partly spent under the open sky due to space constraint, except during rains and severe winter when by turn the four brothers had to manage to sleep inside. From this abode, we pursued our formal education. The three younger siblings did rather well under modern education and did not have to pursue the path their two elders had followed in pursuing the traditional study of Sanskrit formally. I stayed on with the twin-tracks of traditional and modern education, and had also joined the Sanyasi Sanskrit College which was managed by and actually meant for Sanyasis. Only a few non-Sanyasis like me, who were proficient in spoken Sanskrit, were admitted. I was eventually awarded the degrees of "Sahityacharya" from the Sampoornanand Sanskrit University, and Master of Arts in Sanskrit, with specialisation in Philosophy, from BHU.

Kedar Datt Joshi, astrology teacher in the Faculty of Oriental Learning and Theology, BHU used to advise some well-known business houses and conduct religious rituals for those seeking their prosperity regularly in Varanasi. R.P. Goenka was one of his clients for whom two-three persons recited prayers/ mantras on a daily basis for an hour early in the morning under his close supervision in the temple within his residential compound. My elder brother got engaged in this part-time task on a monthly fixed remuneration. I too found similar stop-gap assignments. A younger brother earned some money by providing tuition during his spare time. We were by now nearly self-sufficient; earning while learning.

Alongside my studies, I got an interesting work as a "Reader" and "Writer" for three blind students who studied Sanskrit and modern subjects at Graduate level in an institute for the blind. This enriched me intellectually besides giving me a great amount of inspiration and satisfaction. I did not accept the remuneration offered. In return I asked my differently-abled friends to recite inspiring or devotional songs at the end of my reading and writing sessions with them. They happily reciprocated. One of them played the "Tabla" quite well, while the other two were proficient on the harmonium and flute besides having melodious voices. Regardless of societal discrimination often on display, a divine flame exists inside every human being which only needs an opportunity to get manifest and magnified. I would recall their unique attributes, strengths and talent, whenever later on I chanced upon differently-abled persons in various successful walks of life. My three friends in Varanasi in whose company I found enjoyment in my leisure hours were my seniors in class. Indeed, I opted for political science as a subject at Graduate level simply because I had read from books on political science to one of them. I smile at providence to this day that this friend would score better marks with me as his "Writer" in the University examinations than those I would later on get for myself!

During these years, I was exposed to several seeming dualities in myself and the world around me. In studying Political Science for my graduation degree, I developed a strong liking for Western political thoughts, especially Marxian philosophy which I found inspirational. At the same time every Sunday morning, I unfailingly attended scholarly lectures on the Gita at Malaviya

Bhavan, BHU, which gave me inner strength and confidence. I found the call of Karl Marx and Friedrich Engels in the Communist Manifesto – "*Workers of the World, unite! ... You have nothing to lose but the chains [of slavery]*" – complementing and in resonance with the call of Lord Krishna in the Gita that "*O Parth, there is no fall for him here or hereafter, for none who strives for self-redemption ever meets with evil destiny*":

पार्थ नैवेह नामुत्र विनाशस्तस्य विद्यते।
नहि कल्याणकृत्कश्चिद्दुर्गतिंतात गच्छति॥ (6/40)

I also attended the Shakha of Rashtra Swayamsevak Sangh held early every morning at the play-ground close to our abode before 'Emergency' was promulgated by Central Government. Right through the Emergency, I found myself enjoying heated arguments and company of fellow leftist students, many of whom had become card-holders. The Mantras of *Ishavasyopanishad* and Shlokas of the Gita to me did not convey any clash with those of Communism in essence. I was not matured enough to distinguish their finer distinctions, but was sure that neither the Sanghis nor Communists, individually nor together, represented nor did justice to the rich Indian culture and ethos. I did not join either organisation formally. Being influenced by Dr. Ram Manohar Lohia and other socialist leaders on the caste system which in a way had benefitted me too, even before completing my BA course I removed my surname officially which identified me as a Brahmin.

For some of my new-found friends, I was seemingly living a life of contradiction, enjoying teachings of the Gita, Upanishads and holy scriptures, reading liberal classical Sanskrit literature and performing religious rituals for livelihood on the one hand and participating regularly in discourses with left-oriented intellectuals on the other. It was a journey in education from "knowledge that leads to emancipation" to "knowledge that provides material goods". However, despite the attractions of left-leaning political thoughts, I could not internalise them. Western political thoughts remained an area of interest as did Indian Philosophy with spirituality largely as its core although the latter was qualitatively vastly different from the former. The traditional and modern educational systems I had pursued concurrently gave me a rare insight and advantage which made me increasingly bold and confident in the later part of my life and proved a providential blessing indeed. I had passed Bachelor of Arts narrowly missing the First Division, but at the next level I received a First Division both in Master of Arts at BHU and in "Sahityacharya".

I was not born into a family with a sound economic background. I lived a very hard life from childhood right through to the onset of adulthood. Ironically, my experience and expertise acquired during formative years, despite being my strength, did not have any value in the organised job market. I could do every household and agriculture-related work efficiently. My proficiency in cutting and collecting good fodder for household animals, paddy transplantation, etc. were the envy of village women for whom these were specialised fields of work. In any competition, I could readily score over them even at a very tender age. After completing a 3 km trip carrying a head-load of compost made of cow-dung to our family's farm-land early morning along with my sisters who would return home carrying my empty container, I would proceed directly to my school at Pankhu. Students who failed to report on time for the school assembly for collective prayers, including singing the national anthem, used to be punished. The punishment was to carry a large stone from the nearby rivulet to the school. Stones thus gathered were used for constructing retaining walls for developing the school garden or play-ground. After farm work I would invariably get late for school and thus developed the habit of carrying a large stone in anticipation of punishment to avoid the repeat trek to the rivulet. Collection of bark from certain types of trees in nearby forests, which had medicinal value and selling them to a local trader gave additional income and I generally carried out these chores on public holidays and during any spare time. During the summer vacation when I came home from Varanasi, I did not mind working with labourers engaged in construction of an all-weather road which was to pass through our village. The sport I had mastered in addition to playing Gulli-Danda and Kabaddi was climbing mountains as well as tall trees for cutting branches to meet our firewood needs. Sadly, such skills had little value in a job market, in which candidates who could not speak English were not considered educated. Proficiency in agricultural practices like transplanting in straight lines, though not an easy task, is still considered as 'unskilled work' by the so-called civilised educated professionals. Come what may, I desperately needed a stable job as early as possible after my Graduation.

I developed a craving for a career in teaching, though my relatively poor academic credentials so far and lack of connections put me at a distinct disadvantage. As a backup, during my final graduate year in 1976 I had begun preparing for Provincial Civil Services Examination conducted by Uttar Pradesh Public Service Commission. Luckily, I cleared the examination in my first attempt, but the final merit did not allow me to be selected for the executive branch, the only option I had exercised. I did not have the money required to be deposited as additional fees to opt for other allied services. Thus, in spite of securing marks which could have ensured a place for me in Provincial Police Service or any other allied service, I lost the first opportunity for a good job and felt devastated.

In the meanwhile, I had taken admission in Master of Arts in BHU and also for "Sahityacharya" in Sanyasi Sanskrit College with Sanskrit as the medium of instruction. The Masters course in BHU appeared easy in the light of deeper studies of Sanskrit through the traditional method pursued by me side-by-side. Luckily, soon after passing out my elder brother got appointed as a Religious Teacher classified as a Junior Commissioned Officer in the Army Medical Corps. I registered myself in the Ph.D. Course at BHU and both of us started earning regularly. There was no need to pursue priestly services for subsistence now. I shifted to a hostel in BHU and our three brothers continued to live in the small room at Assi Ghat for some more time. Over time, these three too shifted residences to hostels at the University and to relatively better houses on rent as two of them also started getting University Grants Commission scholarships. The journey had become decidedly easier.

Educationally, these were very heady days. I came in contact with some great scholars and inspiring teachers. I was advised by one of them during my Master's course to remain in academic field, as he had faith in my academic potential and was hopeful of my career in it. Without looking for other career options, I now started focusing on my specialisations in classical literature and Indian philosophy, Adwait Vedant in particular. Having secured the First Division for the first time in my life and that too in dual Masters' degrees from two well-known universities at the same time, I steadily gathered the ambition and hope of securing a teaching job in some college or university that provided education through modern or traditional systems. After all, I had also published about half a dozen research papers written in Sanskrit in reputed journals even before completing my degree in Doctor of Philosophy.

Towards the end of my Ph.D. Course, I was appointed as a Lecturer and Head of Sahitya against a vacancy in the reputed government-aided Sadhuvela Sanskrit Mahavidyalaya of Varanasi. Shastras were taught here in Sanskrit using traditional methods. Though initially appointed on temporary basis, the management had assured me a permanent position in the foreseeable future. This provided welcome additional income to bridge education needs of my younger brothers. My happiness, however, did not last long. The manager of the Mahavidyalaya became unhappy with me when I declined to sign the salary register for the summer vacations after I was told that no remuneration for this period would actually be given to me. I stayed steadfast with my refusal to sign and my post was advertised after a few months. But I did not feel too disappointed by this experience as a candidate more qualified than me was appointed against the post held by me temporarily.

Teaching assignments remained elusive as half-a-dozen job interviews in universities and colleges yielded no positive outcome. Without upfront assurance of permanent absorption, I did not like to take up another temporary appointment as Lecturer offered to me at the Buddhist Research Institute (a deemed university now) at Sarnath, headed by the Rimpoche who incidentally became Prime Minister of Tibetan Government in exile a few years later. In couple of more years of such trials, I would also have lost the opportunity due to age-bar to appear in the Civil Services Examination. My fear of mathematics, even simple arithmetic calculations, precluded me from appearing for any recruitment tests for banking and insurance services as an alternative. This new target was not without its challenges either. Time was short for appearing for this examination. I wrote my Ph.D. thesis within 18 months devoting full energy to it. I locked up the completed thesis, already printed in requisite copies, in a trunk because procedurally it could not be formally submitted in BHU before completing the mandatory period of 24 months. I left for Danapur where my elder brother was now posted after completing his year-long training in the Army, and armed with the blessings of my Guide began to prepare and try my luck once again to join Uttar Pradesh State Civil Services. I added Civil Services Examination to be conducted by Union Public Service Commission (UPSC) to my list of trials. Fortunately, the UPSC had started conducting examinations in regional languages besides in English that offered equal opportunities to non-English medium candidates.

I succeeded again in this second attempt in the State Civil Services Examination, which again did not offer me the executive branch. With Political Science as my subject at Preliminary Examination stage, and Philosophy and Sanskrit in the Main Examinations conducted by UPSC, it was not too difficult to qualify the written tests. But I failed to cross the final hurdle in the UPSC as my marks in the personality test were insufficient. I was indeed most apprehensive about the outcome in the personality test as there were none to guide me. None in my family had worked in the government or organised sector elsewhere either. But I succeeded in the next attempt on both counts. I did not join the State Civil Service when the offer to join came, as by then the results declared by UPSC promised me a place in the Indian Administrative Service (IAS) after a couple of months. It would be fair to say that my joining the civil services was more accidental and compulsive than a planned one.

Incidentally, the member of UPSC who headed my interview board was the same in both my attempts. In my assessment, I had performed better in my first appearance. I had then scanned the list of successful candidates in the newspaper "The Times of India" from the top to bottom confident of finding my name, giving up midway finding myself unsuccessful. On my second attempt, I read the list from the bottom upwards, persevering amidst failed hopes to eventually find that the second paragraph started with my name ranking me at serial number 101 in the combined list of general candidates. For some of my well-wishers, probably it was a blind shot. It took time for them to believe the news. But for me the success was a cumulative effect of the sacrifices made by my elder brother, continuing striving against odds and blessings of my parents, grit and grind nurtured in me by some of my inspiring teachers, and providential kindness. In my heart of hearts, I felt that my son came as '*sikandar*' in my life, born on 2 April 1983 just a couple of months before UPSC's result was announced.

I had negligible to indifferent understanding about the civil services and no great ambition, but one compulsion ruled – I wanted a steady job in order to stand on my feet firmly and be able to support other family members. How could I forget that my mother often went without food in order to feed her hungry children? I also remember well the gloom that would flit on the faces of my parents when a standing crop ready for harvest suddenly got damaged by hailstorm. Looking back, I also rue the day when neither I nor my elder brother studying in Varanasi had the money to pay for journeying to our village to attend the wedding of my elder sister. The curse called poverty, however, did not break the spirit and conviction of my parents, who never allowed us to suffer from any kind of bitterness or to be in the grip of deprivation in any sense. The age-old saying of seers and sages that luck only favours those with venture, courage, forbearance, intelligence, strength and valour guided and sustained me in difficult times. My advice to fellow travellers irrespective of their field is that there is no need to lose the battle before a determined fight as the Sun cannot remain clouded over for all the time.

TRAINING: A VITAL NECESSITY

I formally joined the IAS on 1 September 1983 as a Probationer, when I reported for training at the Lal Bahadur Shastri National Academy of Administration (LBSNAA), Mussoorie a couple of days later than others due to my illness and hospitalisation. I was the proverbial village bumpkin, a fish completely out of water! English, the medium of instruction, was as much a challenge as was the etiquette required to be displayed which included the periodic formal dressing up. I resorted to silence for the most part, but keenly observed everyone. I also took time to find my feet and open up with fellow probationers. My room-mate, a native of Bihar, was from Indian Railway Accounts Service. His father was a renowned professor in a Medical College. My neighbour, from IAS, was the son of a Chief Secretary of another State. I had to forgo active participation due to lack of prior exposure in sports, hobby clubs and cultural activities despite abundance of facilities. I had a fair amount of bookish knowledge acquired in the process of preparing for the General Studies papers, which only enabled me to make some contributions in discussions. The village sports I knew well had no place in the Academy, but I found that I could take up horse riding with ease and here I stood on equal footing with fellow probationers. A week-long trekking about a month later offered me an ideal opportunity to interact more closely with them albeit in a smaller group. The 'Village' visit, another group exercise of about 10 days during the foundation course, broke my isolation in a real sense. But, without doubt I remained an odd man out, particularly in the first three months.

Towards the end of this Foundation Course, I was suddenly made aware that a couple of assignments were to be carried out followed by tests in various subjects, all to be conducted in English. Since the performance would affect my standing in the final order of merit, I expressed my difficulty in writing these assignments and papers in English to a faculty member from Tamil Nadu who appeared to appreciate the linguistic dilemma. However, I was chided by the Academy's Director when I was taken to him by this faculty member. I did not like to get disheartened amidst much smarter fellow officers, many of whom had already presented their skills in various fields, specifically proficiency in English, or flaunted their superior socio-economic background. I felt that articulation was being viewed as a show of competence by them even before appearing in the actual test of public service on the ground, which would start only after completion of a couple of years of training. Sophistry was being taken for sophistication. The only option before me was to work harder and consult the English dictionary frequently. Somehow, I managed to write the assignments and papers in English and passed the examinations conducted at the end of the Foundation Course, though that did affect my standing in the final list of merit.

I became more assertive when the Professional Course commenced. Allocation of Cadre by Department of Personnel & Training (DoPT) towards end of the Foundation Course had brought gloom on many faces for whom their own State or at least the region was preferable. I was surprised to see these young officers greet this news as though they were being deprived; after all they could boast the best of education and could take pride in being a part of the elite IAS. I was happy to be allocated Odisha[1] Cadre, not least because my wife, a classmate from M.A. in BHU, was an Odia. My job experience taught me that it was better to be allotted a State other than the native one because it was easier to work with greater independence and objectivity, without the overhang of expectations and compulsions from near and dear ones. The advantage of learning one more language if the State's language is other than the officer's Mother tongue is actually a welcome opportunity to better understand and assimilate with the socio-cultural diversity of the nation.

I found myself more at ease in this phase of training which had participants only from IAS. The period of training, which included Bharat Darshan, being longer provided an opportunity to know fellow trainee officers better. I improved my English language skill to a greater extent and also ventured into some indoor and outdoor sports. Towards the end of the Professional Course and on the first day of examination, a massive fire broke out that devastated the main building and library of the Academy. I participated in rescue operations and saved a good number of books despite getting injured. Examinations, postponed by a year were cleared by me without difficulty. In any event, unlike the Foundation Course, these results did not affect the standing of trainee officers in the Batch.

I reported at Gopabandhu Academy of Administration (GAA) with fellow probationers of Odisha cadre on 15 June 1984. Four weeks of training gave me, a newcomer to Administration and also to the State, useful grounding in

1. Called Orissa in those days.

its legal framework and socio-economic situation. This institutional training included a week-long Odisha Darshan and upon its conclusion on 12 July 1984, I joined the post now termed Assistant Collector, reporting to Collector, Cuttack for my district training. I was fortunate to get trained under one of the most dynamic, experienced and finest IAS officers at the helm of district administration, the Late Har Mohan Patnaik during the bulk of my district training. Unfortunately, he died young just a few years later due to a sudden asthmatic attack while working as Director in Union Coal Ministry. Besides exposing me to various areas of administration, including management of natural calamities, he assigned to me a few important tasks to be executed under his guidance, such as preparing reports on implementation of priority sector schemes, handling VIP visits, departmental proceedings, etc. In fact, a notable VVIP visit to Cuttack was that of the then Prime Minister Smt. Indira Gandhi, coincidentally made just a day before her assassination. As desired by District Collector, keeping the provisions in the Blue Book in view, I had written an essay on security arrangements for her hugely successful visit.

District training gave a ring-side view of the functioning of administration at the crucial district-level and levels below it. Attachments with judiciary and police offices at times do not fall within the radar of senior judicial and police officers for imparting training to an IAS Probationer aka Assistant Collector. Still, I found the inputs provided during these attachments greatly enriching. I devoured the Police Manual which informs that District Magistrate is the head of criminal administration in the district. I got to visit various police offices and stations to understand the processes followed in policing, without which it is not possible for District Magistrate to function effectively. Training in judiciary is important to learn the techniques used in examining and analysing evidences, which are vital for writing reasoned orders. I acquired valuable insights into the way judiciary functioned and decided litigations.

Thanks to these trainings, notably the grinding I received from Sub-Divisional Judicial Magistrate of Cuttack, almost every order passed by me later on in administrative life withstood the test of judicial scrutiny, whether it was in relation to preventive detention for maintenance of essential supplies or various revenue and commercial laws. It is tragic that many trainee officers now-a-days do not give adequate importance to judicial and police training as they appear to attach more importance to the indifference shown to them. I found it to be in my professional interest to ignore such occasional indifference. I focused on being the inquisitive Assistant Collector before all my trainers. Humility and respect towards trainers are prerequisites in acquiring useful knowledge, particularly when that requires some practical experience for management of processes.

The two most important assignments during district training are those as Block Development Officer (BDO) and Tahasildar. Both are key functionaries at the cutting edge of administration. It is difficult to understand that despite being notified as BDO/ Additional BDO for three months and Tahasildar/ Additional Tahasildar for 30 days, none in our batch was actually given substantive charge of these offices perhaps because of insufficient understanding of the local language among the probationers new to the State. Official business in Block/Tahasil offices is mostly conducted in the State's language. I felt one could learn both the language and substantively only by actively being involved, just as one cannot learn swimming by avoiding the swimming pool or water. With Sanskrit as my background, it was not difficult for me to learn Odia quickly. I was posted to Cuttack Sadar Block as Additional BDO. The incumbent BDO was very experienced and knowledgeable but appeared more interested in my physical comfort. Instead of sharing with me his expertise, he avoided answering questions and rarely liked me to accompany him during field visits. On his work front also, his focus seemed to be to keep the local MLA and other politicians happy even if that required some functional compromises to retain his posting as BDO of Sadar Block. I saw him ignoring warnings of District Collector for his poor performance during monthly review meetings. Despite getting constrained due to the elusive BDO, I made extensive notes on various schemes under implementation correlating them with applicable circulars/guidelines during my Block training. I subsequently used them extensively to write a handbook on Block Development Administration some years later.

Tahasil training was less challenging as the work was largely regulatory in nature, except for calamities when Tahasil administration was on the forefront of rescue and relief operations. Floods and cyclones occurred regularly in Cuttack district, and I closely watched the handling of a severe flood which affected a large part of the district. I studied the State's Relief Code in depth. These helped me in managing massive relief operations some years later as Collector of Ganjam district. Distribution of ceiling surplus and government waste land for agriculture and homestead purposes to landless families in rural areas are an important task assigned to tahasils which is reviewed by District Collector in monthly meetings. Collection of land revenue had been waived off in the State, but collection of cess was an important activity of Tahasil administration entailing regular contact with tenants and seamless updating of land records. I found that record keeping in Block Office was a mess, though in Tahasil office it was better. Revenue Inspectors (RIs) maintained 12 important documents called Jamabandi Registers containing everything in relation to land and land revenue matters. Another important task of Tahasildar was to inspect each RI's circle and make sure that Jamabandi Registers were updated regularly. During my attachment in Cuttack Sadar Tahasil, I found the Tahasildar mostly engaged in law and order duties with hardly any time for revenue work. Naturally, I was rarely satisfied with inputs being given during this phase of training.

Training in Survey and Settlement gave me real exposure to revenue and land administration. Despite deploying seemingly primitive methods, the field work was quite systematic. I internalised all four stages of updating land records – Kishtwar & Khanapuri, Bujharat & Attestation, Draft Publication & Objection Hearing, and Final Publication & Patta Distribution. I attended settlement camps across Cuttack staying in them for about 10 days, some of which did not have sanitation facilities. Deep understanding of the *modus operandi* and state-of-play served me well in my posting as Charge Officer with a supervisory role over revisional settlements, immediately on completion of training. Indeed, I would not have been effective in handling revisional survey and settlement operations of Kalahandi district but for my rigorous training. I could also use the skills acquired to make systemic improvements in land administration two decades later as head of Revenue & Disaster Management Department.

The Collectorate with its various sections and branches is a mini secretariat in the district. Training here provides insights and exposure to a number of administrative processes and procedures followed for examination of a variety of issues on delivery of public services and regulatory administration. There is no harm in challenging the established age-old office procedures when they are found redundant and inadequate to fulfil the current requirements for timely delivery of services. The young blood with a fertile and imaginative mind after studying the systems and procedures in vogue may come up with alternatives that are more relevant and consistent with the prevailing situation. Administration has to be dynamic and cannot be taken for maintaining status quo any more. For instance, I was appointed as an Enquiry Officer later on in a departmental proceedings case which had been pending for more than a decade. My judicial training gave me confidence in its disposal. I had recognized the merits of not prolonging such pendency. Delayed proceedings may eventually result in acquittal of delinquent official for loss of evidence or otherwise, and impact his functioning in the organisation. Timely disposal even if it leads to minor punishment may not only give him an opportunity to improve, but may also work as a deterrent for others. It is important that every trainee officer draws the notice of District Collector any difficulties being faced by administration, which may include inadequate attention to disposal of departmental proceedings. This would also assist the trainee officer once he is in active service in conducting analyses of causes of abnormal delays and take corrective and preventive steps.

Despite taking district training seriously and acquiring skill in the local language, I had to take another shot at clearing departmental examinations on law and Odia language the following year. I took this in my stride and used the opportunity in deeper studies of local revenue laws and serious reading of Odia literature which I really loved. I contributed to amending many of these laws besides applying them extensively in subsequent administrative avatars.

After the year-long district training, we reported back to LBSNAA at Mussoorie. This second phase was rather enjoyable being more interactive and discussion-oriented and was without any worrying clouds of compulsory classroom lectures and tests! Probationers mostly presented their experiences gained during district training. More experienced officers invited from various States and Central Government offered observations and expanded out options to deal with situations narrated by trainees. This phase was also entertaining as some probationers gave expressions to their experiences with dramatic twists as if what they had undergone was unique or unprecedented. Articulations of those seeking to occupy centre-stage at times substituted serious discussions on substantive administrative issues. Talkative ones naturally believed that they were the most efficient. I generally remained an observer even when I was not in agreement with the majority view on suggested solutions. Indeed, often in my career I could not subscribe to the dominant narratives on administrative issues which I felt were less relevant from the point of actual practice or even outright superficial at times. In my assessment, administrators fail to deliver the desired outputs as they rarely believe in what they articulate publicly for impressing others.

It would be a travesty of truth to say that I did not gain from every bit of the training imparted howsoever superficial or incomplete it could be on certain occasions. I can say with conviction that for a first generation professional from a humble background, it was an enriching exposure. I benefitted greatly from academic tutorials and theoretical inputs received at training institutes and also from my own practical observations and insights gained during attachments at district/ block/ tahasil levels. I tried to assimilate and apply these varied inputs in my own way in delivering public services during the days to come in my administrative life.

* * * *

2

First Cut in Revenue, Regulatory, Development Administration

CHARGE OFFICER, SETTLEMENT, JEYPORE, KORAPUT

My first formal posting was as Charge Officer, Settlement, a post considered less significant in the prevailing administrative milieu. Out of 7 officers in my batch allotted to Odisha, 5 were posted as Sub-Collector[2] of revenue sub-divisions; mostly in socio-economically backward districts. At LBSNAA itself, probationers allotted to other State cadres got their posting orders early. But those allotted to Odisha State probably had to wait the longest for their first substantive posting. An early posting order enables the inquisitive trainee to prepare better for handling his assignment by going through State/ District Gazetteers and other relevant documents available in the extensive library of LBSNAA. As I realised over time, the administrative system in Odisha rarely weighs in or values economic and social opportunity costs even in relation to more important policy and administrative matters for which the State has continued to suffer heavily. It is a lesson hardly learnt except in sporadic and episodic instances of individual efforts by a few who believe in quick decisions and invite risks for exhibiting that quality, which suggests that general apathy, and not lack of insights, is the real culprit. Odisha Administration has no option but to change for better results and improve its standing and reputation.

Almost immediately after my posting order, I received a welcoming letter from the officer whom I would succeed at Jeypore in Koraput district under Berhampur Major Settlement forming part of Southern Division of the State. The letter mainly gave a panoramic view of Eastern Ghats highlighting its natural beauty. Addressing me as "Dear Madam", the author mistook me for a lady officer no doubt by reading my name in two parts. I soon found that he was desperate to leave the place and was seeking to lure me to assume charge, perhaps apprehending that I would represent for my posting elsewhere. After serving for some time, I realised that posting of officers from coastal districts in tribal districts of Southern Division was largely considered a measure of punishment!

---

1. Post of Sub-Divisional Officer was subsequently re-designated as Sub-Collector.

I joined at Jeypore on 24 August 1985 and worked there up to 7 October 1985. The tenure was short and workload insignificant. During the rainy season besides preparing for deployment of camps depending upon the size of work plan approved by Director, Land Records, Survey and Settlement, the details collected during Kishtwar & Khanapuri stage are analysed, compared and verified by technical staff. Field operations take place after the rainy season when kharif crops are removed from the land to be surveyed. There were no camps in operation for "Objection Hearing" after Draft Publication. The area identified for revisional settlement largely had Bangladeshi Hindu resettlers under Dandakaranya Project in model villages in Malkangiri area. I did nothing more memorable than visit Malkangiri to be familiarised with the area and took briefs from subordinates on implementing the Plan during ensuing working season. I met senior officers of the Project which was in its winding-up phase. The focus was on making reimbursement for settlement operations besides transferring of its assets to State Government.

The only significant administrative activity was a visit by Settlement Officer from Berhampur. I waited with curiosity for the visit of my immediate boss. The 300 km distance from Berhampur to Jeypore could be negotiated easily in one day. However, his advance tour programme spelt out the arrangements to be made for two night halts enroute at Vijayanagaram in Andhra Pradesh and Rayagada, then a part of Koraput district. Assistant Settlement Officer (ASO), in charge of office administration was required to tie-up these arrangements. On the third day the Settlement Officer reached the Circuit House, Koraput where I was waiting to receive him. After spending a few minutes and exchanging courtesies, he retired to his suite. Though hopeful, I waited in vain for him to appear in the office, his supposed destination. ASO who had accompanied him on the return leg of the journey told upon his return that no work programme was discussed with Settlement Officer. But for my receiving him, the Settlement Officer would not even have realised that I had joined as the new Charge Officer.

TRANSFER TO BHAWANIPATNA, KALAHANDI DISTRICT

On transfer from Jeypore, I joined at Bhawanipatna on 8 October in an inter-change of posts with my other batchmate. The transfer effected was on my representation as my wife who had been working as Lecturer in a College at Cuttack, had been posted by State Government in Government College, Bhawanipatna. State's transfer policy provided for posting of working spouse at a place or in proximity to the extent possible.

Office of Charge Officer, Settlement, Bhawanipatna in Kalahandi district which then included Nuapada (a separate district now) under Sambalpur Major Settlement had been established a few months before my joining. The newly opened office was run from a rented private building in a corner of the town. Survey and other office equipment from Sundhargarh where settlement operations had been completed had been shifted to Bhawanipatna along with the manpower. Though a very old jeep of scrap value had also been brought, the relevant financial rule did not allow its repair. There were allegations of corruption in transportation of furniture and equipment from Sundargarh though it was not possible to verify their veracity as no inventory of articles received in the office had been made at the time of making payment to the transporter. I was also ill-equipped to handle such allegations having no prior experience.

Settlement Officer, Sambalpur who was my immediate boss belonged to Odisha Administrative Service (OAS). He was known to be technically very sound but of doubtful integrity. He would visit Bhawanipatna frequently to micro-manage the field operations. He instructed ASOs who had to work under my leadership, not to bother me with technical details of operations as my tenure in this post was going to be very short.

My immediate task was to undertake recruitment against a large number of seasonal posts, created after assessment of requirements by Settlement Officer on contractual basis, before deployment of settlement camps in a few months hence. Settlement Officer is the only authority below State Government having powers to create posts in Group-C and D categories on the basis of prescribed yardsticks. Amins and supporting staff, such as Chainmen, Process Servers, Cooks and Orderlies, are engaged in bulk during field operations usually carried out between November to June. In consultation with my team of experienced officials, I decided to issue an open advertisement to invite applications clearly indicating that Amins and Chainmen with prior experience of settlement only would be appointed and preference would be given to local candidates. Chainmen, whose job was to carry survey equipment from one parcel of land to another and draw the Gunther's chain for measurement to help Amins during survey work, were as good as Amins in terms of their practical field knowledge and, therefore, could not be recruited fresh from the market. In contrast, persons with cooking skill, Process Servers and Orderlies, could be contracted without prior experience in such operations. The essential qualification common to all was functional literacy and an able body. Before my joining, Settlement Officer had already segregated out ASOs to be deployed at various camps. He had also recommended a few candidates to be recruited on contractual basis to Group-D posts to be filled up.

Difficulties Faced Early On

I constituted a Committee for short-listing candidates with requisite qualifications. Some touts and hooligans visited me to demand appointment of their local candidates considering that Settlement Office was functioning from their locality. They were not happy when the procedure being followed was explained. The local MLA had also forwarded some names. Another list endorsed by Chief Whip of the ruling party, who represented an Assembly Constituency in the district, was handed over to me by District Collector when he called me for a discussion. I conveyed my inability to give any consideration to candidates thus recommended variously. I notified the list prepared by the Committee on the office notice board in addition to informing selected candidates by post. This ruffled the feathers of the rising young leader and politician-in-the-making, who had brought Kalahandi to national and global attention by highlighting alleged starvation deaths and sale of children by poor parents. The bunch of ruffians who did everything short of assaulting me physically in my office, as I learnt later had been sent by him. Threats and choicest abuses showered on me scared my office staff into vanishing from the scene. The ruffians left after warning me of physical harm if their candidates were not appointed within two days. I had never imagined that such a situation would unfold before me simply because I was instituting a fair and transparent recruitment process. It was hardly a month since I had taken charge at Bhawanipatna.

I quietly walked the 2 km distance to the local police station. The police officer in charge, however, refused to receive the First Information Report (FIR) I gave in writing. I hired a rickshaw and proceeded to District Collector's residence seeking his intervention, who I was informed by his personal staff was in siesta after lunch, which as per his instructions could not be intruded into. Finding no option and feeling helpless, I boarded the evening bus for Bhubaneswar to put forth my plight before Pyari Mohan Mahapatra, Secretary, Revenue & Excise Department, well known for his action-mindedness. He agreed to meet me almost instantly. My ordeal narrated, and per chance, District Collector of Kalahandi, who had come to the State capital for reasons unknown to me, entered his room only to receive a thorough dressing down. Without doubt, it was the "Pyari Mohan effect" that my office was sanctioned a new vehicle within a fortnight and criminal proceedings were initiated against those who had threatened me openly. Four years after filing the FIR, I appeared before Chief Judicial Magistrate to depose, but thereafter lost track of proceedings and outcome of the criminal case filed by me against the ruffians. The youthful rising political leader agitating against the Janaki Ballabh Patnaik-led State Government of Congress Party, became an MLA of the rival political party, and finally landed up in the lap of Congress Party itself after some years. In my interactions with him on several occasions in the times to come he remained cordial and respectful towards me. Probably, I had passed his test.

Within a week I faced another incident albeit of a different type. Quite early in the morning, two persons appearing to be students in their early 20s knocked the door at my residence. They narrated their plight attributable to poverty and unemployment, all pervasive in the district. I thought they wanted some financial help, when suddenly one of them took out a bunch of currency notes and offered it to me in lieu of their job appointment! In shock combined with anger, I shouted out but by the time some people gathered, the two boys ran away. This time I did not file any complaint in the local police station but remained more vigilant about all forms of proverbial knocks-on-my-door henceforth.

Exposed to Misuse of Power

I did not face any other external difficulties further as local leaders probably understood that I would not bend rules and procedures to favour the vested interests. District Collector was transferred out. Incoming Collector,Chinmoy Basu, known for his sincerity and hard work was already known to me, as he was Project Director of District Rural Development Agency (DRDA) during the major part of my training in Cuttack. Though not related to my work directly he was always ready to support my initiatives unlike his predecessor.

The problem I started facing now was internal and from my immediate boss, the Settlement Officer. His interference in day-to-day administration was coloured by his supporting corrupt officials posted by him in charge of settlement camps in important circles. Postings at camps had been made by him without consulting me despite my being administrative head at Bhawanipatna. When I transferred some ASOs against whom allegations received were found to be *prima facie* true, he issued orders superseding mine restoring the earlier position.

An ASO, evidently close to Settlement Officer, heading Kesinga town settlement camp which included peripheral villages, was being blackmailed by a local tout-cum-journalist. A news item was found published which averred that lakhs of rupees had been stolen from this camp. A few days later, perhaps in a deal fixed with him, another news item – a corrigendum this time – was found published averring that the theft was limited to a few thousand rupees received by the camp for disbursement of remuneration to contractual field staff.The ASO had not made any claim for any such loss of moneys. During my visit to his camp office, I had seen petitions from married women with thumb impressions/ signatures attested by their respective brothers stating that they had no claims and interest in their parental land. To me these appeared more of a ploy to prepare the Record of Right (RoR) during settlement operations in favour of brothers in violation of succession law. ASO being the competent authority to approve the RoR would indulge in some arm-twisting and his favourite Amins would happily connive with him as they too got their share of the loot.

Corruption was not limited to such instances only. Valuable Government land could be recorded mentioning adverse possession of private persons for more than 30 years in order to facilitate transferring its Right and Title through civil litigation in accordance with the legal provisions on adverse possession. This was happening despite strict instructions prohibiting settlement functionaries from making any mention about adverse possession. There was none objecting to this type of irregularity as loss of land by Government was apparently nobody's concern. As such, despite being carried out in broad day light, survey and settlement operations are mysterious to the public at large due to lack of awareness about legal provisions and procedures followed for preparation of land records.

Lapses being committed by settlement officials were easily verifiable. ASO heading the town-camp was suave with a demeanour of innocence and an overtly helpful attitude in his dealings with the public. The methods followed by another ASO who also enjoyed the confidence of Settlement Officer were crude. He openly demanded a price for the work to be done. People exploited by him were mostly naïve tribals who rarely knew their rights. When my warning was of no use and Settlement Officer was found siding with both of them openly, I invited Deputy Superintendent of Police (DSP), Vigilance to my residence and after narrating the situation requested him to lay a trap to catch these two corrupt officers. I also shared with him the irregularities, including fudging of records, in transportation of equipment from Sundargarh to Bhawanipatna. True to his promise, within a week DSP (Vigilance) was able to entrap one ASO when he was attempting to exploit some tribal tenants. I now wrote to the Settlement Officer reminding him of my warnings which he had ignored and compounded it by cancelling my orders transferring these ASOs. I underscored the possibility of few more ASOs being exposed for exploiting innocent tenants. Settlement Officer did not reply, but definitely cautioned other field functionaries to become more circumspect and careful in their dealings.

In the hierarchy of survey and settlement organization, ASOs and Kanungos are key stones of field administration. They carry out supervisory tasks over the main field work of Kishtwar & Khanapuri done by Amins. The age-old plain table method is used travelling from plot to plot in the village. Up to 10 percent margin of error is allowed. ASOs and Kanungos conduct test-checks at random in every village to ensure maximum accuracy of survey work. At Bujharat & Attestation phase, comparison is made with old cadastral maps and other textual records. In case of doubt, more experienced Amins and Inspectors are deputed for spot verifications. Draft Publication & Objection Hearing stage is most vital as records thus finalised get finally published and pattas/RoRs are prepared and distributed accordingly. Few stakeholders have the means to file an appeal before Settlement Officer against orders passed by ASOs during Objection Hearing. RoRs thus prepared are presumed to be correct unless challenged and changed by competent civil courts. As such, settlement functionaries or revenue officials regardless of the position they hold have no authority to create Right and Title over land.

The vast majority of people in Scheduled Areas of Kalahandi district, namely, Lanjigarh and Thuamul Rampur Tahasils, belonged to tribal communities. Villages under survey then did not have proper road communication networks. Health and educational infrastructure beyond Block headquarters was virtually non-existent. Malaria and diarrhoea were the most-dreaded diseases, which broke out routinely particularly during summer and rainy seasons. It was not unusual to find loss of life also among settlement field staff working at village level. Supervisory ASOs and Kanungos would avoid visiting remote villages which necessitated a night halt. I discovered that some functionaries had resorted to maintaining diaries showing fake records of field visits and test-checks carried out by them. At different stages of operations, yardsticks for daily output stand prescribed for field functionaries starting from Amin to ASO, making it easy to verify the actual work done by them on day-to-day basis.

On a surprise visit to a settlement camp, which was not far from a motorable road, I was told by ASO that the Kanungo, his next in command, had gone to a remote village about 15 km away. I decided to visit the village much to the surprise of ASO even though it involved a 30 km to-and-fro trek on foot through forest hills. Reluctantly, he accompanied me. On reaching the village, the Amin reported that in the last one month none from the settlement camp had visited and inspected his work. The Kanungo's tour diary for the previous week showed check-lines drawn while supervising the work of this Amin. I told the ASO to file a missing person report at the local police station, as the possibility of Kanungo being harmed by wild animals could not be ruled out. The neighbouring forests had bears and elephants, and local people had been attacked and injured by these animals occasionally. Information about the matter reached the Kanungo, who had gone to his native village in Dhenkanal about a week back without taking leave. He appeared before me the next day seeking pardon and promised that he would never repeat such lapses in future. As I found out later, he was not only true to his promise but also transformed himself to become one of the best officers, more knowledgeable than even ASO in charge of the camp. From this Kanungo, I learnt many finer points and technical details of settlement operations. I once overheard the Settlement Officer, inquire about who was educating me on these details.

Survey and settlement field functionaries at village level mostly belonged to the traditionally more educated and enlightened coastal districts. The social atmosphere in Western and Southern Odisha including in Kalahandi was not necessarily cordial for them. The highest authority in revenue administration with quasi-judicial powers, Member, Board of Revenue, B.R. Patel, visited my residence while on tour to Bhawanipatna. He casually narrated an anecdote attributing the local hostility towards people from coastal districts to the mischief done by a settlement functionary leading to transfer of land inherited by an innocent villager to another khata during survey and settlement operations. This villager, when informed, chopped off the hands of the Amin using his axe (usually a weapon of self-defence in remote villages), and returning home stated that his land would now not be able to move to anyone else's khata as he had taken care of the root cause! Local animosity towards people from coastal districts continues to this day, though in a more subterranean latent form.

Skewed Distribution of Land

The most frightening inequity I witnessed during settlement operations was that about 90 percent of cultivable land in the majority of villages was owned by less than 10 percent of families. In some villages, the 'Gomtia' controlled almost all the agricultural land in different names to circumvent the ceiling of 10 standard acres of land per family set out in Odisha Land Reform Act. A marked disconnect between revenue field functionaries and the so-called beneficiaries from this Act was seen. In the absence of demarcations followed by handing over possession, most recipients of ceiling surplus and government waste-lands were not even aware of having been allotted land by the State Government through the local Tahasildar.

In local parlance, landless families were called "Sukha-basis". Though I had experienced poverty in my family, I had never imagined the extent of hunger, malnutrition and deprivation I saw then in parts of Kalahandi district. This situation changed for the better with the passage of time when special programmes for Kalahandi-Balangir-Koraput (KBK) Districts and Indrawati major irrigation project were implemented. Besides providing employment to the landless, Kalahandi became the granary of the State next only to Bargarh in producing marketable surpluses. Disparity between the "haves" and "have-nots" in Kalahandi and its neighbouring districts, however, has continued.

Similarly, KBK Districts remain substantially behind the State's relatively more developed districts. The composition of political power structure coupled with the tendency of the State's leadership to wash its hands simply by highlighting the backwardness have also contributed to this backwardness. If the ground reality is taken to be the real test of land reform laws, it can be safely concluded that those responsible for enactment and implementation of these laws are the ones mainly responsible for breaking them. I could draw no other conclusion after witnessing this reality while supervising survey and settlement operations in Kalahandi.

The progressive provisions of land reform and inheritance laws which, *inter alia,* did not permit ownership of land beyond 10 standard acres nor rights of absentee land-lords who leased out land illegally for share-cropping had been sabotaged by both law makers and officers responsible for implementing them. Mostly these were absentee large land-lords, but were being called upon to give effect to the provisions of the land reform and succession laws. It was a text-book case of the delinquent becoming law maker, administrator and judge. Ignorance among female family members about the legal provisions of succession law, was leveraged by many settlement field functionaries ever ready to turn a blind eye to fabricated and forged documents with fake signatures or thumb impressions of female members, particularly of daughters of the family who were not interested in their parental land. The Charge Officer, Settlement in Kalahandi did not have any statutory powers in relation to preparation of RoRs. Even administrative powers as Head of the Office were not being allowed to be exercised by Settlement Officer for reasons which suggested more than that met the eye. My tenure at Bhawanipatna was of 10 months.

FIRST EXPOSURE TO ADMINISTRATION: SUB COLLECTOR

I was transferred to Balangir Sadar as Sub-Divisional Officer and soon after as Sub-Collector and joined accordingly on 25 August 1986 within two days of receiving the posting order. For an IAS officer, this post provides the first substantive exposure in general administration and prepares the young officer to hold the most important post of Collector & District Magistrate a few years later. Duties and responsibilities discharged by Sub-Collector at sub-divisional level are similar to those of Collector & District Magistrate at wider district level.

Despite being Head of Administration, more often than not the Sub-Collector in public perception is a flunkey of the Collector who simply carries out instructions on matters referred to him. Further, unlike outer sub-divisions, due to the presence of District Collector at the same location, the value of the post of Sub-Collector of a District Headquarters' sub-division stands somewhat eroded. Even for matters to be disposed of at the level of Sub-Collector, people generally prefer to approach the Collector with their grievances. Interference in day-to-day administration by Collector, in case he was more possessive or intrusive, could become another irritant at times. Nevertheless, I did not find the assignment any less challenging and exciting. Balangir was then, and remains to this day, one of the most socio-economically backward districts. Despite being surrounded by large perennial rivers and high groundwater table, the share of agricultural land under irrigation is the lowest in the State. Drought and large-scale labour migration continue to define the district. My assignment brought out vivid experiences and insights in administration of a sub-division in all its colours and it hardly required any prescience to know that it would be of short duration.

Sadar sub-division was known for political resistance primarily initiated by a very popular leader Balgopal Mishra, an independent MLA, whose hold over the public was complete. He seemed ever ready to raise a fight against the ruling dispensation whatever its hue. Officers perceived by him as favouring the ruling party found it difficult to administer as he was prone to challenging them openly and most often using an out-of-control bruising tongue. Organizing the visit of the then Chief Minister J.B. Patnaik to Balangir district was a difficult task for district administration as the protests staged by him and his dedicated band of followers would stretch well beyond the show of black flags. Unlike the District Collector and Superintendent of Police (SP) who in his perception stood identified with the local Minister and State's ruling party, I had joined without any baggage and after some time was perceived by elected representatives across party lines as an unbiased and fair-minded functionary. Or perhaps the aggressive independent MLA simply did not consider my position worth challenging.

How Grounding in Settlement Helped

Theoretical and practical knowledge of revenue laws, particularly of RoRs, acquired during my previous assignment served me well as sub-divisional head of revenue administration. Distribution of government land and ceiling surplus land to the landless was a priority item under the "20-Point Programme" first launched in 1975 and restructured in 1982 and 1986. Besides carrying out fresh distributions, I also gave attention to verifying the appropriateness of demarcation and possession of agricultural land given to landless families in the past.

Based upon my recent experiences in Kalahandi, here too I suspected that official lapses could have happened in distribution of agricultural land to the landless in rural areas, and perhaps to a lesser extent in allotment of government waste land. Inquiries made revealed that paper-work had been done on distribution of land to the landless families, but after passing orders on ceiling surpluses, in most cases effective steps had not been taken to demarcate and hand over possession of the land. This afforded me the opportunity to actively participate in completing the task of land reform which had been undertaken by the administration rather haphazardly. Tahasildars and RIs were asked to give in writing that they had completed the task of demarcation and handing over possession of such land, and also to ensure that no gaps were allowed in future.

But during field verifications what shocked a fledging officer in me the most was to witness first hand some revenue functionaries arrogating to themselves the largesse of land meant for distribution to the landless. Land records mostly stood in the name of head of household who invariably was the senior-most male in the family. The official definition of landless excluded government servants and their families as well as those having certain amount of annual income from other sources. But some functionaries found it expedient to declare their spouse, or any other female family member, as landless in order to get land allotted in her name. I found a couple of cases where the beneficiary was the respective spouse of Personal Assistants to District Collector and of Sub-Collector who had retired in the meanwhile. Revenue functionaries like Amins and RIs usually belonged to the district, and knowingly participated in committing such outright fraud. Taking advantage of their post, some public servants were perpetrating as well abetting crime by snatching away land meant for those at the bottom rungs of poverty by exploiting inadequate understanding of their rights under law. I did my best to ensure justice for numerous beneficiaries by even taking assistance of the police wherever required. A young Additional Tahasildar of Sadar Tahasil who was officiating as Tahasildar assisted me enthusiastically in the exercise. Sadly, he died after some months due to cerebral malaria which was not diagnosed in time.

Under Odisha Land Reform Act, prior permission of Sub-Collector/ Revenue Officer is necessary for transfer of land held by Scheduled Castes (SC) and Scheduled Tribes (ST) to others. These officers in turn are required to ensure that SC/ST owner does not suffer from landlessness as a result of this transfer/sale. I felt then, and continue to do so now, that this provision has all the disadvantages of harassment and hardly any benefits for SC/ST land owners. Any person, regardless of his caste affiliation, is unlikely to sell his landed property without certain advantages or compulsions. In the case of SC/ST land owners, Sub-Collector/ Revenue Officer concerned would doubtless apply his judicial mind to get satisfied that the seller of the land has genuine grounds for the proposed transaction, but this could be of little value to the applicant himself. This condescending official stamp most of times actually hurts the interests of the land owner who runs from pillar to post to seek such permission.

Many years later, as Secretary, ST&SC Development Department, I found another instance of a legal provision hampering the translation of intent to benefit landless STs. Public sector oil companies expressed a genuine interest to invest in developing infrastructure for petrol pumps to be allotted to STs in Keonjhar and Mayurbhanj districts. But this investment benefit, which required ST land to be first mortgaged with the oil company, could not be actualised as the law in Scheduled Areas did not permit transfer or mortgage of ST lands. So, if an educated ST family wanted to sell its land for a better price to a non-ST person or wanted to mortgage it with a bank to raise a loan for investment elsewhere, the law would not permit it. To me this restriction not only appeared absurd, but also amounted to preventing upward-looking people of tribal communities from moving up on the socio-economic ladder. Although the problem is smaller in non-Scheduled Areas where members of SC/ ST communities are at least allowed to sell land albeit with prior permission of Sub-Collector/ Revenue Officer, the procedure was cumbersome amounting to debilitating harassment. This also resulted in clandestine sale and mortgage of land by SC/ STs at lower rates. In most cases where permission had been denied by my predecessors, I did not find any strong ground for doing so. Rather, I discovered that many orders denying permission had been drafted by Assistant/ Peshkar in Sub-Collector's court, which were rubber-stamped by Sub-Collector as if without any application of mind. Considerations for such orders could hardly be based on merit.

Eviction of Encroachments

A serious challenge faced by every administration is eviction of encroachment from government land in both urban and rural areas. This task is usually left to Tahasildar who, based on requisitions received from RI, initiates eviction proceedings in accordance with provisions of the Odisha Prevention of Land Encroachment (OPLE) Act. My experience conclusively showed that eviction proceedings under this law in rural areas were initiated mostly against landless people found encroaching government waste-land in order to raise some subsistence crops during Kharif season. By the time cases reach hearings stage, the crops are harvested. On the basis of another report submitted by the same RI that no encroachment exists on government land at the time of second field enquiry, the case is disposed of. In practice some corrupt RIs threaten and collect bribes from the poor encroacher, and this practice repeats itself the next year.

Performance of Tahasildars in terms of disposal of cases under various laws is reviewed in District Revenue Officers' monthly meeting and thousands of cases are shown to have been initiated and disposed of annually. This exercise becomes largely farcical. Cases against the well-to-do or otherwise important persons in rural or urban areas are rarely instituted. It is rarer still to take such rare cases to the logical end. Land along National/State highways are seen encroached near town areas or growth centres, but officers concerned hardly show any interest in eviction and wash their hands off after informing district administration orally during official meetings. Line departments remain mute spectators in most cases of encroachments on their lands and the tragedy of community land being encroached is seldom taken note of.

Curiously enough, Revenue Officers too are found ignorant about the provisions of laws to deal with encroachments. This ignorance plays into the hands of powerful encroachers, who indulge in forum shopping and playing off the provisions of one law against another. On the face of it, there are overlapping provisions in relation to jurisdiction under OPLE Act and Odisha Public Premises Eviction Act (OPPE Act). Revenue & Disaster Management (R&DM) Department administers the OPLE Act, which applies to the whole State, whereas General Administration (GA) Department is the nodal department for OPPE Act which applies to urban or certain specified areas only. Public premises under OPPE Act include government lands in specified areas and only officers notified by GA Department as Estate Officers are competent to pass orders for eviction. Except in a few important town areas, normally Sub-Collectors are required to be notified as Estate Officers. But the main problem is that GA Department rarely makes these notifications nor lays down the procedure to be followed in handling eviction cases. Much later, as Additional Chief Secretary (ACS), R&DM Department, in consultation with Law Department, I clarified to all concerned that OPPE Act being a special law and limited to specified areas should only be invoked for removal of encroachments in urban areas for which requisitions should be filed by department concerned and subordinate revenue officials wherever required.

In Balangir, I followed a different route to deal with encroachments on State and National highways and in urban areas. Tahasildars and RIs were desired to file requisitions in prescribed formats as per the provisions for dealing with public nuisance under section 133 of the Code of Criminal Procedure (Cr.P.C.). I would pass interlocutory orders as Executive Magistrate quickly for removal of public nuisance on the last working day of the week and go to the site with police force for eviction the next day. District & Sessions Judge, who entertained appeal petitions easily against orders passed by Revenue Officers and Executive Magistrates on land disputes, did not have powers to hear appeal against interlocutory orders passed under the provisions of Cr.P.C. Thus, encroachers did not have enough time to knock at the doors of High Court in Cuttack against such interlocutory orders. Some risk was always there but there is no administrative life without risks! The real test of effective administration for me was in terms of results in the larger public interest.

Encroachments of government land in important municipal areas also, though clearly visible, hardly attract the attention of enforcement administration despite the provisions under municipal laws being much stronger for their removal. Contrarily, elected members of urban local bodies are often seen promoting encroachments on urban lands, with many of them complicit in grabbing it for themselves. The organised encroachments in a locality called Salia Sahi over an area of about 200 acres of forest land and similar land around other planned housing colonies in Bhubaneswar stand testimony of how encroachments are promoted to create a solid vote bank for ruling party politicians in electoral politics. After Independence, though the State Capital Bhubaneswar was developed as a planned city along with Chandigarh, today nearly 40 percent of its population consists of slum dwellers cum encroachers. The tragedy is that encroachments are mostly planned rather than accidental. Since important persons indulge in land grabbing with impunity and the State's political policy as practised encourages encroachments on vacant public land for political gains, the compliant administration remains complacent as though providing immunity from law and blind to the distressing situation.

In Balangir Sadar, a portion of the official residence of Sub-Collector, and adjoining bus stand stood encroached. The office of Collector & District Magistrate, the head of enforcement administration was just across the road. But neither the collector nor police nor my predecessors nor officials of Works Department, though custodian of public premises, had thought it necessary to take steps to remove these encroachments. Their pretext was that such action would amount to inviting law and order problem. I felt that the concept of rule of law was being turned on its head and the very logic of law and order was being applied in a contrarian form, neither of which was acceptable. But before taking any drastic action against encroachers, who were mostly small vendors, action had to be taken against the bigger offenders to avoid allegations of any preferential treatment favouring influcntial encroachers or land grabbers. I called the local young Additional Tahasildar and the RI and desired them to prepare the list of the larger encroachments on public land with complete details of encroachers, particularly on the road-side and in centrally-located highly-priced places in district headquarter town. It would be of interest to share a few of my experiences here.

A part of the biggest hotel in Balangir town, the "Raj Mahal", financed jointly by Odisha State Finance Corporation (OSFC) and Andhra Bank stood on a valuable piece of government land. The influential promoter had received 25 percent capital investment subsidy from State Government. Not even the Revenue Department which is responsible for maintenance and updating of land records had taken note of this road-side encroachment. Though prominent, neither public nor media had reported it. In fact, my immediate predecessor had held his wedding reception in this hotel. I wanted to initiate eviction proceedings, but no government agency was inclined to file the requisition. Finding no other option, I advised the officiating Tahasildar and RI to prepare a report under Section 133 of Cr.P.C. taking the assistance of local police, if necessary, and to file it in my Court. This implied that the encroachment was to be treated as a public nuisance as it attracted a huge number of customers and created inconvenience in traffic movement. The encroacher despite knowing about the proposed action against him failed to gauge that the administration could pass interlocutory orders for removal of public nuisance and execute them thereafter. I had taken District SP on board but had not kept the Collector informed. No government department nor any public body had a heavy machine for demolishing the encroachment. I requisitioned a bulldozer of the newly-established Ordinance Factory at Saitala in Titlagarh sub-division while simultaneously passing interlocutory orders on the last working day of the week.

On a Sunday morning, police started cordoning off the area to regulate the traffic. The bulldozer arrived. Sensing the inevitable now, the hotel owner came to the site along with President of Balangir Bar Association, a top advocate in the district, to protest against my orders describing them as illegal and actions smacking of highhandedness. After citing the relevant provisions of the Indian Penal Code to the President of Balangir Bar Association, I warned both of them against creating any obstruction when a public servant was discharging duties in public interest. The advocate left the spot. In no time the structure on encroached land was raised to the ground with a massive roar echoing in the entire town. Along with my subordinate enforcement staff I then left the site leaving the task of maintaining law and order to the police personnel instructing them to keep me and SP informed about any untoward incident or for any intervention as and when needed. I remember that none other than the hotelier was agitating and indeed people around were celebrating and appreciating the administrative action. People from far and wide started visiting the demolition site as if something good worth seeing had happened. It is usually seen that the society at large applauds just actions taken by administration even if with heavy hands against bigger culprits more than the initiatives in implementing developmental projects. The promoter of the hotel did file a case against me in the High Court claiming damages, and I had to hire a private advocate as Advocate General initially refused to defend me on the ground that I had been made a party in person. Subsequently on instructions from Revenue Department, a senior government advocate helped me in preparing my counter. I don't know as to what happened thereafter as I never received any further notice from High Court.

My next target was eviction of encroachments from the bus stand and adjoining areas including a portion of my own residential compound on which pucca structures had been erected and stationery shops, vegetable vending, etc. were being run. As eviction would affect the livelihoods of some encroachers for some time to come, I made alternative arrangements for their rehabilitation at a corner of the town where the Regulated Market Committee (RMC) headed by me had constructed a market sheds which were unoccupied. Considering their relatively remote location, vendors were not inclined to move to these fully-constructed sheds offered to them at nominal fee. But I was determined to clear the encroached areas. I again took recourse to the Cr.P.C. treating encroachments as public nuisance and personal equations formed with SP worked to get me police support, though normally police personnel remain evasive in taking such risks. Despite the number of affected persons being large, there was no major resistance during eviction operations on the basis of my interlocutory orders. However, some damage was caused to my residential compound in retaliation. The next morning, I woke up to find that the flowering plants had been chopped off, walls were defaced, the main gate including my name plate had been damaged and some dirt, including excreta, had been thrown inside the compound. At the end of the day public at large was happy to find an end to public nuisance and anarchy at the bus stand and its environs.

Precious endowment properties of Gopalji Temple including Rajashri Dharmashala in the centre of town were in occupation of some traders and certain anti-social elements. As Sub Collector, I had been notified as Executive Officer, Endowment, and responsibility fell on me to protect and maintain them. The occupants of these endowment properties had stopped paying monthly rents for more than ten years despite the amount being small. State Endowment Commissioner had not released funds for maintenance of its valuable immovable assets either. I wanted to discuss the matter with the unauthorized occupants, but none was inclined to participate in the talks. Rajashri Dharmashala was a large double-storeyed old building with a sprawling compound. When I went for its inspection, I found a large hall being used as a centre/ adda by bootleggers and gamblers. Anti-social elements were in control of a few other rooms used for various illegal activities, including prostitution. Executive Engineer of Works Department accompanying me stated that the building had become unsafe due to lack of maintenance and agreed to issue a certificate to that affect. I had now a very powerful idea which could be used to rid the Dharmashala from unauthorized occupation on grounds of public safety. Thus, notices were issued and publicised for eviction of occupants who were also directed to pay arrear rents at rates which were revised retrospectively in case they wished to avoid legal actions against them, including seizure of their goods, which included huge quantities of coal, salt, cement, etc. They were given one month's time orally for compliance. As though reluctantly, they paid the arrear rents as per the revised rates which was about ₹ 1 lakh cumulatively. The anti-social elements vanished before proceedings could start against them under the preventive provisions of Cr.P.C. I utilised the services of Block Engineers, under the supervision of Executive Engineer, of Works Department for renovation of this massive Rajashri Dharmashala. The task, including fencing of property by raising a compound wall, was completed on war-footing within two months by utilising the arrear rents.

For reasons not known to me, District Collector who was seen to be identified with the local minister became unhappy with me for the eviction drive I had started, and particularly of Gopalji Temple premises and Rajashri Dharmashala. Finding the new reality, he without consulting me and going beyond his jurisdiction suddenly issued an order allotting the renovated building and its entire compound to a private school, and that too free of cost! I did not know the reasons for the generosity shown by District Collector towards the private school at the cost of endowment department. I would not have objected to the functioning of a public school from the premises on payment of some rent to Gopalji Temple Trust based on due process being followed. I found out later that District Collector was at oars drawn with me because I had evicted an NGO headed by a lady social worker from government land by the side of a Sanskrit college in the town. Students and teachers of this college had brought to my notice that their play-ground had been encroached restricting their physical activities. What really got my goat, however, was receiving a reprimand, incidentally in my wife's presence, from the Collector when we visited his residence on his invitation, a few days later. It became evident that with the support of District Collector, the NGO wanted to remain in control of the land without any right. I was bluntly told to lift my prohibitory orders. I responded that as the senior-most Executive Magistrate in the district, he could review my orders or advise the so-called social worker to approach the court of District Judge to assert her right, title and possession over the land in question. I added that I would not lift the prohibitory order until I was fully satisfied that there was no danger to peace in the locality. I left his residence shortly thereafter and never visited his house again. Not surprisingly his attitude towards me became increasingly vindictive with the passage of time in this posting as well as in my subsequent one.

I remained focused on my duties without being deterred by considerations that had the potential to affect my professional career so early in life. I was informed by some officers that the Collector had recorded adverse observations about me in my confidential Annual Performance Appraisal. But, Revenue Divisional Commissioner (RDC) who had a good impression about me apprised me some time later that he had not supported the District Collector's remarks. As providence would further have it, 25 years later when I was serving as Principal Secretary of R&DM Department, this District Collector visited me to plead for release of family pension to the widow of his younger brother, an OAS officer who had met an untimely death a few years back. The claims of the widow had remained unsettled for years because of large liabilities created while her husband was in service and gaps and complications in his service record. I went out of the way to rebuild the service record and paved the way for payment of family pension to his widow. I did not believe in allowing any past bitterness to colour my professional duties, and always tried to do whatever was humanly possible to ease matters for those in need.

The State highway from Balangir to Sambalpur had been heavily encroached from both sides at a place called Salebhata, which incidentally was the native place of the said aggressive independent MLA. Large contingents of his supporters frequently indulged in extortion and rioting employing various methods. Illicit brewing and trading of country liquor was being done openly, but none from Excise Department could dare to raid this place and initiate action. One day when the MLA visited my office, I apprised him of my intention to evict the encroachments at Salebhata. Since he and government pleader too were found to have encroached some government land, they were also liable for action. He told me to do whatever was considered necessary in pursuance of legal provisions and made it clear indirectly that he too was not happy with the state of affairs created by his foot soldiers at Salebhata. He wanted some advance hint about the date of enforcement to enable him to avoid witnessing any unpleasant situation. Since Executive Engineer, Works Department, was evasive and unwilling to file requisitions for the eviction under Section 133 of Cr.P.C., I again desired Tahasildar and RI to furnish them. During the proceedings in my Court, when the names of the government pleader, whom I had come to regard well over time, and of the MLA were called along with those of others, I had to school myself to show equanimity and remain detached. Within a fortnight of the cases being filed interlocutory orders were passed, and the very next day I was there with police force and district SP to enforce the order. More than 100 structures were demolished. There was hardly any resistance despite some initial verbal threats. Encroachers voluntarily removed their movable assets and there was no need for use of force. I had told the Executive Engineer to deploy enough manpower and materials to immediately start and complete widening of the road and construction of drains on both sides, and on this issue, he effectively utilised the opportunity. After a fortnight, the independent MLA again met me in my office and complimented for the peaceful enforcement and widening of road at Salebhata.

Some houses had been damaged due to heavy hailstorm in Salebhata about a couple of months prior to this drive. But villagers had not been permitting revenue field functionaries to enumerate the damaged houses. They wanted the list prepared by them to be accepted without any scrutiny and grant of financial assistance under the Relief Code to every listed family. This unreasonable demand was unacceptable. Right after encroachment eviction was carried out, their resistance vanished. Enumeration of damaged houses too was smoothly completed. Illicit liquor trade by and large also became a thing of the past.

Eviction drives against encroachers elsewhere did not face any hurdles after the humps were smoothly crossed at Salebhata. Almost all road-side encroachments in Balangir Sadar were cleared without use of force. In fact, people from other parts of the district not aware of limitation of my jurisdiction, started appearing with petitions in my grievance cell for eviction of encroachments elsewhere. I enjoyed public good will and confidence, perhaps more than I truly deserved. Although I spent most of my time in supervising implementation of anti-poverty programmes and revenue (land administration) related work, people were more appreciative of my enforcement work, which at times was painful for me as I found their impression influenced by feudal mindset, a legacy from the colonial past.

Other Revenue Administration Functions

Collection of land revenue (cess) and penalties against encroachments and unauthorised removal of minor minerals were other important functions performed through RIs and Tahasildars. Though the amount collected barely contributed to the State exchequer, the activities enabled revenue functionaries at the village level to maintain contact with the tenants and helped in updating of RoRs. It also helped in ensuring that government or community land was not encroached upon and sairat sources were not illegally exploited by unscrupulous elements. The Sub-Collector's role was largely supervisory with regard to revenue collection. Under Public Demand Recovery Act, he was the senior-most revenue officer at sub-division level to handle larger defaulters, including acting on requisitions for recovery received from financial institutions against loan defaulters.

On a few occasions, I was threatened and intimidated by some influential persons. I had issued orders attaching their immovable properties which were publicized through "beat of drum" in the entire town as required by law. They naturally felt humiliated. I remember a High Court lawyer warned me by recalling that a very senior officer of my service in trouble for being implicated in a corruption case had been successfully defended by him in High Court, and that I should not be over enthusiastic nor overrate my position in administration at such an initial stage of my career. After all, how could I know what lay in store for me! A young MLA-cum-Deputy Chief Whip of the ruling party issued a statement which was comprehensively published in a daily newspaper that I had tried to molest his sister by entering their house when he was away from home. The fact of the matter was that I had never even seen his house. The piece of land owned by him had been attached on the basis of a property statement furnished by Tahasildar. About six years later, this MLA who had by then changed his political loyalty to another party, was my friendly neighbour in Bhubaneswar. I also antagonized the erstwhile ruler of Patnagarh Princely Estate; an important political leader of the main opposition party for attachment of his property. All the three eminent persons had to clear their dues, perhaps recognizing that I had no ulterior motives nor any intention to humiliate them. Revenue field functionaries who had unsuccessfully approached these defaulters in the past felt very happy to witness the administration finally catching up with them. Collection of revenue by tahasils of Sadar Sub-Division registered substantial growth during that year.

Implementation of Priority Sector Programmes

I recognised that the reality of skewed land-holding pattern seen in Kalahandi was hardly different in its neighbour Balangir. It was thus of great interest to ensure implementation of land reform laws including distribution of government waste-land and land confirmed as ceiling surplus to the landless and to deploy other tools in the hands of administration to address some of the problems of the poorest of the poor. The task, however, was easier said than done. In Balangir, the bulk of population belonging to SC and other backward classes was landless and depended upon landlords for livelihood. Many of those resided either in small huts within the residential compound of their masters or in huts constructed on community or government land. They had no choice but to work as captive farm labour-cum-domestic help. To refuse such bondage meant forced vacation of their meagre dwellings and even eviction from the village. They were known as "Sukh Basis" in Balangir too. Migration of landless families in search of labour to other parts of the country continues to be highest in Balangir even today. It was, therefore, necessary to focus on implementing poverty-alleviation and employment-generating schemes where the chances of success were more.

It was a new experience for me in general administration and I was not aware of a different public perception about the post I was holding. Even as I held the weekly court without break and enjoyed the challenges of enforcement administration, my heart yearned for undivided attention to implementing projects leading to creation of durable community assets. I tried to squirrel out more hours in a day to spend my maximum time in field visits to interact with beneficiaries of poverty alleviation schemes and community leaders including elected representatives at Village Panchayat and Panchayat Samiti levels. I also held frequent coordination meetings at Block and Sub-Division levels with officers of line departments and financial institutions.

The most important beneficiary-oriented income-generating scheme was Integrated Rural Development Programme (IRDP). It called for identification of families below the poverty line at village level, sponsoring of their applications by Block/ Panchayat Samiti with viable income-generating schemes to a specified bank branch, and sanction/ disbursement of subsidized loans in the form of income-generating assets for providing gainful self-employment to beneficiaries. As per schematic guidelines, the officer heading the bank branch was required to conduct an appraisal of the scheme before sanctioning the loan. In lieu of loan disbursement in cash a beneficiary would get income-generating assets, and thereafter, admissible subsidy varying from 33 percent for general caste to 50 percent for SC/ST families would get adjusted. Disbursement of loan would happen in what were called 'loan melas' (credit festivals) attended by senior government and bank functionaries besides local public representatives.

My experience in the initial days of implementing IRDP was quite exciting. However, soon enough, I realized that critical gaps made it less viable in more ways than one. Not only was the scheme vitiated by motivated choice of beneficiaries, the absence of both requisite skills and backward-forward linkages needed to be plugged. But the singular message being given by elected representatives to beneficiaries was that there was no need for them to repay the credit sanctioned by financial institutions. This not only led to corrupt practices in sanctioning loans and procuring income-generating assets by purchase committees at Block level, but also made disbursement of full unit cost perpetually incomplete. At times the beneficiaries would not be aware of the amount of loan and subsidy sanctioned and disbursed in their favour. Naturally, recovery of loan was bound to be affected. With regard to skills, Training of Rural Youth for Self-Employment (TRYSEM) was taken up as a sub-scheme of IRDP. Its implementation was constrained by the absence of qualified master trainers. Nevertheless, finding them useful, I tried to organise all possible trainings for masonry, carpentry, plumbing, electrical fittings, tailoring, etc.

There were other schemes under implementation at the same time on the pattern of IRDP. Small and Marginal Farmers' Programme (SMFP) envisaged subsidy of 25 percent for small and 33 percent for marginal farmers for land development, dug-wells and energisation to promote agriculture. Special Central Assistance was received by Blocks for SC/ST families below the poverty line to implement schemes similar to those under IRDP. BDOs had to ensure identification of eligible beneficiaries and sponsor their applications to the banks for the subsidized loan. A State sector income generating scheme called Economic Rehabilitation of Rural Poor (ERRP) meant exclusively for landless poor and released bonded labour was also under implementation. In Balangir, no bonded labourers had been released from captivity of their tormentors. But, a large number of landless 'Sukh Basis' had been identified as bonded labourers who eked out their livelihood by virtually working as captive workers of land-owing class, particularly Gomtias. Sub-Collector had powers to release bonded labourers and punish those who kept them as captives in addition to a supervisory role in implementing the bonded labour rehabilitation programme.

Banking network in Balangir was grossly inadequate. Balangir Anchalik Gramya Bank which had the largest number of branches in rural areas was bordering on bankruptcy. Recovery of loans was negligible. Achievements in implementing income-generating schemes were thus far from satisfactory. When administrative support for recovery against earlier loans was extended, financial institutions commenced sanctioning fresh loans. Balangir Sadar Sub-Division performed far better than the other four Sub-Divisions in implementing all these anti-poverty and rural development programmes. Perhaps for this reason, a few months later on being promoted to senior time scale, I was posted as Project Officer/ Project Director, DRDA, Balangir.

National Rural Employment Programme (NREP) replaced 'Food-for-Work' Programme with enhanced coverage and allocations in 1980. Its primary objectivewas generation of wage employment in rural areas. Workers received wages partly in cash and partly in foodgrains at subsidized rates. This was the period when India was in the process of achieving self-sufficiency in production of foodgrains and the national policy provided for distribution of foodgrains at cheaper rates to the poor who did not have agricultural land and needed to be assured of food security in some form. Creation of community assets of durable nature was its secondary objective. The ratio between cash and material components to be maintained in implementing community projects, which included primary school buildings, was 60:40. A minimum of 10 percent of allocation at district level was necessarily to be spent on social forestry.

I found a large number of cross-drainage works, community centres, primary school buildings, etc. abandoned since they required more than 60 percent cost towards material component leading to infructuous expenditure. I suggested to the six Panchayat Samitis under my Sub-Division that rather than maintaining it project-wise, the ratio of 60:40 on wage and material components should more sensibly be taken against total allocations under NREP. I also suggested that preference should go to completion of incomplete projects while planning for the subsequent year instead of taking up only new projects. This helped us complete a large number of primary school buildings, community centres and cross drainage structures which had remained incomplete or abandoned. NREP with 50:50 cost-sharing between the Centre and State was conceptually sound. The problems, however, were in the implementing guidelines issued by Central Government, which literally straight-jacketed the implementation as if these were provisions of law. The policy makers probably lacked practical field experience and State Government did not have resources to fill the critical gaps. I discovered with heightened distress that earthworks in projects like excavation and renovation of village tanks or formation of village roads which provided more wage employment, were seen to hold out higher scope for fudging of accounts and misutilisation of NREP allocations. 10 percent of the allocation stood earmarked for construction of houses for SC/ST beneficiaries under a sub scheme called Indira Awas Yojana (IAY).

Rural Landless Employment Guarantee Programme (RLEGP) was introduced in 1983 in the Central Sector intended to generate employment. However, it did not permit expenditure for projects of durable nature which generally involved high expenditure on material components. It is difficult to say that RLEGP succeeded in achieving its objective as the limited allocations received could hardly guarantee 100 days of wage employment to one member of each landless family in rural areas. On an average, each Block with a population of about one lakh received allocation of ₹ 10-15 lakh annually. 10 percent funds were to be utilized for afforestation which could be in terms of either fresh plantations or trench-fencing and gap-filling of existing village forests to allow better growth through regeneration. As in NREP, 10 percent allocation under RLEGP needed to be spent for SC/ST houses under IAY.

A major problem rarely visualized at the time of launching of schemes I felt was that no assessment of logistics was made in advance. Many schemes with similar or same objectives were introduced by multiple departments and administration at the cutting edge was not equipped to handle them. This affected the quality of implementation while objectives to be achieved remained almost as distant as ever. I thought there was no need to come up with multiple income generating schemes and rural employment programmes. A better course of action would have been to increase scope and allocations in limited number of schemes while unshackling implementing guidelines. Execution of projects under NREP was done through village committee leaders, whereas under RLEGP line departments held sway. Engagement of contractors was not permissible though smaller contractors were still at work in the garb of village committee leaders.

Indira Awas Yojana (IAY) was merged in Jawahar Rozgar Yojana (JRY) in 1989 only to make it a standalone scheme in 1996. Indeed, JRY itself was a merger of NREP and RLEGP. Curiously enough, the unit cost of a house including sanitary latrine stood differentiated at ₹ 7,500 under NREP and ₹ 6,500 RLEGP despite specifications remaining the same. Implementation of IAY could be done either through Village Committee Leaders or through the beneficiary. Schematic guidelines at that time also provided for construction of a colony with not less 15 houses in one place though it was difficult to find government land for such a large number of beneficiaries at one place inside the main village. Since State Government had a separate programme for distribution of homestead land in rural areas for landless and homeless poor, it was a practice to construct housing colonies for beneficiaries on land allotted to them. This was happening mechanically and at times without consulting beneficiaries. Since land allotted was invariably a bit away from the main village, allottees were hardly interested in occupying the new housing colonies in the absence of requisite infrastructure and alternative means of livelihood. The poor identified under IAY depended upon the relatively better off sections of the village community for sustenance and did not like to move away from the village to stay in isolated houses constructed for them under IAY.

My advice to Panchayat Samitis was to execute houses through beneficiaries as far as possible, and involve them even if execution was done through Village Committee Leaders. There was no point in wasting funds for construction of houses which were not to be inhabited. I also issued clear instructions to Tahasildars to allot homestead land to eligible persons inside the main village or in close vicinity. During survey and settlement operations and formation of revenue villages, it was mandatory to earmark at least 10 percent of total village area for community use which included grounds for easement, cremation, animal grazing, village forest, etc. Since the land-man ratio was not unfavourable, in most villages land earmarked for community purposes was more than 10 percent. I instructed the Tahasildars to also furnish proposals for dereservation of community land in excess of 10 percent closer to main habitations and pending approval by competent authority, to allot it as homestead land to eligible persons. Allotted land needed to be demarcated in the presence of allottees, with pattas (RORs) given to them simultaneously. Once BDOs were on board, this arrangement became effective.

This arrangement was supported by Collector and elected representatives. Serving as Project Director, DRDA Balangir, I could readily extend it to other Blocks in Balangir, and later on in Sambalpur district also. There was no case of houses constructed under IAY remaining unoccupied during my tenure in these posts or even in the district where I served as Collector. It is necessary to have conviction in beneficiary-centric programmes and sincerity to implement them. The officer should place himself in the shoes of the beneficiary to visualize its outcome and internalize the reality rather than implementing it blindly. There is also no alternative to involving beneficiaries for successful implementation. Expenditure-driven, target-oriented, mechanical approach and ulterior motives of officials and non-officials are typically the real causes of mismatch between objectives and outcomes, I sometimes felt.

Public Distribution System and Social Welfare Schemes

Sub-Collector in those days also played a key role in implementing social welfare programmes such as Public Distribution System (PDS), promotion of elementary education, health sector schemes of immunization, small family norms, etc. Misappropriation of essential commodities meant for PDS by retailers and storage agents, most of whom were associated with the ruling party, was common. Sub-Collector had powers to suspend and cancel retailership but could do nothing against storage agents even if they were found conniving wholescale in such misappropriation. Since some wholesalers and storage agents were also involved in procurement of levy rice, it was not uncommon to find them recycling levy rice in the name of procurement and public distribution. Nothing more than reporting such irregularity to District Civil Supply Officer (DCSO) and Collector could be done.I benefitted immensely in understanding the issues in PDS and used this exposure later on as Collector & District Magistrate and further on as Chairman & Managing Director (CMD) of Odisha State Civil Supply Corporation (OSCSC) to deal with such offenders of law.

I proactively participated in promoting small family norms, despite being part of a large family, by organizing sterilization camps and achieved better results than any other sub-division against annual targets. Elementary education always held special interest for me and I tried to improve the conditions of residential schools specially meant for SC/ST students. Their pathetic conditions could also be attributed to delays in allotment and misappropriation of stipend money. Distribution of scholarships among SC/ST students needed to be done through Welfare Extension Officers posted in Block Offices, which I supervised closely through an Additional DWO posted in the office of Sub-Collector. Besides monitoring timely distribution of stipends to SC/ST students, I encouraged sports events and cultural functions in these schools.

Unnecessary Administrative Rituals

Regular visits to villages followed by intensive reviews of ongoing programmes in Blocks and Tahasils exposed me to the gaps between presentation on paper and ground reality. I however, found that field visits and night-halts by some officers were more to enjoy sumptuous lunches and dinners arranged for them by subordinate field functionaries rather than conducting reviews aimed at improving the delivery system and analysing the difficulties or guiding field staff. I had gone through the patently superficial inspection and tour notes of District Collector and other senior officers, which rarely addressed issues deserving attention. "Book Circulars" of State Government, issued in 1950s and 1960s, called for 10 night-halts every month for Collector and Sub-Collector individually in remote villages to address public grievances. Night-halts had become a ritual with the stated objective rarely being achieved. I did not find the necessity nor justification for me to make such night-halts as it took only a couple of hours to return to District Headquarters from any of the villages. I could never understand as to how work that could not be done during the day would be performed better by a visiting officer at night. Some aspects of the Book Circulars had become irrelevant over time with improvements in communication systems, but these were still being required to be followed. Perforce on a few occasions, and only to avoid any adverse observation of Collector for not making night-halts, I left for field visits in the evening carrying my dinner from home to spend the night in some Revenue Inspection bungalow in a remote location. I never wanted my subordinate field staff to make camp arrangements for me and indeed embarrassed the Collector when I had to be present during his inspection of a Block office at Agalpur. To follow this inspection, for lunch the BDO had arranged a lavish vegetarian and non-vegetarian repast. Being habituated to boiled vegetarian food at home, I picked up a few items and paid the official in the presence of Collector. Years later as administrative head of State's R&DM Department, I revised the old Book Circulars making night-halts need-based considering the improved road and telecommunication systems and reduced size of districts after their reorganisation.

In ranking, my sub-division held the top slot in implementing all the important flagship schemes and revenue-related works including disposal of court cases. RDC, Sambalpur found his visits to my sub-division satisfying and commended me. When he became Secretary of Community Development & Rural Reconstruction (CD&RR) Department, I was appointed as Project Director of DRDA of Balangir district on my transfer. Perhaps, this happened without consulting the District Collector who had assessed me adversely or even against his wishes.

FLAVOUR OF FIRST PROMOTION: PROJECT DIRECTOR IN DRDA, BALANGIR

After promotion to senior scale, I had continued as Sub-Collector for a couple of months as the post had been upgraded, until I was transferred and posted as Project Director (titled Project Officer then), District Rural Development Agency (DRDA), Balangir. I joined on 8 April 1987. Since I was already aware of most of the developmental schemes and programmes, having supervised their implementation with interest as Sub-Collector, there was no difficulty in getting under the skin of my new assignment quickly.

DRDA Balangir was created in 1980 by substituting Small Farmers' Development Agency, primarily for implementing IRDP. The DRDA at the district became the nodal body for supervising all the family-oriented poverty alleviation schemes, namely, IRDP, IAY, TRYSEM, ERRP, SMFP, Bonded Labour Rehabilitation, and Development of Women and Children in Rural Areas and the two main employment-generating programmes, viz. NREP and RLEGP. Additionally, a special scheme called Drought Prone Area Programme (DPAP) which covered eight out of the twenty Blocks of Balangir was also handled by the DRDA. The eight Blocks included all five Blocks of Titlagarh and three Blocks of Patnagarh sub-divisions being chronically-affected by drought. The situation was actually dichotomous as the district was home to a number of perennial and semi-perennial rivers, and yet it had the least facilities for irrigation in the entire State. Two mighty perennial rivers of Odisha flowed through it; Mahanadi on one side and Tel on the other. Over and above, the ground water table was quite high, though its exploitation was virtually nil. Thus, the only way to arrest forced migration of even those who had some agricultural land was by laying emphasis on development of irrigation potential, moisture conservation measures and promotion of land-based activities.

All the beneficiary-oriented income generating programmes barring ERRP were sponsored by Union Government. Availability of resources depended upon utilisation of allocations already received. Central Sector Schemes were fully funded by Central Government whereas costs were shared equally in Centrally Sponsored Schemes between the Centre and State. At times, inability on the part of the State Government to provide matching share would result in reduction of allocations to the district.

Overturning Mismanagement and Implementation of Schemes

My predecessor in DRDA was a senior OAS officer, a local man with a decidedly regulatory approach in discharging his work. He viewed the guidelines of schemes with exactitude, and raised objections against any creative interpretations even when these were aimed at improving outcomes. He was extremely conservative in releasing funds to executing agencies which had resulted in piling of funds in savings bank accounts of DRDA and poor achievements in implementing programmes. For every small decision, he sought the approval of District Collector, who was ex-officio Chairman of DRDA. An imbalance in allocation of funds among executing agencies was also seen. Despite norms being fixed for allocations, Blocks/ Panchayat Samitis headed by opposition party leaders stood invariably discriminated. I had not understood this situation fully as Sub-Collector earlier. Balangir district occupied bottom slot in State-wide ranking despite resorting to financial sleights of hand to show expenditures but without implementing income-generating projects and wage employment schemes correspondingly.

Governing Body of DRDA comprised of elected representatives, viz. MLAs, Member of Parliament (MP) and chairpersons of selected Panchayat Samitis. Project Director served as its Chief Executive Officer (CEO). In order to achieve the scheme-wise targets set by the State Government, the main task before the Governing Body was thus to discuss and approve plans and programmes in accordance with the guidelines of specific schemes taking into account the annual budget provisions and allocations of funds. It was required to meet at least once every quarter to review the progress and make changes, as and when required, in the Annual Action Plan.

In reality DRDA Balangir was not habituated to meet as required. When the Governing Body met, a statement containing allocations received under various schemes from Government and released to Blocks and other executing agencies as per approval of District Collector was placed for perusal or ex-post facto approval. Its most aggressive member, an independent MLA, invariably complained that meetings were not being held regularly and that the release of funds was discretionary and discriminatory. But hardly any other member opted to support him. Effective coordination with line departments and banks was missing. Release of funds to Blocks and other executing agencies needed to be done following well set out norms of the scheme at issue taking into account the percentage of SCs/STs, small and marginal farmers, landless labourers, number of identified bonded labourers, relative backwardness, sectoral weightage, etc. However, it seemed that these norms were either not understood or were simply being ignored. Analysis of the resulting allocations showed that undue preference was being accorded to Blocks and areas represented by ruling party leaders. Holding regular meetings of DRDA's Governing Body would at least have ensured release of funds transparently with recourse to discretion becoming difficult, if not impossible. In a nutshell, DRDA was working like a post office or a section of the Collectorate.

In the given circumstances, it was but natural that my predecessor desirous of not being transferred out of his native district could hardly be effective on the job. Neither bank officials nor executing agencies followed his occasional communications to them. Banks were more interested in deposits while executing agencies knew that DRDA had no option but to depend upon them for implementing the expenditure-driven schemes. The result was a mis-match between the targets and achievements on the one hand and significant misuse of funds both by banks and executing agencies on the other. It was virtually left to the effectiveness of Sub-Collectors in supervising the ongoing schemes through Blocks. The details of coverage of beneficiaries, generation of employment man-days, creation of community assets and other achievements reported by Blocks and line departments, were simply transmitted to the State Government, which did not find the results satisfactory. The poor performance of the district, coupled with rampant labour migration and other sufferings due to chronic drought, frequently invited embarrassing criticism, even as substantial funds for implementing poverty alleviation schemes and employment generating programmes remained unutilised.

Streamlining Office and Field Administration

Realizing the enormity and systemic nature of many problems, I worked hard to streamline systems for release of funds to Blocks and other executing agencies and ensured adherence with the prescribed guidelines. As Sub-Collector, Balangir Sadar, I used to hold review meetings at the end of each month in which BDOs, officials of line departments and lead bank invariably participated. After each meeting, I would release a review note indicating achievements and ranking of executing agencies, especially BDOs in my sub-division. Now as Project Director, DRDA, my area of operation extended to the entire district which had five sub-divisions. All the executing agencies were called upon to unfailingly furnish monthly progress reports indicating physical and financial achievements in prescribed formats at the end of every month. I again made it a point to hold monthly review meetings on fixed dates. Review notes which contained performance ranking of Blocks and Sub-Divisions were released within a week of a review meeting. Doubts raised were answered and clarifications sought by executing agencies were provided during these meetings.

These monthly exercises revealed gaps between funds received and physical and financial achievements of executing agencies. Huge balances were found lying with Blocks, line departments, namely, General Manager, District Industries Centre (DIC) for training under TRYSEM, Divisional Forest Officer (DFO) for afforestation, Chief District Veterinary Officer for development of animal husbandry-related infrastructure projects, Odisha Lift Irrigation Corporation and Odisha Agro-industries Corporation for installation of community lift irrigation points and supply of pumpsets for energisation of dug wells, and with Soil Conservation and Minor Irrigation Departments for soil conservation measures and renovation of minor irrigation projects. Even without spending these funds, utilisation certificates had been submitted by my predecessors! The distortions and imbalances were also due to failure in pointing out and in following the relevant norms for release of funds. I discussed the matter with senior officers, including Director, Special Project, in CD&RR Department (now Panchayat Raj Department) and decided not to submit files for release of funds to District Collector for his approval; and instead started releasing funds following the budget provisions and guidelines in time.

In the course of interactions with Block officials and beneficiaries, it was noticed that achievements under IRDP and other schemes were being reported after the release of subsidy to banks but before disbursement of loan or in some cases after its part disbursement. Beneficiaries were being branded as defaulters even without disbursement of the entire unit of subsidised loan. I found a large number of dug wells incomplete on the lands of small and marginal farmers as only the subsidy portion had been disbursed, that too partially, though full achievements had been reported to the State Government. Coverage of beneficiaries who wanted to execute houses directly under IAY was similarly being reported after release of the first instalment and without pursuing actual construction of houses. The practice was to show a higher coverage of beneficiaries than even the annual targets. Compounding these lacunae with lack of monitoring contributed to the so-called beneficiaries often utilising the assistance received by them under IAY for consumption purposes instead. Village Committee Leaders who were de facto contractors and were involved in implementing IAY could not also be held responsible as they did not receive the allocations fully. Blocks, especially represented by other than the ruling party, were found receiving funds far below their entitlements. DRDA was responsible for such distortions and irregularities to a great extent.

I took steps to convene meetings of the Governing Body of DRDA at regular intervals. Agenda notes for discussion were drawn up. I made sure that these provided full details of allocations received or likely to be received by DRDA alongside releases made or proposed to be made to various Blocks and other executing agencies in the district, in addition to scheme wise expenditure incurred during the previous quarters. Annual targets and achievements were placed before it for deliberation. Compliances on decisions taken in earlier meetings were also placed for perusal.

As a result of systematic monitoring and timely release of funds, the performance of Balangir district started improving steadily. The district ceased to occupy the bottom slot in ranking across various schemes. Members of the Governing Body of DRDA appreciated the improvements and transparency in release of funds, cutting across party lines. There was virtually no acrimony or dissenting voice during my tenure barring a few exceptions. Achievements were no longer reported to Government only on the basis of release of funds to executing agencies. Senior officers of CD&RR Department visited the district appreciated the change. Director, Special Project, issued instructions to other DRDAs to follow the monitoring practice adopted by DRDA, Balangir. I felt greatly encouraged.

My effectiveness greatly depended upon timely allocations and in ensuring that no more than 25 percent of extra works including IAY houses were taken up for execution. It was also essential to ensure that the first charge of funds in subsequent releases was on completion of incomplete works. Considering the large number of incomplete primary school buildings under NREP and houses under IAY, there was very little scope for release of funds under these two schemes for fresh works except to a few Blocks that stood discriminated. In a short period of six months, the number of completed and now usable community assets increased substantially and exceeded that of the previous year due to higher attention to completion of works languishing unattended on account of instructions not to spend more than 40 percent of the project cost on the materials component. Across schemes accountability for performance was fixed. Recovery efforts initiated by banks were supplemented by involving Block officials. I also attended a few recovery melas every month which sent a positive signal encouraging financial institutions to remain involved in implementing income generating schemes.

Public administration is never a popularity contest. I had driven this point home with my teams and stakeholders regardless of consequences from the very beginning of my service. My faith in the ability of field functionaries was rarely shaken. Many a times, they performed way beyond my expectations once it was digested that there was no option but to work hard with sincerity and accountability.

I remember an important instance when in a meeting held by District Collector, 56 houses were decided to be constructed within a couple of months under IAY in Nuagaon village of Godvella Block in time for inauguration by Chief Minister during his forthcoming official visit to Balangir district. After seven days when I visited the site without informing the BDO, I saw hardly any activity on the ground. Greatly worried, I proceeded to the Block office reaching there after 8:00 p.m. There was no regular BDO, and the officer in charge was not in good health. I summoned the junior engineer who needed to execute the work departmentally and again proceeded to the construction site reaching there around 10.30 p.m. in pitch dark. The site surrounded by forests was more than two km away from the main village. I was angry with the junior engineer for his negligence and left him at the dissolute site telling him that if he failed to bring all 56 houses up to the plinth level within 10 days and up to roof level in three weeks, he would have to suffer departmental proceedings for major penalty. The next evening when I again visited without notice, the construction site stood transformed to one being developed on a war-footing. More than 100 persons including members of beneficiary families were at work. Heavy earth moving machines were being used for land-levelling. Layout of houses had been given. After interacting with beneficiaries, I left the place informing the junior engineer that I would visit the site every week and that arrangements of workers like masons, carpenters, etc. and construction materials would need to be made to achieve the weekly milestones I had set. The junior engineer, who executed the project departmentally involving the beneficiary families, followed the timelines without deviations. He had innovatively drawn water required for construction from the nearby rivulet using a long plastic pipe and a diesel pump set. A few brick manufacturing units following the conventional method were also put up on the site itself involving some villagers who had requisite expertise. Before the houses were given finishing touches, five new tube wells had been sunk in different locations to meet the consumption need of safe drinking water. Mandatorily, sanitary latrines were constructed, though I found after some time that many beneficiaries were using them for storage of household goods as they felt more comfortable with open air defecation!

The houses were ready seven days before the due date of inauguration. When I asked the junior engineer as to how he had managed when in anger I had dropped him alone in an isolated place at 10.30 p.m. in a dark night, he informed me smilingly that his fellow junior engineer had followed my jeep on his motor cycle maintaining a safe distance to avoid detection and a few minutes after my departure, he had given him a ride back to the Block colony! I complimented the junior engineer for doing a fantastic job of constructing the colony by exceeding my expectations. I found that he too was very happy having demonstrated his potential and conveyed his gratitude for opening his eyes. Over the years, I found him to be one of the best performers who indeed enhanced my confidence in the capabilities of field functionaries.

As programmed, Chief Minister inaugurated the newly constructed colony by distributing "land pattas" and "keys" to beneficiaries. He conveyed appreciation in the open public meeting by stating that this was the best housing colony he had seen and inaugurated. District Collector, while proposing vote of thanks took credit for the entire work though he had never visited the site prior to inauguration. For me, the best reward was the smiles on the faces of landless SC/ST beneficiaries. They had neither homestead land nor pucca houses prior to receiving the keys to their new homes from Chief Minister.

The Drought Prone Area Programme (DPAP) was being implemented in the district through Soil Conservation Department. An Assistant Engineer in charge of Titlagarh Sub-Division was a most efficient and imaginative officer despite being perceived as corrupt. He received the lion share of DPAP funds from DRDA, and had executed some very impressive soil conservation projects which had benefited drought-affected farmers of the area immensely. Due to his proximity with successive Collectors, District Soil Conservation Officer who was his immediate reporting officer remained in awe of him and more often than not simply signed off on all that was placed before him.

Upon my joining this post in DRDA, an interesting story about this well-connected Assistant Engineer was recounted to me. Works Department, responsible for construction, repair and maintenance of government buildings, was finding it difficult to source funds for raising the compound wall of Collector's bungalow, residential office and a large chunk of area partially covered under plantation. It was averred that this Assistant Engineer quietly volunteered to do the work unofficially, only to deny it when an enquiry on allegations about misappropriation of funds was initiated by the Government. None could produce any evidence to show that a large amount of expenditure on raising the compound wall was actually incurred by him. A case of "facts true and no clue" perhaps!

Soon enough, I was deploying his impressive ability to execute projects within timelines in many soil conservation projects while maintaining a watchful eye on expenditures and a safe distance. I was not concerned with his past nor his proximity with Collector-cum-Chairman DRDA although it was amusing to hear once that he was still currying his favour by offering to find a buyer with a good price for his dilapidated old personal vehicle. It is painful to find that sometimes efficiency and honesty are not necessarily complementary to each other in public administration. Soil conservation projects like water harvesting structures, check dams, diversion weirs, etc. executed by the Assistant Engineer had created opportunities for protective irrigation in drought-affected villages of DPAP Blocks which made him both popular and visible in the district. He rarely cared for maintaining records and accounts and had scant regards for rules and procedures. This worked both ways. It invited allegations as well as disabled complainants, as documents could not be produced to substantiate charges against him. His colleagues were impressed with his skill in managing audits and ability to impress senior officers. I made it a point to inspect every single project implemented by him for which funds under DPAP or any other programme were released to him.

Balangir and other western districts of Odisha had a glorious age-old practice of harvesting rain water, rather than allowing run-offs leading to erosion of top soil, and other outstanding works in soil and water conservation. In the absence of controlled irrigation system, the first storage point of rain-water was called 'Kata 'in local parlance. Surplus from Kata flowed into a 'Munda', and from there onto large water body known as 'Sagar'. While Katas and Mundas created potential for protective irrigation during Kharif season besides recharging groundwater, Sagars were permanent water bodies used by communities round the year in multiple ways, including for bathing and drinking. Over time, population pressure was coupled with bias towards large irrigation projects for controlled irrigation. These traditional systems were regrettably forgotten. Promises made by successive governments to provide controlled irrigation remained elusive and the land of traditional water bodies started getting encroached. It was a tragedy of increasing proportions with growing dependence on government which did more harm than good to communities who had been scientifically managing their time-tested traditional irrigation systems. Governmental schemes did not put emphasis on conserving these traditional systems. Regardless, DPAP helped farmers of drought-prone blocks significantly.

It was practically impossible to implement all anti-poverty and employment-generating schemes with the same amount of attention due to variety of constraints. But I saw great opportunities in these schemes to improve the socio-economic conditions of the poor, and thus remained impatient in getting them implemented fast to the point of showing extreme intolerance occasionally against non-performers. The worst witness perhaps was Bir-maharajpur Block. On a visit, I started questioning the intentions and level of understanding about the schemes of an elderly BDO in a bid to ascertain the reasons behind his poor performance. Unable to respond to my queries on every scheme, he turned towards his Extension Officers. Quite harshly, I accused him of enjoying job entitlements without discharging his duties. He fainted and was rushed to the nearest medical college hospital. Fortunately, he recovered soon after being admitted. I felt guilty and apologized to his family members. This incident made me more careful particularly in dealing with elderly BDOs who were overwhelmed by a plethora of schemes to implement. Logistics and infrastructure capacities were not in place and at the fag end of their service many BDOs simply lacked the motivation to comprehend their newer mandates.

Years later, I had opportunities to interact with the Second Administrative Reform Commission. I shared some of my experiences and suggested that the number of schemes should be reduced and logistics and infrastructure needs must be taken into account before launching new schemes for effective implementation. I underlined that since situations varied from region to region, there was no need to follow a rigid uniform pattern country-wide. My observations were heard with attention, but the Commission's report and recommendations, which I had occasion to deal with while working in the Cabinet Secretariat disappointed me.

I had made it a point to avoid harsher language during my interactions and reviews. However, my demeanour was unsmiling, which I later understood created an element of fear in the minds of field functionaries. Despite momentary embarrassment caused by my blunt observations, they did not find me vindictive or biased. Although I never troubled field functionaries for arrangements during my field visits or night-halts, they suffered in a different way as at times while accompanying me for inspection of projects in remote locations, they had to go without food for long hours.

Disbursement of schemes' funds to Blocks and other Executing Agencies by DRDA without taking prior approval of Collector was viewed adversely by him after some time. I did not like his tendency of utilising the interest money of schemes' funds for furnishing his office and residence. Rules were unambiguous that utilisation of interest money needed to be done for the same purpose for which principal allocations under the scheme had been received. I put up a statement on interest earned out of IRDP allocations and expenditure incurred before my joining on purchase of fancy furniture, including a dining table and sofa set, for the residence of Collector-cum-Chairman, DRDA for perusal/ approval of Governing Body. It was the last item in the agenda and had probably escaped the notice of Collector while approving the same before it was circulated. When it came up for discussion, the most vocal independent MLA drew attention to this expenditure describing it as a case of corruption and boycotting the meeting in protest!

My action though not deliberately intended to embarrass the Collector had perhaps touched a raw nerve. A few days later, while on a tour, a news item published in a daily newspaper conveying my transfer was brought to my notice. I did not know whether there was any 'cause and effect' linking it with the Governing Body meeting held a few days prior. Performance of DRDA, Balangir had decidedly registered a substantial improvement during my tenure in implementing priority sector schemes. Both RDC and Principal Secretary of CD&RR Department had appreciated it. I had spent just ten months in this post and I was eagerly waiting to see the assessment for my overall performance during the relevant financial year which was going to end in the next 40 days. And yet, quite unusually, even though the official notification of my transfer had not yet been received and nor had any substitute been posted, District Collector-cum-Chairman DRDA passed orders for my relief with immediate effect on the basis of a news item! I was handed over the relieving orders at my residence upon return from field tour that evening. My next place of posting was Sambalpur in the same post. After relinquishing charge on 8 February 1988, I reported at Sambalpur DRDA on 10 February 1988.

Despite two short tenures, the learning experiences on rural development and general administration in Balangir placed me in good stead to face challenges in the rest of my public life in Odisha. The transfer turned out to be a reward indeed. I got posted in neighbouring Sambalpur, one of the largest districts in the State with green and beautiful sylvan pastures, where I spent the best part of my field posting for more than two years with great degree of satisfaction in experimentations for achieving rural development. The programmes under implementation in Sambalpur were the same as in Balangir.

SYLVAN GREEN PASTURES AT DRDA SAMBALPUR

I came to know after joining in DRDA, Sambalpur, that there was another consideration for my new posting. State Government had been facing flak for its below par performance in implementing priority sector schemes, particularly in large districts with high potential which included Sambalpur. District Collector of Sambalpur, Mohan Kumar, an IAS officer of 1979 batch, had brought glory to DRDA for his systematic and dedicated services as its Project Director for two years on an earlier posting. Now, he was transferred out within 40 days of my joining on account of an unfortunate development used as a ruse. Just a few days before I joined, an encroacher having received eviction notice attempted to commit suicide by self-immolation in front of the Collectorate and succumbed to burn injuries later. Influential politicians wanted to oust the fair and rule-minded Collector who did not accede to their unreasonable demands, and levered this incident and the shortfall in performance of Sambalpur district in implementing priority sector programmes for securing his untimely transfer.

Initial Hiccups in Sambalpur

Chinmoy Basu, a 1977 batch IAS officer, known for his commitment to rural development joined as the new Collector, Sambalpur. In the first meeting of DRDA's Governing Body held after he joined, both of us faced verbal assault from some of the public representatives. Their diatribe against us led by Satya Bhushan Sahu, the ruling party's Chief Whip, contained unwarranted personal attacks and insinuations and actually went beyond what could be deemed acceptable behaviour. The charge was that non-official members of the Governing Body should not be taken for granted nor funds released to executing agencies without their prior approval. The anger was fuelled for funds released by DRDA under Small & Marginal Farmers Programme and for preparatory works including raising of nurseries for plantations under NREP and RLEGP. These needed to be done for timely and qualitative utilisation of funds, a practice we had followed in our respective previous districts.

When the MLA and Chief Whip taunted that we were no more in Balangir and Kalahandi districts where members of the Governing Body could be ignored, I intervened to firmly assert that all actions taken by Project Director and Chairman DRDA were strictly in accordance with the verifiable norms which could be scrutinised by the members. I underlined the urgency for release of funds which had to be utilised in a time-bound manner, and drew attention to Government's serious concern regarding non-utilisation of funds received a year ago. I bluntly reminded the elected representatives that neither Project Director nor Collector-cum-Chairman of DRDA had any vested interest in the District or State, as in their case. The ensuing pin drop silence was broken by Sriballabh Panigrahi, a member of Lok Sabha, and Shraddhakar Supakar, a highly respected politician representing Sambalpur Town Assembly constituency. In their moderate voice, they observed that neither Collector nor Project Director, DRDA should feel personally hurt as the goal was common. They adjured us also not to take otherwise the public pressures and expectations faced by elected representatives in their respective areas, which could get manifest and come to a boil occasionally in such meetings. They emphasised the need to hold regular meetings of the Governing Body. The marathon meeting lasted for 10 hours ending after 8:00 p.m. only after a threadbare discussion on all issues including release of funds which had been questioned.

Improving the Ecosystem

From the first month of the new financial year, Sambalpur district started registering improved performance in implementing priority sector programmes and other schemes. It was ranked first from the first quarter itself while maintaining this top rank as long as I held the post over the next two years. Meetings of DRDA's Governing Body were held with punctuality. Senior officers of State Government started visiting the district to verify the speed with which the turn-around in its laggard status had been achieved and returned fully satisfied.

At the end of the financial year, when news of my transfer as Settlement Officer, Cuttack was reported in a daily newspaper, all the MLAs led by the aggressive Satya Bhushan Sahu protested before Chief Minister and got the transfer order cancelled. Had the transfer order been notified, for sure I would have relinquished charge immediately and left the district without any loss of time. Nevertheless, I felt a bit embarrassed as in matters of transfers and postings, I did not like intervention by others. A few months later, Chinmoy Basu proceeded to undergo foreign training. He was succeeded by Hawa Singh Chahar, an IAS officer of 1976 batch. The new Collector was a fine human being. Unlike in my preceding three assignments, I enjoyed complete confidence of my reporting officers in Sambalpur.

Sambalpur district was truly my first "karma bhumi"; the main ground for me to implement and experiment with various poverty alleviation programmes, which was my passion. The district, with its 7 sub-divisions and 28 blocks, demonstrated paradoxes in many ways– a veritable existence of inseparable and contradictory opposites in socio-economic conditions, factors and ethos. While Bargarh and Sambalpur falling in the command area of Hirakud project were advanced in agricultural practices which made the district granary of the State, there were Tahasils and Blocks bordering Balangir and Kalahandi (now Nuapada) which remained in the grip of chronic drought and resultant materials' scarcity. In particular, Padampur covered under DPAP was in no way different from Balangir or Nuapada and beset with widespread labour migration, acute malnutrition, etc. Kuchinda sub-division had three Blocks with majority tribal population afflicted with poverty and backwardness. Jharsuguda had a few industries and mining areas that had brought relative prosperity to its populace. Debgarh and Rairakhol too had a sizable SC/ST population suffering from high incidence of poverty and backwardness.

The programmes under implementation in Sambalpur were the same as in Balangir. The flagship IRDP was the main vehicle for removal of household poverty. A similar scheme called Integrated Tribal Development Project (ITDP) implemented through Integrated Tribal Development Agency (ITDA) was exclusively for tribal families with a higher percentage of subsidy entitlement. In other words, multiplicity of schemes and executing agencies did not necessarily add up to higher focus and qualitative implementation. Rather, it caused confusion counting a beneficiary multiple times, and occasional misappropriations. Since majority of beneficiaries were illiterate, unskilled and unaware of schematic guidelines, implementation of IRDP and ITDP did not have the desired outcomes. Citing poor recovery position, National Bank for Agriculture and Rural Development (NABARD) had stopped refinancing BAGB, the Regional Rural Bank (RRB) with the largest network of branches in Balangir and Sambalpur. Resultantly, this bank was not able to participate in implementing income-generating schemes which focused more on business and service sectors due to preferences of beneficiaries and easier disbursements.

I held detailed discussions with the top management of the RRB and sponsor commercial bank. It was agreed that business and service sector-related income-generating schemes for which NABARD refinance facilities had been choked up would hereafter draw lower priority as compared to primary sector in sponsoring loan applications by Blocks to BAGB branches. Taking BDOs on board, I devised a strategy to sponsor more applications for income-generating projects which were land-based including dug well energisation, fishery and animal husbandry. This matched the profile and potential of

Sambalpur district which was agriculturally advanced. There was no difficulty in getting NABARD refinance in these sectors. The loan repayment potential of beneficiaries was also higher in primary sector projects.

Simultaneously, I started supervising recovery drives with BDOs in order to support the financial institutions. This twin-pronged strategy yielded results in more ways than one. The quality of implementation of schemes for self-employment improved and financial institutions started participating in them more actively. The District achieved the annual targets under anti-poverty programmes with a far better sectoral balance, which received appreciation from State Government as well as financial institutions.

Chinmoy Basu was a veteran in implementing priority sector programmes. We were simpatico, with shared interests professionally and personally. We started holding monthly review meetings on fixed dates at sub-divisional level in which officers of all line departments had to be present. District Lead Bank Manager and senior officers of other banks too remained in attendance. All aspects of anti-poverty programmes were fleshed out in detail, including selection of beneficiaries, identification of schemes in consultation with banks, sponsoring of applications, pendency with bank branches, sanction and disbursement, recovery of past loans with administrative support, etc. Monthly targets would be fixed again in a participative manner with BDOs, Banks, and line departments. Blocks were ranked according to their performance which included the parameter of facilitating recovery drive of banks. As a result of collective effort, team spirit and effective monitoring, ranking of Sambalpur district improved consistently rising to the top at State level.

Innovations to Redress Deficiencies in Schemes and Programmes

Extensive field visits and reviews at various levels had exposed me to the chasm between reported achievement and ground reality. Closer scrutiny revealed misappropriation of funds released by DRDA Sambalpur for conducting skill training under TRYSEM by General Manager, DIC, who had otherwise tried to project himself as an efficient performer. TRYSEM called for selection of rural youth by BDOs for skill training and self-employment in consultation with DIC. After analysing the gap between number of trained youth and those assisted by banks with subsidised loans for self-employment and verifying the expenditure incurred in the name of training, I drafted a detailed fool-proof charge sheet for misappropriation against him. Ironically, he managed to extricate himself from these proceedings even after the charges stood established against him. I had left the district by that time. Not only did he escape disciplinary action but got promoted as Additional Director of Industries before his retirement. About 25 years later, in July 2013 by when I stood promoted to apex scale and posted as ACS and Chief Administrator, KBK Districts, this former General Manager, DIC, Sambalpur had the audacity to visit my residence along with a retired District Judge carrying a bouquet of flowers to compliment me on my promotion. He then introduced himself as Secretary of an anti-corruption body set up by him and some of his friends!

Development of Women and Children in Rural Areas was a newly introduced sub-scheme of IRDP under which 13 Blocks of Sambalpur were covered. It envisaged forming groups of women below the poverty line for undertaking economic and community activities collectively in villages with financial subsidy of up to 50 percent. Just prior to my transfer from Balangir, I had taken up implementing it extensively across half of the Blocks there. Recruitment of Lady Supervisors as per posts sanctioned under the scheme had been completed and substantial progress had been made in formation of groups to start the economic activities. I found that Block level officials in Sambalpur were not even aware of this scheme, because schematic guidelines had not percolated down. Being already conversant with the scheme, I swiftly initiated action for recruitment of Lady Supervisors, formation of women self-help groups, and construction of training-cum-production centres in each of the 13 Blocks as per the prescribed type plan simultaneously.

Within six months, all training-cum-production centres were ready; the one in Maneswar Block was inaugurated along with a bakery unit as an economic activity by Governor, Odisha. Lady Supervisors were in position in the meanwhile. Women self-help groups became vibrant and a district-level exhibition was organized for promoting their products, particularly of handicraft and handloom sectors. One outlet for marketing the products of these self-help groups was opened at district headquarters by the side of DRDA office. State Government appreciated the promptness of DRDA Sambalpur and cited it as an example while nudging all lagging districts to replicate its achievements in a similarly short time. A useful scheme with tremendous potential had remained unattended for nearly a year in Sambalpur. It was successfully implemented by the very same field functionaries keeping in view the character, specificities and needs of the district within a short time, which adequately proved that it was not lack of capability but the lack involvement and conviction that made the difference.

"Million Wells Scheme" was introduced as a sub-scheme of JRY. Under it, SC/STsmall and marginal farmers below the poverty line received financial assistance for digging open wells that could provide irrigation for half an acre each of their land in addition to generating wage employment for the family. It differed from SMFP in terms of coverage of 100 percent SC/ST beneficiaries with full financial assistance. The scheme was revised later to include up to 50 percent non-ST/SC small and marginal farmers below the poverty line. Subsidy of 33 percent to 50 percent was available for wells dug under SMFP and beneficiaries had the option not to avail of bank loan if they could contribute in the form of voluntary labour or cash equal to the bank loan. Unlike in coastal districts where ground water table was very high and land was suitable for shallow tube wells, Sambalpur did not offer much scope for irrigation through shallow tube wells. I had proposed to State Government to allow open wells under SMFP in the same way as shallow tube wells were enabled in coastal districts. This scheme was more inclusive and permitted larger coverage in terms of its catchment even though assistance available was 50 percent or less than that given under Million Wells Scheme. Alongside digging of wells, beneficiaries were provided with "mini-kits" by local horticulturists for raising vegetables. Deeper excavation during the day required dewatering every morning and the water thus taken out was enough to irrigate the vegetable crops on 10 to 20 decimals of land, thereby adding to the income of beneficiary family even before completion of dug well.

The monitoring grid prescribed by DRDA Sambalpur called for maintenance of registers indicating dates of selection of beneficiaries, issuance of work orders, and progress as per fortnightly milestones. Registers were maintained and updated at Gram Panchayat level by Village Level Workers (VLWs) and Extension Officers for respective villages and Gram Panchayats, and at Block level by BDO. Random verification of progress by Sub-Collectors and DRDA officials was weaved in. Senior officers from State and Central Governments frequented Sambalpur district to see the results of this "Open Well" exception. Managing Director, Odisha Agro-Industries Corporation (MD, OAIC) visited Sambalpur and commended me to his officers asking them to take their instructions from me as far as this district was concerned. OAIC had got good business from Sambalpur being the main supplier of electric pump sets for dug well energisation. The district not only managed to get allocations higher than its entitlements on the basis of achievements but also received additional funds diverted from DRDA Ganjam, traditionally considered the most progressive in the field of agriculture and energisation. Dug well census in Sambalpur had shown less than 10,000 dug wells since inception, whereas in two years of my tenure more than 11,000 dug wells were added together under Million Wells Scheme and SMFP. The new dug wells, deeper in depth and wider in diameter were distinctly marked and a good number of them were energised. Sambalpur became a model for development of micro irrigation system and dug well energization.

Under IAY the situation was found to be similar to that of Balangir. Due to mismatch between allocations and coverage of beneficiaries, disbursement of second and subsequent instalments had hardly happened in time despite the best of intentions. Sub-standard housing colonies constructed departmentally or through VCLs by Block engineers without involving the beneficiaries did not serve the desired purpose. Beneficiaries inclined to execute houses directly had to run from pillar to post for their second and subsequent instalments in a bid to complete their houses. As I had done in my previous district, a decision was taken that first priority would be given to complete the incomplete houses. It was also decided that houses would be constructed involving the beneficiaries mandatorily and no more than 25 percent extra work orders against the allocation would be issued. It was not difficult to track progress and slowly the gap between construction taken up and houses actually completed was minimized. There were no more instances of houses not being used by beneficiaries either. My standard refrain or test was that BDOs and co-workers should work with the same determination and forethought as if these IAY houses were being constructed for own use.

It was felt necessary to demystify the priority sector schemes up to village level and make allocations of funds to Blocks transparent. Bridging whatever trust deficit remained after the initial meeting, Governing Body of DRDA was taken on board in the beginning of financial year itself. It was decided to organise workshops at district-level to sensitise elected representatives, officials and non-officials on ongoing schemes and their governing guidelines. Media was encouraged to report incidents of irregularities, if any, seen by them. Occasionally, DRDA Sambalpur facilitated field visits for journalists to draw them closer to the ground reality and to help avoid false reporting due to misunderstanding of schemes or on the basis of anecdotal evidences. Monthly progress reports were compiled on the basis of verified achievements and circulated to all Blocks showing implementation status and their rankings, which helped in creating a competitive atmosphere. Delinquents were dealt with timely and adequately. Conflicts between officials and non-officials, mainly between BDOs and chairpersons of Panchayat Samitis, which were irritants in many places, were resolved by timely interventions. On my part, I visited each Block every month to ensure desired coherence and fair play. Having personally seen and lived a life in distress and scarcity in my formative years, the opportunity to work and try to make a difference was far more important for me than personal comforts offered by the post I was holding.

Lack of emphasis on creation of durable assets was the main deficiency and reasons of leakages which rendered less effective the implementation of rural employment programmes, viz. NREP, RLEGP and JRY. NREP guidelines expressly provided for creation of community assets of durable nature as its secondary objective subject to no more than 40 percent funds being spent on materials' component. Instead of maintaining this ratio at district level, it was prescribed project-wise. As a result, assets of durable nature like primary school buildings, community centres, cross drainages works including small bridges and culverts which were critically important for rural connectivity were either given lower priority or left incomplete. Non-official members readily accepted my suggestion to apply the wage-material component ratio at district level as a whole and agreed that no project started under employment-generating programmes should be left incomplete under any circumstances. Dovetailing of funds received from other sources including from Education Department under Finance Commission awards, etc., was encouraged in order to accord priority to construction of school buildings under NREP, RLEGP and JRY in Sambalpur. The tendency to anyhow spent allocations in the name of labour-intensive works and report generation of man-days and expenditure was controlled without any substantive deviation from guidelines.

A far-reaching innovation was to lay greater emphasis on water and soil conservation measures for employment-generation. In a unique experiment in Sambalpur, a watershed-led approach for improving groundwater recharge, moisture conservation and to check erosion of top soil was taken up involving Soil Conservation and Agriculture Departments. Once every month, I held meetings with district level departmental heads and Block officials on identified watersheds to be treated and developed scientifically by measures like plantation, contour bunding, gully control, construction of water-harvesting structures, farm pond, etc. Dug wells and energisation followed by suitable cropping practices involving field functionaries of Agriculture Department were essential ingredients of this approach to rural development.

Another significant innovation was avenue plantations to cover all major district roads which helped in beautifying the roads besides contributing to environmental improvement. This was carried out in addition to Block plantations, gap-filling and protection of village forests by involving Forest Department officials and village communities. Expenditure-driven orientation became a bad thing of the past, as the outcomes were effectively monitored and documented for verification. I had to perform an unpleasant task of preparing draft charges against two senior officers of Indian Forest Service for misutilization of funds meant for Block plantations in remote areas which I had unrooted during field verifications.

Six Blocks of Padampur Sub-Division (now in Bargarh district) stood included under DPAP. Buoyed by the confidence reposed by Collector-cum-Chairman, DRDA, Sambalpur, I was in a much better position to leave behind trials faced in Balangir DRDA and facilitate convergence including dovetailing of other ongoing programmes with watershed-led approach to implement DPAP. Dr. D.P. Mishra, Deputy Director Agriculture, Sambalpur, an expert in soil science along with senior officers of Soil Conservation and Forest departments, formed the core team for selection of watersheds in Sambalpur and their development with all possible aspects to create a substantial positive impact. DPAP funds, instead of being utilised as gap fillers for labour-intensive works like water-harvesting structures at the whim of MLAs, were now reoriented and bedrocked in watershed development. Dug wells under SMFP and Million Wells' Scheme were taken up in larger numbers in villages which formed part of selected watersheds. As in the case of open wells, farmers were provided mini-kits by Agriculture Department to promote suitable crops simultaneously in villages around the treated watersheds.

Watersheds were selected from all six DPAP Blocks and funds' utilisation did not deviate from entitlements. Funds received by Soil Conservation Department along with resources of NREP, RLEGP, JRY and SMFP were utilised with maximum possible synergies among them for developing watersheds in drought-prone areas. Indeed, success in dug well programme in some unirrigated areas was also partly a result of watershed development. I was happy to find my innovation and experiment vindicated when a few years later Union Ministry of Rural Development (RD) decided to embed a watershed-led approach in employment-generation schemes in rural areas through out the country.

Correcting the Mechanical Approach and Improper Methodology

The cost-sharing ratio under NREP, JRY and IRDP was 50:50 between the Centre and State. However, Union RD Ministry did not consult States before drafting and issuing their guidelines. Without necessary flexibility, this approach did not offer enough scope for imaginative planning at district level. There was no option but to pick up projects for implementation from the list circulated by Central Government, though on paper this list was cited as illustrative. Non-official members of Governing Body of DRDA often protested when good projects suggested by them which had been recommended by Panchayat Samitis could not be included in the shelf of projects finally prepared at district level by DRDA under NREP, RLEGP, JRY etc. on the ground of those not being permissible.

I had brought up such matters in meetings with Union RD Ministry, which had only made their attitude more rigid. Rajiv Gandhi, then Prime Minister, had initiated holding regional conferences to involve Panchayat Raj institutions on decentralised planning. A Project Director from each State was invited to these meetings and I represented Odisha. In one such National Conference of Project Directors of DRDAs organised at New Delhi, the Secretary, Union RD Ministry, invited the State Governments to be frank and free in suggesting refinements to the guidelines. I raised the concerns of elected representatives about their suggested projects getting rejected due to rigidities in guidelines which indeed went against the principles of decentralised planning. My observations however, fell on deaf ears. At the end of the Conference, I was invited to share views in the presence of Secretary Vinod Pande. While underlining the need to change the rigid interpretation of guidelines, I cited the views of elected representatives once again that "despite Central Government contributing only 50 percent of funds, it was imposing a 100 percent straight-jacket on its directions for utilisation all funds." I called for flexibility in interpretation of guidelines in view of regional variations and risks of imposing uniformity country-wide. In their concluding remarks, Secretary and Additional Secretary took note of my submissions and advised the participants not to go back to their States with any negative thoughts while promising to seriously consider all suggestions received in order to refine the existing guidelines of ongoing schemes.

Arrogant officials who work like mercenaries in States as well as in Central Government have greatly contributed to deterioration in Centre-State relations due to lack of understanding about the ground realities while advising political masters heading their Ministries and Departments. Rural development can never be superimposed through a top-down process and uniformity cannot be the name of the game in the given socio-economic diversity, regional disparities and variations in levels of development in communities living even in the same village what to speak of country-wide. Officials holding key positions should visualize and understand this reality even if they do not have adequate first-hand experience and domain knowledge.

Promotion of Non-Conventional Energy and Other Schemes

Despite sizeable investment in rural sector for sustainable development after Independence through various plans and programmes, results as evident have not been commensurate with expectations. It would, however, be a travesty of truth to disregard the incremental growth and what has been achieved during the last over 70 years. Equally, it can be concluded without doubt that the returns would have been higher but for lack of consistency and coherence in the process of planning and implementation of rural development policies and programmes.

A prime example is promotion of renewable sources of energy. Odisha Renewable Energy Development Agency came into existence in 1980. With Dr. S.B. Agnihotri, an IAS officer of 1980 batch and an environmental engineer by discipline, as its Chief Executive, the Agency performed commendably in promoting solar and wind energy in addition to development of biogas plants in Odisha. DRDAs and Blocks were the vehicles for promoting biogas plants in rural areas. The Agency placed services of their Assistant Engineers in each DRDA besides providing subsidy to beneficiaries of biogas plants. A leading NGO 'Gram Vikas' under the leadership of Joe Mediath was in the forefront of promoting biogas plants in Odisha. It not only provided an additional dose of assistance to farmers having large animals but using its trained manpower, including community motivators, in high potential Blocks it helped in executing biogas plants. Ganjam District, where Gram Vikas was headquartered, consistently achieved the first position in execution of biogas plants.

I saw no reason for Sambalpur District to lag behind. DRDA Sambalpur had started promoting animal husbandry, particularly dairy development, through anti-poverty programmes. Any family having more than four large animals could get a biogas plant virtually free of cost due to inherent subsidies offered by OREDA and Gram Vikas. The biogas plant could meet the energy needs for cooking food for the whole family besides providing power to light at least one bulb in the beneficiary's house. With vigorous implementation, Sambalpur DRDA secured the first prize in performance and achievements consistently for the next two years. Initiatives and interest in development of biogas plants exhibited by Dr. Agnihotri were not taken forward by his successors, some of whom even tried to find fault with what they described as poor track record in maintaining proper accounts. His imaginative and unconventional ways were probably not appreciated. This is also true of many other schemes. Accountability of key public servants has been at a discount in our system of governance in both formulating and implementing coherent and consistent policies and programmes. The net result is a huge mismatch between intention and outcome. Investments and returns do not match either. The situation seems to have deteriorated over time. We cry at spilt milk!

Shifting to the new DRDA Office Building

When I joined DRDA at Sambalpur, the office was functioning from an old and dilapidated building originally owned by a famous Assamese creative genius Lakshminath Bezbaroa. The building along with adjoining land by the side of river Mahanadi and in front of Hirakud Club was in possession of State Government only in part as the remaining land stood encroached. A Marwari businessman had claimed to have purchased the entire property long back from the family of the original owner. Besides larger space needs arising from expanding programmes, the edifice itself had been declared unsafe. There was an urgent need for DRDA to go for its own building. A piece of land partly under encroachment, close to the Collectorate was identified and permission of State Government taken for utilisation of IRDP accumulated interest money now allowed to be spent on office-related infrastructure. Special permission to quickly construct the building departmentally without inviting tenders was obtained. Executive Engineer of Minor Irrigation Department agreed to execute the work and a new double-storeyed office building was ready in six months. DRDA Sambalpur was privileged to be the first in the State to have its own new office building.

It rarely happens in our system that an office building gets started and completed within the incumbency of the same officer. Encroachment eviction was a sensitive issue, particularly given the charged atmosphere created by the self-immolation bid and death of an encroacher a few months back. Luckily the local Sub-Collector, who had worked with me before, managed the eviction smoothly. Development of peripheral area did not give scope for any discontent. Local politicians did not stand by the encroacher this time. Indeed, they were happy to find a nice new office building completed departmentally in record time, which proved the capabilities of public functionaries. It is another issue that such a happy display in execution of own projects was not forthcoming by engineers of Minor Irrigation Department. Timely execution apart from disallowing cost escalations and providing benefits of opportunity cost, also works as a deterrent against corrupt practices. My experience also tells me unequivocally that time-bound implementation of projects without deviation from the relevant technical parameters does not in any way compromise the quality of work.

Time simply flew during my tenure of nearly two-and-half years. In my native village during formative years, I had hardly seen any governmental intervention and here I was in charge of implementing a big basket of income and employment-generating programmes aimed at development of rural areas. I tried to grab the opportunities from everywhere with both hands to deliver tangible and meaningful outcomes by working as hard as possible. Looking back, I consider this tenure most satisfying, with enjoyment of full functional freedom. My experiments with rural development through implementation of a variety of projects as per local felt needs, and collaborative and cooperative endeavour of a dedicated team of colleagues, made me increasingly optimistic about the future of the State and that of society at large.

Management of Homes for the Destitute

My association with NGOs makes me think twice before making sweeping generalisation about their functioning. I found a good number, including grassroot organisations, engaged in social work and in implementing rural developmental projects producing outstanding outcomes without indulging in publicity and propaganda. Providentially, I was associated with a great 'Gandhian' worker Parbati Giri to facilitate the opening of a 'home for destitute' and an 'old-age home' at Phuljaran (on National Highway in Jujumura Block). Construction of building for the destitutes' home, inaugurated by Governor, Odisha, was done by utilising NREP funds. The old-age home was supported by district planning unit and Red Cross.

Having worked towards establishment of these two homes, I often visited them while returning from field visits. I was greatly pained one evening when I entered the destitute home to find a 4-year old child suffering from acute diarrhoea, with his stinking body with sinking health abandoned and kept under a big Sal tree at a corner of the compound. The lady supervisor told me that the child had been isolated in order to prevent outbreak of an epidemic. I felt some movement in the body under the Sal tree and took him to the district hospital with the lady supervisor accompanying me. He was admitted within an hour for intensive treatment and care. Having fully recovered, he was released a week later. I continued to pursue his well-being even after my transfer from Sambalpur till I was informed that he had completed his primary education from the nearby school and was taken home by his relatives in Balangir. I realised that the Head of the NGO, a committed motherly figure besides being a well-known freedom fighter, was not singularly able to manage all her institutions. The lady supervisor, herself a victim of domestic violence and desertion, was untrained and not equal to the task. I supplied the required number of wooden cots to the home for ensuring improvement in living conditions of the unfortunate 50 discarded children and saw to it that they were admitted in nearby schools.

Parbati Giri, the finest unassuming social worker and most dedicated person I had ever met, was also running a "Home" for about 150 destitute girls at Paikmal (Padampur), where she mainly resided. She worked for uplifting those in extreme distress selflessly. Prior to her demise, she had opened another "Child Home" in Patharchepa village (Balangir). I discovered it accidentally years later in October 2006 while on tour as Commercial Tax Commissioner. I entered the building to find 45 destitutes in pathetic condition, perhaps even more so than the dilapidated building with its broken doors and windows and an unsafe roof. On enquiry, I found that the building had initially been constructed by RD Department and stood abandoned before being put to use as a "Destitutes' Home". The same lady supervisor from Sambalpur was now looking after this home and was herself suffering from an incurable disease. After the demise of Parbati Giri, a retired High School Headmistress from Balangir had become Patron of this institution. As the parent body at Paikmal had stopped supporting, it was surviving through small donations, including from District Red Cross Society. I called the BDO and requested him to immediately get 25 wooden cots manufactured and supplied for use at my cost, as I had done for the Distitute Home in Sambalpur, years back. Each cot could be shared by two tiny-tots, who had been somehow surviving in a hopeless condition. I requested Executive Engineer of Rural Works Department to find some savings for the essential repairs rather than declaring the building unsafe as a better option. The Patron of the Destitute Home came to meet me and explained how with great difficulty and by using some of her personal savings she was somehow managing. After assessing the gap, I personally started supporting this institution quitely for the next few years and stopped doing so in 2014 when it started getting State Government assistance.

Community support on a durable basis and government assistance to sustain such institutions are grossly inadequate. A few NGOs with access to donations from foreign agencies support them only if it helps in promoting their overt objectives and sometimes their hidden agenda, with which the assistance is invariably tied. As Secretary, RD Department in State Government in 2009, I could find some savings to get the building being used as "Destitute Home" at Patharchepa (Balangir) repaired as the minor repairs carried out earlier by Executive Engineer were quite inadequate. The poorly-managed Destitute Homes in Sambalpur and Balangir districts continued pricking my conscience besides reminding me of the certain period of my own early life, though I no longer suffered due to acute distress as in the past.

* * * *

3

Decisive District Administration: Ganjam

I succeeded a batchmate as Collector and District Magistrate of Ganjam on 30 June 1990. It was the third largest district of Odisha. Its topography could be broadly divided into two; coastal plains in the East and hills and table land in the Southwest. The hills being quite close to the sea and rivers flowing through though not very long, were prone to sudden floods depending upon the extent of rainfall in catchment areas. The district had a coastline of 60 km. Normally cyclonic disturbances occurred in the Bay of Bengal during April to May and October to December. With laterite soil in the Western regions, a strip of black cotton soil ran through the centre and Northeast close to Lake Chilika.

Historically Ganjam was a part of Madras Presidency during the colonial administration before the State of Odisha came into existence on 1 April 1936. Administratively, in 1990-91 the district consisted of four revenue sub-divisions, namely, Berhampur, Bhanjanagar, Chhatrapur, and Paralakhemundi. The only surviving Cooperative Sugar Mill in the State is in Ganjam district. Unlike compulsive labour migration commonly seen in Kalahandi and Balangir, migration of labour from Ganjam was voluntary despite it being very high, assessed during 1991 at 2.5 lakh or over 8 percent of its population. People migrated mostly to Surat in Gujarat. Coupled with careless sexual behaviour, perhaps this was a key reason for the highest incidence of AIDS in the district. Even so, Ganjam enjoyed a better reputation of hardworking and productive human resource in Odisha. Respect for administration was also high for being administered better. Influence of coastal Andhra and a sizable Telugu population which dominated industries and business in the major town of Berhampur in Ganjam is still visible.

A major paradox was that four out of five Blocks of Paralakhemundi (now Gajapati district) with its predominance of tribal population stood identified with extreme forms of poverty and backwardness generally seen in neighbouring tribal districts of southern Odisha. In the name of promoting social welfare in Paralakhemundi, the unmissable presence of some NGOs supported by Christian organisations had adequately contributed to social fragmentation among various aboriginal communities who had otherwise been living in harmony for generations. Religious conversion led to destruction of traditional tribal art and culture. The only visible change after conversion including in tribal villages under Paralakhemundi, has been a certain change in life-styles and religious practices of converts. Poverty and backwardness continue to follow them as usual.

An Unexpected Students' Agitation

Ganjam offered more challenges and varieties of experiences than I had imagined. Apart from routine important aspects of development and regulatory administration, I faced an unexpected situation within a few months of my joining as District Collector. Union Government, with V.P. Singh as Prime Minister, suddenly announced the implementation of recommendations of Mandal Commission to provide for 27 percent reservation for socio-economically backward castes in government posts and services. State Government of Odisha with the same ruling party and Biju Patnaik as Chief Minister openly opposed these caste-based reservations. Students all over the country, particularly in Northern, Western and Eastern India, mounted a violent protest against the decision of Central Government. Students' agitation in Odisha too resulted in a large-scale destruction of public properties. Tempers were running high in Ganjam and unrest gripped the campuses of Berhampur University and other colleges in the district.

One afternoon a couple of public transport buses were hijacked by students and taken to the campus of Berhampur University. On hearing about the incident from Senior Superintendent of Police (SSP), I proceeded straight to the University to meet student leaders, senior faculty and office bearers, including Vice Chancellor. I had rejected the advice of SSP to be accompanied by him nor taken a security guard in plain clothes for my protection. I had already removed the red beacon from my office vehicle and issued strict instructions to all functionaries, including SSP and SP, to avoid its use except during patrolling activities as per the motor vehicles rules. A detailed discussion ensued till late into the night in the office of Vice Chancellor and resulted in lowering of heat. I could pacify and persuade the students not to damage buses and other public properties, and to instead use the means of peaceful protest. I strongly feel to this day that my impromptu decision to visit the University Campus without accompanying police force and the trappings of power and the simplicity with which I interacted with the agitating student leaders also had some soothing effect on them. I issued clear instructions to all executive magistrates and police officers not to use unnecessary force in handling the students' issues.

A senior Cabinet Minister, Bijoy Mahapatra, was assigned the task of monitoring the law and order situation in the State on behalf of Chief Minister.

I was instructed over telephone by him, as though these were directions of Chief Minister, to take into custody certain student leaders and leaders of the opposition Congress party who according to him were fomenting violence by instigating students. I explained that the prevailing situation did not warrant arrest of political leaders as that would be an unnecessary precipitative action which could only aggravate the existing volatile law and order situation. In my assessment, none of them were participating in the agitation in Ganjam either overtly or covertly. Apparently, Principal Secretary to Chief Minister, Pyari Mohan Mahapatra, was by the Minister's side. The patently angry Minister after warning me that I would be singularly responsible for any loss of public property and lives in the district, handed over phone to Pyari Babu. I reiterated to him that as head of criminal administration in the district, I should be held accountable for any deliberate act of omission or commission on my part and that the Minister could be told accordingly. But any provocative action was not only uncalled for, it would only fan the flames of students' agitation that were being doused in Ganjam. Pyari Babu neither expressed his displeasure nor repeated the Minister's undue warning. He advised me to remain vigilant and to do all that is administratively necessary. Thereafter, regular interaction with office bearers of the University and Colleges, and student leaders served well in handling the volatile situation without any noticeable incidents of violence. Despite an aggressive students' agitation across the State, Ganjam suffered the least damage to public property.

An Unprecedented Natural Calamity

The second development that followed was the occurrence of an untimely natural calamity on 3-4 November 1990, which would perhaps be regarded among the worst days in living memory of the district. A deep depression over Bay of Bengal intensified and moved quickly in a North-westerly direction on 2 November, crossing the coast at Gopalpur and landing on the mainland on 4 November. Heavy rains and resultant flash floods of catastrophic magnitude resulted in all the rivers just after the full moon night of Kartik Purnima on 2 November when tidal waves were at their peak which drastically reduced the discharge of water into the sea. This natural barrier compounded the difficulties of the district administration. Covering 8,948 sq.km. of drainage area, Ganjam had received 25 to 55 cm of rainfall within less than 48 hours.

Rushikulya river right up to Hinjali covering over 1,000 sq.km. received the highest water ever leading to discharge of about 3 lakh cusecs at Aska, the confluence with Bada Nadi. Flood water of Rushikulya, Bada Nadi, Dhanei, Baghua and Ghodahada rivers taken together was about 5.5 lakh cusecs, which networked to cause havoc across the district inundating a large number of villages and towns. The flood broke all past records by attaining the highest level of 87.87 metres, the previous highest being 80.06 metres in 1988. The only silver lining was that rains and floods pounded the district on a weekend when schools were closed. But in the light of the day, when the clouds parted, the Sun God was the unblinking eye-witness to the full extent of human helplessness across the plains of Ganjam.

Going by past experiences, after South-East Monsoon retreats, the possibility of flooding in Ganjam in the first week of November is remote. As a routine exercise, in the District Natural Calamity Committee meeting held on 22 May 1990 by my predecessor, no participant could have apprehended the occurrence of such devastating floods. The focus of its decisions thus lay elsewhere. District Emergency Officer and his staff were new hands with no past experience of handling natural calamities. After the change of State Government a few months back, the new set of officers appointed had not familiarised themselves, and did not appear to be even fully conversant with the district's topography. The most devastating flood in its history laced strongly with rarity of magnitude was faced with inadequate preparedness.

Warning from Indian Metrological Department (IMD) on 2 November had been transmitted by District Administration to Sub-Collectors using wireless messaging system as STD facilities were not available in all important offices those days. The weather warning was not pin-pointed and stated, "*Cyclone storm crossing between Kakinada and Gopalpur on sea today evening or night. Heavy rains with gale 60-70 km per hour. Fisherman not to go into sea*". Subsequent updates were also conveyed to Sub-Collectors and Tahasildars as per the usual protocol, besides seeking reports about damages that might be seen. Sub-Collectors of Chhatrapur and Berhampur had been separately asked over telephone to remain particularly alert as the cyclone would hit coastal areas more than the hinterland. Possible location of the cyclone as per updates received from office of Special Relief Commissioner (SRC) and IMD were also conveyed to Sub-Collectors on 3 and 4 November through wireless and telephonically with instructions to keep a close watch on the weather besides taking preparatory steps necessary for relief operations.

The Rushikulya irrigation project happened to be a century old canal system, actually started in the year 1884. By now, the reservoir and canals had silted up considerably reducing their storage and carrying capacity. Heavy rains and flood water during a very short span of time could not be stored and regulated effectively. Non-existence of protection embankments along the river was also the cause or damage by floods at vulnerable points. At first indication of submergence of some major roads calling for traffic diversion among other actions, the three ADMs were assigned the task of supervision, rescue and relief operations in Chhatrapur, Berhampur and Bhanjanagar sub-divisions. After the residents were moved to elevated locations, during the night on 3 November, Aska town got fully submerged. Wireless messages were sent to SRC and to State Home/ Revenue Secretaries on 3 November itself seeking logistic support, besides providing situation briefs. Requests were also sent to

Indian Naval Ship (INS) Chilika and Air Defence & Guided Missile (ADGM) School, Gopalpur for power boats, rescue teams and other logistic support as the situation was developing menacingly. District Emergency Control Room functioned round-the-clock, though it faced challenges in collecting and coordinating information on rescue and relief operations due to complete disruption of telecom networks as also in the wireless system in some areas, despite SSP at Chhatrapur and SP at Berhampur being fully involved in managing the situation.

Rains practically stopped on 4 November, a Sunday, with markets, offices and educational institutions remaining closed. But flood water started engulfing the national highway, major district roads, and town areas in addition to a large number of villages. It became impossible to visit or deploy teams with relief materials from district headquarters to the most vulnerable places and those already in deep water including the town of Aska. An ADM, who was deputed to Aska, returned as his rubber boat started capsizing when he tried to cross River Rushikulya near Hinjali. The limited number of country boats available proved grossly inadequate before the flood fury of nature. In the meanwhile, locally available senior officers of INS Chilika and ADGM School (Navy and Army units) had conveyed their inability to help without getting clear directions from their respective headquarters. Line departments, especially those connected with sanitation, drinking water, health, PDS, etc. were put to work on war-footing and concerted efforts were made round-the-clock despite limited resources and no immediate help coming from State Headquarters or from other external agencies like local Army and Navy units.

Curiously enough even when the flood situation had taken an alarming proportion, disbelief prevailed in office of SRC and in State Government regarding the seriousness conveyed in district administration's missives until the national media started highlighting it. They probably thought that the frantic wireless messages being sent by district administration conveying the alarming conditions were no more than unnecessary desperate reactions of an inexperienced District Collector, as the month November was hardly the time for heavy rains and devastating floods. It had not happened in the past. Chief Minister had been camping in Delhi to participate in political events after the collapse of V.P. Singh's Government. He rushed back after the calamity was highlighted by the national media.

I recall that I had proceeded to Digapahandi around 8.00 a.m. on 4 November, leaving the Emergency Control Room after receiving a message from SP Berhampur that a Koraput-bound public transport bus had been swept into the waters, but was luckily blocked by a large tree, but had many passengers precariously perched on its roof. Before I reached the site, the flood waters had made further inroads. I assigned the rescue operation to the SP and proceeded to the more affected villages. An ADM who had accompanied me and I soon found ourselves literally neck-deep in rising floods. But being swimmers, we could manage to reach nearby inundated villages and undertake relief and rescue operations first-hand using local resources. I had swum across the River Ganga many times during my student days in Varanasi, and could therefore, disregard personal safety concerns with confidence in these rising tides. ADM too was a competent swimmer and had valuable experience in flood relief works from his previous assignments in flood-prone coastal districts. Luckily, it was not raining during our ordeal. This was a horrific experience nonetheless. But, the full extent of the coordinated dance of death mercilessly executed by the rivers of Ganjam district was still to be seen, standing in naked helplessness without any pretentions before the fury of nature!

Five major bridges, including two over river Rushikulya, were washed away in the flood which constrained relief operations till the rivers ceded ground and waters receded after the next couple of days. Extensive damage to lives and properties were seen particularly in 13 worst-affected Blocks of Aska, Belaguntha, Chhattrarpur, Dharakot, Digpahandi, Ganjam, Hinjali, Khallikote, Mohana, Purushottampur, Sankhemundi, Sheragada, and Soroda. Soroda Block had not experienced floods in past despite providing home to the confluence of rivers Jarau and Padma with river Rushikulya. Due to heavy rains in the catchment of Harabhangi irrigation project, all the rivers and rivulets were in spate by the morning of 4 November. Rescue and relief operations mounted immediately resulted in relocation of 4,000 persons in seven temporary shelters with free kitchens opened in the compounds of Revenue Bungalow, Tahasil Office, Block Office, Schools, and Notified Area Council Office in and around Soroda. Flood water had entered Sheragada area very early in the morning. In between Soroda and Aska town, 15 temporary shelters were opened which accommodated 13,200 persons from worst-affected villages, including of Sheragada. Grassroot community organisations and local NGOs did a commendable job by joining hands with government organisations in these operations.

Flood waters entered Aska town early in the morning on 4 November. Emergency Control Room in AskaTahasil office was functioning since the heavy rains started. Rising waters of Rushikulya and its tributaries took the entire town in its grip, including Tahasil office. Announcements were made by Tahasil officials using the public address system with the help of local people to move to safer locations. These saved lives though there was no way to save public and private property. About 2,000 people of Aska were relocated in temporary camps with provision of free food and drinking water. Rice, including flattened rice (Chyuda), in possession of millers and wholesalers in the district had to be taken over for distribution among affected families to by invoking emergency relief provisions.

There was a threat of strike from 4 November by private bus operators when the entire district administration was fully engaged in flood management. There was no time to engage them in talks. I issued strict instructions to SPs to apprehend any trouble-makers under every provision of law in case they went ahead with the strike. The warning worked, and private bus operators indeed contributed in relief work instead of acting upon their threat for strike.

Damage and Restoration

Human casualty would have been far more than 73 had the flash flooding not occurred during day hours on a Sunday when schools and offices were closed. It was impossible to prevent loss of property, and almost every socio-economic sector was heavily damaged. This included loss over 1,82,751 ha of Kharif crop nearing harvest, of which 14,320 ha had become unsuitable for Rabi crop due to sand-cast.The flood damage included loss of 20,050 ha of vegetable crops, 60 water-harvesting structures, 7 National and State Highways over 380 km, 365 rural black top roads over 682 km, 2,000 km of Panchayat and project roads, 5 major bridges, 170 cross drainage structures, 45 big breaches, 860 lift irrigation points, 660 minor irrigation projects, 10 medium irrigation projects, one major irrigation project and 1,533 school buildings. Besides, 14 drinking water supply projects in urban and 8 in rural areas, 489 tube wells in urban and 1,751 in rural areas were all heavily damaged. Power supply got disrupted in 700 villages. Assets of various government departments and public bodies were damaged in varying degrees.

However, the task of temporary restoration of drinking water projects, including disinfection of open wells used for drinking water purposes, power, telecom connectivity, was completed within 3 to 7 days in the entire district. Essential commodities available with millers and wholesalers were taken over for distribution, deploying also available private transport, and a large number of relief centres were opened. More than 220 NGOs, mostly grassroot/ community organisations actively and voluntarily participated in the operations without which it would have been impossible to restore normalcy in such a short time. Public response remained most positive and constructive, which unfortunately has become a rare commodity with changing social behaviours and political discourse.

I had visited major flood-affected villages and supervised restoration works on a day-to-day basis in the initial days. Normalcy was returning fast as nature itself turned kind and conducive for carrying out reconstruction work. Human resource in the district, well-reputed for its productive and supportive characteristics, completed tasks in days what would have taken weeks elsewhere. I personally monitored PDS right up to the retail point to ensure that scarcity of essential commodities was not felt and people rather than depending indefinitely on relief materials got their entitlements and moved on quickly to lead a respectful normal life.

A number of villages on the banks of river Rushikulya had to be relocated elsewhere on elevated places. It was impossible to resettle the affected families in their original places, many of which looked no different from river beds with houses and other structures becoming traceless. During the cloud burst, heavy rains and resultant flash flood, about 4,000 houses had been swept away, 8,000 houses collapsed, and 98,000 were partially damaged. Fortunately, a proposal sent by district administration a couple of years earlier to State Government to notify a big chunk of revenue land with bushy growth as protected forest had still not been acted upon. I instructed the local Tahasildar to undertake plotting of the area, which was also the choice of displaced families of Sorada Tahsil for their relocation, and allotment to them in anticipation of de-reservation of the land in question. My instructions made ADM holding charge of revenue section quite nervous. He cited provisions of Forest Conservation Act underlining the risks involved in my action highlighting that local DFO had already registered his protest, though informally to the Tahasildar concerned. I analysed the situation and legal provisions again and concluded that there was no option but to allot the said land to displaced families in the given situation. I took Secretary, Revenue & Excise Department, into confidence and sent a letter withdrawing the proposal sent to notify the area as a protected forest. I drafted a reasoned order and handed it to ADM stating that he was at liberty to offer his contrarian views on file, which would stand superseded by my order as drafted and to be pasted after his views. It was added that any delay in plotting, demarcating and allotting land for homestead purpose to displaced families would not be acceptable. Both Tahasildar and ADM mellowed down and completed the task of plotting and distributing land quickly.

As such, some of the affected families had already started constructing houses on the land the status of which was being disputed. I had verbally assured earlier that each of them would be provided 10 decimals of land for homestead purposes. I was willing to take any personal risk on this matter given the distressful situation. DFO who was already vulnerable against a flood of allegations of corruption against him did not carry out his threat, choosing to remain silent when the legal position was explained to him. Additionally, he was cautioned about the consequences of precipitating any action that would only add to the sufferings of people badly affected by floods. While economically better-off families volunteered not to put conditions for moving to the new sites and started constructing houses, the TATA group's relief Committee had agreed to construct about 400 pucca houses there. SC/ST families were given housing assistance under IAY. Work started without loss of time, and construction of houses progressed at a spanking pace worthy of the productive spirit of the people of Ganjam.

In all, 6,119 temporary houses were constructed in different places to accommodate families whose houses had been fully destroyed. Construction of 1,243 houses for flood victims under IAY, 5,000 with HUDCO loan which were subsidised by State Government and about 400 houses with full financial support from the TATA group of companies were taken up within the minimum time possible. A new colony constructed under IAY for relocated families in Ganjam Block was completed within 45 days, which was inaugurated by Lok Sabha Speaker Rabi Ray. Reconstruction and rehabilitation work at this speed was possible only in Ganjam and nowhere else in the State.

The unusual natural calamity exposed the unpreparedness of district administration. Lack of experience of officials involved in handling the situation aggravated their difficulties. However, with limited resources and without any support from other wings of State Government or external agencies, every branch of district administration worked round the clock for about seven days and mounted rescue and relief operations which received support from grassroot organisations and local gentries beyond expectation. No untoward incidents were reported such as rioting and snatching of relief materials (except in some stray cases), which usually happened in other coastal districts during natural calamities routinely faced by them. After the situation was controlled by district administration, trickles of support started flowing in from external agencies like INS Chilika, ADGM School, etc. When the road and telecom networks were temporarily restored, Ministers and other VIPs started frequenting the district and affected areas. I did not have time to meet and brief them about the situation as I preferred to focus on relief and restoration works.

Operational Difficulties

Weather warning received by district administration was too vague to enable visualising the magnitude of the natural calamity that followed inundating even non-flood prone places, let alone enabling rescue and relief operations at least at critical spots. This would hold true even if vulnerabilities to floods in past had given clues. Besides recent large-scale posting of officers from the Block to district level on transfer, a large number of posts still remained vacant as replacement of those transferred had not taken place. No power boats were available in the district and a few country-boats that were deployed could hardly meet the extensive requirements of rescue and relief operations. While power boats of Gopalpur Port were reported to be under repair, facilities of INS Chilika and ADGM School were not available. Although Ganjam's roads network was considered the best in the State, continuous onslaught of heavy rains for two days and the floods devastated it instantly. Destruction of telecom network compounded the difficulties of district administration in coordinating effectively with State Government and field functionaries like Tahasildars and BDOs.

Flood waters submerged the district's granary in no time, which included 1,253 villages and 12 Notified Area Council areas. Air-dropping of dry food pockets in flood-affected places took place only after flood waters had begun receding and was largely for political consumption to manage public perception. Print and electronic media was more interested in covering the political and social turmoil engulfing the country following the decision to implement the recommendations of Mandal Commission on reservations and Ram Janmabhoomi movement. The natural calamity occurred during a festival season. Some persons reported by media as missing or dead during the calamity appeared subsequently as they had either gone to watch "Jatras" or to Ayodhya to participate in the Ram Janmabhoomi "Car Seva" and could not return in time due to heavy rains and floods which had disrupted the communication infrastructure.

Excessive reviews taken at higher levels, a plethora of inconsistent and at times conflicting instructions received from various quarters, and VIP visits were proving counter-productive for relief operations. Senior functionaries who were expected to supervise relief operations during the crisis were called upon to attend review meetings at State and Divisional headquarters. RDC of southern division in particular, started holding meetings twice a week which rather than helping the situation, disrupted and delayed relief and restoration works. When my request to avoid frequent meetings was rejected by him, I had no option but to skip those meetings. He started shooting out letters to Chief Secretary and Chief Minister's Secretary complaining against my so-called disobedience by not attending his meetings.

The tendency to be governed by emotions and impressions invariably hampers relief operations. False assurances and promises that Government would compensate the losses, which were made without regard to provisions on entitlements, only aggravated the difficulties of functionaries engaged in relief work. At times, law and order situation was created due to pronouncements regarding relief assistance by senior leaders, including elected representatives of the ruling party, which could never be kept. Verbal instructions issued during review meetings held by Ministers created more complications when the ground reality was different. Irresponsible statements of the ruling party leaders who had perhaps never even read the Relief Code and who wanted to prove themselves more large-hearted than their predecessor ruling party, led to roadside instances of snatching of relief materials by villagers in a few places which were less affected and caused law and order problems. Such incidents happen when higher expectations are created but not fulfilled.

Misunderstanding and Confrontation

While people at large in the district were appreciating the work being done by district administration, the absence of elected representatives amidst them during the crisis and belated visits by Ministers and other important leaders who tried to find fault with district administration only made them more vulnerable to public criticism. Notably, Ministers of Rural Development and Revenue & Excise Departments were virtually ignored by the public when they tried to pin sweeping blame on district administration, being unaware of the work done and goodwill generated due to sustained services during the crisis. They failed in the usual practice followed by politicians to blame local administration by creating a deceptive impression in a bid to misleading the public. As I was informed by Chief Minister later, unhappy due to my failure to meet them during their district visits, they had spoken adversely against me.

After the natural calamity had been reported by national media, Chief Minister Biju Patnaik had rushed back from Delhi to Bhubaneswar. When entire district administration was then still struggling to control and stabilise the situation, suddenly I received a call from Pyari Mohan Mahapatra, Secretary to Chief Minister conveying that I should not believe in the news item published in some newspapers about my transfer! Later on, I could gauge that this call was in response to the statement made by Chief Minister immediately on his return from the national capital that he intended to shift SRC, RDC, and District Collector for their inept handling of the situation!

I had hardly slept for seven days and focused single-mindedly on relief, restoration, relocation of devastated villages with massive mobilization for providing temporary structures required by a large number of families who had lost their houses completely. Incidentally, I had received a telegram from my sister, elder by a mere two years, conveying the sudden and untimely death of her husband on the same day that the cloud burst and floods had struck Ganjam. I had not shared the news with anyone and worked non-stop to save the life and property of those struggling to survive, choosing not to rush to her village to hand-hold my bereaved sister in her hour of tragedy which had heightened her already desperate situation. Her family included two small kids. She was undergoing treatment for tuberculosis. I failed to fathom the mind of politicians who could go to any length in creating a deception to gain cheap popularity, though their well-tried and tested tricks failed to work this time as they were in complete dissonance with the feelings running large in the public. They simply wanted a scapegoat to extricate themselves from the corner they had been pushed into, due to their absence and inaction during the crisis. The missive they tried to fire on me backfired on them.

Secretary to Chief Minister called me again, this time to say that Chief Minister wanted to visit the district. I advised that the proposed visit could be postponed at least by a week in order to ensure uninterrupted continuation of relief and restoration work. I argued that the visit of Chief Minister would naturally engage and distract district administration which could be viewed adversely by the affected public. My advice was ignored. Chief Minister landed at Sorada, his native place, which was the worst-affected. None in district administration other than local police officials were informed. No sooner his helicopter landed at Soroda, local people greeted him by pelting stones and raising slogans. He was not allowed to come out of his helicopter. The rotary winds caused by the helicopter were blowing away the roofs of plastic sheets of a large number of temporary dwellings constructed on war-footing in the area. I had been visiting these temporary shelters almost every evening to find out and address difficulties faced by hundreds of families living there, in addition to taking steps for providing homestead land in safer locations adjacent to their affected villages in consultation with them. This had generated a huge body of good will for the district administration. They were also angry hearing rumours of my so-called transfer and probably found this protest a means to convey their disapproval. Chief Minister Biju Patnaik who was always greeted with spontaneous public support and applause, had to return without meeting the local people.

Chief Minister visited the district after a week, which had been my initial advice, along with half-a-dozen Ministers of his Cabinet. He held a meeting with farmers, particularly sugarcane growers, in a specially erected pandal in the campus of the Guest House of Aska Cooperative Sugar Mill. In the opening remarks, he asked for a show of hands by farmers who had not received assistance against their sand-cast land. I was seated by Chief Minister's side, as he had desired, and was instructed to respond to farmers' complaints instantly. Having done my homework and supervised each step of relief operations, distribution of sand-cast assistance, restoration work and PDS in the badly-affected villages personally, I was reasonably confident of being able to respond to the grievances of farmers. The local Tahasildar who had distributed the sand-cast subsidy was in attendance with the relevant documents.

One MLA had wanted me to show all the villages of his Assembly Constituency as calamity-affected which I had rejected being factually incorrect. He had brought his band of follower-farmers to this meeting. As anticipated, a farmer got up to complain that his claims had been rejected despite having lost his sugarcane crop. Chief Minister looked at me and I politely asked the farmer to indicate his name, his father's, and that of the village. The moment he mentioned his father's name and village, I presented the register before Chief Minister indicating that his father as head of household had received sand-cast subsidy, which was also confirmed by local Sarpanch present in the meeting. When a couple of other farmers voiced a similar grievance, I bluntly submitted that their village, which came in the Assembly Constituency of the said MLA, had not been affected by floods. Biju Patnaik was known for being instinctive and impatient. He suddenly announced that the meeting was over and that he would make a detailed review in the evening at Berhampur. Thus, I felt that my credibility had been established despite Chief Minister having come to the district with a mind that had been fed and coloured against me by two of his Cabinet colleagues. He wanted me to join him for lunch in the Guest House which I politely declined. One of his Ministerial colleagues informed him that I usually ate only home-cooked food and avoided eating out.

I left Aska to make arrangements for the review meeting at Berhampur announced suddenly by Chief Minister. MPs from Ganjam, MLAs of the district, and half a dozen Cabinet Ministers attended the meeting, in addition to district level officers of line departments. The focus was on impact of floods on agriculture and public infrastructure. Ganjam had two Lift Irrigation Divisions and a large number of community lift irrigation points which provided controlled irrigation. Most of them had been partially or fully damaged. Superintending Engineer started fumbling in explaining the status of damaged projects and plan of action with timelines for their restoration. I was closely monitoring restoration of key infrastructure projects and intervened to provide an overall status. My intervention was not appreciated by Chief Minister who said that I was not technically qualified to respond to his queries. Bijoy Mohapatra, Irrigation Minister considered to be close to Chief Minister, advised me to remain silent. Probably, Chief Minister was still unhappy with me. At the end, he wanted to know from his party leaders about the functioning of PDS. I was again cut short when I tried to explain the availability of essential commodities and their distribution through retail price shops. Fortunately, public representatives present, all speaking in one voice, certified that PDS was functioning effectively. At once, Chief Minister announced that the meeting was over and officials should leave as he would address the media at the same venue. His interactions with media, notwithstanding his unhappiness with me during the official meeting, were pleasant and he said a few good words about the functioning of PDS and work done by district administration.

After the meeting, I was called to meet Chief Minister in the Circuit House briefly. He wanted me to recommend takeover of a privately-managed educational institution, viz. the Sanjay Gandhi Engineering Institute. This famous private Engineering College had been established by a reputed Congress leader, Brundaban Naik. Some supporters of the ruling party had been creating unrest among the students and faculty to trigger its takeover by government. I conveyed my inability to endorse actions of disgruntled elements, explaining my understanding of the situation. In short, the visit of Chief Minister to the district gave him nothing that was politically assuring from my side. I too was not in a mood to present myself submissively.

The dust settled sooner than later. After two weeks of the district being hit hard by the natural calamity, I took casual leave of four days to visit my bereaved sister in her village in Almora district. On my return, I sought an appointment with Chief Minister in his Secretariat office at Bhubaneswar. I had never called on any Minister or Chief Minister in the Secretariat. For the first time I was meeting the top political executive and that too not in a happy frame of mind. He appeared to be aware of the tragedy that had befallen my sister. I expressed my earnest desire to be moved out of the district as despite my hard work performed with utmost sincerity, I had been viewed adversely in handling the crisis situation. I had read about Biju Patnaik during my student days, and he had inspired me for his courage, vision and daredevilry. However, I was quite disturbed that he had reacted adversely in public regarding my handling of the flood situation. Contrary to my expectation, Chief Minister was kind and lavish in his appreciation of my work and attributed his initial reaction to the false perception created by two of his Cabinet colleagues. When I persisted, he said that the decision as appropriate would be taken when the time was right and that I should continue with the good work being done by district administration on restoration and reconstruction.

I did not have any first-hand experience of handling a natural calamity, except for limited exposure as observer during my training in Cuttack about six years ago. The crisis in Ganjam taught me valuable lessons, which I used in multiple ways in the days to come. Almost 23 years later in October 2013, I was ACS, R&DM Department holding additional charge of MD, Odisha State Disaster Management Authority (OSDMA) when a very severe cyclone 'Phailin' struck coastal Odisha with landfall at Gopalpur (Ganjam). My experiences in handling the Ganjam cloudburst and floods in 1990, duly documented on the directions of Chief Secretary Ramakant Mishra, were of immeasurable help to me in knowing that preparatory actions taken in advance could have real and critical value in saving precious human and animal lives. The management of Phailin in 2013 thus marked a rare departure from the handling of such crises in Odisha. In contrast, 'Super Cyclone' that had hit Odisha coast in 1999 had resulted in human casualty of about 10,000 in the absence of preparatory groundwork. More on this later.

Exploitation by Some and Enforcement by Administration

There were a few black sheep bent on exploiting the tragic calamity situation for monetary gain. K. Nagabhushan Senapati, a close friend of a Minister from the district, was a big businessman and storage agent for essential commodities, including highly subsidised PDS rice meant for tribal families of Paralakhemundi sub-division (popularly known as ITDP rice). This Aska-based businessman had opened a free community kitchen for the flood victims and generated enormous goodwill for his charitable work. He had become a veritable hero for his generous acts, particularly when government agencies in the perception of some had failed to fully meet public expectations. A man with deep pockets, he had cultivated friends in Civil Supply administration. Successive Collectors had failed to catch him despite his indulgence in black-marketing of essential commodities meant for public distribution; a widely known story. Any plan to raid his godowns howsoever secretly designed, would reach him in advance and would not yield any evidence against him. I had been informed that one of my predecessors got his sugar godown raided after getting credible information that he had black-marketed a huge quantity of sugar meant for public distribution. As soon as he came to know about the imminent raid from his informers in enforcement administration, the clever businessman had reportedly filled his godowns overnight with sand bags while making sure that the top layers were lined with bags of sugar. As had been planned his godowns were raided, but no 'shortage' of sugar stock could be detected!

I did not involve Civil Supply officials and indeed, decided to detain Civil Supply Officer (CSO) under Prevention of Black-marketing and Maintenance of Supplies of Essential Commodities Act (PBMSA) for his connivance with some black-marketeers, including K. Nagabhushan Senapati. He had not reported shortage of stocks of essential commodities despite detecting the same during inspections by him and his subordinate staff in some cases. The CSO ran away from the district and did not return for as long as I served there. Trucks carrying supplies of essential commodities to Paralakhemundi had to detour over 220 km via Phulbani since the bridge over river Ghodahad near Digapahandi had collapsed. This proved to be a bonanza by way of receiving extra mileage payments for the highly subsidised ITDP rice that was rarely delivered in remote tribal areas except on paper by this storage agent. His modus operandi was to deposit sale proceeds in designated bank branch on behalf of retail centres instead of delivering rice to them, thereby creating a mirage of distribution of stock delivered in the previous month. The bank's confirmation of receipt of sales proceeds enabled him to lift stock for succeeding month. PDS in tribal Blocks was essentially stage-managed.

I decided to track the movement of trucks carrying ITDP rice from Food Corporation of India (FCI) godowns towards Paralakhemundi at different Check Gates and important points using officials of Tahasils, police stations and Transport Department. It was not difficult to catch the culprit when 28 trucks carrying 280 tonnes of ITDP rice on a particular day, instead of heading towards Parlakhemundi, moved towards Cuttack Malgodown and were tracked at Check Gates at Ganjam and Gopalpur (Cuttack). Delivery of these 280 tonnes of rice was made to Secretary of Cuttack Chambers of Commerce, who was one of the biggest wholesale dealers of rice. Regional Transport Officer, Ganjam and a few other reliable officials under him managed to quietly get statements of truck drivers in the form of affidavits. The number plates of trucks carrying ITDP rice were recorded along with the time at which they cleared the Check Gates at Ganjam and Gopalpur. There was now clinching evidence of malpractice. I passed orders under PBMSA for detention of Senapati and also of the recipient of ITDP rice in Cuttack. Somehow Senapati had sniffed out the unusual developments and plan of his detention. I received an inquiry from the local Minister and his friend, Surya Narayan Patra, whether any enquiry or action was being contemplated against Senapati. I feigned ignorance. The businessman-cum-storage agent, however, remained elusive till he responded to a knock at his door at 2:30 a.m. one night. He opened the door to find a warrant for his detention served upon him by a police officer assisted by a local revenue official associated with enforcement work. Senapati was taken to Central Jail at Berhampur without further ado.

Simultaneously I deputed DSP Patnaik to Cuttack to arrest the Secretary of Cuttack Chambers of Commerce. This accomplice and recipient of

28 truckloads of ITDP rice was still not aware of his impending arrest. The strategy to arrest him in Malgodown was executed before the news regarding detention of Senapati could be reported by media. DSP Patnaik was one of the most unassuming, trusted and honest police officers. Along with two police constables incognito he pretended to be a bulk-buyer of quality rice and located the shop of Secretary of Cuttack Chambers of Commerce who was found seated there in the company of two others. When DSP Patnaik not being sure as to who among them owned this shop called for samples of quality rice, he was directed by those two persons towards the owner, who took them to his main godown to provide the samples. After collecting the samples, DSP Patnaik returned to the Police Station at Ranihat and sent his two subordinates to lure the wholesaler there with some more samples for discussion in connection with purchase of rice. The warrant of arrest was served on the wholesaler as soon as he reached the Police Station mid-afternoon. Unexpectedly, some of his friends had followed him to the Police Station found out about his arrest.

Within no time, the news of his detention spread like a wildfire in Malgodown. Traders surrounded Ranihat Police Station, and pulled their shops' shutters down in protest against what was described as high-handedness on the part of District Magistrate of Ganjam whose action for passing detention order was challenged on the ground of lack of jurisdiction against a trader in another district. The powerful body of Chambers of Commerce held an emergency meeting and decided not to participate in sale and movement of essential commodities throughout the State if the detenue was not released forthwith. They also decided that their leader would not be allowed to be taken to Berhampur Central Jail under any circumstances. About half-a-dozen Ministers from undivided district of Cuttack and State's Civil Supplies Minister were approached by them for relief. Office of Collector, Cuttack was also gheraoed. Agitating traders and supporters were told by DSP Patnaik that the detenue would have to spend the night in police custody with other hardened criminals if he was not allowed to be moved to Berhampur quietly, which on being publicised would hurt his reputation far more. Finding no relief coming from any quarters in Government, the traders finally yielded around 11.30 p.m. and Secretary of Cuttack Chambers of Commerce was lodged in Berhampur Central Jail around 3.30 a.m. next morning, almost at the same hour but twenty-four hours after the main culprit K. Nagabhushan Senapati of Aska had been lodged there.

As per the relevant legal provisions, detention orders passed by District Magistrate are required to be confirmed by Government within a fortnight. The grounds leading to detention are also required to be served on the detenue to enable him to make his representation to the Government against his detention. The arrest had been made around 1.30 p.m. A few hours later, I received a call from S.M. Patnaik, Principal Secretary, Civil Supplies

Department, who appeared agitated and blamed me for the outbreak of an unwarranted and embarrassing situation, which according to him was bound to have a serious bearing on maintenance of essential supplies not only in Cuttack but also elsewhere in the State. The Traders' Association was a powerful body and was pressurising the State Government to get the detenue released. When I had meticulously worked for nearly a week before passing the order, I had not visualized exhibition of such nervousness on the part of the senior-most civil servant in Civil Supplies Department. I firmly submitted that there was no need for the Government to succumb to pressure exerted by black-marketeers, and that I had a fool-proof case against both detenues. I was told to meet the next day with relevant papers to satisfy him.

S.M. Patnaik happened to be one of the most upright officers in the IAS cadre of Odisha. Legal orders passed by him after hearing appeal petitions against orders passed by me as District Magistrate under Essential Commodities Act and various Control Orders were always sound and educative. The Government pleader in my Court would rank his orders in quality above even those passed by High Court of Odisha. I was fortunate to enjoy confidence and guidance of this wonderful person throughout my working life in State administration. He was a man of conviction, polite and firm. I met him the following day with all the relevant documents. He now told me that he had recused himself from the case on the ground that the detenue was a distant relative, and that I should meet his Additional Secretary Priyabrat Patnaik to brief him. Accordingly, I met the designated officer, explained the case, and handed over one set of papers to him. Detention orders against both offenders were confirmed by State Government. Their representations were rejected.

Both detenues made subsequent representations as per law before the Advisory Board headed by a reputed Senior High Court Judge, Radha Ballabh Patnaik, with two other retired High Court Judges as members. PBMSA did not provide for a detenue to be represented by legal counsel, and similarly the detaining officer was personally required to defend his orders. But I found both detenues were allowed services of lawyers. In fact,a lady advocate appearing on behalf of detenues of Ganjam district was representing Senapati too. I pointed out this coincidence in the course of my submission. ADM accompanying me predicted that there was no chance of the detention order being upheld after my submissions, which could be viewed as suggesting some form of nexus between the lady counsel and some members of the Advisory Board. The detenue from Cuttack was defended by a top lawyer of Odisha High Court, who surprised me by mischievously submitting that his client was not served with 'legible' copies of documents which were the basis of detention as a result of which an effective representation could not be made by him before the Government. He presented photocopies of vital documents which were indeed not legible. I now realised my mistake in not signing each page of the documents served on the detenue, and submitted before the Advisory Board clear copies of the documents that had actually been served. Although during the hearings I felt that members of the Advisory Board appeared sympathetic to both detenues, I was pleased to find that their orders upheld both detentions. This meant detention for a full six months for each of the two black-marketeers. Obviously, the trick played by the top advocate did not work. He played a similar trick in another litigation, which is discussed later.

I had been passing practically one detention order every month against black-marketeers of essential commodities in Ganjam. This helped in streamlining not only PDS but also checked hoarding and black-marketing of essential commodities there to a large extent. Traders and media started distorting my name to "Terror Datt" for such enforcements affecting black-marketeers and a few transporters. My frequent face-offs with members of Advisory Board in the presence of detenues and their legal retainers were rarely pleasant, although despite my occasional bluntness orders passed by Board upheld my actions. Justice Radha Ballabh Patnaik of the High Court, and Chairman of the Advisory Board, was elevated to the Apex Court some time later. But for his untimely death in a road accident, he would have functioned as Chief Justice of India for a long period considering his young age and legal acumen.

About a month after the detention of Senapati, one day I received a letter from his son containing the disturbing news that his sister's forthcoming marriage to an alumni of Indian Institute of Technology (IIT) had been called off and that he had to discontinue his post-graduate study in the reputed College in Berhampur due to detention of his father. I felt his pain and remembered the plight of my parents when the impending marriage of my younger sister was suddenly called off because of our family's inability to meeting dowry demands. I almost felt guilty as the innocent son and daughter had to suffer social stigma due to incarceration of their father in jail based on my action which had turned their lives upside down. The letter haunted me until about a year later when I received an "invitation card" from him to attend the marriage of his sister. I was working as Director, Tribal Welfare at that time. Although I did not have the courage to attend the marriage, I felt greatly unburdened and sincerely thanked God for the providential kindness.

There are indeed members of our society who go out of their way to help others in crisis. Some deceptively exploit tragedies and have no qualms about depriving or befooling the poorest of the poor. K. Nagabhushan Senapati did it for the money but was punished when caught out. A Minister belonging to his community who later held the charge of R&DM Department when I was ACS there, tried to help him escape punishment. His rival in Cabinet, Ramkrishna Patnaik also from the same district, celebrated the detention of Senapati and complimented me for my action! Although appearing to be so, it was not the case of one being dishonest and the other not being so. Ramakrishna Patnaik had complained to the Chief Minister and sought my transfer as I was unable to meet him when the crisis caused by floods was just unfolding. Now, after this detention he praised me before the same Chief Minister perhaps finding an opportunity to berate his political rival in the district. Paradoxically, a few months later, both of them joined hands when mid-term Lok Sabha elections were announced suddenly, and they became candidates to contest election from the two Lok Sabha constituencies of Ganjam. I had often ignored their unsolicited advice given on administrative matters. Chief Minister, who had earlier turned down my request for transfer out of the district and had wanted me to carry forward restoration and rehabilitation work, now found the new situation expedient to transfer me. How difficult it is to fathom the thinking of politicians, all in the name of public interest! By the way, both these leaders lost the Lok Sabha election, yet did not lose their Ministerial positions as they were inducted in the Cabinet again.

During my limited tenure of about 10 months at the helm of administration in Ganjam, I prioritised implementation of an effective and functional PDS which was critically important, particularly for the landless poor, SCs and STs. Scope for leakage in PDS was inbuilt in the scheme and maintaining absolute purity and integrity was an impossibility. Storage agents were handpicked by leaders of the ruling political party. Fair price shops were managed mostly by workers of the party in power. Officials dealing with civil supplies stood discredited, barring a few exceptions. Storage and transportation charges allowed to storage agents and retailers met only about half of actual costs, leaving them scouring for loopholes to bridge this gap.

It was thus not unusual to find recycling of PDS rice or channelizing it to the open market. Wheat allotted under PDS invariably reached private flour mills. Kerosene oil rarely reached intended beneficiaries. Adulteration of petrol using kerosene oil, besides black-marketing in other forms, did not receive due attention of enforcement functionaries of Civil Supplies Department. Apart from leakages in their distribution, hoarding of edible oils and oil seeds and thereby creating an artificial scarcity in the market was a regular feature that by and large defined traders of essential commodities in the district.

Implementation of Essential Commodities Act, including various Control Orders thereunder and PDS, was in utter doldrums when I had assumed charge of district administration. Prices of edible oil were soaring due to hoarding by wholesalers. Kerosene oil was sparingly available under PDS. Despite substantiation of close links between some wholesalers who openly black-marketed essential commodities and some officials, no action was being taken against anyone. An Inspector of Civil Supplies who had openly tried to influence the election results against a sitting MLA, appeared unusually friendly with a local Minister belonging to the same party. Despite documentary evidence, district administration had not taken action against him. The MLA had met me soon after I took charge only to issue a challenge to me to take action against this Inspector or reject her petition submitted since long on which no action had been taken by my predecessor. After a fast-track enquiry following due process, I imposed a penalty amounting to stoppage of three increments considering that the delinquent was left with only three years of active government service. Immediately after imposition of this penalty, the delinquent official managed to secure his transfer out of the district perhaps with the help of his powerful political patron.

The chain of black-marketing actually originated with storage agents and kerosene dealers selected by Civil Supplies Department, many times by disregarding proposals sent by district administration. The nexus and resulting corruption between the political executive and such agents/dealers did not require any proof. Civil Supplies' officials knew this well and liked to work in a 'win-win' situation even if their functioning went against public interest. To break the black-marketing chain, I decided to deal with storage agents and wholesalers, who enjoyed administrative and political protection. After gathering evidence, which included mismatch of stocks held with records maintained during verifications, hoardings, black-marketing, etc., I invoked provisions of PBMSA, which were similar to those under National Security Act, against serious offenders. I passed detention orders in at least one case every month to prevent artificial scarcity by hoarding essential commodities and picked my targets carefully. Principal Secretary, Civil Supplies Department cautioned me of adverse consequences when I intended to pass orders for detention of CSO found complicit in crime with some big storage agents/ wholesalers, and advised me to take RDC on board if I was determined to go ahead. I opted not to consult RDC, who most of the times worked at cross purposes with me and had written against me confidentially to Chief Secretary and Principal Secretary to Chief Minister highlighting what he considered as my insubordination. The CSO sensing the build-up of action against him absconded from the district and did not reappear until I left the district on transfer. Government did not post any substitute in his place, as no officer from the cadre was probably inclined to work in the prized post of Civil Supply Officer for as long as I was in the district.

I had involved the Establishment Officer of Collectorate, perceiving him to be more reliable and trustworthy, in a particular case of detention. But the case record containing documentary evidence was mischievously misplaced by him after the detention order was passed which enabled the delinquent to go underground before he could be actually detained based on documentary evidence. On advice of government pleader, I had no option but to recall the warrant of arrest issued against the offender which could be done only after following a painful legal process involving the district judiciary. In a blatant manifestation of motivated back-stabbing, the lost case record was presented to me by the Establishment Officer a month later saying that he recovered it from a garbage dump during his morning walk! Before the cunning and misdemeanour of this Establishment Officer, I found myself stymied in this particular case. But I learnt a valuable lesson and hereafter did not involve him in any important matter.

A wholesale dealer of oils and oilseeds, who also happened to be the highest sales tax and income tax payee in Berhampur town, was known for his rowdiness having once assaulted the officer in charge in the police station. Yet no case stood registered against him. ADM in charge of PDS, a native of Berhampur and a very upright officer, had briefed me about previous attempts towards taking action against him which had invariably fizzled out mainly due to mischievousness of Civil Supplies' Officials. Backed with meticulous planning involving the ADM and a few others, the storage godowns of this wholesaler were raided and a cache of hoarded commodities, along with materials for adulteration and incriminating documents, was found. He was put under detention for the next six months under PBMSA. Commercial and Income Tax Departments suffered some loss of tax revenues due to the detention and indeed registered their protests to me!

Enforcement work helped in achieving a substantial turning around of PDS towards better availability at reasonable prices, reduction in hoarding and black-marketing, and checks on adulteration of edible oils in the district. This was appreciated by the public. It was not to gloat that black-marketing or leakage in PDS came to an end, which was an impossibility at the margins offered to storage agents and retailers. In my assessment if about 75 percent of essential commodities could reach fair price shops and be distributed among intended beneficiaries, PDS could be said to be functioning outstandingly. It was also a fact that total allocation of essential commodities to the district was more than the requirement on account of inflated number of beneficiaries. Thus, even if every family actually received their full quota as per entitlement, there could still be enough surplus for black-marketing. The bulk of stocks meant for distribution in tribal districts would flow to the open market at Berhampur which was the main business centre in southern Odisha. Collectors and civil supply officials of tribal districts were inadequately equipped logistically. They were also hamstrung by lack of education and awareness about their entitlements among the poor and innocent tribal families. It was rare to find demands for action against any black-marketeer from them. As people in rural areas were not used to consuming wheat products, the stock mostly reached flour mills and urban consumers not covered under PDS. In a way, black-marketing of essential commodities, particularly of rice and wheat meant for PDS could be found to have helped in stabilising their prices in the open market! I would be more than happy to hear of changing trends over the last three decades since then in PDS.

Rural Development Works in Ganjam

Destruction caused due to the natural calamity propelled me to work harder still on rehabilitation of displaced families and restoration and reconstruction of infrastructure. Support from the public was a big stimulant. Ganjam district regained its glory (from Sambalpur) of holding the top position in the State in implementation of priority sector schemes. It received enhanced allocations for construction of houses for flood-affected families and in an unprecedented short period of three months after the floods, thousands of houses stood completed and the affected families could move on with their lives normally.

Effective monitoring remained an important tool for achieving results and good performers were commended orally during meetings; in writing subsequently. The strategy to execute projects in a time bound manner helped in preventing leakages and saving valuable time in conducting vigilance enquiries to penalise delinquents for lapses and corrupt practices. A performing field functionary would never suffer whereas the one neglecting duty consistently for two months or more was pulled up; getting affected temporarily till his performance improved. To allay any feelings of victimization when the shortfall was on account of factors beyond the control of the field functionaries, they were given the option to undertake to make up the backlog during the succeeding months, and this arrangement satisfied most of them.

I thus held Sub-Divisional Coordination Committee meetings on fixed dates in the first week of every month, regardless of public holidays for systematically implementing and reviewing progress in anti-poverty programmes and rural employment generating schemes. After all, there was no loss of status of being a public servant on public holidays. Apart from reviewing previous months' performance of each executing agency, targets were set for the next month besides discussing logistics and any difficulties which needed to be addressed. In the case of Blocks, progress made scheme-wise, and there was a vast plethora of them, were reviewed at length. Minutes of meetings indicating monthly targets and achievements under various schemes, shortfalls, targets for the next month, Block-wise ranking, etc. were released within two days of holding the reviews.

The basket of poverty alleviation programmes to be implemented under the direct supervision of District Collector was large by virtue of his being head of DRDA, ITDA, Brackish Water Fish Farmers' Development Agency, Fish Farmers' Development Agency, etc. Rather than spending time on all schemes equally, I followed my philosophy honed up in past assignments and exercised options by focusing more on those which in my perception held the potential of yielding better results. Elected representatives usually saw political gains emanating from these schemes and while resisting recovery efforts demanded loan waivers. In short, the outcome in implementing each poverty alleviation scheme was not necessarily satisfactory to the desired extent.

Farming community in Ganjam being progressive and relatively more demanding, efforts were made to focus on SMFP that provided for development of micro-irrigation and energization. Fishery sector was another field which produced relatively better results. Housing for flood-affected families and SC/ST under IAY marked an outright success in the district. District administration successfully resisted pressure from elected representatives to distribute funds among Blocks equally, which would have meant most of the houses remaining incomplete in perpetuity in the guise of larger coverage. Instead efforts were to secure a higher rate of completion of houses under construction.

NGO Gram Vikas supported governmental efforts in promoting biogas plants in the State. In my earlier stint as Project Director, DRDA, Sambalpur district had snatched the position of best performance in implementing this programme from Ganjam. I sought to restore that glory to Ganjam by pushing the programme aggressively in potential villages. Despite sizable losses of big animals due to natural calamity, which impacted the scheme temporarily, the biogas programme picked up again. It was however, not possible for me to see the final results due to my transfer just 10 days before closure of the financial year. Sadly, interest in promoting biogas development has been lost in the State with the passage of time.

Public participation and interest in implementing Developmental plans in Ganjam, which found roots in its socio-economic and cultural ethos, was far better than what I had experienced elsewhere. Efficiency in offices including quality of record keeping was also superior. Despite large-scale destruction of public and private property, and loss of office records, in the floods, I was awarded a medal by Registrar General of India in appreciation of satisfactorily completing the Census operations before any other district in the State. Ganjam district also stood first in mobilisation of small savings, but here inexplicably, State Finance Department shared out 50 percent of the prize money awarded in that financial year with my successor who worked in the district for a mere week at the fag end of the financial year. The district he headed before coming to Ganjam did not stand anywhere in ranking in relation to mobilization of small savings or in implementing any other flagship scheme.

Misunderstanding with RDC

On the one hand I enjoyed tremendous public appreciation for the work done showing solid team spirit by district administration, on the other there was a glaring trust deficit with RDC to whom I reported. Somehow, I remained oblivious about his unhappiness with me for quite some time. The tension surfaced when he wrote to me not to hold Sub-Divisional Coordination Committee meetings for reviewing priority sector schemes every month and to focus on revenue administration. He cited Circulars issued by GA Department (some decades ago) which did not provide for such meetings. In his assessment, the Collector was primarily to be concerned with revenue/ land administration since establishment cost of the Collectorate was borne on the budget of Revenue Department. He did not like my response and started calling me for discussions on the dates fixed well in advance for my meetings. I would request him either to postpone his discussion to another date or to allow ADM to attend his meeting on my behalf. RDC also started giving directions to officers of line departments on restoration and reconstruction works keeping me in dark, besides writing to Chief Secretary and Principal Secretary to Chief Minister about what was construed by him as my disobedience in dealing with him. It would be interesting to recount a few instances which manifested the misunderstanding.

Rampant violation of the provisions of Essential Commodities Act and various Control Orders as explained earlier resulted in detention of a few big offenders and I had to appear before the Advisory Board in High Court premises personally to defend my actions. After my appearance before the Board for the first time, on the way back I made my first call since my posting as Collector, Ganjam on Rama Kant Mishra, Chief Secretary. This meeting was unpleasant. He told me that rather than wasting time in appearing personally before the Advisory Board at Cuttack, I should have deputed an ADM to represent me. He was not convinced when I explained that under the relevant legal provisions there was no option other than personal appearance of District Collector. On return to District headquarters, when RDC inquired about my interaction with Chief Secretary, I had briefed him adding in a lighter vein that I had been interrogated as if by an Investigating Officer in a Police Station! In reality, Rama Kant Mishra, Chief Secretary was the most kind-hearted person in the bureaucracy of Odisha, intellectually-gifted, straightforward, and personally honest. I grew over time to hold him in the highest regard. I was not aware then that RDC's dislike towards me had reached the high bar to the extent that even my words in lighter vein were twisted. He started writing adversely about me in his fortnightly confidential letters to Chief Secretary underscoring my so-called disobedience. It was when none other than the Principal Secretary to Chief Minister, humorously quoted a sentence from my official correspondence with RDC some months later that I became aware of these fortnightly missives to Chief Secretary which were copied to Principal Secretary to Chief Minister.

An interesting development took place a few months after the situation caused by floods had normalized. Chief Secretary conveyed his intention to visit Ganjam and inspect Rangailunda Block. Without keeping me in the loop, RDC deputed his senior-most officer to carry out an advance inspection and to prepare a Draft which would be kept in readiness for use by Chief Secretary during his inspection. Being unaware of this exercise, I too visited the Block office to collect inputs. From my recollection of Chief Secretary's Inspection Report of a Block in Sambalpur district, I drafted the prepared a Draft taking due care to preferences to highlight the developments and achievements using pie charts, histograms, diagrams and tables using the computer facilities in DRDA Office. When I tried to share this Draft with RDC, it was brushed aside. I remained silent.

The dates of Chief Secretary's visit were postponed twice. In this uncertainty, RDC proceeded on a tour of Koraput. I was called by Chief

Secretary himself informing that he would visit Ganjam the following day. When I informed him of RDC's absence, I was directed to inform him not to cut short his tour for this inspection programme. I complied and requested RDC to speak to Chief Secretary also. Recalling my earlier interaction with Chief Secretary, I was quite apprehensive about the visit. I tried to remain as formal as possible, did not open up discussions, and otherwise also tried to maintain the proverbial safe distance during his two days of stay in the Circuit House. Immediately upon his arrival I had handed over the draft inspection note for his personal use. When he visited the Block Office, he ignored the draft prepared by office of RDC handed over to him by Secretary to RDC. He appreciated the progress in implementing ongoing programmes and statistical presentations made in my draft report. After completing the inspection, we proceeded to Berhampur Circuit House for lunch. He appeared very happy, as though a totally different person from the one who had chastised me in his Secretariat office a few months earlier. In fact, he also talked about his affection towards RDC who had taken his district training under him about 30 years ago when he was Collector, Balangir.

Chief Secretary wanted to have a meeting with local gentry and senior officials to assess the post-flood scenario. In the meeting, he received comprehensive feedback which included lavish appreciation of the work done by me much to my embarrassment. Before leaving for Bhubaneswar, Chief Secretary put his hands on my shoulder and stated that he had not wanted RDC to remain present during this visit, and that he would visit the district again to meet my family and to have a dinner at my residence. I felt ashamed that I had not invited Chief Secretary to my house for dinner thus breaking a long-held tradition, and indeed for maintaining a distance with him throughout his stay in Ganjam. His generosity towards me was in full display and I was speechless. My personal relationship with him continues strongly to this day. At the end of my tenure in Ganjam, RDC assessed me adversely. But Chief Secretary, who was the accepting authority, disagreed with him.

S.K. Palit held the post of Member, Board of Revenue, the top regulator in the hierarchy of Revenue and Relief administration in the State. RDC invited him to Ganjam to visit flood-affected areas. Member insisted that I accompany them. The route chart prepared by RDC maliciously sought to expose me by projecting the weakest areas of progress made at that early stage which included inspection of temporary shelters, perhaps to implant memories of unhappy condition of flood-affected families in the mind of an important visitor. Anyhow, adversity always brings out the grit and determination in me to do more. And here, perhaps RDC was not aware that I had been regularly visiting these shelters and interacting with the families inhabiting them to ease their problems to the maximum extent possible. Pucca houses were being constructed involving the affected families at no great distance from these shelters. RDC had probably given some prior negative inputs to the Member. I could see the Member trying to brush away attempts by RDC to frequently whisper in his ear or at having a conversation in their common Mother tongue while we were travelling in the same car. I barely spoke. From the moment the Member started directly interacting with flood victims, perhaps the other side of the story about me coming from the mouths of the affected people cast an indelible impression on his mind regarding the spanking pace at which work was being done.

Later on, after my transfer from the district, when I met the Member to present a copy of Documentation of Ganjam Flood which also contained some critical observations on the role played by RDC, he was kind enough to say that he had not agreed with RDC's assessment about me and attributed his adverse appraisal of my performance to temperamental differences with me. I had not cared to know as to how I was being assessed by my immediate seniors. The authorities above them continued to extend a generous helping hand towards me in many ways. P.K. Patnaik, ACS Finance, was a native of Chhatrapur in Ganjam district. On one visit, he had reminded me quite philosophically, that I should not forget that I have journeyed to Odisha from the high Himalayan mountains where blunt and straight talk may be necessary for survival, but that on the way I have crossed the city of Lucknow renowned for courteous behaviour and politeness of its people. He said that I should, therefore, display diplomacy in handling my senior colleagues! I digested his advice in all sincerity but could not succeed in recasting myself in the Lucknavi tehzeeb till the very end of my innings in public service.

An embarrassing incident which brought into fore my differences with RDC was on the occasion of a 2-day long Divisional Conference of Collectors, SPs and other senior officers of the Southern Division. Held once every quarter, the Conference logistics and arrangements for food, snacks etc. were made by Collectors of participating districts by turn, and now it was the turn of Ganjam Collector. Shunning the practice of sourcing packed food from the most expensive hotel in Berhampur, I suggested that all four Collectors of Southern Division and RDC could go to the Circuit House or nearby Revenue Inspection Bungalow for a simple lunch as arranging food for a large number of officers and their drivers was beyond my ability. Some of the Collectors laughed at me, while one advised me quietly to assign the arrangement to Excise Superintendent or Regional Transport Officer. My inability to arrange the working lunch was not appreciated by RDC who remarked that being head of DRDA, ITDA, BFDA, SFDA etc., I should avoid advancing excuses for an arrangement that would fall upon me only once in a year. A Collector perceived to be closer to RDC asked as to how I made arrangements for Ministers and other VIPs visiting the district frequently. My response was blunt; the money received by DRDA, ITDA, BFDA, SFDA, etc. was for schemes meant for the poor and not for lavish lunches and dinners of officers, Ministers, etc. Earlier when RDC himself had come to inspect a few sections of Ganjam Collectorate, I had instructed Nizarat Officer to serve the food bills on him as per the actual expenditure incurred. Another Collector volunteered to arrange the working lunch on both days for the participants. When the Conference broke for lunch, I quietly left the place to return after the lunch and re-join discussions. This practice continued as long as I served as Collector Ganjam despite considerable embarrassment to me and some others.

Another incident which got publicised extensively was about an agitation by Class-IV or Group-D employees of Ganjam district. The genesis of the strike was gross misconduct by a young Group-D staff who habitually misbehaved with senior officers, and sought postings in offices of his choice. Despite being arrested and in detention for over 48 hours earlier in a criminal case for rape entailing deemed suspension as per the relevant CCA Rule, disciplinary action had not been taken against him. Routinely shifted now to another section of the Collectorate, he protested. Group-D employees are generally not transferred to distant places and are merely moved from one section to another. Now, in the face of this compounding insubordination when he did not join the section of his posting in the Collectorate, I passed a reasoned order transferring the disobedient employee to the farthest end of the district. Along with his supporters, he filed complaints before RDC and a 'dharna' was staged in front of his office by the association of Group-D employees. Minister, Revenue and Excise telephoned me and advised rescinding the transfer. Speaker of Legislative Assembly visited the district along with President of State's Group-D employees' association and pleaded with me to withdraw the order. I explained the character of the employee, his past conduct, and rape charges against him. I bluntly asked the President of State's Group-D Employees as to how he could condone a rape just because it had happened in another family and how he had failed his position as President by arriving here all the way from the State Capital in support of a cause without having full knowledge of the situation. What was more distressing for me was that the agitation by Group-D employees was tacitly being supported by RDC. I had rarely been harsh on Group-D employees and generally remained sympathetic towards them. However, discipline was an article of faith for me; there was no exception here.

The turning point which led to the end of this agitation after a month came accidentally. State Government had issued a circular conveying economy measures which did not permit use of office vehicles on Sundays. Along with an ADM, I had gone to Berhampur by bus for a discussion with a Committee of Odisha Legislative Assembly scheduled to be held in the Circuit House. Once there, I saw a Group-D employee of my office in tears as he needed blood for the surgical intervention on his anaemic wife. She was already mother of five daughters and was expecting her sixth child. When the Blood Bank conveyed inability to help, I hired a rickshaw and proceeded straight to donate blood. After undergoing a safe surgical procedure, his wife delivered her sixth child, a boy! I had not informed anyone, and only ADM and Blood Bank officer were witnesses to this incident. To my surprise, local newspapers published the incident of my donating blood for the wife of a striking employee the following day! I went on to take action against the Blood Bank-in-charge as he was found selling blood irregularly, which action was appreciated. Group-D employees association called off their strike instantly, without bitterness. Chaff was thus finally separated from the grain.

Communal Conflict

Although my tenure as Collector & District Magistrate was less than 10 months, it was eventful and satisfying. Some of my actions, however, invited controversies too. For one, in R. Udaygiri area of Paralakhemundi Sub-Division, communal conflict between Christian converts and Hindu tribals erupted when the festival of Holi and Good Friday coincided. I was informed about a communal incident having occurred at about 8.00 p.m. by SSP. We reached the spot around 10.00 p.m. By this time, two critically-injured persons had been shifted to a hospital at Berhampur. About a dozen persons each from both sides had been apprehended by local police, though still appeared to be straining against their fetters ready to hit out at each other. We met representatives of both communities separately. The Hindu community, including Vishwa Hindu Parishad's representatives, narrated that when people were playing Holi in the forenoon and approached those assembled for prayers in the local Church to join them, they were asked to come in the afternoon after rituals in the Church were over. Accordingly, when they went, they were greeted with bullets and sticks. They also mentioned about killing of a bull dedicated to Lord Shiva by some Christian youth who had thereafter absconded to the nearby forest. I advised them to remain calm and not to take law into their hand as the administration would do all that was required.

The Christian community were led by head of the local Church, a Priest from Kerala who had arrived here about a couple of years ago. He did not allow any of the local people of his faith to put forth their views. Besides, he simply kept repeating himself and blaming the rival group for all the trouble. Local police officials told me that a similar situation had been created last year too during Dussehra festival after which the police force had remained deployed in the area for a long time. It was seen that since his arrival, this head of the local Church had been aggressively propagating his faith and was intolerant of those who disagreed with him. His presence appeared to have catalysed strife between otherwise peace-loving communities who had coexisted for generations in the area. He remained argumentative repeatedly playing his minority card, unmindful of other side of the story.

Perforce, I ended the discussion by reminding him that no religion permitted peace among people to be disturbed. His two years of stay in the area had broken the age-old harmony, which only suggested that he was either a lunatic or devil in the garb of a saint. I warned that he would be taken into custody if arms used during clashes and those responsible for slaughtering the bull failed to surrender within two hours. SSP became nervous after hearing my blunt loud warning. The rival group quietly left the place finding their concerns being addressed adequately by district administration. I also advised SSP to reduce the presence of police which could create unnecessary panic among the simple and unworldly tribal communities. My warning indeed worked. Arms used during the communal clash were brought to the Police Station and the youth who had vanished into the local forest after killing the bull surrendered. Peace was restored in the area in a short time.

My intervention and warning triggered a strong reaction among Christians State-wide. Their leaders sent a representation to Chief Minister accusing me of bias against Christians. DSP, Intelligence Branch, deputed to conduct an enquiry met me and informed that a very senior IAS officer, himself a Christian despite taking the benefit of reservation as a person from SC, had helped to draft the representation. I thanked the DSP for sharing the details with me and advised that he should draw his own conclusions after studying the situation.

About a fortnight later, Chief Minister wanted to visit Paralakhemundi on the request of the Christian community. His office wanted a joint report from District Magistrate and SSP on the situation, which was submitted. Not satisfied with the advice, *inter alia,* not to accept this invitation as the time was not conducive and situation still volatile, Chief Minister telephoned me to state that he did not require advice or permission for his visits. I submitted that as head of district administration, it was my responsibility to inform his office about the situation and administrative assessment, though Chief Minister could always exercise his privilege of rejecting this advice. Paralakhemundi, which became the separate Gajapati District later, had majority of tribal population including 33 percent of Christian faith. With mid-term election for Lok Sabha around the corner, it was not possible for a seasoned politician to resist the temptation to accept an invitation from Christian leaders. At this stage, I was transferred. Many in media attributed my transfer to keeping the Christian community happy. Chief Minister's visit was reported by media as a disaster. Election results too did not show any political gains.

Efforts towards Total Literacy and Exit

Dr. L.D. Mishra, Director General of National Literacy Mission, visited Ganjam and advised that district administration should prepare an action plan for Total Literacy Campaign (TLC) to universalise functional literacy. I argued with him that unless and until requisite infrastructure for elementary education was in place, TLC was unlikely to succeed, particularly in Paralakhemundi where tribal population was in majority and rate of literacy was the lowest in the State. The difficulty in finding volunteers who would go out to spread literacy among those who did not have access to elementary education in their formative years would be acute, even unsurmountable. Dr. Mishra understood the practical difficulties but remained persuasive when he said that the literacy campaign might be taken up in phases. In its first phase, TLC could include areas where necessary infrastructure existed. I found strength in this argument that those who were deprived of elementary education in their formative years could get another opportunity for acquiring functional literacy.

Exercises for building up the implementing environment for TLC were started quickly and systematically in Ganjam. A blue print was prepared indicating the requirement of volunteers and availability of grassroot organisations at village level. Requirement of funds was assessed. A detailed action plan was prepared. I was invited to present the action plan on 20 March 1991 before the Executive Body of National Literacy Mission. The action plan was appreciated and approved. The plan excluded Paralakhemundi due to absence of infrastructure and non-availability of logistics.

In the evening on 21 March 1991 just as soon as I had returned from Delhi, I received a call from Special Secretary, GA Department. Before he could say anything, I asked whether he was calling to apprise me of my transfer. Though I had simply shot in the dark in jest, conveying surprise he asked me as to how I could know when the file containing the proposal was still to be approved formally by Chief Minister. Sobering up, I told him that he had never called me before. Mid-term election had been announced and model code of conduct came into effect from 22 March. Coupled with the fact that both the Ministers hailing from Ganjam were candidates for the two Lok Sabha constituencies in the district, it was not difficult for me to surmise the imminent possibility of my transfer. He confirmed that he had been asked to break the news in advance and also to relinquish charge without waiting for the substitute to join. Deputy Secretary in GA Department, earlier my ADM here, was the one who conveyed the notification number basing upon which I relinquished charge as Collector & District Magistrate instantly. I packed my personal belongings the same night and kept them in a room. The next day my wife and son moved to a room in Revenue Bungalow at Berhampur, while I travelled to Bhubaneswar and reported on 25 March 1991 in Industries Department as Joint Secretary in charge of medium and heavy industries.

Things Which Remained Unattended

I had initiated steps for a healthy development of Ganjam district in sanitation and literacy campaign which were to go hand-in-hand with universalisation of elementary education. Indeed, I had designed to expand the scope of TLC to include awareness about sanitation and universalisation of elementary education. The primary condition for inclusion of a village in TLC was availability of volunteers who were qualified to teach those beyond the school-going age group and ensuring that enrolment in primary schools was universal at the same time.

Sanitation standards in Ganjam were probably the lowest in the State. Road side defecation was common. Water from village tanks was used for bathing and consumption purposes in many places, which frequently resulted in the incidence of water borne diseases. The district had the highest incidence of rabies. Central Rural Sanitation Programme had just been launched by Central Government to provide assistance to families below the poverty line for constructing household sanitary latrines. I was already ensuring that houses under IAY invariably included toilets. The sanitation programme was a most essential need of the district, and NGO Gram Vikas was inclined to be involved in its implementation in a big way. However, my plan remained in my dream. The rural sanitation programme was forgotten after I left the district. TLC stood reduced to mere propaganda, as I found later. I was trying to push these programmes despite the elected representatives having no interest in them. Public support was my main strength for sustaining them.

Berhampur town, a very old business centre for Southern Odisha, was probably the dirtiest in the whole State. Once upon a time, its drains were scientifically linked with the Rushikulya Drainage and Canal System. These old drains now existed only on paper with permanent structures having been constructed over them. In the rainy season, release of water from the town was extremely difficult. The famous Ramalingam Tank, a pride of Berhampur town at some point of time, had become a stinking death trap due to siltation and dumping of garbage. Since the elected municipal body had been superseded and District Collector had been notified as Administrator, I had seized the opportunity to take steps for restoring the Tank by involving all the stakeholders. The plan had received appreciation of all concerned.

Another issue I had wanted to address was in relation to the cremation ground situated on a low-lying area at the outskirts of Berhampur town. To radically change the landscape of this place, I deputed a municipal engineer to Pune to obtain the blueprint of the crematorium "Vaikuntha-puri". I had seen it and found it well organised with aesthetic green cover, neatly maintained, and having a designated centre for collection of ashes a day after cremation. By the time, the work started to replicate the system in Berhampur, and compound walls were raised to secure the area, I was transferred. Neither the restoration of Ramalingam Tank nor the modernization of cremation ground could be ensured despite both these projects being very close to my heart.

Expression of Public Appreciation and Rejection of Favours

My tenure at the helm of district administration was full of excitement, suspense, risks and to some extent unpredictability. Medical community at large remained unhappy with me for certain actions. Chief District Medical Officer otherwise a well-behaved and well-connected official, was suspended when I reported his habit of permitting sale of "opium" on medical ground. My frequent unannounced visits to Primary/Community Health Centres in rural areas exposed absenteeism among doctors who mostly practiced privately in Berhampur town. They were also displeased with me for being reprimanded in monthly review meetings on this account and for poor performance in implementing important programmes like immunization, sterilization etc. I believed in working with anonymity and felt quite embarrassed to witness public emotions pouring in to support my interventions as administrative head of the district during the period of crisis and also in normal times.

On a visit to one of the worst-affected villages to inspect restoration and reconstruction works including under-construction IAY houses in Shergarh Block, I saw that the village seemed largely and surprisingly empty. By the time I returned home, it was well after midnight. I was again surprised, this time to find that my residential compound was chock-a-block with people. I became a bit nervous too. After alighting from my office vehicle at the entrance, and before I could ascertain the reason for such a huge assembly, slogans started reverberating the atmosphere in my support! I was told that their visit in a group was to personally convey gratitude for my intervention, including assistance for construction of pucca houses. I pleaded before them with folded hands not to indulge in sloganeering. I now understood why the village was virtually empty earlier in the evening.

Another incident which was equally embarrassing and widely reported was in relation to a visit to Bhanjanagar to attend a review meeting about a month after the natural calamity. A Minister from the district was also around. Local people naturally like to meet their elected representatives and articulate grievances to their leaders. They went to the Minister in a large number with petitions. On being informed about my visit and meeting being held at Sub-Divisional level, almost all of them deserted the Minister and surrounded me with their grievances and petitions. Perhaps they valued my temperamental impatience and habit of speaking out my mind, conveying clearly what was possible to do, which would be committed quickly along with implementing timelines. Whatever was not doable, would be rejected outright. This proclivity, my DNA, might have displeased a few momentarily, but I was rarely misunderstood. People believed in me more than I believed in myself.

About 10 months after my transfer from the district, I faced a peculiar situation while returning early morning from the field visit the previous day in Koraput district as Director, Tribal Welfare. Since the bridge over Ghodahada river had washed away during floods and construction of a new one had not started yet, I was not sure whether any temporary bridge had been constructed since then. Villagers near the bypass road told my driver that waters had receded and there was no difficulty in crossing the river in the car. This was, as I found soon enough, a trap to extract money. The moment my car approached the river, a few persons found roaming around encouraged the driver to move on till the Ambassador car started sinking and the engine stalled! They now demanded money for rescuing us which had to be agreed. After somehow crossing the river when I offered money as promised, they perhaps saw my face and recognizing me started apologising profusely for the inconvenience. They also refused to take any remuneration for their help saying that their lives had been saved during the floods and that they were not so ungrateful as to accept money from me. They were pleased to see me among themselves once again after a gap of close to a year. I was overwhelmed and felt greatly rewarded for whatever work I had done in ten months as Collector Ganjam.

Chief Minister who at one point appeared unhappy, had become very cordial, occasionally conveying his appreciation over telephone. The perception of Chief Secretary too had changed positively. There was, however, no change in my style of functioning. I recall that an educated youth once appeared before me with a petition seeking his appointment as RI against a vacant post. He said that his family had lost all assets, once in fire and second time in floods, and that he would kill himself if not appointed against a vacant post. It was no coincidence that just before he appeared before me, I had received a telephone call from Chief Minister to say that the petitioner needed to be helped. I had calmly conveyed to Chief Minister that he should rest assured that rules and procedure laid down by Government would be fully complied with in dealing with every case of appointment. In this case, I found that the petitioner was not ready to accept my advice to even apply for the post sought by him when it was advertised. He threatened that he would commit suicide in front of my office, reminding me what had happened in Sambalpur where an encroacher had attempted to self-immolate in front of Collector's office and later succumbed to burn injuries. I knew well that he was trying to blackmail me by leveraging an unfortunate incident, but he had failed to gauge my mettle.

After my transfer from the district, my successor did appoint him as RI. Reorganisation of Ganjam district a couple of years later resulted in the transfer of this person to Gajapati district where he did not want to work. Resultantly he was removed from service. Years later, as fate would have it, he appeared before me when I was ACS in R&DM Department with his appeal petition against the order of removal passed by his appointing authority. The appeal had no merit and was dismissed. The episode highlighted well that an undeserving person had been extended undue favour by brazenly violating the prescribed rules and procedures for appointments, without realising the consequences of such action on the system. Favours granted by functionaries wishing to remain close to those in power and enjoy so-called prized postings which are at best temporary, or out of sheer timidity against pressure, simply exemplifies the old adage of being 'penny wise and pound foolish'.

When mid-term Lok Sabha polls were announced, it was evident that the political parties in power were anxious not to get on the wrong side of T.N. Seshan, the indomitable Chief Election Commissioner. His no-nonsense attitude to maintain purity of the electoral process was legion. Ruling dispensations without exception, are more comfortable with pliable officers occupying key administrative posts. When elections are announced and even more so with a Chief Election Commissioner like T.N. Seshan, political parties swing swiftly to place their chosen ones in position before the Model Code of Conduct comes into play. My strong perception has been that political parties suffer the illusion of being helped, since the end results do not show that the support of such officers necessarily helps them to the expected extent.

Even so, with my moniker of "Terror Datt" which received wide currency in Ganjam for my enforcement works which saw some officials enjoying political patronage take a fall, anxiety among ruling party leaders was highly likely. As if in confirmation that their sense of heightened political anxiety during elections was real, and not a figment of my imagination, soon after the election, I was offered the post of Collector of Koraput, then the biggest district in the State. Had such an order been passed without asking me, I would simply have packed my bags and joined duty at Koraput. But, something about the verbal offer of this posting as though in reward for the work I had done in Ganjam after lobbing me around in the Secretariat rubbed me wrong. I respectfully informed the Special Secretary, GA Deparment that I had not acquired any special qualifications during the intervening period for holding the post of Collector again. In the matter of transfer and posting I have always held that regardless of causes, suitability and quality of orders, it was the prerogative of Government to pick and choose officers for assignments. Consulting the officer concerned was invariably not handled with dispassionate rigour required either by Government or Officer concerned, and the results were seldom in public interest.

* * * *

4

Desk Jobs in the Secretariat and Foreign Training

FIVE WEEKS IN INDUSTRIES DEPARTMENT

I joined in Industries Department as Joint Secretary on 25 March 1991. Posting in the Secretariat was in complete contrast with exciting and eventful field work where one could see with gross anatomy of the eye the results of administrative interventions. A Joint Secretary in the Secretariat with hardly any role in policy planning or decision-making almost amounted to being a glorified clerk. In the initial months of my assignment, I could not perceive any direction, sense of purpose nor urgency. Departmental administration appeared engrossed with routine paper-processing and intermittent fire-fighting depending upon the political priorities of those who mattered.

I was allotted charge of medium and heavy industries. My domain knowledge was limited, but my keenness to get familiarized with functional aspects of the Secretariat in general and those concerning industries in particular was unlimited. To begin with there were difficulties in finding a suitable room for me. A small room without ventilation used as a store-room was vacated and offered to me. I found it unhygienic and started getting headaches frequently. After some time, I was allowed to share a bigger room allotted to another Joint Secretary perceived to be close to Secretary of the Department. I was grateful to him for his kindness.

After a first couple of weeks, I started getting a strange feeling as if my presence was becoming increasingly uncomfortable for the Secretary. Some of the important organizations under the department headed by young and friendly officers, who were initially welcoming and friendly, started avoiding me sensing the mood or indications of the Secretary perhaps. My room-mate mentioned in passing that one such IAS officer taught Physics and Mathematics to the Secretary's son after office hours. Another heading an important Directorate had been researching out material and literature for preparation of a book to be published in Secretary's name. I was perhaps incapable of providing any such useful services.

The seeds of a breakdown were sown when I received Secretary's orders to attend an important meeting and present the State Government's views on a sick industry before the Bureau of Industrial Finance & Reconstruction. I received the file containing the orders, though dated prior to the scheduled date of meeting, after it was over. I came to know soon enough that the previous Secretary had been replaced for tendering advice on the issue which had merit and objectivity, besides being in accordance with the State's Industrial Policy Resolution. The case in brief was that both Ballarpur Industries and Modi Paper Mills had conveyed their willingness by making identical offers to take over the sick Titagarh Paper Mills which had over 600 hectares of land and other fixed assets, on the condition that State Government should grant sales tax exemption and deferment for a certain period after transfer besides supplying raw materials (Bamboos) at concessional rates. However, both offers violated the advice given in Bureau of Industrial Finance & Reconstruction's award. Chief Minister was desirous of accepting the offer made by Ballarpur Industries. But State Finance Department was not inclined to accede to the conditionalities proposed in the offers which violated the industrial policy resolution and also due to likely revenue losses to the State exchequer. Forest Department too did not support supply of raw materials at concessional rates. It was reasoned that after nationalisation of Bamboo even tribal artisans who otherwise had unbridled access to forest produce were not eligible for Bamboo supplies at concessional rates for manufacturing baskets, etc. for sustaining their livelihood.

A meeting was called at the highest political level to resolve the differences among various Departments in relation to these conditionalities in Ballarpur Industries' offer. In addition to Ministers and Secretaries of relevant departments, Chief Secretary, ACS Finance, and Development Commissioner participated. Industry Secretary had assigned the task of recording the meeting's minutes to me. During the formality of obtaining signatures on the attendance sheet, when his turn came Pyari Mohan Mohapatra, Principal Secretary to Chief Minister, instead of signing informed me pointedly that he never signed attendance sheets, not even in meetings held in Delhi. Secretary Industries, sitting next to him, snatched the attendance sheet from my hand murmuring something to him in an inaudible voice. Anyhow, when ACS, Finance supported by Finance Minister and Development Commissioner tried to point out the extant policy of the State on granting tax exemptions, etc, Chief Minister shouted them down calling them "bloody bureaucrats" who had no knowledge of industries and simply enjoyed huge perks without doing any productive work. Views mildly expressed by other participants too were trashed. Industries Department was directed to process the proposal without any further delay so that Memorandum of Understanding (MoU) could be signed with the new promoter within a week or so.

I submitted draft minutes within hours as desired by Industries Secretary, recording them carefully, being my first such experience in the Secretariat.

The record note covered all the important issues raised, including observations of Chief Minister (excluding his rude words). In the evening, I was called by Secretary and asked as to why I was creating difficulties for her, and seeing perplexity in my face, was told me pointedly, "*Didn't you know the Chief Minister and hear his observations during the meeting?*" I politely submitted that the draft had been prepared based on meticulous notes, but Secretary may like to point out or modify if any points discussed were missing. After some more interchanges, I was asked to leave the room when I indicated my unwillingness to withdraw these draft minutes adding politely that there was no need for me to know Chief Minister's preferences as I was being paid by the State to work in public interest and in accordance with laid down rules and procedures.

The next morning an Under Secretary came to me to convey the directions of Secretary to sign the file now carried by him which contained a brief note of one-and-half paragraphs stating that the issue of transferring the sick Titagarh Paper Mills to Ballarpur Industries was discussed in the high-level meeting and endorsed unanimously. The file did not contain the draft "record note" of the meeting I had prepared nor my note endorsing it to the Secretary. When I expressed my reluctance to sign this new note and wanted to know why the papers prepared by me were not in the file, the Under Secretary went away and did not return. A few hours later, I found out that he had signed and issued this revised brief record note. I had no occasion to see that file again.

A couple of days later I found a memo signed by Secretary on my table seeking my explanation as to why I had failed to be present at the time of signing of MoU between State Government and Ballarpur Industries. I was surprised. Neither Secretary nor anyone else had informed me about the event nor verbally advised me to attend it, although the subject matter stood allotted to me. Vice President of Ballarpur Industries, who had called on me in my office the previous day, had also not said anything about the impending signing of MoU! He had instead offered me a gift, which I politely and firmly declined after naively cautioning him to desist from offering gifts to any official as such things had potential to pollute public life besides influencing decision-making, Anyhow, I immediately sent a reply to Secretary refuting her charge besides narrating what had happened the previous day.

Later in the evening, I received a telephone call from ACS Finance, P.K. Patnaik, who asked me as to what was wrong with me. He wanted me to meet him immediately, which I did. He informed me that in his presence Industries Secretary had made a number of allegations against me before Chief Minister which included my non-cooperation, disobedience and challenging the authority of Chief Minister. I was also informed about my imminent transfer from Industries Department. I explained the sequence of events. He was happy to hear my side of the story and said some comforting and encouraging words. Later on, power circles were abuzz with the news that the advocate spouse of

Industries Secretary was rewarded with retainership by Ballarpur Industries with a handsome package in Odisha High Court despite the company having no case to contest.

The following morning at 10.00 a.m. on 3 May 1991, I was served the notification of my transfer as Joint Secretary, Panchayat Raj Department. Without any ado, on a blank piece of paper I wrote my relinquishing charge report. There was no scope to call on Secretary, who had taken leave on that day, probably to avoid a situation that could be considered embarrassing. I was neither happy nor sad to leave a Department I had served in for a mere five weeks. Short or long, as I always considered it unbecoming of a civil servant to question postings or influence them anyway, within an hour I had reported in Panchayat Raj Department

TASKS ASSIGNED IN PANCHAYAT RAJ DEPARTMENT

As I had spent a major period of service so far in the field of rural development, it was not unnatural for me to be posted in Panchayat Raj (PR) Department, which had been called the Community Development & Rural Reconstruction Department earlier. State Government, with the ruling party having won a three-fourth majority in Legislative Assembly, had superseded the rural elected bodies and made newly-elected MLAs in charge of Panchayat Samitis in their respective areas through executive orders. My assignment was to handle vigilance matters related to schemes implemented through departmental field formations. This entailed conducting enquiries on allegations received on past and ongoing works. Other than a personal assistant, I had no supporting hands. As far as personal facilities or entitlements were concerned, I was never demanding, preferring always to make minimum use of my entitlements. I had not been provided with transport facilities in Industries Department and did not care for not getting the same in this Department either, regardless of officers junior to me being provided official transport, or that the Secretary was holding on to more vehicles, including one exclusively for social use of his family. I drove to office on my personal scooter, and once a week I could access an office vehicle for my field visits.

Secretary desired that enquiries should be conducted specifically on matters referred to me by Minister. The procedure for enquiries based on political considerations for selection among various allegation petitions, including prompted ones against adversaries, was difficult for me to accept. I started selecting the allegation petitions at random for conducting enquiries. During my enquiries, I found large-scale irregularities being committed by ruling party MLAs who were in charge of most of the Panchayat Samitis though the larger number of allegation petitions were related to old works executed during the tenure of previous government.

Secretary of PR Department was very popular among young officers for his friendly gestures and intellectual discourses. He enjoyed an image of a widely read officer with an open mind. In informal chats, he would expansively hold forth in a bid to encourage youngsters that they should offer views frankly and fearlessly. In practice, he expected his subordinates to adhere strictly to his writ and that of the Minister regardless of merit. Once when Director, Special Projects, was on tour I was invited, being his stand-in, to a Ministerial meeting with Education Department to discuss their proposal regarding construction of primary school buildings for which 50 percent funds had been received from Central Government. School & Mass Education (S&ME) Minister wanted Panchayat Raj Department to consider dovetailing these funds available in her Department with those of employment-generating schemes. It was reasoned that the balance between materials and wage components could thus be easier to meet and a larger number of primary school buildings could get constructed. Being conversant with both schemes, I pleaded that the proposal merited support being in conformity with prescribed guidelines. But no decision was taken as my Minister and Secretary were non-committal. On his return from tour, Director, Special Project, invited me to his house to convey Secretary's anger and advice to me not to speak out of turn. A few days later, during an internal meeting of departmental officers, the Secretary with his usual friendly façade repeated his usual refrain of fearless speech because "*superior views should prevail and not that of the superior's*". I waited for my turn to speak and paraphrased to agree that superiority and seniority might not necessarily go hand-in-hand and, thus, seniors' views might not necessarily imply superior's views. After the ensuing pin-drop silence, I was reasonably sure that what I said would be viewed seriously.

The scale of my field visits and enquiries started shrinking due to inadequate availability of transport for site visits. In the meantime, Chief Secretary also insisted that I should complete the documentation on the Ganjam floods. I thus utilised a part of my time in compilation of materials and writing the report on the Ganjam floods of November 1990. District Planning Officer of Ganjam was of great help in providing inputs for the documentation. I was candid in my narration about impediments and negative role played by some key functionaries of State Government.

When the results of inquiries being conducted by me did not suit the dispensation, I was useless for all practical purposes to the Department. On a day when Secretary was away from Office, as had happened in Industries Department, I received my marching orders to serve as Director, Tribal Welfare, in Harijan& Tribal Welfare (H&TW) Department. I relinquished the charge instantly, without waiting for the Secretary to pass orders for my relief. I had lasted a full 72 days here, a bit better than 39 days in Industries Department.

However, the administrative process of joining the new post was not as smooth. Unlike in armed and paramilitary forces, transfer orders in civil administration are not followed by movement orders. I realized that a misunderstanding leading to a confrontation between Director, Tribal Welfare, and Secretary of H&TW Department was the immediate cause of the chain of transfer orders. While I was slotted to step into the post of Director, Tribal Affairs, the incumbent was to move to a post of MD of a spinning mills cooperative federation under Industries Department after that post fell vacant with the superannuation of the serving officer on 31 July 1991. Thus, I gave my joining report in H&TW Department on 25 July 1991 and was extended joining time by GA Department. I was able to use these few days to complete my documentation on Ganjam floods. It was not for nothing that R.L. Jamuda of 1981 batch of IAS whom I succeeded, proceeded on long leave soon enough when the problems he started facing with the Secretary of Industries Department became too tough for him to bear.

HEADING A DEPARTMENT: DIRECTOR, TRIBAL WELFARE

I learnt soon enough that my predecessor had fallen out with R.M. Senapati, Secretary in the Department over two matters. In the first, contrary to Secretary's desire, my predecessor was disinclined to initiate disciplinary proceedings against Project Director of Odisha Tribal Development Project (OTDP), Kashipur. More on this later. In the second matter, Secretary had issued an administrative order cancelling my predecessor's order for conducting the audit of accounts of Tribal &Harijan Research-cum-Training Institute (THRTI)[1]. The order for conducting the audit had been issued to enable investigation into allegations of financial irregularities against Director, THRTI in exercise of powers under the provisions of Odisha General Financial Rules. This had complicated the situation for both of them and challenged their harmonious co-existence. Nrusingh Patnaik, Director, THRTI, despite being one of the most reputed anthropologists in the country, was equally well-known for his weakness towards money and materials. He had been very close to successive Secretaries of the Department. When orders to audit the accounts of THRTI were cancelled by incumbent Secretary, Jamuda escalated the matter to the next higher authority on the ground that statutory powers enjoyed by him as Head of Department under General Financial Rules could not be superseded through an executive order passed by Secretary of the Department. In less than two months of my joining the Department, R.M. Senapati was replaced by a great gentleman, D.P. Bhattacharya, an IAS officer of 1964 batch, who joined as Principal Secretary and good fortune smiled happily at me for the next two years that I served under him.

Untangling Knots in OTDP, Kashipur

I found that implementation of OTDP, Kashipur was suffering from internecine dislikes, with actual developmental issues relegated to cold storage and the demoralised lot of field staff could do very little to redeem the situation.

---

1. This Institute was later recast as Scheduled Tribe and Scheduled Caste Research & Training Institute (STSCRTI), Bhubaneswar.

The situation was aggravated by palpable factionalism between Secretary of the Department on the one hand, and Director Tribal Welfare aided by both Project Director, OTDP, Kashipur, and Head of "Agragami" which was the participating local NGO, on the other. The Project was supported financially by International Fund for Agricultural Development (IFAD) for sustainable development of tribal communities in Kashipur Block (Rayagada). It mandated strong community participation and involvement of a leading local NGO, which is how "Agragami" came to be associated with it. Compounding the problem was that this NGO was being run by one Achyut Das, an aggressive person who was considered a megalomaniac by his detractors. Director of NGO Agragami was rather well-connected and stood appointed by Chief Minister also as a member of State Planning Board. At this stage he turned hostile against the Secretary and conveyed his unwillingness to remain involved with this IFAD-supported Project.

Immediately after taking up the assignment, I proceeded to Kashipur to study the situation and look into the allegations against Director of NGO Agragami as well as alleged nexus between him and Ashok M. Dalvai, an IAS officer of 1984 batch serving as Project Director, OTDP, Kashipur. I recalled well that a baseline survey conducted by Ashok M. Dalvai as Sub-Collector of Gunupur sub-division on the prevalence of hunger and malnutrition in tribal communities had embarrassed the previous government as his findings were used politically by the principal opposition party. During my visit, I was impressed by the human resources' development work carried out by NGO Agragami in remote villages which had greatly helped in promoting agro-forestry, horticulture, soil and water conservation, development of critical infrastructure and community mobilisation in Project-villages. The proactive NGO had unsettled the nexus between local leaders, including elected public representatives, and vested interests, which included money lenders and intermediaries. I advised Project Director, OTDP and Director of Agragami to remain in partnership as everything they had done was in accordance with the Project mandate. I did not see any truth in the allegations made against them by local leaders. My report contradicted the findings of the Joint Secretary deputed earlier to Kashipur by the Secretary before I joined the Department.

I also found that the Project was not just a battleground between the principal functionaries, it suffered because of non-deployment of requisite manpower. Vacancies were over 50 percent of sanctioned strength. The administrative department had simply not taken interest to fill up posts. Successive Review Missions had drawn attention to the shortage of manpower while appreciating the human resources' development work done by Agragami in terms of community mobilisation in conjunction with Project staff. I got convinced that the project's implementation suffered due to an unnecessary controversy despite some excellent work initiated on the ground. The Review Missions appeared to have transmitted signals to IFAD as if the State Government was not seriously interested in implementing the Project.

Shortly after my joining, another Review Mission submitted its evaluation report, similarly communicating its dissatisfaction on account of inadequate support to the Project by State Government. The Mission called on Chief Secretary and asserted that much more needed to be done in order to achieve Project goals. When a Mission member stated that the Project could be wound up if the State Government failed to meet its commitment to provide mutually-agreed manpower, Ramakant Rath who had joined as Chief Secretary in the meanwhile, and was not fully aware of the constraints being faced by the Project, was incensed. He observed bluntly that the Review Mission should not remain under any misconception that the State Government was less concerned than IFAD about development of its people and that if the funding agency wanted to wind up the Project, so be it. When he expected me to say something, I confirmed the acute shortage of staff while detailing out other administrative difficulties faced in the past which had now been solved. After the meeting concluded with uncertainty writ large about the Project, Chief Secretary called me and took stock of the situation, which resulted in more than 80 percent posts being filled up. Additional financial incentives were provided to Officers to join in Kashipur in order to overcome lack of facilities during their tenure at OTDP.

Unlike his predecessor, D.P. Bhattacharya gave me free hand. It did not take time to improve the work environment in Kashipur and at State level. The Joint Secretary, whose unfounded adverse report alleging nexus between Project Director and NGO's Director, had contributed to deteriorating relations between Director, OTDP and Secretary was initially side-lined and later transferred. I started visiting Kashipur once a month. Demoralised field staff, including fence-sitters, and the aggrieved NGO were taken on board to work jointly. Infrastructure development projects including roads, bridges, office and residential buildings which had been left unattended or were languishing, picked up speed and completions started getting recorded in record time enabling the execution of more projects being taken up with improved staff strength. Special financial incentives offered to project staff with adequate freedom for imaginative project planning and implementation greatly contributed to the improvement.

A large number of hills left bald by shifting cultivation in and around the Project-villages were required to be covered under soil conservation and agronomy measures including plantation of fruit bearing and agro-forestry species involving local communities. Initially tribals were apprehensive of losing their hills and community lands on which they cultivated minor millets through shifting cultivation. In fact, some of the agro-forestry plantations taken up under OTDP Kashipur were hardly allowed to survive by local communities themselves as they thought that they would lose their land to Government. Sustained training and community mobilisation involving animators of NGO helped in convincing them that they would remain owners of their land, besides enjoying usufructuary rights over agro-forestry plantations. Although the Project Document called for preparation of RoRs of beneficiaries through revisional survey and settlement operations in Project-villages, technical rules did not permit undertaking such operations on slopes of more than 10 degree. I could not succeed in convincing Chief Secretary on the need to amend age-old technical rules by recognising this ground reality.

Even so, agro-forestry works benefited tribal communities. Plantations of fruit-bearing trees like cashew, guava, mango, etc. in addition to forest species enhanced their incomes on a sustained basis with the passage of time. Efforts made dedicatedly by field functionaries of line departments deputed to the Project Management Unit of OTDP, Kashipur and NGO Agragami did not take much time to resurrect the Project from its death-bed and convert the impression of the Review Mission when they visited again after six months. Unfortunately, Project objectives called for scalability and replication elsewhere for larger benefits which could not happen. This tragedy invariably follows most of the plans and programmes of Government. All subsidy-driven priority sector schemes do not perform satisfactorily in equal measure; but those offering better results meet the same fate as the ones faring badly. Temporary political gains are valued more than sustainable results by those in charge of running the affairs of the State.

Tribal Education: Achieving Certification of Merit

Rules framed under Article 166(3) of the Constitution provided for subjects to be handled by different departments in State Government. Elementary education stood assigned to S&ME Department[1]. Education, universally accepted as vital for development and quality of human life, is the first-generation input for tribal communities in Odisha. For this reason, Odisha's "Rules of Business" called for ST&SC Development Department to supplement efforts of S&ME Department in promoting elementary education among tribal communities.

Although SCs are as distinct from STs as other intermediary castes or upper castes, the egregious tendency of opinion-makers and researchers has been to put STs and SCs within the same bracket and view their needs from the same prism. The nodal department for SCs and STs in the State was called Harijan & Tribal Welfare Department, which to my mind indicated a bias towards SCs, in large part emanating from India's freedom struggle and lack of awareness and inclusion of the more remotely-located tribal communities. Tribal families for their very subsistence use their children as economic assets who start assisting their parents from early childhood.

Development of tribal communities is essentially a post-Independence intervention. A good number of exclusive residential schools to promote

1. Erstwhile Education Department.

elementary education for tribals have since been opened in places with predominance of tribal population in Odisha. Due to lack of parental awareness and discipline at home, which are essential ingredients of modern formal education, tribal children at a very tender age are admitted in residential primary schools called Sevashrama/ Ashram opened exclusively for them. Although instructions issued by State Government categorically stated that residential schools under H&TW Department could admit up to 10 percent SC students as boarders in the event of ST students not being available, in reality SC students constituted 50 percent or more in many residential schools meant for tribal children. I tried to implement the rule position as intended and eliminate such distortions. I started visiting tribal schools in Scheduled Areas frequently. DWOs and Headmasters were advised to avoid the soft option of filling seats in residential schools on "first come, first served" basis, which had hitherto made SC students the principal beneficiaries of entitlements of STs. Before admission of new SC students, supervisory officers were desired to certify that there were no unadmitted ST students in the relevant age groups in the catchment villages. Under no circumstances the number of SC students in residential schools for tribals could exceed 10 percent of total strength. Tribal schools being residential, distance was not to be a consideration for admission. I issued clear instructions also for round-the-year admission of tribal students.

Pursuing strict compliance with instructions issued, the imbalance in residential schools got corrected to a large extent in the next academic session, when new admissions of boarders from SC students got restricted from nil to 10 percent. It was ensured that SC students admitted in previous years continued with their placements, as suddenly shifting them from these schools to others was neither possible nor desirable. Even so, while ST MLAs, who were larger in number, were happy with my approach, the instructions on fresh admissions of tribal students caused palpable heartburn among some SC elected representatives. They submitted petitions to Chief Minister and also alleged administrative highhandedness and 'discrimination' on my part. I explained how despite ST population being about 23 percent and SCs being a lower 16.5 percent of the State's population, SC boarders and scholarship holders outnumbered ST students State-wide and also in residential schools meant exclusively for tribal students. Chief Minister understood the obfuscation in the allegations against me. He approved my approach but wanted that instead of disallowing SC students completely, efforts should be to maintain the ratio of 90:10 in fresh admissions in tribal residential schools. This was done.

Elected SC representatives were still unhappy. Chief Minister passed orders to bifurcate H&TW Department into two administrative wings, namely, Department of ST Development and Department of SC Development. In short, it was called Department of ST&SC Development since it continued to function as an integrated office establishment. Paradoxically, establishment matters of tribal education remained with Director, SC Welfare, as earlier. For the seasoned politician, it was a packaging to create a separate block of ST voters who had hitherto stood clubbed with SCs and were perceived to be the vote bank of Congress Party in the State.

Tribal education in the State suffered in other ways too. The nodal Education Department by and large ignored its responsibilities towards tribal education on the pretext that Tribal Welfare/Development Department had already opened a number of residential schools and expanded elsewhere. State's Education Department thus gave greater priority to non-tribal areas in opening educational institutions. Tribal communities actually accounted for more than 50 percent of population in about 45 percent of the State's geographical area, but did not have a strong voice to articulate their concerns against such biases towards their areas. Relatively, SC leaders were more organized in raising own issues. It suited them to be bracketed with STs in order to appropriate a larger share of benefits under schemes meant for tribal communities. This however, does not mean that SC population in the State did not suffer due to development deficits. Within three months of my joining the Department, Director, SC Welfare left for a year-long training. I was given his charge additionally. This gave me greater opportunity to rectify distortions by amending the Recruitment Rules for teachers besides also to take steps to improve the functioning of educational institutions including in admissions and administration of scholarships.

I had already inspected a large number of tribal schools with teachers who were mostly natives of coastal districts. The tendency among such teachers was to manage their transfers or deputations back to their native or neighbouring districts. In the event of such arrangements not materialising, many kept their local dummies on payment of nominal remuneration. They would visit schools occasionally but collect salaries regularly without doing any school-related work. Recruitment Rules under which Director, SC Welfare was appointing authority for teachers were thus amended to make District Collector the appointing authority, and teachers in tribal schools were brought under the respective district cadres. This was essential to ensure recruitment from within the district and also to prevent their inter-district transfers, which had hitherto resulted in increased suffering in backward tribal districts. Finding no justification for written examinations and interviews for appointment of teachers in Ashram Schools, the relevant part of Recruitment Rules was amended. These arrangements thus created more employment opportunities for local candidates.

Unfortunate deaths of boarders occurring frequently in Ashram Schools due to lack of medical faculties hardly came to the limelight or caught the attention of authorities. Government orders at the highest level were therefore, taken for fortnightly visits by doctors of Primary Health Centres (PHCs) to Ashram Schools. Visiting Ashram Schools during lunch/ dinner hours and occasionally taking food with boarders ensured improvement in quality of food and reduction in leakages. I felt hurt right down to my soul to find instances of tribal boys and girls being routinely exploited physically, even sexually, in many remotely-located residential schools. Close monitoring of their functioning, including academic performance, besides frequent unannounced visits helped in improving the overall educational environment. Assessment of Headmasters and teachers on the basis of their performance and initiation of departmental and criminal proceedings against many offenders created a sense of fear and inculcated discipline among teaching and associated care-giving staff.

Better results from residential High Schools started getting recorded in Secondary Board Examinations. Within a year tribal schools which had been spewing out Nil results in this Board Examination swung towards 100 percent results. Pass percentage of tribal students from Ashram Schools, which used to be much below the State average of about 40 percent to 45 percent, surpassed the State average substantially and the number of tribal high schools posting 100 percent results increased rapidly to my personal satisfaction. Headmasters, teachers and tribal students performing better were felicitated at State level by awarding prizes and certificates of merit. Overall, the administrative interventions in tribal education and changes made in running tribal schools and hostels were appreciated by District Collectors, community leaders as well as elected tribal MLAs and MPs. It was now easier to take quick action in filling up of vacancies, enforcing discipline and accountability by decentralised appointing authorities for absenteeism of teachers and other lapses. Tribal schools lagging behind their counterpart general schools of S&ME Department in terms of performance, excelled in producing much better results.

Historical 'Exclusion' of Tribal Development

Historically, a national policy of minimum intervention was followed towards development of tribal communities and areas with predominance of their population. Its roots lay in the moniker "Excluded Areas" and "Partially Excluded Areas", and separate sets of laws and regulations for administering these two areas applied by colonial administration. Conscious efforts had been made by the British to describe the tribal communities as distinct ethnic groups who did not form part of the traditional social order or mainstream of society. In the name of relief work during famine and other calamities, Christian Missionaries were encouraged to work in tribal areas while ensuring least intervention by the administration.

This "exclusion" thus set the tone for a policy of least intervention in all their developmental aspects post-Independence also. "Excluded" and 'partially excluded areas' were now clubbed as "Scheduled Areas" through a Constitution Order of 1950. Tribal communities were similarly notified as "Scheduled Tribes". During the first three decades, there was recognition that Scheduled Areas usually have tribal communities in majority and were increasingly vulnerable to commercial exploitation by vested interests. But the areas barely received any interventions by way of development of road communication, formal education, entrepreneurship promotion, etc. This was essentially due to a felt perception that such interventions would lead to penetration of non-tribals to tribal areas, which would result in destruction of tribal traditions and culture in addition to their exploitation. Exclusion won the day, but at a huge cost to tribal communities. Rather than accelerating their assimilation in the mainstream through development interventions to address the development deficits affecting them socio-economically, national policy planners went by the romanticised views of anthropologists and perpetuated the proselytization interests shown earlier by the British in relation to tribal development.

Tribal communities and Scheduled Areas started receiving some attention at least of Union Government, albeit in fits and starts, only after the Scheduled Tribes Commission, popularly known as Dhebar Commission, was set up under Article 338 of the Constitution in April 1960. Dhebar Commission studied Scheduled Areas administration and welfare of STs and made recommendations to bridge the gap between tribal and non-tribal areas. P. Shilu Ao Committee set up by Union Planning Commission in October 1966, in its report of September 1969, called for vigorous implementation of recommendations made by Dhebar Commission.

A conceptual break was made country-wide by introducing the 'Tribal Sub Plan' (TSP) during the Fifth Five Year Plan, 1974-79. It called for earmarking budgetary provisions in proportion to the tribal population by States and Central Ministries. It focused on identification of tribal-majority Blocks and introduction of ITDPs under an integrated and projectized approach for development of tribal communities and creating appropriate administrative structures. Notably, TSP-approach stipulated non-divertability and non-lapsabilty of budget provisions, provisions for Special Central Assistance as additive to State Plans, and funding investment through institutional finance. Constitutional provisions under Article 275(1) for release of special grant from Consolidated Fund of Union Government formed an inalienable part of TSP.

But, in practice it remained largely a half-hearted budgetary paper exercise. Union Planning Commission seemingly did not have full clarity about formulating the TSP and strategy for development of Scheduled Areas. Majority of Central Ministries too did not earmark budgetary allocations of Plan Schemes/ Programmes under their respective purview in proportion to tribal population. Non-lapsability of budgetary allocations was not adhered to. Non-divertability of budgetary allocations became a notional exercise of merely earmarking allocations. Diversions allowed frequently was mostly on vague grounds that the scheme was not feasible or that absorption capacity was limited. Most of the medium and major projects involving huge budgetary provisions for development of irrigation potential, industries, mining, etc. in natural resources-rich Scheduled Areas exhibited ostensibly under TSP budgetary-heads, more often than not resulted in distress of tribal communities by displacing them while benefits went to the non-tribals of plain areas.

Nevertheless, with the passage of time, the application of TSP-approach to various schemes/ projects did lead to higher investment in tribal-majority areas overall in India from 1980s onwards. Specifically-targeted schemes and flagship programmes started making a visible impact in improving the socio-economic conditions of Scheduled Areas, and tribal communities. It would be travesty of truth to say that nothing has improved over the years, though the large disparity in development between tribal and non-tribal areas exists to this day. The factors include, but are not limited to, a generalised normative approach in formulating and implementing flagship programmes which formed part of what came to be known as "Bharat Nirman". Most of these programmes adopted the population-criterion for selection of villages and projects, which failed to capture the reality that tribal habitats were thinly-populated. Thus, such government interventions could not benefit the Scheduled Areas in equal measure nor make a perceptible dent in their development deficits.

According to Article 244 of the Constitution, provisions of Vth Schedule apply to administration and control of Scheduled Areas and STs. In reality, despite having a sizeable tribal population, I rarely found any Governor in Odisha paying attention to the affairs of tribals or administration of Scheduled Areas. Governors have not exercised powers and responsibilities conferred upon them under these provisions. There are no instances of Governors to direct, by public notification, as to whether any particular Act of Parliament or of Legislature of the State shall apply or not to Scheduled Areas or any part thereof. He could specify exceptions or modifications for implementing such laws or make regulations for peace and good governance in Scheduled Areas of the State. The enabling specificity and flexibility in the application of Plan Schemes thus largely remained on paper.

Further, although various Expert Committees on administration of Scheduled Areas have recommended posting of competent and dedicated government functionaries, in reality it remains egregiously otherwise, with these areas being made sanctuaries for incompetent and delinquent officers or posts being left vacant at best. Extension of Panchayats to Scheduled Areas (PESA) further deteriorated the situation. It diffused the accountability of public servants while the law contained many unrealistic and un-implementable provisions. The TSP-approach combined protective legislation with development intervention calling for a single line of administration with provisions for incentivising the posting of officials in Scheduled Areas which had remained neglected for ages.

ITDAs were set up at sub-divisional level in Scheduled Areas of Odisha, which were headed by senior administrative officers for integrated planning of projects. The legal framework to deal with land alienation, money lending, provisions of reservations in posts and services, etc., were put in place to ensure social justice and remove disparities between STs and others. Special emphasis was laid on education in tribal communities, which was critical for sustainable socio-economic development. These policy interventions, however, did not lead to the desired outcome due to creation of parallel structures and absence of administrative will. DRDAs were created in scheduled areas which minimised the relevance and responsibility of ITDAs. It was ironical that establishment of residential Ashram Schools which were additive, were considered as substitutes for normal schools in tribal areas. It actually amounted to perpetuating discrimination, albeit of a different form, instead of making more substantive interventions aggressively to bridge existing gaps. Laws aimed at protective discrimination got implemented haphazardly and reluctantly. Reservation provisions too were flouted on various grounds. The TSP-approach despite ensuring higher investment in tribal areas in Odisha at times appeared more of a symbolic gesture.

Vested Interests at Work in ST&SC Development Department

I would find myself disconcerted when on occasions the Minister of State and Cabinet Minister in charge of the Department, both representing tribal communities, were seen deliberately or indeliberately acting in ways that promoted vested interests at the cost of their own communities. Cabinet Minister Ghasi Ram Manjhi, a simple man who incidentally had also served in the Cabinet of Biju Patnaik some 30 years earlier, could not catch out attempts to manipulate him. He could not resist interference of his other ministerial and party colleagues in matters of recruitment, transfers or when actions were taken against functionaries found malfeasant and corrupt.

In the initial days, the Cabinet Minister was so pleased with my work that he protested before Chief Minister on hearing about a proposal for my transfer to Finance Department. Soon enough, we were often at crossroads because I broke away from the practice of my predecessor and declined his dictate that being the Minister, he would have to approve all transfers and posting orders of State cadre officers. He contended that while his requests to his colleagues in transfer/ posting matters were honoured by them, he was not able to reciprocate. I cited the Service Code and CCA Rules which empowered the Director as Head of the Department and appointing authority in matters of appointment, transfer, posting etc. for Welfare Extension Officers, Junior Engineers, etc. I maintained a polite but firm stance informing him of my inability to do his bidding in transfers/ postings or in implementing orders passed by him in violation of statutory rules and procedures.

Seriously aggrieved, Cabinet Minister sent a note to Chief Minister underlining what he described was my sanctimonious high-handedness in ignoring orders passed by him repeatedly. It was never my intention to hurt the Minister, a simple person. I was called upon to respond to his allegations before Chief Secretary to whom this note had been forwarded. I gave expression to my side of story and my understanding of extant rules and procedures while seeking guidance. Chief Secretary Ramakant Rath, known for his thoroughness in rules and procedures, called on Minister Ghasi Ram Majhi personally with the relevant file. I was invited too. Explaining the rules and procedures, Chief Secretary suggested that notes sent by Minister on transfers and postings could be viewed by the Department as important inputs in the process of decision-making, rather than taking them as orders and making an issue in terms of powers to be exercised. He made similar observations on the file too, which matched my understanding of rules and procedures.

In the case of promotion of a Group-B officer, I had submitted before the Departmental Promotion Committee (DPC) headed by Chief Secretary that the officer being corrupt did not deserve promotion. He was under suspension pending major penalty proceedings for misappropriating about ₹ 1.0 lakh while on deputation to Tribal Development Cooperative Corporation (TDCC). Despite substantiation of charges against him by Enquiry Officer, this well-connected officer had managed to get himself exonerated without any reasoned considerations behind the decision of the two Ministers. My submission against his promotion was overruled by the incoming Chief Secretary-cum-Chairman of DPC. My "note of dissent" sent with the meeting's minutes was not appreciated by him. Citing that there was no scope for opposing promotion of an officer who stood exonerated, he conveyed his displeasure; informed me that his views as head of DPC were final, and I should withdraw my note of dissent. I reiterated my position of proven misappropriation and that the DPC would be within its remit not to recommend his promotion. I asserted that in any case, Chairman DPC could consider overruling my note of dissent if he found no substance in it. Cabinet Minister got wind of my stand and sent a strong note against me to Chief Minister seeking action against me for disobedience. Chief Minister's office called for the relevant records for perusal and after a few days not only upheld my stand but also reversed the orders passed by Ministers to exonerate the delinquent officer. Naturally it was embarrassing for both the Ministers. I remained respectful towards the Cabinet Minister knowing it well that his simplicity and magnanimity were being exploited by vested interests including some of his private staff.

In another case of misappropriation in the name of a study funded by Union Ministry of Social Welfare[1], the Minister was under pressure from some colleagues and senior officers not to take action against a former Joint Secretary and two others. Funds received from Central Government had been drawn and shown as utilised within the last three days of Financial Year 1989-90. The report submitted on "Shifting Cultivation in Tribal Areas" was practically a reproduction of a study on the same subject conducted by THRTI about 13 years earlier in 1976. An audit of THRTI's accounts ordered by my predecessor, which had not been allowed by previous Secretary, was finally concluded. It

1. Subsequently renamed as Ministry of Tribal Affairs.

highlighted the plagiarism and misappropriation. The Joint Secretary in question had bypassed the then Director, Tribal Welfare, his immediate superior in getting the allocations drawn, released and utilisation certificate submitted within three days and had been promoted and posted as Director, Municipal Administration in the meanwhile. To me it was an "open and shut" case and Principal Secretary, despite being pressurised by his senior colleagues fully agreed that the delinquents deserved to be held accountable. Cabinet Minister, under pressure also from Housing & Urban Development Minister under whom this former Joint Secretary was working now, tried to force through a quiet burial of the matter. Ignoring these pressures, the proposal for departmental action was processed and put up through one of the finest officers, P.K. Patnaik, ACS in supervisory charge of ST&SC Development Department for approval of Chief Minister. When he asked me whether I was sure about the possible outcome, I outlined my understanding without predicting the outcome, elaborated instead the merits of the case against the delinquents. He endorsed the proposal to the Chief Minister after a couple of days when the Minister was on tour to his constituency. The proposal for major penalty proceedings along with draft charges was approved by Chief Minister and the file was returned back to the Department.

Curiously, Pyari Mohan Mahapatra, Principal Secretary to Chief Minister, recalled the file before it reached my table. It was obvious that after the orders were passed, Chief Minister had been approached by his close friends to help one of the delinquents known to him from his college days. After a couple of days, the file came back to the Department with revised orders which excluded the former Joint Secretary from the departmental proceedings! A few months later, this officer on the verge of retirement was elevated to the Constitutional post of State Election Commissioner, an assignment usually offered to IAS officers holding the post of Chief Secretary or equivalent rank prior to retirement. Pyari Babu had been a source of inspiration for many including me for his uprightness, blunt-speak and quick decision-making ability before he joined the Chief Minister's office as his Principal Secretary. His action in protecting and promoting a functionary of doubtful integrity, showed me an image hardly befitting a person I had considered a role model for many years.

The Section Officer included in the departmental proceedings was a key office bearer of the Orissa Secretariat Service (OSS) association. Along with an Under Secretary and a few Assistants, he tried to instigate the ministerial staff when I wanted punctuality to be maintained in the office. Suddenly, one day at about 10:30 a.m., I was surrounded by a slogan-shouting mob, comprising of ministerial staff mainly from other Departments. I was given the first bitter lesson of working in the Secretariat when the crowd, short of assaulting physically, warned me against playing with fire. Some office bearers of OSS Association, with choicest abuses accused me of being insensitive in dealing with subordinates and warned me of serious repercussions if I continued to humiliate them. They wanted me to heed the difference between a Secretariat and Collectorate, the latter being a place where I could play dictator. A copy of a representation sent to Chief Minister by the wife of an Assistant which stated that her husband would commit suicide if I was not shunted out of the Department immediately, was thrown at me. This Assistant was close to the Section Officer against whom charges had been approved. For an hour, my office lay completely siege. A relatively new entrant in the Secretariat, my presence got registered when newspapers gave wide coverage to this incident the next day. Rather than submitting to the intimidations and unruly behaviour, I prepared another charge sheet against Under Secretary, Establishment, and submitted it to Home Department, the cadre controlling department for OSS officers. He was relieved even though orders of his transfer had not been passed. Home Secretary Bhaskar Patnaik, a batchmate and friend of my Principal Secretary had been taken on board informally before the Under Secretary was relieved of his duties. I also filed a FIR against him for misplacing some important office files. Chicken-and-drink parties being held in the department after the office hours ceased and discipline prevailed in the department during my remaining tenure.

Contempt of Court

As stated earlier, the conditions of Ashram Schools and status of tribal education in the State left much to be desired. Recruitment, transfers and postings of teachers at times involved corrupt practices. In a litigation before State Administrative Tribunal (SAT), recruitment of Ashram School teachers which had been concluded about two years back, had been challenged by an unsuccessful candidate. The litigant averred that candidates with lesser marks than his in the written test had been called for interview and appointed. The Tribunal called for his answer sheet for verification along with other records containing marks awarded to successful candidates. Appallingly, the answer sheet of the litigant presented to SAT was tampered with during its custody in Court, probably in connivance with his advocate or some court official. He had been awarded a zero each by the examiner against two questions which carried maximum 5 marks each. The tampered answer sheet showed the litigant candidate having secured 10 marks each! The Advocate of the candidate, well-known for his smart and mischievous skills, managed to convince the SAT that the actual marks secured by his client were suppressed to deny him appointment. This was the same Advocate who had played similar tricks with paper-evidence in defending a black-marketeer against his detention before the Advisory Board in the High Court about a couple of years ago when I was District Magistrate, Ganjam.

The Tribunal set aside the entire recruitment process without verifying the answer sheet carefully and adjudged the story of the litigant's Advocate to be true. Government advocate, who was a bit hard of hearing, failed to bring the mischief to the notice of the Court. The impact of implementing SAT's orders would have been felt by a large number of teachers whose services would be terminated for no fault of theirs, besides resulting in unwarranted disruption of education in Ashram Schools. SAT had also directed that recruitment of teachers to be held afresh should be conducted by Collector, Koraput. I had taken over additional charge of Director, SC Welfare who handled affairs of teachers in tribal schools being the appointing authority, and thus the implementation of SAT's orders fell on me. As I found, the orders passed by SAT were unfair besides being unimplementable. A decision was taken to file a review petition before the Bench explaining how the answer sheet was tampered while it was in SAT's custody and why it was not possible to assign the task of fresh recruitment to the officer specified by SAT without amending the statutory recruitment rules in vogue. Principal Secretary and I personally appeared before the Tribunal to explain the matter. Rather than appreciating our submission, SAT hardened its position and initiated proceedings against us for contempt of Court on the grounds of orders passed by them not being implemented.

Vice Chairman of SAT, earlier Principal Secretary Law, showing outrageous conduct spoke informally to his successor in Law Department, and asked him not to grant permission for filing a Special Leave Petition (SLP) in the Apex Court against SAT's order, and to inform Chief Secretary about our alleged misconduct in open Court. It was simply awful to see a couple of back-dated orders by SAT to buttress charges for Contempt of Court against Principal Secretary and me. Chief Secretary was duly informed by Law Secretary. He also did not delay in rejecting the proposal of ST&SC Development Department for filing an SLP against SAT's order and in turn called for its immediate implementation. Ramakant Rath, incumbent Chief Secretary conveyed more by his serious facial expression than in words. But, after hearing us and going through the file patiently, he directed Law Secretary to convey approval for filing SLP in Supreme Court against unjust orders of SAT and allow the administrative department to hire services of a senior lawyer. Law Secretary was further told in unequivocal terms that we were being unnecessarily hauled up in the name contempt of Court and the Vice Chairman, SAT should be informed that State administration would not allow any serving of warrant to force the officer to surrender before the Tribunal as they have followed the correct procedure.

Supreme Court instantly passed orders to stay SAT's order pending final hearing. A couple of months later, the SLP was allowed with the observation that SAT had exceeded its brief in passing orders and that the answer sheet of litigant candidate should be sent to two independent experts, and after such revaluation if litigant candidate secured marks equal to or above those who had been appointed, he should be offered appointment too, which would serve the interests of justice. After revaluation of his answer sheet, the litigant candidate was found having secured less than the overall marks awarded to him initially! It was, however, not as if there were no irregularities in the process of recruitment of teachers. Indeed, the tabulation sheet had over-writings on marks secured by some candidates. I had been informed by some junior officers about pressures exerted by the then Secretary on Director, SC Welfare, a simple gentleman, to favour some candidates recommended by him during the interview and also at the time of issuing appointment orders. A few such changes made in the 'merit list' and 'waiting list' would seem to testify that. Be it so, SAT had egregiously failed to analyse the statement containing marks awarded to the litigant candidate in the written test and had overplayed its hand after it got carried away by submissions founded in falsehood and manipulation by a clever Advocate.

Implementing Reservation

Odisha was among the first States which enacted a law, the Odisha Reservation of Vacancies (for SCs & STs) in Posts and Services Act 1975, to enforce the provisions of reservation. However, the law remained without implementation in letter and spirit for a long period as far as ST candidates were concerned for two main reasons. First, lack of educationally-qualified tribal youth due to insufficient attention to tribal education in the past; and second, the Rules under this law allowed exchange of vacancies between SC and ST candidates in the event of candidates from either community not being available. Thus, SC candidates being relatively better educated invariably grabbed the posts and vacancies meant for STs. The situation became worse in promotional appointments due to negligible representation of STs in recruitment at entry level. This law also provided for de-reservation if reserved candidates were not available after a special recruitment drive. STs suffered due to lack of self-awareness about non-application of mind by administrators in analysing the root causes.

I quickly took steps to amend the Rules to disallow exchange of vacancies between SCs and STs besides ensuring admission of no more than 10 percent SC students in residential tribal schools under my Department. Line Departments were desired to avoid soft options of submitting proposals for de-reservation without holding special recruitment drive exclusively for reserved category candidates to fill up reserved vacancies. Consequences of failure of appointing authorities and cadre-controlling departments to maintain roster registers were unambiguously outlined. These registers were hereafter regularly verified by inspecting officers of my department. An irrefutable vindication for these measures was found within ST&SC Development Department. Earlier on, incumbent Director, Tribal Welfare, himself a tribal, was found to have signed the initial circulars for laying down the procedures for issuing caste certificates and caste-based reservation after enactment of reservation Act, but had gone on to implement the provisions in his capacity as appointing authority by recruiting some SC candidates against posts meant for ST candidates in the Department!

The only way to deal with distortions in implementing the reservation law was by creating an enabling atmosphere for which promotion of tribal education was essential. Development interventions had to go hand-in-hand with affirmative actions. Political leaders for a long time generally considered STs in Odisha as no more than their vote bank. I repeatedly placed proposals before Tribes Advisory Council and also before Scheduled Caste Welfare Advisory Board for reservation of seats in higher educational institutions, including in government Medical and Engineering colleges, in proportion to ST and SC population which was essential to improve their representation in health and engineering services. But Odisha remained perhaps the only State where reservation of seats in higher educational institutions for STs and SCs was much lower at 12 percent and 8 percent against their population of 23 percent and 16.5 percent respectively. Obviously, State administration and polity were not sufficiently serious about empowering marginalised communities in the actual sense of the term.

Single Line Administration: A Paradox

TSP-approach which was premised upon an integrated strategy for tribal development could not be effective due to multiplicity of administration and finer specialisations, which confused the single command-driven tribal communities. DoPT had called for a single line administration with deployment of more competent and committed officers with financial incentives for administration of Scheduled Areas and other tribal majority pockets suffering from development deficits due to their legacy of relative backwardness. In Odisha, ITDAs were set up in geographical convergence with Revenue Sub-Divisions. Blocks in Scheduled Areas were specified as Tribal Development Blocks, the equivalent of Community Development Blocks elsewhere for implementing poverty alleviation and various welfare schemes. All line Departments involved in implementing them at sub-divisional and district levels were required to participate in planning and executing them under the umbrella of ITDA. In reality, however, hardly any serious attempts were made to translate policy intentions into action. Efforts made by my grand predecessor Mohan Kumar, and now me, towards single line administration faced resistance and setbacks due to narrow departmentalism guiding the senior officials including political executives heading these departments.

It is nobody's case that TSP-approach and ITDAs did not help in improving the conditions of tribal communities. As such, financial investment which used to be around 1 percent of budgetary provisions of Central and State Governments put together increased to 7 percent after introduction of TSP strategy. However, the TSP concept did not work effectively in implementing what had been conceived. Central Government did not give sufficient attention to monitor and translate the TSP strategy into action and operationalisation of single line administration varied from State to State. Neighbouring Andhra

Pradesh made a substantive change and tried to bring all line Departments, including police, under Project Administrator of ITDAs. For some time, young and dynamic officers were posted in tribal areas due to the initiatives of S.R. Sankaran, a seasoned and committed senior civil servant.

In Odisha, despite some initial positive movements, ITDAs did not receive similar attention and after some time became no more than executing agencies for implementing the schemes under Special Central Assistance. Constitution of DRDAs in 1980 diluted the role of ITDAs further. With the passage of time, posts in Scheduled Areas and ITDAs were viewed as expedient parking slots for inconvenient and incompetent officials. Multiplicity in administration increased manifold. Earmarking of budgetary resources became notional. Policy planners and administrators failed to realise that in the absence of an enabling social infrastructure in local areas, development could not be a top-down superimposed process. Corresponding efforts were not made towards education and skill development of tribal communities which made their survival more difficult. Diversion of funds from TSP to general heads also became a common practice. Except leveraging tribal communities for gaining access to benefits politically or financially and extending lip service, development of tribal communities in Odisha to my assessment did not receive the required attention. A former Special Secretary in GA Department, who was on Central deputation in Ministry of Tribal Welfare when I was holding this post of Director, Tribal Welfare was found to be more interested in getting funds received under Special Central Assistance by ST&SC Development Department in the name of preparing "integrated action plans" for ITDAs through his NGO! Rather than releasing any more funds to his NGO, I made efforts to effect recoveries as hardly any work had been done against funds released to it over time earlier.

Junior engineers and assistant engineers posted in ITDAs had limited powers to accord technical approval to projects to be implemented by them. Similarly, powers for granting administrative approval of Project Administrators and Collectors were also inadequate which caused abnormal delays in implementing projects. To facilitate faster development, I took up revision of their powers. Senior engineers of Irrigation, Rural Development and Works departments posted at the district, division and State level were made competent to grant technical sanction for projects which were beyond the sanctioning powers of engineers posted in ITDAs. Administrative powers in full were delegated to Governing Bodies of ITDAs. Seeking of administrative approval of ST&SC Development Department for any project to be implemented by ITDAs was thus eliminated. After all, the department had hardly any qualified technical manpower to scrutinise project estimates, and referring such projects for administrative sanction could only delay implementation besides leading to cost escalation.

Another intervention which I found necessary for local participation in implementing projects was in terms of providing 10 percent price preference or advantage to local tribal youth over non-tribal contractors/ executants. Lack of participation of local communities was evident in implementing even small infrastructure projects in tribal areas like check dams, diversion weirs, irrigation channels, water harvesting structures, small village roads including cross drainage works, school and hostel buildings, etc. With some hand-holding and facilitation by ITDA engineers, it was not difficult to get many such projects executed by local tribal people.

Critical gaps and casual attitude were manifest in the functioning of ITDAs and Micro Projects. At times, it was seen that Special Central Assistance was utilized like a discretionary grant by Collectors who were Chairpersons of ITDAs. Neither Project Administrators of ITDAs nor Project Officers of Micro Projects were found to have gone through and understood the guidelines issued by Union Ministry of Social Welfare. Annual action plans were prepared casually without adequate prioritisation or assessment of community requirements. It was as though the programmes were meant for helping contractors and a few local leaders! I started holding monthly zonal-level meetings with Project Administrators of ITDAs and Project Officers of Micro Projects which were also attended by senior engineering personnel and DWOs. Detailed circulars were issued explaining Special Central Assistance guidelines for selection of beneficiaries and projects to be implemented. Outcomes were reviewed regularly.

Unlike SC families, tribal communities did not suffer due to landlessness despite increase in cases of surreptitious alienation of their land. Emphasis was therefore laid on land-based activities for implementing family-oriented income-generating schemes and infrastructure projects which were incidental to such income-generating schemes. As tribal regions happened to be origins of many perennial semi-perennial rivers and rivulets, developing irrigation potential was prioritized by constructing low cost micro irrigation projects. Tribal communities were involved both in identification of such projects as well as their execution.

Tribal areas did not have adequate banking network. I devised land-based schemes with a group approach where individual tribal beneficiary families could contribute labour equal to the loan amount and amount of subsidy utilised for development of land and irrigation potential. In the process, hilly land used by tribal communities for cultivation of minor millets under rainfed conditions or shifting cultivation by the primitive "slash and burn" system of cultivation, could now be terraced for settled agriculture. Head works of minor irrigation projects could be constructed utilising the admissible subsidy and field channels could be constructed by beneficiary families through voluntary labour contributions. This strategy yielded good results.

In Odisha, 13 tribal communities stood specified as Particularly Vulnerable Tribal Groups[1] (PVTGs) on the basis of their lower human development indices. Female literacy rate was 1 percent among PVTGs as per 1981 census. 17 Micro Projects (the number has now increased to 19) for development of these groups had been established. In the initial years, anthropologists heading these Micro Projects promoted romanticized views on tribal development. They were slowly replaced by young officers from OAS and State Welfare Service. This opened more windows for development interventions in villages inhabited by PCTGs many of whom carried "bows and arrows" which sometimes scared the public servants. Micro Projects received funds separately from State Government out of Special Central Assistance in addition to those spent by ITDAs and Blocks for executing schemes under other priority sector ongoing programmes.

Each Micro Project catered to a population between 2,500 to 4,000. PVTGs living in relative isolation slowly started visiting Micro Project offices to ventilate their felt needs to staff who were now able to understand their dialect. I had to initiate departmental proceedings against a Project Officer for misappropriation and misuse of funds but did not allow him to suffer further after finding the misutilisation unintentional. The young OAS officer heading the Micro Project got into the Indian Police Service subsequently.

During my tours, I invariably made night-halts in Micro Project offices many of which were not even electrified. It was noticed that officials hardly visited them nor executed any of their departmental programmes in such villages. Schools under the purview of S&ME Department in these areas mostly existed on paper though teachers drew salaries regularly. There was no existence of primary health services. Substantive programmes under State Plan for socio-economic development of PVTGs were the responsibility of line departments. Despite being an additionality to the State Plan, Special Central Assistance routed through ITDAs and Micro Projects in reality became substantive. Before visiting remote villages mostly on foot, I had not imagined that such places existed in the State. Considering the apathy of development functionaries of various departments and detachment of mainstream administration, at times I felt as if tribal villages and PVTGs did not form part of the State; otherwise the administration could not have been so insensitive.

It tore my heart to find that rather than reaching out to PVTGs to promote development and work for their assimilation into the mainstream, administrators mostly avoided them due to their baseless fears of possible physical harm if they visited their villages. These fears were largely founded on some yester year colonial documents which cast the behaviour of some PVTGs as fearsome. "Bondas" of Malkangiri and "Lodhas" of Mayurbhanj in

1. Known then as Primitive Tribal Groups; subsequently renamed Particularly Vulnerable Tribal Groups.

particular were considered violent. Racial prejudices of British administration were on outrageous display in branding certain tribes as criminal by birth in Criminal Tribes Act, repealed by Parliament after Independence. But the same mindset continued to prevail among some post-Independence administrators thus victimising the victims further. The innocent tribal communities, particularly PVTGs, suffered the most. Interactions with PVTGs during my visits to their habitations despite language barriers increasingly humbled me with the realization that one could find in them creation of the Almighty in the purest form.

In the course of my sustained tours, I found that six schools reportedly opened by State Education Department in villages inhabited by Bonda tribes in Malkangiri did not exist despite teachers drawing salaries from Block office at Khairput. I had no difficulty in getting admitted more than 350 boys from Class I to Class X in the residential High School at Mudulipada, the heartland of the so-called dreaded Bonda tribe. In Andrahal, the biggest Bonda village, ITDA Malkangiri constructed a new school building exclusively for local tribal students and admitted 150 children aged 5-10 years with mid-day meal facilities specially run by the local Micro Project. The mid-day meal scheme in operation currently did not exist in the State then. The school was run by animators engaged by Micro Project. I felt blessed to enjoy the bliss of watching the children reciting prayers before starting classes during one of my surprise visits. I also got to test my skill in the "bow and arrow", the traditional weapon carried by Bonda males. While I could not hit my target, "a big jack fruit" hanging at the nearby tree, Bonda menfolk could aim at an object perfectly at a distance of 20 meters! Just before my departure from ST&SC Development Department, P.K. Patnaik, Development Commissioner paid an official visit to Mudulipada, probably the first visit by an officer of such seniority and recorded his appreciation for the work in progress.

As elsewhere, land development for settled agriculture on terraced land had been started in villages under Bonda Micro Project. Some masons belonging to Soura tribe, known for their expertise in settled agriculture had been brought from Rayagada and Gajapati. They were paid minimum wages, and engaged alongside Bonda people who were to be paid 50 percent wages for working on their own land, the rest being their contribution of labour, in accordance with the guidelines I had issued earlier to be followed uniformly by all ITDAs and Micro Projects throughout the State. After completion of the all-weather motorable road, RDC Southern Division, under whom I had suffered an educative experience of official scrutiny when I was Collector, Ganjam, paid a visit to Mudulipada. He now alleged discrimination in payment of wages calling it a violation of law of minimum wages and sent a report to Chief Minister's office underlining that I was the officer responsible for triggering such lapses. He had found another opportunity to settle old scores with me. I came to know about it when Bijoy Kumar Patnaik, a senior IAS officer who had been told to enquire into the matter by Chief Minister's office visited me to ascertain my views on the allegation. No case could be made out against me, but after the enquiry commenced, land development programme in Bonda villages was discontinued to avoid further controversy.

Seventeen years later when I was holding the post of Secretary in ST&SC Development, I received an unexpected telephone call early morning from Ramakant Mishra (a former Chief Secretary) who as stated earlier was fond of the RDC under reference. I was indeed shaken when told about the sudden demise of this recently retired officer. I proceeded to his house instantly and called a few of my trusted aides there for extending assistance, although it was a holiday with all government offices closed. We learnt that the officer had enjoyed Durga Puja quite happily till late evening but had succumbed to a sudden asthmatic attack later on. Except his wife, who probably informed Ramakant Mishra, none was at home. I did my best to help in his last rites and complete formalities like obtaining the death certificate. I had remained respectful to him throughout the working life, though occasional thoughts continue to puzzle me to this day as to why some people identify themselves with the so-called high positions they hold temporarily and misunderstand their colleagues. Ultimately, death alone defined life.

FOREIGN TRAINING: FIRST OVERSEAS EXPOSURE

I was nominated for a year-long training course of Master of Arts in Rural Social Development at the University of Reading, UK under the Colombo Plan by DoPT. The course which started mid-September 1993 got completed end-August 1994. My group of 30 students included six from India and the rest drawn mainly from NGOs or those who sought their career in non-government sectors and originated from various African countries, Germany, Japan, Nepal, Pakistan, USA, and even domestically from within the UK.

The excitement of my first exposure to studies overseas died swiftly in the face of biases, inadequacies, and irrelevance of course content coupled with a teaching faculty, substantially drawn also from international NGO fraternity, whose priority and focus thus lay in NGO-related activities. In the case studies and documentaries, besides including just a few from India, the emphasis again lay more in highlighting failures of governments in developing countries and to present NGOs as better alternatives, which would also not cost the exchequer of these developing countries. Not that I could not benefit from gaining valuable insights which could address the felt needs for more substantive NGO-related interventions for rural development in India. But the attempts were to restrict the teaching to a narrow channel of activities and practices which had limited relatability to the Indian rural scenario and ethos. Had the substantive training been fulfilling, I might not have been left feeling the bitter taste to this day of the behaviour of our contact person in the British Council, a Portuguese lady who was anything but polite or sympathetic whenever we approached her for guidance and advice in the initial days at Reading.

This was a course I did not enjoy nor find useful and in hindsight. I would have foregone it had I known what would be taught and how. Probably, before nominating officers for foreign training, DoPT had not paid sufficient attention to the course being offered by University of Reading. It appeared that assistance for overseas students through such courses by the British Government was an important way to support their own educational institutions. After internalising the situation, I was left with a compulsive feeling that there is never a case or justification for availing the charity of a donor country if the training inputs did not add value to the existing skills of officers. Without doubt, the number of opportunities available for experimentation and work in the field of rural development in India had no parallel in the rest of the world. Indeed, the training and educational institution derived more from the participation of Indian officers as far as inputs on rural development were concerned.

All was not a wash-out academically though. The Master's Degree course included writing a dissertation on particular themes of rural development. It gave me an opportunity to introspect and recount my experiences of tribal development in Odisha which was well-received. After some years, I expanded the dissertation and published it in the form of a book titled *Tribal Development in India with Special Reference to Orissa*[1]. What had actually gladdened my heart was the extensive library facilities at the University. I spent hours there, devouring books on Indology, anthropological studies in relation to tribal communities in India, and all manner of subjects which I could now lay my hands on, all of which I had yearned to read in India. I also took full advantage of the facilities by taking photocopies of some rare books from the library besides acquiring computer literacy which helped me in the days to come.

Life in Reading, coupled with travels to other places in the UK during weekends and even to neighbouring countries during Christmas and Easter breaks, most convincingly brought out the civic sense, work culture and discipline in the British society and other West European countries. My exposure to the systems deployed by developed countries across all socio-economic segments of life has been memorable to date.

Initial adjustments towards developing a taste for vegetarian British food (an oxymoron) and its infamous and unpredictable weather notwithstanding, overt and covert racism and portrayal of superiority by some of our erstwhile colonial masters could not be avoided in social behaviour and interactions in the University campus and elsewhere. Such experiences of other course mates from India were no different. We learnt not to get provoked by pin-pricks.

Perhaps there is no pain more hurtful than one which is self-inflicted or by those with whom one is somehow associated. And here I allude to a shameful

1. Gyan Publishing House, New Delhi (2001).

incident involving my three compatriots-cum-IAS colleagues, two of whom were at Reading undergoing the same training course as me and one at the London School of Economics also undergoing training under the Colombo Plan. I remained unaware of the matter until the details unfolded during the enquiry conducted by the British Council. It appears that the officer undergoing training in London was accompanied by his wife and two sons, and had been drawing social security benefits allowed by the British Government to children of their citizens, and also to those residing in UK for more than 6 months. The amount for each child was £50 per month and was perhaps permissible if both parents were professionally occupied. When the application of one senior officer in Reading, whose wife and two school-going children were staying with him, was rejected, it seems that he had filed a complaint, not in his own name but in that of the second fellow officer at Reading alleging discrimination by drawing attention to the social security benefits being availed by the officer in London. The spouse of neither of the two officers was professionally occupied in the UK. The actual complainant appears not to have given any consideration to the fact that the officer in London had been a long-standing friend with whom he had studied at the prestigious St. Stephens College, or even more egregiously, that he himself had been married into the most illustrious Indian family of the late Mahamana Pandit Madan Mohan Malviya, who had fought the British Empire in India and founded BHU where I had studied for more than seven years. Having been brought up imbibing the immeasurable contributions of Pandit Malviya, and now hearing about the enquiry being conducted, even though I was nowhere involved in the entire chain of events I felt as though shamed to my very core due to the shenanigans of my fellow trainee-cum-senior officers who had mortgaged their morality for a mere £100 per month.

MASS EDUCATION: MY LEAST PRODUCTIVE ASSIGNMENT

On my return after foreign training, I served as Director, Mass Education for a little more than a year from 20 September 1994 to 9 October 1995. Although my heart had craved for a posting in the field of education, having been benefitted immensely only due to my educational attainments, I had never disclosed this desire to anyone. Paradoxically, this was the only post held by me for one year which was least eventful and hardly productive in my entire service career.

The assignment gave me the mandate to promote functional literacy among adults who were not fortunate enough to access elementary education during their early phase of life. Adult education programme by now had almost stopped receiving funds from Central Government for running Literacy Centres in villages. Some unutilised funds from earlier years for procurement of reading and writing materials for Literacy Centres and village libraries remained held in banks due to allegations of misappropriations against some past expenditures.

Probably for this reason, my immediate predecessor had allowed funds to remain unutilised. Many creative writers and publishers; past beneficiaries of procurement of books written and published by them were seeking financial support or commitment for purchase of their books to meet the requirements of neo-literates. According to them, they had prepared new manuscripts on requests and assurances by senior officers of S&ME Department including Directorate of Adult Education.

After introduction of "Total Literacy Campaign" (TLC), a new scheme, by Union Government, a separate component of adult education in a conventional sense had become irrelevant and was discontinued. Literacy campaigns for adult literacy were now to be steered by District Collectors, who headed their Zila Saksharata Samitis. They were required to submit action plans to National Literacy Mission directly for approval and allocation of funds. The post of Director, Adult Education, had been renamed as Director, Mass Education, whose role was limited to forwarding the action plans prepared by District Collectors, which was also just a ritual and not mandatory.

My illustrious predecessor was famous for her literary attainments as a creative writer and was the first Collector in the State who had introduced TLC in Sundargarh, a tribal district. Before the TLC was concluded in that district, she was transferred and posted as Director, Mass Education. Ganjam was the second district for which TLC was approved by the National Literacy Mission when I was Collector. The action plan for TLC prepared by me provided for simultaneous universalisation of primary education and adult functional literacy. It is another matter that it became a tool of propaganda in course of implementation after I left the district.

TLC in Kalahandi district launched by a young and enthusiastic Collector had practically fizzled out in the absence of enabling logistics. SCs&STs constituted about 40 percent of the population and the existing low literacy rate in the district made it impossible to find volunteers to run literacy centres. Elementary education in the district was in doldrums. Collector of the district had submitted a supplementary action plan for revival of TLC and it was difficult for me to endorse the same to the Executive Body of National Literacy Mission for consideration and approval for additional funds. I forwarded the supplementary action plan with my assessment of the situation. As Director General of National Literacy Mission himself favoured the proposal, the supplementary action plan was placed before the Executive Body. I was invited to the meeting in which Collector, Kalahandi made a presentation on the supplementary action plan. Having already made my views known to the Collector, when asked to present views of the State Government, I had no option but to place my critical assessment, which resulted in a somewhat embarrassing situation.

I wanted the Executive Body to take a realistic view stating that without creating requisite infrastructure by opening new primary schools and without filling up large scale vacancies in existing ones, it would be difficult to convince adult illiterates in villages to come to the literacy centres or to find qualified volunteers for imparting functional literacy. It was easier to bring a limited number of illiterates into the literacy fold after universalising elementary education as in that case male as well as female volunteers with required qualifications would not be in short supply. Through campaign mode, adults would be afforded another opportunity for acquiring functional literacy. I added that Ernakulum (Kerala), the first district in country, was declared fully literate as this district already had a literacy rate above 85 percent before TLC was launched there. By definition, a district was considered fully literate after achieving 90 percent literacy as 10 percent of the population (in 0-5 age group) were not expected to be functionally literate. In contrast, Kalahandi with 40 percent ST&SC population and existing literacy rate among them being less than 20 percent and 30 percent respectively, there was no possibility of finding volunteers. The response to my submission from DG, National Literacy Mission was that he would send a report against me to Chief Secretary, Odisha for my negative views to which I happily agreed. At the end of the day, the supplementary action plan though approved, failed in achieving any amount of success in reaching the stated objective.

I tried to nudge Collectors of coastal districts where the rate of literacy was high and comparable with advanced States, to create the environment for TLC but to no avail. During my field visits to Sundargarh, Ganjam and Kalahandi which were covered under TLC, I found the allocations received from National Literacy Mission being spent as contingency funds for furnishing offices and residences of Collectors, procurements of a variety of equipment including air conditioners, computers, engagement of domestic helps, etc. These allocations were not subjected to audit scrutiny and were kept in banks since they did not constitute part of the State budget requiring involvement of district treasury for drawls and disbursals. It was easier to prop up NGOs and grassroot organisations in tribal and backward districts to organize meetings and conventions to give an appearance of mass participation in TLC. I was uncomfortable to support this publicity-oriented campaign which was poor in substance due to inherent reasons. My colleagues who as Collectors of tribal and other educationally-backward districts were interested to do so misunderstood me.

* * * *

5

Deep Plough: Agriculture & Food Production

I joined as Director, Agriculture & Food Production (A&FP) on 10 October 1995 and held the post for three years. It was a challenging assignment during a difficult period. In a post conventionally held by the senior-most subject specialist of Odisha Agriculture Service barring exceptions, I ploughed in without any academic credentials in agricultural science. My childhood farming-skills acted as my intuitive guide. My predecessor Dr. D.P. Mishra, a well-known soil scientist and author of several books, had virtually faced an ignominious physical eviction from the Directorate due to an agitation against him by office staff, which had tacit support of some technical officers from a rival group of his service. He had opted to stop attending office for more than three months. Waking up to this reality after such a large hiatus, Government transferred him to the post of MD, Odisha State Seeds Corporation (OSSC) from where he retired a year later.

Albeit a large office and a huge field establishment of over 14,000 Specialists, Agriculture Engineers, Extension Officers, and Village Agriculture Workers (VAWs), etc., Directorate of A&FP was functionally in no good shape. I found elaborate arrangements, guidelines and instructions, including clearly laid down standard operating procedures (SOPs), defining verifiable duty charts of each field functionary under the World Bank supported "Training and Visit" system of agricultural extension in vogue. Extension functionaries, including VAWs, hardly resided in their headquarters in remote locations. Residential quarters in many places were unoccupied or illegally encroached upon. "Training & Visit" programme called for Agriculture Extension Officers (AEOs) and VAWs to regularly visit farmers to convey the "Lab to Land" message, and to maintain a daily diary accordingly. In reality, many of them were maintaining false diaries. Farmers visited their offices only sparingly. Progressive farmers in agriculturally-advanced irrigated areas did not really require their services as they were equally or better aware of advancements in agriculture than VAWs. They were more concerned about Minimum Support Price (MSP) for marketing their surplus. In other places, for farmers dependent on rain-fed agriculture or protective irrigation through other semi-perennial irrigation sources, the efforts for remunerative agriculture including promotion of High-Yielding Variety (HYV) seeds were inadequate or non-existent. Majority of farmers with felt need for services of extension functionaries and subject matter specialists, particularly in remote tribal areas, were hardly aware of their existence. Senior officers from Directorate, including subject specialists, rarely visited farms beyond the district and sub-divisional headquarters and places which were agriculturally advanced. The vast majority of extension workers were from coastal districts for whom posting beyond their native or neighbouring districts was akin to punishment. In a nutshell, except in the command areas of major and medium irrigation projects, beneficial effects of the much publicised 'Green Revolution' were largely invisible.

Sorry State of Agriculture in the State

The seed replacement ratio then was about 2 percent. Production of seeds, mainly paddy, in farms under the Directorate and Seeds' Corporation was around 2,500 tonnes during Rabi and Kharif taken together. Paradoxically, less than 50 percent area under paddy was recorded to be covered by HYVs. More HYV seeds were procured from outside, mainly Andhra and Madhya Pradesh, without meeting suitability criterion in local agro-climatic conditions, than produced within. Similar mismatch was seen in pulses, oil seeds, etc. It is for this reason, in spite of seeds being supplied to farmers at highly subsidised rates, they were remaining unutilised and had to be disposed off as non-seeds or destroyed as unfit for human consumption being chemically-treated.

Odisha's farm mechanisation was perhaps the lowest in the country even though share of agricultural engineers at various levels was higher. Overseers at village level, Junior Engineers at sub-division level, Assistant Engineers at range level, Executive Engineers at regional level and in implement factories, and Joint Director/ Additional Director at State level were running parallel administration with mainstream agriculture extension. Large number of subsidised Small Scale Industrial (SSI) units engaged in production of agricultural implements had become sick as these implements manufactured under advice of agriculture engineers were not being popularised by extension field staff. Specialisation-based narrow departmentalism was harming the cause of agriculture rather than helping it.

A number of district and range-level senior officers were under departmental proceedings for misappropriations or incurring huge expenditure for destroying seeds which had invited serious objections from Controller & Auditor General (C&AG) in their audit reports. This held up departmental promotions across all levels. Litigations compounded the stagnation, further demoralising the officers who held out little hope of realising their promotional prospects during their remaining service. Frequent agitations and absenteeism had created anarchy which practically defined field formations of Agriculture Department. Some officers fearing adverse audit paras had avoided disposal of unutilised seeds, which crowded out fresh seeds from scarce storage facilities in many places. Prolonged storage of unutilised seeds, pesticides, and chemical fertilizers had degraded some storage facilities beyond use.

Office of DA&FP did not present a healthy environment for effective functioning either. From the day of its relocation to an imposing landmark building housing Heads of Departments, records had not been consigned. Broken doors, windows, unserviceable almirahs, broken furniture, damaged electrical fittings, stinking washrooms, etc. made it difficult for officers and staff to remain seated in office and work. Painting, white-washing, carrying out repairs, etc. had not been done in the past many years by Works Department responsible for maintaining Government buildings. Some ministerial functionaries virtually sat on piles of files and frequently resorted to agitations seeking better facilities.

Streamlining Administration: A Pre-Requisite

I was granted freedom to streamline administration and work towards transforming the system of agriculture extension. I kept a time-frame of six months for streamlining office and field administrations. B.K. Patnaik, Secretary of the Department and J.B. Patnaik Chief Minister who himself held the agriculture portfolio, fully supported my initiatives. Luckily, I did not suffer resistance from office or field staff. Ministerial staff was persuaded to cooperate in consignment of over four truck-loads of old files in less than six months. Unserviceable furniture and other items which had cluttered spaces besides rendering the office environment unhygienic were disposed of. Broken doors and windows were repaired or replaced for better ventilation, electrical fittings were replaced, and walls were painted nicely, all to give the office rooms a fresh, hygienic and welcoming ambience. Personnel of other Departments housed in the building became envious of the hitherto much-maligned Agriculture Directorate.

In parallel, subject matter specialists and general experts holding various positions volunteered to help me understand the nifty-gritty and technicalities in agriculture. I succeeded in persuading officers after meeting them in groups and individually not to pursue litigation in their own interest and especially not for staying matters or seeking other succour from courts. In return I assured them swift disposal of departmental proceedings, revision and updating of gradation lists, and holding of DPC meetings, all without any bias or favour. Thus, departmental proceedings held up for years were systematically disposed of within two to three months as planned.

I followed up by getting stays vacated, which had been obtained by officers earlier against various government orders in relation of gradation lists, promotion etc., and prepared revised provisional gradation lists to facilitate departmental promotions. DPCs were held despite a formidable Joint Secretary in Department of Agriculture advising the Secretary not to hold them on the basis of provisional gradation lists and what he averred were hurriedly concluded departmental proceedings when litigations were still pending in Courts even if stay orders had been vacated. It was my strategy to keep minutes of DPC meetings ready along with proposals for posting on promotion on the same day lest any aggrieved officer approached the Courts to obtain a stay order. It worked. Large-scale promotions of officers, many of whom were on the verge of retirement, recharged them.

Within a year of my joining, District Agriculture Officers (DAOs) holding temporary charge of the office of Deputy Director got progressively elevated to the post of Deputy Director and Joint Director, Level-1 and Level-II. DAO and officiating Deputy Director, Agriculture, in charge of Cuttack range, became Additional Director getting four promotions in less than 24 months. Another DAO similarly placed, facing departmental proceedings for reporting huge expenditure in destroying chemically-treated maize seeds in the forest 40 km away from the seed-storage godown in Keonjhar, got similarly elevated after proceedings were concluded with imposition of a minor penalty. My aim at that time was to energise administration and secure the future instead of deriving satisfaction by simply getting delinquent officers punished and allowing agricultural development to suffer and be stymied indefinitely. My approach was to afford officers an opportunity to improve by getting such proceedings which were not very serious concluded fast with some leniency as the officers had already suffered sufficiently, and more importantly the agriculture administration had suffered on the ground far more.

Although 'Agriculture' is in the State List constitutionally, almost all schemes implemented by State Agriculture Department were either in Central Sector or Centrally Sponsored. Odisha's financial condition was quite grim, so much so that allocations released by Central Government for implementing schemes were being released to DA&FP only notionally at the end of the financial year to avoid surrendering budget provisions. This allocation would be desired to be kept in Civil Deposit to maintain a balance in the State's "ways and means" position. State Government had financial difficulty in releasing its share of Centrally Sponsored Schemes also. In double jeopardy, it was DA&FP which would be asked to explain the failure in utilising funds when proposals for release of funds from Civil Deposit were submitted to Finance Department at the start of subsequent financial year. Since utilisation certificates against allocations made by Union Ministry of Agriculture in preceding years had not been submitted, fresh allocations of funds had almost stopped. This issue had to be addressed to justify a meaningful existence in the Directorate.

Interestingly, in 1990 soon after the ruling Congress Government was replaced by Biju Patnaik-led Janata Dal Government, gross and net cropped area under various crops were brought down from 90 lakh hectares and 60 lakh hectares to 60 lakh hectares and 50 lakh hectares respectively through a notification issued by Planning & Coordination Department. Cropping intensity too was brought down from 150 percent to 120 percent without any ground verification. Strangely, per hectare consumption of chemical fertilizers (23 kg in NPK terms) reported earlier on the basis of gross cropped area, which was higher by one third, was accepted as such by this Department! Logically, a lower gross cropped area of 60 lakh hectares should have had a fertilizer consumption figure of 35 kg per hectare. The corresponding national average during the period (1995-96) was 72.13 kg per hectare.

Low use of chemical fertilizers, more or less controlled commodities those days, nevertheless impacted directly on production and productivity. Considering the marginal contribution of Odisha in the national pool of agricultural production, the State always suffered by getting lesser allocations of chemical fertilizers despite higher demand. Central Government had a policy of allotting more, particularly urea, to States that produced more foodgrains. Whatever amount of urea was allocated and received, was channelized through State Cooperative Marketing Federation to primary co-operative societies in the name of preventing black-marketing. Scarcity of fertilizers in reality promoted black-marketing besides creating regular law and order problems during Kharif and Rabi seasons. Ironically, Paradip Phosphate Ltd. and Oswal Group, manufacturers of Di-Ammonium Phosphate (DAP) located in Odisha, supplied their products to other States virtually ignoring the State's requirements. Rourkela Steel Plant (RSP), a Central PSU, also had a fertilizer manufacturing unit in Odisha which produced a mixed fertilizer containing useful micro-nutrients called 'Calcium Ammonium Nitrate'. Though in high demand for growing vegetables, it was routinely supplied to other States with only limited supply for farmers in Odisha. It was necessary to handle producers and suppliers of chemical fertilizers with firmness, besides persuading Central Government to provide higher allocations.

J.B. Patnaik had become Chief Minister for the third time just six months prior to my joining as Director A&FP. No politician in Odisha to my assessment was more knowledgeable and concerned for the State's development, despite widespread allegations of some of his personal proclivities that tarnished his image. He appeared genuinely interested to leave his foot-print by developing agriculture. He wanted a new Agriculture Policy to be prepared, and promised release of funds from State Plan to encourage farm mechanisation, ground-water exploitation, commercial agriculture, etc. besides releasing funds held in Civil Deposits. On being briefed, he met Union Agriculture Minister Dr. Balram Jakhar and persuaded him not to withhold release of allocations to the State while promising that utilisation certificates against earlier allocations would be expedited.

In accordance with the direction of Chief Minister, the new Agriculture Policy was ready within a few months. A strong case for higher allocations of urea and complex fertilizers like DAP and muriate of potash was made before Union Government considering the State's potential for increased agricultural production. I urged local manufacturers and suppliers to ensure guaranteed supplies so as to meet the requirements of farmers, warning them that instances of black-marketing due to inadequate supplies would make them vulnerable to action under the Fertilizer Control Order and other relevant laws. As a licensing authority at the State level by virtue of holding post of Director A&FP, I posted Quality Control Officers at Paradip Phosphate Ltd. and RSP empowering them to stop movement of railway rakes transporting DAP and Calcium Ammonium Nitrate to other States without meeting the requirements of farmers in Odisha. This annoyed Union Department of Fertilizer, but I was not inclined to compromise the interests of Odisha.

I was also convinced that black-marketing of urea resulted from the monopoly of cooperatives, which were in effect selling it through smaller private retailers and at times indulged in creation of artificial scarcity. I convinced the State Government to issue orders against the monopoly of cooperatives over urea and to allow market forces to operate. Union Ministries of Agriculture and Fertilizer both agreed to enhance allocations of urea subject to timely lifting and payment to suppliers. I could manage to get Railway rakes for timely movement of urea by influencing Chairman, Railway Board, whose daughter was a colleague and Collector in an agriculturally-advanced district in Odisha.

Thus, with some amount of arm-twisting or pleading, enhanced allocations of urea by Central Government by about 30 percent year-on-year were achieved for all three years of my tenure as Director A&FP in Odisha. Black-marketing of urea became a thing of past. When annual consumption of NPK in the country grew by less than 10 percent , in Odisha it grew by over 25 percent continuously for the next three years. The share of cooperatives after removal of their monopoly rights for distribution of urea and complex fertilizers came down to less than 30 percent , but overall use of chemical fertilizers took a quantum jump though the State average per hectare of NPK consumption remained far below the national average.

Achieving High Yields in HYV Certified Seeds

The new Agriculture Policy aimed at 10 percent seed replacement ratio and self-sufficiency in production of quality seeds of HYVs involving progressive farmers through motivation and incentives. It was believed that *ceteris paribus*, replacement of local variety seeds by quality HYV seeds helped in increasing crop production by 15 percent. Seed production chain required procurement of breeder seeds from State Agriculture University and other research institutions which had developed those seeds, their multiplication to produce foundation seeds in seed farms of OSSC and Agriculture Department, and finally distribution to progressive farmers for production of certified seeds.

Odisha being a predominantly rice-growing State, requirements of paddy seeds matching its agro-climatic conditions were very high. Progressive farmers were, thus, identified in villages around State Seed Farms, and a "Seed Village Scheme" was worked out. Generally, FCI procured major quantity of paddy/ rice from 2-3 districts in command areas of Hirakud through rice millers, and paddy growers rarely got full MSP. Farmers were told that OSSC would procure seeds from them at prices 20 percent more than MSP for paddy, provided their seeds withstood quality tests and got certified by Odisha State Seed Certification Agency. They were pleased to sign a MOU with Agriculture Department/ OSSC in this regard. Many farmers also liked the offered option of getting their seeds processed in seed-processing plants established in seed production farms of OSSC and Agriculture Department at nominal energy charges if they wanted to get them certified for direct sale to fellow farmers and earn more profit.

The main challenge faced under the Seed Village Scheme, however, was limited capacity of seed processing and conducting quality tests prescribed under the relevant law. Only a few bigger State Seed Farms had seed processing plants, but of limited capacity. There were a large number of agriculture engineers who could ensure civil construction of buildings for installing seed processing plants and storage godowns. Land and electricity were readily available and there was no dearth of trained manpower. As such all existing seed farms had officers-in-charge to exclusively manage them for producing seeds. At this stage my experience gained in DRDAs came in handy. Guidelines of IRDP provided for expenditure of up to 10 percent of total allocation for development of infrastructure incidental to income-generating schemes for families below the poverty line. The only condition was that line department seeking funds had to provide 50 percent matching share. It was possible to get funds from DRDAs of respective districts for installing seed processing plants provided that more than 50 percent of beneficiaries of Seed Village were small and marginal farmers below the poverty line. Funds were to be released centrally by Panchayat Raj Department if the proposals were found to be feasible. Directorate of Agriculture had sizeable unspent amount received under a Centrally Sponsored Scheme, with matching State share, for construction of godowns under a groundnut promotion scheme, albeit kept as Civil Deposit.

Godowns were required in the State for storage of seeds, be it groundnut or paddy. Without going into any further questions, I committed availability of funds and agreement of Agriculture Department to contribute 50 percent of the cost of infrastructure projects to be sanctioned out of IRDP funds to Panchayat Raj Department. With the intervention of Chief Minister, funds from Civil Deposits were released and with the support of my friend G.V.V. Venugopal Sharma, who was Director, Special Project in Panchayat Raj Department, all my proposals got approval despite Secretary of that Department being initially reluctant. A manufacturer from Ambala selected through a short-tendering process agreed to supply and install seed processing plants within six months in a phased manner provided payments were made by agreed dates. Civil construction work started departmentally was completed in a record time of three months in all the departmental seed farms. The supplier of seed processing plants kept his word. Indeed, after his inspecting the buildings, delivery and installation schedule of seed processing plants was advanced especially as he was also receiving payments well before agreed timelines. In record time of about six months, 20 seed processing plants got commissioned which were ready to be used before the next Kharif season.

Seeds of early variety of paddy which were produced on a limited scale under Seed Village Scheme in 1995 Rabi season for use in the following Kharif were processed in some of the newly installed processing plants, which enhanced the confidence of seed growers. State seed farms were rarely known for efficiency. In the name of production of quality seeds despite huge expenditure being incurred on inputs, production was very low with sizeable quantity failing in certification tests.

Posting in departmental seed farms was prized due to facilities available and opportunity to make money through unfair means. In the majority of farms, cost of inputs was higher than sale proceeds of seeds. In agricultural farms with large area under fruit bearing trees such as guava, mango etc., counter-intuitively I found that returns from sale of fruits were zero. In farms in coastal districts, beautiful water bodies existed for irrigation and pisciculture. Yet income from pisciculture was also invariably shown as nil or nominal. After visiting these farms, I initiated departmental actions against farm superintendents for falsely showing zero or nominal income from orchards and water bodies. I saw no reason for State seed farms managed by agriculture experts with optimal use of inputs in controlled conditions to produce less than 4.00 tonnes of paddy seeds per hectare. Barring a few, departmental farms were reporting average yield of around 2.5 tonnes per hectare. Steps for fixing accountability in a few cases and closer monitoring resulted in quantum jump in production of seeds from departmental farms. Similiguda farm (Koraput) with a guava orchard over 25 acres reported income of ₹ 1.25 lakh by putting the produce to auction; income in preceding year was zero. Deras farm, near Bhubaneswar whose Superintendent had been proceeded against, reported income of ₹ 1.00 lakh from mango orchard over an area of about 10 acres as against zero in earlier years. Certified seed production from departmental farms and seed farms of OSSC increased by more than 50 percent in addition to meeting the requirement of foundation seeds for growers under Seed Village Scheme.

TURNOVER IN SEEDS OF ODISHA STATE SEEDS CORPORATION

When I joined Agriculture Department, total production of all seeds was about 2,650 tonnes (from State government and OSSC's seed farms). When I left 3 years later, it exceeded 27,500 tonnes, which included about 23,000 tonnes produced through seed growers under Seed Village Scheme. It excluded seeds produced by progressive seed-growing farmers for own use and direct sale to fellow farmers. Within a couple of years, seed replacement ratio in the State increased from 2 percent to 15 percent , well beyond the target set out in the Agriculture Policy.

OSSC, which had never supplied more than 5,000 tonnes of seeds to farmers, half of it procured from agencies outside the State, supplied more than 25,000 tonnes of seeds during the 1998 Kharif season without any outsourcing. It was the happiest moment for me as Director, A&FP holding additional charge of MD, OSSC, to supply seeds worth about ₹ 70 lakh to Andhra Pradesh and Madhya Pradesh, signalling that for OSSC the wheels had taken a turn for the better. OSSC's turnover rose from ₹ 6 crore per annum, crossing ₹ 25 crore during my tenure. Commercial banks hitherto reluctant, started offering cash credit facilities to OSSCs. Executive Director of Allahabad Bank met me with a request for OSSC to avail cash credit of ₹ 8 crore from his Bank without any sovereign guarantee by State Government.

Production of quality seeds was extended to pulses and oilseeds, in particular groundnut seeds. Though in high demand, these were available only in limited quantity and mostly by way of imports from National and other State Seeds corporations. Odisha depended on Maharashtra for truthfully-labelled groundnut seeds. The only dehumidified godown for storage of groundnut seeds at Chandaka near Bhubaneswar lay defunct since its construction with World Bank assistance a few years back. Trading in seeds procured from outside had made OSSC officials happy and complacent, and they were not interested to repair and operate this defunct godown. Storage facilities of OSSC for other seeds too were quite limited. Conditions of other seed godowns in the State were such that quality certified seeds would become non-seeds if stored beyond a limited period!

Serving as MD, OSSC, I got the old machines from derelict cold storages in Bhubaneswar disposed off. Buildings were renovated and converted into godowns for storage of certified seeds. Technical flaws in dehumidified groundnut godown were addressed and the facility was used to the fullest for storing groundnut seeds produced under Seed Village Scheme. OSSC did not have to depend on governmental funds anymore for renovations and augmentation of additional storage infrastructure. Farmers' representatives who were members of OSSC Board of Directors were pleased to find the financial turnaround of OSSC and its proactive support to farmers in more ways than one.

Aggressive Push to Farm Mechanisation

Analysis revealed that paddy cultivation over one hectare of land required 220 labour man-days. After adding cost of other inputs like seeds, pesticides, etc., average productivity of 15 quintal of rice per hectare did not offer any profit to a farmer even when there was no adverse impact of natural calamity during Kharif season. Cultivation of paddy was thus hardly attractive, particularly in coastal 'rice bowl' districts of the State, after factoring in increased cost of cultivation when natural calamities made these farmers most vulnerable. For going beyond subsistence agriculture based on primitive practices, thrust on farm mechanisation was a must. By reducing disguised unemployment and applying quality inputs used scientifically, the potential to enhance productivity and make agriculture more remunerative was large. Utmost thrust was thus given to these areas with drives and initiatives.

Although agriculture engineers were qualified and competent, they too stood demoralised due to stagnation. Internecine turf war between them and mainstream agriculture specialists and extension functionaries had caused a large share of subsidy available under Centrally Sponsored Scheme for tractors, power tillers, etc. to remain unutilised. Additional Director, Agriculture Engineering in DA&FP, did not like to report to Director, A&FP, the Head of Department. I visited departmental implement factories with him, when he showcased experimentations and activities for production of prototypes of useful small agriculture implements for various crops. But customisation by popularising and mass producing these prototypes had not occurred to him. Of course, a few progressive farmers in agriculturally-advanced areas, being better informed anyway, did not require support of extension functionaries including engineers. It was largely a case of agriculture for subsistence in the major part of the State with less than 50 percent of farmers growing HYVs.

I held meetings with manufacturers of farm equipment, Agriculture Engineers, and agriculture extension officers to direct them to aggressively and collectively contribute to raise the level of farm mechanisation without generating any misunderstandings. Focussed interventions with visible improvements were required. For marketing farm implements, except the bigger ones like power tillers and tractors, departmental "sale outlets" for seeds were involved. These "sale outlets" were mostly managed by Agriculture Overseers, and sometimes by VAWs. Keeping in view that incentives for mechanisation in State's new agriculture policy in the State Plan and unutilised funds towards subsidy for tractors and power tillers under a Centrally Sponsored Scheme, targets were fixed for each district to be achieved jointly by Agriculture Engineers and Extension functionaries. Agriculture Engineers were made responsible to make farm implements available in sale outlets. Odisha Agro-Industries Corporation (OAIC) was roped in for supply of tractors and power tillers besides other farm implements. By chance, I was kept in charge as MD, OAIC which made coordination and quicker delivery easy.

The new agriculture policy envisaged setting up 'Agro-Clinics' run by Assistant Agriculture Officers (AAOs)/Junior Agriculture Officers (JAOs) in clusters of villages. Progressive farmers and young entrepreneurs in and around Agro-Clinics were encouraged and incentivised by offering subsidy to procure tractors, power tillers, and other implements, which could be hired by smaller cultivators. It was the unanimous view of agriculture experts that considering the soil conditions, power tillers should be popularised among farmers of coastal districts and tractors elsewhere. Departmental implement factories had developed some prototypes and a large basket of useful agriculture implements were developed by SSI units on the basis of inputs given to them by agriculture engineersand extension functionaries. The drive for popularising agricultural implements benefitted farmers and manufacturers equally. SSI units who had defaulted in repayment of loans, not only resumed repayment but also started promotional activities which encouraged extension field staff including departmental sale outlets, thereby registering manifold increase in distribution of farm implements.

Large-Scale Soil Testing

The scale of business took a quantum jump and manufacturers of farm implements were now ready to share 1 percent of their profit to promote soil testing in a big way. Hitherto, with only three Soil Testing Laboratories State-wide, it was not possible to complete and communicate all the soil testing reports in time and many samples sent by field functionaries remained unattended. It was, thus, decided that each Agriculture extension officer would be provided with a "soil testing kit" to profile farm land in villages under his jurisdiction. The cost of each standardized soil testing kit was ₹ 1,000/-. Profits shared by farm implement manufacturers were enough to purchase about 1,000 of them for as many AAOs including JAOs.

Each AAO/JAO was thus enabled to inform the farmers instantly about the major nutrient status of their agricultural land. Stratified soil samples from farm lands were delivered to them by VAWs. AAO/JAO then wrote out the soil status after testing samples along with suggested soil amendments, suitable cropping and dose of NPK to be applied for the recommended crops. AAO/JAO could also provide guidance to farmers by carrying out instant soil testing during their field visits. VAWs who delivered the soil health cards containing soil test reports of AAO/JAO as per prescribed formats to the farmers concerned, were also required to explain out the recommendations of AAO/JAO for improved productivity. This decentralised assignment of responsibility for soil testing on a large scale kept agriculture field staff engaged round the year and also raised expectations of farmers making them more assertive and demanding. It was now difficult for field functionaries to run away from their respective headquarters. The targets and achievements of extension functionaries were reviewed with accountability for shortfalls in the zonal meetings held every month.

Micro-Irrigation

In a glaring dichotomy, agriculture in Odisha suffered due to excessive rains leading to floods during certain periods besides drought in the same season elsewhere. Groundwater table was very high yet its exploitation was abysmally low. Counter-productively, Agriculture Department had also rarely been taken on board for promoting either micro irrigation projects or management of bigger community lift points or minor, medium and major irrigation projects. I was convinced that the policy for promoting micro irrigation projects like shallow tube wells and bore wells could not be implemented successfully without involving agricultural field staff. After all, no other Government department, barring School & Mass Education, had man-power at village level like the Agriculture Department.

Thus, it was decided to go for largescale shallow tube wells in coastal districts and borewells in other parts of the State in accordance with the new agriculture policy. Up to 50 percent subsidy was envisaged subject to a ceiling for micro irrigation projects along with water-lifting devices. Initially, field functionaries resisted their involvement and accountability in implementing what they had never done in past. This was not surprising as conventionally, under the World Bank assisted "Training and Visit" system, the only task assigned to extension functionaries including VAWs was to transmit knowledge from 'Lab to Land' and furnish feedback. Despite this assistance being no longer available, the field functionaries insisted on continuing with the same practice regardless of limited success of that project in promoting HYVs, farm mechanisation and overall improvement in foodgrain production in the State. Now, it was made clear to all concerned that functioning and performance of extension workers, VAWs and Overseers would have to be assessed in measurable terms henceforth. This could happen based on their across-the-board achievements in ensuring production of quality seeds under Seed Village Scheme, promotion of chemical fertilizers, soil testing, number of micro irrigation projects, farm mechanisation, crop diversification, etc.

Voluntarily or reluctantly, extension functionaries fell in line to promote micro irrigation projects. A new office of 'Agriculture Promotion & Investment Corporation Ltd.' was set up at State level which inter alia channelized subsidy for shallow tube wells, bore wells, etc. My extensive field visits and reviews at district/regional levels helped greatly in bridging the deficiencies. Depending upon season-wise potential, monthly targets were fixed for each district and every agriculture extension officer in a consultative process depending upon the potential of his/her area. In monthly review meetings, VAWs/JAOs/Assistant Engineers would report their performance in prescribed formats which were consolidated by their supervisory officers at district level. Supervisory officers (DAO/ADAO/Deputy Director) were required to test-check at least 10 percent of achievements' reports at random, before furnishing their consolidated monthly progress reports. Functionaries failing to achieve targets without convincing explanations would face departmental actions for minor penalty instantly. Proceedings initiated against poor performers and reluctant workers would be dropped after a month in case the targets, including backlogs, were achieved during the succeeding month. This practice though perceived a painful measure by a few, made sure that extension personnel stayed in their respective headquarters and visited farmers in villages under their jurisdiction proactively. Soon enough field functionaries got used to working in high gear for time-bound results and started enjoying their multifarious works. Results were visible within months.

Diversification of Production

Odisha being the origin of "Indica" variety of rice, historical bias of famers in raising paddy crops for subsistence even on uplands without adequate water or moisture was difficult to break without a persuasive and forceful extension exercise. Experts in the Directorate consulted experts in Orissa University of Agriculture & Technology (OUAT) to identify potential crops in non-coastal districts which could give better returns to cultivators. Cotton and maize were identified as two thrust cash crops after experts advised that black cotton soil, with limited controlled irrigation facilities, of Balangir, Gajapati, Kalahandi, Nabarangpur, Nuapada, and Rayagada districts was most suitable for raising cotton and maize crops under rainfed conditions in Kharif season. On ground, except in Umerkote (Nabarangpur) where Bengali resettlers, and in Chandragiri (Gajapati) where Tibetan resettlers cultivated cotton and maize, other farmers elsewhere with similar black cotton soil and agro-climatic conditions had remained biased towards paddy and for that reason not prospered. Requisite infrastructure for processing and marketing cotton was also not in place, which discouraged the conservative farming communities from taking risks and venturing into cash crops. Through forceful extension drive, farmers suffering crop losses regularly due to recurring drought were persuaded to diversify, and the collective efforts yielded results.

State-wide land covered under cotton crop of less than 5,000 hectares jumped to more than 50,000 hectares in two years, despite many farmers in Umerkote replacing cotton crop by maize. Area under maize cultivation increased manifold in other districts too. Finding superior quality of cotton now produced in rainfed conditions, Indian Council of Agriculture Research (ICAR) held its first ever all-India Conference in Bhubaneswar on Cotton Research and announced setting up a Cotton Research Station in Odisha. Cotton Corporation of India too got persuaded to intervene in procuring cotton. In no time ginning units started coming up in Rayagada and Kalahandi. Unfortunately, a large upcoming ginning unit with sizable private investment in Umerkote got sabotaged by vested interests which discouraged cotton growers of that area. In the absence of marketing intervention by State agencies for procuring cotton and maize, private players started procuring the surplus.

Despite not getting MSP fixed by Central Government, farmers preferred raising cotton and maize which offered superior returns with much less risk anyway.

Concerted extension efforts on a sustained basis by agriculture extension workers hold sufficient potential to bring about a change in behaviour of farming community for their betterment despite their inherent resistance to change and limited risk-taking nature. Unfortunately, extension functionaries in Odisha had been less forthcoming in areas where their services were required more and whatever lip-service was provided, it was largely limited to relatively agriculturally more advanced areas.

SWIFT REVIVAL OF ODISHA AGRO INDUSTRIES CORPORATION

As in other big States, in Odisha too, the Agro Industries Corporation had been established for promoting agro-processing activities, micro irrigation systems, farm mechanisation, supply of agro inputs, etc. In reality, this corporation had failed miserably in pursuing its mandate. With the passage of time besides providing employment to a few, it became a parking place for some politician as its chairperson or non-official Head. Apart from share capital and grants provided from time to time by State Government, it sustained itself largely by misutilising subsidies received both for processing units and installing community lift irrigation points, dug well energization, etc.

On joining as Director, A&FP, the corporation was found to be practically defunct with negative cash credit account in State Bank of India by more than ₹ 3 crore. It had consumed the sanctioned cash credit for business activities towards meeting salary and establishment costs. Its liabilities to suppliers of fertilizers, pump sets and other agro-inputs were huge. In order to make OAIC financially viable and not to force farmers to remain at the mercy of market forces, subsidy provided under State-sponsored energisation scheme was being administered by DRDAs through OAIC. Diesel and electric pump sets supplied by OAIC were more expensive due to higher margins charged for such services. Even then, it could not execute orders in time which forced the State Government not to insist on supply of water-lifting devices through OAIC for subsidised energisation under priority sector schemes. OAIC having misappropriated the subsidy and sale proceeds, bulk suppliers of agro-inputs had stopped their supplies. About 400 OAIC employees had stopped receiving salaries, after Government agencies, private suppliers lost faith in it. Senior Government officers were not willing to work as its MD principally to avoid being heckled by employees for their 'entitlements'. The senior-most OAIC employee, while officiating as MD, had got himself absorbed as Joint Secretary using his clout, which enabled him to draw his salary from the Government. He would never visit OAIC office, having no interest in an organization on its death-bed with unpaid employees. The lending bank was in the process of invoking sovereign guarantee given by State Government for cash credit.

I was assigned additional charge as its MD at this stage. Having worked as Project Director in two DRDAs that had given huge amount of business under the energisation scheme, some employees of OAIC were known to me. As Director A&FP was the Licensing Authority at State level for manufacturers and suppliers of fertilizer, and farm mechanisation besides micro irrigation projects were thrust areas under the new agriculture policy, I hoped to revive OAIC. On my first day itself, a few well meaning employees agreed to work without immediate returns when I asked them whether they would work diligently to generate business and without agitation for some time to regain the confidence of farmers and suppliers of agro-inputs. With their agreement I issued circulars stating categorically that remunerations would be paid in proportion to the profits generated by them in their respective districts. Employees posted at head office in large numbers were deployed to respective districts. Annual targets, disaggregated month-wise, were fixed for various business activities depending upon the potential of district branches. Instructions were issued to heads of OAIC branches and banks that salaries would be released by head-office to branches separately based upon performance of district branches, thus discontinuing both drawl and disbursal of subsidy and sale proceeds for payment of salaries at branch level. I convinced Panchayat Raj Department to issue instructions to DRDAs and Blocks not to discriminate against OAIC in placing orders for supply of pump-sets under the energisation scheme if OAIC branches were able to execute timely orders in competition with private dealers. State Bank of India too was requested to allow a few months before taking the extreme step of invoking the sovereign guarantee.

The revival strategy started yielding results. Vendors agreed to resume supplies if time-bound payment against fresh supplies was made, with clearance of past liabilities in a phased manner. They also undertook not to sell their products through private dealers at unit costs lower than those offered to OAIC. In fact, as long as their payments were not held up, they had no difficulty in offering further discounts to OAIC which was a bulk buyer. Agricultural operations being season-bound, it did not take time to significantly increase OAIC's business. Despite lower margins, fertilizer and other agro inputs contributed in huge measure to this increase. Since suppliers had agreed to make products available on credit for a reasonable time, OAIC with its network at district and village levels, got the active support of agriculture field functionaries. Monopoly of cooperatives in distribution of urea/ fertilizer had already been broken and availability position of fertilizer had greatly improved due to higher allocations by Union Government. After Kharif season, execution of micro irrigation projects was taken up on a large scale that generated sizable new business for OAIC. The Corporation was given monopoly of subsidised supply of tractors and power tillers which offered higher margins. SSI units manufacturing agricultural implements also offered higher discounts to it. Without showing any bias towards OAIC in terms of pressuring suppliers at the cost of farmers' interest, my position as Director, A&FP helped OAIC to a great extent. DRDAs and Blocks resumed placing orders for execution of community lift irrigation projects and supply of pumpsets with OAIC. The sinking ship came afloat and picked up speed.

Within six months after my promise to them, employees of OAIC started getting full salaries. Cash credit account with State Bank of India now showed a surplus of more than ₹ 3 crore. In less than a year past liabilities were wiped out and OAIC became a vibrant organisation. Margins being charged by OAIC in supply of products to farmers were reduced and quality of services improved despite manpower remaining the same. Quick interventions and departmental actions against some senior officials who had indulged in misappropriation and instigation brought a sense of discipline and accountability.

However, no sooner had OAIC started looking up and doing business vigorously with performers holding key positions in district branches and at State level, I was suddenly replaced. A senior General Manager known for his manipulative skill and corrupt practices, and marginalised by me in Head Office, was posted as regular MD by State Government. This official informed me over telephone about his posting when I was on tour to Kalahandi primarily in connection with work of OAIC, and even joined the post without waiting for my return! I had no interest in ascertaining the reasons for appointing an official of doubtful integrity when the organisation had turned profitable.

My experience as MD of OSSC and OAIC, posts I held additionally for about a year, established the strength and potential of Government corporations in helping the public besides raising the volume of business in a competitive environment despite being weighed down with excessive manpower. These bodies had inherent business advantages and strengths linked with State-sponsored schemes which invariably entailed subsidies. Dealing from a position of strength and support of public institutions, such bodies had a captive market and there were no reasons for their sickness if healthy business practices were followed and minimum moral standards with average accountability was benchmarked. It was not at all the case of public sector corporations not getting full functional freedom. They got overstaffed only when their administrative heads were pliable and thus, got influenced by political functionaries heading them as chairpersons.

Sorting Out Convoluted, Unseen Dimensions of Agriculture

Eastern India in general is endowed with rivers, plenty of seasonal precipitation and groundwater resources, and soil ideally suited for growing paddy and many other crops. Odisha has eleven big perennial rivers with annual precipitation of 150 cm on average. Ground-water potential extends to 50 lakh hectares. In spite of natural advantages, rice yield is quite low compared to other rice-growing States. Unlike agriculturally advanced States like Punjab and Haryana where foodgrain production and productivity of some crops have reached saturation point, their levels in Odisha remain below the national average. An analysis of the agricultural scenario throws up some interesting causes that impede growth of this sector.

Low farm production and productivity in Odisha is attributable to three main factors: climatic, technological, and sociological. Despite high rainfall, its distribution is uneven and erratic. A delay in onset of monsoon with intermittent dry spells leads to belated agricultural operations and moisture stress at critical stages. Continuous downpour at times leads to excessive inundation and water logging, particularly in coastal districts where it is almost a regular feature of monsoon season. More than 65 percent of net cropped area sown is rain-fed. No water management exists in these lands. Precipitation on highlands is lost by runoffs, seepage and percolation and agriculture suffers from water scarcity even as there is water accumulation in low lands. In the remaining 35 percent area, continuous flow in canals with inadequate control structures and mismanagement of distribution points results in excessive inundation and water logging, but has water scarcity at the tail-end. Thus, even in certified irrigated areas, both availability of water and yield rate become low. Improper crop management practices which include varietal mismatch, unscientific plant population, late transplanting, inadequate use of fertilizers, ineffective pest and disease control, limited farm mechanisation etc. lead to low productivity. Predominance of small and marginal farmers and share-croppers, fragmented and widely-scattered operational holdings, insecurity of tenancy, poor progress in consolidation and sense of complacency are a few sociological constraints that stand in the way of achieving higher yield.

When in 1990 agricultural statistics were revised suddenly in the State, without conducting any study, it was reasoned that State Government had been losing Plan assistance annually by about ₹ 600 crore under the Gadgil-Mukherji formula by showing higher income from agriculture! Successive Finance Commissions had been recommending devolution of Central tax revenues to States giving higher weightage to 'income distance factor' or relative regional backwardness. Probably, Chief Minister on the advice of some key advisers thought it better to rewrite the agricultural profile of Odisha to access greater amount of Central funds. Production and productivity in the years to come remained suppressed which created a situation whereby the State hardly figured in the priority of national procurement, marketing or storage agencies like FCI and Central Warehousing Corporation. This invariably led to distress sale, and even smuggling of surplus rice to neighbouring States and Bangladesh within active knowledge of Government agencies despite restrictions on inter-State movements under the relevant control order. State Government did not take any noticeable steps for developing agriculture marketing infrastructure including storage godowns on its own and only played the 'victim card' against the Central Government for not making procurements of Odisha's stocks through FCI.

It was thus hardly surprising that Directorate of Economic & Statistics reported a lower production of 58 lakh metric tonnes (MT) of rice in 1997 Kharif than even that of 1991 Kharif (60 lakh MT) despite a normal monsoon and manifold increases in supply of HYV seeds, fertilizers etc. After registering a record production of 90 lakh MT in 1989-90, production of rice was shown as hovering around 56 lakh MT in normal monsoon years with peak production of 61 lakh MT in 1993-94. Area reported under paddy was also frozen between 42-43 lakh hectares and yield rate unchanged at around 1.4 tonnes per hectare. Weather conditions, except in 1996-97, remained congenial after 1993-94 with similar distribution and intensity of monsoon. In fact, it was better in 1997 than in earlier years of Kharif season for obtaining higher yield. Increase in areas under HYVs, improved irrigation, farm-mechanisation, higher seed replacement ratio, and higher use of plant nutrients in the assessment of Directorate of Economics & Statistics had no significant impact on food grain production. In 1989-90, when rice production increased to 90 lakh MT, it had been attributed to increased area under HYVs, higher fertilizer consumption, besides good monsoon.

Despite the fact of duly documented higher input usage and crop-cutting data of DA&FP, which suggested increased production in almost every district, Directorate of Statistics and Economics was not inclined to accept improvements in those very factors since then. By their own admission, area under high yielding varieties and controlled irrigation had increased considerably, along with quantum jump in use of other agro inputs, namely, quality certified seeds, fertilizer, farm-mechanisation, etc. Even procurement of surplus rice by FCI through miller agents, which was around 3.50 lakh MT in 1989-90, had increased by three times in 1997-98 to reach 10.00 lakh MT as per FCI's report, in spite of rampant distress sale and smuggling of rice to Bangladesh and neighbouring States. In fact, because the procurement limit of FCI had been breached, farmers who were still left holding surplus stocks started agitating.

After working hard for more than two years which resulted in substantial increase in seed replacement ratio, more than 90 percent coverage under HYVs against around 50 percent earlier, higher availability of agro-inputs, and no major natural calamity or reasons for crop loss, it was frustrating to find the wrong projections based on so-called crop-cutting experiments. I insisted that the crop-cutting data needed to be verified. On perusal, it was seen that major crop losses had been shown in Ganjam and Bargarh which were actually agriculturally the most advanced and where farmers were on the war path for not being able to market their surplus due to limited intervention of State marketing agencies. Even Sonepur and Balangir districts, though having lesser area under controlled irrigation, had harvested bumper crops due to timely and evenly distributed monsoon during the Kharif season. Despite increase in distribution of HYV seeds and fertilizer by multiple times, lower yields had been reported by Statistics & Economics Directorate. For example, seed replacement ratio under HYVs in Balangir had increased from less than 2 percent in 1995 to 15 percent in 1997 Kharif, NPK consumption had also increased three times (from 2,000 MT to over 6,000 MT) and there was no drought, flood or pest attack during the season. Yet, production of rice had been shown by them as less than in three earlier years. There was no plausible explanation to justify this situation. I was convinced that production data had been fudged. I, therefore, suggested joint reality check by a team of experts from both the Directorates in a few districts.

Crop-cutting data collected by DA&FP through its well-trained Statistical Investigators revealed yield status to be totally different from what was being reported by Directorate of Economics & Statistics. More than once, I had underlined the need for joint crop-cutting experiments by field functionaries of both Directorates to the Government in past. It was known to everyone who mattered in Planning & Coordination Department that Directorate of Economic & Statistics did not have Amins and Statistical Investigators even at Block level to undertake crop-cutting experiments on the basis of stratified random samples for high, medium, low, irrigated and non-irrigated areas during the harvest season. Yet there was no desire to work out production estimates in a scientific manner. This was beyond my comprehension.

Finding a very high degree of variation in yields reported for Ganjam, Sonepur and Boudh, I now succeeded in getting a joint team organised to verify the samples of crop-cutting. It included the Chief Statistician, DA&FP, an officer committed to purity and authenticity of data, and a Deputy Director from Directorate of Economics & Statistics. Names and signatures of farmers in crop samples reportedly collected by Amins engaged by District Statistical Officers upon verification were found to have either not existed or in some cases had expired long back. It appeared that rather than visiting the farmers and collecting samples before the harvest, these Amins had collected names of farmers from old revenue records of some villages and prepared fake reports. They had not even realised that harvesting time for short, medium and long duration paddy was different! Egregiously, even after being thus exposed, Directorate of Economics & Statistics stuck on to their crop-cutting data. Convoluted justifications were attempted averring lack of Amins in every Block and where these had been engaged, they were not properly trained and equipped to do the job! Whatever may be the reason for the Directorate, the justification for State Government suppressing crop production and productivity data was simply to seek higher allocations under Central Plan assistance and devolution of tax revenue by Finance Commissions over time!

Agriculture marketing in Odisha did not have an existence beyond paper. Hardly any efforts had been made to develop infrastructure as in other progressive States. In the absence of functional market yards or mandis, procurement of surplus rice in Odisha was made solely by FCI in those years.

FCI in turn operated through rice millers serving as their agents. Farmers had to make delivery of their surplus at the milling point and accept the price offered as per millers' assessments of the quality. A few small market yards constructed by Regulated Market Committees (RMCs) in certain areas were either defunct from day one or were of little use. RMCs were generally dens of corruption, while State Agriculture Market Board remained a captive body under Cooperation Minister, whose writ ran wild and large in transfers and postings of Inspectors.

Food security, vital for overall security of the State, rarely received the required support of State Government in a befitting and sustained manner. Interventions for promoting agriculture, barring those under the new agriculture policy, remained limited to Central Sector or Centrally-Sponsored programmes. Political gains rather than actual interest in development of farms and farmers governed non-revision of water rates in command areas of irrigation projects, waiving of irrigation cess levied nominally in the name of natural calamities, subsidy for seeds using calamity relief funds received from Central Government which made them cheaper than ordinary foodgrains, declaration of areas as affected by drought for waiving land cess charged nominally and for crop insurance claims, etc.

A major factor impeding growth of agriculture, as mentioned earlier, was rampant prevalence of share-cropping. Although land reform law of the State did not permit share-cropping barring a few exceptions, in reality most farmers, particularly in coastal districts were cultivators for namesake. Since share-cropping was thus practised illegally, neither adequate quantities of quality seeds nor appropriate dose of fertilizers could be used by share-croppers due to lack of access to institutional finance. It would be just to say that share-cropping kept the real cultivators at subsistence level. Actual land owner, who went on changing share-croppers regularly to confirm their continuing possession over land, remained satisfied with share of 50 percent of produce without spending any money. Assistance given by Governments for crop losses and insurance claims in the event of natural calamities, brought the absentee landlords returns which were far more than the value of his usual returns from share-croppers in a normal year.

Irrigation is the lifeline of agriculture. Conventionally almost 30 percent of State's Plan resources were set apart for irrigation projects. In the process, large numbers of major, medium and minor irrigation projects were initiated. Barring a few bigger projects such as Hirakud and Indravati, major irrigation projects including Rengali, Subarnarekha, Lower Indra, and Lower Suktel, have been awaiting their completion for decades. What is witnessed clearly in implementation of these projects is evasion of responsibility, and probably corrupt practices too. Keeping these projects perpetually incomplete on some ground or other serves interests of engineers, bureaucrats and politicians alike. Costs of all of such projects have increased more than 10 to 20 times, but there is no urgency on the part of the department concerned, to take them to the logical end within specific timelines. Despite huge amount of funds being spent every year and commitments made repeatedly in public to bring 50 percent of State's arable area under controlled irrigation, area under irrigation is either shrinking or remains stagnant. Among major States, Odisha has the distinction of less than one percent power consumption in agriculture sector.

Agricultural production in the country in areas considered to be the granary has already hit the ceiling. Adverse effect of excessive use of chemical fertilizers and pesticides is not only affecting soil health and fertility but also polluting the ground-water and thereby causing a variety of health hazards. Excessive and unscientific use of water, including over-exploitation of groundwater, in some parts has caused salinity in soils which is badly affecting the quality of production and soil productivity. On the other hand, States in eastern India, including eastern Uttar Pradesh, Bihar, Odisha and Assam, despite their tremendous potential have failed to register the desired degree of success in crop production largely due to State-induced lethargy, inadequate policy support and lack of desired administrative interventions.

Odisha certainly deserves a progressive upward-looking policy in agriculture, which is vigorously implemented. This can easily happen if State Government takes due interest in creating enabling physical infrastructure and puts in place requisite legal and administrative framework. These include development of agriculture marketing infrastructure such as market yards with cold storages, other storage godowns, quality control, mechanism for generating awareness about grading of agriculture produce at farmgate stage, agro-processing units, development and completion of major, medium, minor and individual micro irrigation projects in a time-bound manner, assured power supply to promote regulated exploitation of groundwater and crop diversification. The list seems long but is eminently doable as the disciplined State's operations in my tenure of a mere three years showed.

Tribal communities and backward regions have received far less attention of Government in agriculture as compared to relatively advanced areas. It would not be far-fetched to say that the technology underpinning the 'green revolution' had been biased against tribal farmers since hardly any research has been done in India to develop HYVs of minor millets and other subsistence crops cultivated by them in rainfed conditions. Agricultural extension services favoured farming in plains and irrigated areas which mainly produced rice and wheat. Further, large areas of Odisha with predominance of tribal population still do not use chemical fertilizers and pesticides primarily due to lack of awareness. But, in the absence of technology to certify and differentiate their organic agricultural produce, these resource-poor farmers do not receive remunerative prices. State support in this increasingly attractive area to health-conscious Indians and western countries is completely missing. Promotion of natural or organic produce definitely needs attention. Besides, although the presence of agriculture extension functionaries has reduced due to non-recruitment against mounting vacancies, tribal farmers still need extension support services. It is, thus, desirable that extension support services are relocated from agriculturally-advanced areas to tribal areas to help the tribal farmers and avoid further deteriorations in their farming condition. It is easier to register higher growth in agriculture in tribal areas than elsewhere with some amount of handholding support.

In order to maintain quality of agricultural produce with simultaneous improvement in production and productivity, it is necessary to avoid indiscriminate use of chemical fertilizers and pesticides. A realistic mix of organic and chemical fertilizers deserves to be promoted on the basis of unbiased scientific studies. It is often seen that agricultural universities and research institutions fall pray to foreign companies who fund their research studies while promoting their agenda-driven goals for production of chemical fertilizers and pesticides all in the name of increasing foodgrain production. For example, promoting MOP for higher productivity of rice needs to be studied further. Odisha is a stellar example, unable to improve rice productivity substantially despite increasing use of imported MOP as recommended by agricultural scientists. Punjab marched ahead to register the highest productivity in rice without using MOP. National policy on use of chemical fertilizers appears flawed as it creates dependence on manufacturers abroad and foreign suppliers in the name of balanced use of NPK. The fertilizer subsidy bills increased by two times within a year of Central Government accepting the recommendation of a one-man committee of a former Union Agriculture Secretary without corresponding jump in foodgrain production.

The other issue that needs to be given attention is diversification not only in relation to crops, but also in seasonal production practices by farming community. Promoting cultivation of cash crops like cotton and maize in rainfed uplands and medium lands would reduce vulnerability of farmers growing paddy on these lands in case of deficient seasonal rains during Kharif. Cropping intensity can easily be enhanced by taking up light duty crops on unirrigated low-lands except during the last three summer months of Rabi season. In low-lying areas of coastal districts, there is limited scope of crop diversification during Kharif season. Paddy is probably the only crop which can withstand flooding and submergence in water during rainy seasons. There is no point in using higher doses of chemical fertilizers in raising paddy during Kharif on low-lying areas which only enhances risks to human and as marine life. Paddy plants do not absorb nutrients from chemical fertilizer fully. Thus they flow along with flood waters and fill up village tanks used for bathing and pisciculture besides traversing down the rivers to the Bay of Bengal affecting marine life along the path. A better option is to promote agriculture including paddy crops in such areas in Rabi season when there is hardly any fear of floods or heavy rains. Networks of micro irrigation projects by exploiting groundwater and water from perennial rivers and water bodies can be helpful for remunerative and higher production of crops including paddy in Rabi season. All it requires is will-power and determination of the ruling party and accountability of administrative functionaries at various levels.

Pressures of industrialisation and urbanisation have led to increasing use of agricultural land for non-agricultural purposes since land is not an expandable resource. Farming operations with increasing labour and other input costs are forcing farmers out of agriculture or keeping them at subsistence level. This scary situation needs urgent attention by making forceful efforts for converting subsistence agriculture into commercial agriculture. The only way to ensure food security is through enhancing cropping intensify and improving productivity. These can be achieved *inter alia* by incentivising and mechanising agricultural operations. The current approach of State Government towards the future of agriculture does not appear to be inspiring. Undue emphasis on populist schemes aimed at providing food and foodgrains at nominal prices which are not complemented with substantial efforts to create opportunities for gainful employment would only immiserise farming communities and poor consumer-beneficiaries alike besides taking away their pride of achievement. Back-breaking work builds and defines the character of a national population, but backbones are broken with doles.

Hybrid Seeds and Cultivation of a Scam

Odisha accounted for 11 percent of the country's total rice area and 8 percent of total rice production in 1995. Rice within the State contributed 80 percent of total foodgrain production. The Green Revolution ushered in the mid-1960s and early-1970s, which saw a significant breakthrough in rice production nationally by cultivation of dwarf varieties only in the mid-1980s, had a limited impact on rice production in Odisha. Since the early-1990s, rice yield achieved a plateau in large part due to reduction in gross and net cropped area. Considering the rice-eating food habits of a growing population of the State, a demand for rice by the turn of the century of over 90 lakh MT was estimated whereas total production officially recorded in 1995-96 was only 62 lakh MT. In other words, increase in local production by 150 percent was required. The yield potential of rice had increased from 1.06 tonnes/hectare to 1.4 tonnes/hectare in the preceding decade. But increasing use of agricultural land for non-agricultural purposes did not leave scope for expansion of area under rice crop, except during Rabi season which would require huge investments for development of irrigation potential. The biggest challenge, therefore, was to produce more rice on less land, which could be met by scientific crop and land management. This called for promotion of hybrid rice.

Hybrid varieties exploited the phenomenon of hybrid vigour, otherwise known as heterosis. Heterosis is all about producing a crop by crossing two genetically different parents showing superiority in growth and yield over the parents and ruling HYVs. Its successful display in maize during the 1930s had prompted researchers to promote commercial exploitation of heterosis in crops like sorghum, cotton, sunflower and vegetables. Although heterosis in rice had been known since 1926, its commercial exploitation with an increase in yield by 20-30 percent using hybrid rice over semi-dwarf varieties was shown for the first time in 1976 by Chinese scientists. Area under hybrid rice in China increased from 0.15 million hectares in 1976 to 17 million hectares in 1991 constituting about 55 percent of rice producing areas and representing about 66 percent of their total rice production. This breakthrough led to comprehensive R&D of hybrid rice in countries like India, Indonesia, the Philippines, and South Korea.

Given the superiority of hybrid rice technology, ICAR identified hybrid rice research as its top priority and in 1991, a project titled "Development and Use of Hybrid Rice Technology in India" was launched with assistance from United Nations Development Programme (UNDP) and Food & Agriculture Organisation. This national research network in centres across the country, with Directorate of Rice Research at Hyderabad as the Coordinating Centre, released four rice hybrids in 1994 for commercial cultivation, viz. APRH-1 and APRH-2 for Andhra Pradesh, MGR-1 for Tamil Nadu and KRH-1 for Karnataka. Subsequently two hybrids were released, viz. NRH-3 for West Bengal and DRRH-1 for Hyderabad. Yield advantage of these hybrids over the best ruling varieties (check varieties) ranged from 16 to 44 percent. Simultaneously, eight new hybrids of rice developed by private seed companies came to the market, the most popular among which were PHB-71 from Pioneer Overseas Corporation, 6201 from Hybrid Rice International, and MPH-516 and MPH-517 from Mahyco Seed Company.

Hybrid rice yield potential was a well-established fact, duly observed and evaluated by scientists in India including those at ICAR and Central Rice Research Institute (CRRI), Cuttack, besides those at International Rice Research Institute, Manila. Cultivation of hybrid rice started in Odisha during 1995-96 based on a decision taken after discussion between Chief Secretary and Director (International Business Development), Pro-Agro Seeds Co. The letter dated 1 July 1995 of A. Rath, Chairman, OSSC, a very senior IAS officer, to Commissioner-cum-Secretary, Agriculture Department, referred to a discussion held on 22 March 1995 by Chief Secretary stating that Pro-Agro Seeds Co. would supply 1.0 tonne of hybrid paddy seeds to OSSC, which in turn would supply these seeds to Director, A&FP for adaptive trial in government farms, OSSC farms and also in the fields of some progressive farmers during the ensuing Kharif season. DA&FP was told to monitor crop development at each stage, record yields, and also conduct a cost-benefit analysis. Should the result be very satisfying compared to yields of popular HYVs, Government would launch a massive extension programme for popularising hybrid paddy seeds from the next Kharif season.

Accordingly, OSSC procured and supplied 0.99 tonne of hybrid Pro-Agro-6201 paddy seeds and field functionaries under DA&FP organised cultivation during Kharif 1995 season. Despite a late transplanting situation, its yield performance notified by Central Seed Committee on 1 May 1997 was found encouraging; average yield being 4.8 MT/hectare compared to below 3.0 MT/hectare of check HYVs. During Rabi 1995-96 (after my joining as Director A&FP), this hybrid variety was again cultivated in different field situations. Yield performance over check HYV was more than 25 percent. This result stood duly documented formally.

Task Force on Seeds chaired by Commissioner-cum-Secretary, Agriculture Department, reviewed the performance of hybrid rice Pro-Agro-6201 at its meeting held on 23 March 1996. It was decided that OSSC should arrange to supply 20 tonnes of hybrid seeds in the ensuing 1996 Kharif season. Accordingly, MD of OSSC sought an indent from Director A&FP for supply of 20 tonnes of Pro-Agro-6201 hybrid paddy seeds, which was complied with. OSSC supplied 19.98 tonnes to Range Deputy Directors of Agriculture for conducting demonstration under the Integrated Cereal Development Programme for which Union Ministry of Agriculture had given allocations, and also for bulk sale to farmers in Odisha. The results were monitored closely. Performance of hybrid paddy in multi-location field trials, demonstration and also on farmers' fields reported by Range Deputy Directors was far superior at an average yield of 6.5 MT/hectares compared to less than 2.14 MT/hectare achieved by ruling check varieties.

When demands for more hybrid seeds were projected by field officers, it was decided to expand the area under hybrid rice in the agriculture strategy meeting which included Range Deputy Directors, DAOs and other rice experts. Projections were made to cover more land in different agro-climatic situations all over the State. Against the requirement of 200 tonnes of hybrid paddy seeds indented, OSSC supplied 151.81 tonnes of Pro-Agro-6201 and 18 tonnes of NPH-303 hybrid paddy seeds for 1996 Rabi seasons. Since availability of Pro-Agro-6201 was less than indented, NHP-303 seeds were supplied stating that seeds of this variety were already being sold to farmers directly by Nuziveedu Seeds Co. of Andhra Pradesh and growers were finding it far more productive than comparable HYVs. Trials of NPH-303 hybrid paddy seeds had not been held in the preceding year in any farms supervised by field functionaries. Unlike Pro-Agro-6201 hybrid, of which yield advantage had been certified by CRRI through demonstration in their farm, NHP-303 was supplied by OSSC in the name of farmers' choice. Secretary, Agriculture Department, who was ex-Officio Chairman of OSSC during that period, was of the view that it could be questioned if hybrid paddy seeds were procured only from a single producer. The results of both hybrids according to OSSC revealed average productivity of 7.30 MT/hectare with about 20 percent sterile paddy grains in Rabi season.

For 1997 Kharif, a programme to cover 30,000 hectares under hybrid rice was drawn after extensive consultations, feedback from field functionaries, and endorsement of scientists from CRRI and OUAT. On behalf of CRRI, Prof. P.J. Jachuk, Principal Scientist (Genetic Resources), wrote to DA&FP on 3 March 1997 that "*hybrid Pro-Agro-6201 had yielded between 6.50 to 7.00 tonnes/hectare at CRRI during 1995-96 and 1996-97 having an yield advantage of 1.5 to 2.00 tonnes/hectare over the check variety*". CRRI Newsletter, April-June 1997, wrote as follows: "*During the dry season of 1997, the recently developed hybrid Pro-Agro-6201 produced a grain yield of 6.551/ha. when planted with 20-days old seedlings and balanced use of fertilizer dose of 120 kg N applied in three splits (of 50 percent at planting, 25 percent at 25 days after planting and the rest at panicle initiation stage), 50 kg P_2O_5 and 20 kg K_2O/ha (applied at planting). The additional application of another 30 kg N and 10 kg K_2O/ha during heading further boosted grain yield of this hybrid up to 7.65/ha. These findings indicate that rice hybrid Pro-Agro-6201 has a good potential for cultivation during the dry season in Odisha*".

Supply of NPH-303 hybrid in 1996 Rabi by OSSC had created discomfort in my mind. I drew the attention of Secretary, Agriculture & Chairman OSSC to the risks as NPH-303 had not been put to adaptive trial in the State. It had also not been recommended by OUAT or any ICAR institution. Noting my misgivings, Chairman OSSC took a meeting with rice scientists of OUAT on 23 May 1996 after visiting their research plots. Besides MD, OSSC, the meeting was attended by Prof. Bhagirathi Senapati, Dean Research, Dr. D.P. Ray, Associate Director, Research (Seeds), and Dr. S.R. Das, Rice Breeder. Though Director A&FP was not invited, minutes of the meeting which were conveyed to his office stated, *inter alia,* that "*the State of Orissa may go for use of hybrid paddy seeds of types used during Rabi/Summer 1996-97; namely, Pro-Agro-6201 and NPH-303 at the ratio of 70:30. This was recommended considering the productivity and duration from seed to seed, which according to OUAT Scientists was 130-135 days in case of 6201 hybrid and 115-120 days in case of NHP-303*".

Development and multiplication of proprietary hybrid seed being the exclusive right of seed-producing company, OSSC did not feel it necessary to purchase hybrid seeds through tender in 1995-96 and 1996-97. However, as indented requirement increased substantially in the subsequent season, official tenders were floated for its procurement. The response to the tender, however, came only from Pro-Agro Seed and Nuziveedu Seeds. OSSC procured 345.895 tonnes of Pro-Agro-6201 and 145.9 tonnes of NPH 303 hybrid paddy seeds to cover 30,000 hectares under hybrid rice during 1997 Kharif. Procurement price, duly approved by OSSC's Board of Directors, was ₹ 7,885/quintal for Pro-Agro and ₹ 7,800/quintal for NPH 303. Union Ministry of Agriculture, by way of encouraging Odisha to promote hybrid rice by accessing seeds from available sources, had approved demonstration of certified hybrid seeds over an area of 3,000 acres in 314 Blocks during 1997 Kharif and made necessary financial allocations for this purpose. Andhra Pradesh, Tamil Nadu, and West Bengal had also been given similar support. However, NPH-303 did not come under the 'certified' category.

Although area under hybrid rice had been increasing steadily, high percentage of sterility in the case of hybrid paddy was reported in some places by media. Overall productivity remained much higher compared to check HYVs in 1996 Rabi, albeit with about 20 percent sterility, despite inadequate application of nitrogenous fertilizers and exposure to high temperature due to delayed transplantation by some farmers. In 1997 Kharif, incessant rains during flowering stage affected performance of hybrid rice, in particular NPH-303 in some places of coastal districts. Performance of both hybrids showed variation depending upon soil and climatic conditions, input usage, and crop management practices. A farmer of Keonjhar achieved the highest yield at 11.80 MT/hectare. Total area covered under hybrid rice remained constant at 22,122 hectares against programme requirement of 30,000 hectares. Un-utilised seeds were taken back by suppliers. As many as 8,993 crop-cutting experiments were carried out and compiled meticulously at State level. These showed that State-wide average productivity was 3.9 MT/hectare against 2.0 MT/hectare of non-hybrids. Considering the lower performance of NPH-303, farmers preferred Pro-Agro-6201 during 1997 Rabi and an area of 2,200 hectares was covered under this hybrid with yield conforming to expectations.

Hybrid rice production had been introduced carefully and after extensive consultations. Pro-Agro-6201 hybrid seeds had been put to adaptive trials in State farms and farmers' fields, initially in 115 Blocks covered by Integrated Cereal Development Programme before expanding cultivation to all 314 Blocks. The package of practices to be followed had been laid down clearly underlining that progressive farmers with controlled irrigation facilities should only be involved in cultivating hybrid rice. Extension functionaries were required to visit and interact with hybrid paddy growers regularly and monitor their cultivation practices. Hearing about the yield advantage, some over-enthusiastic farmers purchased hybrid seeds from private dealers besides government outlets but did not follow attendant crop management. Many farmers cultivated hybrid paddy in low-lying areas and uplands under rainfed conditions in coastal districts in anticipation of better returns despite clear instructions to field functionaries to identify farmers and farm-lands carefully. Yield results were thus bound to be uneven. FCI exhibited reluctance to procure hybrid rice on the ground that the classification norm to pay support price for hybrid paddy had not been prescribed by Central Government. This made it difficult for farmers having marketable surplus to dispose of their produce without distress sale.

Controversies surrounding Chief Minister J.B. Patnaik, who held charge of Agriculture Department, and groupism within his own ruling party gave fodder to his opponents to highlight below par performance of hybrid rice in a few cases, particularly of NPH-303, and blow it up to the maximum extent possible for political gains. In order to avoid further criticism, State Government decided not to promote hybrid paddy in 1998 Kharif. Since Government outlets did not distribute hybrid paddy seeds, farmers on their own bought it from private dealers. Ignorantly, some farmers used hybrid paddy produced by them during the previous season as seeds, which was bound to fail as hybrid seeds could not be multiplied like HYV seeds. This aggravated the problems of Government in terms of adverse publicity. Promotion of hybrid rice in the State which was picking up fast, got sabotaged due to dirty politics.

I was asked to officiate as MD, OSSC, from 18 January 1998 to 14 September 1998. I had already sensed something unusual in inclusion of NPH-303 hybrid, which became unpopular due to higher proportion of sterility. As I did not find adequate records containing technical justification except minutes of a meeting taken by Secretary with OUAT experts to go for NPH-303 hybrid rice, I pointedly asked Chairman OSSC-cum-Secretary, Agriculture Department, who was widely held to be a go-getter and trusted officer of Chief Minister, as to how and why a sudden decision was taken to procure this uncertified NPH-303 variety. I was told that the nephew of a former Chief Justice of India, an old friend of Chief Minister, had triggered its purchase from Nuziveedu Seeds Co.! This person, Advocate by profession considered to be close to J.B. Patnaik at that time, joined the Biju Janata Dal some 10 years later and became a Lok Sabha Member representing the party which was in the forefront of protests against what was called a seed scam of ₹ 100 crore involving J.B. Patnaik, the then Chief Minister!

State Government constituted an Expert Committee headed by Dr. P.J. Jachuk of CRRI on 27 March 1998 to look into the alleged poor performance of hybrid paddy during 1997 Kharif season and to advise the remedies. It included both Additional Director (Extension) and Joint Director (Farm & Seeds) of DA&FP. Procedurally, after defining an imprecise and incomplete "failure" and "success" of hybrid rice cultivation, the Committee visited 13 out of 30 districts from May to July 1998 and interacted with 325 farmers brought to the offices of range Deputy Directors. It curiously neither interacted with former MD, OSSC, nor with DA&FP. The Committee had pronounced that hybrid paddy was introduced in a hasty manner without proper trials in diverse ecologies of the State which resulted in failure!

The report was hardly an objectively conducted examination. The Chairman, a reputed plant breeder who earlier had given an opinion in writing to certify the yield advantage of Pro-Agro-6201 paddy hybrid over check HYVs and recommended its cultivation. Hypocritically, as Chairman of the Expert Committee he damned the State for promoting hybrid rice! Additional Director and Joint Director of A&FP had never recorded their advice against hybrid rice in the run-up to its popularisation in the State. Having been outsmarted by their rival colleague to the post of MD, OSSC, the duo found an opportunity to settle scores against their detractor. Other Members of Expert Committee were from OUAT. They appeared to have kneeled before State authority vested in two disgruntled members by rubber-stamping a report prepared unscientifically and placed before them.

I also came to know about the report well after I had demitted the office of Director, A&FP. B.K. Patnaik, Agriculture Secretary between 1995 and 1998, called upon to offer comments on the report, showed it to me. In one plain reading, I could make out that instead of meeting its terms of reference, the Committee from its constitution till submission of report, worked to achieve its aim of sabotaging hybrid rice cultivation in Odisha. Substantively it could not be deemed anything but unscientific, drawing its analysis from factual inaccuracies and prejudices of its members. Amongst farmers ostensibly interviewed by them, the Committee had failed to draw any distinction between growers of Pro-Agro-6201 and NPH-303, as well as between actual growers, share-croppers or absentee landlords. None of those farmers whose details stood documented were interviewed by the Expert Committee. No mention was made of crop-cutting by field officers meticulously covering 8,993 hybrid paddy growers during 1997 Kharif, some of whom had received yield up to 11.00 MT/hectare. The report curiously also ignored the 1996 and 1997 trials and production during both Rabi and Kharif seasons. In what could only be termed motivated ignorance, it opined that hybrid rice was taken up for the first time without any trial.

At first glance, I had seen inconsistencies and contradictions between some tables in the report. What to speak of veracity of categorisations, even arithmetic sum of total number of samples analysed did not tally. Conclusions drawn from analytical tables could not be correlated. The programme was called a failure despite recording that in 94 percent of samples drawn from 3,790 locations, hybrid yield was either higher than or as good as check HYVs. Grow out tests conducted earlier were either selectively used or ignored. Conspicuously, records were summarily rejected wherever superintendents of departmental farms and farm management specialists did not agree to manipulations in their recorded data.

The report also failed in responding to the terms of reference which desired the Committee to recommend the remedies after going into the details of alleged failure. The report recalled to my mind opposition of some agriculture scientists to introducing dwarf variety wheat in India for which seeds had been received from Mexico just prior to the launch of Green Revolution. In his Book "*Bitter Sweet*" by B. Sivaraman, Union Agriculture Secretary when trials had been carried out in Rabi 1964 in 14 locations, has written that trial results showed that in 12 locations dwarf varieties had done badly compared to local varieties as per reports submitted by agriculture scientists in charge of those stations. When they were asked to furnish all records of trials indicating the package of practices followed and reminded of consequences in case of deviations in timely use of prescribed dose of inputs, the true state of the results was revealed and resistance against introduction of dwarf wheat type method vanished[1]. In Odisha, the two disgruntled officers, who had earlier participated in promotion of hybrid rice including multi-locational field trials while officiating as range Deputy Directors prior to 1997, had conveniently changed their position. Along with some other scientists from OUAT, and head of Expert Committee, who had otherwise failed to make any headway in developing hybrid rice, found it an ideal situation to sabotage the promotion of hybrid rice to justify their relevance. Achievements of agriculture scientists of OUAT and CRRI did not travel beyond development of HYVs.

I left the Department of Agriculture in September 1998, and B.K. Patnaik, the Secretary, a few months later. J.B. Patnaik was replaced as Chief Minister by Giridhar Gamang, through machinations spearheaded by Basant Kumar Biswal, now Deputy Chief Minister and Minister of Agriculture. He did not waste time to embarrass his former mentor-turned-adversary J.B. Patnaik in every possible way. His newspaper 'Samaya' published fake and fabricated reports to keep the political pot boiling. Lies were recycled by leaders of the principal opposition party to describe hybrid paddy promotion as a ₹ 100 crore "seed scam" by J.B. Patnaik! With Assembly elections approaching, Naveen Patnaik, the budding new face in the political firmament inheriting the political legacy of his father, the late Biju Patnaik, declared that the 'seed scam' along with other scams of J.B. Patnaik would be handed over to Central Bureau of Investigation (CBI) if his party came to power. Thus, hybrid paddy cultivation which was progressing steady in the State for three years became a casualty.

Seeds of an Investigation by CBI

The ruling Congress party suffered a humiliating defeat in State Assembly election held in February-March 2000. Naveen Patnaik took charge as Chief Minister on 5 March 2000. True to his declarations pre-election, CBI investigation was ordered by his Government as soon as he occupied the seat of power. Although none, either in the embedded media nor in political circles, had written or spoken against my role in procurement of hybrid paddy seeds, all of a sudden, I found SP, CBI Branch Bhubaneswar at my residential doorstep in New Delhi in October 2000. I had joined the Union Home Ministry on Central Deputation on 1 August 2000. He handed over a questionnaire to me stating that though I was not involved in any wrong, the investigating agency had to complete the enquiry for which questions framed for me needed to be answered. I answered but was not surprised to find that the investigating officer who had perhaps framed questions did not have understanding of scientific

1. B. Sivaraman, P. 302.

aspects nor of Central Government's schemes for popularising hybrid rice nor of seed laws in the country.

Towards the end of 2002, I received a letter from Department of Agriculture in Odisha to submit my comments on the report furnished by CBI to State Government. I was expected to peruse it by visiting Bhubaneswar. I wrote back requesting that a copy of the report should be sent to me and if that was not possible, the State Government could take action as appropriate without seeking my views. I was told verbally that CBI had not found any evidence of criminality. Government was to dispose of the matter administratively which necessitated comments of all concerned then – MD OSSC, Secretary Agriculture & Chairman OSSC, and Director A&FP. I remained in utter ignorance about what happened thereafter till a decade later in 2012, when my empanelment as Additional Secretary in Central Government did not happen in the first round on the ground that State Government had not intimated the outcome of the so-called administrative action in this matter to Union DoPT. There was no official communication to this effect to me. I was merely apprised by a friend who happened to be Additional Secretary in DoPT about what was a surprising omission to him given my outstanding performance record in the empanelled officers list. On my request made now, State Government headed by Naveen Patnaik sent a report to DoPT that it did not find the matter deserving any administrative action and had been closed.

Thus, CBI did not find any truth in the so-called 'seed scam'. Curiously, the investigating agency had failed to make efforts regarding the sudden inclusion of NPH-303 hybrid paddy seeds which had not given satisfactory yield performance besides having contributed to a higher percentage of sterility. The work of extraneous considerations in the supply of this hybrid could not be found out even at this stage, despite my resistance conveyed in writing. With the change of party in power, B.K. Patnaik was appointed Commissioner-cum-Secretary in Department of Water Resources of which Chief Minister Naveen Patnaik was the Minister. After completion of his long innings as Secretary, Water Resources, he became Secretary/ Principal Secretary to Chief Minister for the next five years. Superannuating as Chief Secretary to State Government, he was given two successive post-retirement appointments, the last as Member of State Human Rights Commission. The politics on the so-called hybrid seed scam had no adverse effect on his professional growth.

End of My Innings in Agriculture Department

I could never agree with some of my seniors who were ever ready to remain pertinent or indispensable to the ruling dispensations by changing their positions as though sensing the political winds and requirements. It seemed that they were proving that the socio-economic development in the State could never take place through governmental efforts and that thus there was no need to show too much enthusiasm in implementing the ongoing programmes. If only the exception to this could withstand the tests of time instead!

When I requested release of funds received from Union Agriculture Ministry for crop demonstration and other components, one of the friendliest senior officers who happened to be a degree holder in Agriculture and was ACS Finance told me once that crop production depended solely upon farmers and rains over which Governments had no control. I had written to him explaining how delays in release of funds till the season was over could result in misappropriations when officers had to report funds' utilisation in a hurried manner at the end of the financial year. I had suggested that it might be useful to draw and keep the allocations in a bank for use during the next working season by relaxing the provisions of the State's GFRs. I outlined the embarrassing dilemma faced by Directorate of Agriculture. When its proposals for release of funds were submitted, since the very Finance Department which had been unwilling to release funds mandated to be parked in Civil Deposits, would now seek justification for low utilisation of allocations. Finance Department invariably rejected the proposals deepening the injury by justifying its decision on the grounds that Directorate of Agriculture had not satisfactorily explained the reasons warranting drawl from Civil Deposits!

On another occasion, in my statement before Public Accounts Committee as Director A&FP I had bluntly apportioned blame at the door of Finance Department. The Committee was considering a C&AG report albeit for a period unrelated to my tenure. I had notified my intention to tell the truth in advance to ACS Finance. Responding to their direct query, I had said that in order not to strain the "ways and means" position, State Government had been unwilling to release allocations received from Central Government. Thus, it was not that Agriculture Directorate was unable to meet the desired objectives of schemes, but that unutilised funds lay parked in Civil Deposits of State Government. I had subsequently conveyed my statements made before the Public Accounts Committee in writing to Finance Department to its discomfort. I had to leave Directorate of Agriculture after this incident, which affected my plans to continuously pursue farm mechanisation, crop diversification, seed multiplications, vigorous implementation of micro irrigation projects, etc. Time would tell whether this resulted in a slowdown.

Chief Secretary and his two batch-mates who successively worked as Agriculture Production Commissioner appeared to be more interested in matters concerning transfers and postings of their chosen ones from the tribal areas to coastal areas. I had been resisting such moves and had already invited their displeasure more than once. Chief Secretary was particularly unhappy with me at this point of time as I had just conveyed my inability to implement his request given to me initially through Secretary, Agriculture and later on by calling me to his office personally, for cancellation of transfer order of an officer from Cuttack to Malkangiri. It could not be acceded to as such requests attracted precedents. Perhaps my submissions to the Public Accounts Committee were the proverbial last straw on this camel's back.

Rightly or wrongly, I believed in the ability of individuals and organisations working under the Government in efficient and effective delivery of public services and in creating an enabling atmosphere to facilitate faster socio-economic development. I did my best to grab opportunities with both hands and expected others to do so with conviction and without being afraid of risks. I felt adequately rewarded for my close to three years' tenure as Director, A&FP to find that as a result of vigorous implementation of the new comprehensive agriculture policy, (i) seed replacement ratio increased from 2 percent to more than 15 percent ; (ii) fertilizer consumption went up from 23 kg; NPK to more than 36 kg (which translated into about 54 kg/hectare if calculated taking into account the gross cropped area maintained by Directorate of Economics & Statistics and Planning & Coordination Department); (iii) micro irrigation through shallow tube wells, bore wells etc. created irrigation potential over one lakh acres at a minimal subsidy of ₹ 7,200/acre; (iv) about 50,000 hectare of land was brought under hybrid cotton cultivation and similar area under hybrid maize cultivation; (v) 20 new seed processing plants were installed in State seed farms which helped in making the State not only self-sufficient in meeting its requirements of paddy and groundnut HYV seeds, but was also able to sell HYV paddy seeds to neighbouring States; (vi) area coverage under HYV paddy was increased from 50 percent to 90 percent ; (vii) despite distress sale, procurement of surplus rice increased hugely from below 4 lakh tonnes to more than 10 lakh tonnes; and (viii) massive farm mechanisation had not only helped cultivators but also had led to revival of sick SSI units which were engaged in production of farm implements. There was all-round appreciation for the work done by the team of officers, including extension functionaries from villages right up to those at State level, though some disgruntled elements did try to create pinpricks occasionally.

Speaking of individual abilities and values, I recall that Sikandar Alam, singer luminary retired honorably after faithfully discharging official duties as ministerial head of his section in the Directorate. In sharp contrast, I was constrained to dismiss Subash Chandra Das, another eminent singer, from the post of Assistant for neglecting his obligations. It surprised me when in a chance encounter, Prafulla Kar, a top musician, lauded this official action.

Sovan Kanungo was one of the most reputed officers holding post-retirement assignment as Chairman, Odisha Public Service Commission, when I chanced to meet him for the first time in Odisha Bhawan, New Delhi. He held my hand and took me to his room. He asked me as to how I could avoid revolt from field functionaries despite so many departmental proceedings I had drawn against them. I explained that the field strength exceeded 14,000 and number of persons under such proceedings with reformative objectives and quick disposal was perhaps around 1 percent. He not only loved my explanation but also complimented me by saying that he liked my clear orders with cogent arguments and adequate justification and thus awarded penalty or punishment instantly. He underlined that most of the senior officers in matters of departmental proceedings only endorsed noting of subordinates without applying their mind, and I did not follow that pattern. I recalled that the orders passed by the Commission would largely uphold mine. Now, I felt flattered to hear the kind words of Sovan Kanungo.

In another incident after about seven years of demitting the post of Director A&FP, on my return from Central deputation in 2005, when I stood posted as Commercial Tax Commissioner by State Government, I had to travel by train from Koraput to Sambalpur. At Kesinga (Kalahandi) two businessmen boarded this train for Howrah. I could make out from their talks that they were on their way to Malaysia on business, and could not help but listen in when they spoke with other 2-3 persons who had also got onto the train at Rayagada about the working and business environment in Kalahandi district where I had once served. They started explaining about the transformation in the agricultural economy in Kalahandi district due to extensive coverage under HYV paddy which had made the district foodgrain surplus and how the number of rice mills had increased, providing useful downstream value addition. The success for this was attributed by them to one 'Taradatt', who they said was Director A&FP of Odisha some seven years back. I felt humbled and at the same time acutely embarrassed to overhear this. Throughout the journey I remained cautiously quiet fearing to be recognised. However, after a few hours when I got down at Sambalpur, I found a high spring in my step and felt adequately rewarded for my sincere and selfless work as Director A&FP. No appreciation in my ACRs/ APARs, which was aplenty, could have been more satisfying than this.

* * * *

6

A Bit of Everything

ONCE MORE IN PANCHAYAT RAJ DEPARTMENT (VIGILANCE)

I joined as Additional Secretary, Panchayat Raj Department on 15 September 1998, where I was given the task of vigilance, the same area I had held way back in 1991 for a mere 72 days. A small room along with a personal assistant was given to me and a Mahindra Jeep was committed for my field visits as and when I required, subject to availability. I had never complained about lack of administrative amenities, including transport from residence to office, and did not do so now either. I was quite happy to walk the stretch from my office to residence. My two-wheeler was enough to meet other limited needs.

Nothing had really changed functionally. Within days I realised that Minister Habibullah Khan wanted me to selectively conduct enquiries in constituencies/ Blocks held by his opponents. My reaction again was that I was not available to be used as his mercenary to help settle his political scores. I again started picking up petitions containing serious allegations at random for field enquiries on the alleged irregularities. One of the first such cases happened to be in the Assembly Constituency of Minister himself where large amounts of funds of IAY had been allegedly spent for construction of houses in favour of ineligible beneficiaries. On enquiry, I found that not only was there a mismatch between the records on physical achievement and expenditure, it was reported by BDO that IAY houses on Government land had been taken up at the direction of Minister! More than 200 houses were being constructed within the urban area of Nabarangpur in brazen violation of IAY guidelines which permitted assistance to ST and SC families below the poverty line in rural areas only. The beneficiaries here were Minister's captive voters. I gave a detailed report suggesting departmental action and recovery from Block officials concerned. As expected, no action was taken on my report.

After conducting a few more enquiries and submitting reports, I knew well the futility of my exercises howsoever painful for me. I put up a long note to Secretary outlining what I felt was necessary for efficient implementation of priority sector programmes including wage employment and housing schemes. I urged taking more steps towards creation of enabling administrative infrastructure and effective monitoring mechanism at State, District and Block levels for better outcomes. There was little point going for post-mortem to punish officials concerned after the damage had been done. I called for additional logistics support to Blocks and Gram Panchayats for timely and orderly implementation of schemes, which would automatically reduce corrupt practices. I reasoned that it was always better to avoid bringing an additional element of vigilance-based enforcement which brings a high risk of negative impact. I also indicated that Government had not taken any action on my enquiry reports submitted earlier without assigning any reasons and that Secretary might consider bringing my note to the notice of Chief Secretary and Government at the highest level.

I had worked as Project Director, DRDA Sambalpur, when the incumbent Secretary had been District Collector. During my previous short posting in this Department, he had been Director, Special Projects. He came to me after reading my note and tried to explain his limitations. To drive home the point that effective monitoring, including frequent field visits by senior officers, were better alternatives for successful implementation of special projects, I recounted our collective experiences in Sambalpur. He agreed that enhanced allocations to Panchayat Samitis and Gram Panchayats called for strengthening these institutions, but that could not be done instantly. As regards action on my enquiry reports, he said that I should also put up detailed draft charges along with enquiry reports against the delinquent officials as the section in charge of departmental proceedings was not equal to the task. He agreed to assign atleast one Junior Engineer to me for technical verification of development projects meant for generating wage employment to make the charges more specific and sounder. Projects to be enquired into were mostly under the Employment Assurance Scheme (EAS). I made it abundantly clear that vigilance enquiries to be undertaken would have to be acted upon or rejected stating the reasons, which was agreed. My enquiries covered officers of Blocks, Departments, DRDAs and Collectors some of whom I found had directly or indirectly helped in misappropriation of EAS funds variously.

In this tenure of seven months, I conducted 149 enquiries and submitted as many reports along with specific draft charges against delinquent officials. It was an unpleasant thing without corresponding gains in improving quality of implementation. The problem was that EAS guidelines did not permit expenditure on engagement of requisite technical manpower and State Government did not have own resources to support the personnel required to effectively supervise the projects. The expenditure-driven rural employment programme without any obligation towards creating assets of a permanent nature was bound to be misutilised by public functionaries whose morality was easily sold at a huge discount. Those for whom morality was simply not for sale remained in a minority and were at times considered inefficient.

Habibullah Khan was replaced by Kanhu Charan Lenka as Minister Panchayat Raj after J.B. Patnaik was replaced by Giridhar Gamang as Chief Minister. The new Minister was equally selective in accepting my reports. Under EAS, assistance was provided to raise horticultural plantations on lands of beneficiaries and on the community land. Apart from seasonal employment to beneficiary families, it could give them a sustainable source of income after a gestation period. After verification of horticultural plantations for which more than ₹ 100 crore had been released during past three years by DRDAs to horticulturists and other agencies, I found that in reality, many of the so-called beneficiaries were not even aware of what had been done in their name. A few had received seedlings and limited wage employment for pit-digging work. Plantations of fruit-bearing trees existed sparingly on their lands and community lands even though horticulturists concerned had been released funds regularly for maintenance including casualty replacement by DRDAs for the second and third years running.

During my enquiry in Ganjam district, when nothing was found to exist at the sites referred to by Collector-cum-Chairman, DRDA against crores having been released for maintenance and casualty replacement to develop horticultural plantations, shockingly he told me to see those in the Circuit House and his residential compound! From the files maintained by DRDA, I found that Project Director, DRDA had pointed out inadmissibility of such expenditure under EAS, but District Collector by arrogating to himself discretionary power he never had, had passed orders for diversion of EAS funds meant for works in rural areas exclusively for horticultural and general plantations in urban areas. Although two horticulturists under him were placed under suspension, despite my enquiry report no action was taken against the Collector who it seemed was close to various powers. A fair-weather traveller, he held a key position in the office of Chief Minister after the party in power changed. In my experience, fixing accountability against such a resourceful officer is rarely possible while smaller functionaries without Godfathers can be roasted easily even if mistakes committed by them are without malafide intention. In Ganjam my other enquiries, despite liberally assessing the reported earth works for renovating tanks under Rushikulya irrigation system, estimated the extent of misappropriations to be as high as 75 percent of allocations of EAS funds to Executive Engineers of Water Resources Department. Draft charges were prepared against the Engineers concerned. My job done; I did not care to know the final outcome of those proceedings over time.

I also found that Mayurbhanj Collector had misappropriated sizeable EAS funds ostensibly for raising lemon grass to sustain a SSI unit, which incidentally had been funded by OSFC when he was the General Manager. Lemon grass hardly existed. In this district too, my various reports were acted upon in terms of departmental actions against horticulturists for malafide in the name of assisting development of horticultural plantation on lands of families below the poverty line from tribal communities. However, Collector and Project Director, DRDA who were no less responsible for this malfeasance remained protected by the Minister. Such discrimination in dealing with delinquents after my enquiry reports were submitted was hugely hurtful, even though I did not care for consequences having discharged my assigned duties.

Project Director, DRDA of Keonjhar, who got posted as Collector subsequently, was found to have spent EAS funds for beautification of a large temple compound with decorative plants and ornamental grass, besides raising mango plantations with expenditure on their maintenance on private and community lands. Although here I could find actual existence of some mango plantations, albeit not in good condition, misappropriation of large sums was obvious. I furnished a detailed report along with joint draft charges against former Project Director, DRDA as well as horticulturist. The main culprit, now Collector, had been a favourite of Principal Secretary, Panchayat Raj Department. The charge sheet submitted against him was rejected by GA Department on the technical ground that he belonged to an All India Service and could not be 'jointly' proceeded against with the horticulturist who was from State cadre service. In vain I submitted a separate charge sheet, which were approved. But the officer managed to get himself extricated soon enough to qualify for further promotions.

In the course of enquires, I found large-scale misappropriation of EAS funds in Angul, Dhenkanal, Kalahandi, Kendrapada, and Sundargarh too. Respective horticulturists were placed under suspension and proceeded against. In Kendrapada I found expenditure incurred in the name of "ber" (Jujube Plum) plantation on land affected by salinity! In Kalahandi, mixed horticultural plantations, which included mango, guava and "ber" on the banks of River Tel, did not exist at all despite annual maintenance cost getting released and spent. On books, seedlings for such plantations were reportedly brought all the way from Maharashtra! Mismatches between species selected and agro-climatic conditions were as evident as robbery in broad day-light. DRDA Project Directors and District Collectors had forgotten their supervisory responsibilities after releasing funds to horticulturists. Another reason for such malpractices was limited absorption capacity of Blocks and pressure on DRDAs and executing agencies to report higher expenditure without which release of funds by Union RD Ministry would not take place. Physical achievement in terms of coverage of beneficiaries was nothing more than a calculation game as none would verify the reality. The trend seems to be continuing even today in different forms.

The maximum misutilisation in Blocks and Gram Panchayats I noticed was in the name of renovation of village tanks in low lying areas and in construction of houses under IAY. Vigilance enquiries into allegations of misappropriations in about 50 cases each in Pipli and Kanas Blocks (Puri) against Block officials and local influential public representatives revealed that work orders had been issued between 25-28 May and final bills passed within a fortnight between 10-15 June after check measurement, knowing fully well that Government circulars did not permit earth work during the rainy season thereafter right through till end-September. It was difficult to verify the actual work done after the rainy season. Measurement of earth removed from tank beds and stacked on bunds was the only way to assess the size of misappropriation, as the so-called renovated village ponds were full of rain water. I allowed up to 25 percent erosion of earth stored on bunds/ embankments due to rains and yet found about 75 percent misappropriation. Muster rolls had been fabricated. As a practicality it was simply not possible for two Junior Engineers and BDO in a Block to supervise renovation of 50 tanks within 15 days all at once and take up measurements and check measurements which needed to be entered in Measurement Books before making payment to the executants. I found that Measurement Books for some projects were missing, while those available contained fake entries in most of the cases. It was difficult for Government to place every Junior Engineer and BDO under suspension on the basis of my enquiry reports and draft charges. Anyway, I had no say in such matters and just soldiered on. But the discomfort in the Department due to my reports was discernible.

In Bhadrak, I found misappropriations to the tune of 80 percent to 90 percent of IAY allocations. The so-called beneficiaries recommended by an influential and aggressive MLA had received no more than 10 percent to 20 percent of the cost of houses allotted to them. Many households shown as beneficiaries were not even aware of the assistance shown to have been given to them. The manipulated and fabricated case records suggested that lion share of unit costs was cornered by the MLA, with the rest distributed among Sarpanches of Gram Panchayats and Samiti members and some Block officials. The MLA and his followers got furious when I started the enquiries.

Implementation of EAS, IAY and other priority sector schemes did help some of the poor despite lack of correspondence between expenditures and achievements of stated objectives. I found more mismatch in coastal districts where level of awareness about schemes was higher! What was worrisome was the decentralisation of corruption and its institutionalisation in implementing priority sector schemes. People at large did not revolt against corrupt practices taking place so openly. Hardly anyone would come out openly to share the truth during field enquiries. Indeed, many allegation petitions were filed with the motive of settling scores with political rivals, and not for the sake of finding the truth and to fix accountability.

Centrally Sponsored Schemes to some extent became a trap for State Governments, which had to bear the operating costs. Staff recruited after a scheme was discontinued had to be paid even if there wasn't sufficient work for them. Trained staff also generally resisted moving on to learning and moving to new ones. Governments periodically announce populist schemes without providing for fresh recruitments nor taking steps for filling up existing vacancies. Quality of implementation becomes a casualty with schemes becoming increasingly expenditure-oriented. It was not difficult to find the same village roads or village tanks being repaired and renovated and the same family below the poverty line being shown as assisted under similar schemes at the same time, year after year.

I once heard a Chief Secretary announce in a meeting that he wanted go-getters rather than unproductive honest officers. I had retorted that the assumption of honest officers being unproductive was misplaced. Go-getters were simply those who could report higher expenditure but hardly achieved higher quality outputs. In his Approach Paper to Tenth Five Year Plan (2002-07), N.C. Saxena, Secretary, Planning Commission had stated that about 250 schemes were under implementation at Block level as schemes introduced once did not get formally closed. At any point of time, 30 schemes are being implemented simultaneously in a Block, many with only nominal allocations. Increasing allocations without strengthening Blocks and Gram Panchayats aggravated misutilisation. In my assessment, corruption consumed about 50 percent of overall allocations, particularly under employment-generating programmes. After replacing Planning Commission by NITI Aayog, rationalisation of schemes and programmes taken is a step in the right direction but the jury may still be out whether the situation on the ground in State Governments is any different today.

I did not enjoy my assignment as Additional Secretary, Vigilance, in Panchayat Raj Department as my task could hardly contribute to improving the system. I had been posted due to my name being associated with some fear for being relentless against the corrupt, and perhaps because some of my seniors wanted to see me out of Directorate of Agriculture. State leadership wanted to package my posting to get some mileage politically, though the real reasons I felt were different. Chief Secretary and his close friend in Finance Department wanted to isolate me in the periphery as I had bluntly conveyed my inability to carry out their wishes including in matters transfers and postings. Secretary Panchayat Raj and Director Special Project who were among the sincere officers in the State besides being friendly to me were increasingly uncomfortable as my reports could not be faulted nor rejected outright, but could be taken as a reflection on their functioning at the same time.

It was not that I did not consider enforcement work including vigilance enquiries and framing of draft charges against delinquent officers an essential part of official responsibilities. Indeed, hundreds of departmental proceedings were initiated and disposed of by me as Director, A&FP in three years. But the difference was that more than 90 percent of those proceedings, disposed of within 90 days, were for minor penalties and were aimed at improved performance of field functionaries. Improvement in performance seen after initiating departmental proceeding, assured the official no more than an administrativc warning at its conclusion. I would not mind recommending exoneration to the appellate authority against the penalty imposed by me if the punished delinquent officer was found to have improved his performance substantially with the passage of time. Letters of appreciation were issued to performers. But in Panchayat Raj Department there was no scope for me to replicate this model which delivered positive performance-linked outcomes. As I had no role in either monitoring schemes or handling establishment matters here, what I was doing could hardly help the cause of public service. There was no question of taking any action against corrupt politicians as they did not sign any office papers and could not be pinned down. I was transferred from Panchayat Raj Department without substitute on 20 April 1999, which was expected as my critical reports had become quite difficult for the new Minister to handle. My new post was MD, Odisha State Civil Supply Corporation (OSCSC).

HITTING BULL'S EYE IN OSCSC

I joined as MD, OSCSC on 21 April and was soon re-designated as Chairman & Managing Director (CMD) on 10 May 1999. The choice of my new posting came as a surprise to me and quite a few others considering that the corporation did not enjoy a high reputation for its dealings which made me *ab initio* a misfit. Perhaps the new Chief Minister and new Chief Secretary wanted to present a fresh image of a Government free from fresh taints.

Conventionally, Secretary of Civil Supplies Department functioned as ex-officio Chairperson of OSCSC, and its MD served as Chief Executive with functional freedom. MD, OSCSC was responsible for handling day-to-day administrative matters, including delivery of essential commodities under PDS at specified points through storage agents appointed for each district. From there, retailers would lift stocks for distribution to identified beneficiaries. In reality, Civil Supplies Department exercised authority in selecting storage agents who were mostly affiliated to the ruling party or chosen ones of Civil Supplies Minister.

Storage agents would lift rice, wheat and sugar from storage godowns of FCI or Central/ State warehousing corporations depending upon monthly allocations received from Government. Similar procedure applied to lifting of kerosene oil for distribution under PDS. I had studied the functioning of PDS carefully as Ganjam Collector, and was aware that it was impossible to run the system with purity in letter and spirit, primarily because their operating costs were at least 30 percent to 50 percent more than the margins allowed by State Government depending upon location of storage godowns and fair price shops. Market rates for transportation and storage were much higher than those allowed by Government. Persons involved in running fair price shops, storage and transportation were not Saints eager to pay from their own pocket to bridge gaps in PDS expenditures. Being affiliated with the ruling party or loyal to its leaders, misappropriation of essential commodities at various levels by them was rarely viewed seriously by administration. My track record in administration of essential commodities including in running the PDS as Collector hardly rendered me suitable for the assigned job in the given situation. After all, I had booked a number of storage agents and wholesalers under PBMSA and was on the verge of detaining District Civil Supply Officer for connivance with storage agents when I was Collector, Ganjam.

I did not like to do anything abruptly that could disrupt the functioning of PDS. I knew that bulk lifting of stocks happened towards month-end. In order to regulate these appropriately, I started by calling upon important participants to ensure lifting of stocks as per prescribed timelines in the beginning of the month to ensure timely availability of PDS commodities at fair price shops. Prescribed procedures called for storage agents to furnish accounts of lifting and delivery for the previous month prior to their lifting stocks for the succeeding month, but there were many instances of non-submission of such accounts. I instructed the Chartered Accountant in OSCSC to put up a statement containing details of lifting and delivery of essential commodities by storage agents in previous months. Many District Managers, working as District Civil Supply Officers were not furnishing updated accounts stating that storage agents had not furnished the details. This failure was either an act of blackmail or clear admission of misappropriation of PDS commodities. I issued a strict warning to District Managers to abide by their responsibilities.

About a week after my joining, a statement was put up to me informing that a storage agent in Cuttack, Nanu Agrawala, had not submitted accounts for years altogether, and yet had been allowed to lift essential commodities every month for two coastal districts. When the facts were brought to Secretary's notice, I was informed that this agent had once assaulted the Financial Advisor in the presence of senior officers of the department. The storage agent indeed enjoyed a strong bonhomie with the former Secretary was amply borne out by the leniency for him even when he physically assaulted Financial Adviser of the department and the incident having been widely reported in print media. As though to build on his folklore of intimidations, a former MD, OSCSC narrated to me that his wife received threatening midnight calls when he tried to enforce discipline among storage agents. Ultimately, he had to exit after a short tenure. I was not worried by these stories. In my assessment, based also on experience, criminals who meant business would execute their plans rather than announce them over phone eerily to family members. I had received many such threats as Director A&FP. My habit of spending night hours in travelling, even when visiting southern insurgency affected districts, in order to save day hours for reviews and inspections was well known. I had no doubt in my mind that some disgruntled officials facing departmental proceedings portending to be leaders of Naxalite groups were behind the threats I received periodically that my vehicle would be blasted or I would be murdered. Such threats never deterred me as I had never tried to harm anyone with a vindictive mind.

Nanu Agrawala was found to be otherwise also well-connected. Apart from handling a contract of Water Resources Department worth crores for construction of a ring road in Sambalpur, he was the sole supplier of *dal* (pulses) under a feeding programme for pregnant women and lactating mothers of Women & Child Development Department. When I asked for auditing of accounts of Cuttack branch of OSCSC for the preceding three years, I was again apprised of threats issued by the agent. For protection of the audit unit and District Manager, I got a section of police force posted in front of his Office. Cuttack Collector readily agreed to promulgate prohibitory order around District Manager's Office under section 144 of Cr.P.C. till audit was completed. District Manager reported that some Registers containing details of transactions had been misplaced. I got these reconstructed by tracking actual transactions of the storage agent and verifying them. The special audit was completed within the specified timeframe of 45 days. Total stocks of essential commodities found to have been misappropriated by the rogue storage agent amounted to more than ₹ 8 crore. Total liability after adding interest burden was assessed at ₹ 13 crore.

After going through the audit report and getting satisfied, I wrote to Chief Secretary to instruct all the departments with whom Nanu Agrawala was conducting business not to release his dues till he cleared all liabilities to OSCSC. A copy was also marked to the two departments known to have contracted his services, with the request to deduct the dues of OSCSC before making any payment to the defaulter. Any conscientious Collector of Cuttack or Secretary of Civil Supply Department should have passed detention order long ago against the delinquent storage agent who had for years openly indulged in black-marketing of PDS commodities. But long-standing inaction coupled with support received from the highest level in Civil Supplies Department had only emboldened him to spread his tentacles to other departments. I did not share office matters with the media directly or indirectly in my administrative life. But my letter got somehow leaked to media and was widely publicised. State Government headed by J.B. Patnaik earlier had been facing criticism for alleged corruption. His adversaries in media and elsewhere did not leave any stone unturned to sensationalise any unpleasant reports against then ruling party. My actions against Nanu Agrawala which thus received wide publicity naturally affected his business and so-called reputation in society. He filed a case against me in High Court and obtained orders staying the actions suggested in my letter.

Personally, I believe that higher judiciary, barring aberrations, has contributed greatly in protecting individual rights and enforcing rule of law. I firmly hold that but for the watchful higher judiciary, fundamental rights of citizens would not have remained protected and if the political leaders of the ruling party of the day had a mandate to draft the Constitution today, perhaps fundamental rights might not form part of it. However, the judicial intervention in this case suggested a lot more to it than meets the eye. The suspended storage agent was represented by a leading Advocate in High Court. This leading Advocate was assisted by the daughter of a former Civil Supplies Minister. The Bench was headed by acting Chief Justice who happened to have worked as his subordinate when this Advocate had served as Advocate General for the State. The acting Chief Justice knew me personally for more than 12 years, having defended me in High Court after government's intervention when I had been implicated in person for my actions as Sub-Collector of Balangir Sadar sub-division. It is the very same senior Advocate, the then Advocate General who had initially declined to defend me, and was now defending the storage agent. The Bench took no time to direct the State Government not to take action on my letter and sought my personal presence every week on a fixed date only to adjourn the matter to the next date after noting my presence, and without passing any order till I was transferred from OSCSC after about two months.

In another case of misappropriation of a large quantity of essential commodities involving a storage agent of Balasore, the offender's petition against my orders for his removal as storage agent got listed before the same Bench. In this case, local Tahasildar and Sub-Collector had already been departmentally proceeded against on the basis of a report submitted by me for their wrongly showing a valuable piece of Government land in the name of the storage agent for issuing a solvency certificate to render him eligible for storage agency. When the storage godown of the offender was inspected by me, shortage of huge quantities of essential commodities were detected leading to immediate suspension of his license. In reality someone else was operating as storage agent on behalf of the offender, who appeared politically well-connected. The High Court Bench again stayed my orders. It was even more intriguing that the son of the second Judge in the Bench served the copy of Interim Court Order on Balasore District Manager of OSCSC the next day, a public holiday! The suave District Collector, who left the administrative service after some years to join greener pastures appeared to be playing a dubious role. Indeed, I was hardly surprised when this IAS officer after 20 years was nominated by the ruling parties in the Centre and State to Rajya Sabha.

Chief Minister Giridhar Gamang rung me twice requesting to defer action against this storage agent fearing that the ruling party would lose heavily in Balasore town in the ensuing general assembly election as assessed by his party colleagues. The simple and guileless tribal leader was being manipulated by crafty politicians from this coastal town. His fault lay in unwillingness to disbelieve their stories. I told him that he would be rather better off in taking credit for coming down heavily on black-marketeers and for enforcement work to streamline PDS, but it was difficult for him to handle the pressure mounted on him. This was evident when he again called me even as I was holding a meeting of District Managers and ADMs of coastal districts in Cuttack. I humbly reiterated that it would be unthinkable for me to reverse my orders against the offender, who indeed deserved preventive detention for his misdeeds. Giridhar Gamang and his new Chief Secretary after taking charge had publicly announced a transparent and a corruption-free administration. In reality, quality of administration deteriorated as Giridhar Gamang having never worked in State administration was being taken for granted by the same politicians of coastal districts who had succeeded in displacing his predecessor from chief ministership. Two Special Secretaries appointed by him in his office were relatively less experienced officers who did not enjoy the confidence and respect of the vast majority of civil servants in administration.

I was transferred from OSCSC on 13 October 1999. Less than two months later, Giridhar Gamang too was replaced as Chief Minister. Chief Secretary in J.B. Patnaik government was brought back. Giridhar Gamang had been a Lok Sabha Member since 1972 without interruption and a Central Minister for a considerable period. He had been sent to take over the reins of State administration to bring better fortunes for the grand old party whose Chief Minister in Odisha was being perceived in public domain as a corrupt leader with many personal vices. The experiment did not work as evident from the developments that followed, including election results in February/March 2000.

PDS in Odisha has rarely received the attention it deserved, except in recent years, that too in a limited way after introduction of rice, initially @ ₹ 2/kg and later @ ₹ 1/kg, essentially for electoral gains. Deliberately or otherwise, the design of PDS has been defective, which made misappropriation and black-marketing of essential commodities as if inevitable. Civil Supply Officers responsible for inspection and enforcement administration of essential commodities are notified as District Managers of OSCSC in a clear case of conflict of interests. The fundamental principle that prosecutor could not be the judge was violated in a more aggravated form as the officers who were to work as prosecutors against the offenders were also officiating as business managers at district levels and down below. They forgot their regulatory role and many joined hands with black-marketeers and became the veritable black sheep that contributed heavily to erosion of administrative integrity. The size of the black-market could be gleaned from the fact that the cost of rice in the open market at times would be found to be 20 percent to 25 percent lower than the all-in-cost price which included MSP and other permissible operating costs of essential commodities like rice and wheat procured for PDS.

I also found a few cases of storage agents and wholesalers being the same which made recycling of essential commodities easy. In one case, I had found that to meet the scarcity situation, OSCSC had purchased 500 tonnes of rice from a miller in Bargarh at market rates after the miller had reportedly met his levy rice quota. State Finance Department at the level of Principal Secretary had approved the cost of purchase. On enquiry, I found it was a paper transaction. The stock of 500 tonnes of rice was reported as delivered at a godown about 50 km away on the same day when the said godown was already packed to the brim with FCI rice. It was equally telling that only one truck had been engaged for transporting the rice from the miller's godown to the State Warehousing Corporation's godown. I submitted a detailed report to the Government calling for stringent action, but it was all in vain.

An interesting feature of PDS is that people usually do not make complaints about leakages. The main reason, besides inadequate awareness, is that the number of ration cards in circulation are far more than actual number of beneficiaries. Thus, the vast majority of eligible beneficiaries are by and large able to receive essential commodities, particularly rice. The number of ration card holders in Nabarangpur, which at one point of time was represented by Civil Supplies Minister, was more than 110 percent of the total families! The matter was enquired into after the change of Government and Secretary, Civil Supplies, who was also Chairperson of OSCSC, was proceeded against. A retired Chief Secretary working as Inquiry Officer in the departmental proceedings conveniently recommended acquittal of the delinquent officer years later. The officer in question had already taken voluntary retirement and moved to greener pastures elsewhere. Incidentally, the flow of PDS commodities to the open market also helped in stabilising their cost and availability in the open market!

Posting in OSCSC gave more comfort to officials whose integrity stood mortgaged to the ruling dispensation, political or administrative. It was not that senior departmental functionaries were lagging behind in taking undue advantages by leveraging their positions. When I directed the Administrative Officer to submit the office inventory, he put up a statement containing names of senior officers including a former Secretary of Food & Civil Supplies Department who was shown to have been supplied expensive furniture for use at his residence, which had not been returned even years after his transfer. I directed the Administrative Officer to issue notice for recovery to the said senior officer and he reported compliance. A few months later when I was on deputation to Central Government, I received a midnight distress call from this officer, who had also been transferred after some months. He stated that orders were about to be issued for his suspension at the behest of the said senior officer. The case against him was his failure in taking follow-up actions on the special audit report on misappropriation of essential commodities by storage agent Nanu Agrawala. The real reason he said was that the senior officer had now become Principal Secretary, Finance, and wanted to teach him a lesson for having the temerity to issue a recovery notice. Despite my nature not to hark back to my past assignments, early next morning I called Jugal K. Mohapatra, Secretary to Chief Minister, and requested him to examine the matter carefully before issuing suspension orders. With his intervention, the Administrative Officer could be saved from being suspended. The said senior officer became Chief Secretary and got appointed to a constitutional post for five years post-retirement. Administrative Officer, OSCSC, retired as Director, Municipal Administration.

Kerosene oil got black-marketed the most. Villages in remote areas which were not electrified rarely received kerosene. In Bhubaneswar alone, supply of kerosene was over three times its requirement despite the town having 100 percent electrification and nearly 100 percent supply of cooking gas to consumers. PDS kerosene was mostly misused for adulteration of petrol or for industrial purposes, with administration a passive spectator. Wholesalers and sub-dealers of kerosene were mostly ruling party loyalists. Inspecting officers of Civil Supplies Department rarely called for action either for black-marketing of kerosene. OSCSC had hardly any authority except signing the allocation orders issued by Civil Supplies Department. I could do nothing more than bringing the rampant black-marketing to the notice of State Government for action.

An incident which occurred in front of my office room around 10:00 a.m. one day, that unnerved me momentarily, was an attempt to commit suicide through self-immolation by a youth using kerosene oil stored in some containers lying in OSCSC office building in Bhubaneswar. This incident probably highlighted integrity issues of some senior officials. Sensing commotion outside my office room, luckily my personal staff and a few other officials reached the place quickly, intervened, and saved his life. When I asked the youth to explain the reasons for his extreme step, I learnt that he had been coming to the office for many days to find the officer to whom he had paid bribe by selling his only piece of property on promise of some employment. Not being able to find him, in helplessness, he wanted to end his life. I was in no position to help him recover his property, but I reported the matter to the local police. None in the office could tell me about the culprit who had taken the bribe. Possibly, the person had been transferred out of OSCSC or someone had faked the identity of an OSCSC officer and tricked the victim.

Public distribution of essential commodities is a most critical intervention of the welfare State to ensure that the poor and landless do not suffer starvation. The system designed to support the weakest in the society, however, is sometimes managed through some of the most corrupt public servants at various levels who are seen enjoying confidence and protection of powerful politicians. Random enquiries during my field visits and inspections revealed a large number of fake and non-eligible beneficiaries of PDS while many eligible ones were unaware of their entitlements or were being deprived outright for localised political reasons. Although catching culprits was the easiest task, but those holding key positions in administration with powers to punish the offenders tended to look the other way. Corrupt functionaries in the chain included officials of FCI, Central and State Warehousing Corporations, and

State Civil Supplies Department in addition to storage agents and retailers. A well-meaning regulatory functionary does not have to be a marksman to take aim at the 'bull's eye' to catch the culprit; the target is as visible and as large as the bull itself. It is, however, also true that margins allowed to storage agents and retailers towards operating cost need to be realistic to properly implement PDS and to avoid the organised loot.

A SHORT CREATIVE TENURE IN GAA

I joined as Deputy Director General (DDG) at GAA, the State's apex Training Institute on 1 November 1999, after availing of sick leave of 18 days having suffered from a slipped disc suddenly which warranted complete bed-rest and prevented me from taking up an assignment that required field visits or other official tours even though I enjoyed grassroot level interactions immensely. My transfer from the post of CMD, OSCSC, was to the post of President, Board of Secondary Education at Cuttack. But medical advice did not permit the daily commute from Bhubaneswar. For the second time in my administrative life, I made a representation for modification of my posting order, but this time for a physically less taxing assignment in Bhubaneswar. In popular perception GAA was a parking place for inconvenient or incompetent officers. Despite being a diffident speaker in private, I loved taking lectures and holding forth on developmental and regulatory aspects of administration. From the feedback of trainee officers, I found that they too enjoyed my lectures with empirical content.

GAA had shifted a few years back to a new building, though poorly maintained, at its sprawling campus at Chandrasekharpur. Upon joining, shortage of manpower due to vacancies was tackled by outsourcing expertise. A directory of resource persons willing to deliver lectures at GAA was prepared. I tied up with Director of Regional Plant Resource Centre to help in beautifying the campus and maintain its sprawling vistas. Within a few months, the appearance of GAA was transformed. Improvement in its internal and external ambience contributed to allotment of the first short-term training course for All India Service Officers to GAA by Union DoPT.

The Library, which was a disordered mess of uncatalogued books, was organised systematically. New books were procured from savings in training courses sponsored by Central Government. Senior State Government officers, some of whom had since retired, had reportedly taken a large number of books, including rare ones, years back, and forgotten to return them. Since records of transactions were not maintained properly, it was difficult to recover them. In order to avoid such anarchy in future, norms were laid down for issuing books for a limited period with a fine for not returning them in time. Issuance of books no longer available in the market was stopped. The practice of issuing books to outsiders was stopped pending development of a robust system of guaranteed recovery in the event of loss of books.

It was made mandatory for training course coordinators to compile reading materials for every short-training course handled by them, besides seeking a summary of lecture to be delivered by each guest speaker. The Academy started publishing a quarterly journal containing articles on various aspects of administration. Dr. K.J.S.Chatrath, the Director General of GAA, himself a creative mind, encouraged the faculty and senior administrative officers to contribute to the journal. I was sad to find that it was discontinued after my departure from the Academy.

Having worked in rural development including tribal welfare for over ten years, I was keen to document my own administrative experiences which could be useful for officers in formative stages of their administrative career. I found that GAA provided the academic ambiance with its adequately stocked library to write a book on tribal development in India[1] and another one Block Development Administration[2], both with specific reference to Odisha. These two books were published some time later when I was on Central deputation and posted in MHA.

My tenure at GAA was short and sweet. After four months and nine days, I was transferred by the new State Government on 5 March 2000 to serve as Commissioner-cum-Secretary, Fisheries & Animal Resources Development (FARD) Department. I had already been promoted to the super-time scale with effect from 1 July 1999. However, I continued to hold additional charge in GAA as I was required to complete a training course of two months on Total Quality Management jointly organised with LBSNAA, Mussoorie and British Civil Service College, Sunningdale Park, UK.

STYMIED AND STALLED IN FISHERIES & ANIMAL RESOURCE DEVELOPMENT

I succeeded M.M. Mohanty of 1968 batch of IAS as Commissioner-cum-Secretary, FARD Department on 10 March 2000. Although a new sector for me, I was aware of its huge potential given Odisha's 480 km long coast-line which offered a rich diversity of marine and brackish water fishery. Being home to a large number of perennial and semi-perennial rivers, sweet water fishery offered no fewer opportunities. Improving the breeds of small animals through artificial insemination deserved due attention. A large number of fodder farms stood underutilised. Animal farms with large chunks of land and other infrastructure had not been receiving sufficient budgetary support due to resource crunch. I felt it desirable to explore the possibility of private or joint ventures for a more productive management of these farms. Odisha was almost

---

1. *Tribal Development in India with Special Reference to Orissa*, Gyan Publishing House, New Delhi (2001).
2. *Development Administration in an Indian State: Guide Book for Block Development Officers in Orissa*, Uppal Publishing House, New Delhi (2002).

entirely dependent on neighbouring States for poultry products and fish seeds etc. which too needed to be looked into with a sense of urgency.

I went through the inventory of infrastructure which were screaming out loud to be put to productive use in short and medium term even with limited budget provisions available. I was surprised to find that despite having its own breeding farms and water bodies in large numbers, the State quite heavily relied on West Bengal and Andhra Pradesh for supply of fish seeds, and fingerlings to fish farmers. It was easily possible to produce fish seeds in departmental breeding farms which required minor repairs. Progressive farmers could also be involved in production of fish seeds which did not require a high degree of specialisation. The State had simply failed to leverage the Central Institute of Freshwater Aquaculture in close vicinity at Bhubaneswar. A reputed ICAR institution for training of fishery officials and progressive farmers, I visited it immediately after joining the department and held long discussions with fishery experts. I came across many innovative methods and technologies developed by them which were being replicated in other States to improve fish production and productivity, but not in Odisha. I was told that productivity in pisciculture in Odisha at about half that of Andhra Pradesh, was the lowest in the country. The massive potential for meeting consumption needs locally, besides exporting surpluses to realise valuable revenues for its poor fishing communities, was just begging to be grasped.

Despite my recent and still tenuous recovery from slipped disc, and unmindful of the doctor's words of caution, I started inspecting departmental fish-breeding farms one-by-one. I got prepared a comprehensive plan for their revival after detailed discussions with stakeholders with the determination to produce and supply quality fish seeds to all fish-farmers in time during the ensuing season. It was vital to assess requirements and initiate preparatory works without loss of time. Provisions made in the Vote on Account Budget by the previous Government, except for salary and establishment charges, could be released only with prior approval of Finance Department. The departmental breeding farms did not have powers to utilise own sparse resources generated from sale of fish and fingerlings. I quickly submitted a proposal to Finance Secretary, who having earlier worked in the post held by me was well aware of the time-bound operations of seasonal schemes, to release the Budget provisions to enable undertaking preparatory works including repair and renovations of fish farms and procurement of inputs. Although he agreed, I found that some insensitive officers of Finance Department had opposed my proposal on the grounds of lack of resources and fear of triggering similar demands from other line Departments!

The straight-jacketed mechanical approach applied by Finance Department not only exposed their intellectual hollowness but also harmed season-bound schemes, potential for developing the sector and growing the overall economy. After all, major infrastructure departments like Public Works, Rural Works, and Water Resources, could make up for lost time by executing their projects vigorously after the rainy season. But the schemes of season-bound sectors like inland fisheries and agriculture could not be implemented if allocations were delayed. Thus, budgetary objectives not only got defeated, but scope for corrupt practices multiplied. The programme for production of fish seeds too would suffer due to this negative attitude. The Secretary was unwilling to overrule his subordinates.

I was as usual impatient acutely conscious of the time ticking away before onset of monsoon. Officers in Directorate of Fishery and field functionaries perhaps understood the futility of advance exercises I was forcing upon them. Finding none to appreciate my worries and hurries, I felt as if caged and chained as the opportunity to do something tangible was slowly slipping away. Minister was heading a couple of other Departments deemed meatier, and I could barely catch his attention to my near desperation. Surrounded by the great waters of the Bay of Bengal and sweet waters of the network of rivers, I nevertheless felt like a fish out of water. The reason for performing poorly in a sector with the highest potential was as obvious as daylight for me to visualise now.

A World Bank-assisted project for development of brackish water fishery at Jagajjor (Jagatsinghpur) was in the throes of disputes and controversies. The project, if implemented effectively, was designed not only bring prosperity to beneficiary fish-farmers within a short time, but also transform the economic conditions of coastal fisherman if replicated elsewhere. Spread over 25 hectares, identified families were to receive fully developed tanks, each over Ac. 0.10, for production of prawn. Quality inputs free of cost and technical supervision by fishery experts round the year were ensured in the first year. Pump houses with heavy duty pump sets had already been installed and were to be operated by a fish farmers' society for management of collective assets and other affairs. Demonstrations conducted by project authority headed by Director of Fisheries had conclusively established the economic potential of this project. Allegations of corruption and cloudiness in awarding of contracts against my predecessor were substantive to my assessment. Selection of beneficiaries stood widely contested leading to in-fighting and rivalries in the project village which resulted in some damage to project structures, with some disgruntled persons having gone to the extent of outright sabotage by quietly releasing poisonous substances in a couple of tanks. Construction of drainage system which had been designed scientifically for drawing water from the sea and its regular replenishment had remained incomplete due to such conflicts although substantial works had been completed. In the meanwhile, environmental activists had become over-active, opposing the project which was surrounded from three sides by Bhitarkanika Sanctuary for its impact on biodiversity and harming the associated eco-system by destroying mangrove plantations. As I found later, the project was finally abandoned. Earmarked land was handed over to Forest Department for raising mangrove plantations. The World Bank loan in multiples of crores went down the drain due to disputes, controversies, corruption and environmental activism. None was held accountable.

The situation on animal husbandry side was even more disturbing with a thoroughly demoralised and demotivated set of officers at district level. Many were on the verge of superannuation. They had lost interest in work having faced abnormal delays in their legitimate promotional appointments. I kept my promise given in the first interaction with them and succeeded in organising DPC meetings, though their recommendations were kept pending for about two months by the Minister despite my repeated reminders. The proposals finally forwarded by Minister to Chief Minister's office were received back with approval by the department belatedly when some senior officers expecting promotion had retired. I felt personally embarrassed for not being able to keep my assurance despite doing everything within my control as fast as possible and incessantly reminding others in the hierarchy.

Departmental fodder farms needed to be opened up to the private sector as per Government's policy decision. After collecting the relevant details strenuously, I prepared a comprehensive proposal to privatise a few fodder farms without changing their objectives. The proposal submitted for approval remained unattended in spite of Minister being regularly reminded. He was the senior-most leader of BJP, a coalition partner, and perhaps did not like to give importance to fisheries and animal resources development being pre-occupied with two other major Departments and with political management under his belt. It was also possible that certain factors and considerations unknown to me were playing in his mind, which were not being fulfilled by my proposals, including those for the artificial insemination programme.

I was in hurry to make the maximum use of time and opportunities, but it became difficult for me to handle such road-blocks to discharging professional responsibilities from early on in FARD Department. I had made extensive tours at personal health risk and drawn comprehensive road-maps for action. Yet I was unable to move forward, and felt stymied and stalled at every turn. It was not possible for me to pray for a posting elsewhere due to my utter helplessness here. I decided to opt for Central Deputation to work in Government of India. Luckily, GA Department did not delay forwarding my application to DoPT. Within about a month, my deputation materialised and after being released by State Government on 31 July 2000, I reported in the Union Ministry of Home Affairs the next day.

* * * *

7

Central Sojourn: Handling Home Affairs and AYUSH

RINGSIDE VIEW OF FUNCTIONING OF CONSTITUTION: HOME AFFAIRS

I held post of Joint Secretary, Zonal Council Secretariat with office in Jamnagar House, Man Singh Road. As Director (State Reorganisation) I functioned from the North Block simultaneously. Although Ministry of Home Affairs (MHA) was considered a dry Ministry and IAS officers generally preferred postings in socio-economic ministries, and more so at the level of Director and below, I was immensely pleased to be there for three reasons. First, three major States, namely, Bihar, Madhya Pradesh, and Uttar Pradesh were reorganised immediately after my posting and I was getting an unmissable opportunity to get involved in drafting three State reorganisation laws and participating in their implementation. Second, I was interested to understand the constitutional scheme of Centre-State relations and from MHA, which included Department of Justice at that time, the functioning of Constitution in that sense could be felt in flesh and blood. Third, it was difficult to work effectively in State Government in the absence of a national or unitary sense of priorities and direction, even though grassroot level opportunities were far more. Since the new political leadership in my cadre State appeared somewhat indifferent in matters of development, I felt a bit suffocated and opted out for the time being rather than turning into an outright cynic.

During discussions on the Report of States' Reorganization Commission, Prime Minister Jawaharlal Nehru had proposed to group the States into four or five zones with 'Advisory Councils' to inculcate cooperative working among them. It was probably considered necessary to minimise tension and possible damage due to linguistic pattern followed in reorganising the States. Risk of turmoil endangering the core and fabric of our nascent nation was large. India with a live history of more than 5,000 years was never a political unit as it became on 15 August 1947. Cultural factors had mainly held the Indian nation together as a geographical unit for thousands of years. The concept of a Nation State became a reality after hundreds of years under foreign subjugation and half a century of struggle for liberation involving voluntary sacrifices made by public at large and leaders representing each section of society in every part of India. Democracy underpinned by cooperative federalism was the only option to sustain political unity considering the humongous diversity which was so pervasive that what might be felt to be right and closer to reality in one part, the reverse was equally true elsewhere. As an antidote, it was vital to set up high-level Councils to handle any adverse impact of hostilities and create a healthy Inter-State and Centre-State environment with a view to solving problems of the States and fostering a balanced socio-economic development of the different zones.

Functioning of Zonal Councils of States

Provisions had been made to set up five Zonal Councils (Northern, Central, Eastern, Western, and Southern) in Part-III of the States Reorganisation Act, 1956. The sixth North-Eastern Zone and its Council was created only in December 2002. A single Secretariat for all Zones came into existence in the National Capital in 1963 under administrative control of MHA. While Section 17(1) of the Act laid down procedures and timelines for holding meetings of the Zonal Council, Section 19(1) specified the staffing pattern to manage its affairs. Union Home Minister was ex-officio Chairman of Zonal Councils whereas Chief Ministers of States forming a part of each Zone became Vice Chairpersons by rotation. All the Chief Ministers, and two Ministers of each State to be nominated by Governors of the Zone, were included in the Council besides two members of Union Territories of the Zone. The Council also had an Advisor nominated by Union Planning Commission and Chief Secretaries of respective States. Although Zonal Councils did not have specific powers for enforcing their recommendations, they played a vital role in achieving the desired objectives of (a) harmonious assimilation of States into national mainstream, (b) arresting negative growth of acute State consciousness, regionalism, lingualism and particularistic tendencies, (c) enabling the Centre and States to cooperate and exchange ideas and experiences, and (d) establishing a climate of cooperation amongst them. Zonal Councils could discuss any matter of common interest in socio-economic planning, border disputes including linguistic minorities and inter-State transport, and issues connected with and arising out of reorganization of States under the Act.

It was ironical that with the passage of time, Zonal Councils started meeting less frequently. They had met 100 times since their inception in the year 1957 to until 2000. These provided an excellent platform for discussing and amicably solving inter-State and Centre-State issues. Standing Committees consisting of State Chief Secretaries of respective zones also failed to meet regularly to firm up agendas for Zonal Councils, taking a cynical view that they had hardly any powers to enforce their resolutions. Union Government was equally responsible in not taking their recommendations to the logical end. During my tenure as Joint Secretary, Zonal Council Secretariat, from 1 August 2000 to 23 December 2001, several dates were fixed and elaborate agenda notes prepared for holding Zonal Council meetings. But meetings got postponed, invariably due to preoccupation of Union Home Minister with other urgent matters.

Nevertheless, Zonal Council had contributed greatly in terms of suggesting policies and interventions in various areas including internal security, coastal security, policing, sharing information on crimes and criminals, prison reforms, communal harmony, and resolution of socio-economic problems. When India started facing challenges, particularly after liberalisation of economy since 1991, its meetings on addressing common issues confronted by States became less frequent as Union Government started suspecting the intentions of assertive States and felt it best to avoid discussing motivated agenda items received from them. I recall Union Home Minister expressing discomfort when a proposal of a Southern State calling for greater industrial and commercial cooperation within the Southern Zone was received for inclusion in the agenda. Central line departments had not fully endorsed this proposal either. In my view, ignorance-based highhandedness on the part of narrow-minded senior officials in Central and State Governments have indeed caused more harm to Centre-State and inter-State relations. Rather than analysing issues and their ramifications objectively which require thorough understanding and critical scrutiny, most of the bureaucrats holding high positions tend to tender advice as per the predilections of their political masters, many times based on guesstimates, to hold on to their so-called important positions. Resultantly, more frictions are created instead and constitutional and statutory institutions get undermined. New mechanisms are then sought to be created to deal with the situation, which leads to weakening of time-tested and stabilised structures.

Reorganising States is not about size; natural resources matter

My tenure gave me immense exposure to State reorganization matters and issues of Centre-State relations. The processes involved in creating three new States of Uttaranchal[1] (from Uttar Pradesh), Jharkhand (from Bihar) and Chhattisgarh (from Madhya Pradesh) educated me not only in understanding Parliamentary functioning in terms of legislative requirements but also to the complicated work of division of physical assets and liabilities, institutions and administrative resources, i.e. All India Service and State Service cadres of parent States.

The Acts provided for apportionment of assets and liabilities between the successor States on an "as is where is" basis. In the event of dispute, a reference was to be made as per legal provisions by either State to Central Government

1. The name was soon changed to Uttarakhand.

whose decision was binding on both States. Even so, any apportionment was an exercise which involved occasional bitterness between them as if they had no shared or common past. Bifurcation of State funds and devolution of Central funds, including of Finance Commission awards, invited controversies too. No successor State would be interested to accept liabilities of the parent State. Meetings held at State and National capitals, with Government of India as an arbitrator, would turn acrimonious at times. It was as if negotiations were being held between divorcees holding adversarial positions, although the main participants formed part of the combined erstwhile State cadre.

While division of State cadre services and pension funds between Chhattisgarh and Madhya Pradesh was relatively easy due to excellent record-keeping, it was most difficult between Bihar and Jharkhand as employee service records and provident fund accounts of State cadres were in a mess. Majority of employees were desperate to join Jharkhand fearing that the successor Bihar would not be in a position to pay salaries and pensions after bifurcation. Almost 90 percent of commercial assets and resources of erstwhile Bihar went to Jharkhand. Some All India Service officers albeit with an upright image were not lagging behind in influencing the process of division of the Cadre in a blatant exercise to get allotted to Jharkhand. Parties in power in successor States being different with an adversarial relationship, division of State cadres and apportionment of assets and liabilities was all the more difficult.

Although the party in power was the same in the case of Chhattisgarh and Madhya Pradesh, Chief Minister of Chhattisgarh Ajit Jogi supported by his compliant bureaucracy did not care to wait for either an amicable settlement with Madhya Pradesh nor for orders of Union Government on division of statutory bodies and body corporates. He issued orders throwing legal provisions, prudence and caution to the winds in an attempt to grab the units of key commercial organisations, particularly those engaged in generation and distribution of power. Most of the power plants of parent Madhya Pradesh were situated in Chhattisgarh region, and such high-handed actions would create immiserising effects for successor Madhya Pradesh. Thus, surplus power was offered to Madhya Pradesh only if it was willing to offer the highest rate by participating in commercial bids floated by the new Chhattisgarh State Electricity Board. This Board was also not willing to take apportionable manpower and past liabilities of the parent Electricity Board.

The situation between Uttar Pradesh and Uttarakhand was typically different. There was no bitterness in division of State service cadres and All India Services. Successor Uttar Pradesh conveyed willingness to embrace employees who were not willing to go to Uttarakhand. On the other hand, Uttarakhand was willing to accept whatever was agreed to and offered even if it was in violation of legal provisions. It accepted a proposal of Uttar Pradesh to make available about 50 percent of hydro-electric power generated in the State at generation cost, which was less than ₹ 0.40/unit at that time, whereas purchases in return by Uttarakhand of power produced from thermal power plants in Uttar Pradesh would be at seven times this rate, i.e. at generation cost of about ₹ 2.80/unit! This agreement clearly amounted to exploitation of the tiny State of Uttarakhand, besides being in violation of provisions of Uttar Pradesh State Reorganization Act under which assets and liabilities needed to be transferred on an "as is where is" basis. Uttarakhand had also agreed to pay the cost of special repairs of Government buildings in Dehradun which had become its Capital besides costs of an erstwhile State Bhavan in New Delhi. In brief, Uttarakhand Government was comfortable to be treated like a colony of successor Uttar Pradesh. Senior officers allocated to Uttarakhand, most of whom joined reluctantly, either did not read the provisions of the Act on apportionments within and outside the erstwhile State of Uttar Pradesh or probably apprehended loss of their personal assets created in the parent State Capital and elsewhere. Political leadership of the nascent State lacked maturity and appeared convinced that antagonising Uttar Pradesh by making entitlement claims would harm their State which remained dependent on its big brother for its survival being land-locked.

I made an analysis in a tabular form showing responsibilities and broad entitlements of assets and liabilities of successor States under various sections of the Act. During my visits to State Capitals, representing MHA I pointed out the relevant legal provisions to stakeholders. Finding their agreement on distribution of electricity between Uttarakhand and Uttar Pradesh to be clearly against the legal provisions besides rendering Uttarakhand *ab-initio* anaemic, I advised both States to refer the matter to Union Government for a decision. Similar advice was given in relation of cost of repairs of buildings in Dehradun and proposed transfer of one of the State Bhavans in Delhi. I verbally reported the disquieting developments to Union Home Secretary Kamal Pande who was from Uttarakhand by birth and was allocated to that State cadre. He was cautious not to be seen as biased and remained indifferent. Indeed, I was misunderstood by a few officers of Uttar Pradesh who accused me of favouring Uttarakhand whenever I pointed out any legal provisions. I had reiterated the same legal provisions to officers of other successor States during their meetings at the respective State Capitals.

Union Home Minister took a meeting on Uttarakhand and Uttar Pradesh, when both sides agreed that the question of reimbursing costs of repairs and renovations of office buildings at Dehradun which preceded formation of Uttarakhand did not arise. The smaller Uttar Pradesh Bhawan at Chanakyapuri in New Delhi was decided to be transferred to Uttarakhand without charging any cost. As regards exchange of hydro and thermal power between them, it was agreed that one or both successor States would make a reference to Union Government for final arbitration. Since the legal provisions were clear and left no scope for discretion, in a subsequent meeting held by Union Power Secretary, it was decided that hydro power plants situated in Uttarakhand would be transferred to that State. However, Uttarakhand could make surplus power, if any, available to Uttar Pradesh as per rates to be agreed upon mutually. The decision on Tehri Power Project which provided 10 percent power free of cost to the State in which the project was located and 25 percent at generation cost in accordance with the equity contribution of parent State of Uttar Pradesh was postponed. This was done deliberately. Madhukar Gupta, Chief Secretary of Uttarakhand, I was apprised later by my counterpart in Union Power Ministry, requested Union Power Secretary privately not to ignore the demand of Uttar Pradesh considering that Uttarakhand could not afford to antagonize the neighbourhood big brother. Madhukar Gupta, a hard-working bureaucrat who became Union Home Secretary a few years later, appeared to be more interested in promoting the interests of his native State of Uttar Pradesh but without being seen to be doing so.

Creation of Uttarakhand, and indeed smaller States in general, was never an administratively viable proposition. Such States did not have adequate means for generating tax and non-tax revenues to meet their developmental needs after meeting heavy establishment costs. Creation of new institutional structures like Legislative Assembly, Secretariat, and High Court, entail a huge financial burden. Allocations made by Central Government even for Central Sector and Centrally Sponsored Schemes, Finance Commission awards, etc. for developmental projects got diverted to meet establishment costs in tiny States. A clear case in point is that Uttarakhand region of erstwhile Uttar Pradesh had been receiving higher budgetary allocations than annual budget provisions made by successor Uttarakhand State immediately after its creation. Potential for industrial development being limited in its hilly districts, youth were invariably employed elsewhere, including in armed and paramilitary forces. Since entry in these forces was based on what was called 'male able-bodied ratio' of States, youth from hill districts of erstwhile Uttar Pradesh had benefitted from the advantage of parent State's bigger population followed by relaxation in physical parameters for them. Bifurcation of the parent State implied shrinkage of employment opportunities affecting the new State's 'money order economy'. It is probably for this reason that senior political leaders from Uttarakhand had not favoured its creation. Overall situation of Chhattisgarh and Jharkhand, however, was different. Geographical area, size of population and potential for economic development in these mineral-rich regions justified creation of separate States. Administrative viability was never in doubt.

It is not at all a case that Uttarakhand region was ignored completely when it was part of undivided Uttar Pradesh. Indeed, leaders from the region like G.B. Pant, H.N. Bahuguna and N.D. Tiwari had headed Uttar Pradesh Government more times than from the rest of the State. None of these leaders had supported the idea of a separate hill State. By all indicators of human development, hill districts fared better in comparison to those in Central,

Bundelkhand and Eastern regions of Uttar Pradesh. What triggered the agitation for a separate State was enforcement of provisions of caste-based reservations in schools and colleges recommended by Mandal Commission. Hardly any caste of hill districts found place in the list of Socially & Educationally Backward Classes (SEBCs) of Mandal Commission. But almost all educational institutions there were of State Government where admission of SEBC students from plain areas would entail rejecting local students holding higher ranks in merit. The students' agitation changed its course when a group of women were raped and molested by Uttar Pradesh Police at Muzaffarnagar. Higher aggression among agitators resulted in lathi charge and firing by police at several places causing several deaths. Ensuing revival of an old demand for a separate State by students at this stage forced the political parties under compulsion of electoral politics to start supporting it. Agitation driven by momentary emotions finally led to the birth of Uttarakhand. Narrow political considerations defeated durable regional interests. The winners were a handful of politicians and bureaucrats who got elevated to positions in State Government, which they might never have imagined while remaining part of the behemoth Uttar Pradesh. Despite unusual growth in State's gross domestic product and per capita income due to investment in a few big industrial units by corporate houses in a couple of plain area districts, the employment situation in Uttarakhand has actually worsened as I had expected. The State has become debt-ridden despite enjoying special category status.

It is paradoxical that in spite of improved communication infrastructure, which has reduced time and distance to State capitals from remotely-located places, and decreasing dependence on the State for employment etc., demands for creation of smaller States continues to be raised to create political space and secure positions in the power game. Interestingly, creation of Telangana along with three other States did not materialise in the year 2000. Despite the Bill being drafted, Chandrababu Naidu, Chief Minister of erstwhile Andhra Pradesh supported the government in the Centre, but opposed the proposal. It is not to deny regional disparities or negligence of certain regions by those ruling the nation and States, but a more viable strategy is to find ways and means to address such disparities in the larger national interest.

Centre-State Relations – Window Dressing

I was also involved in handling other aspects of Centre-State relations including processing of recommendations made by Sarkaria Commission, formally known as Commission on Centre-State Relations. Union Government had already set up the Inter-State Council under MHA on 28 May 1990 as per provisions of Article 263 of the Constitution. The other recommendations had remained unattended for a long time. Prime Minister A.B. Vajpayee and Deputy Prime Minister & Home Minister L.K. Advani desired that they be processed, having raised questions against high-handedness of the party in power while in opposition. That this Council was virtually defunct and had become a parking place for unwanted civil servants is moot.

It would be of interest to recall that the Commission chaired by Justice R.S. Sarkaria, with B. Sivaraman and Dr. P.C. Sen as Members, had been set up in June 1983 to review Centre-State relations. In the first two decades after Independence, most States had been ruled by one political party. After 1967, other political parties or their coalitions started ruling some States with different visions and ideologies which did not always go hand-in-hand with that of the ruling party at the Centre. These parties started articulating misgivings against the one in the Centre. There was no institutional mechanism to settle disputes between neighbouring States either. Frequent invocation of Article 356 (President's Rule) by Central Government in States ruled by political rivals started aggravating the tension between the Centre and States. The situation warranted setting up the Sarkaria Commission with the following mandate: (i) look into and advise upon disputes which may have arisen between States; (ii) investigate and discuss subjects in which some or all States or Union and one or more States have a common interest; and (iii) make recommendations upon any such subject and in particular, recommendations for better coordination of policy and action with respect to that subject. The Commission submitted its report in January 1988. As recommended, Inter-State Council chaired by Prime Minister with Chief Ministers of all States, Chief Ministers of Union Territories with Legislative Assemblies, Administrators of Union Territories without Legislative Assemblies, six Central Cabinet Ministers including Home Minister to be nominated by Prime Minister and Governors of States under President's Rule was set up. Its mandate was the following: (i) as much as possible, decentralise powers to States; (ii) arrange devolution in such a way that the States can fulfil their obligations; (iii) transfer more financial resources to States; (iv) advance loans to States related to 'the productive principle'; and (v) deploy Central Armed Forces in States either on their requests or otherwise.

Not a single meeting was held for a long time, although the Council was set up in May 1990. NDA Government revived it and meetings were held every year. Sarkaria Commission's recommendations were brought up for deliberation. I was fortunate to participate in examining and processing them. In all there were 247 recommendations on vital issues, especially on legislative matters, role of Governors, and use of Article 356 of the Constitution. No drastic changes in existing scheme of things had been recommended, and most of the recommendations were thus accepted without inviting controversies in deliberations in the Council. In its meeting held in August 2003, the Council called for incorporation of safeguards in the Constitution in relation to imposition of President's Rule as a last resort. On the appointment of Governor, the Commission's recommendation was not accepted by Government. Ironically, the institutional mechanism of Inter-State Council for improving

Centre-State relations which became vibrant for a brief period, has become dormant again. Though headed by a Secretary rank officer, in the Secretariat of Inter-State Council hardly any business is being transacted.

I was formally assigned additional charge of Centre-State relations with effect from 24 December 2001. I was summoned to assume charge with immediate effect while was attending a training course at IIM, Bangalore. It had been obvious that the incumbent Director was not found equal to the task, since Joint Secretary R.K. Singh had been involving me informally and occasionally in processing action plans received from State Government in implementation of two new non-plan schemes of Modernisation of State Police Forces and Prison Reform.

I recount here the tale in circulation that preceded introduction of State Police Forces' modernisation scheme with cost-sharing between Centre and States. Bureau of Police Research & Training had identified deficiencies in State Police Forces and recommended MHA's financial support to raise all State Police Forces to a minimum level of standards. The interventions covered essential residential facilities for forces at cutting edge level, accommodation for Police Stations including coastal policing, transport, communication equipment, and weaponry. At a National Conference of State DGs of Police, Prime Minister A.B. Vajpayee had announced the extension of financial support for modernising State Police forces. But when a proposal containing details of the 5-year non-Plan scheme of ₹ 1,000 crore per annum was drawn up, it was summarily rejected by Finance Ministry on the grounds of resource crunch. The financing envisaged 50 percent States' own share, and 25 percent loan and 25 percent assistance from Central Government. Unofficial note from Union Home Minister to Finance Minister Yashwant Sinha failed to reverse their rejection. Indeed, Finance Minister took the lead in opposing the scheme. Finally, Union Cabinet approved it with unheard dissenting comments of Finance Ministry. It seems that although Finance Minister was well armed with arguments against the proposal, he did not get an opportunity to present them as at the outset Prime Minister conveyed his anguish for delay of six months in implementing his announcement! Cabinet meetings are held maintaining confidentiality and details of deliberations are not recorded. Approval for the proposal was received within days of the Cabinet meeting. After some time, the Cabinet was reshuffled and Jaswant Singh became Finance Minister. MHA submitted another proposal for a non-Plan scheme involving annual expenditure of ₹ 500 crore for modernising prisons along with a note to Finance Minister from Home Minister. Within three days, I was called by B.P. Mishra, Additional Secretary, Expenditure, to explain it and the scheme received financial concurrence within a week!

I visited various States independently and many times with Special Secretary, Home, to review the implementation of these schemes, which gave varied experiences. Gujarat performed the best by creatively implementing police modernisation with more police flats constructed than the approved units by simply adding floors vertically in several places, while remaining within the same financial allocations and without compromising quality of work. Southern States, by and large, were quick to utilise the funds. Northern States, and in particular Uttar Pradesh, Bihar and West Bengal, occupied bottom position despite having more compelling infrastructural deficiencies to bridge. The main problems faced in these three major States was that the respective State Governments were unable to provide matching State share. Senior police officers of these States expressed helplessness and suggested that rather than releasing funds to States for purchase of vehicles, equipment including weaponry, MHA should make the procurements centrally and supply the same to State Police forces. Maximum misuse of funds was seen in Jammu & Kashmir. When I wanted to see the buildings constructed and those in progress, I was shown some abandoned incomplete structures. The State also received funds separately under a scheme for strengthening the State Police to fight militancy. Some works were found being reported twice. Records were not maintained for audit and verification. With regard to the scheme on prison reform, at Leh I could not find any prison building although funds had been shown spent for a new prison building. Incidentally, Leh at one point had been a zero-crime district, but I saw two murder-accused persons, one each from Jharkhand and West Bengal, who had murdered a co-worker after drinking heavily, housed in a rented room. Diversion of funds meant for Police Station buildings and residential quarters for officials below the rank of Police Inspector where satisfaction level was low, was found in Punjab too. The scheme stipulated a review after two years of implementation. Special Secretary, Home was assigned the task. I drafted a detailed report suggesting changes which included waiver for cost-sharing by States. It was suggested that Centre should bear 75 percent of the cost with State share limited to 25 percent in the form of Central loan. My tenure in MHA concluded at this stage.

Handling State reorganization matters and Centre-State relations including modernisation of State Police Forces and Prison Reforms afforded me opportunities to access the national archives, besides frequent interactions with senior officers of various States. Monthly reports of Governors to Union Home Minister from some of the States revealed alarming law and order situations which rarely figured in public domain. I recollect that one such report gave a vivid description of a case of kidnapping for ransom in Danapur, Bihar. It highlighted how a prominent ruling party leader, negotiating the release of two young daughters of a businessman who had been kidnapped, played his role with some concession for himself.

I compiled a statement to document each case of imposition of President's Rule in States after 1950 along with reasons after going through the old files preserved in National Archives. President's Rule has been imposed 116 times after 1950. The first occasion was in June 1951, the reason being internal dispute in Indian National Congress which then ruled the Centre as well as Punjab. I was surprised to find that on many occasions, proclamations had been made even before taking the approval of Cabinet. One of the most celebrated ICS officers serving in Union Home Ministry for about five years was seen to have obtained orders of Prime Minister to impose President's Rule on a few occasions before the matter was sent to the Cabinet. An analysis showed that barring exceptions, Article 356 has largely been invoked on account of political considerations by dispensations in Union Government. The exceptions include internal disputes within ruling parties, reorganisation of States, and a few very strong protest movements in some States leading to constitutional break-down. Political considerations for invoking Article 356 were defections (prompted), law and order situations, break-up in coalition partners and State's ruling parties losing in Parliamentary (Lok Sabha) elections.

A Minor Personal Disappointment

The process of empanelment in Government of India had been delayed whole-scale by two years due to a sudden decision to increase the age of retirement from 58 to 60 years. My batch was thus empanelled to super-time scale towards the end of December 2002. By March 2003, barring a few officers of the batch who probably wanted to exercise options, all of those already on Central deputation had been elevated to promotional posts as Joint Secretary or equivalent. The extant rule provided for such posting in the same Ministry in the event of vacancies arising, and if not so, making officers available for posting in other Ministries and informing DoPT accordingly.

The post of Joint Secretary in Foreigners Division of MHA was to fall vacant towards the end of March 2003. I was given to understand that I would be posted there. The request for extension by three months of the incumbent had been turned down by Cabinet Secretary, who incidentally was Home Secretary earlier. Out of the blue on his last day extension of six months was granted to him. Home Secretary N. Gopala Swami called me to say that he would like to retain me in MHA against another vacancy which was to arise in May 2003. However, when the time came another officer was posted. I was on leave when this was done. There was no possibility of another post of Joint Secretary falling vacant in MHA in the near future and thus, DoPT was informed to indicate my availability to other Ministries for posting. While I had no difficulty in waiting, what pained me was that Home Secretary continued to give me an impression as if he was genuinely interested to retain me in the Ministry. DoPT could have been informed about non-availability of a post in MHA for my posting elsewhere, months back.

It was not surprising to find the same Home Secretary, after being appointed as Election Commissioner, seeking favour for cancellation of transfer of his relative, a doctor of 'Siddha', when I was posted as Joint Secretary, AYUSH. The doctor after continuously working in Chennai for more than

20 years under Central Government Health Service had been posted to Delhi only about two months back. As had been my long-held principle of non-interference with rules on transfers and postings, I respectfully conveyed impossibility of the officer being posted back to Chennai. Election Commissioner's possessive words that he would speak to Minister D. Raja who was from Tamil Nadu I felt were aimed at putting unwarranted pressure on me by a constitutional functionary but did not yield the outcome he had desired.

AYUSH: APPEARANCE AND REALITY

On 22 September 2003, I joined as Joint Secretary, Department of AYUSH[1], with Sushma Swaraj as Minister. The department had been created in March 1995 by restructuring Ministry of Health & Family Welfare (H&FW). It was only during the Ninth Five-Year Plan (1997-2002) that AYUSH got some visibility as a separate Department, particularly after Sailaja Chandra took on the mantle of Secretary. I was informed that her immediate predecessor intended to bring AYUSH sector to the mainstream of health services, but was unable to do anything visible as her sole Joint Secretary, considered negative minded, clashed with her on every administrative issue. This did not augur well for growth of AYUSH sector. Finally, both exited the department.

Shailaja Chandra developed a number of schemes for promoting AYUSH sector which were included in the Tenth Five-Year Plan (2002-2007). However, by the time things started looking up, she was appointed as Chief Secretary of National Capital Territory of Delhi. Her successor Malti Sinha had a limited tenure and was unable to match her predecessor's vision and effectiveness. Development of Formulary and Pharmacopeia of Ayurveda came to a standstill. Traditional Knowledge Digital Library (TKDL), a project initiated in collaboration with Council of Scientific & Industrial Research (CSIR) also did not progress. A number of schemes devised to develop AYUSH sector remained unimplemented.

With my Sanskrit background and ability to easily understand texts of Ayurveda and Yoga originally written in Sanskrit, it was easy for me to deal with Advisors of Indian medicine and experts on Yoga. With seven months of financial year 2003-2004 in hand, I told my colleagues that they could give their independent and objective views on matters to be handled by them but should not suppress proposals and files on any ground. TKDL project, which was suffering in multiple ways for lack of co-ordination with CSIR and in the absence of direction, was put back on track. Though my predecessor had blocked almost all proposals for release of funds to State Governments for development of infrastructure and promotion of Indian medicine and

---

1. Renamed from Department of Indian System of Medicine& Homeopathy (ISM&H) in November 2003.

homeopathy, at the end of the year with strenuous coordination with all concerned, the department was able to fully utilise annual plan provisions of about ₹ 175 crore. Utilisation in new schemes during the previous financial year had been a mere ₹ 50 crore.

Secretary Malti Sinha retired within three months of my joining. She was succeeded by Shekhar Dutt an IAS officer of Madhya Pradesh cadre who happened to be a friend and batch-mate of the Joint Secretary repatriated prematurely due to his running battles with Secretary, AYUSH. His representation against adverse entries on annual appraisal report had been rejected. He had also not succeeded to get them expunged through CAT. Shekhar Dutt desired to help his friend and wanted that another representation made by him be processed and put up. After going through relevant records carefully, I found that adverse observations made against him stood substantiated with a robust documentation. I firmly told the new Secretary that there was no point in reopening the matter and to seek to submit a *suomotu* report to DoPT to contradict documents-backed position taken by his grand predecessors. Further the fresh representation from the officer was also too late, the matter having been closed more than two years back. Unhappy with my position, Shekhar Dutt called for the file directly from Director Administration and took inputs from other senior officials. None endorsed what he desired. Shekhar Dutt, otherwise an amiable person, got annoyed and himself drafted a letter addressed to Secretary, DoPT only to be rejected despite the cadre controlling department being headed by another cadre mate of his. Obviously, efforts to help his friend were seen as a case devoid of merit and therefore, an exercise in futility.

Holistic Reforms and Mainstreaming Indian Systems of Medicine

Department of AYUSH had a number of national institutes and research councils, which were infrastructure deficient and headless. Despite budgetary provisions, construction of buildings for National Institute of Siddha at Tambaram (near Chennai) had not progressed. I ensured that the entire building complex including a 250-bed hospital, hostels, classrooms, etc. was constructed within one-and-half years at a lower cost of ₹ 35 crore against estimate of more than ₹ 50 crore. Morarji Desai National Institute of Yoga in Delhi which was running from a temporary structure got a state-of-the-art complex within the same period along with a new Director. Directors were also appointed to National Institute of Naturopathy in Pune, National Institute of Unani Medicine, Bangalore, and Central Council for Research in Homeopathy and Central Council for Research in Yoga & Naturopathy both in Delhi. The new National Institute of Unani Medicine was established with impressive infrastructure in Bangalore during my tenure. Planned budget provisions for the three National Institutes of Siddha, Yoga, and Unani Medicines which had remained untouched were fully utilised within a period of less than two years. Vacancies in all the National Institutes were filled up in a time-bound manner.

Government of India through CSIR had spent more than US$ 0.5 million in a legal battle of over 2 years to get the patent for wound-healing usage of turmeric granted by United States' Patent and Trademark Office to a private firm years ago revoked. A CSIR study revealed that about 14,000 patents stood granted for medicinal usages of plants found in India to various individuals and firms by patent offices in USA, Japan, and European countries. Medicinal usages of these plants stood vividly described in Ayurveda texts many-many centuries ago. Such knowledge in public domain for long did not warrant grant of patents. The only way to arrest misappropriation of Indian traditional knowledge was by digitising and sharing it with patent offices of various developed countries with adequate protective provisions.

TKDL was a government-supported initiative through Department of AYUSH in that direction. The library was being prepared in five major languages, English, Spanish, French, German and Japanese, which accounted for 99 percent of patents granted globally. CSIR would enter into agreements with patent offices of various countries permitting access to TKDL at the time of scrutiny of proposals for grant of patent to the claimants of original research and innovations, subject to safeguards on misuse. But the project had failed to progress. Substantively, formulations digitised did not cite original sources correctly in all cases. I caught this aspect, when Project Coordinator of CSIR gave a presentation on the status of TKDL. I found that the source of knowledge on anti-fungal property of Neem (Margosa) plant was attributed to a book/ translation of 20th Century, whereas Charak Samhita written two thousand years back had recorded it in detail. Neither of the two Advisors of Ayurveda in the Department nor consultants appointed in CSIR who were being paid to certify the purity of translation including referencing had pointed out such gross inaccuracies. In fact, the Department had limited its responsibility to releasing budgetary provisions to CSIR for the digitisation project. The first phase of TKDL was completed by year 2004-end containing digitisation of about 70,000 formulations from ancient Ayurvedic texts. The second phase involved digitisation of Unani medicinal formulations in addition to yogic postures. I completed my tenure when the second phase of work started. Negotiations were at advanced stages with European and US Patent and Trademark Offices for allowing them conditional access to TKDL. I represented India at the international conference on Traditional Knowledge organised by World Intellectual Property Organisation (WIPO) in Geneva early in 2005 and made a presentation on TKDL.

Central Council of Indian Medicine (CCIM), a regulatory body for standardization of education in Ayurveda, Siddha and Unani medicine, was set up on the lines of Medical Council of India for Allopathy or modern medicine. But it suffered due to whimsical practices and loose standards. There was hardly any discipline country-wide in granting permission for opening new colleges or standardising the educational system in Indian medicine. My first priority was to address a host of regulatory and legal issues. I got drafted a comprehensive Medical College Regulations, 2003 in consultation with CCIM and national institutes for respective medicine streams in order to standardise requirements before approvals were accorded for educational institutions of Indian medicine. After resolving some protests and reluctance, CCIM adopted these regulations which were issued under the Indian Medicine Central Council Act. Similarly, rules were amended under Drugs & Cosmetics Act to disallow manufacturing of drugs without complying with Good Manufacturing Practice (GMP) standards. Amendments to Indian Medicine Council Act further provided that only Vaidyas or their equivalents having essential qualifications or recognised degrees and duly registered could dispense Ayurvedic medicines. The department drafted a new Bill for standardisation of nursing education under Indian systems of medicine and homeopathy. After it received Parliamentary approval and became law, regulatory provisions were thus formalised. There had earlier been no law that regulated such nursing education and practices.

Turning towards implementation of statutes, it was found that hardly any pharmacies producing drugs were GMP-compliant. Pharmacies in government sector were provided financial support for upgrading their existing infrastructure for manufacturing drugs and were clearly directed that supply of drugs in government dispensaries would not be accepted from any pharmacy which was not GMP-compliant. State Drug Controllers, through whom these were to be ensured, were simultaneously desired to take action against non-GMP compliant pharmacies under the Drugs and Cosmetics Act.

The newly created provision of GMP and essential qualifications for practising Ayurveda were challenged in Kerala High Court by Kerala-based Association of Vaidyas, many of whom were practicing without recognised degrees. Kerala High Court initially passed orders staying operation of GMP rules and qualifications. In the final order, the Court directed AYUSH Department to hear the litigant association before rejecting their claims of practicing Ayurveda without holding degrees and preparing drugs without complying with GMP. I examined their representations and heard the representatives of the Association in person. The reasoned draft rejecting the representation of Vaidyas was approved by Secretary, and it also withstood legal scrutiny of Kerala High Court. Enforcement of GMP now became mandatory in all government pharmacies. State-supported pharmacies were provided financial support for upgrading their manufacturing infrastructure under a Centrally Sponsored Scheme.

Introduction of GMP in manufacturing of quality drugs and new regulations for standardising educational institutions, including course curricula, required sustained and multi-pronged initiatives. Besides developing Pharmacopeia and Formularies, drugs manufacturing facilities had to be upgraded making use of the latest available tools of technology. Given the traditional practices in vogue, it was not easy to achieve a break from the past. Laws and regulations alone could not be the instruments of change. As a result of enforcement of regulations for standardising the course curricula under Indian systems of medicine, a large number of old institutions with inadequate and substandard infrastructure started closing down or losing recognition. The Department which had failed to utilise even ₹ 50 crore during the first year of the Plan, utilised more than ₹ 360 crore in the third year in creating a conducive eco-system for further development of Indian systems of medicine and homeopathy. Vigorous implementation of schemes and programmes resulted in full utilisation of Tenth Five-Year Plan provisions by the end of the third year itself. Planning Commission and Department-related Parliamentary Committee appreciated the physical and financial progress made which led to an increase in annual plan provisions.

Ministry of Defence was persuaded to open Ayurveda clinics at Army's Command Hospital, Delhi, and subsequently in Pune, which became so popular that army doctors practising modern medicine felt threatened and started opposing further expansion. After a few months, with change in the party in power in the Centre, both these clinics were closed down. Sekhar Dutt, Secretary AYUSH became Secretary Defence. Having once taken credit for opening of Ayurveda Clinics in Command Hospitals in Delhi and Pune, he did not care to reopen these clinics after he became Defence Secretary!

Statistics maintained in Ministry of H&FW showed that in 2004, the number of qualified doctors in AYUSH was more than those in allopathy. However, vested interests within and outside Government establishments would not permit integration of AYUSH into National Health System. The lure of so-called modern medicine or allopathy which promoted chemical products for instant and temporary relief ruled despite long-term harmful side-effects seen many a times. Indian systems of medicine place greater emphasis on preventive and promotive health with its curative side accounting for less than 30 percent of the discourse. These experience-based systems which had been in practice for thousands of years suffered systematic neglect after Independence and were pushed out of national mainstream of public health management. Ironically, practitioners of AYUSH also started dispensing allopathic medicines as they found it as an easier option for better business. Qualified doctors in allopathy were not available adequately. The adoption of allopathy as the mainstream of national health management was thus virtually taken over by quacks in rural and semi-urban areas as registered and unregistered practitioners of the so-called modern medicine.

The newly announced National Health Policy in 2005 called for integrating AYUSH in mainstream national health management. In reality, nothing substantive happened. At every forum, I suggested that integration in medical education systems was essential at the primary stage to achieve integration at functional level. After all, anatomy and physiology courses taught across all disciplines did not differ from system-to-system and diagnostic tools were equally common. A country having about 10 lakh registered practitioners each of allopathy and AYUSH could serve the society better if services of these 20 lakh doctors were utilised in an integrated manner rather than in silos or at cross purposes. China had already produced a model of how traditional and modern medicines could be practised hand-in-hand holistically at affordable cost to the public thus creating win-win situations. Integration at educational level would ultimately also help in improving quality of education in traditional medicine itself. Simply prescribing a few medicines of Ayurveda, Siddha, Unani and Homeopathy under National Health Mission, the current bulwark of integration of AYUSH into mainstream national health management system, was unlikely to yield tangible results or benefits.

National Health Mission as it was being conceived did not help in preventing fragmentation and was paying lip-service in the guise of mainstreaming AYUSH. I was misunderstood by Secretary H&FW when I suggested to him to avoid inserting an additional layer of Accredited Social Health Activists (ASHA) with educational qualification of VIII-Standard at village level. I suggested strengthening existing structures of Anganwadi Workers, Auxiliary Nurses and Midwives. I reasoned that about half of the villages in some States, including Odisha, which had a high share of ST/SC population, VIII-Standard passed women ASHA workers could not be available. Those somehow recruited from outside would not find performance-based nominal incentives attractive enough to work to achieve the goals of National Health Mission. After some time, ASHAs formed associations and agitated for regular remuneration like Anganwadi workers. In Odisha, tribal villages did not find ASHAs with requisite qualifications.

In my experience, distortions in national health management system were the outcome of lack of political and administrative will and predominance of vested interests including influence of multinational pharmaceutical companies. The situation is unlikely to improve without ransacking and replacing existing biased methods followed in treating various recognised systems of medicine. There is no harm to learn from the Chinese experience here, rather than aping the Western system.

Embedding Standards in Educational Institutions

I had no doubt in my mind that standards of education in AYUSH educational institutions needed to improve to establish the credibility of underlying systems of medicine. Support for infrastructure development and incentivising appointment of specialists in upgraded departments of government and government-aided educational institutions could make a difference in maintaining better quality and standards. Private educational institutions that failed to maintain prescribed standards needed to be given definitive timelines for upgrades and derecognised if they failed to fulfil minimum requirements thereafter.

There were more than 400 AYUSH institutions that provided four-year degree courses in the country in 2003, with the vast majority of them in the private sector. In contrast, about 300 medical colleges for Allopathy existed predominantly in government sector. Department of AYUSH apprised State Governments unambiguously that in case their educational institutions failed to do the needful in accordance with the provisions of the new regulations, they faced sure-shot closure. They were allowed financial support liberally without calling for cost-sharing to facilitate development of infrastructure and salary support for five years in relation to specialised courses. A massive inspection programme launched involving CCIM and Homeopathy Council of India had revealed deficiencies in educational institutions such as inadequate hospital facilities, absence of hospital equipment, shortage of teaching and other technical staff, the same teaching faculty being shown in more than one institution, and limited library facilities. Those private institutions and some government ones that failed to develop the requisite infrastructure were barred from taking admission of students.

At the same time, I did not endorse the policy followed by my predecessor not to grant permission for opening new institutions which had requisite infrastructure, facilities and faculty, and could meet regulatory requirements. He had kept himself busy in seeking explanations and passing strictures against Directors of Research Councils and Advisers in the Department. I found that this was done by suppressing and misrepresenting facts before the competent authority. In a glaring instance I was surprised to find that though departmental proceedings initiated by him against the Director of Central Council of Research in Unani Medicine had been disposed of with orders for his exoneration passed by the competent authority, my predecessor had suppressed the disposal by not issuing Government orders to that effect. Instead, he had taken fresh approval of Minister against the Director for initiating departmental proceedings with the same set of charges. By chance the suppressed file had not been destroyed and I found it in the drawer of the office table after assuming charge.

Administrative Affairs in AYUSH

Minister of H&FW, Dr.Anbumani Ramadoss, an Allopathy physician by education, did not like the change in the department's name to AYUSH by the previous government and wanted to restore the earlier one. Incoming Secretary, Palat Mohandas, was not happy to find his junior batch officer holding the post of Secretary H&FW and cancellation of his posting as Tourism Secretary at the last moment. Responding to Minister's instructions, I highlighted the factors that lead to the change in nomenclature, outlined the procedure mandated for restoring the old name, and opined that there were no pressing substantive reasons for change. Secretary without recording any opinion endorsed my note to the Minister. Disapproving it, Minister sought approval of Prime Minister for his proposal, which was turned down. Later on also, instead of working towards improving systems, the political executive as head of the Ministry showed a proclivity for narrow-minded considerations only because he did not like Ayurveda and Yoga to be mentioned in the name of the Department.

After a few months, Palat Mohandas moved on to become Chief Secretary in his parent State of Kerala. His replacement Uma Pillai, a nice and competent officer who as Tourism Secretary had suffered the wrath of her Minister Renuka Chaudhary, reposed full confidence in me. Despite frequent changes at Secretary's level and my relatively short tenure of about two years, Department of AYUSH did not slow down nor cease to function proactively.

Being the only Joint Secretary, I faced enhancing workload and despite my repeated requests, successive Secretaries did not accept files from Advisors holding equivalent rank or from Directors/ Deputy Secretaries even during days when I was on tour. Taking leave even for attending to urgent personal work became difficult. I submitted a proposal for creating another post of Joint Secretary by surrendering a higher post equivalent to Additional Secretary to be filled by a technical officer. It was approved, but by the time the newly created post was filled, my tenure had ended.

A second baseless CBI Investigation

As mentioned beforehand, my predecessor had opted to reject every application for opening new AYUSH institutions or upgrading institutions for starting Post Graduate courses. It had resulted in litigation. A few applicants approached Delhi High Court for giving directions to Central Government to consider their applications in accordance with extant regulations. The new regulations brought in by AYUSH Department called for a time-bound schedule for processing applications from receipt to disposal. My batchmate from Indian Forest Service working as Director continued to follow the path of my predecessor, favouring rejection of fresh applications without examining them by simply citing 'mushrooming growth of sub-standard educational institutions' in the past. I advised him to follow the prescribed procedure. Under the law, there was no option but to refer applications to CCIM for causing inspection and eliciting their considered views. A section in CCIM was also unhappy with the new norms laid down which contained timelines for disposal of applications as this had minimised the scope for manipulations and malpractices. No queue-jumping had been allowed and there were provisions for fixing accountability. Applications made, however, without the required documents and fee, had to be rejected summarily, with the rejection to be duly communicated to the applicant.

An example of what happened when applicable provisions and procedures were implemented fairly is given here. A trust headed by a professor of a

Medical College in Karnataka wanted to establish a new College of Ayurveda prefixing the word "Bhima" in its name. The application was incomplete. It neither contained details of land and other infrastructure nor recommendation of State Government. Prescribed fee had also not been deposited. When his application was rejected, he first visited my office and then represented before Minister alleging bias in favour of upper caste applicants by overlooking deficiencies in their applications while victimising lower castes and classes. He cited the case of Sri Sri Ravishankar whose Trust had been granted permission to admit 50 students in the first year of a new Ayurveda College. It was another matter that the application of Sri Sri Ravishankar's Trust was recommended by CCIM, whereas the complainant's application being incomplete had been rejected outright. Minister Dr. Ramadoss went through the relevant file and was fully satisfied with the course of action taken earlier in the matter with his approval. He appreciated how norms had been followed rigorously. The Minister was sympathetic towards his cause and wanted to help him to set up the institution. But he got angry when the complainant openly alleged caste-based discrimination. The matter ended there. It was 2004. I left the Department after completing my tenure mid-2005.

Curiously, I received a call in 2010 from Deputy Inspector General (DIG), Anti Corruption Branch of CBI, Bangalore, when I was working as Joint Secretary in Cabinet Secretariat on Central deputation. It was said that a preliminary enquiry had been instituted to examine my role in granting permission to Sri Sri Ayurveda College. I was asked to appear before him. Though surprised by the call, I requested him to send a questionnaire for my response and to go ahead with what was considered necessary thereafter. Separately, I requested Department of AYUSH to send me a copy of the relevant file notes, including inspection reports submitted by CCIM and by a team of experts, and Government orders in the case. After a fortnight, a DSP from this CBI branch met me in my office and handed over a questionnaire seeking some general information. I sent my response almost immediately. I was told that there was nothing against me. The enquiry had been started against the College based on allegations made by a couple of former students who had failed to get jobs. Their petition alleged that at the time of admission for which capitation fee of ₹ 2 lakh each had been paid, they had received an assurance from College authorities of absorption after completion of four-years' Bachelor's Degree course. The assurance was not met by the College and due to sub-standard education, they were unable to find jobs elsewhere.

I remained puzzled as to how my role could become the subject matter of examination till I was told well over a year later by Shekhar Dutt, serving then as Governor of Chhattisgarh, that the foundation of the proposed enquiry was political. Shekhar Dutt had been Secretary AYUSH when permission to admit 50 students in the first year of the four-year Bachelor degree course had been given to the College. I also came to know later that a list of institutions had been prepared centrally in 2010 for random inspections and enquiries, which included this College. The mist cleared. CBI seem to have been asked to somehow reach and embarrass Sri Sri Ravishankar through a public servant, who had processed the matter and thus could possibly have favoured him, by invoking the Prevention of Corruption Act. Unfounded allegation of caste bias had been levelled against me at the time of granting permission to the College. Petitions from the two jobless ex-students of the College were in all probability engineered. The matter had been blown up to become the immediate tool in the hands of Government to settle scores with Sri Sri Ravishankar for his participation in "India against Corruption" movement in 2010.

Since I had provided my response but had heard nothing more for well over a year, I thought the matter being baseless stood closed. In the meanwhile, I sought repatriation to my State cadre for personal reasons and accordingly got relieved from Cabinet Secretariat on 13 January 2012 to get back to my parent cadre. Unexpectedly, I got a telephone call on 1 February 2012 from a senior Indian Express journalist seeking to know whether my repatriation to State cadre was due to the request of CBI for permission of Government of India to investigate my role in a case of alleged corruption concerning Sri Sri College of Ayurvedic Sciences and Research, Bangalore. I told him that my return was purely on personal grounds and that he could verify this position with Cabinet Secretary. I also asked him to judge for himself and sent him a copy of my replies to the questionnaire given well over a year back. I asked the journalist to give my side of the story also based on this information in case his newspaper decided to proceed to publish a story on the matter.

The telephone call from the journalist had shaken me a bit. I did not know him. It was not difficult to guess that a story was in the making, to deflect attention from corruption charges against important Ministers of the beleaguered Central Government headed by Prime Minister Man Mohan Singh. Supreme Court in their judgment delivered just a day prior had set aside allocations of 2G spectrum holding the Union Government responsible for gross irregularities and corrupt practices. The nervous Central leadership which was receiving brick-bats from all sides probably wanted to divert attention by pretending to show its intolerance towards administrative corruption and my completely unrelated repatriation was being considered opportune to give credence to the fake story. I had requested the journalist to verify my credentials in Odisha as well as in all the Central Ministries I had worked before ruining my reputation by bringing out the story he had been handed over. True to his words, he informed me subsequently that there was no question of bringing out any news item on the issue and that all my seniors and colleagues in the State and Central Governments had spoken everything good about me, my integrity and my uprightness.

It was quite surprising that CBI opted to place reliance solely on views expressed by Director, Ayurveda, an officer revealing his negative mindset in recommending rejection of every single application. CBI had failed to take cognizance of the clear views recorded on file which had been given by Department of Legal Affairs after examining all aspects, including holding discussions with Director Ayurveda, as well as recommendations of CCIM. They also ignored the approval granted by Secretary, Minister of State and Cabinet Minister, just to victimise me six-seven years after I had left Ministry of H&FW. Decision-making in Government being a participatory process, for CBI to conclude that a Director was the last word in making decisions made a mockery of the whole system of governance.

It had appeared from CBI's questionnaire that they were in a hurry to assume that the College lacked infrastructure and perhaps without fully digesting the legal and regulatory provisions introduced on 15 March 2004. CBI wanted me to justify admissions in subsequent years too, when I was not even in the department to handle the matter. After receiving the questionnaire, when I informally checked with a few senior officers of Government of Karnataka in charge of Ayurveda, I was told that Sri Sri College was the first choice of students consistently for 5-6 years. The details of teaching and hospital facilities, etc. including building infrastructure, received by me now showed an impressive development of the institution. Sri Sri Ravishankar himself appeared fully aware of the CBI investigation and named an important politician close to UPA Chairperson conspiring against his organisation to defame him intentionally, nationally and internationally. My assessment was that his participation along with that of Baba Ramdev in the campaign by "India Against Corruption" had brought their organisations under Central investigation scanners. Persons like me got targeted simply to achieve some political and nefarious goals. This so-called preliminary enquiry by CBI too fizzled out.

* * * *

8

Taxing Life: Administration of Commercial Taxes in Odisha

I reported to Government of Odisha for my next posting on 1 August 2005 and joined as Commissioner of Commercial Taxes (CCT) when my posting was notified on 22 August 2005. Tax administration was new to me. Chief Secretary conveyed his confidence in me saying that my image of 'Terror Datt' had already unnerved some dealers/ tax evaders and officials. He added that it would hardly take time for me to settle down and be in command of commercial tax administration. I was grateful for his kind words.

Administrative Difficulties in Implementing Value Aid Tax (VAT)

Bulk of tax revenues of State Government came from Sales Tax, Central Sales Tax and Entry Tax. Professional Tax being deducted at source by respective drawing and disbursing authorities, did not require specific collection effort. Realisation from Entertainment Tax was on a decline as theatres were either closing down or seat-utilisation waxed and waned after the spread of television and Internet-enabled entertainment.

Sales Tax country-wide had been replaced by Value Added Tax (VAT) a few months back riding on expectations of simplification and enhancement in tax base. So far not much had changed in reality. Sales tax collection at the first point had been the norm. Under VAT, Tax Identification Numbers registered right through the value chain were expected to increase. But these had remained largely static with more than 90 percent of tax coming in from less than 1 percent of registered dealers. Hardly anything had changed in tax collection pattern either. Going by age-old practice, advance taxes had been collected during the last quarter of previous financial year. These were adjusted against tax liabilities of dealers in the first quarter of succeeding financial year. None appeared concerned that retailers collected VAT from consumers by selling commodities at tax-included maximum retail price, but appropriated it rather than paying it to the State. Central Government had committed to compensate Sales Tax loss as a result of introducing VAT for three years. The new law did not permit grant of concessions to attract investors and investments, such as exemption or deferment of taxes for setting up new industries or expanding existing ones. At the time of introduction of VAT all States had voluntarily agreed to maintain the same tax rates for commercial products, not to extend concessions under their respective industrial policies, and to maintain healthy rates of VAT.

The Empowered Committee of State Finance Ministers constituted at national level met every month, with their Commercial Tax Commissioners and representatives of Union Finance Ministry, to sort out Centre-State and inter-State issues. Since rates of Sales Tax on taxable commodities stood reduced in most States and uniformity needed to be maintained, almost every major State was reporting losses in collection of VAT and seeking compensation. Not having a strong or wide tax base, dealers and tax payers in Odisha too did not like to be pursued by tax officials in light of compensation provisions. Official approach was no different.

Odisha's Finance Minister Prafulla Chandra Ghadei appeared unconcerned that Sales Tax officials were soft against dealers regardless of tax evasions, arguing that non-cooperation on their part would only hurt the State's revenue interest. It was a needless self-injury when compensation of tax losses was assured. Across products, Sales Tax rates in Odisha were arguably much higher than the national average. Surcharge of 10 percent of tax payable was also levied prior to introduction of VAT. Reduction of tax rates, introduction of uniformly approved rates for all the States, and abolition of surcharge were bound to impact revenue collection, if tax on value added downstream along the chain was not collected effectively. Input tax credit could be claimed under VAT law. Sales Tax collection was assessment-based, but compliance under VAT was largely voluntary. Inspections of 20 percent accounts of dealers needed to be done every year. In case violation is detected, tax penalty was 200 percent.

Creating Healthy Office Conditions for Healthy Tax Collections

Office of Commercial Tax Commissioner, located in the ground floor of a three-storeyed building on the left bank of River Mahanadi in Cuttack, did not offer a healthy or congenial environment conducive for work. It was prone to flooding during heavy rains. Stinking and unpalatable condition of rooms virtually throughout the year were typical of the ground floor, as the river bed was higher than the drainage system in Cuttack town. The ground floor ceiling leaked due to improper drainage on the first floor. Naturally, office attendance used to be thin.

State Government had made budgetary allocations to Works Department for a new multi-storeyed office building, including Tax Tribunal's office, at a better location in nearby Cantonment area. Construction work stood assigned to a contractor through the Industrial Infrastructure Development Corporation

(IDCO). The contractor, chased by police on tender-fixing charges related to some past contracts, had gone underground. Dispute between Revenue Department and IDCO on demarcation of plot was a convenient excuse for not releasing funds to IDCO by Works Department. Budget provisions were being surrendered regularly for the last two years. The attitude of Works Department, facing the heat of allegations of tender-fixing, was evasive and unhelpful. Digging deep, I found that more than anything else it was a situation created due to clash of egos of officers heading Revenue Department and IDCO. MD, IDCO wanted full cost to be released in advance before starting construction and was unwilling to invest IDCO's resources in anticipation of reimbursements. Works Department insisted that funds' releases would be made in a phased manner once the construction site was handed over depending upon progress achieved and utilisation certificate submitted.

MD, IDCO and Revenue Secretary, themselves batch-mates, were my good friends. On the plea that Commercial Tax Department should not suffer the consequences of narrow-minded departmentalism or any communication gaps between their respective juniors, the dispute regarding the plot of land was quickly settled in a meeting. The site was demarcated within a day under the supervision of Collector, Cuttack and handed over to IDCO, a day thereafter. Secretary, Works Department agreed to release the budgetary provisions in one go. IDCO agreed to get the work executed through over-ground workers of the underground contractor. Commercial Tax Department enjoyed vast influence in Finance Department due to its role in revenue collection which sustained the functioning of various departments. I found it surprising that it had been suffering due to apathy by some of those very departments.

I drew up a detailed time-bound plan, with fortnightly milestones, involving officers of IDCO, representatives of contractor, Works and other line Departments like Public Health and Energy, and fixed-day monthly meetings to review the progress made on construction. The target was to complete it within a period of 10 months. Activities of line departments for drainage, removal of existing power, telecom and other pipelines, laying new lines, sand-filling of low-lying area, etc. were also reviewed simultaneously. I visited the site every fortnight with IDCO officials and was amazed to see the fixed milestones being achieved in advance with the same officials in position. This beautiful landmark building in Cuttack was completed within the agreed timeline. I was transferred before actual shifting of office could take place.

In the interregnum, I felt it necessary to get existing office space made more conducive for functioning. Works, Public Health and Energy Departments were requested to address the problems. I found that Non-Plan budget provisions had been made every year for special repairs only to be surrendered at year-end. I fixed a timeline of three months to complete the special repairs and renovation, including sand-filling and concreting of vacant space in front and around the office block to prevent standing rain-water, reconstruction of drainage, special repairs of toilets on the first floor to prevent leakage from the ceiling and resulting stink, fresh electric wiring, painting, etc. To release office space, a plan was chalked out for destroying unwanted old records and transferring relevant ones after labelling them properly to the Record Room, besides disposal of old almirahs and other unserviceable furniture. Finance Department, which was generally allergic towards Non-Plan grants to other departments, did not question the proposal of Commercial Tax Commissioner for funds to meet additional establishment requirements, including cost of computerisation, which was my top most priority. Within a short period of two and half months, the office environment stood transformed due to visible changes made to the internal and external atmosphere. There was a marked improvement in punctuality, not least because I would invariably reach office half-an-hour before the scheduled time, and subordinates could not afford to be late.

Finding that the Works, Public Health and Energy Departments had rendered yeoman services for renovation of my office and compound, officers and staff staying in residential colony of Commercial Tax Department pleaded with me to pay a visit to their colony in Cuttack town to witness the pathetic condition in which they were living. Overhead tanks and drainage had become defunct and residential quarters had not seen repairs and maintenance since their construction. I visited the residential colony with senior engineers of concerned line departments who promised to do the needful. The colony witnessed a sea change within two months thereafter. My credibility as head of the Commercial Tax Department family concerned with the well-being of staff and their family members also helped in improving the functioning of the office.

Overcoming Staff Stagnation and Demoralisation

I also realized that tax officials from top to bottom of the pyramid suffered from a complaints' psychology which resulted in a low tax base and lower tax collection. Their promotions had been totally held up for 5-6 years due to litigations after State Government had ordered reservation in promotional appointments with consequential seniority. Assistant and Deputy Commissioners officiating against higher posts for years had virtually given up all hopes of their promotion. Posts of non-judicial members in the Tax Tribunal were vacant as officers of eligible seniority were not available for posting. Some senior officers had even stopped writing their confidential annual self-appraisal reports, perceiving it to be an exercise in futility. The next important problem to be addressed therefore was stagnation and filling up of vacancies through promotional appointments.

Accelerated promotions of ST/SC officers with consequential seniority was the result of Constitutional amendments carried out by Union Government. Accordingly, on the recommendation of a Committee of Secretaries from Law,

Revenue, and GA Departments, State Government had introduced reservations in posts above Junior Class-1 rank. This decision, which had been backed by the State's Advocate General, had created a stalemate as the revised gradation list had been challenged in a court of law. SAT and High Court had stayed promotional appointments on the petitions of litigants from both sides.

I carefully studied the legal provisions in relation to State Government's decision. In my understanding, the relevant Constitutional amendments for accelerated promotions and consequential seniority were enablers on the basis of which State Government could affect corresponding changes in its reservation law. Rather than taking steps for amending the law, Odisha Government had constituted a committee of three Secretaries who in turn had recommended what had already been provided for through Constitutional amendments which had received validity of Supreme Court of India. The impasse created due to Government's decision had resulted in the suffering of officers eligible for promotion to higher ranks. I opted to address this problem frontally.

After discussing the matter with senior officers of all categories, I took their assurance not to resort to litigation emphasising that all would gain if promotional appointments were made subject to the outcome of litigations pending in SAT and High Court. I met the senior officers of Finance Department, the cadre controlling authority of Odisha Finance Service (OFS), and devised a strategy to convince Advocate General and pray for vacation of stay orders passed by High Court. Chief Secretary agreed that he would chair the DPC meetings immediately if Advocate General reversed his previous stand. For preparedness, he also agreed to issue instructions to the officer in GA Department in whose custody the Annual Confidential Reports (ACRs) of senior officers in the zone of consideration for promotion had been kept, to make them available to hold DPC meetings. Special Secretary, GA Department, had to be bypassed as he had reiterated that it was an infructuous exercise. Joint Secretary, Confidential Section, having worked with me earlier took no time to supply the ACR dossiers of OFS officers. Special Secretary, Finance Department, a former OFS officer promoted to IAS, agreed to accompany me to meet the Advocate General and to persuade him to modify his earlier advice.

Bijoy Mohanty, an expert in commercial tax laws, had enjoyed a roaring practice before being appointed Advocate General of the State. He had appeared before some of my predecessors here. In a case involving the State's revenue interests, even though an Advocate General now, he had taken the side of his former clients i.e. certain SSI units. He made a submission before High Court knowing well that State Government held diametrically opposite views. Without placing before him his earlier advice given in writing, I submitted my analyses of the State's reservation law with which I was fully conversant. The position we were taking was not unreasonable and indeed was the only way to break the impasse which had affected all Government Departments. As expected, he agreed that in the given situation and pending amendment in State's reservation law in conformity with Constitutional amendments for "accelerated promotions and consequential seniority" of ST/SC employees, it would be possible to plead in High Court for vacation of stay orders and making promotional appointments subject to the outcome of pending litigation. He also appeared sympathetic towards officers of Commercial Tax Department many of whom were known to him personally. Having succeeded in persuading him to revise his earlier views, it was decided to make a formal reference seeking his modified advice in writing. Accordingly, a reasoned note was put up to him for advice after firming up the issues to be clarified citing provisions of Odisha Reservation of Vacancies (in Posts & Services) Act, Supreme Court rulings in Indra Sahani case, and administrative problems faced by Commercial Tax Department due to large scale vacancies at higher levels of administration. I also prepared a draft which he could modify and give shape of his considered advice. After another lengthy meeting, as the draft he was dictating was not an unequivocal piece of advice I had wanted, the alternative draft was placed before him for his consideration. He was gracious enough to accept and approve it with minor changes. Thus, in fitness of things, High Court could be requested to vacate the stay orders pending passing of final orders to which promotion would be subjected to. In the next hearing after a few days, High Court agreed to his submission and vacated the stays granted earlier.

In consultation with Special Secretary, Finance, I had already prepared the agenda note as well draft minutes of three DPC meetings to be held back-to-back. Proposals for posting orders consequent upon promotions had also been drafted as it was felt necessary to avoid any legal challenge which could reduce the whole exercise to nullity once again. I went to Chief Secretary with the fresh advice of Advocate General and the latest order of High Court which enabled us to go ahead with holding these DPC meetings in accordance with provisions and procedures followed in the past. Special Secretary, GA Department, unaware of intervening developments, again started opposing my proposals for holding DPC meetings for OFS officers' promotion. On being updated, he suggested that promotion of officers of OAS, of which GA Department was cadre controlling authority, which too had been held up for years, should be taken up first. Chief Secretary firmly brushed aside his attempt to jump the queue ahead of those who had done all the leg work. He agreed to hold the DPCs the next day and advised me to keep the draft minutes ready, which I had already done. All went as planned. DPC meetings were held and minutes put up for approval of Chief Minister along with proposals for postings without loss of time. B.K. Patnaik, Secretary to Chief Minister under whom I had worked earlier was approached by me personally with the files endorsed by Special Secretary, Finance in agreement with his Principal Secretary. Approval of Chief Minister was obtained without delay. Finance Department issued orders of promotion and posting of officers at three senior levels as soon as they received the files from Chief Minister's office. Officers who had been promoted were informed telephonically and posting orders were sent by fax so that they could join their new posts without availing joining time. Despite some apprehensions, none challenged these promotions thus made on the basis of the old gradation list subject to the final outcome of litigations pending in High Court. It was a win-win situation for all categories of officers in the given situation.

Another proposal for rationalisation of OFS cadre was prepared by involving K.C. Badu, Special Secretary, Finance. Two posts equivalent to Special Secretary would be created and the number of posts of Additional/ Joint Commissioners were to be increased, besides enhancing strength of entry level posts by 225. This was necessary considering the increasing number of dealers under VAT law which also provided for audit of 20 percent dealers every year. Principal Secretary, Finance Dr. U.C. Saratchandran was not willing to enhance establishment cost by creating additional posts without showing actual additional revenues when the proposal had been discussed with him in the past. Providentially, he was on a long leave with Special Secretary, Finance holding charge. By the time he returned from leave, the proposal for rationalisation of OFS cadre had already been approved by State Government.

Twin Tracks: Tax Mobilisation and Enforcement

On the revenue collection front, I was confident that tax net could be widened substantially after introduction of VAT which was a consumption-based tax. A smaller State like Kerala had more than two lakh registered dealers paying VAT. In Odisha, less that 20,000 of about 68,000 registered dealers had been paying VAT. For sure VAT was not being collected from all eligible retailers. Collections were limited mainly to a few organised retailers like Big Bazar and super markets. This placed honest tax payers at a disadvantage. A number of bigger dealers preferred to leverage the legal system to avoid or delay their tax liabilities. This included many public and private sector companies. I called for registration of all unregistered dealers. Commercial Tax Officers (CTOs) and Assistant CCTs heading offices at Circle and Range levels were advised to initiate a time-bound drive to widen the tax net. I fixed monthly targets in consultation with them for doing so. Every month on fixed dates, region-level meetings were held with them not only to review progress in revenue collection but also to take stock of other emerging issues due to implementation of VAT Act including registration of new dealers. I felt it was vital to lay a strong foundation by enhancing the tax net to benefit the State.

In every meeting with tax officials and chambers of commerce, my continuing refrain was that evasion of taxes would never allow investments by honest investors to be hounded by tax officials. Evaders would enjoy the relative advantage by using unfair means, which would not be in any one's long term interest. Tax collection could not be seen as extortion in any form.

There were certain powers and functions which defined the State and differentiated it from other bodies. These included the power to tax, besides policing and land administration. I did not agree with the position taken by associations of traders and manufacturers that in view of compensation provisions in VAT against loss of overall revenues for three years by Government of India, dealers should not be coerced to pay taxes every month. Claiming compensation from Central Government for me was not the option to be exercised for Sales Tax losses as I was confident that such a situation would never arise. Lower tax rates invariably lead to better compliance with tax provisions. After extensive interactions with stakeholders and tax officials, I reached the conclusion that tax evasion in the State was as high as tax collection. Many larger dealers including multinational companies and public sector companies were found denying their tax liabilities by misrepresenting facts and obtaining stay orders from the High Court.

Minister's Restlessness

Within three months of my assuming charge as CCT, I found that Finance Minister Ghadai had become somewhat restless. Although I had not met him, he would frequently telephone me to advise that I should not be too strict in dealing with officials and dealers since the provisions for compensation by Central Government would meet the State's tax losses. He felt that the lower collection of VAT in the State was due to reduced tax rates. I got first wind of his acute restlessness with me when Principal Secretary, Finance called me for a meeting. He said that Finance Minister was aggrieved that I was misbehaving with dealers and officers, becoming abusive, and showing highhandedness for which both dealers and officers were turning hostile. It was apprehended that this situation would ultimately affect tax revenues of the State adversely. He said that Finance Minister had made similar complaints to Chief Secretary also more than once. Dr. U.C. Saratchandran, himself a fair officer with a high regard for rules, was fully satisfied with my pro-active approach which was beginning to bear positive results. He readily agreed with my request that a meeting with Finance Minister could resolve his grievance, and thus together we met the Minister soon enough.

In the meeting, without any introduction Principal Secretary Finance bluntly reproduced what Minister had said about me. He then asserted that professionally he was satisfied with my work and approach, adding that to ensure efficient functioning and better outcomes it would not be in anyone's interest to provide room for misunderstandings. He asked me to address the apprehensions and grievance of Minister. Perhaps Minister had not expected him to bat quite so straight. Before I could respond, he became defensive and apologetic stating that people had probably misinformed him about me. He said his only concern was that Odisha's revenue interests should not be affected due to any negative message about my functioning.

I responded that I had no desire to hold the post of CCT if Minister actually believed in the loose talk being indulged in by some vested interests known to him. I clarified that while I may appear serious and grim at times, I have never used abusive or unparliamentary words in dealing with anyone. I believe in discipline, but hold firm conviction in fairness towards all before law. I requested Minister to recount any instance of my so-called highhandedness and abusive behaviour. He failed to respond, and we left his room within 10 minutes of entering it. Principal Secretary Finance did not display any emotion as we left. Being a man of few words, he did not opt to dissect the meeting. But I was left with the feeling that nothing untoward had actually happened. Dr. Saratchandran was a remarkable officer, tall in every respect. He led an unusually austere life, travelling using an old Maruti 800 as his office vehicle. He had turned down a proposal for purchase of a high-end car for official use of Chief Secretary. I too believed in a similar style of functioning. All that mattered at the end of the day was achieving unprecedented growth in tax collection in the short time that I served as CCT. I remember that this austere, tall officer was extremely happy to see this growth in tax collection and expansion in registered dealers' network, and greatly appreciated my work.

Tax Brushing Some Well-known Industrial Enterprises

Having addressed promotion-related issues of senior and middle level officers, I gained their confidence and full support. Offices of CTOs and ACCTs also progressed well in getting modernised, with simultaneous activities of consignment of old records, disposal of old and unserviceable fixtures and furniture, and cleaning up of office compound. Officers at all levels started sharing genuine difficulties in handling certain well-connected influential dealers known to indulge in tax evasion, but largely succeeded in achieving the monthly tax targets fixed in consultation with them in regional, circle and range meetings. I started dealing with the so-called influential dealers, some of whom behaved as if they were doing a big favour by paying VAT, Central Sales Tax and Entry Tax. A few approached the High Court when notices were served on them, besides showing their influence in many other ways. I visited those offices of CTOs and ACCTs more frequently where the dealers had been attempting to dictate terms and misbehaved with tax officials. It would be of interest to recall some instances.

The soft drinks' company Coca-Cola had obtained an order from High Court against collection of arrear tax liability of ₹ 25 crore using coercive measures. On scrutiny I found that the multinational company was leveraging the judicial system to delay auditing of their production and sales transactions and thereby avoid legitimate payment of taxes. I called their senior officials to understand their problem. Their standard refrain was that they have always acted upon the advice of their legal consultants and chartered accountants. I explained that the law provided for 200 percent tax penalty. Their legal luminaries were not authorised to interpret law, which could either be done by those responsible for its implementation or by judicial courts of law. For nurturing a healthy relationship with tax laws, I gently advised them to pay their past liabilities and to also consider withdrawing unnecessary litigation. In case the business transactions were not allowed to be audited, the company should be prepared to face its dealership being suspended sooner rather than later. Methods available with tax authority which included 'best judgment' assessment in the event of detailed accounts not being made available for audit, and taxing of retailers throughout the State were elaborated. Senior Vice President of the company and senior chartered account from its Gurugram office who came to meet me were also informed that ultimately their Headquarters in Atlanta, USA, would be apprised in writing about their tactics to evade tax.

Initially, they protested against my warning for suspension of their manufacturing license besides actions against their franchises all over the State if they did not pay VAT on the basis of 'best judgment' assessment deeming it to run counter to the orders of High Court. But when I further said that I would apply the provisions of law in a most transparent manner, and once the bullet was fired it would not be possible to restore it to the barrel, they sought a week's time to look into the issue afresh. Within a week, they reverted with a proposal promising payment of prospective taxes regularly in addition to clearing arrear liabilities in three equal instalments over a period of three months. They wanted assurance that their dealers and sub-dealers would not be asked to pay taxes and that interest on arrears should be waived. I informed them that as I had no authority to waive interest liability on arrears; they could seek the desired relief separately from High Court after withdrawing their main litigation. But I did assure them that their dealers and sub-dealers would not be troubled if the company's accounts were presented for audit whenever required and taxes paid as per actuals. The company kept its word. Arrear taxes were paid, and they got interest waiver from High Court. They started paying monthly tax at prescribed VAT rates regularly. Collections became 50 percent higher than what the company had been paying earlier.

Under 'Dhirubhai Ambani Exclusive Club' scheme, M/s. Reliance Communications had distributed mobile handsets to consumers on which Sales Tax had not been paid. Their plea that they had not 'sold' handsets but merely supplied them to their customers without charging a one-time cost, stood rejected. The company had been assessed for tax liability including penalty of about ₹ 12 crore for past years based on purchase price of handsets as per invoices. Their Vice President came from Mumbai and tried to overwhelm me. He stated that the company accounted for about 10 percent of India's GDP and contributed to the growth of economy in more than one way. He said it was their policy not to pay taxes in such promotional schemes. He also flaunted his own credentials including academic qualifications and genealogy, emphasizing that his father had retired as DG of Police, Maharashtra. I went straight to the brass-tracks stating that his credentials and those of the company were irrelevant before law. His plea for tax avoidance on the grounds that it was company policy could not be upheld. I suggested that the company could get temporary relief if it paid 50 percent of assessed liability including penalty pending conclusion of litigation. Immediately after he left my office, I received a call from a Secretary in Government of India with whom I had worked a few years back. Citing reference to my meeting with this Vice President, he requested me to extend a helping hand to the extent possible. I reiterated my position. The next day a senior advocate appeared in my Court and undertook to pay 50 percent of tax liability including penalty within three days, which was allowed. However, I became aware that the time of three days sought by the company was a mischievous ruse. Within two days the company got an order from High Court staying the proceedings in my Court pending disposal of their Writ Petition. But the trickery fell flat on their face because High Court directed the company to pay 50 percent of tax liability including penalty for considering their Writ Petition, which was the exact proposition on tax relief that had been ruled by CCT! The senior Advocate representing the company before my Court who had executed the trickery now reappeared and apologised saying that the company had suddenly changed its stand and approached the High Court.

The case of National Aluminium Company (NALCO) was of a different kind. This PSU evaded Central Sales Tax by showing inter-State sales of its customised products to major clients as "branch transfer". I advised their CMD a native Odisha to be fair to his State which provided every possible support to the company despite its major market/ large clients being outside. Legally, products subjected to branch transfer could not be taxed provided the branches were specified and mentioned in dealership license. NALCO had not disclosed their branches or stockyards outside the State as per terms and conditions of dealership license. I cautioned them that audit of their so-called branches or stockyards could lead to imposition of heavy tax penalty and consequences in the event of transactions being found manipulated. Business organisations usually go by the advice given to them by their legal and tax consultants. NALCO was no exception. I started the audit exercise of time-bound verification of their transactions, including inspection of so-called stockyards in two major cities of neighbouring West Bengal and Andhra Pradesh. The verification report was on expected lines. A case was instituted indicating detection of Central Sales Tax evasion of ₹ 60 crore. In light of solid evidence which substantiated manipulations in inter-State transactions, the leading advocate hired by them to appear before me, was clearly told that his client might not get relief from High Court which in such cases usually directed the dealer company to pay 40-50 percent of assessed liability just for its Writ Petition to be entertained for consideration. The Advocate, Indrajit Mohanty, known well for his razor-sharp mind, who subsequently was elevated as a

Judge in the High Court a few years later, understood the case and message. He advised NALCO wisely. The company paid the amount of Central Sales Tax excluding penalty, pending disposal of freshly raised litigation. I was informed by a senior executive in NALCO later that their auditors would have objected had they paid taxes earlier and not contested the case! They were indeed happy to pay taxes regularly thereafter. Annual payment of commercial taxes by NALCO which used to be ₹ 40 crore increased to ₹ 120 crore during my tenure of a year as CCT.

The cases of RSP and Steel Authority of India Limited (SAIL) were more or less similar. Sanak Mishra, MD of RSP, appeared to be a very clever and deceptive personality. On the verge of retirement, he promised that his company would fully pay Central Sales Tax by stopping branch transfers during meetings with Finance Minister. But he never acted upon his assuring sweet words. Despite a booming steel sector, payment of VAT and CST by RSP during his incumbency had reduced substantially. I met his successor who explained that sales were handled by Sales Branch of Corporate Head Office and he did not have any direct control over transactions. Nevertheless, he agreed to convey the State's concerns to his Corporate Office. I had also got some inter-State transactions of RSP/ SAIL verified through commercial tax intelligence unit and informed senior officials of the consequences if the company continued to ignore its actual tax liabilities. At the same time, I wrote to CMD, SAIL, and met him in Delhi to explain the unfair practices being followed in the name of branch transfers. A case had to be instituted to raise the demand. The company cooperated finally and contributed more than twice the previous-year's taxes.

Defence Ordinance Factory in Balangir had been avoiding paying taxes on the ground that it was a PSU under Ministry of Defence and supplied products for defending the country. The company neither responded to notices nor allowed entry of commercial tax officials in their premises for audit/ inspection. My considered views were that PSUs claiming prime positions must be assessed more rigorously in matters of enforcing legal provisions and for setting an example for similar standards to be followed by others. When the company's General Manager declined the notices repeatedly, the 'best judgment' method was applied for assessing tax liability, and a tax demand of ₹ 25 crore was raised. MD, Ordinance Factories' Board and senior officers from Department of Defence Production wrote to Chief Secretary against what they called unwarranted and unprecedented action of CCT. I ignored those communications. The factory paid tax for the first time in the State to avoid attachment of accounts. If only Ordinance Factories' Board had applied a cool mind to the issue, they would have realised that there was no need for them to seek to evade taxes on products sold by them to captive buyers. They could have saved themselves the ignominy of receiving tax notices with penalties. I learnt later that the General Manager was transferred for accepting the tax liability even though he had done so reluctantly.

The case of Hindustan Aeronautics Ltd. (HAL) in Sunabeda (Koraput) was slightly different. HAL had been paying only nominal taxes by misleading my predecessors and those in State Industries Department to present limited liabilities. It virtually ignored notices issued by local CTO to make their transactions available for audit. I found this situation unacceptable. Ultimately the company's accounts had to be attached, which held up their transactions including salary disbursements. HAL approached the High Court and pleaded for relief before my court. The company dangled their status due to their high-end products and invoked national security considerations to overwhelm tax officials, which I felt was irrelevant. Partial relief secured from High Court was inadequate. They requested me to visit Sunabeda. My visit coinciding that of their CMD. I felt deeply pained when Russian technicians engaged in testing a Sukhoi engine shouted at HAL engineers on finding them standing close by. During discussions, I explained the provisions of input tax credit under VAT which helped reduce their tax liability substantially. I clarified explicitly that there was no tax exemption for HAL and any confrontationist approach to avoid paying full taxes was misplaced. Instead, they could include the tax element in costing of their products. CMD HAL attributed their lack of understanding to a senior official who probably simply followed past practices instead of trying to understand the new VAT law. I advised HAL not to misunderstand tax officials who were not insensitive towards our national security concerns. CTOs would not mind travelling the extra mile to help HAL in every possible way in understanding and calculating its tax liability. HAL became amenable to pay tax as per the law without claiming immunity again signifying harmonious resolution.

Industrial development in Odisha received visibility after the year 2000 though the seeds had been sown when the Indian economy was liberated from 'license/ permit raj' by Central Government in 1991. Private companies which invested in mineral-based industries included Jindal Steel and Jindal Power headed by two brothers. I found both companies indulging in tax evasion by misinterpreting State and Central Tax laws, besides compounding the matter with attempts to leverage their political and administrative clout. Concessional Central Sales Tax rates existed in law to procure capital goods and raw materials to be used for new products to be manufactured by investors. But Jindal Steel had purchased cement from neighbouring States at concessional rates for use in construction of residential houses, office buildings, compound walls, swimming pools, etc. and avoided 12 percent VAT. It reluctantly produced records for inspection by CTO in the presence of their advocate. The advocate who attended my court conceded the mistakes but pleaded helplessness in advising payment of VAT liability including penalty exceeding ₹ 6 crore. He sought time for submitting the company's reply. The sister company faced a tax demand of ₹ 10 crore for past evasions. I was on leave for attending to the last rites of my father in my native village, when I received a phone call from Naveen Jindal, MP (Lok Sabha) who wished to discuss the tax liability. I declined politely advising him not to try to influence officers on such matters through calls or otherwise. Fearing actions from tax authorities, the company approached the High Court. Under orders of High Court, it paid ₹ 5 crore, being 50 percent of tax liability including penalty, under compulsion. The sword of balance payment hung over the industrial unit till such time as High Court passed its final orders.

About a year later, I had gone to attend a week-long training at LBSNAA, Mussoorie on "Ethics in Administration". Naveen Jindal, MP (Lok Sabha) stood invited to take a session. He had publicised what he called his victory on the matter of use of the National Flag, "the Tricolour", on the rooftop of his office premises. Before the session commenced, I was requested by the Course Director to propose a vote of thanks at the end of his session. I agreed to do so provided that none would mind my sharing experiences with his tax evasion including his attempt at putting pressure. The Course Director got nervous and withdrew his offer. During the interactive segment, when a participant asked Naveen Jindal as to how his company handled 'difficult' government officials who did not cooperate, he answered that in a few cases such officers had to be transferred on his request by State administration, and cited a case in Chhattisgarh to that effect. I felt sad that we were being taught 'ethical' governance by those who brazenly admitted to having discounted their morality.

The case of Bhushan Steel was identical with that of Jindal Steel in dodging tax officials and avoiding taxes. The *modus operandi* followed was also similar. It also tried to exert pressure through a powerful functionary of the ruling party in the State, who was the last word in transfers and postings of senior government functionaries.

Mangalam Timbers in Nabarangpur had benefitted more than once under the State's Industrial Policy. Land was provided at a nominal rate besides a higher capital investment subsidy and tax exemptions, deferments, etc. for setting up an enterprise in this industrially-backward district. Just before the tax liability arose, the unit had declared itself sick and got further tax benefits for revival and expansion. The dealer wholly exported its products, but was unwilling to pay Central Sales Tax despite the exemption period being over. Sales were shown as 100 percent 'branch transfers' without disclosing the branches in other States. Intelligence enquiries revealed that supplies were customised and sold mostly to captive customers in Kolkata. Records were found of the same truck carrying finished goods, and delivering the product at several outlets. When a case was instituted, a senior advocate met me with message from a retired Chief Secretary, talked of as the most industry-friendly officer. I did not like to verify whether the advocate was truly conveying his wishes to overlook the tax liability of a defaulter and simply conveyed my inability to extend undue benefits. The dealer did what other similarly-placed defaulters had been doing. Under orders of High Court, it paid 50 percent of the tax liability including penalty and was to await the final orders on its Writ Petition.

The most famous bullion trader in the State Capital, Lal Chand Jewellers was known for his proximity with some senior civil servants and important politicians. Wielding influence on commercial tax officials, the dealer was not paying taxes for his sales transactions or would pay nominally as if to retain his Tax Identification Number. The specious argument for non-payment of taxes was that only shapes and sizes of old ornaments of his customers were being changed by giving them a modern look, and the dealer was realising no more than conversion charges which did not require payment of Sales Tax or VAT. The dealer had not been audited nor correctly assessed in the past perhaps due to his good equation with those who mattered. Based on advance information collected through the departmental intelligence unit, I felt it essential to verify his accounts and deputed a large team of commercial tax intelligence officials, which the dealer had not expected. Within no time, tax evasion was detected with records showing procurement worth about ₹ 100 crore during the past one year from merchants in Mumbai, Hyderabad, Jaipur, etc. The dealer proprietor who had gone to Delhi returned immediately and appeared before me submitting that he would lose his social reputation if the tax raid on his premises was publicised. He agreed to pay VAT with penalty on the discoveries immediately and without contesting the case.

Tata Iron & Steel Company (TISCO) with a huge presence in the State was also the largest importer of coal through Paradip Port. Imported coal after washing was used in its Sponge Iron Plant in Keonjhar, and also sold within and outside the State. Though Entry Tax law provided for tax liability @1 percent for causing entry of goods in the local area, the company avoided paying it stating that their legal consultants had advised them not to do so. An importer of coal, who had changed his business in the meanwhile, had confidentially informed me about tax evasion by virtually all importers. After gathering information from Custom officials at Paradip Port, which took almost six months, it was found that average landing cost of imported coal exceeded ₹ 3,000/tonne, while VAT was paid by importers by reflecting a transaction value ranging between ₹ 1,000-1,200/tonne. I called a meeting of all importers advising them to clear their actual tax liabilities of previous two years within a week gracefully to avoid adverse actions and cautioned them about tax evasion in future. The head of TISCO in the State was informed that although his company took pride in claiming to be tax law-compliant, the reality did not bear it out. He was advised to be ready for suspension of licence of the Sponge Iron Plant in Keonjhar within a week if the company failed to discharge its Entry Tax and VAT liabilities against imported coal as per actuals. He was also told that a note would be sent to Chief Minister's office to inform Ratan Tata who was scheduled to meet Chief Minister on 6 September 2006 that his company in Odisha was indulging in tax evasion. The State representative of

TISCO was in tears probably fearing loss of his job and sought more time for response, which was turned down on the grounds that it was my job to protect State's revenues but not his job. This meeting with all coal importers was held late afternoon on 30 August 2006. Exactly 24 hours later, at around 5.30 p.m. on the next day, I received a telephone call from Special Secretary, GA Department that I now stood transferred and posted as Commissioner-cum-Secretary, ST&SC Development and OBC & Minority Welfare Departments with immediate effect. When requested to fax the transfer order to enable me to leave the place, I was informed that the orders were going to be issued within an hour or so as the file was yet to reach his office from that of Chief Minister. I was also asked not to wait for my substitute and relinquish the charge immediately.

The tendency to evade taxes appears widespread. Yet sometimes I felt compelled to ponder, perhaps unnecessarily, that some of the biggest industrial groups including the TATAs who indeed contributed in nation-building immensely in terms of generating employment, capital formation, institution-building, promoting education and research in fundamental sciences and social sciences, sports, etc. found nothing wrong with evading taxes. I remained curious to know whether this was an unstated policy of these prominent industrial groups or the minions working for them voluntarily indulged in such ventures to show their loyalty and to deliver more than the system legally permitted. I found a similar tendency, though to varying degrees, in most of the industrial houses in relation to land acquisition and hoarding, with grossly inadequate regard for resettlement and rehabilitation of families displaced due to their industrial projects as elaborated in a later Chapter.

In my professional life, I did not resist transfers and postings and felt that it would be unethical to question them on any ground. I firmly believed that whatever be their considerations it was the prerogative of Government to decide as to where they would like to utilise the services of public servants. To me the administrative life of a public servant was defined by transfers, postings, periodic promotions, and finally, superannuation. Yet, wherever posted, I felt tempted to draw up a three-year plan as the stated policy of State Government was to generally give substantive assignments to officers for a period of three-years in a post. Considering the potential in Commercial Tax Department, I had drawn up a plan in consultation with my team of officers to double revenue collection by making the tax administration more accountable, dealer-friendly, predictive and transparent. Exactly after one year of my tenure as Head of Commercial Tax Department, the annual growth of tax collection including VAT was a huge 35 percent. In hindsight, in order to achieve my mission, I should have been patient rather than going hammer and tongs at some of the influential big dealers who were found to be indulging in evasion of taxes. However, it went against the grain to chase and hound the smaller fish for a pittance of tax evasion while letting the big fish swim away with crores. Even so, as in the past, I had no regret at leaving this Department suddenly either.

I enjoyed the confidence of the bulk of field functionaries as I had tried to help them in personal and professional matters despite being firm about performance milestones and even harsh on discipline. I stood by them whenever they faced threats and there were a few such cases. I was informed that mercenaries had come to the residence of a CTO of Jharsuguda Circle to eliminate him simply because he took his duties seriously, but his wife suddenly intervened and got stabbed to death. Successive CTOs worked in fear, and a number of large dealers had not been paying taxes at all, but no action had been taken against them. I called a meeting of the traders' association in the office of CTO during one of my visits and ordered audit of accounts of a couple of big dealers since they had openly refused to file tax returns. The traders physically manhandled tax officials when they went instantly to their business premises to comply with my instructions. Tax officials had to retreat to escape bodily harm. Upon hearing about these happenings, I proceeded to the site after informing the local police personnel. By that time, the traders across the town had pulled down their shutters to register protest. I ordered sealing of those two establishments where tax officials had been manhandled. Finding the District SP not available over phone, I proceeded to her office with the FIR which I had signed myself as the CTO and others who had gone for the audit were afraid for their lives recalling past incidents. FIR though registered, a few months later after my transfer, I received a letter from the district police office that a final report on my FIR had been filed and that I could contest it if wanted to. I was not surprised.

On that visit, I had proceeded to Rourkela and found that office of ACCT had been surrounded by an unruly mob of traders to show solidarity with their counterparts in Jharsuguda! Unlike in Jharsuguda, the office bearers of the local Chambers of Commerce, however, appeared polite and agreed to get engaged in discussion. I explained to them the situation in Jharsuguda and problems caused by a couple of dealers who had created a culture of threat and intimidation and advised them not to side with such elements to claim legal immunity perpetually. Subsequently I found that the traders in Rourkela had indirectly been instigated by the local ACCT and a CTO, neither of whom enjoyed a good reputation for their integrity. The traders demand in Rourkela was that Commercial Tax Department should not undertake inspection of their business establishments till VAT got stabilised and they understood the law. They also wanted that Odisha too should avoid pursuing revenue collection vigorously, since possible losses on account of introduction of VAT were being compensated by Central Government and all major States were claiming it. I advised the dealers not to seek relief beyond the legal provisions and to abide by the law in their own interest. They were required to pay taxes collected from consumers, but had a right to claim input tax credit. A number of SSI units having Sponge Iron Plants in Sundargarh complained that their input tax credit claims had not been accepted. I found some claims to be true and issued instructions to the CTO on the spot to accept such input tax claims which had been submitted with corroborating documents and to take into account those claims at the time of collecting VAT/CST on their finished products. The traders promised to cooperate and dispersed.

The incident of Jharsuguda was raised in the Legislative Assembly after a week by the local MLA Kishore Mohanty, who was also the Chief Whip of the ruling party. I was sitting in the Officers' Gallery during the question hour. Suddenly, the MLA while asking a supplementary question on commercial taxes alleged that because of the highhandedness of the arrogant CCT, traders of Jharsuguda in particular and Western Odisha in general had passed resolutions not to pay taxes. I was not surprised to face the wrath of the ruling party leader. Finance Minister did not utter a word in my defence either.

Bhubaneswar and Cuttack Club or Cabal?

Bhubaneswar and Cuttack Clubs had stopped paying Sales Tax/ VAT justifying that they no longer held a dealer's licence. The President of Bhubaneswar Club was an IAS officer of 1976 batch, well known for his flamboyance. His father-in-law, a senior IPS officer, was the President of Cuttack Club. Traditionally, Bhubaneswar Club used to be headed by Chief Secretary, with majority of All India Services' officers as its members. It was said that the Club's character had changed since the incumbent President had taken over. He was the real force behind its expanded activities through mobilisation of funds from various sources. The Club continued to function from a Government building, which had been renovated and expanded massively. Notwithstanding the Club deregistering itself as a dealer under Sales Tax/VAT law, it was incumbent upon it to pay VAT with a right to claim input tax credit. I personally tried in vain to contact the President. None in IAS or outside dared to join issues with him knowing his aggressive response at the slightest provocation. Finding him unresponsive to my calls, I sent the local CTO to the Club to assess VAT liability. Club officials refused to cooperate and did not present records. The only option left was to assess the tax liability by applying the 'best judgment' method. The current VAT liability including penalty was assessed for an amount of about ₹ 26 lakh and a demand notice was raised accordingly.

Instead of paying or challenging the demand notice in the appropriate appeal forum, the Club's President pasted a notice on its Notice Board stating that "*officers of Commercial Tax Department would not be allowed to use Bhubaneswar Club and that CCT Taradatt stood ostracized for all the time*". The notice got widely publicised in print and electronic media. Perhaps I was the only IAS officer in the State who had not taken membership of Bhubaneswar Club. I had gone to the Club only once in the past to attend a meeting of IAS officers' association when the supersession of four senior most IAS officers by a relatively junior officer was to be discussed. I now sent a letter to Chief Secretary, attaching also a copy of the said Notice, but underlining that the

Club stood on prime Government land and building. I highlighted that despite the majority of its members drawing from senior officers, judges and other high-ranking public functionaries, it violated the State's own tax laws and intimidated tax officials. I suggested stringent administrative action, but failed to receive any response. In order to realise VAT including penalty, its accounts were attached. The Club challenged it, but had to be pay 50 percent of assessed liability including the penalty as per interim orders passed by High Court against the attachment order. What happened subsequently was quite disturbing.

Under extant law, the Club's tax liability including penalty of 200 percent was again assessed by applying the 'best judgment' for previous two years for an amount of ₹ 2 crore including penalty. Orders for attachment of accounts which were challenged by the Club again were temporarily vacated by High Court subject to payment of about ₹ 30 lakh. However, before the amount could be realised, I was transferred from Commercial Tax Department. As I was apprised by the CTO, my successor who was a batch-mate of the President, did not allow him to realise the amount. After my successor's transfer when the amount was realised by giving effect to the attachment order read with the order passed by High Court by the CTO in position, he was thoroughly admonished by incumbent CCT who happened to be my own batch-mate. The CTO, in tears, shared it with me during a chance meeting in a train a couple of years later.

Having exhibited courage by passing orders for audit of the Bhubaneswar Club, I too faced threats and intimidation. I was in the habit of taking a morning walk regularly starting early morning at 4.30 a.m. in Biju Patnaik Forest Park adjacent to my residence. One morning a few days later when I came out of my house, I was shocked to find the decomposed body of a dead animal dumped on the doormat along with piles of human shit in the portico and veranda. All the small trees in my compound had been chopped off and flower pots broken. The malevolence was scary, the environment stinking, and destruction of nature devastating. I called DCP, Bhubaneswar who visited my residence after an hour to see the carnage. He collected the FIR from me and promised action as fast as possible. A couple of other police officials with a dog squad came and inspected the site. Investigation of the case was assigned to the Officer-in-charge of Capital Police Station who too visited my residence to inspect the site of crime along with his team. The incident was reported in the media extensively. State's Home Secretary telephoned me during the day to say that as per his inputs, President of Bhubaneswar Club had used his goons to commit the crime at my residence. He wanted me to take security guards for protection. In disbelief, I declined his offer for security cover.

Further developments were more intriguing. DCP continued to assure me that the police were about to nab the culprits. After some time, he suddenly left on Central deputation to CBI. When I called the Investigating Officer to ascertain the status, it was informed that the former DCP had supervised the case himself and had desired to file a final report stating 'facts true but no clue'. This Investigating Officer too got transferred to Cuttack thereafter! I was told that both DCP and Police Commissioner formed part of the inner circle of President of Bhubaneswar Club. A Judo Coach reportedly also close to the President was murdered by a rival gang leader in broad day-light leading to a public outcry about the law and order situation in the State Capital, which finally led to transfer of Police Commissioner too. A senior officer and member of the Club mentioned to me about a year later that the murdered Judo Coach was the mercenary engaged for causing mayhem at my residence by the Club's President out of sheer revenge and in order to scare me. He described the murder as a case of poetic justice. There was no need for me to waste time again for the reality check.

Resisting Interference in Transfers and Postings and Other Matters

Office of CCT and those of important field functionaries are vulnerable to external influence. ACTOs, the foot soldiers, who were specially gazette officers, managed to get transferred to the place of their choice using their connections despite CCT being their appointing authority. This was happening regularly and round-the-year qua a circular issued by GA Department. After the general period of transfer (between May-June), transfers would be given effect to only with the approval of next higher authority. This circular, to my understanding, had to be read in relation to general delegation of powers according to which the appointing authority delegated its power to the next authority below and exercised it after the specified period of general transfer. Exercise of the same power concurrently at two levels could lead to anarchy. GA Department had rightly indicated the period of general transfer by the authority exercising delegated powers, which then stood withdrawn after that period was over, and was exercised by the appointing authority on administrative ground or otherwise throughout the year. Without drawing the distinction between exercising delegated powers and inherent powers, the common practice was to allow transfer and posting of ACTOs at Finance Minister's level. I made it clear in writing to Finance and GA Departments that the power of transfer and posting of functionaries appointed by CCT was not a delegated power and thus, any order passed by Government would only have advisory value. On posting of senior officers, proposals submitted by me as CCT were largely approved by Chief Minister who usually did not permit changes desired by Finance Minister.

I was not deterred by some adverse developments around me or occasional provocation as my focus was squarely on transforming the work culture and making tax administration more transparent and giving less scope for exercising discretion or favour. I worked assertively and objectively in accordance with my plan of doubling the revenue collection in the next three years by plugging loopholes in the system and making it predictive and dealer-friendly. It was in the interest of tax administration to widen the tax net by granting dealership licence to everyone in business or who intended to do business. But many shops and commercial establishments were engaged in business without any Tax Identification Number and avoided their tax liabilities. I was thus deeply disturbed that CTOs and ACCTs were extremely conservative in granting dealership licence. The maximum complaints I received were in relation to delays and rejection of applications for dealership. S.M. Patnaik who had retired as Chief Secretary when I joined Odisha cadre, once telephoned me and complained that his grandson had been running from pillar to post to run his business in electronics but was unable to get a licence for dealership. The norms were publicised and Licensing Authorities were instructed to invoke the penal provisions invariably if anyone in taxable zone of income was found to be in business without dealership. As a result of proactive approach, the dealers' network increased from 68,000 to more than 91,000 within less than a year with more than 30,000 dealers paying taxes regularly against less that 20,000 earlier. Revenue collection had also increased by 35 percent at the end of my year-long tenure as CCT. Substantial progress was made in modernisation of main check gates and commercial tax offices. In brief, one could witness a substantive change in the internal and external environment which improved performance and inculcated a sense of self-respect among the functionaries.

Finance Minister after his initial reservations about me were allayed had become cordial. I was aware of his vested interests to some extent though pretended to be ignorant whenever matters related and relatable to him were brought to my notice. One of the interesting episodes which disappointed him was about seizure of a truck transporting electronic goods from Kolkata to Rourkela on the basis of an intelligence input after it had bypassed the border check gate in Mayurbhanj. The driver presented papers showing transport of potatoes! A nephew of Finance Minister was working with the transport company involved in this clandestine operation. ACCT Balasore in whose jurisdiction the truck had been seized informed me about the pressure being mounted on him by Minister. I bluntly reminded him of the consequences of succumbing to pressure. He was instructed to say that action against the transporter was being monitored by CCT. I left for Delhi to attend a meeting of State CCTs, which was followed by a meeting of Empowered Committee of State Finance Ministers. Thus, the next day when Finance Minister came to Delhi to attend his meeting, he sought my intervention as according to him the job of his nephew was at stake. I told him that appropriate orders would be passed on the matter after returning to Headquarters and he should rest assured that nothing unfair would be done. It seemed that the transporter had paid the maximum penalty to get his truck released and the proposal put up to me by Additional Commissioner was for approval to release the truck. It was clear that the Minister had influenced the decision-making process at every level below. I rejected the proposal and passed order for auction of the seized truck which obviously the Minister did not appreciate.

I was convinced that tax administration required a major overhaul and radical reforms. Long stoppages for inspections of trucks carrying goods at major check gates till the issues were settled to the satisfaction of officers of Commercial Tax and Transport Departments were not always for legal compliances. Check gates were breeding centres for corruption and places of prize posting. For sure, evasion of taxes could not be arrested by imposing penalties at check gates alone. There were other ways to track commercial transactions which could be achieved by higher degree of automation and transparency in processes, cooperation with other States and Central tax agencies, and by way of passive surveillance. To some extent tax officials were also responsible, even though the tendency to evade taxes was all pervasive. An honest dealer suffered more while a dishonest one could have his easy way out. In my experience, the most tax-compliant professionally-managed dealer company in the State was Larsen & Toubro. The company at times succumbed to pressure of tax officials who raised undue demands just to show higher tax collection. In a case, I found it to have been subjected to unfair assessment, which was contested by it subsequently. I passed orders for tax refund and advised tax officials to remain fair and objective in assessing liabilities.

Non-disposal of claims of dealers who had been over-assessed but were still forced to pay to avoid the wrath of tax authorities had created a trust deficit between them. I resisted this bad practice heavily. My own disposal of appeal petitions in a year was 373 as against 162, 18 and 30 respectively by my predecessors in the previous four years. My monthly reviews of pendency of cases in the courts of Additional and Joint Commissioners also helped in increasing overall disposal. For modernisation of Commercial Tax offices, Oversees Development Assistance from the British Government had been used. Their Deputy High Commissioner who visited ACCT Office of Bhubaneswar Range could hardly believe its transformation since his visit a year back. The highest growth of tax revenue during my tenure was indeed the sum total of cumulative efforts made collectively and concertedly in various aspects of tax administration in the entire State.

* * * *

9

Equity and Equality: ST&SC and OBC & Minorities Welfare

On 1 September 2006, I joined as Commissioner-cum-Secretary, Scheduled Tribe & Scheduled Caste (ST&SC) Development and OBC & Minority Welfare Departments, which was substantively familiar territory for me. STs&SCs were perceived to be the traditional vote bank of Indian National Congress. Biju Patnaik as Chief Minister during 1990-95, had split H&TW Department into two, ST Development and SC Development Departments, to capture and wean away the political constituency of tribal communities from his rival political party. No new programmes for development or welfare had been added. The two departments got integrated again. Naveen Patnaik-led Government created a separate OBC & Minorities Welfare Department without adding any new scheme for their welfare or development. Functionally, both departments worked as one.

STs constituted about 23 percent , SCs 17 percent and OBCs roughly another 50 percent of Odisha's population. Minority population of about 4 percent formed part of OBC/SEBC list by and large, although a section of tribal communities despite being converted to Christianity continued to maintain its social identity as earlier. Central OBC list did not include a few dominant intermediary castes which stood included in Odisha's OBC list, for which leaders of those castes had been agitating.

Magical Development of a Thousand 100-seated ST Girls' Hostels

Chief Minister, Naveen Patnaik, had suddenly announced that one thousand ST girls' hostels of 100-seated each would be opened within a year about two months prior to my assuming charge in the Department. Without making enabling budget provisions, ST&SC Development Department had been directed to implement the scheme.

Paradoxically and senselessly, educational institutions run by the Department stood excluded by State's School & Mass Education Department in its implementation of Sarva Shiksha Abhiyan (SSA), the Centrally Sponsored

Scheme which provided financial support for construction of additional class-rooms, appointment of additional teachers in single-teacher schools, teachers' training support, etc. Odisha's lower literacy rate stemmed largely from its sizeable ST&SC population which had historically suffered for inadequate attention to socio-economic development including elementary education. Yet, even now institutions of elementary educations set up exclusively for these ST&SC communities to address the historical deficits were being denied support under SSA. I explained this to Collectors of tribal districts who headed the society for implementing SSA at district level. They also played a vital role in running educational institutions, mostly residential, meant for ST&SC students. I advised them that additional class-rooms and appointment of teachers (Shiksha Sahayaks) for ST&SC Schools should be given higher priority under SSA in order to meet the additional requirements arising from opening 1,000 ST girls' hostels to honour the announcement made by Chief Minister. I similarly requested Secretary, School & Mass Education Department, who had rather casually proposed opening 1,000 ST Girls' hostels, and that too within a year, to Chief Minister during a meeting to discuss the sad state of affairs in ST&SC literacy.

I preferred to rely on my first-hand feedback in matters of policy planning and administrative decisions. After a month of assuming charge, I went on a long series of field visits to tribal districts of Southern Division and reviewed the functioning of residential schools managed by the Department. Collectors and District Education Officers informed me about instructions issued to them by Director, Odisha Primary Education Promotion Agency (OPEPA) against providing any SSA support to educational institutions of ST&SC Development Department. This to me was in brazen disregard of SSA objectives. Not only this, School & Mass Education Department had been focusing more on opening new primary schools in non-tribal areas. The pretext was that ST&SC Development Department would take care of tribal education. It was a case of double whammy against tribal communities already suffering from marginalisation.

Immediately after returning from these field visits, I sought a meeting at highest level to discuss the issue of tribal education and status of 100-seated 1,000 ST Girls' Hostels in particular. Chief Secretary, Development Commissioner, Principal Secretary to Chief Minister, Secretary for School & Mass Education, and Director OPEPA, were present in addition to Chief Minister when I drew out the grim ground reality. I explained that if ST&SC population was excluded in estimating literacy levels, Odisha would be found comparable with Kerala and Tamil Nadu. I underscored how more-needy schools exclusively meant for ST&SC students were being excluded and deprived of SSA support. SSA was intended to bridge the chasm in elementary education among educationally-less advanced sections and other areas. If the current approach continued, SSA would defeat its own purpose. It would end up widening this divide. I stated that in sharp contrast to Odisha, States like Chhattisgarh and Madhya Pradesh where proportion of tribal population was equally high, ST&SC schools rightly received higher priority under SSA. In response, Director OPEPA quoted a letter of Union Ministry of Human Resource Development (HRD), which according to him did not allow what I was suggesting. Other senior officers present were stoically silent. Chief Minister appeared supremely indifferent.

Allocations received from Union Ministry of Tribal Affairs under various schemes like SCA, Assistance under Article 275(1) of the Constitution, and Assistance for ST Boys and Girls Hostels had remained unutilised for years. As utilisation certificates had not been submitted, the Department suffered from no fresh allocations. Support for SC Boys and Girls Hostels from Union Ministry of Social Justice & Empowerment (SJ&E) had also stopped. My predecessor managed to get some allocations after submitting utilisation certificates on the basis of funds released to ITDAs. In reality, over ₹ 1,000 crore was found lying parked and unutilised by ITDAs in various commercial banks across districts. The bulk of it was meant for developing infrastructure, including schools and hostels. My field visits revealed that infrastructure project proposals sent by ITDAs to the department had been awaiting administrative approval endlessly. Year-after-year, they answered queries and sent revised proposals and estimates. Years back, when I was Director, Tribal Welfare, instructions had been issued decentralising administrative approval, and need for seeking approval of project estimates at State level had been removed. As I found out now after a gap of 13 years, those instructions had been recalled making it mandatory to seek administrative approval of State Government for projects costing ₹ 10 lakh and above. I quickly restored the earlier position.

I further found that Collectors in Southern Division had enough funds under Backward Region Government Fund (BRGF) and Revised Long-Term Action Plan for Development (RLTAP) for KBK Districts, which could be utilised for constructing ST girls' hostels. Collectors of Sundargarh, Keonjhar, Mayurbhanj, etc. were not lacking in resources under BRGF and other schemes either with enough flexibility in provisions and guidelines to utilise them. Some tribal MLAs too were inclined to contribute 50 percent of cost of hostels in their respective constituencies from their Local Area Development (LAD) funds if remaining 50 percent was mobilised from other sources. Union Ministries of Tribal Affairs and Social Justice & Empowerment were approached and found willing to support hostel infrastructure if utilisation certificates against allocations of previous years were submitted considering the losses Odisha had suffered by being deprived of its legitimate entitlements due to inactions in the past. Private sector funds were forthcoming too. A few big mineral-based industrial units were desirous to contribute funds towards Corporate Social Responsibility (CSR) for constructing ST girls' hostels.

I got on the job innovatively at war-footing. Plans and estimates for constructing 1,000 ST girls' hostels were prepared through ITDA engineers. Execution of task within six months was assigned to ITDAs in districts which had their presence. In non-ITDA districts, it was given to Blocks under the overall supervision of DRDA Project Directors. District Collectors were in any event on board being chairpersons of ITDAs and DRDAs. Competence to grant technical sanctions for hostel complexes beyond the technical powers of engineers in ITDAs and Blocks rested with senior engineers of RD Department. Full powers for administrative approval were delegated to Collectors and governing bodies of ITDAs/ DRDAs to avoid delays entailed by referring a proposal to State Government. ST girls' hostels were for students from Classes I to X. In the case of departmental schools not being in position in some places, arrangements were made for admission of ST girls studying in schools of School & Mass Education Department in the upcoming hostels. ST girls unable to pursue study as day scholars due to poverty and distance factor needed to be admitted in such hostels.

In addition to using available resources, I furnished proposals for creating ST&SC girls' hostels to Union Ministries of Tribal Affairs and SJ&E. Though both Ministries under their new schemes provided 100 percent assistance for ST/ SC girls' hostels, I persuaded them to give 50 percent Central share as per the old norms for a higher number of hostels rather than providing 100 percent assistance for a limited number. The remaining 50 percent was the contribution of State Government or MLA/MP LAD funds, CSR, etc. Having worked in Commercial Tax Department earlier, I had developed sufficient goodwill within State Finance Department to persuade Budget Officer and Special Secretary to accede to my request for providing at least ₹ 25 crore under the State Plan at Supplementary Stage which could be used as the State's share matching 50 percent Central share under Centrally Sponsored Scheme for ST&SC Girls' Hostels. As had been agreed, Union Ministry of Tribal Welfare released financial support for 266 ST girls' hostel and Ministry of SJ&E for another 188. The cost of each hostel building was between ₹ 15-20 lakh.

Facilities for drinking water, toilets, compound walls, etc. were created under other schemes which permitted such projects. The leverage of ST&SC Development Department lay in its role in influencing allocations and utilisations under Tribal Sub Plan (TSP) and Scheduled Caste Component Plan (SCCP). No line department could avoid its scrutiny to ensure setting aside prescribed allocations in their budgets in proportion to ST and SC population separately under TSP and SCCP. The Department's concurrence was necessary for diverting any funds from TSP and SCCP heads to other budget heads even for genuine reasons. The entire State Plan thus could not get approved by Planning Commission without its endorsement and certification on earmarking of TSP and SCCP funds by each line department.

Despite initially failing to persuade School & Mass Education Department to provide SSA support, I was determined not to give up. Frontal challenge was mounted against discrimination between their own elementary educational institutions and those under my Department for which the opportunity came by earlier than anticipated. Rajeev Ratan Shah, Member Secretary, Planning Commission, held a meeting with a few key officials to discuss the thrust areas of the State Plan. Citing failure to provide adequate resources for development of infrastructure, he chided Principal Secretary, Finance for acting as an agent of the ruling party by ignoring core areas that required urgent interventions. He also underscored areas of concerns, which included unsatisfactory socio-economic development of ST&SC communities, particularly their lower literacy rate in Odisha. It was a perfect setting for me to explain what the State Government intended to do for promoting elementary education among tribal communities, particularly for ST girls. While highlighting the recent initiative to set up 100-seater 1,000 ST girls' hostels, which would add the number of ST girls in schools by one lakh, I emphasized the flawed implementation of SSA in the State where support was being denied to the educational institutions exclusively meant of ST&SC students due to discriminatory instructions issued by Union HRD Ministry. Rajeev Ratan Shah instantly telephoned Secretary for School Education & Literacy. He asserted that Central Government had no role in deciding whether schools were run by one or two Departments in States. The objectives of SSA would be defeated if any such differentiation-based discrimination was made. He desired that a meeting between the Joint Secretary of that Department and myself should be arranged to sort out the misunderstanding prior to the impending full house meeting of Planning Commission.

During the meeting, Vrinda Swarup, the Joint Secretary showed me a letter written to her by Director OPEPA, Government of Odisha, seeking approval for exclusion of elementary schools of ST&SC Development Department stating that those institutions did not require any support and were also not under his functional control. This proposal had simply been approved by Union HRD Ministry. It was now abundantly clear that Director OPEPA, for reasons best known to him, had been misrepresenting that it was the Central Government which had not permitted SSA assistance to ST&SC departmental schools. Vrinda Swarup immediately spoke to Director OPEPA to convey her grief at being reprimanded for approving his proposal. She instructed him to give more attention to educationally-backward areas and communities to fulfil the objectives of SSA. Speaking to me at the same time, an apologetic Director OPEPA agreed to modify the instructions to enable inclusion of ST&SC departmental schools in the annual actions plan of each district on priority. On return to the State, I helped to prepare this clarificatory letter. The letter issued also instructed all District Education Officers and Collectors to prepare supplementary Action Plan for their respective districts within three months to meet the requirements of additional class rooms, drinking water, toilets and teachers or Shiksha Sahayaks considering the enhanced students' strength of tribal schools with the opening of these 1,000 hostels. With sustained and persuasive efforts, it was thus possible to mobilise resources, including manpower, for both tribal schools and girls' hostels within a very short period.

Exactly after one year, ST&SC Development Department published a guidance book showing 1,004 newly-opened 'ST Girls' Hostels' with new buildings and boarders, indicating venues, affiliated schools, and other informative essentials. Copies of the book were sent to all Panchayat Samitis, MLAs, MPs, etc. with a request to visit these hostels whenever possible and point out further improvements needed after their reality check. Chief Minister asked me how I had performed this "magic" when the task status on his announcement was presented through this book in a meeting held by him with Chief Secretary and other senior officers in attendance. During the Annual State Plan Meeting, Chief Minister presented this book crediting me for the work which was appreciated by the full house of Planning Commission.

An innovation in 100-seated 1,000 ST Girls' Hostel scheme was that in each hostel, over and above 100 seats of ST girls, 10 seats were earmarked for SC girls. The effective strength of boarders became 110 in each hostel. The number of seats for SC girls in 188 hostels for which 50 percent assistance had been received from Union Ministry of SJ&E was higher. Most of these hostels were located in non-Scheduled Area districts. Curiously enough, about a year after I had left this Department, some officials from that Ministry came to inspect the hostels supported by them at random, as allegations had been made that I had utilised assistance received for SC girls' hostels for ST girls and thereby violated prescribed norms. After their visit, they concluded that what I had done was most appropriate as there were hardly any exclusive schools for SC students and all tribal residential schools had admitted 10 percent SC boarders in about 1,500 ST hostels.

Maintenance of 1,004 hostels involved a huge amount of expenditure towards stipend of boarders and remuneration of 2,008 cook-cum-attendants appointed on contractual basis. I had made it a point that local ST ladies only were engaged as cook-cum-attendants for girls' hostels. To the extent possible, lady teachers were appointed as hostel superintendents. Since the amount of stipend sanctioned was only ₹ 300/boarder, it was difficult to manage hostel expenses. Finance Department agreed to enhance the stipend to ₹ 400/boarder. I also persuaded Government to make rice available at the subsidized rate of ₹ 1/- per kg in these hostels in line with PDS rates for families below the poverty line. In order to avoid misappropriation of stipend and maintain transparency, a menu with unit costs of food items was specified. It was made compulsory to exhibit it with other entitlements of boarders on the notice board. Savings from the stipend, if any, needed to be deposited in savings bank accounts of boarders. Visits at random to hostels, including those attached to schools administered by School & Mass Education Department, resulted in the arrest of a couple of teachers and Hostel Superintendents for misappropriation. Such incidents were publicised sufficiently to inculcate fear, discipline and deterrence. In tradition-bound tribal communities, the progeny, particularly girls were considered economic assets as they started helping parents in collection of minor forest produce, shifting cultivation, etc. for subsistence rather than going to schools in their formative age. Elected tribal representatives were happy to find a large number of hostels coming up in remote areas in a record time for the poor families that had hitherto not been able to send their girl-child to schools which now also gave some sense of food security.

Building Educational Complexes for Particularly Vulnerable Tribals

My past experience and credentials enabled me to remain involved in matters concerning tribal affairs even when I was working elsewhere. While working as Joint Secretary in Ministry of H&FW, I was associated with drafting Scheduled Tribes & other Traditional Forest Dwellers (Recognition of Forest Rights) Act, 2005, popularly known as Forest Rights Act. I was also a member of the Working Group set up by Union Ministry of Tribal Affairs to study and make recommendations for promotion of elementary education among Particularly Vulnerable Tribal Groups (PVTG), which had very high female illiteracy rates. The Group recommended, *inter alia*, establishment of 'Educational Complexes' exclusively for PVTG girls in the age group of 6-14 years. I grabbed the opportunity under this specific scheme with 100 percent Central assistance by submitting, comprehensive proposals for opening 19 Educational Complexes before other States could understand the scheme.

Some innovation was called for as the scheme for Educational Complexes did not provide funds towards cost of buildings for schools and hostels. I had taken advance actions for constructing hostel buildings by using funds received under Article 275(1) of the Constitution, BRGF, etc. Population of PVTGs in 15 out of 17 Micro Projects was within 2,500 to 5,000 each and within 7,500 each in the remaining two as per latest data. Every girl-child within the age group of 6 to 14 was identified and admitted in these Educational Complexes. Running expenses, which included remuneration of 6 cook-cum-helpers, 8 contractually-appointed teachers, and cost of fixtures including cots, TV sets, monthly stipend, provisions for annual excursion, contingency, etc., could be managed using liberal Central allocations. Only female workers were appointed contractually to run these Educational Complexes. An Educational Complex was envisaged in Malkangiri's"cut off" area badly affected by left-wing extremism. It was opened in a building complex originally constructed by district administration for a new Tahasil Office by spending 2 crore of RLTAP funds about five years back although there was no government approval to that effect. The building included a few quarters constructed thoughtlessly only to be abandoned later. These structures were now utilised after suitable repairs to run the new Educational Complex with admission of 240 ST girls.

As a result of fast-paced developmental works undertaken on Educational Complexes, Odisha ended up cornering nearly 40 percent of first-year's budget of Central Government for the scheme. State's PVTG population was a fraction of its tribal population, which in itself was only about 10 percent of tribal population in India. Other States were caught napping due to lack of preparedness to develop and furnish proposals. I always held that instead of claiming allocations from Central Government as a matter of entitlement and somehow reporting expenditure, it was better to claim more, or even less, depending upon absorptive capacity for quality expenditure. It was for a similar thought that I had enforced VAT law seriously on dealers instead of turning a blind eye to tax evasion, in the certainty of Centre reimbursing VAT losses. Central allocations based on absorptive capacity coupled with due enforcement of tax laws, for enhancing collections by States were intrinsic to a more progressive management of overall pool of Central resources across developmental schemes in States.

The newly-opened Educational Complexes admitted practically every ST girl who had been left out from the existing school system including from residential schools. I frequently visited these complexes to ensure fulfilment of schematic mandates. It tore my heart when I found that almost 25 percent of PVTG girls out of 250 enrolled in Educational Complex at Tumba in Ganjam district were reportedly born to unwed mothers, a result of hideous sexual exploitation of naïve and trusting tribal communities in remote places. It heartened me that we were opening up a world of opportunities to tribal girl-child through education.

Ekalavya Model for Tribal Residential Schools

During the Tenth Five Year Plan, Union Ministry of Tribal Affairs had introduced a new Scheme of 'Ekalavya Model Residential Schools' (EMRS) for tribal boys and girls from Classes VI-XII. Odisha was allotted 10 EMRSs out of 100 country-wide, which was in proportion to the overall tribal population ratio. The sanctioned students' strength of each EMRS was 420, with equal number of girls and boys. The schools were to be run by an autonomous Odisha Model Tribal Education Society (OMTES) constituted for this purpose at the State level.

Although the scheme was launched three years before my joining this Department, only 2 EMRSs, at Bhawanipur(Sundargarh) and Dhanghera (Mayurbhanj) had been made fully functional with their own buildings. Construction of school and hostel buildings, including residence of the Principal, had been assigned to IDCO, a body corporate under State Industries Department, and to Odisha Construction Corporation (OCC), a PSU under

Water Resources Department. Construction of EMRS complexes appeared to be their last priority. They were also demanding cost escalation for the already-delayed construction of buildings. Construction of EMRS complex at Pallupai(Rayagada) stood abandoned at the ground-floor roof level because the site was stated to be infested with snakes, mosquitoes and Naxalites, and a high-tension electric line was passing over it. The contractor had been paid ₹ 50 lakh to settle his arbitral claims out of the total cost of ₹ 2 crore of EMRS complex. So far EMRSs had been running from existing residential schools of the Department by admitting a limited number of students in lower classes. Admissions after Class X had not been done due to space constraints, except at Bhawanipur and Dhanghera. Appointment of teachers had not attracted any priority. All the model schools were expected to be affiliated with Central Board of Secondary Education but no initiative had been taken for that.

I called a meeting of heads and Engineers in charge of executing agencies. They were given a time-frame of six months to complete all the complexes, except for the building at Pallupai (Rayagada) abandoned after incurring infructuous expenditure of ₹ 50 lakh. Alternative site for this EMRS was identified near Rayagada and OCC was given one year's time to develop the complex. In the meantime, estimated cost of this new EMRS complex had increased to ₹ 3 crore against availability of ₹ 1.50 crore. Additional funds were mobilised from RLTAP, BRGF and Article 275(1) of the Constitution to execute the scheme. The same executing agency which had heavily defaulted in the past, completed EMRS complexes within the revised timelines which only established that there were no capacity constraints. What was lacking was the desire to implement the projects with a sense of accountability. I had warned executing agencies that in the event of further delay, the officers in charge should remain prepared to face charges of atrocities against STs under the relevant provisions of SC&ST (Prevention of Atrocities) Act. I also took steps to make contractual appointments of teachers to fill up vacancies in all EMRSs. It ensured that functioning of these model schools commenced as soon as developmental works were completed. Since EMRSs were largely in remote locations, it was felt essential to construct quarters for teachers too, for which funds received under Article 275(1) of the Constitution, BRGF and RLTAP were utilised.

Within six months, all 10 EMRSs started functioning from their own premises. Although the EMRS complex in Rayagada was not fully completed, the model school started running from the new location as soon as 50 percent of the complex (ground floor) was completed. It was a much better option than running the school from an existing residential Girls' High School of the Department which had limited space. Finally, this complex turned out to be the best among all.

A sad side of the EMRS at Pungar (Koraput) was that the contractor had to abandon the ST girls hostel building and run away as he could not fulfil the demands of the son of local tribal MP, who himself was an important elected office-bearer of Zila Parishad. I had to warn the MP and his son with a clear message that the matter would be brought to the notice of Chief Minister if they ever visited the site or approached the contractor anywhere before the hostel was completed. The warning worked. The hostel along with a boundary wall was completed in a record time of six months involving a new contractor.

I felt rewarded when a student from its very first batch of EMRS Pungar (Koraput) secured 3rd position in Joint Entrance Examination for admission in State's Government Engineering Colleges. Coming from a poor economic background, the advance deposit money of ₹ 50,000 for appearing in counselling session was raised by local ITDA officials through voluntary contributions. SBI,Jeypore of was requested to sanction him a loan, which could be repaid when he started drawing regular scholarship after admission.

Another innovation I could bring in EMRS Schools was additional remuneration of ₹ 2,000 per month to teachers of Science, Mathematics and English provided that 20 percent students succeeded in qualifying the entrance examination for admission in Engineering and Medical courses. Subject matter teachers of these schools which did not provide Arts and Commerce subjects were required to take extra classes after school hours to prepare the students for the joint entrance examinations. As Chairman of OMTES, I had also issued instructions that teachers should be allowed free cooked food in the hostel's mess, which hardly resulted in extra cost, but helped in improving food quality. It was always possible to feed 15 teachers within the meals prepared daily for 420 students and other attendants.

In spite of original delay in making EMRSs fully operational, Odisha became the first State to complete all 10 EMRSs in the country. Since the Government of Assam failed to implement the scheme, Union Ministry of Tribal Affairs diverted the two EMRSs of this State to other States. Odisha benefitted in getting another EMRS in the process. I proposed opening it in Sukinda(Jajpur), where 13 tribals had been killed in police firing when in order to protect their land they had agitated against the construction of a compound wall by TATA Group for their proposed steel plant. I felt this would assuage their feelings and found a suitable patch of 25 acres of land adjacent to the Nilachal Ispat Steel Plant. Revenue Department and district administration were requested to alienate this land in favour of the proposed EMRS. Interestingly, the local MLA and Finance Minister under whom I had worked as Commissioner Commercial Taxes seemed to have vested interest in this piece of Government land. Villages around the land were dominated by SC population who were used as a tool of protest against transfer of this land for the proposed model school exclusively for tribal students. I sent a blunt message through District Collector to the Minister that in case his supporters continued to create problems, the matter would be brought to the notice of Chief Minister. As funds for the new EMRS were yet to be received, I persuaded a friend and colleague Ashok Mahadev Dalvai heading Odisha Mining Corporation (OMC) to contribute CSR funds of ₹ 25 lakh for raising a compound wall to protect the land. Soon enough funds were also received from Central Government. My time in the Department was over when about 70 percent of construction work had been completed.

From Elementary to Higher ST/SC Education in 8 KBK Districts

State Government had decided to upgrade 8 departmental residential high schools, one each in 8 KBK districts to Higher Secondary level in Science and Commerce subjects but without earmarking budget provisions. No serious thought had been given to recruitment of qualified teachers nor to development of other logistics, such as additional class rooms, laboratories, hostels, and library. Simply admission of Class-X pass-outs of existing Secondary Schools along with few others had been made in Class-XI. One such school in the worst Naxal-affected Bandhugaon(Koraput) did not have facility of even adequate drinking water in the high school which was proposed for upgrading. The existing school building itself was on private land and the son of the original landowner had refused to believe that his father had actually donated the land to Government orally for opening the high school years back. The problem was solved by offering contractual appointment to the land owner.

I visited all 8 upgraded high schools and saw to it that a regular Headmaster was posted in each. Proposals for creating posts of Principal, subject teachers, laboratory assistants, hostel cook-cum-attendants and other associated posts were got approved from Finance Department after pursuing them on a day-to-day basis. I got building plans for additional classrooms, hostels, laboratories, etc. prepared and issued instructions to ITDAs of tribal districts to execute these projects departmentally at break-neck speed. In Nuapada, Balangir and Sonepur, construction of new buildings, including hostels, was similarly taken up through respective Blocks under the supervision of Rural Works Department. In these cases too, Finance Department, usually very conservative in creating new posts, was quick to approve my proposal for creating new posts on the condition that the proposed appointments should be made on contractual basis. Within a short time, subject teachers were in position. Although reservation law did not apply to contractual appointments, recruitment was made in accordance with reservation provisions wherever ST&SC candidates were available. Another creative solution applied was to maintain the overall reservation ratio against total number of posts, but not subject wise.

Each KBK District received about ₹ 25 to 30 crore under RLTAP besides almost an equal amount under BRGF. These schemes had inbuilt flexibility in funds utilisation. It was thus not necessary to depend on State Plan separately to create infrastructure for upgrading educational institutions. Special provisions were made for granting stipends to students and remuneration of teachers under RLTAP and other Non-Plan schemes. Within a period of less than a year, the desired missing logistics were put in place. The ratio of 90:10 between ST&SC students was maintained for admission. More SC students were allowed in Sonepur as the school was located in a non-tribal SC populated area. As in the case of EMRSs, provisions were made for residential accommodation of teachers as rented houses in remote places were difficult to find. Teachers were given the option to have free food along with students in hostels, although there were not many takers. Those teaching Science, Mathematics and English were offered additional incentive of ₹ 2,000 per month for extra classes if at least 20 percent boarders qualified the joint entrance examination for medical and engineering courses. The educational environment of upgraded high schools improved steadily. A few students got into engineering and medical courses after a couple of years. After I demitted office, I was told that my successor discontinued the incentives introduced during my tenure for otherwise poorly-paid teachers.

I believe that it is in the interest of STs/SCs to get educated in an inclusive and competitive educational environment, especially after secondary level, in order to get assimilated in the mainstream with broader mindsets. Since the Department did not have expertise to administer higher education, I proposed supporting more hostel facilities for ST&SC students in colleges under Higher Education Department and to provide funds for extra subject teachers, if necessary, for special coaching. Luckily, Chief Secretary liked my proposal which was also approved by Chief Minister Naveen Patnaik unhesitatingly. It was decided not to upgrade Secondary Schools of ST&SC Development Department any more.

54 Residential High Schools for ST Girls Usher Parity with ST Boys

Exclusive residential high schools for ST boys stood established in all 118 Scheduled Area Blocks of Odisha. But, 54 of these Blocks did not have any residential high school exclusively for ST girls. I took in-principle approval of Chief Minister and also managed to get ₹ 25 crore at supplementary stage to start construction in one go of 54 schools along with hostel buildings. Additional funds were mobilised from other ongoing programmes. Standard plans for classrooms, hostels, teachers' quarters etc. were prepared and circulated to ITDAs to execute the work departmentally, if capable contractors were found unwilling to complete the building complexes within 6 months. Strength of boarders from Classes VI-X was capped at 50 per class. Additionally, 10 percent SC girls could be admitted. This raised the total strength of ST&SC boarders to 275 per school and 14,850 across all 54 new schools.

As had been decided, the new residential ST Girls High Schools became functional from the next educational session, except three in Kandhamal district, which had been terribly affected by ethnic conflicts and communal violence.

More on the ethnic and communal violence anon. When approval for the one-time capital cost of ₹ 25 crore at the supplementary stage had been taken, I had consciously avoided mentioning the recurring liabilities to operate the new institutions which called for creation of new posts. As a back-up, Director OPEPA had already been persuaded to sanction posts of Shiksha Sahayaks for departmental ST&SC schools after factoring additional requirements, including those of upcoming residential ST Girls' High Schools at a pupil-teacher ratio of 40:1. I succeeded in my strategy and Finance Department approved the proposal for creating teaching and non-teaching staff when the new institutions became functional. Earmarking posts of cook-cum-attendants for STs in all the new schools and hostels created some heartburn among SCs and other intermediary communities considering that in old residential schools, these posts had been appropriated by them. President of cook-cum-attendants association, an SC, threatened to go on strike with his followers, though on a different ground, i.e. demanding 100 percent increase in remuneration to ventilate his anger for hiring cook-cum-attendants from STs only.

Rationalisation of Admissions in Hostels

In addition to establishing new educational institutions and stabilising existing ones, it was necessary to rationalise admissions in the large number of departmental residential schools called Sevashrams, Ashrams, Kanyashrams and High Schools. These institutions had been opened in the past with varying strengths of boarders. In some residential schools, boarders' strength from Classes I-VIII was 50 on average. In others, it was up to 100 in Classes I-X, while in a few others it was more than 300. In consultation with Headmasters, District Welfare Officers and Project Administrators of ITDAs, I got the number of boarders in each Class and every institution rationalised. The norm would be 50 boarders in each Class. Depending on number of teachers and hostel capacity, the number of boarders could be enhanced.

It was also resolved that residential schools would allow boarding to students enrolled in Classes I-V if there was no school within a kilometre, and in Classes VI-VII if their native village was more than 5 km away. For Classes IX-X, the hostel eligibility norm was a distance of 10 km or above. This decision, along with implementation of schemes for opening new 100-seater 1,004 ST Girls' Hostels, 54 new ST Girls' High Schools, 11 Ekalavya Schools and 8 upgraded higher secondary schools led to enhancing the total strength of ST boarders across all residential schools in the State taken together by more than 100 percent. The number of boarders in tribal schools crossed 3.5 lakh, signalling a massive jump within a period of less than two years.

Hard Landing of Soft Skills Vital to Promote Tribal Education

Mentoring and support was provided voluntarily by officials of ITDA, Koraput to enable a meritorious tribal student ranked third to handle the counselling sessions successfully to secure admission in engineering course. It was symptomatic of the need to systemically supplement the merit of tribal students with soft skills and financial wherewithal. They might not benefit from reservations for them in technical education if special arrangements are not made to meet large financial deposits' requirements for participating in counselling sessions before admission. I, thus, proposed creation of a corpus of ₹ 2 crore for eligible tribal students desirous to study in engineering and medical courses. The scheme proposed interest-free advance towards counselling fee to those qualifying the entrance examinations refundable by them on receipt of post-metric scholarship subsequently. This could help in merit-based utilisation of seats reserved for ST students appearing for engineering and medical courses.

Mobilisation of ₹ 2 crore was not difficult. Local heads of Central PSUs agreed to make CSR contributions for this noble cause. For administering this fund, a separate society headed by Secretary for ST&SC Development would be constituted. The proposal was appreciated when Tribes Advisory Committee considered and approved it. Subsequently, Memorandum of Association and Bye Laws of the Society were drafted and put up for approval of Chief Minister after obtaining concurrence of Finance and Law Departments. Despite repeated reminders, it remained unattended for more than six months. In the meanwhile, unable to withstand the delay, I got the Bye Laws of OMTES amended through a resolution at my level to provide temporary advances to students from a separate fund proposed to be created. Shortly after this, the proposal submitted for approval of Chief Minister came back with some needless queries when the whole exercise had become futile. Eventually the scheme I had proposed suffered a premature death after my departure from the department.

Launching Innovative Tribal Education: Ramakrishna Mission

Socio-economic development of tribal communities in the State despite being a stated priority had not attracted attention to the desired extent. Interventions of NGOs barring a few exceptions were louder in words but in substance amounted to no more than skimming the surface at best or serving hidden agendas at worst. For a large number of NGOs, the cause of tribal communities remained a source of their own livelihood. Their superficial and flowery articulation was often taken for action by their donors which included Central Government.

Rama Krishna Mission (RKM) was a stellar exception to this generality. When I was Director, Tribal Welfare during 1991-93, I had requested them to either open or take up management of some tribal residential schools. RKM had expressed inability due to lack of manpower and decreasing number of youngsters joining RKM order. When I revived my old proposal after taking over as Secretary for ST&SC Development, Swami Vishokanandji in charge of Puri RKM Math agreed. RKM President and General Secretary at Belur

Math in Kolkata also agreed after their initial hesitation. To open a residential school from Classes V-XII exclusively for tribal boys in a district of Southern Division, suitably placed land needed to be given to them.

After inspecting various sites, Swamiji chose Hatmuniguda village (Rayagada). It had 100 acres of Government land classified as 'Parvat' which was not useful for agricultural purpose. Bhaskar Sharma, Collector Rayagada enthusiastically submitted a proposal for change in the classification of land to Member, Board of Revenue, besides initiating the lease proposal to be sent to State Government. Such proposals did not usually draw official attention with a sense of priority. I met Santosh Kumar, Member Board of Revenue, a stickler for rules and allergic to external influence, seeking his attention. He got it examined quickly which was followed with a number of objections. Compliances were arranged. As soon as approval for change in classification of land was obtained, R&DM Department sought approval of Cabinet for its long-term leasing to RKM for the stated purpose. Union Ministry of Tribal Affairs was impressed with the work I was doing, particularly on tribal education. Soon after G.B. Mukherjee, who had served as Chief Administrator of KBK districts, took charge as Secretary, a new scheme had been introduced for Innovative Projects to be fully funded by Central Government under Article 275(1) of the Constitution. I detailed out the innovative aspects of the proposed RKM fully residential educational complex for tribals. Union Ministry examined the proposal from all angles and for conformity with notified guidelines on innovative projects. They liked the idea and suggested adding vocational components for any school drop-outs. A Detailed Project Report (DPR) was prepared, with cost estimated at ₹ 17 crore. The proposal got approved almost instantly. With the complete support of Collector Rayagada, construction of approach road, drawl of electric line and installation of a bore well got done within two months under on-going programmes. Local MLA Dambarudhar Ulaka, although from the opposition party, contributed the cost of transformer from his LAD grant.

I now requested Swamiji to open the school from academic session of the year 2008. Despite Swamiji's initial apprehensions, it was decided to put up temporary structures for classrooms and dormitories to accommodate two sections of 40 students each in Class-V and an Office-cum-Guest House for teachers and staff. It was agreed that tribal students to be admitted would be from all four districts of Rayagada, Koraput, Nabarangpur and Malkangiri equally i.e. 25 percent students from each district. They would be selected for admission through an entrance test only from families below the poverty line. The school with English as medium of instruction would be affiliated with Central Board of Secondary Education.

As planned, temporary structures were ready in time. Chief Minister Naveen Patnaik, as requested by RKM management was approached for inaugurating the school on 19 July 2008. He agreed subject to weather conditions allowing landing of his helicopter on the site. Though the date had been fixed and invitation cards printed in consultation with his office, just three days before the inauguration I was called upon to explain as to how Chief Minister's name was printed on the invitation card without his consent! It was outrageous. I had personally discussed the matter with him and he had happily agreed to attend. Only thereafter Secretary to Chief Minister, B.K. Patnaik had told me to go ahead with printing of invitation cards. Officers in his office rather than reminding Chief Minister about his commitment had issued a letter in bad taste to seek my explanation. I sent a reply stating facts and stopped distribution of invitation cards. It was a clarion call not to take political leaders at face value.

Chief Minister Naveen Patnaik in my assessment was not negative in matters of development, though nonchalant many a times. Observing actual progress on ground, he became exceptionally enthusiastic in the matters of opening of 100-seater 1,004 ST girls' hostels. He would be happy and supportive if any work done by his officers added to his popularity. He would allow functional freedom provided such liberty did not invite any embarrassment or controversy for him. I liked this attitude which gave me complete control of any situation even if Minister of the Department did not like any scheme or proposal. On file he would invariably approve my proposals and reject changes, if any, made by Minister. The risk which I was willing to take happily in the event of any action leading to adversely impacting his carefully cultivated image of being ruthless against corrupt officials suited me perfectly. What made me happy and got me going was the opportunity to work on rural and tribal development projects. I did not like to postpone the inaugural function to another date and General Secretary of RKM from Belur Math came to grace the inaugural function and blessed the 80 tiny-tots who had enrolled for admission in Class V from remote villages of the four tribal districts. Development of permanent infrastructure i.e. hostels, class rooms, etc. got going rapidly simultaneously.

I was transferred mid-November 2008. As I was told, my successor did not care to visit the upcoming institution situated in the heart of an area hit by left wing extremism. Only a few senior officers ventured to visit remote tribal districts those days. State Government too did not like to place senior officers at risk of Naxal-misadventure. District Collector was head of Governing Body of the Society created for running the school, with Swami-in-charge of local RKM Centre as its Secretary, as per Memorandum of Association and Bye Laws. Till Bhaskar Sharma was transferred from the district after a year the school's development did not suffer. His successor wanted SC students to be admitted in the school, which the Bye Laws did not permit, besides which financial support from Central Government and allocation of land by State Government was also for residential education exclusively for tribal students.

In November 2009, I left for Delhi on Central Deputation but remained in touch with the Swamiji of RKM. My two successive successors in the Department were indifferent to this innovative project. I tried in every possible way to prevent the tiny-tots from suffering due to inadequacies of an indifferent State administration. As I was informed by Swamiji, the new Secretary scoffed at difficulties faced by the governing Society and initiatives that needed to be taken with his callous observation that with the princely sum of ₹ 17 crore, he could have arranged quality education for tribal students at Duke or Harvard University. He declined to endorse a proposal for an additional ₹ 5 crore to meet enhanced cost of buildings and additional works like staff quarters to Union Ministry of Tribal Affairs. The new District Collector and ex-officio chairman, ITDA, Gunupur through which funds were channelized for executing the project, was not as prompt as his predecessor. I called him to explain in a non-invasive manner the school's objectives, provisions of Bye Laws, and specific Government order which did not permit non-tribal students to be admitted in this residential school. He saw sense and became prompt in release of funds thereafter.

In the face of resistance in endorsing the funds' proposal to Union Ministry of Tribal Affairs, I spoke to my counterpart there requesting him to explain to incumbent Secretary ST&SC Development in the State to reassure him that allocations for innovative projects were not from the usual share of State Government and that the revised estimates could be sent with the caveat that the amount sanctioned to RKM school should not be from Odisha's normal share of allocations. At the same time, I called the Secretary to request him to visit the school to be convinced that there was no better institution for quality education of tribal students in the State. He was told to forward the pending proposal for additional grant to Ministry of Tribal Affairs with whatever reservations, besides verifying that support to RKM in Odisha was mere peanuts compared to what was provided by State Governments in Tripura, West Bengal and Chhattisgarh for educational development of tribal students. My advice was heeded. Additional requirement was sanctioned by Central Government without delay. I was happy that incumbent Secretary, ST&SC Development became positive after his visit to the RKM facility. Field visits help in internalising the realities and conceptualising policies.

I returned to Odisha cutting short my Central Deputation in January 2012, and over a year later in 2013, got posted as Chief Administrator, KBK districts. Further development of this institution was taken up which included sports facilities, vocational training centre, health centre, etc. with more resources allocated by Ministry of Tribal Affairs and under RLTAP, besides CSR funds of corporates mobilised by Swamiji. State Government started contributing to partly meet its recurring expenses. I was happy to see the problems of naxalism in the area diminishing and the institution contributing immensely to tribal education. I had been inspired by the work of RKM in education in the most difficult areas in other States, recalling in particular my visit to their school for tribal students near Agartala established during the peak of insurgency in Tripura. This institution with residential facilities exclusively for tribal students entrapped by insurgent groups during dark days greatly contributed to mainstreaming them. Tripura arguably became and remains the most peaceful State in North East Region since then. In Narayanpur(Chhattisgarh) too, RKM ran one of the best schools exclusively for tribal students. Alas, the attitude of Odisha was hardly similar to the pioneers in other States. Officialdom remained unenthusiastic towards the eager students, innovative institution, and its proactive monk manager in its formative phase. The situation changed with the passage of time, though much more remains to be done.

Partial Success at Rationalising Student Scholarships, Staff Remunerations

In July 1991, monthly pre-matric scholarship for ST boarders was revised to ₹ 150 for boys and ₹ 155 for girls by State Government. The respective amount was revised to ₹ 200 and ₹ 225 in 1994 and to ₹ 300 and ₹ 325 in 1999. I now pleaded repeatedly to raise the amount at least to the same level as offered to destitutes in State-supported NGO-managed orphanages (₹ 500/ month). Despite recognising its gross insufficiency to meet the boarding costs and irregular releases by Finance Department, State Government revised it to a mere ₹ 400 for boys and ₹ 425 for girls. I tried to supplement the cash with kind and managed to get my proposal approved, despite resistance from Secretary, Food Supplies & Consumer Affairs, for making PDS rice available to all residential schools and hostels for ST&SC boys and girls at the same rate as to families below the poverty line. I had been unsure of being able to assure that improvement in tribal education with investment in cheaper rice for ST/SC boarders would bring corresponding political dividends. Thankfully, the matter got settled at the level of Chief Secretary.

Central Government had set up Sachar Committee to look into the relative backwardness of minorities and to make recommendations to address their historical deficit. The Muslim and Christian population in Odisha taken together was about 4 percent of the total. For their socio-economic development, in pursuance of one of its many recommendations, merit-based monthly pre-matric scholarship of ₹ 600 per student was introduced by Central Government with cost sharing of 75:25 between Centre and States. Since a good number of tribal boys and girls in residential schools and hostels were from the Christian community, it was utterly discriminatory to have two rates of pre-matric scholarship for two sets of ST students. Political controversy was also inevitable as BJP which was a ruling partner could communalise the discrimination. Central Government did not have any pre-matric scholarship scheme for STs/ SCs. I did not hesitate in putting forth my assessment. I advised Secretaries in Union Ministries of Tribal Affairs and SJ&E that it was vital to introduce a merit-based pre-matric scholarship for ST/SC students on par with minority students. My advice remained unheeded despite being appreciated. Only Union Secretary of Minority Welfare chided me for what he said was perverted thinking on my part!

I presented my analysis before State Government and proposed that monthly pre-matric scholarship for ST/SC boarders should be raised on par with minority students. Alternatively, monthly rates for scholarship to ST/SC boys/ girls should be raised from ₹ 400/425 to ₹ 500/525 respectively with availing of pre-matric scholarship for minority students too at the same rate. My alternative proposal was approved by State Government. It did not like to be seen opposing schemes meant for minority communities introduced by Central Government in pursuance of recommendations of Sachar Committee. At the same time, it would not have been expedient to support higher rates of scholarship for students of minority communities than for those belonging to ST/SC. Indeed, almost the entire Christian population in Odisha consists of ST/SC converts, and barring a few isolated cases, their socio-economic conditions have not undergone any visible improvement after conversion. Odisha followed the middle path without inviting any controversy. It became one of the first States to quietly implement Central schemes aimed at addressing the development deficit of minority communities.

The experience with opening residential schools and hostels for tribal students showed that financial implications are not visualised credibly, what to speak of with exactitude, particularly when politically-expedient decisions are suddenly announced. Moreover, recurring costs rarely receive attention of planners even as physical infrastructure could be created by utilising the unutilised funds, and by dovetailing and accessing resources under various programmes supported by Central/State Governments. In the cases of ST and SC girls/ boys' schools and hostels, there was no way to avoid recurring cost towards scholarship and other establishment charges. Maintenance of residential schools and hostels required appointment of a cook-cum-attendant for every 50 boarders. In older residential schools and hostels, almost all attendants were male and mostly non-STs. This had resulted in exploitation of innocent ST boarders in many forms. There were instances of ST girls being exploited sexually by hostel attendants and superintendents. I had handed over a couple of teachers officiating as hostel superintendents, who in connivance with cook-cum-attendants had misappropriated pre-matric scholarship by showing false enrolment in hostels, to the police.

I, thus, issued strict instructions for appointment of ST candidates from the local area as cook-cum-attendants. For ST girls' hostels, hostel superintendent had to be a lady teacher and cook-cum-attendants ladies only from tribal communities. This action displeased vested interests. Office bearers of association of cook-cum-attendants who were mostly non-STs, raised alarm at discontinuation of what they believed was a legitimate prerogative of members of their castes. They represented before Chief Minister alleging discrimination against SCs in the appointment of cook-cum-attendants. While mismanagement in hostels in the past had never been raised, now with appointment of ST males/females as attendants it suddenly became a chorus. The attendants who were being paid monthly remuneration of about ₹ 3,200 besides free food had been generally happy. But now through their association, they raised a demand for minimum wages of ₹ 7,000 per month. In the consideration of this demand, politics now was played out.

With the date of General Elections approaching, I was asked by Chief Minister to process the proposal for enhancing monthly remuneration of cooks-cum-attendants from ₹ 3,200 to ₹ 7,000. The proposal for marginally enhancing remuneration for these workers had been turned down earlier by Finance Department with the approval of Chief Minister. Labour Department after examination had observed that attendants did not work for more than six hours a day to be qualified for minimum wages in terms of the relevant legal provisions. In my examination, I observed that trained graduates appointed as Shiksha Sahayaks and teachers engaged contractually to manage elementary educational institutions were being paid a mere ₹ 1,500 per month. Existing inverted disparity with cooks-cum-attendants getting paid monthly remuneration of ₹ 3,200/- besides free food, would become even more stark and unjustifiable. About 2,500 fresh ST men/women who had recently been appointed as attendants were happy with the present remuneration. I recommended to Government that remuneration of temporary teachers/ Shiksha Sahayaks should in no case be less than those of cooks-cum-attendants and submitted a proposal accordingly. Labour Department remained neutral and Finance Department maintained stony silence this time. Chief Minister did not approve the proposed remuneration of Shiksha Sahayaks and temporary teachers, but approved the proposed remuneration of cooks-cum-attendants, which thus became more than four times higher than those of trained graduate teachers appointed temporarily. Such penny wise, pound foolish decisions taken for assumed political gains are available in dozens for just a dime. Hollow words and tokenism in tribal education in particular have ruled for many a decade.

Misunderstanding with Minister, déjà vu

Chaitanya Charan Majhi, Minister for ST&SC Development and OBC & Minorities Welfare, was a seasoned tribal leader with more than 40 years' political experience. He had worked as Deputy Minister in Indira Gandhi's Council of Ministers in the early 1970s. Although he was very happy to welcome my posting, his erratic behaviour became too pronounced to be misunderstood after a year had gone by. Besides voicing his displeasure against Director for Tribal Welfare who was actually an energetic and experienced officer fully committed to his duties, Minister frequently wrote to Chief

Secretary and Chief Minister seeking his transfer. When I argued in the Director's favour by drawing out his excellent credentials, he thought I was extending undue protection to him. I met and explained my understanding of the situation to Chief Secretary when my opinion on his transfer was sought. I emphasised that in case the transfer was a must in order to stem the growing disquiet in the department which was liable to diffuse the focus away from tasks on hand, the transfer should not be taken as a measure of the officer's incompetence or punishment. He was transferred, only to be substituted by an officer known more for his vices than virtues! His back-biting habit and loose morals endeared him to the Minister's office more than his ability to work. Soon enough I found the Minister far more adversarial towards me, perhaps emboldened by the posting of an officer of his choice as Director, Tribal Welfare, even though he was aware that I enjoyed the confidence of Chief Minister. In transfers of a senior field functionary, Chief Minister in variably approved my proposal, rejecting any change suggested by Minister. This was possibly hurting him more though he had never made any direct observation to me.

Construction of 100-seated 1,004 ST girls' hostels neared completion and 54 ST girls' high schools were in full swing. Despite having approved the sites earlier, Minister wanted to change some of them on political considerations. He also passed orders in a few cases to stop the functioning of a few newly-constructed hostels in villages in and around his constituency in Mayurbhanj. I did not want to join issues with him as I was sure of vested interests at play to influence his simple-mindedness. More so also, any frontal confrontation would lead to derailment of a large number of projects under implementation. Thus, wherever it was feasible to change the sites of new projects, I had no problem in heeding his directions.

In the case of a new residential ST Girls' High School, when Minister instructed the Project Administer of ITDA concerned to change the site, the local MP from Jharkhand Mukti Morcha, filed a Writ Petition in High Court. To uphold Minister's wishes, I ensured that construction work was taken onto the new site so fast that by the time the case came up for hearing after about three months, ground-floor slab-casting of school and hostel buildings had been done. Advocate General presented a status report along with photographs of the site in the Court. Orders of 'status quo' passed by High Court on opening of the new school, did not prevent further construction as the position taken by the department was that construction work had progressed considerably when High Court passed orders against change of site. I also personally spoke to the litigant MP, who agreed not to pursue his case in Court. I had argued that opening of the school in this other village would benefit ST girls from the earlier site to be admitted as boarders in the residential school. Work proceeded ahead smoothly.

In a note to Chief Minister, Minister had cited certain ST girls' hostels and a few residential schools, which according to him were in bad shape. Curiously, he also complained that I was forcing field officials to complete hostels without giving them adequate time! These insinuations were irrational and without foundation. In monthly review meetings held at regional level, progress of each project was gauged while fixing milestones to be achieved during the next month. I had issued clear instructions to executing agencies to keep records of the sites of new school and hostel buildings, before starting and after completion. They furnished visual proof through photographs of monthly progress achieved during their presentations. It was, thus, easy for me to explain the status of infrastructure that had been added as compared to what existed earlier against each institution cited by Minister in his instant communication to Chief Minister. The photographic evidence of construction of schools and hostels at sites sought to be shifted by Minister elsewhere gave a compelling picture of why these could not now be closed having already spent a huge amount of money to make them functional. I humbly pointed out that rather than calling for faster execution of infrastructure projects for schools and hostels, Minister was unnecessarily disturbed by work being done in a time-bound manner. Office of Chief Minister did not pay any heed to Minister's complaint. At least I did not receive any adverse reaction for my proactivity.

Minister had never uttered any misgivings to me directly about implementation of projects. When his surprising communication to Chief Minister came to me for comments, I realised that his personal staff, some outsiders, and even his elder son-in-law, who happened to be a non-tribal advising in office matters without any formal job assignment to him, were prone to take his signature on drafts without explaining the content to him. The new Director, Tribal Welfare who had to leave the Department after some months when I was about to put up draft charges against him, was found aggravating the situation. It was ironical that the simple-minded tribal leader was in the grip of vested interests, which meant that some of his actions were against the interests of his own community. Noting that I was not able to endorse or implement every belated and irrational order, he assumed that I was tacitly supporting his political opponents. I felt a strong déjà vu, as though my experience as Director, Tribal Welfare about 13 years back was repeating itself. The Minister on that occasion too was simple and honest, albeit misguided.

Making a Cooperative Corporation Stand on its Feet

State ST&SC Development Finance Corporation became defunct when the central funds were stopped due to lack of recovery of past loan assistance. The State Government was also unable to provide support from its own resources. Tribal Development Cooperative Corporation (TDCC), an organisation critically important for marketing Minor Forest Produce, upon which the traditional tribal economy rested historically, had become defunct too. Employees were not being paid. A good number had availed benefits under a voluntary retirement scheme introduced with British aid. Others anticipating its revival, and some involved in misappropriation, had remained with TDCC. Chairperson TDCC, a political appointee, was at loggerheads with the MD, an Indian Forest Service officer, whose salary was being paid by the department due to inability of TDCC to generate business and incomes. Another officer was persuaded to join as his substitute, but only after giving her a clear assurance that Chairperson would not interfere in day-to-day administration and the Department would leave no stone unturned for TDCC's revival. After bamboo was nationalised by State Government, tribal artisans subsisting on bamboo craft had lost their livelihood substantially as procurement of raw materials at commercial rates was not economically viable. State Government had delegated powers for fixing support price for other Minor Forest Produce to Gram Panchayats. Each Gram Panchayat would fix its own price differently from others, while many were not even aware of this responsibility. State Government had stopped supporting TDCC in its procurement of Minor Forest Produce from tribal communities.

I found that Central Government had announced a new scheme to incentivise participation of State agencies in procuring surplus foodgrains for PDS. State Government was providing highly subsidised rice under PDS which made it incumbent to make higher procurement of paddy/rice from producers to meet the need. FCI, with its limited presence in the State, had agreed to take rice procured by State agencies. Sensing emerging opportunities for business given the presence of TDCC branches in remote areas of predominantly tribal districts, I persuaded Food Supply & Consumer Welfare Department to involve TDCC also in procurement of paddy/rice, which offered a good margin. Collectors of tribal Districts were called upon to extend logistic support to TDCC branches to ensure timely delivery of rice procured from farmers and payments to producers as soon as moneys were received from FCI. This arrangement worked like magic and that too without requiring any investment. Within a year, TDCC started paying full salary to its employees. Banks were now willing to extend cash credit facilities without Government guarantee. The new lady MD, originally from Nagaland, meticulously monitored procurements and TDCC became vibrant once again. With improved cash flow and profits, TDCC started intervention in other areas like procurement of organic turmeric and ginger from tribal growers. It was no more dependent upon State Government support for existence or to run its business.

Two Vital Schemes for Economic Development

Two main schemes under which the department received sizeable financial allocations from Union Ministry of Tribal Affairs were SCA and Assistance under Article 275(1) of the Constitution. In reality, allocations under these two schemes had shrunk due to failure in utilisation of funds received in earlier years. Senior officers in charge either out of ignorance or otherwise incurred expenditure as if allocations were discretionary grants at their disposal. Plenty of opportunities existed to bridge the critical infrastructure gap under Article 275(1). There was also enormous scope for forming Self-Help Groups to implement income-generating schemes under the SCA with the support of financial institutions. Yet, unspent balances remained, notwithstanding that ITDAs had been spending funds in the name of community lift irrigation projects and sprinkler irrigation sets and 100 percent subsidy was being given without giving attention to feasibility of such schemes and by ignoring the relevant guidelines. Tribal areas being the origin of a large number of perennial and semi-perennial rivers and rivulets, it was desirable to utilise maximum amount for developing minor irrigation projects like diversion channels, check dams, water harvesting structures, etc. followed by land development for terraced cultivation. These projects helped in generating self-employment and wage employment. In villages with no access to institutional finance, beneficiaries could contribute labour equal to the loan for land-based projects whereas the cost of material components not exceeding 50 percent of projects could be met from SCA. Importantly, transparent procedures were laid down for documentation in order to avoid fudging or manipulation of accounts.

In a hitherto untried move, I had initiated a massive capacity building and training programme for tribal youth in contract management in order to involve them in implementing smaller infrastructure projects and reduce dependence on non-local non-tribal contractors. I got a manual for training tribal youth in contract management drafted in consultation with engineers from State RD Department. With some hand-holding by engineering personnel of executing agencies, it was possible to ensure local participation which in turn served to bring about sustainability of developmental interventions. After gaining experience, status of these contractors could be upgraded.

A key factor responsible for mismatch between outlay and outcomes was lack of correspondence between theoretical framework of plans and implementation on ground. Administrators and advisors involved in conceptualising programmes lacked field exposure and understanding of ever-changing risk-prone environments. Supervisory officers in charge of programmes at State level did not perform regular field visits for reality check in implementing projects which ultimately became expenditure-driven. Misappropriation of funds could not be ruled out. For instance, I found large volumes of sprinkler sets worth crores having been procured in the name of promoting micro irrigation and use of plastics! This served hardly any productive purpose. No amount of post-mortem by fixing accountability could help if course correction did not take place structurally at regular intervals. The real test of any project or programme is indeed its ease of implementation in accordance with the defined objectives.

My attitude in administration had been target and accountability driven in every posting which also implied 'action for inaction'. Monitoring of projects to be implemented in a time bound manner was an essential pillar. I never felt that quality and quantity could be achieved by compromising one, but rather that the two were inter-twined. It was easier to achieve better and quicker results in tribal areas as the element of political and administrative interference was almost non-existent and sky was the limit for good work or improvement. Effective coordination with DRDAs, BDOs, etc. helped not only in avoiding repeating schemes and beneficiaries, but also in dovetailing of funds for developmental projects wherever possible with a transparent record keeping system.

Implementation of projects at times by tweaking rules and procedures and by reposing confidence in field functionaries gave wonderful results within a short time. Completion of new and also old/abandoned incomplete projects was ensured without resorting to departmental actions against officials in charge of those projects which inspired them to work harder. Odisha, which was considered a laggard at National level due to its poor track record on tribal development came to the forefront and started receiving allocations from Union Ministries of Tribal Affairs and SJ&E way higher than its normal entitlements. The same executing agencies shed their weaknesses and started travelling the extra mile to finish projects ahead of schedule and without compromising on quality. Luckily Secretaries in both Central Ministries concerned with my sector happened to be either Odias or from Odisha cadre and I enjoyed a good working relationship with them. Joint Secretaries and officers in these Ministries too became supportive once the change in indicators of development became visible in the State. The reality of 100-seated 1,004 ST girls' hostels, 54 new residential ST Girls' High Schools, 10 Ekalavya Model Schools for tribal students, 8 new higher secondary schools in KBK districts, and 19 educational complexes for girls of PVTGs could materialise within a period of less than two years.

Rural development in general and development of tribal communities and backward areas in particular was a subject which had been close to my heart. While working in the department earlier, I had submitted some proposals based on felt needs which included a Tribal Museum, Library building, and Auditorium within the compound of ST&SC Research-cum-Training Institute (STSCRTI) in Bhubaneswar, besides a Drip Irrigation Project to revive citrus plantations of tribal communities in Gajapati, and a critical road from Tumba(Ganjam) to Kainpur (Gajapati). Ministry of Tribal Affairs had approved and allocated funds for these projects but just prior to my leaving the department. My then successor had released funds for at least three of them: for the said critical road to RD Department, for Tribal Museum to IDCO, and for Drip Irrigation project to ITDA, Parlakhemundi.

After more than a decade I returned to find that the road had not been constructed though utilisation of funds had been reported! Funds for Drip

Irrigation stood misutilised leading to criminal/ departmental proceedings against a senior officer. The building for Tribal Museum had been constructed but the roof was leaking and walls had suffered due to seepage of water during rains causing heavy damage to artefacts inside. Tribal Museum project had caught the interest of CM Naveen Patnaik, but he was unhappy to see its deteriorated condition. He desired me personally to give attention to the Museum. I requested both MD and Chief Engineer of IDCO which had executed this project in the year 2000 to renovate it without charging any additional amount. They were asked to complete the renovation work to the satisfaction of Chief Minister who would review the status after six months. Perhaps, this was the only occasion when I used the name of any higher dignitary to extract work from an executing agency. Renovation work was taken up in right earnest and was completed within the specified time-frame. Repairs and painting of the compound including plantations and placement of flower pots was done tastefully using maintenance grant of STSCRTI. CM became happy to see the transformation. The Tribal Museum has since become an important land mark of Odisha's tourism.

After reviewing the other projects and visiting sites, I came to the conclusion that nothing could be done to revive the Drip Irrigation project. I wrote to both Chief Engineer, Rural Works and Secretary of RD Department to either refund the amount received for developing the critical road or face criminal charges for misappropriation and false utilisation certificates. Within a couple of months, the allocation was refunded! Allocations received for Auditorium and Library buildings had remained unutilised as civil deposits even after 12 years! Turning my attention to them, I managed to get civil deposits released from Finance Department. The old and dilapidated Library building was replaced by a new one, and Works Department also completed the Auditorium, both within 10 months. An unwilling department now completed these two projects within a record time without any cost escalation. There was no lack of capacity in executing projects in time. The real problems indeed were lethargy, lack of accountability and absence of appreciation for quality works. It could hardly be inspiring when manipulators with PR skills were rewarded routinely with appointment to key positions and risk-takers who batted straight were either found inconvenient on some nebulous count and side-tracked or made to suffer in a myriad of vindictive ways.

Dead Against Social Discrimination of SCs

The social problems faced by SCs, which constituted about 16.5 percent of State's population were different from those of ST population. SC population suffered far more due to landlessness than tribal communities. There were no major exclusive Central Sector Schemes or programmes for economic development for SCs, except for some allocations of SCA, which were a fraction of that received for tribal communities. SCA received was meant for family-oriented income-generating schemes in line with other similar ongoing income-generating schemes implemented through Panchayat Raj Department. SCCP was largely notional, being a budgetary mechanism for earmarking of funds in proportion of SC population. There was no exclusive major programmes or schemes of the State Government either. Post-matric scholarships granted to SC/ST students and incentives for inter-caste marriages involving SCs were administered under Centrally Sponsored Schemes.

The worst debilitating factor that affected SCs in the State, and perhaps elsewhere in the country too, is social discrimination. It is not difficult to observe that the parties in power had been more interested to use STs and SCs for political gains by providing lip service, treating them for years as if they were identically placed. It is important to understand that the hallmark of the caste society is its structural stratification. Historically, occupational specialisations and cultural variations had been the main reasons for caste segmentation. SCs traditionally known as "Harijans", bore a clear identity. Their social status was determined by persistence of stigma of untouchability, an easily identifiable phenomenon in society. Poverty and educational backwardness were concomitant, but not determinants of social discrimination against them. In traditional society, SCs did not receive the services of Brahmin priest, village barber and village washer man. Their entry into temples was resisted by conservative elements in society which belonged to higher castes. The test for specifying tribes were different from those applied to SCs. A community to be considered as ST was required to possess characteristics such as primitive technology, pre-literate language, cohesive social organisation, and community life limited within a small area and small population. A "Tribe" was treated as a 'social group' having fundamental features like definite territorial affiliation, comprehensive culture and mutual interdependence. Unlike SCs, STs did not suffer social discrimination of the same order and kind. A person could claim to be from SC or ST by birth alone.

Our Constitution did not permit practising untouchability and social discrimination in any form and those indulging in such atrocities could be proceeded against. In reality the vast majority of victims lacked awareness about legal and constitutional provisions and a few, though aware from both sides were often seen to be misusing or ignoring them. In an age-old practice in Keradagarh(Kendrapada), SCs were not allowed entry in Jagannath Temple and holes had been made in the compound wall from where they could see the temple deities. When on being mobilised by an NGO, SCs started opposing such brazen discrimination, all caste Hindus got united to confront them leading to serious unrest. District administration remained passive rather than invoking legal provisions against those rooting for continuance of discrimination. Government at political level looked the other way as if nothing was happening. Political leaders cutting across parties maintained neutrality in the fear of loss of their captive voters. As administrative head of ST&SC Development

Department, I entered into a dialogue with both sides to find a solution and to restore harmony. Though the upper caste leaders admitted in private that what was being practiced by them was a legal offence, they felt constrained to suddenly abandon the age-old practice. I succeeded in breaking this impasse. It would be hypocritical to think that similar humiliating practices were not being followed elsewhere.

An example of a diametrically opposite extreme was found in Angul where the upper caste Headmaster/ Principal in a departmental residential High School, a Group-B officer, was arrested for an alleged atrocity on the complaint of a SC District Welfare Officer holding equivalent status. The Headmaster did not offer his own chair to the visiting officer who treated this as her insult and filed a case of atrocity. She added that the Headmaster had washed the chair offered to her when she was leaving his office as a measure of purification which constituted atrocity against an SC officer. The Headmaster had to languish in jail without bail for about six months. As I came to know later, it was a case of misuse of legal provisions.

The worst example of social discrimination I saw being practiced by none other than State Government itself a few years later. An SC officer working as RDC of Central Zone, Cuttack was transferred within a few months of his posting as the famous Rath Yatra of Jagannath Puri was approaching. Under law, RDC was required to perform certain rituals which temple priests would not have allowed by an SC officer as apprehended by State Government!

OBC Politics in the State

About 50 percent of Odisha's population stood specified as SEBCs/ OBCs but practically no programmes existed exclusively for them. Despite creating a separate Department for OBC & Minorities Welfare, hardly any budget provisions existed for socio-economic development of these communities. State OBC Development Finance Corporation existed only on paper. Funds received from Central Government for construction of hostels for OBC students' years back had remained unutilised which rendered the State ineligible for further allocations. I managed to utilise those past allocations and having furnished utilisation certificates, became eligible for allocation of more than ₹ 4 crore by Union Ministry of SJ&E for opening new OBC hostels in Utkal University, University of Culture, P.N. College, Khordha, etc. OBC students did not receive scholarships under a Centrally Sponsored Scheme as State Government did not agree to budget provisions to provide matching State share. Indeed, many a times State Government was unable to provide the State share in Centrally Sponsored Schemes for boys and girls hostels meant for ST/ SC/ OBC students too.

A couple of interesting developments worth mentioning occurred after my joining the department. On the issue of reservation, particularly for SEBCs or OBCs, Biju Patnaik as Chief Minister, Odisha during his second term (1990-

95) having opposed implementation of Mandal Commission recommendations for SEBC reservations initially, took an about turn towards the end of his tenure. His Cabinet passed a resolution to provide 27 percent reservation for SEBCs in all State Government services in addition to 39 percent reservation already existing for STs/SCs put together. Supreme Court in the landmark Indra Sahni case capped reservation at 50 percent , but as a result of 27 percent reservation for SEBCs and 1 percent for physically handicapped, the total reservation percentage in Odisha had gone up to 67 percent.

Biju Patnaik did not win the next election to State Legislative Assembly, but it was unthinkable for the successor Government headed by J.B. Patnaik to reverse his decision on OBC reservation of 27 percent. The resolution was challenged in courts; initially in SAT which found reservation beyond 50 percent as *ultra vires*. State Government's appeal against the orders of SAT lay pending in High Court for long as a result of which fresh recruitments remained held up. Vacancies in different departments had increased as any recruitment with provisions of reservation beyond 50 percent on being challenged had been stayed by SAT and High Court.

ST&SC and OBC & Minority Welfare Departments being nodal in relation to reservation matters, had received references seeking clarification regarding actual ceiling on reservations. None had been issued by my predecessors. I examined the matter in consultation with Law Department after going through relevant judgments of the Apex Court, particularly Indra Sahani and Nagaraj vs. Union of India cases. Both judgments were categorical about the ceiling on reservation at 50 percent. I, therefore, issued a clarification to all departments citing these judgments and Article 141 of the Constitution according to which orders passed by the Apex Court became the law of the land. In the clarification, it was clearly mentioned that SEBC reservation had to be capped at 11 percent as 39 percent reservation for STs/SCs was already provided by Odisha Reservation of Vacancies in Posts and Services (for SCs & STs) Act in force since 1975. This circular issued under my signature on being presented to High Court by a litigant resulted in disposal of pending appeals and other petitions stating that the matter did not require further hearing as State Government had already conformed to the law laid by Apex Court! A full paragraph of my circular was reproduced in its Order by the High Court.

The clarificatory circular created a political storm of sorts despite having paved the way for fresh recruitments in various State Government services held up for many years. OBC MLAs cutting across party lines represented before Chief Minister against me alleging that I had exceeded my brief by setting aside a Cabinet Resolution that provided 27 percent reservation for SEBCs. I had not escalated the matter to Chief Minister for his approval or that of his Cabinet before issuing the clarification as it would have been impossible for political leadership to alter its earlier position. My only interest was to put the Constitutional position in perspective and pave the way for fresh recruitments as governance was suffering due to increasing vacancies. I took the risk as there was no doubt in my mind about the Constitutional provisions on reservation. Politics won over the Constitution as State Government still did not allow fresh recruitment with 50 percent ceiling for reservation until the General Elections of 2014 were held. Vacancies had increased to unmanageable levels despite contractual reappointment of a large number of retired employees to manage governmental business. Interestingly, in spite of facing abuse from the floor of Legislative Assembly and various other fora, I continued to enjoy Chief Minister's confidence. Minister despite having approved the clarifying circular, abdicated himself from all responsibility by telling the Legislative Assembly that senior officers of his department had issued the circular without informing him about the implications and ramifications!

When asked to suggest options before the Government, I cited the case of Tamil Nadu where reservation in State Government services was 69 percent and State reservation law formed a part of Ninth Schedule to the Constitution. It had not been subjected to judicial review despite Supreme Court holding in a judgement that any law if found to be against the basic structure of the Constitution even if it was a part of the Ninth Schedule was liable to judicial review. The basic structure included a general reservation ceiling not exceeding 50 percent. I was asked to prepare a draft Bill on the pattern of Tamil Nadu's reservation law which was complied with quietly and quickly. I stood transferred soon after its introduction in State Legislative Assembly, where it was passed later. But State Government did not approach Union Government proposing its inclusion in Ninth Schedule to the Constitution, which implied that it was all politics of reservation and nothing more. For more than 10 years, State administration suffered due to non-recruitment and its impact which would continue to be felt for years to come.

The second issue in relation to SEBC reservation was that certain castes in State's list claiming SEBC status did not find place in Central SEBC list. Under law, inclusion or exclusion of OBCs could be considered only on the recommendation of SEBC Commission after examination of representations made by claimants. Leaders of a dominant land-owning caste "Khandayat" in State SEBC list, with a few other denominations were pressing for their inclusion in Central list. Law makers from this caste had aggressively represented against me for issuing the clarification on ceiling on reservation in State Government services. Justice S.R. Pandian, Chairman, National SEBC Commission held a 2-day public hearing at Bhubaneswar on claims for inclusion in Central SEBC list. I was required to remain present. Leaders of the Khandayat caste argued vociferously for reconsideration of their claim. A leader highlighted its historic contribution to the expansion of Kalinga Kingdom from the banks of River Ganga to River Godavari. He added that it was only due to the unmatched bravery of solders of this caste that colonial administration had faced heavy resistance in extending control to areas defended by Khandayats. He found it an injustice to exclude a caste with such glorious credentials from the SEBC list prepared by Central Government! When Justice Pandian sought my views after the public hearing, I respectfully submitted that he should go by his own assessment and I had no views on the matter. He said that it was not possible to reconsider claims without fresh data or evidence about the relative backwardness of the caste. The claim was rejected again.

Office Reforms

In my tenure of two years and two months as Secretary in the two Departments, I tried my best to bring improvements in the functioning of the two integrated Departments. The office environment was hardly conducive to effective functioning. There was space constraint besides conditions being unhygienic. Since consignment of old files and other records had not taken place for many decades, heaps of them with thick layers of dust occupied virtually half the floor space along with unserviceable equipment and broken furniture. Some ministerial staff could occasionally be found sitting on piles of files! It was only providential kindness that kept the employees generally healthy.

I drew up a four-months plan for consigning old records and disposing old and unserviceable furniture. Truck-loads of old records were either destroyed or transferred to Secretariat's record room after verification and marking their utility following the provisions of relevant record manual. Works Department engineers in charge of Secretariat maintenance were called to undertake necessary repairs, painting and varnishing, etc. The room occupied by a Deputy Secretary exclusively was converted into a 'washroom' for female employees. Almost 50 percent extra office space had become available for use. Desks of Assistants, Section Officers etc. were re-arranged to give a modern look and all concerned were requested to maintain cleanliness and punctuality. Office environment was transformed within four months.

It was my habit to come to office half an hour before the time and go around to routinely see cleanliness and other arrangements. I would also be among the last to leave the office. One morning, I was distressed to find a newly-painted wall discoloured due to spitting of chewed tobacco-laced beetle leaves. I came to my room and returned after an hour with a brush and bucket of water to wash the place when ministerial staff had occupied their respective seats. When I started, the employees gathered and begged apology for what had happened. Till I remained Secretary there, no such incident came to my notice thereafter. Everyone was happy to see the change. Principal Secretary, H&FW, whose office was on the ground floor of the same block came, saw the changes, and tried to replicate them in his office without equal success. Female employees were happier. A small initiative on my part by involving all concerned gave the office a transformed look.

Handling Ethnic Conflict in Kandhamal: No Easy Task

I tried to stretch myself to the maximum. Occasional differences with Minister could be taken in one's stride, especially since I enjoyed the full confidence of Chief Minister. Lack of sincerity and absence of serious political will to address the difficulties of ST/SC communities and their exploitation continued to deeply trouble me. Finding the State failing to fulfil some of its obligations, a number of NGOs had become active in tribal areas as if to fill up the vacuum created due to governmental inactions. For some NGOs, poverty and under-development of tribal communities was a major source of self-survival. A good number having access to foreign funds operated with hidden agendas in Kandhamal, a tribal district affected by ethnic conflict, which was given communal colour. Ethnic conflict invariably attracted adverse publicity, nationally and internationally.

Historically, 'Kandha" STs in Kandhamal district in particular, and more generally in Southern Division of Odisha, had been traditionally exploited by three social groups known locally as 'Kumuti', 'Sundhi' and 'Pana'. Kumutis ran the business of money-lending and procuring tribal produce whereas Sundhis were engaged in manufacturing and selling country liquor to tribals. Panas, who knew the tribal dialect known as 'Kui' besides Oriya, worked as intermediaries enabling Kumutis and Sundhis to transact with tribals. Initially, Panas enjoyed the confidence of tribals as they conversed with them in Kui. In the times to come, Panas improved their socio-economic profile despite being largely landless and working only as intermediaries, whilst that of tribal communities who were the traditional rulers of Kandha hills deteriorated rapidly. So much so that Panas started replacing Kumutis/Sundhis and started doing business with tribals directly. With the penetration of Christian NGOs in hinterland of Kandhamal and inducements to convert, a large number of SCs became Christian. Together they also persuaded a section of tribals to get converted. Constitutional provisions made SCs ineligible for reservation if they converted into other non-Hindu religions which did not practice untouchability. STs remained STs even after conversion and, thus, there was no loss of reservation for them after their change of religion. Access to education offered by missionaries made the Panas who had been converted in larger numbers more suitable for employment in Government and outside.

During the first Survey and Settlement operation in the late 1960s, Panas also got lands recorded in their names, particularly those which were in some sort of possession of tribal communities for generations. Unaware of modern land record system and ignorant about RoRs over their lands, tribals did not apprehend any mischief and made no appeals before settlement authorities. Converted Panas also started presenting themselves as STs in land records, which were to be the primary documents to be relied upon for issuance of Caste Certificates by the competent authority. Apart from asserting claims over tribal lands on the basis of RoRs prepared during the survey and settlement operations, Panas also started purchasing land from the tribals at cheap rates, and often clandestinely. Many Pana converts suppressed their change of religion in order to grasp the benefits of SC reservation. Indeed, many went a step further by presenting themselves as STs as they conversed in the 'Kui' spoken by local tribals. By elbowing out the tribals, they could also appropriate reservations in Government posts and services meant for STs.

When such practices went beyond stray incidents, Kandhas started opposing Panas to protest against their loss of land and benefits of reservation meant for tribals. They had also started resisting the demographic changes that had clandestinely and concertedly taken place during the last three decades through inducements and pressures by Christian organisations. Christian population had already increased by a huge 626 percent in the district, numbering about 16,247 (or a share of 4 percent of total) in 1961 to more than 1.19 lakh (or a share of 18 percent of total) by 2001. During the same period, comparatively, Kandhas increased by 57.34 percent from 2.14 lakh to 3.37 lakh. Between 1981 and 1991, Christian population had increased by 78.87 percent as against 0.46 percent increase in tribal population. In villages with majority of converts, Hindu families including Kandhas felt insecure and threatened if they declined to convert. Since a number of tribal families had been converted, the cultural and religious divide thus created a sense of alienation and fragmentation within tribal communities. The role played by certain Christian NGOs, who enjoyed administrative patronage, aggravated the social divide and ethnic tension. Ethnic conflict in Kandhamal district started recurring more frequently. State Government had passed the Odisha Freedom of Regions Act in 1967. The law empowered District Magistrate to require persons engaged in propagating religion to disclose the source of aid in cash or kind and notify conversions in advance, but was not implemented in reality.

A time came soon enough when State Government reduced its role to a silent spectator of demographic changes. A few highly ranked officers holding key positions in civil and police administration contributed directly and indirectly to changing the situation irreversibly. Hindu organisations, in particular Vishwa Hindu Parishad (VHP), became active. Swami Lakshmanananda Saraswati led non-Christians in a campaign against conversion and cow slaughter. Apart from an Ashram, he opened a couple of schools for ST girls and boys and was working for uniting tribal communities and others against conversion and cow slaughter. His unorthodox methods included a life style similar to that of local communities, sharing food with them and conducting religious rituals in their houses, which brought him closer to indigenous communities as upward mobility or process of Sanskritisation was also at work. His increasing popularity among tribals and a section of SCs had become a challenge for Christian NGOs. Ethnic conflict started appearing on the surface with regularity. His cold-blooded murder on 23 August

2008 on the night of Krishna Janmashtami celebrations undoubtedly brought matters to a head and aggravated the already ethnic conflict brewing in the district for long. Thus, it was clear that a number of socio-economic factors contributed to the disquieting social disharmony between the two dominant ethnic groups of Kandhamal, namely, Panas (SCs) and Kandhas (STs). Kandhas were indeed hurt by alienation of their land, misuse of provisions of reservation, continuing backwardness, fragmentation of tribal homes and sense of bewilderment due to changes taking place within the community on account of conversion, etc. But the conflict could not be reduced to a rift between followers of Christianity and Hinduism, although conversions under inducements and pressure had also become a major issue in the recent past. Giving it a communal colour also suited certain hidden agendas which could then attract the full force of international might in what would otherwise have been a district, State or national issue at most.

Kandhamal had earlier witnessed large-scale ethnic violence in the year 1994. The causes identified by administration were three-fold: First, Kandhas became conscious that they were being cheated by Panas who were buying their Minor Forest Produce and agricultural produce like tamarind and turmeric at low prices while making big profits by selling them to traders outside. Panas also grabbed tribal lands through money lending business. Second, Kandhas were angry with Panas as political space was monopolised by them since both Lok Sabha Member and Phulbani MLA were from Pana caste in spite of tribal voters being in majority. Third, the rift between two local political leaders aggravated the Pana-Kandha conflict.

The ethnic conflict in 2007 was painted as a clash between Hindus and Christians. It was triggered after an NGO '*Phulbani Kui Jan Kalyan Sangh*' founded by Panas filed a Writ Petition in High Court claiming ST status. The NGO reasoned that the Presidential Order for STs as amended in 2002 showed 'Kui' community as ST and since Pana caste people spoke 'Kui'(a tribal language), their social identity needed to be changed from 'Pana' (SC) to Kui (ST). Odisha High Court in their Order dated 12 July 2007 while disposing of Writ Petition at admission stage, directed State Government to look into the matter and make necessary correction in RoRs as per the Presidential Order of 2002. Using this High Court order, the NGO started a campaign with publicity that all those recorded as SC (Pana) in revenue records of Kandhamal district would be treated as ST (Kui) in future. It was reportedly being guided by a Rajya Sabha Member, himself being a Pana Christian, who could find traction readily having earlier worked in State and Central Government in key administrative positions.

In counter reaction, tribal communities under the banners of '*Kui Samaj Seva Samiti, Phulbani*', '*Nikhil Utkal Kui Samaj Union*', '*G. Udayagiri Kui Kul Samiti, Baliguda*', '*Kandhamal District Kui Samaj Coordination Committee, Baliguda*' and others organised rallies. Their demands included cancelling registration of NGO 'Phulbani Kui Jan Kalyan Sangh', deleting 'Kui' from Presidential Notification of 2002, and making certain administrative changes in the district. Office bearers of Zila Kui Coordination Committee, an umbrella organisation of various tribal groups of Kandhamal were not satisfied with Government's clarification that communities mentioned in Presidential Order of 2002 at Entry 31 were in relation to 'Khand/ Kand/ Kandha' in terms of synonyms and sub-groups which included 'Kui'. There was no scope to read "Pana" in it which is a SC in another Presidential Order for SCs vide Entry No. 69. The situation created by "Phulbani Kui Jan Kalyan Sangh" had vitiated the atmosphere. Tribal leaders were in no mood to hear anything other than acceptance of their demands. Members of Kandhamal Kui Samaj Coordination Committee led by Lambodar Kanhar had given a call for 36-hours bandh in Kandhamal district on 25 December 2007. Not being amenable to change their position despite persuasive efforts and assurance by district administration, agitators in large number blocked all district roads by felling about 1,000 trees at several places or using boulders. The agitators guarded their road blocks armed with traditional weapons including spears, bows and arrows, sickles and swords.

Another incident led to a second bandh call. On 24 December 2007 at Brahmanigaon village, communal tension erupted when Hindus protested against erection of arches by Christians as part of Christmas celebrations at a place where Hindus used to observe Dussehra festival. Having heard of the incident, Swami Lakshmanananda Saraswati proceeded to the place from his Ashram. Along with his followers, when he was assaulted by a group of about 350 Christians at Dadingibadi village, VHP gave a call for State-wide Bandh on 25 December 2007.

Two Bandh calls and massive road blocks brought the entire Kandhamal district in the grip of ethnic, communal tension. Baliguda sub-division was worst-affected. State law enforcement agencies despite best efforts could do little to avert the situation as it was far more than a law and order problem. Moreover, tribal leaders had lost confidence in district administration as their demand for transfer of District Collector was not accepted. After a series of meetings with tribal leaders, State leadership took note of their demands and promised to revisit about 500 cases of appointment in Government posts and services which though reserved for STs had been arrogated by Panas. As the enquiry started revealing later, the number of fake and false caste certificates obtained for employment in Government only increased hereafter. It was painful for me to terminate the services of a SC lady of Kandhamal district after having served for about 28 years against a post reserved for ST in my department. Paradoxically, the appointing authority in that case turned out to be a tribal IAS officer! The demand to deregister NGO 'Phulbani Kui Jan Kalyan Sangh' was also accepted by State Government to contain further ethnic flare up in the district.

As usually happens, instead of taking note of the brewing disturbing situation for years, State leadership took pride in announcing grants of temporary relief to affected families after loss of lives and property. Dignitaries, journalists and activists started visiting the affected-areas to find platforms to publicize their superficial observations and findings. Sane voices got drowned in the cacophony that followed. Vested interests did everything possible to exploit the tragedies for their political gain. The visit by M.P. Pinto, Vice Chairman of National Minority Commission, was an exception to the rule. Without fan-fare, he had a paid a quite visit and made observations which were measured and useful. The second visit made by two members of the same Commission, namely, Dilip Padgaonkar and Zoya Hasan on 6-8 January 2008 appeared to be less about fact-finding and more aimed at blaming VHP. Both members came without leaving their prejudices and were reluctant to hear anything other than what they considered to be the truth. Dilip Padgaonkar during his interaction with senior officials in the Secretariat after a flying visit to Phulbani Circuit House, saw in the tribal leader Lambodar Kanhar the makings of a famous Maoist leader leading insurgency in Nepal. Chief Minister would not go beyond making announcements of relief and compensation to the violence-affected people. A famous Pakistani Human Right Activist Asma Jahangir met Chief Minister in the presence of senior officers including myself during her visit to gather information about the ethnic conflict. In course of discussion, the response of Chief Minister turned more towards the prospects of his old friend Imran Khan in Pakistan's political firmament.

Ethnic tensions continued to prevail, though in some places in latent form for some time. As if in retaliation against the disturbances during preparations on 24 December 2007 towards Christmas celebrations, on the auspicious Krishna Janmashtami festival on 23 August 2008 at about 7.55 p.m. a group of around 25-30 persons forcefully entered Jaleshpeta Ashram and fired at its inmates killing Swamy Lakshmanananda Saraswati and a few others on the spot. Utter mayhem and large-scale destruction of life and property followed district-wide as a consequence of allegedly pre-planned killing which had no parallel in its history. Followers of Swami Lakshmanananda Saraswati reacted with a vengeance as the cold-blooded killing of their revered Saint was difficult for them to digest. The total death toll became 38. Villages and families which followed the Christian faith suffered the most. About 30,000 people whose houses and properties got damaged were kept in temporary shelters/ relief camps and almost all of them happened to be Pana Christians.

Worse was still to come after deployment of State Police and Central Reserved Police Forces who occupied residential schools meant for tribal boys and girls. In the name of containing violence and controlling the situation, indiscriminate arrests were carried out and even minor ST students were picked up when they went out for easement, on their way to school or farm-land/ forest area. Regardless of whether they had played any role or not in the communal violence, whoever was named or fingered by the Christian community was arrested without any verification. Innocent tribals started withdrawing their children from schools and running away to forests to avoid arrests. I visited some residential schools and hostels run departmentally which were forcibly occupied. I spoke and wrote to Home Secretary and Director General of Police (DGP) to issue instructions to police forces in Kandhamal not to harass innocent people, which in the long run could be counter-productive. I also requested officers leading Central Paramilitary forces to vacate schools and hostels in order to reopen them and begin their school functioning which would help normalise the situation.

Ramakant Rath, an award-winning writer and a former Chief Secretary, who incidentally had worked as Collector of Phulbani district about 40 years back, visited Kandhamal in the third week of October 2008. He sent his pithy and to-the-point observations and suggestions to the State Government. He called for action against those who actually participated in crimes observing, "*Man folk in a number of tribal villages, apprehending arrest by the Police have absconded to hills and forests. Those left behind are woman and children. They have hardly any food and absolutely no help for the sick. Harvest time is not far away and if tribals cannot harvest their crops, their misery would be acute in long term. In my view, the fear of large scale and indiscriminate arrests needs to be dispelled at once*". He appreciated the prompt steps taken by me in the department by issuing clarification in relation to the status of SC and ST in the relevant Presidential Orders which needed to be followed strictly by district administration and all concerned. In order to find a durable solution to recurring social conflicts in the district, he underlined the need for restoring tribal land, expediting inquiries into bogus caste certificates, correcting land records, reviving Agency Marketing Cooperative Society at Tikabali, disclosing financial aid by those engaged in conversion in accordance with the provisions of Odisha Freedom of Religions Act, etc.

The district was seeing violent confrontations between SCs, mostly converted, and STs who had lived in harmony for generations and had become enemies of each other now. Instead of implementing the solutions thus outlined, the focus of State Government alas was episodic and one-sided, more towards fire-fighting, announcement of ex-gratia relief and rehabilitation package besides maintenance of relief camps. Christian NGOs raised their pitch nationally and internationally depicting the ethnic conflict as a Hindu communal carnage against peace-loving Christians leading to their demand for a separate territory within Kandhamal for Pana Christians as they could no longer feel safe in the "Mal" (hills) of "Kandhas". No State leaders were willing to visit the district to assuage the hurt and fear of the people affected by the worst unrest in its history. They simply wished to avoid being seen taking sides that could have electoral ramifications. Senior officers too avoided visiting the district, as though afraid of being misunderstood about their assessment in case it differed from the political view and apprehensive of adverse action against them in case the situation deteriorated after their visit. State administration had become increasingly spineless and sycophancy or silence was the preferred strategy for most of the bureaucrats in proximity of the power centre. SP in the district had been suspended and his substitute was happy to play to the gallery. He occupied himself in making security arrangements for visitors from outside the State. Knowing well that Chief Minister Naveen Patnaik would go along with administrative advice given to him by bureaucrats heading the departments, I tried to do whatever was possible for me to do.

A young IAS officer Dr. Krishan Kumar had been posted as Collector of Kandhamal in the meanwhile. Government could have done this much earlier as tribal leaders had been repeatedly stating their unwillingness to have any dialogue with the previous Collector. Incoming Collector had to get busy in maintaining relief camps and meeting visitors. My advice to him was to bring community leaders and other stakeholders to the table for discussion as the communities at war against each other had to coexist in the district. Relief camps should be closed as soon as possible by giving priority to repair and reconstruction of damaged houses. Touts roaming in and around relief camps were instigating dwellers and even dissuading them from expressing the wish to go back home. This was being done to prolong publicising the unfortunate incident nationally and internationally, as if to prove that Christian minorities were not safe. I was a witness to a tragic tutoring and drama enacted during one of my visits to a relief camp. Women were found being tutored to greet the visiting dignitaries with tears, cries, words of hopelessness and despair. Attempts were made by some touts to manhandle me when I asked one of the crying women to give me her coordinates, name, address etc. so that administration could address her problems quickly. This happened in the presence of senior district officials including police.

District Collector agreed that it was essential to establish a dialogue between the two warring sides but his own attempts made locally might not yield the desired result. As I had been visiting the district regularly, he wanted me to preside over such meetings in which leaders of various groups could be requested to participate. I agreed and asked him to also invite local MLAs, Zila Parishad Chairperson, etc. State Election Commission had appointed me as Observer in connection with elections of Urban Local Bodies of Gopalpur and Berhampur in neighbouring Ganjam district. Usually, as per the laid down practice, I would undertake district visits after approval of Chief Secretary. Not being sure that my plan to visit and discuss issues of Kandhamal district with factional leaders inimical to each other would be approved in the given situation, I did not inform the Chief Secretary about my meetings in advance.

After Urban Local Body elections were concluded, I proceeded to Pulbani, the headquarters of Kandhamal district instead of returning directly to headquarters. Kandhamal Collector had made arrangements for the first round of meetings on 20 September 2008 with tribal leaders and NGOs in addition to visiting relief camps. It was an open-ended meeting to break the ice. Amongst others, local Lok Sabha Member Sugreeb Singh (a Pana), tribal MLAs, President of Zila Parishad and senior district officials including the Collector were present. Tribal leaders ventilated their grievances aggressively in the beginning but promised at the end that they would not turn violent if assurance was given to look into their legitimate demands and false cases instituted against innocent people by police were withdrawn. The demands made by them included restoration of their land; recognition of their forest rights; fresh survey & settlement to prepare RoRs in respect of land in their cultivating position; restoration of their land occupied by others; action against those who had misappropriated reservation meant for them; banning of Christian NGOs in the district who according to them were responsible for social fragmentation and disharmony; nabbing of killers of Swami Lakshmanananda Saraswati; release of arrested innocent tribals; and focus on socio-economic development of the district. I persuaded them not to be unreasonable in dealing with Pana Christian families with whom they had coexisted amicably for many generations. I had also requested them not to get unnecessarily aggressive when a joint meeting would be held during my next visit.

After the meeting, I visited two major relief camps at Tikabali and G. Udaygiri which housed about 1,500 people each at that point of time. I had been informed about the highly charged situation in these camps. I found a sizeable number of inmates in both camps eager to return home. In the course of interactions with some of their so-called community leaders who appeared very aggressive, one of the demands put forth was that an exclusive settlement of Pana families to be named as "Panas' Land" should be carved out as a separate geographical territory in Kandhamal as it was impossible for them to coexist with Kandhas and other tribals. I requested these leaders to help in resolving the problem and implementing rehabilitation packages which were in the best interest of all concerned. When I visited some of the affected villages thereafter, it surprised me to find some old houses being demolished. On enquiry, I was told that this was being done to claim higher assistance announced by Government for fully damaged houses. The tragedy was indeed being exploited in more ways than one.

On return to headquarters, I gave a detailed note to Chief Secretary about the situation in Kandhamal district containing what needed to be done on the basis of my feedback. I also underscored the need for segregating negative elements from relief camps which would help in restoring normalcy including early return of affected families from relief camps. I underlined the need to avoid unnecessary arrests of innocent tribals, particularly school going students, and provision of alternative accommodation for personnel of central para military forces who had occupied schools/hostels without prior permission of district administration. Chief Secretary appreciated my initiative and complimented me for courageous steps taken by me.

As planned in consultation with District Collector, on 28 September 2008, I held two meetings, one with representatives of Christian community, and a second in the afternoon with leaders of Pana caste. Public representatives also attended these meetings, as they had earlier, along with District Collector and other senior district officials. Discussions were again free-wheeling and were intended to allow release of pent up feelings. A third joint meeting scheduled on 29 September 2008 was intended to be more structured.

In the meeting, representatives of Christian groups asserted their contribution in the fields of education and health besides articulating grievances against elements envious of their community. They aggressively demanded higher relief and higher rehabilitation package including financial support for reconstruction of damaged churches, besides deployment of armed police and para-military forces for their protection. Some participants appeared extremely provocative and aggressive while majority appeared in favour of reconciliation and restoration of peace and harmony as early as possible. A participant went to the extent of claiming that Christianity was the only religion for salvation and enlightened Christian NGOs had a responsibility to work to realise this ultimate goal! I had to tell him to leave the meeting venue if he was not able to control his emotions and contribute to improving the situation. It was also asserted by a Christian leader that State Government having admitted to the role of Maoists in the murder of Lakshmanananda Saraswati, should take strong action against those indulging in propaganda holding Christians responsible for the killing. They held local administration responsible for allowing the procession carrying mortal remains of Lakshmanananda Saraswati through Christian majority villages and churches with provocative speeches. At the end, urgency for restoring peace and normalcy in the district was unanimously endorsed.

In the afternoon meeting, representatives of Panas who had not been converted to Christianity expressed their anguish for depicting them as grabbers of tribal land. They called for action to prevent disinformation depicting Pana community as thieves and land grabbers who had also cornered Government posts meant for STs; time-frame for verification of land possessed by Pana families; settlement of land disputes once and for all; action against outsiders occupying tribal land; action against outsiders involved in instigating simple-minded tribal communities against Panas and Christians; and reservation in Panchayats for SCs in proportion to their population by amending the existing law under which posts of chairpersons of Panchayats in Scheduled Areas had been reserved for STs only. Many participants observed that Panas and Kandhas had been favourable to each other since time immemorial but that some outsider businessmen (Sundhis and Kumutis) had created the rift between them for which they needed to be dealt with heavy hands. They wanted ST&SC

community leaders to sit together to discuss all issues and resolve differences created by vested interests and outsiders. This meeting with leaders of Pana community was held in a congenial atmosphere.

The crucial joint meeting on 29 September of all the groups at loggerheads with each other, held out the potential to be an explosive one in case emotions were not kept in tight rein. District Collector indicated his inability to attend it. I was aware of consequences if the situation slipped out of hand, and yet I did not like police personnel to surround the meeting venue. I started by frankly briefing participants about my separate meetings. I requested them to address the issues to be raised by them to me, and not to each other, and to keep in mind their long-term interests as they had coexisted in harmony for generations and would have to do so for times to come. I also requested them to avoid extreme and provocative expressions and that for durable peace emphasis should be on finding solutions to problems surrounding both sides of the divide. Although leaders representing different communities and religions agreed to maintain discipline, there were serious moments when tempers reached sky-high as though the heated arguments could explode through the roof-top of the Conference hall! When one participant representing the Hindu segment wanted the induced conversions to be stopped, the response from a young Christian leader was that he had converted to Christianity after studying Hindu scriptures and Sanskrit, and that Christianity was the only path for human salvation. Constitutional provisions were cited to claim freedom of religion by way of conversion. I cautioned religious leaders that such extreme elements had contributed to the cracks in harmonious relationships, which were now wide chasms almost unbridgeable, among inhabitants as they did not understand the value of peace which was at the core of all religions. There was unanimity on restoring peace and normalcy but consensus on causes and methods remained elusive.

The issues raised by various interest groups clearly underscored that socio-religious conflict was the result of multiple factors. The immediate trigger now was the brutal killing of Swami Lakshmanananda Saraswati who was very popular among Hindu segments of both STs and SCs. Many suggestions on restoring goodwill were thrown up, which were acceptable uniformly and deserved attention of administration at district and State level. I, therefore, sent another long note to Chief Secretary, a copy of which was marked to District Collector proposing action on the commonly acceptable issues in addition to summarising the discussion. My proposal focused on positive trust-building steps to be taken with emphasis on vigorous implementation of development projects, rehabilitation package without discrimination, fresh survey and settlement operations, enquiries into land disputes and alleged misuse of reservation provisions in a time-bound manner. Additionally, I recommended suspension of all gun licenses; scrutiny of outsiders allegedly indulging in instigations; relocation of police and paramilitary personnel from educational institutions; and release of ST students who had been arrested while travelling to their schools, among other things.

I had held meetings with factions having serious frictions without bothering to know about the thinking of the inscrutable State political leadership. Senior officials in close proximity of the leadership remained guarded and non-committal. The only discernible priority appeared to be to maintain status quo. Anyhow, I made regular visits with district administration on board as it was necessary to break the ice through dialogue followed by vigorous implementation of rehabilitation package without discrimination and developmental projects were the most important means to move forward. I did not allow the media to know about my meetings. Those who came to know about them were politely requested not to report anything. Since Chief Minister had expressed his appreciation about my work in the field of tribal welfare at various forums including before the Planning Commission, I was inclined to gauge that my visits to the district without consulting the senior officers around him were not being viewed negatively. I did not like to follow the 'wait and watch' policy of State Government which had resulted in closure of an Express Highway for years following tribal unrest in Jajpur district after police firing while providing protection to an industrial house engaged in construction of compound wall. Fortunately, my visits and meetings with stakeholders started yielding positive results. Police officials now agreed to allow movement of trucks carrying construction materials and equipment for implementing developmental projects including ST Girls' High School buildings.

The dilemma of State leadership to my mind was also on account of the fact that the political ally BJP was known for its proximity with VHP which was aggressively campaigning against Christian NGOs in Kandhamal. Indeed, after a few months of the socio-religious conflict and well before the General Elections held in April-May 2009 the coalition broke apart. Chief Minister was quick to dump the political ally of more than 10 years in the State and nationally to distance himself from the party with whom VHP was perceived to be associated. He also started announcing his secular credential more loudly than before.

Odisha Scores High on Conferring Land Rights to Tribal Families

One of the principal demands by tribal community leaders in Kandhamal and also elsewhere was restoration of lost land and implementation of Scheduled Tribes and other Traditional Forest Dwellers (Recognition of Forest Rights) Act, 2006. Survey and settlement operations conducted in the past did not include areas having slopes higher than 10 degrees despite the land remaining in cultivation of tribal families for generations. The limited amount of plain land held by them had transferred hands over time. Implementation of Regulation-2 of 1956 in Schedules Areas, like Land Reform Act in the rest of the State, had not received the desired attention of revenue administration to prevent alienation of tribal land.

Notwithstanding my reservations with regard to some of the provisions of the Forest Rights Act, I was made member of the Committee set up by the Union Government in Ministry of Tribal Affairs under the chairmanship of S.R. Sankaran for drafting the rules to lay down the procedures for implementing the law under reference. It provided for non-transferable heritable rights over forest land up to 4 hectares each in occupation of tribal communities as on December 2005. Implementation of the law became the responsibility of respective State Governments. No sooner were the rules notified, I issued detailed guidelines explaining the procedures to be followed for recording forest land in possession of tribal families. A format in accordance with the law and rules thereunder was devised to show the land coordinates, though loosely, for recognizing the heritable rights of tribals on the said forest land. There were problems in providing the geographical coordinates of forest land over which titles needed to be granted to the tribal families, as forest land had remained unsurveyed. I persuaded State Forest Department to use GPS instruments to find out the correct coordinates of land claimed by tribal families. Since Forest Department officials had expressed inability to procure GPS instruments due to lack of financial resources, I had obtained approval of Union Ministry of Tribal Affairs to provide funds from SCA for it. Officers of Forest Department became part of the mechanism developed for conferment or recognition of right on forest land at village, block, sub-division and district levels. I started holding monthly meetings of tribal districts at regional level to review the progress made and to sort out problems on the spot. Odisha became the top performer in implementing the Forest Rights Act. More than two lakh tribal families in Odisha got benefitted within less than three years of the law being enacted. More than 35,000 tribal families in riot-hit Kandhamal district got title deeds recognizing their forest rights.

Interestingly, I was holding a meeting of officers of Southern Division on the issue of forest rights at Berhampur, when I was telephonically informed about my transfer. As I was informed later by an officer in Chief Minister's office, the transfer was on account of some articles and speeches of my wife on the killing of Swami Lakshmanananda Saraswati, of which I was completely unaware. I closed the meeting instantly and returned to headquarters to immediately demit the charge.

Did It Have To End This Way? Some Embarrassing Moments

Elections to Bhubaneswar Municipal Corporation were notified to be held in November 2008. Suddenly Chief Secretary Ajit Kumar Tripathy came to my office telling me that State Election Commissioner S.C. Hota wanted my services as Election Observer and I should not say no. I had always held that it was the prerogative of Government to utilise my services without consulting me. I said that there was no question of my saying no to any order of Government.

A couple of incidents that followed my assignment as Election Observer made my end of tenure in the ST&SC Development Department far from pleasant. One afternoon while on duty, I found Chief Minister's motorcade in front of his house leading to a place of meeting with more vehicles than permissible. It was a momentary embarrassment for me to stop the motorcade with Chief Minister remaining stranded on the road for about 5 minutes till the vehicles beyond the permissible limit were separated and challaned to the police station. This incident figured prominently in daily newspapers the following day. Another relatable development occurred when having received a complaint about violation of Model Code, I reached a place for inspection which was close to the residence of Pyari Mohan Mahapatra, who was widely held to be running the show for the ruling party. I got a call from him on my mobile conveying displeasure for unnecessary interference by me in campaigning by political parties and candidates. He objected to my actions which according to him impeded the process of democratic franchise, buttressing it by recounting his expertise and experience in election matters as Chief Electoral Officer while in service. When I read out the legal provisions and a paragraph from the Model Code and asked him as to what he would have done in my place, he promptly put down the phone. The next day my attention was drawn to a news item in a daily newspaper commenting that I was favouring BJP, a partner in State Government, but contesting election separately. It also alleged that I was unhappy with my transfer which took place after my appointment as Election Observer!

For violating the Model Code of Conduct, I had issued orders for seizure of about 50 vehicles of Biju Janata Dal, 45 of BJP, and 40 of Congress party. Other parties too faced similar action for violation of laws and Model Code. Elections to Bhubaneswar Municipal Corporation were concluded smoothly. All concerned at the end of the day were happy with the fairness of their conduct. I had relinquished my charge as Secretary to Government in ST&SC Development and OBC & Minority Affairs Departments immediately after transfer but assumed charge of the next posts on 14 November 2008 after completion of elections.

* * * *

10

Multiple Hats: Cooperation, Excise and Rural Development

COOPERATION DEPARTMENT

I joined as Commissioner-cum-Secretary in Cooperation Department, with concurrent charge of Excise Department. Logically and for administrative ease in case another department was to be assigned, the combination with Agriculture may have gelled better with its symbiotic twin Cooperation. As a loyal soldier, I waded into my two disparate charges handling them for the next about 8 months. I was soon given charge of Director, Agriculture Marketing too. I had cherished the subject of agriculture and drew advantage from having worked as Director, A&FP about a decade back. Surama Padhi from BJP, a coalition partner, was Minister of the department. File work was sparse. I had more opportunity to focus on field-work on issues of crop-financing and agriculture marketing.

The main activities included ensuring smooth supply of agricultural inputs like credit, seed, fertilizer and pesticides, in addition to facilitating marketing of agricultural outputs through regulated markets. About 80 percent of agricultural credit in the State was availed of by farmers from District Central Cooperative Banks (DCCB) through Primary Agriculture Cooperative Societies (PACS) and Large-Scale Agriculture Multi-Purpose Societies (LAMPS). While PACS catered to the needs of farmers in major parts of the State, LAMPS met the requirements including that of marketing some agricultural produce of farmers in Scheduled Areas. The societies disbursed crop loan in the form of cash and kind. Supply of fertilizer, pesticide and seeds were usually distributed in kind as B-Component of loan sanctioned by DCCBs which in turn would be financed by State Cooperative Bank subject to repayment. State Cooperative Bank got refinanced by NABARD.

From my frequent field visits as Director A&FP a decade ago, I had discovered that farmers who could access crop loan were mostly from irrigated areas. The other fact I had verified was inordinate delays in sanction and disbursement of crop loan. Fresh loan in favour of farmers depended upon recovery of earlier loans. On paper, farmers with membership of PACS and LAMPS could access B-Component, which was supplied to societies by State Cooperative Marketing Federation (Mark Fed), an organisation under Cooperation Department. As Director A&FP and Licensing Authority for chemical fertilizers at State level, I had worked to break the monopoly and black-marketing practices of Mark Fed. I had also ensured that seeds were supplied through outlets of Agriculture Department or authorized private dealers reducing the scope for paper transactions by cooperatives. However, cooperative societies had continued to show crop loan disbursal to their members partly in cash and partly in kind as B-Component of loan sanctioned.

Anarchy in Crop Loans and Paddy Procurements

Logically, crop loan sanction and disbursement, even if done in a phased manner, during Kharif needed to be completed between June to August. But, the statement on Kharif loans in the year 2008-09 put up to me by MD of State Central Cooperative Bank indicated that disbursement of loan had started in July and continued till end-October even for paddy. This strengthened my suspicion that crop loan transactions existed mostly on paper. Before raising my concerns about the mismatch with bank officials, I went on extensive field visits across districts. I inspected loan and recovery ledgers of PACS and LAMPS. It was hardly surprising to find that most of the farmers in various districts shown to have been sanctioned crop loans were the same and percentage of recovery shown during each season ranged between 69 percent and 71 percent against total loan sanctioned and disbursed, year after year also indicated a similar pattern. There were rare cases of fresh loans being disbursed. Recovery ledgers showed that farmers were sanctioned loans of a few hundred rupees more than the amount to be repaid by them within one to three days of their reported repayments. It was practically not possible to identify defaulters who according to these ledgers had stopped availing of loans for many years! This only implied that loan transactions shown to have been made were incorrect. In brief, it was a case of evergreening crop loans through paper transactions. It also suggested that loan waivers occasionally announced by Governments and recapitalisation of Cooperative Banks mostly legitimised manipulations.

Policies and pronouncements of State Government too contributed to such transactions. Interest subventions as notified were not acted upon. Rescheduling of crop loans and orders against recovery efforts on the grounds of recurring calamities such as drought with resultant crop losses benefitted mostly irrigated area farmers who indeed reaped a bumper profit during drought being beneficiaries of controlled irrigation system. The suffering of farmers in irrigated areas was indeed more due to distress sale of their produce as State

Government had not given any attention to development of agriculture marketing infrastructure which made the system of MSP infructuous.

I also verified storage facilities for agricultural inputs like fertilizers, pesticides, seeds, etc. to find that hardly any functional storage godowns existed with PACS and LAMPS. The only visible side of crop loans was that unlike in other States, farmers distressed due to accumulation of agricultural loans did not take extreme step of committing suicide in Odisha as disbursement and recovery of crop loan were exercises largely confined to ledgers maintained by PACS and LAMPS! Farmers at large were hardly aware of what was happening.

State Government had involved cooperative societies in procurement of paddy/ rice. During my visits, I found that PACS got some margins besides operating cost as offered by Central Government for procurement. In reality they merely functioned as intermediaries for FCI and State Civil Supply Corporations on the one hand and millers on the other. In the absence of storage godowns, societies only directed farmers to deliver their surplus paddy at specified milling points in their area for custom-milling. Producers were paid belatedly at millers-determined prices depending upon quality of paddy delivered at milling points personally or through aggregators. This practice continued due to lack of regulated market yards with necessary infrastructure and lack of facilities to certify 'Fair and Average Quality' of agricultural produce (paddy) to get MSP. Farmers in Odisha thus rarely got MSP for their produce.

No more evidence was required to prove my apprehension about crop loans. In a meeting with District and State cooperative bank officials, I shared my findings about crop loans reportedly sanctioned and disbursed by societies. The situation did not differ anywhere so that I could verify and analyse the difference. There was no satisfactory explanation from any participant. The dividing line between officials of cooperative banks/societies and politicians was extremely thin. Despite State Central Cooperative Bank having sanctioned funds for computerisation of records and office automation, hardly any attention had been given to this work, which had potential to expose fake transactions. Anarchy and vagueness suited all.

State Government at the highest level had been making occasional announcements for appeasing the farming community by lowering crop loan interest rates, compensating farmers having suffered crop losses, etc. In reality, it was a façade of concern for their well-being. Capacity building of organisations including Mark Fed was not in the zone of governmental consideration. I was not surprised to get back a file from Chief Minister's Office relating to State Warehousing Corporation that had been submitted by my great grand predecessor about five years back. When I met Secretary to Chief Minister in his office and asked how he remained so calm and cool when his office looked like a record room with files jumbled up all over, he responded with a broad smile stating that he could not force the horse to drink water after walking it to the river. The boss across the corridor he said was allergic to files! I tried to enforce some discipline for timely sanction of crop loans and issued instructions to avoid disbursement after the sowing and transplanting season to avoid misutilisation but with limited success.

Quirks of Fate Secure Completion of Market Yard for Fish at Chilika

Development of marketing infrastructure was top most in my mind. For collecting market fees, entire State/ districts stood notified as 'market yard' with no attention paid for developing agriculture markets in key locations where farmers could bring their surplus produce and State agencies or traders could buy, as was the practice in other major States. Union Agriculture Ministry was willing to provide financial and technical support to develop agriculture marketing in the State. The indifference on the part of State's officials was evident from the fact that I received a letter from my immediate predecessor who was now Secretary of Agriculture Department for utilisation certificates against an amount of ₹ 40 lakh which had been released by Union Agriculture Ministry for development of a market yard at Chilika for fish farmers about four years back! When information was sought regarding this allocation, I was apprised about its release to RMC, Balugaon but nothing was known beyond that. I visited the development site to be told that 25 percent of allocations had been spent on earth works which was a sheer waste as it got washed away due to heavy rains. As reported to me, construction of market yard could not be resumed due to opposition from fishermen of Chilika Lake. There was no trace of any work having been done.

Having worked as Secretary, FARD Department years back, I knew their senior engineers. On my request, they prepared a detailed plan for market yard at an estimated cost of ₹ 80 lakh and also agreed to supervise the construction. Work started concurrently. I shared this development with Principal Secretary, FARD Department, who coincidentally was my grand predecessor having served a long tenure in Cooperation Department. Allocation for the market yard from Union Agriculture Ministry had been received during her tenure. After receiving the funds, she had done nothing more than releasing them to RMC. She did convey her happiness at hearing about the fast-tracked implementation of the project pending technical sanction. But she saw to it that her department's senior engineers did not give technical sanction nor were permitted to continue supervising the work which was progressing at a fast pace. I finally utilised the services of engineers of RD Department to get the project completed. I was transferred to RD Department after a few months, but before completion of market yard. As though a quirk of fate, having initiated its execution while heading Cooperation Department, I got it completed after joining RD Department. All said and done, it was difficult to fathom the minds and actions of some of my predecessors. The unutilised amount would have remained as such had I not received a letter by chance reminding me of the delay in transmitting proof of utilisation of an allocation made years back by Union Agriculture Ministry. Utilisation certificate was furnished within four months of getting the letter by when the project had progressed substantially and the amount got utilised.

Chilika Lake supported thousands of fishermen livelihoods of Puri, Khordha and Ganjam districts surrounding this beautiful blue water lagoon. Export of marine products were more than ₹ 400 crore annually. Local RMC could have easily got a market fee of more than ₹ 4 crore annually (@ 1 percent of cost of marketed produce) with timely development of market yard. Based on a petition from exporters and some big fishermen, collection of market fee had been denied by an order of High Court, reasoning RMC had failed to develop a single market yard and had no right to collect it. In my meetings, fishermen and others having adjoining land all conveyed their support, and underlined the need for it. The only request from those owning the adjoining land was for provision of proper drainage to prevent water logging in the rainy season. It was a genuine demand and win-win situation for all stakeholders.

Success in Democratising Institutions; Infrastructure Remains a Dream

Odisha Agriculture Produce Markets Act, 1956 provided for constitution of markets and RMCs. Every market committee was to have 17 members, which included 4 elected by licensed traders from amongst themselves; 8 to be elected by organisations of agriculturists in the market area recognised by State Government, and where no such organisation existed to be nominated by District Collector; and 2 to be elected by local authorities within whose limits the market area existed, which included one member to be elected by Municipal Councillors and another by Gram Panchayat. Remaining 3 members were to be State Government nominees. I felt it was absolutely essential to constitute the Committees as per the statute and take them on board for growing the development plans. Neither State Government nor officers heading RMCs were inclined to hold elections. Possibly they feared bringing in democratic control and accountability over their functioning. Despite political and administrative resistance, for the first time in the history of RMCs, elections were held to elect members. It was a big achievement for me to get the elections to RMCs completed notwithstanding law and order problems created in some areas and petitions filed in court to prevent holding elections.

Since I stood appointed additionally as Director, Agriculture Marketing, it was easier for me to prepare a comprehensive plan for development of infrastructure for agriculture marketing in the State. Senior officials of Union Agriculture Ministry had promised necessary technical and financial support. They had organised my exposure visit to a modern market yard developed scientifically near Jaipur in Rajasthan. A comprehensive plan was prepared to develop a 3-tier network of market yards at district, sub-division and Block levels, while at village level agriculture marketing could be handled through Gram Panchayats. RMCs in various districts had fixed deposits in cooperative banks and other financial institutions of more than ₹ 100 crore. According to my quick estimates, it was possible to generate ₹ 100 crore annually towards market fee if leakages and corrupt practices could be minimised substantially.

Sub-Collectors were *ex-officio* chairpersons of RMCs at sub-divisional level in most places. Their administrative support helped in collecting market fee from check gates erected on roads from State agencies, traders, and millers, who were bulk buyers of agriculture surplus. A few market yards stood developed with limited infrastructure by some RMCs in irrigated areas, though these were grossly underutilised. Market fees were also collected from other weekly *haats* where trading of domestic animals and other agricultural produce was held. Marketing Inspectors of Directorate of Agriculture Marketing were Secretaries to RMCs, who would keep their chairpersons in good humour by providing fancy furniture, air conditioners, extra vehicles, etc. and occasionally facilitate their tours outside the State. In the year prior to my assuming charge, about ₹ 50 crore had been collected, but net saving was only about ₹ 10 crore due to large administrative overheads, which should have been no more than 10 percent of collections.

In order to streamline administration of RMCs, I displaced the Secretaries of RMCs who had spent more than three years at a place. Many of them were holding positions in higher revenue-earning RMCs for more than five years with the blessings of Cooperation Minister who was chairperson of State Agriculture Marketing Board. Past Directors for Agriculture Marketing, despite being the appointing authority for these Secretaries had abdicated their responsibilities and allowed Minister to effect their transfers and postings at will. Naturally, Minister was perturbed when I started exercising these powers, besides taking disciplinary actions against those who had not performed satisfactorily unmindful of whether they enjoyed proximity with Minister. One day, not finding my actions in consonance with her requirements, Minister called me to her Secretariat Office for a one-to-one discussion. She was very respectful as always but complained that my actions were causing her embarrassment in the eyes of her colleagues and party circles. I explained to her the statutory rules about transfers, postings and disciplinary actions and assured that no action of mine would be guided by any angularity nor personal likes and dislikes. I further asserted that reform in agriculture marketing was a mission for me, with very high potential for improvement including in generation of revenues by minimising leakages in collection of market fee. As such, collection of market fee had doubled after my assuming charge of Director, Agriculture Marketing. But, instead of being interested in developing marketing infrastructure, Minister was singularly focused on her position ahead of ensuing General Elections to the State Legislative Assembly. RMCs, I guessed, were means for mobilising resources to fight elections and show favours to fellow travellers. I finally told her that the option available to her was to approach Chief Minister for my transfer as I was not in a position to match her expectations and left her office. After the Kandhamal communal conflicts, when relationship between the coalition partners had strained, within a few months all BJP Ministers, had to quit the Government.

I continued to work on my plan for developing the 3-tier structure of market yards in all 30 districts at an estimated cost of about ₹ 1,000 crore. Market yard at district level was to be spread over an area of 50 acres with separate sections for grains, fruit and vegetables, and animals. Land needed at sub-divisional and Block levels was about 30 acres and 20 acres respectively. Blue print of proposed market infrastructure was being developed in consultation with experts. After appreciating my initiatives, Union Agriculture Ministry pledged financial and technical support. More than ₹ 100 crore was already lying in banks, and I was confident of generating at least ₹ 500 crore within a period of four years from market fee. After all, collection of market fee had already increased exponentially during the 8 months of my tenure to ₹ 112 crore, and cost of establishment was curtailed at 10 percent of revenue generated.

I approached Revenue Department for land. Based on the blue print of my agriculture market infrastructure plan, G.V.V. Sharma, Secretary R&DM, was quick in issuing instructions to Collectors to identify and alienate required government land in favour of Cooperation Department. Alongside, I outlined the proposed infrastructure directly to District Collectors, contacting each one of them personally. As a result of persuasive efforts, including meetings with Collectors, Sub-Collectors and Tahasildars, I started receiving positive responses on identification of land for market yards. In Cuttack and Sambalpur districts, it did not take much time as two stand alone market yards had been identified earlier.

On another democratic front, after Surama Padhi demitted office, Chief Minister Naveen Patnaik remained in charge of Cooperation Department for a couple of months. In the meanwhile, General Elections to State Legislative Assembly were concluded following which one of the senior-most politicians of the ruling party Dr. Damodar Rout became the Minister, Cooperation. RMCs had been used as milch cows by successive Ministers through transfers and postings and by Sub-Collectors heading the committees. When things started looking up and moving fast, I was transferred to RD Department. This was hardly surprising. What the earlier Minister could not do probably due to cracks that had developed between coalition partners, her successor succeeded in getting done within two months of taking charge. My grand plans for developing a holistic 3-tier network of agriculture marketing infrastructure across all 30 districts in the State remained an exercise in futility, a distant dream.

So Close to Refunding Depositors' Dues of a Collapsed Bank

The saga of Bhubaneswar Urban Cooperative Bank which had collapsed with depositors losing their deposits which the bank had attracted by offering an unbelievably high annual interest rate of 13 percent may be of interest. The bank branches had generously advanced loans to about 400 borrowers without verifying their credentials and coordinates. This happened with the active involvement of some senior officials of the Department. Retired employees across Government departments had put their savings and General Provident Fund as fixed deposits to earn super-high interest in this Cooperative Bank. But when they went to withdraw their deposits, there was no money to return. The limited recovery made by bank staff was consumed towards their monthly salary. It was most shocking that though some of the bank officials had been placed under suspension, no efforts had been made to file cases against defaulters; many of whom had not given proper addresses at the time of availing of loans.

Depositors were naturally restless and approached me with their complaints when I assumed charge. State Government had desired to transfer the management of the bank but there were no takers of the liability created by misappropriation of deposits amounting to about ₹ 15 crore. I started reviewing the situation on a weekly basis fixing recovery targets and for filing cases against more than 225 defaulters, some of whom though were known faces but were not receiving notices as addresses given by them were incorrect. The pressure put on bank officials by me improved the recovery position. Reserve Bank of India (RBI) had issued directions to stop all transactions by the bank. The local RBI head now agreed with my proposal to refund the principal amount to depositors in proportion to recovery which had increased from less than ₹ 5 lakh per month to about ₹ 30-50 lakh per month. The fear of civil and criminal actions against bank officials and borrowers alike had started yielding results but the depositors' hope to get their money once again became short-lived.

Chief Secretary Ajit Kumar Tripathy appreciated the proactive role I was playing in the recovery drive. Some of his friends who had lost all hope were able to get back a portion of their principal deposits. Some time after my transfer when I asked him that if he had really appreciated my work, what was the hurry in shunting me out, he replied with sadness that he himself had not been aware of my transfer order till it was issued! Chief Secretary not being consulted or informed about transfer and posting of a senior officer of his team seemed to have become a new normal of State administration! For me, it did not make any difference as RD Department offered no less opportunities in a field so close to my heart.

Investments and Losses: Finger-Pointing at Erstwhile MD, OSCB

I handled an interesting case of certain loss-making investments by Odisha State Cooperative Bank (OSCB). On the basis of a Special Study by NABARD, RBI had recommended criminal investigation by State Government, in addition to imposing a personal fine of ₹ 5 lakh, on the MD of OSCB, on the grounds that RBI Regulations did not permit the cooperative bank to make such investments. These actions had been brought to the notice of Chief Minister, but left unattended after that by my immediate two predecessors.

The case in brief was as follows: OSCB had been investing its surplus in non-statutory liquidity ratio (SLR) bonds/ securities from time to time for generating profit. In the special study of the investment portfolio of OSCB for the period from 1 April 2006 to 31 October 2007 conducted by NABARD, it was found that the bank had purchased coupon bonds and zero bonds worth ₹ 152.97 crore mostly from counter-parties, the value of which was assessed at ₹ 120.24 crore. RBI thus concluded that the bank lost ₹ 32.73 crore in these transactions which could have been avoided had the purchases been made either through prices quoted in Stock Exchange or through Yield-to-Maturity (YTM) based prices. RBI had further observed that OSCB's transactions were in violation of their guidelines issued during September 1992 and June 1996 and provisions of Banking Regulation Act 1949.

In response to the show cause notice MD, OSCB had submitted that Treasury Management Cell of the bank had been purchasing bonds/ securities mainly for trading with the objective of augmenting profits from treasury business. Thus, the bank could not give importance to YTM in transacting the deals and market prices of securities/ bonds could not be ascertained and compared, as they were not listed on the Stock Exchange. Zero coupon bonds had been regularly purchased and sold by the Cell without NABARD auditors or statutory auditors pointing out any deficiencies in trading of non-SLR bonds. As such, the Cell had earned a profit of ₹ 52.34 crore between 2000-01 to 2006-07 including ₹ 4.09 crore during the year 2006-07 by trading in government/ non-SLR securities. It had been averred that the bank had built up an emergency deficiency reserve fund which stood at ₹ 32.99 crore and was enough to meet the purported loss of about the same amount in the later period.

I studied the previous inspection reports of NABARD and Registrar Cooperative Societies of Odisha, and the audit reports of Treasury Management Cell by statutory auditors as required by RBI. I found that no major deficiency in respect of investment activities had been pointed out in any of these reports. Indeed, NABARD's inspections of previous years had praised the treasury operations of OSCB with the observations that "... *the significant expansion of the portfolio was due to increase in the treasury business*", "*the bank was trading in Government/ other securities in the secondary market*", "*the bank has followed the accounting procedure, valuation of investments etc., as per RBI norms and provisions made thereon towards depreciation/ loss*", etc. Due to volatility of the market, the value of many securities had come down. The bank had apportioned an amount of ₹ 411 lakh out of profits for the year 2004-05 towards 'Investment Depreciation Reserve Fund' and during the subsequent year an amount of ₹ 0.31 lakh had been written off towards depreciation in securities. I found that the special study report of NABARD had wrongly called for provisioning on Government of India securities held by OSCB which clearly indicated that the officer who conducted the special study was not well conversant with the relevant guidelines and procedures.

It is not as if OSCB's treasury transactions were strictly in accordance with RBI's guidelines which had been served along with the show cause notice on MD, OSCB before imposing penalty that had already been paid by the bank. The fact of the matter was that OSCB had never seen those guidelines and had framed its own guidelines in the year 2002 on the basis of guidelines issued by RBI to Commercial Banks. This was not being viewed by NABARD or RBI adversely. Incumbent MD when the guidelines were framed was a different person. As the source of price and discounting principle were not known to OSCB personnel nor were they pointed out in earlier inspection reports of NABARD, at the time of purchase price discovery was not made and YTM was not calculated. The price was negotiated by the Cell with counter-party banks on the basis of calculation of simple yield without taking into account YTM. However, there was no evidence of *malafide.* As such, previous inspection reports of NABARD had encouraged them to continue with the same policy finding it in accordance with RBI's laid down norms till RBI imposed the penalty and called for criminal investigation.

This I found was a case of highhandedness as it singled out one MD only and ignored previous reports of NABARD, statutory auditors, etc. In my assessment, he was one of the most upright officers in the entire cooperative organisation. One of his predecessors had caused heavy losses to the bank by lending a huge amount in violation of the banks primary mandate to some industrial units which were declared sick after some time. Since Executive Director of RBI in his letter to Chief Secretary, Odisha had requested for investigation from vigilance angle, I suggested to the State Government that RBI should be requested to share materials in their possession, if any, on the basis of which vigilance probe had been proposed by them. This was approved. In response, RBI forwarded copies of NABARD's special study report and show cause notice that had been issued by them to MD, OSCB. These documents and more had already been studied by me earlier. Special audit conducted by a reputed firm in the panel of NABARD and RBI had found nothing to reveal any serious lapse on the part of OSCB warranting further vigilance probe. OSCB had already discontinued investment transactions on non-SLR securities. Thus, I recommended that this chapter should be closed by State Government without further action on the issue, which was approved.

Cleaning Operations

Office conditions in Cooperation Department too were not conducive for effective functioning, besides being unhygienic. A time-bound plan was drawn up to introduce total quality management in the office. Old records were separated and classified in accordance with prescribed procedure, and the task of consignment completed within two months. Unserviceable furniture, etc. too were disposed of. Office rooms were painted afresh and repairs of broken windows/ doors, etc. carried out. The entire office staff cooperated in reorganizing their seating arrangements which gave a pleasant look besides enabling better systemisation of processes. Usually senior officers remain concerned only about their own amenities. In all my assignments, I did not change furniture and fixtures in my office, but invariably made it a point to improve the arrangements, including amenities, available for others right through the hierarchy. This paid dividends in many ways.

Office of Director, Agriculture Marketing, and Odisha State Agriculture Marketing (OSAM) Board were functioning from a few rented rooms. Despite funds lying parked in banks, no attention had been paid to complete the office building under construction for many years. Land purchased for it was partly under encroachment. The under-construction building had become a milch cow for the contractor and engineers of OSAM Board as changes in specifications and cost escalation were the only regular activities. I got the design frozen and wanted the building to be completed and office to be shifted to the new building within six months of my taking charge. At the end of the day, everyone was happy to see a new office building for OSAM Board and Director, Agriculture Marketing being completed, besides encroachers getting evicted, though I got transferred immediately thereafter.

STATE'S EXCISE POLICY AND ITS IMPLEMENTATION

There was no surprise in my getting additional charge of Excise Department, though I neither had any prior understanding of the subject nor a taste for hard drinks. Indeed, I rarely if ever drank tea or coffee either. Minister in Excise Department had ruined his health due to excessive drinking, though as an individual he was one of the most decent politicians I have worked with. File work in Excise Department was limited to preparing the State's Excise Policy, taking approvals for prices at which shops were to be put to auction, setting up enquiry commissions, implementing recommendations of commissions that enquired into liquor-induced tragedies in which lives had been lost in the past, and establishment matters. By virtue of being Secretary to Government in Excise Department, I was also heading Odisha State Beverage

Corporation (OSBC) as its chairperson. Posting in Excise Department educated me about the various brands of Indian-Made Foreign Liquor (IMFL), beers and other admixtures. I found the assignment quite interesting.

On assuming charge, I found that almost 50 percent space in the rented office of OSBC was locked up and out-of-bounds due to long pending vigilance and departmental proceedings against the first MD of OSBC. Procurements made by him which included furniture, computers, office vehicle, labelling materials, etc. had been questioned, and had remained stacked in sealed rooms and outside, as the criminal cases filed against him had not been concluded. After studying the relevant papers, I did not find any justification in allowing the office to look like a dumping ground for old computers, furniture etc. I also did not find enough force in charges framed against that MD who incidentally was the topper of 1982 batch of IAS. He had been arrested and imprisoned for a considerable period, which to my understanding was more on account of his personal animosity with certain senior officers who succeeded in fixing him up. Indeed, his successor in OSBC who himself had misappropriated a huge amount of funds temporarily escaped action probably because he allowed himself to become a tool in the hands of those who wanted his predecessor to be fixed.

Liquor Guzzling Godowns: Improving Delivery Systems

In my capacity as Chairperson, OSBC, I inspected all major storage godowns where manufacturers of IMFL, beer, etc. stored their products, and which served as distribution points to licensed dealers in different districts. It was beyond my imagination to find long queues of trucks, which I was told was a regular feature in storage godowns at Balasore, Berhampur, Khordha, and Sambalpur. It would require days to take delivery of stocks supplied by manufacturers. Owners of 'On' and 'Off' shops too had to wait for days to take delivery from these OSBC godowns. Surprisingly, despite long queues, rioting or law and order problems were rarely reported by managers in charge of these storage godowns!

On inspection, it became clear that half of each storage godown was occupied by stocks of beer and liquors whose shelf-life was over with expiry dates having passed or the brands were no longer in circulation. The practice of piling crates of fresh stocks vertically on top of old ones also resulted in older stocks remaining unsold. Suppliers were only interested in dumping more and more. Managers of regional godowns had not taken steps to dispose of older stocks before selling new ones, due to difficulty in separating new stocks from old. Since inception of OSBC none had given attention to inventories and proper management of these godowns. As per terms and conditions of agreements with respective suppliers, unutilised stocks after their expiry dates or stoppage otherwise of their circulation needed to be taken back by them. Prescribed rules and procedures called for destruction of such stocks in case the suppliers did not take them back. Manufacturers of IMFL and beer were also required to pay towards rental for delay in taking back their unutilised stocks. After discussing it in OSBC Board, it was decided to issue notices to suppliers of unutilised stocks and publish those notices in national dailies. In case of no response from them within a fortnight, further action could be taken. Managers of regional godowns were directed to hire labour to segregate old stock within a month. All godowns stank due to breakage of some liquor and beer cases/ bottles stacked one above the other up to the ceiling and their spilt contents.

Except one or two manufacturers/ suppliers which included Kingfisher, others did not respond to published notices. It appeared that most of the companies who had supplied beer and IMFL earlier, had changed their brands or closed business and were disinclined to accept any liability for old and expired stocks. Finally, lakhs of beer and IMFL bottles had to be emptied in huge pits dug within godown compounds in accordance with prescribed procedure. It took almost four months to complete this exercise. Very old IMFL stocks and beer with expired date which had occupied almost half of each godown were disposed of finally and records maintained accordingly. A new procedure was laid down for storage and issue under which older stocks prior to their expiry date had to be issued to dealers before, or along with fresh stocks, to avoid accumulation of inventories. The new arrangement started working efficiently and queues of trucks for delivery and receipt reduced substantially.

Replacing Degrading Poly-Packs: Bottling Country Liquor at Aska

Aska Sugar Factory was the only authorised manufacturer of country liquor in the State. There was a huge mismatch between demand and supply, but State Government would not agree to involve private companies in manufacture and supply of country liquor apprehending loss of employment and business at Aska. It was more to do with dependence on generation of cash, not from sugar but from molasses that produced the spirit which would be converted into country liquor. Aska Sugar Factory would buy spirit produced by Shakti Sugar Mill in Dhenkanal too for producing country liquor, yet the demand would remain unfulfilled. This led to illicit brewing of country liquor with its consumption resulting in human casualties at regular intervals. Patra Commission of Enquiry, which went into the liquor tragedy in Ganjam in 2004, had found that some people engaged in illicit brewing had taken out the spirit from tankers carrying it from Shakti Sugar Mill in Dhenkanal to Aska Sugar Factory in Ganjam. Illicit country liquor produced from this spirit turned poisonous and killer of many of those who consumed it.

Country liquor manufactured by Aska Sugar Factory was marketed through authorised distributors in poly-packs of 200 ml each. Workers' pressure did not allow State Government to modernise the packaging. In spite of procurement of bottling equipment, these were not utilised fearing labour unrest in the factory. To me, it was quite unsightly to see consumers of country liquor awkwardly drinking it from cheap plastic packets. On calculation, I found that country liquor packaged in small bottles would cost extra no more than ₹ 2.50 per unit. Drinking from glass bottles, as in case of IMFL, added some respectability to consumers, besides being more environment-friendly. I decided to go for bottling and finalised procurement of bottles for packaging country liquor at Aska. I visited the factory and spoke to workers, mostly women engaged contractually for manual packaging. It was promised that none of them would be retrenched, and their services would be utilised differently. There was no option but to utilise the bottling plant and change the packaging system failing which it was difficult to retain the consumer base in the long run. Almost all the workers committed to cooperate in packaging country liquor in bottles. Within a fortnight, the bottling plant which had been procured a couple of years back, became operational. The cost did not exceed my assessment.

Tragedy with Liquor: Hooch Deaths

The loss of human life due to production, distribution and consumption of illicit liquor visited Odisha State quite regularly. Hooch deaths of 1992 were 550 in Cuttack district. Biju Patnaik, the then Chief Minister had then famously and remorselessly not only refused to visit the affected families but had also commented that he did not care for lives of those who consumed liquor without knowing its ingredients and quality. People in the business of illicit production of country liquor were usually connected politically. A weak administration lacked will power and wherewithal to deal with offenders with severity and strictness.

Commissions were set up to look into illicit production and distribution of liquor largely to manage the momentary public anger. After years and months, reports submitted by Commissions headed by malleable retired Judges were consigned to the office almirah. In the scratchy report of Patra Commission on Ganjam hooch tragedy of 2004, there were indications of highly-placed officials being involved though its conclusions were different. The Commission had recommended, *inter alia*, capacity building measures in terms of setting up laboratories and sanction of technical manpower. Though State Government had accepted most of the recommendations, proposals for budgetary provisions for creating requisite infrastructure had been routinely turned down by State Finance Department.

The role of influential politicians mostly from the ruling party in illicit trade of country liquor also became evident when excise auction and opening of IMFL shops were not allowed in high-potential areas on artificially-created grounds including prompted agitations. Recurring loss of human life due to consumption of non-standardised illicit liquor, besides uncontrolled and unregulated consumption of alcoholic products, affected the society particularly poor women in multiple ways. It led to a demand for ban on alcohol, which despite leakages and unauthorised sale was one of the main sources of State's revenue. A couple of States did ban sale of liquor without achieving success at the cost of revenue. Paradoxically in those States in spite of laws enacted for complete prohibition, active and retired personnel of military and para-military forces were allowed to lift and consume their entitlements of IMFL every month. Consumption of liquor procured from neighbouring States surreptitiously also continued unabated. Under Chief Minister Bansi Lal, Haryana had tried to enforce complete prohibition, but loss of revenue and surreptitious procurement of liquor from neighbouring States forced his successor to do away with prohibition after four years.

In tribal areas, consumption of country liquor is associated with cultural traditions of indigenous communities who are legally allowed to brew up to a certain quantity of country liquor in Odisha. It is possible for the State to spend a certain percentage of excise revenue in strengthening regulatory infrastructure for enforcing laws to disallow production and consumption of alcohol beyond permissible limit instead of imposing outright ban which cannot be enforced to prevent people from drinking in these circumstances. Almost all allopathic medicines contain a specified alcohol content. Complete prohibition cannot succeed in the given and developing social trends even if it is imposed country-wide. In the name of popular protest, liquor shops are not opened or ordered to be closed in certain places, which at times is only to enrich vested interests and illicit sale. As such general policy does not permit opening of liquor shops within a certain distance of educational institutions, places of worship, highways, etc. What is critically important is enforcement of rule of law, which if done sincerely and honestly would amount to holding accountable some of those responsible for enactment and enforcement.

A fragile political and administrative atmosphere is manifest in terms of uncertainties and delays in approving the excise policy and its implementation including omission of potential areas. Even so, during my incumbency as Secretary, Excise and additionally holding charge of OSBC, the growth in collection of excise revenue exceeded 20 percent over the previous year. It gave me some degree of satisfaction to get godowns of OSBC cleaned of aged useless stocks and systematise and transform management of inventories. Operationalisation of bottling plant at Aska and packaging changes introduced there were a win-win for all stakeholders.

Exposing Rampant Cultivation of Cannabis

A monumental problem faced by Excise administration was unauthorised cultivation of Cannabis (Ganja) in some districts. In Chhendipada and neighbouring Blocks in Angul district where a very high groundwater table encouraged farmers to grow seasonal vegetables in the past for higher profits, cultivation of Ganja in the last few years had become rampant. In a few other remote and tribal districts, Ganja cultivation had also increased.

A standard or perhaps convenient explanation for this dangerous trend offered by enforcement functionaries was that some Naxalite groups active in those areas were forcing farmers to cultivate Ganja as this was the main source for their financial sustenance. Excise and Police personnel conveyed their inability to visit those areas adjoining or surrounded by forests stating that they were not adequately equipped to confront Naxal groups who allegedly protected Ganja cultivators. I did not believe this excuse having visited Naxal-infested areas extensively in my earlier assignments. I was sure about connivance between local leaders, police, revenue and excise personnel in illegal cultivation of Ganja and, therefore, wanted to visit villages under large-scale cultivation of Ganja. Commissioner, Excise drew up a programme for my visit and advised me to request district SP to provide police force to supplement Excise Police. I spoke to district administration of Angul and took on board the SP who agreed to accompany me during raids that had been planned.

During my visit to villages in and around Chhendipada Block of Angul district, which were not very far from the National Highway, I found the SP conspicuously absent having found an excuse to go out of the district. Local police officials and Revenue Inspectors in addition to Excise Police force, including Excise Commissioner, accompanied me from village after village where the best farm-land under vegetable crops a few years back was now being used for Ganja cultivation, involving supply of inputs and complete buy-back arrangements with agents from Jharkhand. The agents also provided protocols of cultivation practices to be followed. The profits generated reportedly were very high which encouraged farmers to grow more. To avoid exposure, maize cultivation had been undertaken as shields encircling the plots under Ganja. Small open wells provided controlled irrigation for the crop. Cultivators who were guarding their crops ran away finding themselves surrounded by police force and other enforcement officials. Although standing Ganja crops were destroyed to the extent possible during the raids, I was convinced that police officials of local Police Stations and outposts, revenue inspectors, excise officials and local elected representatives could not have been unaware of Ganja cultivation at such a large scale. After all, with just one visit, I had discovered field after field prolific with Ganja cultivation.

The impression given to me before visiting the area was that cultivation of Ganja was taking place in forest villages infested by Naxal groups. I went to visit such villages also. After covering a considerable distance inside the forest, excise and forest field functionaries could not show me an inch of land in forest villages under Ganja cultivation. I had just wanted to call their bluff and succeeded. Cultivation of Ganja systematically and scientifically in controlled conditions as I saw on fertile lands during the visit, was impossible to be carried out on forest land or forest villages inhabited by tribal communities which did not have irrigation facilities through dug wells or otherwise, nor fertile lands. It was not difficult to identify the cultivators of Ganja and suppliers of inputs who also happened to be the buyers, if the local administration wanted to take action against them. My tenure in Excise Department was a short eight months, co-terminus with Cooperation Department. It was thus not possible for me to handle the issue of illegal cultivation of Ganja holistically and effectively within this short period.

An interesting experience during my incumbency in Cooperation and Excise Departments was in relation to my performance appraisal. Having two concurrent Reporting Officers one each in two departments, I was curious to know as to how they assessed me. I, therefore, submitted my self-appraisal reports to them separately. When disclosure was made as per extant rule, Chief Secretary as supervisory officer in Cooperation Department gave me a 10 out of 10. Development Commissioner who was my Reporting Officer in Excise Department gave me 9 out of 10. It was a case of two examiners assessing the same candidate differently at the same time. Subjectivity overtook objectivity, though I have never yearned for the perfect 10.

TENURE IN RURAL DEVELOPMENT: HOISTING FLAGS OF FLAGSHIP SCHEMES

After transfer from Cooperation and Excise Departments on 2 July 2009, I worked in RD Department upto 13 November. 2009. Three Centrally-funded critically important flagship schemes – PMGSY, Rural Sanitation, and Drinking Water projects – were being implemented in addition to a few other smaller programmes in rural areas. State Plan for rural connectivity included construction of a few bridges financed by NABARD under Rural Infrastructure Development Fund. RD Department received funds from other line departments too for construction and repairs of their buildings which were not situated in urban areas, besides smaller allocations as additional SCA, Finance Commission grants, RLTAP for KBK districts, etc. for a few projects.

Prime Minister's Gram Sadak Yojana (PMGSY)

Under PMGSY, villages with population of 500 each and above were required to be connected by all-weather standardised roads. To cover the thinly populated villages of tribal and hilly regions, the population norm stood relaxed to 250 for a cluster of villages. In the first phase of the programme, Central Government wanted to cover villages each with a population of 1,000 and above which stood relaxed to 500 each for tribal and hilly areas. I found this norm strange as it did not give priority to remotely-situated villages and ST&SC habitations beyond main villages. It also ignored the fact that almost every road to be constructed for connecting distantly-situated small villages necessarily covered bigger villages on the way. Same was the case under village electrification and drinking water supply programmes. Smaller villages in scattered and thinly-populated tribal areas always suffered due to this 'big bias' among planners and policy makers of India. As a result, 45 percent geographical area of Odisha where tribals constituted more than 50 percent of the population suffered the most. Existing fair or all-weather roads were included under PMGSY for execution with improved standards for villages with higher population of coastal and other relatively more developed areas. For example, Kandhamal with about 2,500 revenue villages had only 250 villages with population of 250 each and above. Obviously, only a few villages of this district could qualify for connectivity under PMGSY. This also suited engineers of RD Department who would not like to work in remote locations which lacked creature comforts.

The first thing I highlighted in every forum was directed at rectifying the flaws in planning process prescribed by Union RD Ministry. Per chance Cabinet Secretary visited Odisha and sought a note when I reacted adversely to the "one size fits all" approach which ignored the problems of relatively more backward areas. I pointed out that tube wells for drinking water-deficit villages are found on the road side far away from identified villages, simply because heavy rigs could not reach the target areas in the absence of roads. Union RD Ministry finally accepted my contentions, albeit reluctantly, and called for DPRs for covering clusters of villages with population of 250 each in tribal districts. I had already initiated action for preparation of DPRs in anticipation of norms being revised.

Another situation I noticed was that the guidelines clearly stipulated that roads requiring forest clearance and land acquisition should not be included in PMGSY action plan. Yet, roads under PMGSY were seen left incomplete at some places on account of private and forest lands falling in its path. State Governments were required to bear cost of land acquisition or alternative land for afforestation, wherever required. Only after making undisputed land available, DPRs for PMGSY roads could be submitted. Somehow, State RD Department had submitted DPRs and obtained approval for roads requiring forest clearance or involving private land by non-disclosure of the ground reality. Majority of such roads which had been abandoned after completing construction on undisputed portions were in tribal districts.

All such roads were identified during my reviews and field visits. Plans for their completion with timelines were drawn, failing which engineers concerned were to be held accountable. I could persuade senior officers of Forest Department at district and State levels not to "split hair" and instead to extend cooperation in completing the incomplete road stretches which did not necessitate felling of trees. The problem was that in tribal districts survey and settlement operations had been taken up in the past only in a limited way. All un-surveyed land, with or without tree cover, was being interpreted as forest land in accordance with certain rulings of Supreme Court. Such interpretations made it impossible to provide all-weather connectivity for a large number of tribal villages. In this situation, construction of roads without felling trees offered a 'win-win' situation for all stakeholders. As regards private land required for construction or completion of roads, the option I suggested was either to persuade the land owner to gift the land in the larger interest of village community or persuade the contractors to pay the value of land from his profits without any cost escalation from sanctioned project funds. Efforts made accordingly indeed helped in addressing the problems confronted by executants to the extent that almost all the incomplete PMGSY roads due to land disputes, got completed within a few months as a result of meticulous monitoring.

When I wanted to focus on thinly-populated scattered villages of tribal districts, Union RD Ministry had advised me to first complete ongoing roads languishing for years after approval. This was a reality and had to be tackled. The worst situation I found was again in tribal districts, particularly of Southern Odisha. I started inspecting the incomplete roads one-by-one and as frequently as possible to address the bottle-necks. It was found that the majority of contractors here were from outside the State. My experience, however, had convinced me that it was easier to handle contractors from outside the State if their dues were cleared in a timely manner and obstructions faced by them in implementing projects were handled sincerely. When I analysed the causes of abnormal delays specifically in Koraput, Malkangiri, Rayagada and Nabarangpur, which accounted for the bulk of pendency, it became clear that contractors had abandoned those roads after been paid 30 percent to 35 percent of estimated cost. In most cases, existing Panchayat Samiti or Gram Panchayat roads were being widened and brought to PMGSY standards, which did not involve much investment for road formations through earth works. Obviously, payments made to contractors in the name of initial road formation and cross drainage works were far more than the value of works actually done on the ground. As compaction work had not been done, incomplete roads had become much worse for use due to incisions caused by heavy rains, etc.

Senior engineers in charge of road projects accompanied me when I conducted inspections. I gave them no choice but to bring back the contractors to ensure completion of remaining work and timelines along with milestones were decided in consultation with them accordingly. They were directed to inform me directly if any hurdles were faced. Construction materials were sufficiently available. Heads of district administration had assured that they would facilitate by rendering all possible logistics support. Engineers were also clearly informed that vigilance enquiries will invariably be conducted in case the correspondence between volume of work done and payments made was not found. My main objective was to get incomplete works completed by giving the engineers one more chance along with necessary administrative support. Criminal or departmental actions following vigilance enquiries could only delay the projects further and, thus, had to be the last option.

After returning from a field visit in Koraput and its neighbouring districts, I suddenly received a telephone call from Principal Secretary to Chief Minister wanting me to meet him immediately. Monsoon Session of Legislative Assembly was on. When I met him, he informed me that the ruling party's Chief Whip who represented Jeypore Assembly Constituency in Koraput had complained to Chief Minister that I was putting unnecessary pressure on engineers to complete roads without giving them adequate time and without understanding their genuine problems! What I had apprehended turned out to be true. The leader under reference had a good hold over government functionaries and contractors of not only his constituency but also of neighbouring areas. It was a clear corroboration of what I had been told by senior district officials that during State Legislative Assembly and Lok Sabha elections held a few months back, the Neta had most probably taken support from contractors and engineers, and here I was now fixing timelines for completion of roads without cost escalation. The standard practice followed after getting paid for profitable earth works was to leave the incomplete roads and retender them after some time adding some more villages and distance to present fresh DPRs for sanction as new projects. PMGSY guidelines did not permit cost escalation normally. Fresh DPRs were the way out. This trick being played was unacceptable. Even without any problem from left-wing extremists except in a few places, abandonment of works was thus being attributed to their threats.

I reasoned with Principal Secretary that logically elected public representatives should be happier if developmental projects like roads were implemented in their areas with speed and quality as they could take credit for such works. The time-frame of up to one year for implementing PMGSY roads was already over. I shared my earlier experience with the Principal Secretary when the Chief Whip had similarly opposed expeditious execution of residential schools and hostel buildings for tribal students in and around his constituency. I was Secretary for ST&SC Development at that time. B.K. Patnaik, Principal Secretary to Chief Minister did not react beyond giving me a wide smile, as if to say that he had fulfilled his formal obligations to convey Neta's complaint. In the next review meetings, I warned senior engineers in charge of PMGSY roads not to indulge in political games and to focus on completing ongoing projects in their own interest. The message delivered, most of the abandoned road works started progressing fast.

In Lanjigarh Block of Kalahandi, I inspected a road project on which more than ₹ 3 crore had already been spent, and had been shown to have been completed whereas it was more than 50 percent incomplete. Nothing more than road formation and granular sub-base had been constructed. I found that a couple of kilometres had been added by including a few more villages to the same road project with a new nomenclature in revised DPR approved by Union RD Ministry. Project cost stood revised to about ₹ 10 crore! The contractor executing the extended road was also the same. Executive and Superintending Engineers who had accompanied me reported that the project in modified form was being implemented in accordance with the directions of Chief Engineer, Rural Works. I asked the Executive Engineer to send the case records of both projects to me along with an explanatory note. The volume of work in my eye-based estimation was far below the reported expenditure.

After returning to State headquarters, I called the Chief Engineer to know the reasons of what had appeared to me a cleverly committed fraud. His explanation was that DPR originally presented and approved for the road shown as completed had not estimated the actual cost realistically. The previous secretary, according to him had advised verbally to prepare a fresh DPR with a different nomenclature for the same road with some additional distance! I advised him to get the matter recorded by approaching the former Secretary failing which I would have to bring the matter to the notice of Chief Minister for action against the delinquent officers. Finding no response even after seven days, I prepared a self-contained note for the perusal and approval of Minister and Chief Minister to act against the delinquents. Minister B.K. Arukh, a decent politician, had been briefed by me on the matter in presence of Chief Engineer before putting up the note. I also spoke to Anup Patnaik, Director, Vigilance on the course of action from vigilance angle. He advised to refer the matter to him and assured action at the earliest. I sent the details to him demi-officially, separately. Curiously, nothing happened. The file containing my proposal for action submitted to Minister/ Chief Minister had not returned till I left the department a few months later.

The case of another PMGSY road in Keonjhar was even more distressing. The contractor had filed a case in Arbitration Tribunal for his claims. On receiving the notice, as no information on the matter was available in my office, I called Chief Engineer, Rural Works to find out about the case. He narrated a curious sequence of events as follows: Junior Engineer in charge of this project was suspended for taking a bribe from the contractor as per enquiry conducted by the area Superintending Engineer. It appeared that even after taking gratification, the Junior Engineer had not recommended payment of legitimate dues of the contractor to his superior. The work did not proceed further due to this non-payment. In the meantime, a flash flood destroyed the entire work that had been executed and more. The contractor subsequently refused to complete the project at the same cost. He approached Arbitration Tribunal for payment of his dues and damages. On the basis of a spot enquiry report submitted by Superintending Engineer, Junior Engineer had been suspended. Executive Engineer who was politically well-connected was transferred to a better location in Cuttack. While major penalty proceedings were pending against the Junior Engineer, Chief Engineer was told to reinstate and revert him to his parent Water Resources Department. Later on, he resigned from his post and was given a ticket by the ruling party to contest the State Legislative Assembly election that followed. He won the election and became a law maker!

I moved out of RD Department shortly, but two years later I had a chance meeting at IGI Airport, New Delhi with Pyari Mohan Mahapatra who was then a member of State Ruling Party in Rajya Sabha. To my surprise, unprovoked he raised the matter stating that he regretted having given a ticket to that former Junior Engineer to contest the Assembly Election in 2009 adding that he had been ignorant of the corruption charges against him. I recalled that a few months after those elections, as Secretary of RD Department I had submitted a detailed report against this former Junior Engineer notwithstanding his new status as a law maker. I had been a bit taken aback when the controlling authorities permitted the delinquent official to resign. I had asked Secretary, Water Resources Department and his Engineer-in-Chief as to how the resignation of an official under major penalty proceedings could be accepted? Both had repeated what had been said to me by Chief Engineer, Rural Works, that Pyari Babu had pressurised them personally to accept his resignation and they had complied! It was in bad taste on their part to abdicate their responsibility and hold someone else responsible for failure in implementing statutory rules and procedures. The irony was that Pyari Babu, who then remote-controlled the State Administration, in his bureaucratic innings had seldom held such officials in high esteem. Whatever may be the reality, the recollection of the case by Pyari Babu clearly suggested that my report put up to RD Minister had indeed reached him instead of Chief Minister. In the face of such shenanigans, I never enquired as to what happened to my findings and to arbitration proceedings.

Rural Sanitation and Drinking Water

Rural sanitation scheme was meant for families below the poverty line. Financial support was provided to the target group for construction of household sanitary latrines. In my assessment and priority, it was one of the most important schemes, but which had been messed up more than any other programme. In its first avatar as Central Rural Sanitation Programme, the scheme had been introduced in 1991 by Union Government without attracting enough priority either in Central or State Governments. The scheme required mass mobilization at village level with the involvement of Gram Panchayats and village level functionaries under the technical supervision of Block level officials. It was difficult to fathom why the task of implementing it, earlier assigned to Panchayat Raj Department which had the network capacity, got suddenly transferred to RD Department which had hardly any presence in all Blocks. The revised arrangements could thus signal lack of Government's interest in rural sanitation. The net result had been inaction on the ground and misappropriation of funds by submitting false physical and financial achievements. During my field visits, lack of awareness among villagers emerged everywhere. In a few villages where some efforts had been made to construct toilets for beneficiaries of IAY, sanitary latrines had become partly or fully defunct due to inadequate availability of water. As such, it was essential for sanitation and drinking water supply schemes to go hand in hand to succeed. It however, did not mean that both schemes should be implemented by the same department.

Rayagada district had reported an exceptionally high achievement under sanitation scheme during the previous year. I wanted to understand why performance of relatively more advanced districts was poor, when this predominantly tribal district had done so well. Under the drinking water supply scheme too, Rayagada district had registered better performance than others. I drew a tour programme to visit the district to analyse the success. After hearing about my tour, the Executive Engineer on deputation from Urban Development Department, suddenly got himself repatriated without informing RD Department or the posting of a substitute. I had no reason to suspect anything out of the ordinary at that stage. I visited a good number of villages where higher achievements had been reported under both schemes. It was shocking to find that villagers were not even aware of the sanitation programme. The so-called beneficiaries of sanitation did not exist and false reports had been submitted showing expenditure of about ₹ 10 crore in the name of individual household toilets!

Tube wells for drinking water had been sunk without platforms, drainage, soak pits and in many cases, they were without even hand pumps. No information regarding their depth and water yield including its quality was available. Many had become defunct even before being completed. I submitted a report to Government explaining what had happened. The former Executive Engineer after repatriation to his parent department proceeded on study leave immediately. State Government passed orders to place him under suspension just before I demitted office. Failure of sanitation scheme was primarily due to lack of interest and thrusting it on RD Department which was not equal to the task. When performance under a scheme is judged by expenditure alone, misappropriation is a sure outcome.

Implementation of drinking water scheme included piped water supply projects for clusters of villages. The scheme had some contradictions in policy planning and implementation. The minimum unit of families for a tube well in a village was 50. There was no alternative if the only tube well in the village went out of order or yielded inadequate or bad quality water. Odisha had about 50,000 revenue villages on record, with more than 1.42 lakh habitations. Tribal villages in hilly and forest areas were tiny and scattered and did not qualify under population norms for tube wells or supply of drinking water in other forms. Besides, lack of road communication to a large number of smaller villages, particularly in remote areas, made it extremely difficult for a heavy rig to be transported there for sinking tube wells. Many a time, tube wells were installed by the roadside 3-4 km away from such villages as if sunk for the benefits of contractors. Safe drinking water was reported to have been made available and targets achieved.

It was a quirk of nature, almost confounding, that the State which received an average annual rainfall of about 150 cm and accounted for more than 10 percent of the country's sweet water resources suffered drinking water scarcity in large stretches of its land. Tribal regions being the origins of a number of perennial and semi-perennial rivers, it was easier to supply piped water to remotely located villages which suffered regularly due to epidemics and other water-borne diseases due to consumption of unsafe and contaminated water. It was ironical to find the State Government not inclined to spend funds from its own resources, but rather found it generally expedient to blame Central Government for allocation of inadequate funds to meet safe drinking water requirements of even villages deserving serious attention. As the policy was biased towards bigger villages, piped water supply scheme and tube wells for drinking water ensured better coverage in thickly populated villages. Requirements of remote tribal villages remained suppressed and largely unattended. Allocations from State's calamity relief fund for new tube wells during extreme summer when existing drinking water source dried up, rarely benefitted far-flung badly-connected tribal villages.

Political considerations and cheap populism in implementing piped water supply scheme resulted in haphazard implementation which defeated its objective. In order to show higher coverage within limited allocations, piped water supply scheme largely excluded provisions for overhead tanks which were essential for controlled distribution in a cluster of selected villages. Project components included bore well, construction of pump house, laying of pipelines, and a few stand posts in villages. Drinking water would be available only when the pumps operated for a couple of hours in the morning and evening. Water supply invariably got disrupted if the contractually-appointed operator could not run the pump for lack of power supply in the village or it broke down and required repair. Water rarely reached stand posts at the tail end. Within six months of execution, piped water supply projects usually became defunct and there were no provisions for repair and restoration. At any point of time, about 50 percent of piped water supply projects remained out of operation. Guidelines called for involvement of village community in identification, execution and maintenance, but the projects were executed through contractors without any public participation. Villages remained dependent on tube wells or other traditional sources for meeting their drinking water requirements.

I was, however, successful in convincing the Minister that no new piped water supply project should be implemented without provision for an overhead tank. I also pleaded for constructing overhead tanks in projects that had already been executed, but State Government needed to provide required funds for this component as Central Government could not contribute towards projects reported as completed. The only option to contain further damage was not to allow execution of new projects without provision of overhead tanks to regulate distribution of water. Nothing could be done for the huge infructuous expenditure already incurred. The executing agency did not follow the prescribed guidelines and hardly believed in accountability.

Tube wells for drinking water needed to have provisions for elevated platforms, drainage and small soak pits to regulate the wasted water in order to maintain proper sanitation. In reality, except in few villages with demanding gentries, most of the tube wells stood executed in violation of prescribed specifications. There was also no transparency in execution. Quality and discharge of water along with depth of tube well remained shrouded in mystery. This happened due to lack of direction, accountability and attention. Short-term gains by far overtook long-term interests. Even villages by the sides of perennial rivers and other water bodies suffered due to non-availability of safe drinking water. About half of Nuapada district suffered due to heavy fluoride content in the groundwater which made tube well water unfit for consumption. There were two big water bodies and a few rivers that flowed through the district. Yet villagers did not find drinking water except through tube wells contaminated heavily. One could feel the pain of finding a 15-year old youth appearing as if an old man of 75 years of age, and men and women with stunted growth unable to bend their bodies. This was nothing short of criminal negligence on the part of State Government. Since financial support of Central Government under the drinking water scheme was limited to tube wells and smaller piped water supply projects, State Government remained insensitive to the problem which was maiming or killing upcoming generations slowly and steadily. Even villages relocated for implementing lower Indra major irrigation project, did not have access to safe drinking water. It was difficult to understand what prevented the State Government, which spent thousands of crores annually on irrigation projects that remained perpetually incomplete, to spend a few crores for potable water to save lakhs of lives.

During a meeting at the highest level, I brought to the notice of Chief Minister the alarming toll on human health due to consumption of fluoride-contaminated water in the absence of any other alternative. I suggested that State Government should provide funds and timelines for supply of drinking water from upper and lower Indra major irrigation projects through pipelines to the affected villages as there was no other option. I was directed to approach Union Government for funds and ensure that piped water projects were implemented in affected villages within a definite time-frame. Chief Minister perhaps thought that like the 100-seated 1,004 ST girls' hostels, projects for drinking water could also be executed quietly without making corresponding budget provisions. When I met the Secretary concerned in Union Government, I was chastised for the State Government having done nothing more than writing letters to Central Government. I was bluntly informed that it was not possible to provide funds under Centrally Sponsored Scheme for projects that required heavy investments and that too without the State committing to contribute its matching share.

Majority of piped water supply projects in the State were becoming defunct within six months to one year of execution as they were mostly left incomplete and there were no provisions for repair and maintenance. The quality of materials used was also questionable. Procurement of materials centrally or at divisional level involved corrupt practices leading to allegations and enquiries which further affected execution. The scheme provided for community participation and contribution in implementation of projects. After completion, projects needed to be maintained either by respective Gram Panchayats or by local committees constituted for this purpose. Since individual household connections were not being provided, none cared to maintain the stand posts put up in villages using sub-standard materials.

On the other hand, Gram Vikas, a leading NGO operating in some tribal districts had implemented a good number of piped water supply projects which were being maintained by village communities. Repair and replacement of pipes in the event of damage due to natural calamities, etc. was done by village committees which collected monthly subscriptions. After hearing about the good work done by the NGO, Chief Minister himself had invited and wanted it to be involved in implementing drinking water projects in some tribal districts. I invited Joe Mediath, head of the NGO who was known to me for more than 20 years, for his participation in executing piped water supply projects only to be told that he had not received money spent by his organisation for implementing many projects in the past in accordance with decisions taken at the level of Chief Minister. As such a few projects, which the NGO had taken on promises of funds to be made available, were still incomplete. On enquiry, I found that what the NGO had said was factually correct. The dues for work already implemented amounted to more than ₹ 5 crore. Rural Water Supply and Sanitation officials in RD Department holding key positions had taken the NGO as a rival rather than involving it in executing projects in a cost effective and sustainable manner. They had indulged in a mudslinging match. Resultantly, the NGO had quietly withdrawn. I issued instructions for clearing the dues after verification in order to complete the incomplete projects and for taking up fresh ones. After my departure from the department, I was informed that the NGO was again ostracised by my successor who had been my predecessor.

* * * *

11

Highest Office: Cabinet Secretariat and its functioning

I took charge as Joint Secretary in Cabinet Secretariat with its office in the grand Rashtrapati Bhavan on 18 November 2009. It marked a second but last departure from my practice not to intervene in a governmental decision regarding their perceived suitability or desirability in the matter of my posting. I had applied for this second Central Deputation with a view to conclude my administrative innings in Central Government, though providence decreed it otherwise. I was informally apprised in advance of my posting in Ministry of Minority Affairs. Although it rarely happens in civil administration, but my experience as Secretary OBC & Minority Welfare Department in State Government might have tilted the scale in favour of this selection. I was blunt in my instant response that this was not a posting I could do substantive justice to. During an official tour to Delhi I met both Secretary and Establishment Officer in DoPT to say that despite my eagerness to join the Union Government, I would prefer to suffer being debarred due to my inability to take up the proposed assignment if the proposed posting could not be modified. When I indicated my inclination to submit the reasons in writing, I was advised not to do so and that the proposal would be put up for reconsideration. Thankfully, my situation was internalised by those involved in the process of selection and posting in DoPT. The order was revised by Appointments Committee of Cabinet with placement of my services in Cabinet Secretariat.

I had reasoned that some of key recommendations of Sachar Committee being translated into various Centrally Sponsored Schemes by Ministry of Minority Affairs were divisive and held potential to disrupt our fragile social fabric, besides creating disharmony when compared with schemes for ST&SC populations. It was vital to suitably modify or harmonise them with the schemes being implemented through Ministries Tribal Affairs and SJ&E for ST&SC. I was emphatic that socio-economic indices of some minority communities, particularly Muslims, were low and in many instances comparable with those of SCs, but were above those of STs. I had cited, for instance, that it may be better for Central Government to introduce a merit-based pre-matric scholarship scheme for STs/ SCs in line with the one being implemented for minorities. This scholarship for minority community students @ ₹ 600/- p.m. had created difficulties in Odisha as for ST/ SC students pre-matric scholarship was as low as ₹ 15/- p.m. for day scholars and ₹ 400/- p.m. for boarders. Christian community, mostly of ST&SC converts, was less than 2 percent of Odisha's total population. Unlike converted STs, converted SCs *de jure* lose the benefits of protective discrimination upon conversion. It was unreasonable to allow pre-matric scholarship at these unjustifiably different scales, particularly when applied to boarders in the same schools to STs, SCs and minorities. Such discrimination could potentially be interpreted as incentivising conversion of STs and SCs besides leading to an unnecessary controversy. Thus, I had advised State Government to revise pre-matric scholarship for ST/ SC boarders to either the same scale as for minority community students or at least ₹ 500/- p.m. in which case for minority community students also the amount be limited similarly for maintaining parity. State Government had approved the latter proposal. Since then Centrally Sponsored Scheme of merit-based pre-matric scholarship for minority community students was being implemented in a slightly modified form in Odisha to which Union Ministry of Minority Affairs had no objection. In this situation, it would be unacceptable to reverse my reasoning and to implement the scheme, and others like it, while holding a key position in Union Ministry of Minority Affairs.

Cabinet Secretariat is under the direct to control of Prime Minister and its functioning had to be aligned with Prime Minister's Office (PMO). In the past, there had been occasions of Cabinet Secretariat headed by senior-most civil servant and viewed as Chief of all Services being marginalized by power-chasing Secretary or Principal Secretary to Prime Minister. That situation had changed a bit when I was in Cabinet Secretariat with incumbent Prime Minister, an academician and hardly a conventional politician, who valued the considered views of Cabinet Secretary K.M. Chandrasekhar despite such views not necessarily going hand-in-hand with the final decisions taken.

Cabinet Secretariat is the Secretariat for and services Cabinet/ Cabinet Committees/ Groups of Ministers (in some cases). This vertical is responsible for Allocation of Business among various Ministries/ Departments and for Transaction of Business by Central Government. Thus, Cabinet Secretariat resolves policy and implementation issues raised by a Central Ministry through issues-specific Committee of Secretaries (COS) chaired by Cabinet Secretary. Political approval for policy is initiated by the Ministry/ Department concerned by way of a Note for Cabinet/ Cabinet Committee which is appropriately placed on the agenda and further serviced through Cabinet Secretariat. The proposals contained in such Notes are more often than not given final shape through deliberations of a COS.

A very lean establishment, requirements of work were substantially different from development and regulatory administration I was used to in my career till now. Work largely entailed inter-departmental coordination on cross-cutting policy or administrative issues where line Ministries were not able to reach consensus by themselves. Oversight of handling of disruptions in public order and situations of man-made and natural crises and disasters on priority basis was also a standing responsibility of Cabinet Secretariat. This was discharged through various High-Level Standing Committees headed by Cabinet Secretary – COS on Anti-Aircraft Hijacking, Strategic Policy Group, Special Protection Group, Joint Intelligence Committee, National Crisis Management Group on Cyber Security, National Information Board on Cyber Security, National Committee on Maritime and Coastal Security, Task Force/ Review Group on Left Wing Extremism, Review Committee on Interception of Communications, National Crisis Management Committee, etc.

Work was allocated amongst Joint Secretaries along functional lines – economic, social and political. States/UTs were also by and large grouped under them based on preponderance or immediate priorities of such Centre-State issues being raised by States/UTs. For each vertical, Joint Secretary was the frontline functionary exercising on his behalf the authority vested in Cabinet Secretary and assisting him directly in disposing of policy and implementation issues elevated to his level by various Ministries/ Departments of Central Government or by States/ UTs. Secretaries heading Ministries were also required to furnish fortnightly/monthly reports conveying important decisions and developments including actions taken to implement earlier ones. Cabinet Secretary was regularly briefed about them on file. Routine day hardly mirrored another. Timelines were vital to keep. In brief, a Joint Secretary in Cabinet Secretariat was comparable to a 'backroom' trouble-shooter.

Posting in Cabinet Secretariat thus provided a birds' eye view of the entire horizon of policy-making and challenges faced in implementing the decisions taken at the highest of all levels. It also provided deep insights into subject matters handled by functional verticals because only the trickiest of issues requiring intermediation of Cabinet Secretary were brought to a COS before its consensus-based recommendations were included in the Cabinet Note. A Director/ Deputy Secretary supported by a Cell is assigned to each Joint Secretary for this subject-specific work, who also prepares draft minutes of meetings of COS, no easy task as often the nuances of consensus reached between Secretaries took careful handling.

A second opportunity to study the final proposals from a political perspective arose when the Note for Cabinet/ Cabinet Committee was examined for its suitability to be submitted for decision to the polity. The Secretariat for Cabinet/ Cabinet Committees serviced every Joint Secretary on procedural aspects of Cabinet Notes pertaining to him, thereby leaving him to his own on substantive examination of proposals contained in each Note and to his recollections of the issues handled at COS stage. The fact that the Ministry fielding the Note is practically at his beck and call to clarify factual matters is of enormous help most of the times. But on some crucial or complex matters where the Ministry's position may not be straightforward, the Joint Secretary is on his own in sifting out the wheat from the chaff. The Notes for COS or indeed for Cabinet/Cabinet Committees would be received just a few days prior to the meeting, which meant that time was invariably a constraint. Functioning of Cabinet Secretariat is regulated by Official Secrets Act to a large extent, though enforcement of Right to Information Act, 2005 had led to large overload of work on furnishing information sought by Indian citizenry as many Ministries found it expedient to pass the buck by averring that it was the prerogative of Cabinet Secretariat to defray information on Cabinet decisions and on issues cutting across Ministries. Be that as it may, it would not be appropriate on my part to write about the telling, and at times titillating, details about matters involving secrecy.

I found my assignment unusual but interesting, despite having experienced my own share of disappointments on some occasions. I found many a time that important decisions taken by the authority at highest level were not necessarily based on merit. K.M. Chandrasekhar, Cabinet Secretary, was suave, erudite, polite, and a hard taskmaster, but one who allowed full functional freedom to his subordinates. He expected officers under him to remain thoroughly well-versed with the subject matter and brooked no slack in examination of proposals. Results of this scrutiny covering financial, economic and substantive implications and administrative ramifications were required to be presented by Joint Secretary in an insightful, incisive, and pithy brief along with recommendations to Cabinet Secretary. Since Cabinet/ Cabinet Committees met every week at least once, on a fixed day he would hold his meeting with Joint Secretaries to take up all Cabinet Notes on the agenda during that week. It would not be an exaggeration to call it a "weekly test" for Joint Secretaries. Scope of the test changed every week depending upon 4-5 subjects and issues covered in the Notes that fell in the Joint Secretary's lap that week. He had to be literally 'master of all'! Observations made by K.M. Chandrasekhar in a soft but firm voice, if he did not find that the Joint Secretary equal to the task could be the most unpleasant experience. I witnessed him underlining inadequacies in the briefing provided by a Joint Secretary; it was a virtual admonishment before peers. Similar experiences undergone by a predecessor were also legion. Fortunately, I did not suffer such embarrassment, and indeed, enjoyed the best of times and his confidence during my tenure in Cabinet Secretariat. I was often given additional work, unrelated to subjects I was formally assigned, which too was thoroughly enjoyed by me.

Initially, I was allotted social sectors, which required engagement with Ministries covering HRD, H&FW, Women & Child Development, Tribal Affairs, SJ&E, Minority Affairs, Labour & Employment, Environment, Forest

& Climate Change, Sports & Youth Affairs, Telecom & IT, etc. The Director, from Central Secretariat Service, was very thorough in rules and procedures. I did not know that he had been handling service matters and proposals for postings under Central Staffing for a long time, to be suddenly replaced due to his excessive orientation and implacable position on rules and procedures. Despite having a sharp mind, his understanding about social sector and development-related issues was not very good which I realised after a couple of meetings of COS. In fact, the only time I felt a bit embarrassed was when Secretary, H&FW pointed out that her statement in a COS meeting had not been found suitably reflected in the minutes which already had approval of Cabinet Secretary. A corrigendum was issued. It was a lesson for me after which I made it a point to take notes of COS discussions carefully and draw up the minutes myself till my charge was swapped with that of another Joint Secretary, which naturally resulted in the change of Director and other subordinate officials.

Steely Resolve Underpinned Auctioning of 3G Spectrum

An important development which was drawing a lot of attention when I assumed charge was ensuring that impending allocation of 3G spectrum did not repeat the mistakes of 2G spectrum. The procedure followed by Telecom Department in allocation of 2G spectrum on 'first come, first served' basis and a piece-meal approach were being widely criticised in public domain. Central Government at the highest level on the advice of Cabinet Secretary had taken a policy decision to auction 3G spectrum in one go transparently. Cabinet Secretary was very particular in reviewing progress in this regard. Total availability of 3G spectrum was 65 MHz which included 25 MHz in control of Defence Ministry. A MoU had been executed between Telecom and Defence Ministries according to which spectrum in possession of Defence Ministry could be vacated subject to a time-bound implementation of commitments, which included exclusive optical fibre networks for Air Force, Navy and Army to provide them safe and protected communication systems, each costing about ₹ 10,000 crore. An Empowered Group of Ministers headed by Finance Minister Pranab Mukherjee, with Defence and Telecom Ministers as members, had been constituted to review and maintain oversight over implementation of the MoU. Cabinet Secretary was a part of it as well. Despite the overt leaning of Sam Pitroda towards telecom, in the face of his attempts to reinterpret the MOU, Defence Minister A.K. Antony did not want him to be involved in the process. The telecom Czar was, thus, kept at arm's length in 3G spectrum allocation process.

Without doubt there were differences in interpretation of clauses which contained time-bound milestones for exclusive optical fibre network projects for armed forces between Telecom and Defence Ministries. Telecom Department had drawn up its own plan with an accompanying software package containing timelines to handle auction of 3G spectrum which did not fully correspond with the MoU. But Defence Ministry insisted to strictly follow the MOU in letter and spirit, and outright rejected assurances of Telecom Department to make up for delays in placing orders for procuring equipment to implement the defence project component. There came a time when Telecom officers and experts held that auction of entire 3G spectrum in one go might not be possible. Telecom Joint Secretary came to my office and informally handed over copies of office notes containing views and advice of Wireless Advisors and others in his Department, all proposing piece-meal allocation of 3G spectrum considering the inflexible stand of Defence Ministry in relation to implementation of the MoU. He advised me to persuading Cabinet Secretary accordingly. My advice to him was not to change the goal-post by advancing any alternative course, but rather to take course correction themselves and urgently take up measures for implementing the MoU in letter and spirit. Wading into this tightly drawn opposites, Ratan Tata of Tata Group had met Cabinet Secretary with a representation that Government should go for open auction of 3G spectrum in one go. I reported these internal developments in Telecom Department, backed by their internal file notes, to Cabinet Secretary. As expected, Cabinet Secretary's resolve became stronger. He succeeded in convincing the Empowered Group of Ministers. Finally, auction of the entire 3G spectrum was carried out in one go.

Total yield to the exchequer from the auction was more than ₹ 1.32 lakh crore which exceeded everyone's expectations. When I conveyed my view that he was singularly responsible for this achievement, Cabinet Secretary shared with me that Prime Minister himself was not convinced about his assessment that this auction could fetch about ₹ 30,000 crore. Realisation of 3G spectrum yield was taken into account to simulate presumptive losses of about ₹ 1.75 lakh crore by C&AG in allocation of 2G spectrum in a piece-meal manner by Telecom Department. That led to a huge embarrassment for Central Government. I was a bit surprised when Telecom Joint Secretary who had wanted me to convince Cabinet Secretary otherwise tried to take credit and proposed his own nomination for Prime Minister's Award for Excellence for the success of 3G auction! With inquiries into 2G spectrum allocations still in the making, it is anyone's guess what would have happened if change had not happened for 3G spectrum allocation. I felt happy to be involved in the process of 3G spectrum allocation in a small way by assisting Cabinet Secretary who demonstrated his mettle and steel without succumbing to any manipulative and pressure tactics. A performer public servant is known for his work carried out far away from publicity and image-building exercises. Alas that anonymity could remain the hall mark of civil servants as it once was the case in the past!

24x7x365 Handling Defence, Security, Intelligence Work

Within about four months of joining Cabinet Secretariat, my assignment was modified. Cabinet Secretary had closely watched my work for some time. Recognising that I had worked as Director in MHA for about three years and dealt with subjects concerning Centre-State relations, the sensitive charge of political, internal and external affairs was assigned to me. Ministries/ Departments now handled included External Affairs, Overseas Indian Affairs, Home Affairs, Defence, Atomic Energy, Space, Law & Justice, Election Commission, National Disaster Management Authority (NDMA), National Security Council Secretariat, etc. Most of the High-Level Standing Committees also came under my purview, besides the border-States of Jammu & Kashmir, North-East, island-States/ UTs and Naxal-affected States. The Joint Secretary with whom this charge was swapped was senior to me in service and had spent more time in Cabinet Secretariat. He was however, happy with this change, as he had interest and experience in social sectors, particularly health and education.

The nature of my work changed and calls to report to work within 15-30 minutes for handling crises, law and order, political and security matters meant that work consciousness became 24x7x365. Crises are unpredictable. Their management, particularly at rescue and relief stages, is overseen through National Crisis Management Committee headed by Cabinet Secretary at national level on a daily basis for the duration it is required, which in the cases of Jat agitation and Manipur road blockades took weeks and months. Daily report needed to be sent to Prime Minister on important developments within the country and abroad. I was happy to remain in readiness, and also not to claim any weekend or public holiday as a matter of right, and worked through them as often as the situation demanded.

I remember that it was a Sunday evening when a massive earthquake devastated Sikkim. Within an hour, I could successfully organise the meeting of National Crisis Management Committee and within three hours two Air Force AN-32 and IL-76 planes with trained personnel of National Disaster Response Force (NDRF) along with equipment reached Bagdogra on the way to Gangtok. A massive cloud-burst, which devastated Leh in Jammu & Kashmir earlier, was another such crisis which happened just before winter had set in. In this case, apart from rescue and relief stage, some post-devastation developmental work on the hospital, schools, and pre-fabricated houses which could help the locals withstand the biting cold of winter was also monitored. I recall organising instant meetings to deal with breakdown of public order, handling disasters, and crises management in varied situations such as hacking of Indian cyber infrastructure, Jammu & Kashmir stone pelters' law & order situation, Manipur economic blockade, piracy and hijacking of Indian merchant vessels/ crew by Somali pirates, evacuation of overseas Indians from Libya, massive bomb blasts in important places, cyclones 'Laila' and 'Thane', oil spills in Mumbai harbour due to collision of MV Khalija and MSC Chitra and sinking of MV Rak Carrier, and aerial defence of Delhi. 'Rail Roko' agitations demanding reservation in educational institutions and public sector jobs, separately held by Jats and Gujjars had taken a violent hue, besides causing blockage in rail and road transportation at many points across Haryana, Uttar Pradesh, Delhi and Rajasthan. These called for intensive Centre-State interactions besides coordination with MHA and intelligence networks. Political agitations for separate statehood of Telangana leading to frequent breakdown of law and order, and various Naxal attacks on Central Para Military Forces with sizeable casualties and kidnapping of DM, Malkangiri by left-wing extremists were some other complicated matters requiring close monitoring and discreet interventions.

In this assignment, for the first about eight months due to certain sensitive requirements, I was required to put up Submission Notes from Cabinet Secretary to Prime Minister every evening before close of day after gathering intelligence inputs on the day from Indian Embassies/ High Commissions abroad, besides military, civil, financial and commercial intelligence inputs from various and multiple quarters. The periodicity changed to twice a week thereafter, though inputs received from all had to be scrutinised every day and any crucial matter therein was submitted instantly. Some Standing Committees had a mandate for fixed reviews as well, apart from the ones which were called when the need arose. I remember that global initiatives were being led by India to contain the menace of high seas piracy in the Indian Ocean, particularly along the Somalian coastline, and these entailed frequent meetings of National Committee on Maritime and Coastal Security and close coordination with Defence Ministry, Indian Navy and Indian Coast Guard, apart from our Embassies abroad. The Director who assisted me in this assignment was one of the most competent officers I have ever worked with. Without delving into them, suffice to say that the task of handling top secret sensitive matters was most educative and exciting. Besides formally assigned functionalities, I was given additional assignments which I felt were indicators of Cabinet Secretary's growing confidence in me.

Commonwealth Games-2010: Making it Happen Finally

XIX Commonwealth Games (CWG), an international multi-sports landmark involved the participation of 71 teams (Fiji having been suspended from Commonwealth) in 21 disciplines and 272 distinct events. The Games were to be held for the first time in India, the second time in an Asian country, and the third time by a developing country, from 3-14 October 2010 at New Delhi. There was a huge buzz around this event. Independent India had only hosted the two Asian Games way back in 1951 and 1982. In November 2003, India had managed to win the bid to hosting of CWG-2010 by the skin of its teeth after ousting Canada. CWG-2010 was meant to herald and showcase that India could successfully host such mega events.

I handled matters concerning Ministry of Sports & Youth Affairs, but not CWG, during the first four months of my tenure. Soon after the launch of

Queen's Baton Relay with official launch of CWG-2010 in October 2009, the report of Indian Government on preparedness showed that two-thirds of Games venues were way behind schedule as though the years had simply gone by since 2003 when the bid had been won. Serious concerns were expressed by CWG Federation, whose President Mike Fennell stated that slow progress of preparations was a serious risk to the event. The Government appointed Jarnail Singh, a retired IAS Officer as CEO of CWG Organising Committee in a move to redress matters. But a crescendo on lack of preparedness, delays, unhygienic conditions, and enormous cost overruns and associated perception of large-scale and unbridled corruption picked up in the media. A few participating countries added to the woes by hinting that India as a developing country was perhaps not up to the mark to host the event of such mega proportions.

This turn of events, with about 9 months to go, had virtually shaken the Central Government at the highest level. Finding the Chairman of CWG Organizing Committee difficult to handle, Prime Minister instructed Cabinet Secretary to informally take charge. Cabinet Secretary drastically changed the tempo of his review of preparedness and ensuring inter-departmental coordination in meetings of COS on CWG-2010 from the occasional intervention whenever a concern was brought to his notice, to holding regular weekly meetings, and later on to daily ones. Since Cabinet Secretary was not completely sanguine about the way the Cabinet Secretariat itself was dealing with the subject, suddenly one day I was asked to replace the Joint Secretary concerned and to assist him more proactively.

It was already end-April 2010 and just 5 months to go. I started visiting the 12 Games venues and 5 other sites connected with CWG, starting my official day at dawn. I used to submit daily notes containing details of projects which gave my own assessment of the situation and what needed to be done. The heat and dust of Delhi, with temperatures soaring to 42°-44° Celsius, were my difficult companions who could not be brushed aside, what to speak of evasive contractors, engineers and officials responsible for developing the Games' venues and sites. They were on the backfoot and anxious not to be hauled over burning hot coals for the tardy state of affairs. Cabinet Secretary started appreciating my detailed, but honest and blunt assessment about the physical preparedness. It was the true picture based on on-site field visits, in sharp contrast with the verbose feedback being given by Secretary Sports and other senior officers in his meetings of COS based on heresy. It also overwhelmingly contradicted the rosy picture of accomplishments based on expenditures being incurred by CWG Organising Committee that had been fed to him previously. The charge of CWG-2010 along with Department of Sports was formally added in my portfolio.

Serving in State Government earlier, execution of projects as per prescribed timelines was my forte. I brought my past experience fully into the fray in order to deliver on CWG requirements, as befitting its international spotlight and knowing that upholding national prestige was a priority. Cabinet Secretary was happier with my proactive functioning. He found comfort that multifarious works at 17 sites were all now under strict and comprehensive scrutiny with milestones and timelines mapped out and being adhered to. With no alternative in hand, I had to play a lone wolf role that reminded me of actions of mine as Collector & DM, Ganjam, that had first led to the moniker "Terror Datt", which barring a few colleagues from Odisha, perhaps few were aware of in Lutyens Delhi.

Handling CWG-2010, early on I came to realise that the malaise lay deep in time. In fact, it was a dastardly and false lesson that could be drawn of how a hapless and nervous Prime Minister at practically the last hour simply transferred the entire responsibility of ensuring preparedness and execution of the Games till their finale to a hair skin-thin establishment run by Cabinet Secretary. It also showed how he could not rein in and hold responsible for the mindless and enormous delay any of the six senior officers who had held the post of Sports Secretary ever since India won the bid for hosting CWG-2010 in 2003. He was inexplicable diffidence in holding to account anyone in Indian Olympics Association (IOA) headed by Suresh Kalmadi. This covered up the failure of IOA to recognize its own role required to be played vis-à-vis the administrative establishment, so that the available time could be used to optimal advantage in a cost-effective manner to prepare for the Games.

It is worth recalling that the first meeting of Group of Ministers (GOM) on CWG- 2010 headed by HRD Minister Arjun Singh was chaired by Prime Minister himself in October 2005. The blue-print prepared by Department of Sports was an excellent one which had flagged issues that were critically important to be decided upon by GOM. One of them was the need to set up an Organizing Committee for the organization and oversight of the entire process up to the smooth conduct of CWG in October 2010. In the meeting, GOM unanimously decided that the Organizing Committee would be headed by Sports Minister Sunil Dutt. Minutes of meetings were recorded and sent for approval of Prime Minister through Cabinet Secretary B.K. Chaturvedi. Curiously, when the minutes were issued it was seen that the decision of GOM to appoint Sports Minister as chairperson of CWG Organizing Committee stood modified! A surprised Sports Minister wrote a long letter to Prime Minister reminding him about the unanimous decision on his appointment taken by GOM, and very gently suggesting that perhaps an unintentional error had occurred in omitting this decision in the minutes that had been issued. In the meanwhile, an Office Memorandum signed by Joint Secretary Pulok Chatterjee was issued from PMO directly stating that Prime Minister had passed orders appointing Suresh Kalmadi, President of IOA, as Chairman of CWG-2010 Organizing Committee! This dark turn of events way back in 2005 was suggestive of what may be expected to happen in the years to come until

2010. It was the beginning of what pushed the Government of India on complete tenterhooks five years later and indeed brought India to the brink of reneging on its commitment to host the CWG-2010 in a timely manner. The attendant infamy and embarrassment of charges of corruption and lack of preparedness were heaped on the whole nation. Jarnail Singh, CEO of Organizing Committee, a retired IAS officer who had served two successive Prime Ministers in PMO as Joint Secretary, both mild-mannered and decent was unequal to the task of handling the unpredictable chairman-driven Organizing Committee on his own.

It was not as if Government bodies, including Delhi Government, which were involved in developing CWG-related infrastructure had completely neglected or prevaricated on their work. The main problem was that even well-meaning senior officers in charge of developing multiple Games' venues had not been getting the briefs on specifications submitted by sports bodies. Under the system that was operating, these briefs were being routed through IOA before final approval was accorded by CWG Organizing Committee, whose Chairman would habitually change them whimsically and that too frequently at the last moment. This invariably resulted in time delays and cost escalations of items, especially those involving imports. Also, a plethora of brand ambassadors were appointed by the Organizing Committee on heavy payment, in addition to hosting numerous parties for celebrating the forthcoming Games. There was little political will to question, let alone control, projections of expenditures and changes in specifications. It is interesting that total expenditure estimated for hosting CWG-2010 barring the cost of sports infrastructure before the award to India was projected around ₹ 210 crore whereas the final projection made just for two Opening and Closing Ceremonies was about ₹ 450 crore! Finance Minister Pranab Mukherjee had to put his foot down by limiting expenditure on these ceremonies to about ₹ 250 crore.

When the dates of the Games approached, efforts to publicize them also received momentum. At this stage, a prominent media house wanted to be associated as a co-sponsor but expected to be paid for lending its name/participation. As I was informed by DG, Doordarshan, the amount this media house wanted to be paid being sizable, its request failed to find favour. The media house soon enough took centre-stage in leading the doubting brigade on lack of preparedness, besides writing about allegations of corruption. A whirlpool of adverse publicity and aggression was generated when other media houses joined in, none wanting to be left behind in the race for exclusive reporting, particularly since allegations of corruption and governmental misdemeanours had become the flavour of the season. Organising Committee and its leadership failed to muster credibility to counter the narratives against them, despite many of them being false and conjectural. This made the task of executing agencies implementing the projects on sports' infrastructure increasingly difficult. They remained wastefully engaged in issuing clarifications to clear the air of confusion, thus crowding out precious time to be spent on development works. More meetings of GOM and COS on CWG also started consuming time that needed to be devoted in delivery of results. Unable to contain the Organizing Committee's Chairman, a largely apolitical Prime Minister placed higher reliance on his Cabinet Secretary who was to retire in the middle of June 2010. He was granted a year's extension of service in advance, which caused a lot of heartburn in aspiring candidates some of whom were his friends and cadre mates.

My main responsibility was to trouble-shoot and issue clarificatory instructions on the spot problems faced by executing agencies developing 17 Games venues – sports' complexes, practice venues, Games Village, Media Centre, and other projects. While submitting drafts for ratification of Cabinet Secretary subsequently, I was also expected to bring immediate interventions required to the notice of Cabinet Secretary. Construction of flats by Delhi Development Authority (DDA) at Vasant Kunj for accommodating national and international technical officials, and a number of flyovers for easing traffic, were seriously lacking progress. Cabinet Secretary started reviewing such projects proactively in meetings of COS on CWG by involving heads of organizations under Central and Delhi Governments. Lieutenant Governor of Delhi too started holding parallel meetings resulting in more confusion in decisions, diffusion of accountability, wastage of time and finally the blame-game. None, however, had authority nor courage to question and suitably restrain the unbridled whimsicalities of Chairman, Organizing Committee. He continued to enjoy his epicurean lifestyle and added additional financial liabilities by delaying approvals on event-managing logistics, a situation exploited by national and international vendors, charging many times more than the actual cost.

Finding the Cabinet Secretary quite active, the Organizing Committee set up to conduct the Games, became more passive. It remained reticent and reluctant even to take possession of Games venues and other facilities till a mere a week before the Games. At this stage when Cabinet Secretary was driving the last hour preparations, removal of Chairman of Organising Committee was not an option even if Government wanted to do so. Memorandum of Association and Bye Laws of Organizing Committee did not provide for removal of Chairman, who seemingly arm-twisted a helpless Central Government in many possible ways. Senior officers of Ministries of Sports and Youth Affairs, Finance, Urban Development were members of various committees including on Finance, but they had to comply with his whims as the only objective before Government at that stage was to somehow ensure CWG-2010.

It was also strange to find that some executing agencies were failing in completion of works assigned to them, and yet projecting a performance nearing completion in dissonance with ground reality before Cabinet Secretary. Renovation of Connaught Place, construction of Shivaji Stadium, construction of DDA flats at Vasant Kunj and a few flyovers were such projects. Lieutenant Governor of Delhi who was also Chairman of DDA displayed confidence about timely completion of Vasant Kunj flats and related infrastructure, which was not borne out by my assessment given to Cabinet Secretary. After assessing carefully, I suggested that since completing the flats looked an impossibility, alternative accommodation had to be found. In the GOM, headed by Minister for Tourism & Culture Jaipal Reddy, when Lieutenant Governor conveyed supreme confidence regarding completing these flats in time, Cabinet Secretary drew attention to my assessment which projected manpower requirements, including carpenters, electricians, plumbers and masons, required to work in three shifts every day if the flats were to made accommodation-worthy by end-September 2010, while current deployment was hardly 10 percent. Even if manpower was somehow arranged, supply of electricity would be vital. But here too, work had not even started on installing transformers and underground electrical cables, erecting poles for street lighting, etc. for instance, had not even started. Being in possession of full facts, it was embarrassing for me to contradict the Lieutenant Governor before a shocked GOM. After some time, this component was given up, except for housing national technical officials in a few one-room DDA apartments which were segregated from the main area. International technical officials had to be accommodated in hotels.

Connaught Place in May-June 2010 looked like a place ravaged by war. Repair and renovation works spread out extensively were moving at a snail's pace. Yet, Chairman of New Delhi Municipal Corporation (NDMC) responsible for execution of work continued to present a rosy picture in the weekly review meetings. I suggested that scope of work needed to be limited to over-ground renovation and closed. At least another year was needed to complete underpasses and car parking at the prevailing speed of work. My assessment was based on hard facts and detailed feedback from NDMC site engineers, who were perhaps not consulted by their administrative head before making tall commitments in review meetings or before GOM. Shivaji Stadium, a practice venue for hockey, had no hope of being completed before the Games, but again NDMC Chairman was misleading all by giving false hopes that he would ensure completion in time. Sports Secretary, being from his cadre and predecessor in NDMC, chose not to expose him. I presented the detailed ground work done over last two years being less than 30 percent , concluding that by no stretch of imagination remaining 70 percent of Shivaji Stadium could be completed in next four months. Senior officers heading the executing agencies had mostly avoided site visits so far, and seemed to have formed their assessment as though based on superficial reports by some sycophants in organizations headed by them. There was no other plausible explanation for the mismatch with my assessment.

Cabinet Secretary agreed to visit some sites to verify the stark gaps between my assessment on doables and those of heads of executing agencies. I had also wanted him to draw his own conclusions since exaggerated cynical projections by media were at variance with my practical way forward to complete the job on war-footing basis. He visited Connaught Place, Jawaharlal Nehru Sports Complex and Barapullah flyover. He appeared fully in agreement with my assessment and indeed started me calling his 'eyes and ears' on matters concerning CWG. I invariably put up drafts for his consideration wherever his intervention was required. Besides approving them, he would call and instruct senior officials concerned to do the needful and report with updates regularly. It was paradoxical that Cabinet Secretary could find time to inspect some Games' venues during these fire-fighting operations, but Sports Secretary opted to depend only on feedback received from others.

Some flyovers being linked to CWG, though unconnected and at initial stages of construction, had to be separated out in order to focus specifically on essential ones. By end-June 2010, Shivaji Stadium had progressed to only about 40 percent, when NDMC Chairman started showing nervousness. Ultimately Shivaji Stadium was excluded from CWG schedule. It took about two years to complete post-CWG. The scope of work was drastically reduced on renovation of Connaught Place, focussing attention on over-ground work such as repairs, painting, beautification, lighting, etc, all aimed at restoring the aesthetics of one of the most visible architectural landmarks of Lutyens Delhi. Underground work was conceptually desirable, but its slow pace of execution thus far made it a hostage of time. The preparatory period was not the right time to fix accountability of officers at decision-making levels in executing agencies for abnormal delays and misleading presentations thus bringing both embarrassment to the Government and ignominy to the nation. But, after the Games were over it would certainly have been possible. Administration without accountability is anarchy of sorts, which was at display in adequate measure in the preparatory first five years of CWG-2010.

With regard to crucial Games' Venues, incumbent Sports Secretary Sindhushree Khullar and other senior officials had made colourful presentations in April 2010 suggesting that 90 percent to 95 percent of works had been completed and that only final touch up or finishing works remained for which there was enough time. Such conclusions made on the basis of reported expenditure based on booking of procurements concealed more than what they revealed. After visiting Sports' complexes everyday initially and then at least once every alternate day, I started countering these projections, and could show clearly that despite the spanking pace shown after April, even by end-June the corresponding physical progress could not touch 90 percent. During field visits, I found that site engineers were blissfully unaware of exaggerated projections being made by their departmental heads on the status of their projects. The real problems being faced by them were neither being reported nor addressed.

By way of examples, Delhi Police did not permit movement of heavy vehicles carrying construction materials and equipment during the day time. These vehicles remained stranded in the name of security checks causing large avoidable delays. Organizing Committee had not given the approved brief for "play of field" which triggered further delays in other fields of works. For laying cables, multiple agencies were doing the same work one after the other, instead of synchronizing their works at the same time. I carefully noted such problems and on behalf of Cabinet Secretary brought them to the notice of agencies concerned in addition to briefing my boss and highlighting problems solved in COS meetings. Perhaps feeling acutely on the defensive after a series of such meetings, Sports Secretary Sindhushree Khullar once called me to the room of Secretary Coordination after a COS meeting. I was told by her that many of her senior colleagues were unhappy with me and were heard saying that I would be dealt with appropriately once the Games were over as the protection of Cabinet Secretary I enjoyed would not be there for all the times to come. The underlying threat that I would have to face a rough official weather was clear as crystal that once incumbent Cabinet Secretary retired. I simply submitted that my only mission was to assist her in conducting a successful CWG-2010 and that this was not possible without highlighting the realities. I also requested her to consider taking some field visits for a realistic self-assessment of the works at hand.

Incumbent Sports Secretary had been Additional Secretary, Economic Affairs, a key associated department when 2G spectrum allocation painted as 2G scam by media had taken place. She was now facing the dubious distinction of being part of what was projected by media as CWG scam. Before getting posted there, she served as NDMC Chairperson and had awarded CWG-related works worth crores as records revealed later on, on nomination basis perhaps without application of mind though she was a sharp-minded person. Shunglu Committee set up to look into CWG-2010 irregularities had pointed out the lapses committed by NDMC under her chairpersonship. Her warning to me could not materialize as I cut short my Central Deputation and returned to my parent cadre for personal reasons within about 15 months after CWG-2010. She being a well-connected and all-weather veteran, improved her position in the corridors of power. After her posting as Secretary, Planning Commission, when Planning Commission was abolished by the successor Central Government, she became the first CEO of NITI Aayog and enjoyed post-retirement extended tenure as such. This perhaps proves that in matters of appointments to key positions, merit is defined in terms of ability to manage contradictions and keeping political powers happy by exhibiting expertise in pliability.

My daily brief to Cabinet Secretary showed that pace of execution had substantially improved in four months since April 2010 due to proactive role played by him. About four weeks prior to the Games, apart from myself who held the overall coordinating assignment, nine senior officers holding the post of Joint Secretary/ Additional Secretary in various departments were formally identified by Cabinet Secretariat. Designated as 'Special Officer', each officer was made in charge of a specified Games venue, with two of them in charge jointly of Games Village. Their tasks were to oversee, co-ordinate and tie up loose ends with delegated responsibility to take decisions on the spot in matters which did not involve any financial implications. Recognising that the general system of command and control across Department of Sports and others had broken down, these officers were told to remain in touch with Sports Secretary and Cabinet Secretariat in order to raise any matters requiring the latter's intervention. Cabinet Secretariat had been in mission mode, more akin to crisis-management mode, for the last nearly five months, the only objective being to somehow complete preparations and to manage the Games event.

In-your-face adverse publicity by media had drawn attention of many participating countries. Through their High Commissioners, some started questioning the ability of India to ensure safety, security and hygiene of their sports' persons, a case of adverse perception created nationally and internationally about abnormal delays, poor quality of works and charges of corruption. Some also started throwing tantrums, casting doubts about participation of their athletes. They desired safety certificates to be presented to Commonwealth Secretariat and verification of competition venues and Games' Village. Tragically, media reports, which egregiously mostly contained dated photographs or photo-shopped images rather than those reflecting the latest status of Games' venues, had alone formed basis of their apprehensions. It was humiliating to hear such presumptive concerns in meetings held by Cabinet Secretary when their apprehensions were required to be laid to rest. K.M. Chandrasekhar's second extension of tenure as Cabinet Secretary was now considered vital in order to ensure the smooth conduct of CWG-2010. National prestige was at stake and Government at the highest level had no other reliable option. Accountability had become a casualty in Sports Department; probably one reason for it was frequent changes of its administrative head. Six officers had held post of Secretary after the Games were awarded to India in November 2003.

Games Village, near Akshardham temple at the banks of River Yamuna, was on a low-lying land. Floods due to unprecedented rains had led to an overflowing river, which left no outlets for release of rain water from the Village into the river. Heavy rains lasted right until 26 September, as though nature was determined to hamper the finishing and final stage of works at some Games Venues, and particularly at Games Village. There were occasions when an atmosphere of hopelessness and helplessness became all pervasive. It even started affecting the morale of Cabinet Secretary who had valiantly soldiered on with the heavy burden cast on his shoulders in the last six preparatory months by Prime Minister. The unusual heavy rains in September thus worked as fuel to the fire emitted by an increasingly belligerent media.

Secretary, Co-ordination Ajit Seth was one of the most-friendly officers I had seen. Although Cabinet Secretary expected his more active participation by visiting Games' venues regularly to resolve problems on the spot, his only visit to the Games Village materialized towards the last week of September when heavy rains and resultant flash flood in River Yamuna had inundated the Games Village completely. Basements of residential Tower Blocks for athletes got fully submerged and flood water in some places reached four feet high. It was a highly exasperating and confounding situation since furnishing of quarters was in the last throes of completion. For some time even after rains had ceased, the flooded shafts of some lifts caused inconvenience to athletes who had also begun to pour in by now for practice, acclimatisation, and familiarisation with Games' venues. After returning from the Games Village, in the meeting held by Cabinet Secretary late in the evening, Secretary, Coordination narrated his assessment stating that all the lifts in 22 Towers of Games Village were dysfunctional; there was no power supply due to submergence of basements; and that there was widespread water-logging on the grounds even though it had been a sunny day. Cabinet Secretary for the first time showed frustration, and bluntly asked whether he should request Prime Minister to consider cancellation or postponement of the Games. I too had just returned from the Games Village and was quite dismayed to find a hopeless picture being painted by Secretary, Coordination after his flying visit earlier on during the day. I presented the latest status refuting much of what had been portrayed and submitted that powerful pump sets had been operating round-the-clock; dewatering of basement had been completed and that lifts were now operating in 18 out of 22 Towers. The remaining four were expected to become functional within a couple of hours after I had left the Games Village late evening. Power supply had been fully restored. There was no reason for pressing any panic button when we were on the verge of crossing the finishing line. The facial expression and demeanour of Cabinet Secretary changed instantly. He reiterated that only I should accompany him to the GOM meeting.

The situation was completely transformed in a prodigious brinkmanship when heavy rains stopped end-September. Dark clouds lifted to reveal that all infrastructure projects including 3 km long flyover on Barapullah Nala stood virtually completed. Cabinet Secretary emboldened by the happier picture of the Games Village accepted my request to visit both the Games Village and Jawaharlal Nehru Stadium, the site for the inaugural ceremony for his own satisfaction and to convey appreciation for the good work done by NDMC, MCD and Delhi Government functionaries. At Jawaharlal Nehru Stadium, I showed him the front-page story published in "The Times of India" that inaccurately contained a large photograph of an incomplete Stadium. Obviously, the newspaper had not carried out any ground-level verification and had pejoratively published an old photograph unmindful of the deeper impact on national prestige. Such reporting had not only embarrassed the Government of India in public perception but also misled participating countries into believing in their shrill, exaggerated and false 'breaking news' emanating from across various news rooms in India. Perhaps the competition among media houses to publish titillating stories that cast the nation in poor light was tougher than the sporting competition among athletes of 71 participating countries!

More was to come. Commonwealth Secretariat suddenly insisted that completion and fire safety certificates for all sports venues and Games Village must be forwarded to them. Some High Commissioners had already visited some sites and complained about unsatisfactory performance of fire-fighting systems. I was surprised to find that as a matter of routine, in complexes constructed by DDA and other Government departments in NCR of Delhi, rarely any attempts were being made to fulfil mandatory requirements of issuing completion or occupancy certificates by the competent authority. These were issued after a lengthy process based on a prior detailed inspection by relevant regulatory departments and agencies, such as Fire Services, Delhi Urban Arts Commission, NDMC, MCD, Delhi Electricity Regulatory Authority, Central Public Works' Department, etc. To enable issuance of completion or occupancy certificates for all Games Venues, with the approval of Cabinet Secretary, I invited their authorised officers to Cabinet Secretariat and got the prescribed formats for such certificates signed and issued instantly since the luxury of time to go through the processes of site inspections by each of the bodies was hardly available. These certificates were handed over to senior officials of Organizing Committee for transmitting them to Commonwealth Secretariat. High Commissioner of Australia, incidentally of India origin, who had been amongst the most vocal critics, finally appeared to have been left with nothing more to say.

CWG-2010 should be remembered for the spirited participation of athletes of all the participating countries, including from India and its neighbouring countries, and the international acclaim India finally won for the smooth conduct of a vibrant international event of mega proportions. India achieved its best ever medals tally and sports hereafter became more than just cricket. India stood proud not just of its athletes, but also of two other 'teams'. The security and police establishment ensured that all high risks and threats of disruption of CWG-2010 were duly mitigated without allowing any distractions or divergences from the high celebration of sportsmanship by athletes sent by 71 countries, not all of whom saw eye-to-eye with each other politically. The second 'team' comprised of nearly 20,000 artistic performers at the Inaugural and Closing Ceremonies, who were forced to play out their final act without even once having done a 'dress rehearsal' at the venue, the vast arena of Jawaharlal Nehru Stadium. These performers per force practiced their role and event far away at the Army Parade Ground, as the grounds of Jawaharlal Nehru Stadium were being readied for the sporting events and any damage to the central turf and tracks for athletics could not be put to risk especially since heavy rains right through till September had thrown more than infrastructure out of gear. A single full-dressrehearsal for Inaugural Ceremony at the Stadium would have provided one opportunity to the performers to familiarise themselves with their positions and get their bearings in the network of underground passages from where they would enter the field. It is hardly documented anywhere that this rehearsal, scheduled to be held on 1 October 2010, was cancelled because the Stadium was clamped down for security purposes four days prior to the event by Home Minister in the face of heightened security risk. The synchronised performance of these performers, most of whom had never been inside the Stadium in their lives, was matchless in many hidden ways too minute to be recorded here. The spectacular Inaugural Ceremony displayed well India's diversity and culture artistically.

Not to be outdone, Delhiites and many sports lovers and aficionados across India scripted their own important footnotes for readers to read and applaud. They had stood a mute witness to the adverse media blitz for months and international criticism of India. But, throughout the Games' they showered whole-hearted applause on participating athletes, hardly jostled or broke queues. They kept Delhi clean by exhibiting a remarkable civic sense, even traffic discipline. No ugly quarrels or unruly behaviour of fans marred CWG-2010.

Most touching and heart-warming for me was the full support showered as though in one voice by all India which rose in resounding applause in Jawaharlal Nehru Stadium when the Inaugural Ceremony commenced after the National Anthem was sung. It was as if India valued the last five-six months of intensive work done day-in-and-day-out by the core preparatory, organising, and engineering teams and thousands of workers who never gave up and toiled through heavy rains, but made CWG-2010 happen without cancellation or postponement. That night after months I slept most peacefully.

Closing my remarks on the Inaugural and Closing Ceremonies, I would be remiss not to mention the giant 'Aerostat', a technological marvel which stood suspended mid-air at Jawaharlal Nehru Stadium for ease of wonderous 360-degree displays. Its import, along with the gas used to balloon it out and suspend it mid-air, had challenged the administrative machinery across various States which gave it passage after it arrived on the Indian seashore. Our small team of Cabinet Secretariat had monitored its passage from UK to Delhi with bated breath, and also it being hoisted at the Stadium. No serious back-up or alternative display was envisaged should it have failed somehow. Perhaps many wonder to this day what the fate of this Aerostat was after the Games concluded. To me, its one-event usage at no mean cost of more than ₹ 40 crore was a waste of taxpayers' hard-earned money.

Investigative Aftermath of CWG-2010: Public Deserved Better

My sense has been that without doubt the estimated cost of CWG-2010 when India staked its claim to host the event way back in 2003 was unrealistic and more of a back-of-the-envelope calculation. It cannot be refuted that corruption thrived, but it would also be difficult to conclude that the Games involved a 'gigantic' scam with an excessive and inexplicable expenditure of ₹ 70,000 crore. A key element which led to this inflated figure of expenditure was that Central and Delhi Governments erroneously included the costs of all infrastructure projects being executed in and around Delhi as though every work being undertaken was related to CWG. For instance, although desirable to be completed before the commencement of CWG, the cost of expansion of Metro Rail amounted to about ₹ 30,000 crore. Costs of a number of flyovers, widening of roads and beautification of National Capital which were not in the vicinity nor provided direct connectivity of Games' venues also stood included in the package of CWG expenditures. Actual irregularities committed were hardly known to media which had started throwing this figure around. It took the Shunglu Committee to point out some of these errors after CWG was over, though arguably this investigation too was largely done superficially.

Germane to the allegations was perhaps the lavish lifestyle and Games' related promotional activities of Suresh Kalmadi, Chairman of Organising Committee, and his unguarded often loose statements on what was being done to showcase CWG. Preparations for CWG were undertaken in the movement against corruption building up more generally also for some other non-transparent commercial decisions of Central Government which included allocation of 2G spectrum, award of National Highways' projects, etc. These ended up over-shadowing the unprecedented face lift of Delhi in the run-up to CWG-2010. It was deeply felt in some quarters in the real know of the reality that the Government, instead of being credited for extensive infrastructure development and making Delhi CWG-2010 the best ever event in the history of CWGs held across the globe which was unflinchingly acknowledged by athletes community and international observers, got egregiously identified with everything ignominious.

Realpolitik being played out was through selectivity. Many CWG-related procurements, activities and processes were awarded and outsourced at excessive costs, often at the last moment under compulsion due to delays and changes in specifications. There was lack of coordination among various departments and PSUs, lack of accountability of Organizing Committee, and failure of leadership in timely interventions, all rarely highlighted by superficial nagging media. Central and Delhi Governments did not work concertedly. Heads of many executing agencies were thoroughly incompetent and got away by bluffing a system which being in fire-fighting mode to meet the deadline, opted to bypass them rather than getting distracted by calling out such bluffs. By the way, 55 million seedlings were claimed to have been procured and planted for greening and beautification of Delhi on the eve of CWG. During my site visits it was not difficult to notice stacks of plastic bags containing drooping young seedlings thrown around road-sides, vacant corners, below flyovers, etc. Whatever be their numbers and life span, they must have been consigned to garbage dump soon enough.

A shaken Central Government facing charges of corruption appointed V.K. Shunglu, a retired IAS officer of 1962 batch who had worked as C&AG from 1996-2002 to head a two-member Committee known as the Shunglu Committee to look into alleged irregularities in CWG-2010 soon after the event was over. Shantanu Consul, retired Secretary, DoPT, was the other member. Investigation was launched in the aftermath and euphoria of the resounding success of Games. As multiple agencies like C&AG, CBI, and Chief Vigilance Commissioner (CVC) were expected to play their part by looking into various aspects of alleged irregularities, it was felt necessary to draw up the "terms of reference" in consultation with C&AG and CVC to avoid any possible misunderstanding or contradictory conclusions on the same matter to be looked into by them. I was, thus, asked to informally show the draft to C&AG Vinod Rai and CVC P.J. Thomas before approval of Prime Minister was sought. Coincidentally, C&AG, CVC and Cabinet Secretary all belonged to Kerala State cadre of IAS. I faced no problems in securing their audience and suggestions. Prime Minister was on a State Visit to Japan. He wanted the draft to be faxed to him for his approval in order to make the Shunglu Committee functional before he returned to India. Indeed, similar promptness on his part to leash the Chairman of Organizing Committee who was taking many things for granted may have turned out to be the proverbial stitch in time which obviated the subsequent need to set up the Shunglu Committee!

What I could sense at that stage was that the entire exercise of administrative enquiry involving V.K. Shunglu, appointed as C&AG when incumbent Prime Minister was serving as Finance Minister in Narasimha Rao Government, was to quickly clear the smoke and dust of the so-called CWG scam. Unlike statutory audit and enquiry by C&AG and CVC which would take longer time, an administrative enquiry could be completed swiftly, with perhaps a more predictable result. The Committee was tasked to investigate weaknesses in management and alleged misappropriations, irregularities, wasteful expenditure and wrong doings in the conduct of the Games. I compiled two big volumes, one containing the notes and minutes of GOM on CWG from inception, and the other containing minutes of meetings taken by Cabinet Secretary from day one. The first volume also contained important decisions taken at the highest level from time to time including Prime Minister's order on the appointment of Suresh Kalmadi as Chairman of Organizing Committee, and not Sunil Dutt. I handed over a copy of each volume to C&AG and CVC in addition to Shunglu Committee for their perusal and use.

The Shunglu Committee rapidly submitted its report in six parts, one after the other, related to (1) Host Broadcasting; (2) CWG Village; (3) City

Infrastructure; (4) Games Venues; (5) Organizing Committee; and (6) Organising and Conduct of CWG-2010, with the first being received on 31 January 2011 and the last one by end-March 2011. The first report on alleged irregularities in awarding broadcasting rights, unlike the remaining five, was handed over to a fellow Joint Secretary for review. Therein strict action stood recommended against suspended CEO of Prasar Bharti B.S. Lalli and then DG, Doordarshan, Aruna Sharma under the IPC and Prevention of Corruption Act, for alleged act of omission and commission, while referring some other matters relating to alleged forgery, falsification, record creation to CBI and Directorate of Enforcement. I examined the remaining five reports, summarized them and indicated action points in the submission notes sent by Cabinet Secretary to Prime Minister.

I found that the five reports of Shunglu Committee had by and large skimmed the surface and drawn up its findings on the basis of its discussions held with some officers associated with CWG and scrutiny of a limited set of papers and computer records handed over to it by the private consultancy firm. Incidentally, this firm was selected without any competitive bids on nomination basis for a hefty fee, largely for scanning the computers of Organizing Committee. In its various reports, the Committee had cited instances of irregularities, procedural lapses particularly in awarding contracts, delay in execution of works, financial loss to Government, favouring contractors, use of sub-standard materials and purchase of materials at higher cost, irregular appointment of various staff and consultants, lack of supervision and control over contractors and staff, etc. In some cases, it recommended investigations by various agencies.

CBI did register some five cases related to Overlays, Queens Baton Relay, Timing, Scoring & Result System and Merchandising and Licensing, variously against 14 officials of Organising Committee including its Chairman Suresh Kalmadi. Some cases were registered in matters related to Shivaji and Talkatora stadia against some officials of NDMC, Central Public Works Department, and some private entities. In a case pertaining to Lawn Bowls venue at Jawaharlal Nehru Stadium action was registered against some officers of DDA, Central Public Works Department, and a private company. In the Barapullah Project of Delhi Government, a case was registered against some officials of Public Works Department of Government of Delhi and some private companies and individuals. In the matter of Street Lighting project, a case was registered against some officials of MCD and a private entity. Apart from CBI and Enforcement Directorate, Income Tax authorities and CVC also investigated the alleged irregularities. Some recommendations of the Committee which related to corrective actions were taken up for detailed examination by Government in consultation with Ministries concerned.

Shorn of verbiage, the Committee essentially had pointed out instances which were not serious enough to categorise them as a big scam. It made general observations in addition to recommendations for fixing accountability against some Central and Delhi Government functionaries. I recall that in its second report, corruption and delays by DDA were quantified to have led to a loss of ₹ 220 crore to the exchequer. The Committee had made strong observations against Lieutenant Governor for his role as DDA Chairman in favouring the real estate company EMAAR MGF in the bail-out or buy-back package of about ₹ 730 crore in residential flats constructed by it in CWG Village. It also found that issues of conflict of interest had been ignored in engaging valuation experts. The recommendations for action naturally infuriated the Lieutenant Governor who in a detailed letter to the President and Prime Minister disputed the charges against him and attributed his actions to decisions taken in Cabinet Secretary's COS meetings. Interestingly, when I had initially put up a draft Submission Note on Shunglu Committee report containing these adverse observations and seeking action against Lieutenant Governor, K.M. Chandrashekhar who had worked under him as Joint Secretary in Commerce Department, had unusually and perhaps in an indirect indication of his softness in the matter referred it to Secretary, Co-ordination for his views. I recall that he had by chance hinted towards a long-standing professional rivalry between V.K. Shunglu and Lieutenant Governor Tejendra Khanna. When both had worked as Secretaries, the latter held the more significant portfolio besides being a batch senior in service. The latter had been a strong contender upon retirement for the post of C&AG, but here V.K. Shunglu piped him to this post as his case was reportedly supported by cadre-mate A.N. Varma, Principal Secretary to Prime Minister Narasimha Rao.

K.M. Chandrasekhar had impressed me by his style of functioning to a great extent, being largely objective in his assessment and allowing full freedom to his team. No occasion to consult him was required of me before writing notes, howsoever critical and sensitive they might be. I was a bit surprised to find his softness towards his former boss, though the facts cited appeared to substantiate the allegations against Lieutenant Governor regardless of possible motivations for recommending action against him in the report. Separately, I had witnessed Lieutenant Governor giving instructions to senior Police and DDA officials showing his softness towards EMAAR MGF by allowing them to operate from areas inside the Games Village which could have security implications during the event. About a week after referring the file to Secretary Coordination, Cabinet Secretary called me suddenly and showed me the letter of Lieutenant Governor, which had now been forwarded to him by PMO for comments. Lieutenant Governor held that as head of COS, Cabinet Secretary was responsible for the decisions which were being attributed to him by Shunglu Committee and he had only ensured further follow up actions. Given the facts recorded, Lieutenant Governor's response was devoid of truth. He had taken a decision on his own to pay the cost of a certain number of flats at Games Village in advance to address financial constraints supposedly confronted by EMAAR MGF. DDA Vice Chairman had informed COS about that decision later, and the same had been recorded verbatim in the minutes of the meeting. Cabinet Secretary was anguished to read the letter and asked me to put up my draft Submission Note immediately. On being reminded that he had referred the matter to Secretary, Coordination, I was asked to locate it or submit another one instantly. The instructions were complied with, and he approved the Submission Note which was self-contained and factual.

I do not intend to single out any particular recommendation of the Shunglu Committee, which was in any case not the last word on these matters. The distressing fact for me was that despite a spectacular CWG-2010 show, the credibility of Central and Delhi Governments had hit another rock bottom. In a bitter taste or aftermath, media channels succeeded in enhancing their ratings with stories on so-called scams, highlighting the Shunglu Committee's recommendations and other unrelated scams one after the other. These continued long after the public's enjoyment of the show itself had been overtaken by others. Governments were thus not allowed to take any credit or indulge in self-glory for conducting the CWG successfully. From the bitterness of its preparatory phase, only the orientation had changed. The two Governments were constantly put under pressure desiring that the guilty be punished and were regularly reminded of assurances made publicly that action would be taken against the culprits after completion of administrative enquiries.

I had examined five reports of Shunglu Committee on the basis of which actionables had been identified and reported to PMO. Naturally, some senior officers including a few Secretaries were worried about what could happen to them. It was not easy to hold the Organizing Committee's Chairman singularly responsible for each lapse, even though he had created situations in a number of cases which apparently forced the hands of senior officer or precipitated decisions on their recommendation. In the Cabinet Secretariat, many senior officers apprehensive of adverse actions were seen approaching Secretary, Coordination to ascertain the developments. I was once called by him and asked sarcastically as to what was being cooked and whether he could be allowed to see my Notes. I was taken aback since there had been no intention on my part to hide anything from him. Sensing now that he was probably feeling helpless when faced with queries of senior friends in administration, I placed a set of all five Submission Notes that had been sent by Cabinet Secretary to PMO for his perusal.

After K.M. Chandrasekhar demitted office in June 2011 and Secretary Coordination slipped into the saddle as Cabinet Secretary, another three-member GOM was constituted under the chairmanship of Defence Minister A.K. Anthony, with Ministers of Sports & Youth Affairs and Urban Development as members. Its mandate was to (i) consider the views expressed by Central Ministries, Government of NCT of Delhi, and their agencies concerned on the findings and recommendations contained in the reports of Shunglu Committee and arrive at a considered view on the various recommendations;

(ii) recommend the future course of action on each recommendation, which could include disciplinary, criminal and civil action against persons/ agencies/ contractors indicated in the reports; and (iii) recommend policies and guidelines for future conduct of similar events.

I was asked by the new Cabinet Secretary to service this GOM being conversant with the subject matter. It was not my nature to say no to any new or additional assignments as I loved grabbing the opportunity to work more and to deliver to the best of my capability. But in the instant matter, I firmly declined the assignment and highlighted the reasons for doing so. First, it was a case of conflict of interest to appoint Ministers in charge of departments involved in the irregularities to the GOM for taking decisions on the reports of Shunglu Committee. Second, the desirable course of action would be to seek explanations of government servants and private agencies/ individuals indicted and to initiate action against them if their explanations were found to be unsatisfactory by the competent authority. I bluntly stated that this GOM appeared to me to have been constituted with the intention of defeating the administration of justice and in the light of how things were developing, it was not possible for me to service such a body and be part of the cover up. In any case, I had already examined the findings contained in five out of the six reports, commented upon its recommendations, and it would hardly be possible for me to take a different position now. Another Joint Secretary, who by his own admission was once part of the "fan club" of former Finance Minister P. Chidambaram, displaced from Department of Economic Affairs by the successor Finance Minister Pranab Mukherjee and parked in Cabinet Secretariat without any substantive charge was finally given the task of servicing the GOM to take final call on the findings of Shunglu Committee. Showing marked paranoia of his 'phone being intercepted' by investigative agencies (though I had seen no evidence of such interceptions during the reviews on the matter), he was more than happy to take up the assignment. I was called to attend a couple of internal meetings held by Cabinet Secretary to look at the statements containing assessments of the said Joint Secretary before transmitting the same to GOM. After I contested his assessment on some of the substantive findings which I felt were in dissonance with the facts on records, I was not called to such meetings thereafter. I felt greatly relieved as my presence in those meetings was perhaps being viewed differently.

My involvement in the affairs of CWG at a critical juncture of preparations was a great learning experience for me in spite of unintentionally causing grief to a number of my senior colleagues in administration. I had spent more than 50 percent of my time, starting from 5:00 a.m. in the morning to late at night, in matters connected with the event till the end of the Games, selflessly digesting threatening and sarcastic comments of some of my potential bosses simply because I valued national prestige more than anything else. While some of my close friends, colleagues in Cabinet Secretariat, and seniors in other

Ministries wanted complimentary passes to watch the Inaugural and Closing ceremonies, I had rejected the offers of Organizing Committee Chairman to provide complimentary passes for seating in prized rows for my friends or near and dear ones. Indeed, my close family members who had come to watch the cultural extravaganza during the Inaugural Ceremony were disappointed as tickets for sale had already been exhausted and I declined to arrange passes for them. I had also refused to accept a complimentary kit containing an umbrella, track suit, etc. sent by CEO of Organizing Committee. The resounding success of CWG-2010 was the greatest reward for me followed by the confidence reposed by Cabinet Secretary.

My experience in CWG-2010 is used in South Asian Games-2016

I voluntarily left Cabinet Secretariat mid-January 2012 for my parent State of Odisha despite some reluctance of the new Cabinet Secretary to allow me to leave. Sometimes in October 2015, I received calls from Director General, Sports Authority of India (DG, SAI) and Secretary, Sports in Central Government, to accept their request to be Principal Advisor for South Asian Games (SAG) scheduled to be held at Guwahati and Shillong during 5-16 February 2016. On their insistence, I conveyed my willingness subject to State Government agreeing to spare my services. Government of Odisha acceded to the request of Central Government in November 2015 to spare me for the next three months subject to the condition that my additional assignment should not disrupt my regular work under State Government. Thus, Central Government thought to use my past experience in ensuring preparedness and conduct of SAG-2016. I spent the next three months shuttling between Bhubaneswar and Guwahati-Shillong until the close of SAG in mid-February, and returning regularly to Bhubaneswar to discharge my regular responsibilities.

Preparations of SAG had suffered primarily due to lack of effective coordination between Central and two State Governments. The proposal of Central Government to the two State Governments, ruled by a rival political party, which would be hosts of SAG had been rejected. Thereafter an Organizing Committee which included senior officials of these States was constituted. A senior IPS officer who had retired as DG of Police in Meghalaya stood appointed as CEO of Organizing Committee. But he was unable to break the ice at Guwahati where most of the sports events were to be held, including Opening and Closing ceremonies. Finally, his assignment was curtailed to a few sports events to be held in Shillong. DG-SAI, who had also served as Joint Secretary in Union Sports Ministry during CWG-2010, besides being my batchmate and a dear friend in Odisha cadre, now got additionally designated as its new CEO.

Sports infrastructure, including swimming pools, indoor and outdoor stadia, developed way back in connection with National Games held in

Guwahati and Shillong in the year 2007 were found to be in dilapidated condition. These required concerted efforts and heavy amounts for special repairs and renovations. Assam was willing to spare the Games venues and extend administrative support only if financial requirements were fully borne by Central Government. Erstwhile CEO had engaged a large contingent of professionals and other personnel, who appeared directionless, relaxing in hired offices and hotels in Shillong and Guwahati. Services of many officials and consultants engaged in CWG-2010 were found to have been outsourced again for SAG-2016. The situation on the ground appeared to be anarchic, indeed in worse shape than what CWG-2010 was six-months prior to that event. All seemed to be in a standstill until and unless Central Government released funds to meet the costs projected by the two State Governments. They also wanted advance payments for meeting security-related Games' expenditure, including procuring security and communication equipment and vehicles. Assam Sports Secretary who had been designated as Additional CEO of SAG was not attending the meetings of Executive Council of Organising Committee in Guwahati. Others, including State's Chief Secretary and ACS, nominated to the Organising Committee, were also equally evasive and indifferent. Government of India was seriously contemplating postponing the Games, as I was told by the new CEO, if the situation did not change quickly.

I proceeded to Guwahati in November 2015 to assess the situation. I felt that the task of renovating sports venues was possible provided funds were released and works were executed in two shifts a day without interruption. I advised Central Government to immediately convey its financial commitment and release funds without loss of time so that State executing agencies could start renovation works on war-footing. Projections of funds made by State Governments were realistic and there was no reason for Central Sports Ministry not to accept them. I requested Assam Chief Secretary and ACS, who were known to me to issue instructions to line departments to commence repair and renovation works in high gear in anticipation of funds. I assured them of my support for their claims and not those of Central Government on SAG-2016 if ever any such necessity arose in the event of disputes.

As planned, things started moving on the ground faster than expected. Although my role was that of Principal Advisor, I worked as a *de facto* Executive Head. State Government officers did not mind my possessiveness in laying down strict time-lines for adherence in executing various works. For holding pre-final football matches, including a semi-final event, a new football stadium was being taken up at a conversion cost of about ₹ 3 crore on the existing cricket ground. I was apprehensive of getting this project completed in time because the onset of winter would delay the grass turf to stabilise. I advised CEO of Organising Committee, early in January, not to schedule football matches on this new ground under preparation. As I had predicted, all other Games venues became ready before SAG was to start, except this new football ground on which maximum expenditure had been incurred.

Strict adherence to timelines for special repairs, renovation of sports complexes and construction of a new Squash Court at Guwahati, due to effective monitoring, made what was considered almost impossible at one point, possible. National prestige was at stake here too, and realizing the seriousness and limited time in hand, the State's administrative machinery also got recharged. Assam Chief Minister Tarun Gogoi who had been a reluctant partner having rejected Central Government's proposal to Chair the Organizing Committee, now started taking rounds of stadia and found them fully ready with 7-10 days to spare. I complimented him for the fantastic performance of his officials when he visited the Swimming Complex under renovation stating that he had every reason to be proud of them. He felt inspired to hear my lavish words and instructed his officials not to leave any stone unturned to make the Games a resounding success. The Swimming Complex was the last and biggest hurdle to make it competition-worthy. It suffered damage in the heating system, pumps, and drainage, and was finally got ready just two days prior to the event. Assam's ACS had in fact suggested to call off the swimming event finding the situation too difficult to handle. Local Assamese labour was unwilling to work on this risky venture. The much-despised Bangladeshi workers braved all risks and bore the stink without complaints, working throughout the night to clear the mud to unchoke the underground tanks and drains. I personally supervised the work throughout the night till it was completed.

Prime Minister inaugurated SAG-2016, an international sporting event which became an acclaimed success. I was happy to play my part. After a year, when I was asked to accept another assignment as CEO for the Games of Himalayan Countries in Guwahati, I politely turned down the offer. These Games were finally cancelled. The only conclusion I can draw from my experience in connection with CWG-2010 and SAG-2016 is that those holding so-called key positions in Government and associated implementing agencies are more eager to take credit for success but hardly anyone likes to bear the responsibility and risks. It is not that there is dearth of competence. What is lacking is confidence, commitment and team spirit. We work in silos for securing personal and individual success and tend to fail miserably in working collectively as a team. Packaging is considered more important by the so-called efficient performers than the substance and quality of their products. Consistent hard work with sincerity while maintaining anonymity is no more considered a strength.

Some Other Tasks Performed in Cabinet Secretariat

When asked by K.M. Chandrasekhar to suggest measures for improved functioning of Cabinet Secretariat, I had pleaded for office automation through the electronic mode for processing files to reduce the use of paper besides enabling easy monitoring and tracking of progress on consideration of issues and proposals. I had visited the Secretariats in Andhra Pradesh and Gujarat earlier on to find out how office automation had worked there. After a meeting with National Informatics Centre (NIC), and review by Cabinet Secretary, electronic processing of files including digitisation of old records was taken up progressively in Cabinet Secretariat. Despite initial resistance by some senior officers, who felt more comfortable to find physical files stacked on their tables, quite rapidly all routine and administrative work shifted to the electronic mode. Slowly and steadily after suitable safeguards were developed even confidential matters were covered, excluding top secret matters and Cabinet proposals. None could display resistance once Cabinet Secretary ruled out other options emphatically. Inter-departmental communications electronically were, however, not introduced as NIC had limited capacity to produce a versatile software universally applicable. Government did not consider hiring a big private IT company to build a robust common platform for all Ministries.

I had also underlined the need for maintaining punctuality in attending office as flexibility allowed to functionaries in Cabinet Secretariat to my assessment created indiscipline elsewhere in Government departments too. It was hard for me to accept the reality that sweeping staff came to clean my room after 9.00 a.m. and I had to inhale more dust only because I reached office on time. I insisted that cleaning and dusting must be over before 9.00 a.m. or it be done the previous evening after office hours. Some senior officers were taken aback to hear my suggestion that discipline and punctuality as a general practice should not be based on choice and those responsible for framing of rules should not be seen to be violating them at will. K.M. Chandrasekhar with a smile on his face accepted my suggestions desiring that all officers and staff should reach office in time. He introduced a biometric system to monitor arrival and departure of all officers and staff, besides tracking their movements from office during the course of the day, since biometric recognition was required to open the main gate to the building. He started holding his usual meetings at 9:30 a.m. On a few occasions, he firmly instructed officers who were habitual late-comers to maintain punctuality.

Close at the heels of 2G spectrum scam condemned for high-level of corruption, I recall processing a brief for Cabinet Secretary in mid-2010 in connection with a proposal placed before Space Commission on certain costs of the delayed development of satellites GSAT-6, and GSAT-6A to be built and launched by Indian Space Research Organisation (ISRO). This proposal was being made in continuation of one considered and approved in 2005 on GSAT-6 satellites. When I could lay my hands on that 2005 proposal, what struck me as inexplicable was that it had averred that the costs would be met in large part by leasing out its transponders for which as stated "several expressions of interest" had been received by ISRO/ Department of Space. I dug deeper to gauge the nature as well as cost-benefit of such expressions of interests. It was discovered that the proposal had been a *fait accompli*, and that the matter of the decisions of Space Commission taken in 2005 and contract already entered into by Antrix Corporation, the commercial arm of ISRO, with Devas Multi-Media had not been reflected when the approval of CCS had been sought. Basically, two satellites were to be built by ISRO predominantly to service an agreement already reached in January 2005 by Antrix with Devas Multimedia. Under it, Antrix would lease out 90 percent of transponders in GSAT-6 and GSAT-6A satellites which would be built by ISRO in due course with sale of about 70 MHz of the scarce and strategic S-band spectrum to this private company in order to establish a hybrid satellite and terrestrial communications network to supply wireless audio-visual, broadband and mobile internet service across India. This was a clear case of suppression of facts before the Cabinet Committee, especially about a "commercial" transaction already agreed by Antrix. Compounding this was the discovery that Space Commission, which was headed by Space Secretary-cum-Chairman ISRO and which included Cabinet Secretary, Principal Secretary to Prime Minister, Minister of State in PMO, Expenditure Secretary, etc. had also already deliberated upon the matter then while recommending the building of these satellites to the Cabinet Committee. Indeed, Antrix was required to pay compensations for delay which had already occurred in placing these satellites in orbit as per this agreement.

I took the 2005 approved proposal to Cabinet Secretary for his perusal personally and could see a sense of surprise on his face when he went through the papers. Issues related to the strategic and security concerns were pointed out, as also the fact that some former senior personnel from ISRO, Antrix and Department of Space held investment and/or employment interests in the newly formed Devas Multimedia (India) Pvt. Ltd. which also had a complex foreign investment angle. Cabinet Secretary quietly received and retained the Note, probably to explain the matter to Prime Minister. In the meeting of Space Commission held in July 2010 the Devas-Antrix deal was discussed and a series of decisions were taken. Subsequently a difficult decision to cancel the contract, which prima facie appeared ultra vires, was taken by the Government in February 2011 by when the draft Report of C&AG on its audit of Department of Space was also available.

Media had gone into frenzy calling the Devas-Antrix deal another big scam. Allegations of discrepancies, including non-compliance with rules, financial mismanagement, conflict of interest, and favouritism were bandied about. Media cited various audit paras raised by C&AG and internal reviews on the deal, besides sound bites by Devas Multimedia, Deutsche Telecom and other investors who threatened to invoke expropriation clauses in their highly profitable venture. Prime Minister constituted a "two-member committee" under the chairmanship of B.K. Chaturvedi, Member, Planning Commission to review the technical, commercial, procedural and financial aspects of the agreement between Antrix and Devas Multimedia taking into account the internal review that had been conducted by Department of Space after the discovery of the breach. Setting up a Committee under the chairmanship of B.K. Chaturvedi to me was clearly an attempt to cover up. He had been Cabinet Secretary and Space Commission Member since 2004-05 when the proposal for launching the satellites had been approved by Space Commission and proposal was steered through to its approval. I felt as if the accused was being made the investigator and conveyed my assessment to a fellow Joint Secretary who had been brought to Cabinet Secretariat by B.K. Chaturvedi himself. Although I was handling the Space Department in Cabinet Secretariat, the matter concerning Devas-Antrix deal and enquiry reports of B.K. Chaturvedi Committee and Pratyush Sinha Committee subsequently set up were assigned by Cabinet Secretary to another Joint Secretary.

My time in Cabinet Secretariat was exciting and satisfying as long as K.M. Chandrasekhar was there. I found him a soft spoken, hard task-master and a leader who could draw rational decisions from defused discussions in COS meetings taking all on board. He would take up issues with Government up to a point and gracefully accept and implement orders even after holding a different view point on administrative matters. In a particular case of appointment to a constitutional post of Chairman, National Commission for Scheduled Tribes, credentials of the person proposed for appointment by Ministry of Tribal Affairs needed to be verified as per the laid down procedure. Intelligence Bureau was thus asked to furnish required inputs. In its report, the Bureau had given details of criminal record of the candidate including his indulgence in bigamy and illegal religious conversion in Jharkhand. The candidate, a retired IPS officer, had worked as Deputy Minister in Ministry of Tribal Affairs for five years since 2004. The Submission Note thus prepared and approved by Cabinet Secretary to Prime Minister contained inputs which were adverse; the intelligence report was attached. However, after about a month a brief communication from PMO was received stating that Prime Minister had approved the proposal of Ministry of Tribal Affairs and desired that the same should be endorsed for approval by President. When the proposal containing approval and endorsement along with the adverse inputs received from the Bureau was again put up to Cabinet Secretary for his endorsement to President's Secretariat, he appeared reluctant. He asked whether the procedure allowed us to repeat those critical intelligence findings as Prime Minister having been explained the position had already approved endorsing it to the President. Upon being advised that the Submission Note for President was in accordance with laid down procedure, he approved the same. I recall that President's office after receiving the proposal had queried as to whether Prime Minister was aware of the critical findings about the candidate, and on being told in affirmative, the proposed appointment was approved by the President.

K.M. Chandrasekhar encouraged free and lively discussions on important issues, although on certain matters his assignment of tasks to unconnected officers was inexplicable to me. In COS meetings which were coordinated by Joint Secretaries of Cabinet Secretariat, he would take note of useful observations and suggestions made by them. I remember a COS meeting on tackling instances of piracy in the Arabian Sea and Indian Ocean off the coast of Somalia involving an Indian merchant vessel. The Indian Navy had actually taken lead in ensuring safe passage by providing escort to convoys of merchant vessels. However, on specific instances of coming ship-to-ship with a pirated vessel, and when fired upon by pirates, I had suggested that the Indian Navy should consider firing at pirates in self-defence. When Defence Secretary wanted orders in writing, I responded by saying that no orders were required for drawl of admissible emoluments and the same held good for self-defence or defence of national assets. K.M. Chandrasekhar supported my interjections. In a meeting taken by the successor Cabinet Secretary on the same subject, when Home Secretary suggested strong action against pirates, he was inclined to follow a softer line of action suggested by Foreign Secretary who happened to be his batchmate. I had referred to my record note of that earlier meeting of COS to buttress the need for strong action. But incumbent Cabinet Secretary was not inclined to approve the minutes of this meeting and kept them pending with him till I left Cabinet Secretariat. K.M. Chandrasekhar, his predecessor, had never liked delay in preparation and issuance of minutes of meetings containing diverse views.

Progress in construction of 73 strategic border roads which stood approved since 2002 was far from satisfactory. Two major reasons were abnormal delays in forest clearance and inadequate air efforts for transportation of heavy equipment. Average time taken for forest clearance was 24 months for a road project. Cabinet Secretary wanted timelines drawn up for granting forest clearance and air efforts to execute those roads as fast as possible. In a few COS meetings, Secretary Environment & Forest was asked to work out the timelines with milestones for a two-staged forest clearance. If that was not possible, he was asked to propose a draft Bill to provide for superseding the provisions of wildlife and forest conservation laws for strategic border roads in Himalayan belt from Leh to Arunachal Pradesh and in critical Naxal-affected districts. He furnished tentative timelines for stage-wise forest and wildlife clearances and promised that no abnormal delays would be allowed to become road-blocks.

I was asked to assess requirements of "air effort" in consultation with Border Roads Organization (BRO) and other relevant agencies. In the next COS meeting on strategic border roads, 5,000 hours of required air effort was projected. Defence Ministry conveyed its inability to meet anything beyond 20 percent of this due to deployment of Army and Air Force helicopters on more critical operations. MD, Pawan Hans Ltd. was asked to project the financial implications for hiring helicopters from reliable sources within the country or abroad for transportation of heavy machines and materials to bridge the gap in air efforts, which were agreed to. In a subsequent meeting, Defence Ministry/BRO was required to indicate specific sites prepared for landing of helicopters, storage points, etc. to Pawan Hans Ltd. who had been told to go ahead with hiring the helicopters.

Cabinet Secretary wanted me to visit some of these construction sites particularly in Arunachal Pradesh along with Joint Secretary of Department of Border Management which was the nodal department for budgetary provisions relating to strategic border roads. Chief Minister Arunachal Pradesh himself accompanied us along with BRO commanders to show some critically important roads which had been held up. Citing the much better progress in respect of roads allotted to them for execution, he felt that these strategic roads should be assigned to the State Government. After undertaking aerial surveys and visiting some project sites, along with Joint Secretary (Border Roads), I held detailed discussions with commanders of BRO to ascertain the status of each strategic border road in Arunachal Pradesh and specific problems faced by them which were leading to delays. BRO commanders in brief conveyed that the working season was less than six months for climatic reasons. Due to non-availability of equipment and other materials during this working season, work of road formation already done in some cases also suffered heavy damage on account of rains and landslides. They pleaded helplessness as the procurement process according to them was highly centralized and was in the hands of Defence Ministry with hardly any delegation of powers to BRO. State Government could not be assigned the task of constructing roads close to borders, we were told. Through the next day we visited some more roads which had been held up half-way and the situation was no different. Work force engaged by BRO was mostly from outside the State and wages being paid much higher than normal rates. In the absence of non-availability of even smaller equipment like drilling machine which did not necessarily require air effort, progress of work was held up and cost escalation was inevitable. We found roads with lengths of 10 km or less each having taken more than 6 to 8 years and yet were not fully completed.

Having reviewed status of each border strategic road, I prepared a report and placed it before Cabinet Secretary. He found it disturbing and commended it to Defence Minister A.K. Antony. I was invited to a meeting called by Defence Minister with Defence Secretary, Special Secretary in-charge of procurement and DG, BRO in attendance. When I highlighted specific instances of abnormal delays in procurement of even smaller equipment like drilling machines, Special Secretary handling the subject had no explanations. Defence Secretary Pradeep Kumar advised me not to press the issue further as the Ministry according to him had already taken note of what I had highlighted in my report.

In the next COS meeting, MD of Pawan Hans indicated the steps taken by him for air effort, and reiterated his request for details of places for lifting and delivery of equipment and materials, including petroleum products, which needed to be stored for use round the year. Senior officers of Defence Ministry, including DG BRO, took an about turn stating that they had already worked out the logistics, and services of Pawan Hans were no more required! The requirement of air effort according to them had come down by more than 50 percent , which the Ministry could manage internally. K.M. Chandrasekhar was to demit office in the next less than two months and I got a feeling as if senior officers of Defence Ministry wanted to buy time to avoid being questioned. After his departure, his successor did not show any interest in this area at least till such time as I was there.

Joint Secretary (Administration) was on tour during the week preceding the superannuation of K. M. Chandrasekhar mid-June 2011. As his link officer, I oversaw the preparations for his farewell. I requested all officers in Cabinet Secretariat to contribute voluntarily for the farewell dinner and a memento to be presented as a token of our respect. The nearby Conference Hall of Defence Research & Development Organization was requisitioned for the farewell meeting. I made these arrangements despite being told by other colleagues that the farewell function of the previous Cabinet Secretary had been held with grandeur on the open lawn of Rashtrapati Bhavan by creating temporary tented structures with hired air conditioners involving expenditure four years ago of about ₹ 1.50 lakh besides unaccounted courtesies extended by CPWD towards arrangements. I had not participated in any farewell functions at the cost of State exchequer in the past and it was against my principles to get involved in such extravaganza now. My seniors initially resisted my move mildly but accepted it reluctantly. Appointment of Secretary, Coordination as his successor had already been announced about a fortnight back. Thus, the farewell function of K.M. Chandrasekhar was also to be an occasion to formally welcome the old hand in Rashtrapati Bhavan in his new incarnation. The simple function was followed by a dinner at India International Centre.

Stress and Strain

After taking up reins on 14 June 2011, incoming Cabinet Secretary did not like to disturb the team of officers. His style of functioning was discernibly different from that of his predecessor. Joint Secretaries handling affairs of various Ministries/Departments earlier prepared briefs on each Cabinet Note explaining and reasoning out the proposals, and Cabinet Secretary thereafter made short notes himself. The successor wanted short notes too to be prepared for him. Strict timelines for disposal of important office business insisted by the predecessor, were replaced with an easy-going style as if with unlimited time in his hands. Even minutes of COS meetings lay pending on his table for weeks. He did not want files to be submitted to him electronically. K.M. Chandrasekhar never hinted that he should be consulted before putting up notes on critical or sensitive matters. His successor now expected to be consulted on important matters before submitting office notes to him on issues he considered critical or sensitive. For a person temperamentally impatient and perpetually in a hurry, it became difficult to withstand his unlimited patience and mysterious ways of functioning, although he continued to remain most approachable, with a smiling and amiable face in Cabinet Secretariat. After about four months of his taking over as Cabinet Secretary, I wanted to be repatriated to my parent cadre on personal grounds. I was well aware of provisions barring me from future assignments on Central deputation. Initially, he did not agree stating that it was difficult for him to find a substitute for me as I had a raised the bar high, though I was sensing his discomfort in dealing with some of my notes on important issues, which was never the case with his predecessor. On my persistence, he finally forwarded my request to PMO which was approved.

A couple of instances conveying discomfort of the new high priest in Cabinet Secretariat would be of interest. Pulok Chatterjee, a cadre and batch-mate of Cabinet Secretary had been appointed Secretary to Prime Minister in place of T.K.A. Nair in the meanwhile. A Joint Secretary in PMO, verbally asked Joint Secretary concerned in MHA to process a proposal to place the new Secretary to Prime Minister above Cabinet Secretary at tenth position in the Warrant of Precedence. The prescribed procedure called for examination and recommendation of any proposal for inclusion or change in the Warrant of Precedence by a specified COS before approval of Prime Minister and President's consent. This proposal initiated by MHA at the prompting of a PMO official was duly endorsed by Home Secretary who formed part of the COS. It was received in Cabinet Secretariat sometime in October 2011 and was processed by the same Joint Secretary who had been assigned the task of servicing the GOM on the Shunglu Committee report after I conveyed my unwillingness. On my return from a week-long training at Shimla, when the file was put up to me for further action, I was surprised to find that all the relevant norms to be examined had been side-tracked and the only justification given in support of elevating the new aspirant in the Warrant was that the former Principal Secretary to Prime Minister T.K.A. Nair had enjoyed that position.

The approval and endorsement of Cabinet Secretary to place Secretary to Prime Minister above that of Cabinet Secretary in the Warrant was contrary to applicable rules. It was also against the order passed by Supreme Court of India a few years back that any change in the rule and placement in the Warrant that interfered with the positions of Chief Justices or Judges of Supreme Court and High Courts had to be done only with the concurrence of Chief Justice of India. Since the Secretary to Prime Minister was positioned at 23 after Secretary to President and before other Secretaries to Government of India, this proposal to position him at number 10 would affect both Chief Justices of High Courts and Judges, including Puisne Judges, of High Courts variously positioned at

14, 17 and 20. Additionally, apart from being appointed as Principal Secretary to Prime Minister, T.K.A. Nair had also been given the status of Minister of State by Prime Minister himself. The fact that he was senior to the then Cabinet Secretary by seven years by itself did not entitle a change in the Warrant. His placement above Cabinet Secretary was also *ad personam* to him as per the order that had been passed rather surreptitiously. It appeared that without taking concurrence of Chief Justice of India, Cabinet Secretary B.K. Chaturvedi, in the last fortnight of his tenure, had quietly facilitated placing T.K.A. Nair above Cabinet Secretary. The decision to allow T.K.A. Nair's successor the same position as enjoyed by his predecessor was also contrary to a decision taken earlier that no change in the Warrant would be considered in the normal course in future as it would open a veritable Pandora's Box. A large number of requests for amendment to the Warrant had been kept in abeyance in MHA on this count alone. These included the request of Chief Information Commissioner, who enjoyed status equivalent to a Judge of Supreme Court, through his letter to Prime Minister and reminders to MHA and Cabinet Secretariat. The new Secretary to Prime Minister had not even been designated as Principal Secretary to Prime Minister and there was no order of Prime Minister to allow him rank equivalent to Minister of State either.

I resubmitted the file to Cabinet Secretary explaining the rules and procedure stating that any surreptitious amendment in the Warrant was not only fraught with risks, it also compromised the institutional sanctity of office of Cabinet Secretary. Before resubmitting the file, I had shared my understanding of the rule position with both Joint Secretary (Administration) who was quite close to Cabinet Secretary and also with the Joint Secretary who had processed the proposal in my absence. Both had advised me against my plan to resubmit the file as according to them such an action on my part was embarrassing and undesirable. I did not like to be a party to such a manipulation and went ahead with my understanding as my colleagues could say nothing substantively contrary to what I understood on the issue.

The atmosphere in Cabinet Secretariat used to be free, frank, and friendly and Cabinet Secretary was never inaccessible. I had never been asked to put up any note in a certain manner while processing proposals. It was not the first time I was resubmitting a proposal for reconsideration in relation to a proposal of MHA. Indeed, I had put up and resubmitted notes suggesting return of proposals involving some procurements for Central Para Military Forces, which had been sought to be put up for perusal of the relevant Cabinet Committee pointing out anomalies and contradictions. Those notes had been approved without being viewed otherwise, not even indirectly. The Officer in position now took exception to my action.

After about two weeks of receiving the file, he called me wanting to know as to what motivated me in raising issues on a proposal he had already approved, and why I had not discussed the matter with him before submitting it in black and white? He charged me with embarrassing him, and rendering it difficult to explain the matter to Secretary to Prime Minister, the intended beneficiary. I was a bit puzzled having never expected an amiable soft-spoken Cabinet Secretary to charge me of embarrassing him before a junior of his own batch who appeared eager to get elevated to a higher position in the Warrant without any formal communication having been issued from PMO to that effect. I responded by reiterating the rules and added that it would be impossible to justify the decision in the event of information being sought under Right to Information Act. I also submitted that it was my bounden duty to point out serious anomalies amounting to compromising the institutional integrity of the office of Cabinet Secretary. No more was exchanged verbally in the matter.

The proposal which had come from MHA was returned to Home Secretary for his views again by Cabinet Secretary. After a few days, the same proposal was resubmitted by Home Secretary with reiterations in longer note now reinforcing the earlier position without any convincing argument or material for justification. I again elaborated with greater details and stronger force the position that had been explained earlier. I did not hear about this proposal again nor did I care to know what happened next. Some months later when I was back in my parent State of Odisha, I read a news item in "The Hindu" that Cabinet Secretary Ajit Seth did not yield to the pressure on change in the Warrant of Precedence to place the Secretary to Prime Minister above him! I did not mind being misunderstood earlier as my professional duties had never been guided for temporary gains, sense of importance or agenda-driven angularities. In fact, my batchmate in PMO who prompted the proposal and had also worked in Cabinet Secretariat when B.K. Chaturvedi was Cabinet Secretary, once broached the issue with me. I had said in a lighter vein that while holding important positions, we should not behave like monkeys occupying treetops and consider ourselves superior to those on the ground. He did not like my analogy. I felt no regret nor did I wonder whether he had shared my views with his boss who was craving, without being seen to be doing so, to get himself placed above Cabinet Secretary.

Another issue on which I invited the wrath of incumbent Cabinet Secretary was in relation to grant of Padma awards soon after MHA had written to the Cabinet Secretariat among others seeking proposals or recommendations. After discussing the matter internally, I prepared a proposal suggesting the name of former Cabinet Secretary K.M. Chandrasekhar for Padma Vibhushan. On being asked, I had given details of previous Cabinet Secretaries who had been given similar awards after their retirement. I also prepared the citation draft enumerating the distinguished services rendered by him, including his contribution in holding the much-maligned CWG-2010. Special Secretary in Cabinet Secretariat suddenly came to my room to personally return the file. I was told that Cabinet Secretary did not like my action and I should not resubmit the proposal again. I was taken aback as the proposal had been firmed up in consultation with Special Secretary and Secretary, Coordination. A few days later, I was told by Cabinet Secretary that I had again embarrassed him. There was something that had happened, which I guessed he did not want to share with me. I had not intended to annoy or embarrass him in anyway. He had always professed highest regard for his predecessor and it was beyond my imagination that he would have disliked the proposal. I did not resubmit it.

Prime Minister had wanted the new Cabinet Secretary to pay a visit to Jammu & Kashmir along with Secretaries of some key departments to review the implementation of the financial package announced for faster economic development, including creation of gainful employment, apart from reviewing the security situation in the valley. I accompanied him on this 2-day visit. I was asked to particularly take note of discussions on security issues and put up draft submission note immediately on return. Accordingly, I prepared and submitted a note summarising the discussions, actionables, recommendations, etc. the same evening on return. In spite of urgency underlined earlier, the draft languished with Cabinet Secretary for a fortnight. Secretary, Coordination later informed me that this was on account of inputs not having been received from other departments as Cabinet Secretary was no more inclined to approve a stand-alone submission note on security matters. Submission notes on security issues, invariably sent on a standalone basis in the past, involved a high degree of secrecy, urgency, and sensitivity and were prepared most carefully and confidentially.

The prevailing view was that the working environment in Cabinet Secretariat had changed. The centre of gravity of decision-making had moved away from it once again. The incumbent appeared to be apprehensive and more concerned about the likely response of his political masters, rather than offering inputs and critical perspectives whenever felt necessary, frankly and objectively. Perhaps he was also diffident due to his lack of administrative experience of handling any significant department either in his parent State of Uttar Pradesh or in Central Government. Success unfortunately at times is measured by the ability to be a pliable all-weather bird in order to meet non-administrative requirements of political masters. Incumbent Cabinet Secretary got an extended tenure of two years, of which one year was granted by the successor NDA Government followed by a post-retirement assignment. It was not for nothing that the UPA Government in its closing years was known for policy paralysis.

Reluctance on the part of Cabinet Secretary to relieve me even when Prime Minister's orders had been obtained on file approving my voluntary return to Odisha forced me to protest. I asserted that my needs were pressing, and my departure should not be held hostage to delay in finding a substitute. On his repeated insistence to suggest my substitute, going against my practice of never interfering in matters of postings, my own or those of others, I reluctantly indicated the name of one of my batchmates to succeed me which was finally approved by him. I was relieved on 13 January 2012 and I left for Odisha the next day.

It would be of interest to elaborate the developments immediately following my return to Odisha that momentarily shook me. Central Government was under assault from crusaders against corruption under the banner "India against Corruption", a campaign which had taken root in 2010. A nervous and functionally shaky Central Government on 2 February 2012 faced the veritable nail in its coffin when Supreme Court of India pronounced its judgment on 2G spectrum case setting aside all 122 allotments made by it on grounds of irregularities. That very evening, I received a phone call from a senior journalist of a leading national daily newspaper asking me, without revealing his source, whether I had been repatriated prematurely due to charges of corruption leading to a CBI investigation against me! I did not know this journalist and was shocked to hear his question. I requested him to verify his facts with all those associated with approving "my" request for repatriation made at least two months prior to being relieved. These included Cabinet Secretary and other officials in Cabinet Secretariat, DoPT and PMO. I added that his verification before publishing his story was vital, because otherwise it would rob me of my fair name which was the only asset I had earned through selfless public service over a period of nearly three decades. I had urged him to also verify my entire track record in public service using a magnifying glass and blow his story up to any limit if there was an iota of truth in the reason being cited by him for my repatriation. He promised that he would verify facts before publishing any news.

After I came out of my stupor, I began to cast my mind on what could remotely be the issue. I was suddenly reminded of a questionnaire I had received more than a year back from the Anti-Corruption Branch of CBI's regional office at Bangalore in relation to the opening of Sri Sri College of Ayurveda for which permission had been granted when I was Joint Secretary in Department of AYUSH way back in 2004. I had answered the questionnaire. DSP, CBI who had visited me thereafter without any ambiguity had informed that there was no case against me in person. A preliminary enquiry was intended to be initiated on the basis of petitions filed by two former students who had alleged that the institution had taken donations for admission, and they were unable to find employment due to substandard quality of education received by them there. The matter had been referred to CBI to ascertain as to how permission was granted by Department of AYUSH to the institution which allegedly did not have the required infrastructure prescribed by CCIM. As I have mentioned elsewhere the real reasons were to hound Sri Sri Ravishankar for his 'misadventure' in supporting "India against Corruption" campaign against Central Government. I had heard nothing about the so-called preliminary inquiry CBI intended to take up on the matter. The news story sought to be published now appeared to be a desperate attempt at damage control by the Central Government after Supreme Court's verdict by deflecting media attention towards my repatriation on alleged corruption in association with one of those supporting "India Against Corruption"! I had also sufficiently annoyed Cabinet Secretary and Secretary to Prime Minister, what to speak of the blunt threats I had received from some important senior officers during preparations for CWG-2010. After all, they had warned of action when Cabinet Secretary K.M. Chandrasekhar's protective shield no longer covered me, and this was a ploy to defame me by settling scores.

When these thoughts were invading my mind, I called this senior correspondent of Indian Express and informed him about my recollection of having received a questionnaire from CBI branch office at Bangalore about a year back to which I had also responded. I requested that if the national daily was determined to bring out the proposed story on my repatriation, they should also present the facts as I had narrated in my response to the questionnaire. I forwarded a copy to him by email. The senior journalist called me again late in the night and said that he had made enquiries about me in both State and Central Government departments in which I had worked. Having heard everything good about my integrity, he said that there was no question of any baseless story on my repatriation being published by him.

The only way to start investigation for corruption against a private institution under the Prevention of Corruption Act was by involving a public servant who had handled any matter relatable to it. This was explained to me by a former CBI Director later when I asked how a preliminary enquiry could be started against a public servant on the basis of allegation petitions by students against a private institution for paying capitation fee and not being employed by the institution after passing out. I now understood the game and consequences of my actions in perhaps defying Cabinet Secretary and his all-powerful batchmate in PMO who wanted to enjoy a higher position in the Warrant of Precedence and would have succeeded but for my resistance. Perhaps some of those associated with CWG-2010 scams also had access to such corridors of power. I immediately made a representation to Cabinet Secretary, with copies to Secretary DoPT and CBI Director, against what was being done to defame me soon after I had returned to my parent cadre. Central Government's permission was essential under the relevant rules for any enquiry against officers holding rank of Joint Secretary or above. It was not required if the officer had ceased to work in Central Government. This rule position was being exploited now.

Being curious about the subject matter of preliminary enquiry, I met Additional Secretary (Vigilance) in DoPT during my next visit to Delhi. He showed me the file which contained nothing more than the two allegation petitions of students. Curiously, my response to the questionnaire did not form part of the proposal for a preliminary enquiry against me for which permission had been sought by CBI Joint Director of Hyderabad regional headquarters.

When I narrated the development to Cabinet Secretary over phone, he conveyed surprise. On meeting him face to face, he remained as pleasant and courteous as earlier professing ignorance about the development. There was nothing to worry he said, and promised that he would ensure action on what he called "my well drafted representation". I received a call from Joint Director CBI at Hyderabad a few days later conveying regret for the mental strain I had gone through, adding that there was nothing against me. For the sake of formality, I needed to pay a visit to the CBI branch office at Bangalore whenever a notice to this effect was received by me, after which the matter would be closed as far as I was concerned.

It was now clear that as per rules, views of my extant employer, which was Cabinet Secretariat in Central Government had been sought just prior to my repatriation to State Government on the request of CBI to start a preliminary enquiry against me. Perniciously, Cabinet Secretariat waited a few days till I left, thus responding to DoPT saying that I had returned back to my parent cadre. Now an unpleasant side of the pleasant Cabinet Secretary, who had professed ignorance to me about any preliminary enquiry against me, was revealed. When he telephoned me to seek help in the case of his friend who was facing some difficulty in selling his landed property in Odisha, I wished that he hadn't. Had his friend approached me directly, I would have been happier to have helped the aggrieved person in larger public interest. Heading R&DM Department at that time, I had been taking initiatives to eliminate pendency. In this case also, I did not mind calling for examination of the matter and facilitating its quick disposal after I found that the transaction of the said property was needlessly pending for years for some clearance at district level. It did not bother me even after being told by his friend that Cabinet Secretary had been helped by his son-in-law in arranging the US Visa for his daughter. The call made to me was probably to pay back that debt. It seemed that he had no problems in leveraging his position selfishly while dealing with me dubiously.

A little while later, I received a call from a batchmate and dear friend conveying surprise that my name had not been cleared for empanelment to the post of Additional Secretary which he had heard from his source in PMO. He advised me not to remain silent as something other than merit seemed to be influencing the decision-making in my case. Initially, I ignored his call as I had no desire to serve again in Central Government. I had already been promoted to the Apex Scale as ACS in State Government in the meanwhile. However, when the next day Cabinet Secretary had called me for seeking the favour mentioned above, on my gentle enquiry about my empanelment he had said that I should not worry considering my outstanding track record. When I was reminded by this friend again a few days later urging me not to remain complacent, I spoke to Cabinet Secretary to ascertain the truth. He remained evasive but hinted at some missing vigilance clearance. When I spoke to

Additional Secretary (Vigilance) in DoPT, I was informed that Secretary, DoPT, had personally handed over a copy of Vigilance Clearance to Cabinet Secretary as the communication sent by DoPT earlier was reportedly misplaced. GA Department in State Government too confirmed having sent the required vigilance clearance for all officers of my batch in one go from Odisha. In the meanwhile, I appeared before CBI office in Bangalore and was told by DIG in charge of local branch that the chapter of preliminary enquiry against me stood closed. I was categorically told by DoPT officials that lack of vigilance clearance could not be the reason for my empanelment being blocked, and there was more to it than met the eye.

My annual performance appraisal reports were up to date with outstanding grading each year without exception, with numerical scores of 10 out of 10 from the year this rating system started. K.M. Chandrasekhar had given me 9.99, appreciating my performance lavishly while explaining that he was not giving me the perfect 10 as no human being could be perfect to deserve that score. I met Cabinet Secretary Ajit Seth for one last time during a chance official visit to Delhi. I asked him bluntly why he had not shared the truth with me. He dished out his earlier platitudes adding that the technical hitch would be overcome within a fortnight.

Interestingly, I was now informally told by a senior officer in Cabinet Secretariat that the so-called seed scam had been resurrected. Before clearing my name, they were awaiting a response that the outcome of that CBI investigation had finally been closed! This new angle was too much to digest. Well after State Government had ordered this CBI investigation, I had worked twice in Government of India. After serving as Director in Home Ministry for three years, I had been empanelled and posted as Joint Secretary in 2003. In the year 2009, I had been appointed as Joint Secretary in Cabinet Secretariat and was handling the most sensitive and top secret matters there. If I had been under CBI scanner, there was no way I could have been taken on Central Deputation or empanelled. Clearly a game was being played although that hardly affected me in terms of my entitlements. I made a representation evidencing upfront that (a) the State Government of Odisha, the competent authority to dispose of the CBI matter, had been consistent in furnishing my vigilance clearance; (b) it had promoted me to the rank of Principal Secretary and most recently also to the rank of Chief Secretary; (c) CVC itself had not reported anything adverse against me; and (d) DoPT had given information regarding my vigilance clearance in time for my empanelment to be taken up. It would be unjustifiable that grant of such vigilance clearance by the competent authority was deemed by the empanelment process in my case alone to be piecemeal, and not full clearance as on that date.

I requested Cabinet Secretary as the Chief of Civil Services to be objective in assessing the officers of administrative services and prevent any discouragement and demotivation and, ultimately, harm to well-meaning upright officers from extraneous factors. I had bluntly concluded that *"to be empanelled or not is not the only issue I am raising through this representation. Internally, I don't like to care whether people praise or abuse me, as either is equally irrelevant at the end of the day. In public life, however, I attach the highest value to my reputation of absolute integrity, probity and sincerity of purpose. Unsubstantiated allegations are now being used to defame me and to deny what I merit and deserve. I have always believed that statutory provisions and procedures were to protect innocent, sincere and hard-working public servants, and to hold those guilty, accountable. I have tried to measure up to all real tests of time, personal and professional. The illogical and completely unfounded allegations against me now after selfless service for 30 years and subversion of due process of empanelment for unknown reasons seem unreal and have placed me before a hidden force working negatively in this case. This amounts to challenging the very institution of government, much more than the individual at issue. I am placing these facts and thoughts before you for expeditious and suitable disposal."*

Cabinet Secretary Ajit Seth had taken his time to agree to my repatriation as he would frequently say that he was not finding my substitute as I had raised the bar very high. When even after obtaining Prime Minister's order, my relief was being delayed I had to bluntly point out that my hard work and sincerity could not be used against me to delay my repatriation. My views on the issue of "Warrant of Precedence" which were difficult to overrule had annoyed both him and his powerful batchmate. Supreme Court's judgment on 2G spectrum case gave those at the helm of affairs with a strong inclination to appease political masters a perfect platform for deflecting public attention away from the misdemeanours of the pliable and corrupt who were otherwise of use to them in multifarious ways. They opted to maligning my reputation to make a public display of the "honesty quotient" of Central Government using the embedded media tool. Indeed, I was not the only one to be thus used to deflect the public's attention away from the real pain points felt by the then political and administrative establishment when their corruption or other political interests were at risk of being exposed. Instances of successful skirting out of dirty deep political waters can be found throughout the historical times of governance. Obviously, efforts were on to replay the old dirty trick.

Hardly surprising, a few months after my representation, I was informed about my empanelment as Additional Secretary. It was meaningless. At best, it was a message that any rule-bound positions taken by officials were fraught with risks that could have a bearing on their career prospects in government. I always believed that I had got far more than I deserved in the service. I was never attracted towards creature comforts nor spoils of power that posts in Central or State governments entailed. I seriously felt that there was never a need to treat monkeys occupying tree-tops as superior to those on the ground.

Despite working in State Government when my administrative innings were coming to close, Central Government sought my services for SAG-2016 when the situation had gone out of hand, and I gracefully accepted the challenge. After retirement, my services were sought for another similar event which I politely declined.

* * * *

12

Saving Precious Lives: Revenue and Disaster Management

On return from Union Government, I joined as Principal Secretary, R&DM Department on 13 February 2012. After quickly internalizing its functioning, I decided to focus on three most critical issues concerning land administration: first, completion of settlement and consolidation operations in 2,281 pending villages; second, implementation of National Land Records Modernisation Programme (NLRMP); and third, retrieval of government land from land grabbers. Despite being vital, the Department appeared to have slumbered over these issues for unknown reasons, waking up occasionally to tinker a bit. If addressed systematically, effectively and simultaneously, I felt that the Department itself could get recharged to make its presence felt, and would function thereafter as if on auto-pilot. No sizeable budget provisions were needed to vigorously pursue them.

Completing Land Settlement Operations Left Undone

Land administration, which necessarily included regular updating of land records, concerns every household, rich or poor. Hardly surprising that a couple of IAS officers in every batch were posted as Charge Officer, Settlement, just as I was in my formative years, to be groomed as specialists for handling land-related policies later while holding higher positions in State Government. This practice stood discontinued after 1984. Alongside, conduct of revisional survey and settlement operations, hitherto a regular exercise carried out in districts with a 20-30 year periodicity, was virtually discontinued. Field functionaries like ASOs, Assistant Consolidation Officers (ACOs), and Amins, were withdrawn from field formations and redeployed in 1990s to Board of Revenue, Collectorates, Tahasils, and head offices of major settlements. Contractually-appointed Group-D personnel were either relieved permanently or regularised in accordance with High Court's directions.

My exposure to field work and hands-on insights in land matters in my first posting proved invaluable. Taking stock now, I found that about

10,000 villages had been notified for survey and settlement and consolidation operations in the late 1980s. A majority was denotified in late 1990s as satisfactory progress had not been achieved for various reasons, including inadequate manpower and lack of attention. In respect of 2,281 villages of which 1,751 were under settlement and 531 under consolidation, it had been decided to conclude ongoing operations as field work of kishtwar and khanapuri had been completed and process of 'Draft Publication & Objection Hearing' was on the verge or had started. But, after withdrawal of large chunks of manpower without assessing requirements to complete the remaining work, residual work had thus remained incomplete for nearly 12 to 20 years. At my request, Member Board of Revenue agreed to hold a meeting on 29 February 2012 to consider a time-bound plan of action to conclude the revisional operations in the pending villages.

A comprehensive exercise was undertaken in Directorate of Land Records Settlement & Consolidation (LRS&C) to assess field staff requirements to complete pending works as per prescribed yardsticks in 2,281 villages within 15 months. Daily work to be done by each field functionary was quantified. There were about 1,600 Group-D employees, including contractual ones, of which about 600 had been deployed elsewhere. In the meeting, attended by all senior officers including Settlement and Consolidation Commissioners, it was unanimously decided to withdraw all employees deployed elsewhere and complete the unfinished work. A village-wise 'work plan' was prepared and additional requirement of about 1,100 staff worked out. After assessing financial implications, I took concurrence of Finance Department headed by J.K. Mahapatra, ACS to create these 1,100 posts for a period not exceeding two years to execute the work plan. Government decision to discontinue revisional operations had been taken about 13 years back when he was Secretary, Revenue Department. Contractual appointments against newly-created posts were taken up by engaging retired field staff, within 65 years of age, willing to work in positions they had held before their retirement. Against agreed time-lines for each major activity, formats for submitting monthly progress reports against targets of major settlement and consolidation ranges were drawn up.

All hell broke loose when orders were issued by Director, LRS&C, for reversion of existing staff. After all, many officers and field staff, including 600 contractual Group-D workers awaiting regularisation, were being used as office peons and domestic help by senior officers, including in Board of Revenue and secretariat offices of R&DM Minister and Chief Minister, and even at the residence of my predecessor. Consolidation Commissioner who had been appreciative of renewed initiative to complete pending field work in the meeting, realised the fuller implications and was incensed that 12 out of 14 Group-D employees deployed mostly at his residence had been ordered to be withdrawn! He allegedly provoked leaders of Group-D workers by now accustomed to an easy life to agitate. Settlement and Consolidation

Commissioners also stopped holding their courts stating that ASOs/ ACOs used by them as Court Officers had been withdrawn, though no such sanctioned posts existed.

In various invisible and covert forms, affected officers and field staff both mounted an aggressive campaign against Director, LRS&C. His very survival in Board of Revenue became difficult, when Member was found unwilling to intervene to stem the agitation of rowdy advocates similarly instigated to boycott the Revenue Courts on grounds of withdrawal of so-called Court Officers. Consolidation Commissioner went so far as to call Director, LRS&C to his office to instruct him to recall the reversion orders. When he conveyed his inability, he was asked to negotiate the issue with agitating employees. Consolidation Commissioner calling in leaders of agitating Job Contract Employees Association inside his office before quitting his room after stating that being an aggrieved party, he could not help in defusing the situation! Director, LRS&C remained gheraoed without food and water throughout the day. He managed to call me from the office wash room around 10:00 p.m. to describe his situation. I immediately spoke to Police Commissioner, who sent the police force to rescue him from rowdy agitating workers. Police action resulted in arrest of a few union leaders and their suspension. Job contract employees started sending anonymous allegation petitions to various quarters including to State Vigilance, State Human Rights bodies and Government against Director, LRS&C and other senior officers to divert attention. Chief Secretary knew well by now about the brain behind those petitions.

Another problem arose. Job contract employees had already been relieved. Even though instructions stood issued by Directorate of LRS&C to pay their monthly entitlements, this required them to report for duty at their respective new locations. On the basis of writ petitions filed in High Court by staff and orders passed thereon, orders were issued for release of their salaries, pending disposal of their representations to be made within a specified time-frame, by the next higher authority. When these employees did not represent within the time-frame, their salaries remained unpaid. Now, a letter was sent on their behalf to a Judge of High Court who admitted it as a petition for Contempt of Court against Director, LRS&C! The most disturbing aspect was that these contempt proceedings were reportedly being guided by the brother-in-law of the Judge, on the verge of his retirement, who had once worked closely under Consolidation Commissioner. But, in their machinations, it was overlooked that Director, LRS&C was not the drawing and disbursing officer and since the earlier court order for release of salaries was not directed at him, he could hardly be held in contempt. Director, LRS&C, directed to appear personally before the Judge, was humiliated badly in open court and reprimanded besides being issued a warning that he should remain in readiness to go to jail. I had specifically requested Advocate General to defend him. He too was given an identical warning when he tried to defend the Director explaining that there was no cause for contempt of court proceedings against him. Director, LRS&C took leave to go to his son posted in Chandigarh and got hospitalised there. He returned back only after he was transferred and directly joined duties at his new post. The High Court Judge dropped contempt of court proceedings and retired a few days later. Having undergone a similar experience, I was not surprised to find the Director at the receiving end for no fault of his.

There was still no question to giving up without trying all options. I put up a draft to Chief Secretary to advise Member, Board of Revenue to intervene and counsel Consolidation Commissioner appropriately, which he ignored with a broad smile. I also requested him to consider transferring Consolidation Commissioner to a more significant post, as he had worked long enough on a post often considered a black hole or an entrapment with no escape to mainstream administration. I met Principal Secretary to Chief Minister to make the same plea, who like Chief Secretary laughed at my proposal. He added that this officer had to be kept as far away from the Secretariat as possible as he had a habit of creating trouble for his seniors by writing anonymous allegation petitions against them and that Chief Minister was totally allergic to him. I was momentarily disappointed when my request to the two most important officers of Government became futile. My assessment was that Consolidation Commissioner had suffered in service perhaps like none other, as he was arrested and incarcerated in jail in a vigilance case when he was first CMD of OSBC. I have dwelt on this under my narratives on my years serving as Secretary, Excise Department and Chairman of OSBC, when I had found that the charges against him had related only to some procedural irregularities, for which he did not deserve such harsh treatment. He got victimised due to his personal rivalry with an officer who called the shots in Vigilance Directorate. The bitterness in his heart against some senior officers who did not help him out probably translated to his engineered anonymous allegation petitions against them.

Pending revisional operations nevertheless got going. Permanent field staff joined duty and fresh recruitment against sanctioned posts was also undertaken to the extent possible. Job contract employees whose services were being utilised elsewhere reported to their original establishments. After contempt of court proceedings which were without any substantive grounds were dropped, I called the office bearers of employees' association, who agreed to call off the strike and cooperate fully if they were promised permanent absorption against retirement vacancies in Group-D posts in offices under R&DM Department. I found this demand in consonance with long held directions of High Court, and not only got a Circular issued accordingly with government's approval, but also saw to it that it was fully implemented. The going now became smooth and work started progressing fast.

Work was completed in about 20 months in more than 2,100 villages with final publication and patta distribution. About four months were lost due to initial stiff staff resistance, which also refused to completely peter out, and headwinds from undue judicial interventions. Some delay was inevitable due to shortage of manpower as the required numbers of retired employees were not available for contractual appointment against 1,100 temporary posts. Maximum difficulty was faced in 51 villages of Bhubaneswar and Jatni Tahasils. Some senior officers of GA Department, besides land grabbers, did not wish to see old land records being updated. An ASO of Odisha Revenue Service (ORS) in Bhubaneswar Tahasil was found hand in glove with a known member of land mafia who ran a number of educational institutions, including a medical college and an engineering college in the outskirts of Bhubaneswar. Departmental proceedings were drawn up against him for illegal favours showered on vested interests. He tried to turn the tables on me by getting a writ petition filed in High Court insinuating that as administrative head of R&DM Department, I was the one who had issued instructions to ASOs to record private land in government khata! In my counter, I drew attention to illegal orders passed by ASO for which he stood placed under suspension after due process. He now filed an affidavit responding that the wrong orders had been passed by him on my oral instructions! Fully exposed and having failed to draw sympathy of High Court, ASO was removed from service. Ultimately settlement operations were completed in 50 out of 51 pending villages of even Bhubaneswar and Jatni Tahasils. In Sampur, despite work being completed, final publication of revised ROR and patta distribution could not be done during my tenure, due to a stay granted by High Court on the basis of petitions filed by vested interests.

I thus fully utilised my early experiences and expertise in survey and settlement in nearly completing work pending for decades. ASOs/ACOs after closure of field camps were posted as Additional Tahasildars against vacancies that existed for long due to lack of direct or promotional recruitments for years. Group-D staff were reverted to their controlling offices and the practice of drawing salaries from one place while working elsewhere was discontinued.

Land Records: Transforming and Modernising Offices and Systems

The Centrally Sponsored Scheme NLRMP for modernising revenue offices and updating land records had not received the required attention in Odisha. Under the scheme, up to 75 percent of financial requirements were met by Central Government. Allocations received for digitisation of cadastral maps lay deposited since long with Odisha Computer Application Centre (OCAC), while those for hi-tech survey using aerial photography or remote sensing data lay with Odisha Remote Sensing Application Centre (ORSAC). Computerisation of RoRs had been virtually stopped after some initial movements. OCAC opted to apportion blame on R&DM Department, but

ORSAC sat back quietly after spending over ₹ 6 crore on purchase of remote sensing data from National Remote Sensing Centre (NRSC) for 4 districts (Cuttack, Ganjam, Keonjhar, and Khordha). Steps vital for updating land records by comparing remote sensing data with existing cadastral maps and field verification were pending. Central allocations had stopped.

I again found my settlement background useful in marching ahead. It was first necessary to establish a legal framework for hi-tech surveys by using aerial photography and remote sensing data. Traditional systems of survey and settlement in Odisha and Bihar were similar. I found that Bihar had enacted a law regarding hi-tech surveys recently. I deputed a joint team from R&DM Department and Directorates of Land Records & Settlement and Consolidation, to Patna to study their system. Thereafter, we drafted a Bill in a refined form and proposed promulgation of an Ordinance to make it effective immediately in Odisha. Chief Secretary B.K. Patnaik supported it. The Ordinance went on to become Odisha Special Survey & Settlement Act 2012 in the next six months. The new law also mainstreamed survey and settlement operations. A separate hierarchy of settlement and consolidation organisations was no longer necessary for large-scale updating of land records. Tahasildars/Additional Tahasildars were vested with powers of ASOs. Sub-Collectors/Additional Sub-Collectors exercised powers of Settlement Officers in districts covered under hi-tech surveys. Powers of revision, hitherto exercised by Commissioners and Member Board of Revenue, were delegated to Collectors and ADMs. Processes were simplified and updating of RoRs became a concurrent exercise. Earlier Tahasildars stopped updating RoRs through mutations during revisional operations when this task was performed by authorised settlement and consolidation functionaries. The new law had no such restrictions.

After the Act came into force, there was no excuse to avoid undertaking hi-tech surveys. The sole prerequisite was completing digitisation of cadastral maps for comparison and verification of remote sensing data. Facing continuing prevarication by OCAC, funds deposited with them along with accrued interest were withdrawn. The task was assigned to private vendors through open bidding involving Directorate of Land Records & Settlement. When General Manager, OCAC in-charge of digitisation, showed unwillingness to return the cadastral maps, I prepared and submitted a note on the role played by him along with detailed draft charges to Chief Minister. Working transparently, I kept my counterpart in IT Department informed about it. He protested in writing stating that I had no right to charge-sheet a senior officer of an attached organization under his Department. Chief Minister, however, showed no hesitation in approving my proposal. I got cadastral records back from OCAC. Digitisation of over 1.21 lakh cadastral maps was completed by vendors within 6-8 months under technical supervision of ORSAC; competent for certifying their accuracy. ORSAC scientists usefully suggested necessary rectifications before certifying the accuracy of digitised cadastral maps, a task thus completed at costs lower than those being charged by OCAC. What had not been done in more than two years was done in less than eight months with accuracy.

The process of linking digitised cadastral maps and computerised RoRs could be taken up only after completion of both components. Odisha was among the first States to initiate computerisation of RoRs in the country. But soon enough with less than half of it done, work stopped despite receiving financial support from Central Government. On being desired to complete the work with a sense of urgency, some District Collectors cited manpower shortages while others projected shortage of funds. Shockingly, many were not even aware that funds were already available. Seen from their point of view, it was perhaps unexciting dry work. District Collectors were mostly occupied in fire fighting events like distributing relief after natural calamities, implementing priority sector programmes and maintaining law and order. I opted to take it up directly with the next rung in districts. Through monthly video-conferencing with Tahasildars, Sub-Collectors and ADMs, I started reviewing progress against monthly targets for computerisation of RoRs Services of Data Entry Operators were outsourced. The abandoned work proceeded hereafter as though for battle-readiness. RoRs of more than 2,100 villages where settlement and consolidation operations had been carried out were issued in computerised format, which could be uploaded to Bhulekh data-base hosted centrally in NIC server. Sustained pressure on Tahasildars for over a year ensured computerisation of more than 90 percent of pending work. Additional funds required were released happily by Central Government after assessing the progress. My proposal for covering all the districts in a phased manner under hi-tech surveys was also approved by Central Government.

Computerisation of old case records in Tahasils, and modernisation of all 317 Tahasil Record Rooms and 188 Registration Offices, were taken up with financial support from Central Government with a sense of urgency. Chief Secretary visited a Tahasil office of Rayagada, a tribal district, after a year-and-a-half of my taking reins of R&DM Department, to find it unbelievably transformed. I felt rewarded when computerisation of all existing RoRs was completed and spatial data (digitised cadastral maps) were integrated with textual data (RoRs) with full support of NIC before I left R&DM Department. Odisha was perhaps the only State to achieve this milestone despite some teething problems and need for refinement. My past experiences had taught me well not to start a work which could not be taken to the logical end. I had been transferred more than once just when I was on the verge of reaching my goalposts. From media reports or chance remarks in meetings or informally from colleagues, I could sense that the wave-length of my successor many times did not correspond with mine, which resulted in derailment of works I had initiated or that they were taken forward haphazardly.

After digitisation of cadastral maps, it was easier to process the remote sensing data procured from NRSC for four districts. Simultaneously, I proposed to cover the remaining 26 districts under hi-tech aerial surveys. My understanding based on academic studies and experience of Andhra Pradesh and Bihar, was that accuracy with resolution of 10 cm of aerial photography was far better than that of 50 cm by remote sensing satellite. Scientists in ORSAC too favoured aerial surveys. It was finally decided to undertake a pilot based on aerial survey in 5 districts first, viz. Debagadh, Jharsuguda, Sambalpur, Sonepur and Sundargarh, and after comparing the merits of both systems, hi-tech surveys could be taken up in remaining 21 districts. Aerial survey was assigned to a Hyderabad-based agency selected through open tendering, which also had valuable experience having participated in a pilot district of Andhra Pradesh. The task of fixing primary, secondary and tertiary points for survey and field verification was completed quickly. To progress the verification of remote sensing data, Amins, RIs and Tahasildars of the four districts were trained in these hi-tech survey techniques.

Ensuring posting of dedicated and qualified revenue functionaries in Tahasils was vital, but recruitment had not taken placed in OAS since 2006. The number of Tahasils had increased from 177 to 317 after making them coterminous with Blocks in 2008 without creating requisite infrastructure or providing manpower. Odisha Revenue Service (ORS with sanctioned strength of 1,100 had been created in the same year, but recruitment had not happened due to litigation regarding share of reservation. According to Cadre Rules, 50 percent post in ORS were to be filled up by promotion, rest by direct recruitment. I requested Member, Board of Revenue to convene DPC meetings for recommending promotional appointments for 200 ORS officers. In parallel, requisition was submitted to State Public Service Commission for undertaking direct recruitment of another 200 officers. All departments were requested to forward the required details of employees in the zone of consideration for such promotion. Collectors were persuaded to undertake direct recruitment to fill up posts of RI and ARIs. As a result of systematic monitoring, it was possible to fill up vacant posts through promotional appointment of about 200 ORS officers. The newly recruited officers were trained in hi-tech survey after designing a bridge-training course for them. While proposing their posting to hi-tech survey districts, orders of Chief Minister were taken not to displace them from their respective places till these special operations were completed except on serious administrative grounds.

Picking up momentum steadily, aerial survey was completed in all 5 pilot districts within a year. Along with, processing of data started with test checks on accuracy, field verification of land parcels and ownerships with reference to old cadastral maps and RoRs. Processing of remote sensing data of 4 districts procured from NRSC progressed well simultaneously. At this stage, I was transferred from R&DM Department.

Retrieving Government Land from Bellicose Bulls, while Bearing Risks

The third important area of attention was recovery of large chunks of government land in Puri-Konark, Cuttack, Kalinga Nagar, Berhampur and in/around Bhubaneswar. Just prior to my assuming charge, a Special Cell had been set up tasked with identifying Government land in important locations in possession of land mafia. The practice of setting up Committees, Commissions, Task Forces and Special Cells usually came to denote nothing more than a symbolic expression of intentions, an image-building exercise before the public. A retired OAS officer stood appointed as a Senior Consultant, but without necessary support staff. R&DM Department itself was functioning with about 60 percent of its sanctioned staff strength.

Notwithstanding logistics' limitations, I saw a great opportunity in recovering Government land by coupling the Special Cell with Tahasil and district administration in an effective mechanism for identifying land grabs and land grabbers. It was indeed not a case of garnering expertise to hit the bull's tiny eye as land and its grabbers stood identified in most cases; it was a clear case of hitting bellicose bulls. Land grabbers were largely influential people, many of them affiliated with the ruling party or holding high posts in State Government. Some were intimately connected even with families of judges, while yet others belonged to well-known organizations, including bureaucracy and media. Whispers about many land grabbers having armed thugs guarding their interests, especially in construction industry, resonated loudly in R&DM Department's corridors. I was conscious that it would not be easy to take back land illegally held for years in prime locations by these mafia, armed with influence or bullets. They posed enormous though variegated challenges and risks, foremost of which was about ensuring the safety of enforcement teams taking land in their possession by demarcating and posting boundary pillars or fencing. Besides, judicial fora were available to be leveraged by them which was enough to cause delay and or outright sabotage.

I involved two senior government advocates in High Court in consultation with Advocate General. Besides remaining alert on happenings in Court, they attended my weekly meetings and gave valuable inputs in strategizing actionables for retrieving land, particularly in sensitive cases and those involving larger tracts. The results were there for everyone to see. Within a period of three years of my tenure, more than 15,000 acres of valuable Government land in illegal possession of land grabbers was identified, of which 7,500 acres were fully demarcated by posting boundary pillars or fencing. I ignored threats and personal risks in this mission against influential land mafia.

One such land grabber in Bhubaneswar, with reported political links cutting across political parties, used his daily newspaper to campaign against me in person. Perforce I filed civil and criminal defamation cases against him and the Editor. When criminal defamation case against him was admitted, he removed the Editor and got the case against himself stayed by High Court by arguing that the Editor was singularly responsible for the defamatory news report. His perfidy knew no bounds as soon after his removal from the job the Editor had died and could hardly defend himself. Recovery of a big chunk of land from another owner of a reputed daily newspaper who also happened to be a MP was rather a smooth affair.

When action against another political heavy weight was being pursued with full rigour, I survived an inexplicable road accident in Bhubaneswar soon after I left my residence enroute to the office. My office car was hit by a speeding vehicle from behind. The influential politician was earlier Minister in State Government and had been elected to Rajya Sabha. His rival in the ruling party and a Minister, cautioned me that the accident probably was a design to eliminate me and not a coincidence. Special Cell had recovered more than 5 acres of land near Bhubaneswar from his family, in addition to 70 hectares near Kalinga Nagar (Jajpur) on which a farm house stood constructed amidst lush cashew plantation. None had done anything for years to recover this publicly-owned land brought under cashew plantation. Now local Tahasildar and Collector on being warned about action against them, not only revealed the benami ownership of the politician but also took steps to demolish the farm house. This former Minister was found to have used Government funds to construct the approach road on forest land even to the house constructed by his son, a serving MLA, in an urbanised village adjoining Bhubaneswar. I never cared to think about the veracity of claims of the rival leader, and thus taking it all with a pinch of salt, firm in my conviction that nothing could stop it when the end of life became inevitable, I continued to quietly and faithfully restore land grabbed illegally to Government's account. Publicity was also the last thing I craved.

Violence was overt when anti-social elements in Puri hurled crudely-made bombs at local Tahasil officials engaged in raising barbed-wire fencing on about 3,000 acres of land in Shipsarobali village on which cashew plantations had been raised. Instead of engaging in instant retaliation against protesters mobilised by local land mafia, the police force withdrew tactically to avoid untoward incidents. I was present at the site along with senior IGP to supervise the successful operation as local Tahasildar had reported threats to his life and lack of support from Collector and district Police. The mafia had been hardly ashamed to use innocent women and children as shields. After all, they were deriving a good income from Government land they had grabbed on which cashew plantations had been raised by State Soil Conservation Department. For sure, State leadership would not spare the enforcement functionaries them in the event the situation at recovery went out of control or by standers suffered injuries or casualties as a result of police action. But it was hardly credible that district administration was not aware of the land grab. The situation is clearly tragic whenever district administration at its helm chooses to be swayed or guided by its own tainted perception that somehow State leadership is more sensitive to and concerned about adverse media coverage even if it is temporary than about vital matters of maintenance of law and order and enforcement of law of the land in order to protect valuable public assets.

In the first phase, Special Cell focussed on land encroachments in Puri, Cuttack, Jajpur and Bhubaneswar. It examined volumes of lease records and made field visits, which led to detection of 15,841.16 acres leased out fraudulently, in addition to about 1,000 acres of Government land encroached by land grabbers. With sustained work involving huge amount of risk, an area amounting to about 7,500 acres was duly demarcated and partially fenced rapidly to confirm restoration and recovery. It was found that multiple transactions had taken place on the basis of fake case records in and around Bhubaneswar amounting to 4,082 acres. Of these, 1,001 acres, including 153 acres in Shampur and 606 acres in Gothapatna villages, were restored to Government. In Puri, 2,419 acres were restored out of 7,089 acres detected. In Cuttack, 94 acres were restored out of 834 acres detected. In Jajpur 2,395 acres were restored out of 3,734 acres detected.

There was hardly any appreciation for the work done by Special Cell, although progress achieved was being brought to the notice of R&DM Minister and Chief Minister regularly. When Chief Minister came for inaugurating the Revenue Officers' Training Institute in Bhubaneswar and was informed by me that the building stood on the land recovered from land grabbers, he maintained a stoic silence as if to convey his lack of interest and indifference. Curiously, about 5 acres of Government land by the side of this Institute had remained in possession of an influential person, which could not have happened without connivance with some field functionaries of R&DM Department through the years. The land grabber had succeeded in obtaining High Court orders in support of his claims to the land. On the basis of a Supreme Court decision that the law of limitation would not apply to fraudulent transactions detected at any point of time, the Apex Court had upheld actions against many land grabbers earlier. In the instant case, however, the SLP filed by the department had been dismissed due to default on the part of State Government's Advocate on Record in Supreme Court. Market value of 5 acres of prime Government land being more than ₹ 25 crore, a Review Petition was filed after removing the said well connected Advocate on Record and a senior advocate was appointed in consultation with the Law Department to handle the case. I got transferred just a few days before the Review Petition came up for hearing. Later on, I was appalled to learn that the said senior advocate who had agreed to defend the Review Petition and the new Advocate on Record suddenly changed sides a day before the hearing. Instead of defending the State Government as had been agreed, they now represented the land grabber. Review

Petition was dismissed as I was informed later by the officer in Special Cell. A few months later this senior advocate got elevated as a Judge to the Supreme Court!

After my transfer, the Special Cell became defunct. Senior consultant who was sincerely helping in recovery of Government land too was removed in no time. After a few months, I was apprised about abolition of Special Cell itself! Towards the end of my tenure, R&DM Minister advised me not to pursue the action I was initiating against a big builder who had constructed massive Towers and an approach road in an urbanised village near Bhubaneswar partly on Government land. He cited the sufferings of consumers who had paid the cost of apartments which were nearly completed. I conveyed my inability to stop the action, despite concerns of Minister being not without foundation. Another case in my radar then was benami occupation of a large piece of land at Chandrasekharpur, the market value of which was around 30 crore. This occupation was evidently linked to an influential serving Minister. Restless land grabbers naturally celebrated my exit.

Exposing and Disposing Fraudulent Government Land Leases

Dual control over Government land was exploited by land grabbers in Bhubaneswar and villages at its periphery. Actual control over land for deciding its usage and allotment stood with GA Department which hardly had any domain knowledge on the subject. Tahasildars and other field officers of R&DM Department were custodians of land records and responsible for their updating, though they hardly stood informed of allotments of land by GA Department. The problem was accentuated when land mafia started fabricating lease records and taking orders of Civil Courts asserting right and title over such land. In connivance with some corrupt functionaries in Tahasils, as though these were two peas in the same pod fake lease case records had found indistinguishable place in Record Rooms alongside genuine ones. Beneficiaries of fake leases would apply for issuance of RoRs with the passage of time, and if unsuccessful approach the local Civil Court for it. District Collector and other revenue functionaries, what to speak of GA Department, rarely knew about orders of Civil Courts allowing claims of petitioners. Special Cell recovered many fake lease case records, which did not require any further evidence to establish multiple frauds that had been perpetuated. In many cases, I found dates of orders on Note Sheet of fraudulently created lease case records preceding printing and supply of those Note Sheets by Government Press. The numbers were far too large to bluff anyone that these were mere typographic errors!

Under Odisha Government Land Settlement Act, Tahasildars had powers to grant lease up to one standard acre each in rural areas to landless families below the poverty line for agricultural purposes or up to 10 decimals for a homestead with the approval of next higher authority. It was found that despite Government wasteland not being suitable for agricultural purposes, some

Tahasildars had misused their powers by lavishly granting leases in villages around Bhubaneswar which changed hands to reach land mafia and builders. Classification of land and ownership both were changed furtively. A very senior OAS officer known for his doubtful integrity who had retired after holding the crucial post of Additional Secretary in GA Department, had worked as Tahasildar, Bhubaneswar. During his incumbency, a large number of leases were found to have been granted fraudulently. I had to perform the unpleasant task of getting him arrested when it was discovered that he had granted lease of a large chunk of land fraudulently to his relatives about 30 years back. This land had since become part of the State Capital and changed hands in the meanwhile. Buyers got orders from High Court directing the local Tahasildar to mutate land in their favour. On my instructions when incumbent Tahasildar did not allow the mutation, he was hauled up for contempt of court. Even though State's Advocate General advised Government to allow mutation to save him from being punished against proven violation of High Court order, I had my way in getting the matter transferred to Crime Branch for urgent investigation. High Court had admonished the Tahasildar twice and was to pass order less than a week hence. Crime Branch investigation, pushed for early completion by me with Additional DG of Police resulted in the arrest of this former Additional Secretary instead! His arrest, effected just a day before the contempt case came up for hearing, got widely publicised. Despite taking a strong view in earlier hearings, no adverse view was taken against incumbent Tahasildar by High Court in light of the crucial reality which had reached the public domain in the nick of time.

Government lands in vast magnitudes had been allotted regularly after their creation to Bhubaneswar Development Authority (BDA) and Odisha State Housing Board (OSHB) for development of residential colonies and associated infrastructure. Deliberately or otherwise, these bodies left unutilised some portions of land in developed colonies, which was sure to be grabbed either by outsiders or allottees of houses and plots. Peripheral lands even though classified as "forest", became slums duly encouraged by the elected representatives of the local urban body. No steps were taken to inform revenue field officials about land allotted and actually put to use by them for the purpose it had been allotted for updating land records. The left hand of Government did not know what its right was doing. Land grabbers took full advantage of this chasm.

I have mentioned earlier about completing revisional settlement in 50 out of 51 villages of Bhubaneswar and Jatni Tahasils. During my visit to Settlement Camps after I got the incomplete work resumed, ASO of Jatni Settlement Camp showed me copies of a set of fake records reported to have been maintained by some functionaries during 'Kishtwar and Khanapuri' stage. These reflected long-standing possession by claimants over a number of government plots. The copies had been presented to him during 'Objection Hearing' by claimants. Luckily, original records including diaries of Amins written during 'Kishtawar and Khanapuri' had still not been destroyed. On my instruction, ASO filed criminal cases against claimants besides rejecting their claims. This frightened the claimants, who probably had paid for alternative sets of fake records maintained by Settlement Amins during 'Kishtawar and Khanapuri' stage about 20 years back. They did not pursue their so-called claims anymore and land in their wrongful possession could be restored to Government's khata.

State Government on the advice of Central Government had adopted a policy of allotting land to families of defence personnel who had participated in 1962, 1965 and 1971 wars. It provided for allotment of up to five acres of Government wasteland to eligible beneficiaries. Considering the heightened demand, Revenue Department had issued instructions in mid-1980s that applications of intended beneficiaries would thereafter be disposed of by Tahasildars. But, powers of Tahasildar stood limited to leasing agricultural land under Odisha Government Land Settlement Act up to one acre only. Neither Tahasildar nor any other authority below Government had powers to be exercised under Government Grants Act, 1895 to lease land. There were no provisions for delegation of powers to any other authority below Government either. Thus, this unfounded delegation of powers in mid-1980s mostly benefitted retired officers in armed service during the defined period. Large chunk of Government land in villages under Bhubaneswar and Jatni Tahasils changed hands. With rapid urbanisation taking place, jurisdiction of BDA was being extended to villages around Bhubaneswar. Land given for agriculture purpose to retired armed forces' personnel started reaching builders for development of new colonies. Increasing numbers of applications from retired army personnel, widows and power of attorney holders, seeking land in villages around Bhubaneswar started getting filed with State Government. Those who did not get land, alleged discrimination and sought relief from High Court.

Scarcity of land for allotment led to an alternative scheme for financial incentives disbursed through Home Department to eligible retired army personnel. But, their applications for allotment of land were simply forwarded by Home Department to Revenue Department in order not to be seen to be thwarting High Court directions. After examining the scheme in consultation with Advocate General, I obtained Chief Minister's approval for clarifying that delegation of power made under Government Grants Act, 1895 was illegal and, thus, stood recalled. Home Department was called upon to dispose of claims by providing financial incentives as land for lease was not available. An affidavit was filed in High Court accordingly. Though it was the correct course of action legally besides being an effective tool to prevent further land scams, it invited criticism of highhandedness on my part. However, I had found too many instances of fraud to be deterred. In a noteworthy case, when I visited Jatni Settlement Camp for inspection, I found that a retired army officer had received five acres of land twice in a village where these ten acres of land had undergone several transactions thereafter, and on a portion of it a multi-storeyed building stood out prominently.

Skylines of Bhubaneswar started changing rapidly with economic liberalisation in the 1990s and associated boom in mining in Odisha. With the advent of Naveen Patnaik, it was also becoming an educational hub in eastern India. Like Bengaluru in 1980s, large numbers of institutions offering vocational training in professional streams of engineering, IT, medical sciences, and management, started coming up in and around Bhubaneswar in addition to business establishments and multi-storeyed apartments. Job work of organisations like BDA, OSHB and IDCO was practically taken over by private players. Some heads of these organisations went out of the way in providing land to them despite it being earmarked for different purposes at the time of allotment. In an instance, BDA, which had been given land for developing colonies for middle and lower-income groups, had transferred 10 acres at a nominal price to a well-known land grabber who had thereafter set up a number of educational institutions on it. During settlement operations, I also found large quantities of land in Jatni Tahasil allotted to a number of engineering colleges, many of which had barely existed or were on the verge of closure. I was told that a senior officer in State Government was the real holder of land allotted at nominal prices ostensibly to a group of Non-Resident Odias to set up an engineering college, which had closed down practically for all intents and purposes.

Another *modus operandi* to grab Government land was by way of encroaching peripheral areas by allottee. Owner of a private University, who had received 15 acres of land in Jatni Tahasil at a highly subsidised rate from IDCO, encroached another 15 acres of adjoining Government land. He flaunted his proximity with many, including successive Chief Secretaries, an ACS, and Principal Secretary to Chief Minister in order to get approvals on his proposals for funds from various departments in the name of vocational training in addition to silencing junior and middle level officers. Jatni Tahasildar lacked courage to initiate eviction proceedings against this well-connected person who had the temerity to also illegally arrogate and steal laterite stones from this land to raise a compound wall as though to stamp his claim over 15 acres of encroached land. On being warned of dereliction of duty by me, JatniTahasildar pursued eviction proceedings. The land grabber tried to leverage the judiciary by pleading in High Court that it was only a case of wrong demarcation of land allotted to him. High Court, while staying eviction proceedings, passed orders for fresh demarcation using GPS methodology for accuracy, costs of which would be borne by petitioner. The encroacher refused to pay up till the matter was directed to be brought to the notice of Court. Reported attempts to get rid of me from R&DM Department failed as J.K. Mahapatra, perhaps the only exception as Chief Secretary who could not be influenced by this land grabber, advised Chief Minister against my transfer. The encroacher gained over Government Advocate who declined to bring GPS survey findings which confirmed encroachment to the Court. The brief given to him to handle the matter had to be changed by Advocate General on his complicity being exposed by me.

Finally, when the writ petition was found to be devoid of substance and was going to be dismissed, the encroacher succeeded in playing his last card. He prayed for High Court to pass orders for directing State Government for a personal hearing to him by the new Chief Secretary before taking coercive action for eviction. High Court gave 45 days time to consider a representation submitted by him to a pliant secretary in Higher Education Department, which had nothing to do in land matters. Chief Secretary quietly instructed the Secretary, Higher Education to file an affidavit to seek another four weeks for personal hearing and disposal of encroacher's representation. I was transferred in the meanwhile. After my departure, Chief Secretary heard the encroacher and directed IDCO to apply to R&DM Department for transfer of encroached Government land and hand it over to the encroacher in return for some land allotted to him which was described as less useful. The whole exercise was to legitimize the encroachment. The law did not allow transfer or lease of encroached land before eviction of encroachment had been carried out and there were no provisions for exchange of land either. Moreover, land allotted for the private educational institution had been developed and utilised by him with nothing left for the so-called exchange. Besides, the size of encroached land was about the same as that allotted for the institution. It was a clear case of facilitating grabbing of valuable Government land.

Khasmahal land admeasuring 20.808 acres in Cuttack had been leased out to Odisha Olympic Association for a period of 20 years to construct a stadium along with a playground. It provided interesting revelation of institutional land grab, with pointers towards nexus and negligence on the part of some senior functionaries in the past, which even received attention of Supreme Court. Lease period had been extended for another 20 years up to September 1989. But lease terms and conditions had been brazenly flouted by the Association's long-serving General Secretary by constructing a number of commercial buildings and structures on it despite the lease not having been renewed after September 1989. Collector, Cuttack's order recording the land in favour of the Association had been set aside by RDC, Cuttack. But the Association filed a writ petition in 2002 in High Court challenging this order. Another area admeasuring 2.70 acres had also been leased out by Government in 1969 for constructing an Indoor Stadium and a dormitory for athletes. Since this land had not been utilised for the given purpose, it was resumed subsequently. Digging deeper, I found that Revenue Department had also leased 1.94 acres for constructing a swimming pool and restaurant in 1951, but the Association had failed to enter into a lease agreement within the stipulated period and yet remained in possession of 1.22 acres which it fraudulently got recorded in own name in 1988 during settlement operations. This land however, was seen to have been restored to Government later by orders passed by the competent Revenue Court. Egregiously, Odisha Olympic Association still remained in illegal occupation.

The rule position and ground reality revealed a different tale altogether. Section 15 of Odisha Development Authority Act, 1982 disallowed construction over government land without written permission of competent authority within development area. But the General Secretary had constructed commercial complexes including Kalyan Mandaps without approval. His family and close relatives were beneficiaries of the commercial operations. Cuttack Development Authority (CDA) had remained a passive spectator. Perhaps his ability to foster close connections with ruling dispensations over time by shifting loyalties enabled his continued enrichment and that of favoured few.

Supreme Court had passed orders directing State Government to file lease orders in original, and an affidavit duly sworn in by competent authority, along with photographic evidence, giving nature of commercial establishments constructed on Government land. This provided a golden opportunity for Special Cell to go to the roots of the matter. Not to be outdone, the General Secretary somehow obtained approval for the building plans from CDA. RoRs for land admeasuring 20.802 acres specifically provided term of lease up to 1989 as remarks. But the Association while applying for approval of CDA for the plan to construct the stadium gallery produced a manipulated RoR showing a blank remarks' column! CDA officials without verifying the documents granted approval vacuously, exposing their unholy nexus with key office bearers of the Association. I asked CDA Vice Chairman to fix accountability.

On the direction of High Court, CBI investigated allegations of fraud in alienation, illegal and unauthorised occupation of Government land in Bidanasi area of Cuttack. Based on its report, orders had been passed directing State Government to recover land held by encroachers and submit compliance. Collector, Cuttack was tasked to remove encroachments, even as R&DM Minister was found batting for their regularisation. No visible steps appeared to have been taken by District Administration against either smaller encroachers or large land grabbers for recovery of land. I made a couple of visits to Barabati Stadium and other sites to review encroachment cases and obtained the status of organised land grabbing by well-connected persons. My last review was on 17 April 2015 before I was transferred on 21 April 2015.

Instances cited here are illustrative, but show the lust and greed for land and support land grabbers received from their well-placed friends. In order to discourage it, I had studied how progressive southern States handle such situations. I found that Andhra Pradesh had enacted laws to make grabbing of public land a cognizable crime. A Ministerial Group under R&DM Minister constituted in Odisha suggested measures for arresting land grabbing, including stronger laws. With active support of Special Cell, I got approval of State Cabinet for promulgating the Odisha Land Grabbing (Prohibition) Ordinance, which became law soon after I left R&DM Department. It foresaw punishment ranging between 1-7 years of imprisonment, made land grabbing a non-bailable cognizable offence, and defined land grabber and land grabbing to exclude the innocent poor if found to be in possession of public land for subsistence or survival. It is, however, another story that Special Courts and Tribunal envisaged under the law with civil and criminal powers are yet to be set up and remain unlikely in the near future given lack of political will to implement the enacted law coupled with a risk-averse and increasingly domesticated bureaucracy.

Bringing Discipline, Accountability in Land Acquisition and R&R in Law

Land acquisition and rehabilitation & resettlement (R&R) were important and sensitive issues requiring greater attention along with administrative reforms. Key and critical role played by Tahasils, the oldest administrative units, had ceased to be important since long now. With the advent of Block/ Panchayat Samitis as focal points at the cutting edge of administration, Tahasils stood relegated to the background. Revenue and development branches could no longer function hand-in-hand. Land acquisition, R&R of displaced families, lease and sale transactions of land, and relief operations during and after incidents of natural calamities received occasional attention. Land reform, including modernisation of land laws, had ceased to be the flavour of changing times. The trend was disturbing. There were big gaps in R&R despite a good policy in place. R&R was lost sight of soon after land acquisition for mining and industrial projects got completed. I was surprised to hear from HR Head of a renowned industrial house after my joining full details of sections and officials empowered to issue notifications in relation to pending land acquisition proposals for his company!

R&DM Department had released about ₹ 1.50 crore for developing an application software for online monitoring of land acquisition and R&R of project-displaced families. Specific industrial projects had been selected on pilot basis in Angul and Sambalpur to test and customise the software being developed. Selection of firm had been done as per recommendation of OCAC under IT Department. Funds release was linked to progress made against prescribed milestones set out in the contract. However, I saw that the firm had received full funds ignoring the prescriptions on the recommendation of Director (R&R), Revenue Department who stood transferred as MD, OSDMA a couple of months prior to my joining the department.

I found that the IT firm had submitted a design which did not fulfil the requirement. It demanded additional funds for further work. Since funding support from UNDP was exhausted, expenditure incurred became a sheer waste.

OCAC simply walked away. I called the firm and sought corrective measures as they had deviated from prescriptions and there was no possibility of software design being of any use for online monitoring. But the firm reiterated its demand for extra money. On enquiring into its credentials and competence, I found that the firm had managed to get assigned most of the Government's IT projects and cornered the bulk of annual budgetary provisions for IT projects year after year despite hardly any among them getting completed to be put to use. Ironically, the objective of various departments remained utilisation of budgetary allocations regardless of end results. This firm appeared to have perfected its design of public relations to grab funds for IT projects. Needs kept changing and successor heads of departments were more interested in awarding new projects rather than achieving closure on existing ones. Accountability and work rarely went hand-in-hand. I could do nothing beyond seeking Chief Secretary's intervention for action against the firm. Nothing happened.

It was impossible to find details of land acquired in the previous 10 years or current acquisition process at different stages in different districts in one place. In earlier assignments I had found NIC experts quite competent in designing application software for monitoring projects. NIC did not charge for costs incurred either. I called Director NIC and gave my requirements for online monitoring of land acquisition and R&R. In consultation with R&DM officers, the application software for online monitoring was developed by NIC and was put to use by land acquisition sections in different districts and in the Secretariat simultaneously. Land Acquisition Officers in districts were allowed to use contingency funds received by them to outsource services of Data Entry Operators for regular data entry and updates. It was possible to generate monthly reports for providing updated project-wise status of land acquisition at various stages along with actual R&R of displaced families. Time-bound notifications to be issued as set out in various provisions of Land Acquisition Act could now be tracked easily. Delays or selective attention for issuance of notifications became a thing of the past. I was happy that industrial houses no longer flocked the corridors of R&DM Department.

Online monitoring also detected a number of irregularities in issuance of notifications without fulfilling prerequisites in the past, which in some cases appeared to have been done to bestow favours to a few industrial houses. For instance, the final notification for acquiring land meant for ESSAR in Jagatsinghpur had been issued for all project villages even though less than a third of the compensation amount legally required had been deposited by project proponent. IDCO which had a facilitating role appeared to have misled R&DM Department to get the final notification issued without the pre-conditions having been fulfilled.

Public projects too were tarnished with irregularities. In a number of cases, some officials of Water Resources Department were found to have taken possession of land from tribal farmers for irrigation projects without payment of compensation and indeed, before issuance of required notifications. In some other cases, some farmers had been compensated only in part, and when project implementation started years later, these farmers demanded the balance compensation at the latest higher rates. Those having received full payment years back got the opportunity to refuse to hand over possession of land without being paid additional amount to maintain compensation rate parity with others. It also appeared that some officers were seeking to lay the blame on R&DM Department for delay in land acquisition and somehow justify delay in their own project implementation which invariably involved cost escalation. The fact remained that the relevant law did not permit payment of compensation in the same village in phases spread over years. In a district, more than ₹ 50 crore was found to have been misappropriated in the name of payment of compensation for a major irrigation project and the Land Acquisition Officer had gone underground. It became difficult to suppress such facts after online monitoring of land acquisition was introduced. None could now get away with blaming R&DM Department for delay in land acquisition either.

Historically, large-scale land acquisition in Odisha was mostly limited to projects of State and Central Governments. Compensation to displaced families was paid most conservatively. Prior to 2005, there was no robust R&R policy and besides displaced families lacked awareness of their entitlements. Concept of public interest litigation (PIL) had not developed sufficiently for public-spirited activists to approach courts of law holding a brief for displaced families. It was shocking that a number of displaced families of Hirakud Project and RSP, having received only nominal compensation, were still agitating for their entitlements and rehabilitation. After the mining sector of natural resource-rich Odisha was opened up following reforms introduced in 1991, private players made a beeline to set up mineral-based industries including power and steel plants. As the State continued to follow the old procedure of assessing value of land to be acquired taking into account returns from agricultural activities, families dependent upon subsistence agriculture having lost their land did not find either alternative land or employment elsewhere. Their only alternative was either to perish or retaliate.

Biju Patnaik had successfully sold his dream of a second steel plant to the electorate. When he came to power in 1990, about 5,000 acres were acquired in Kalinga Nagar (Jajpur). Foundation laying ceremony, held with great fanfare, attracted a gathering of over 50,000 people, generating hopes for employment and economic growth of coastal districts. Indian-origin British-promoter Swaraj Paul attended the ceremony, only to back out after sometime. The acquired land finally got transferred after 5 years to the Tatas. Tribal farmers had been paid compensation at the rate about ₹ 25,000/acre in early 1990s, with hardly any prospects of employment even after a decade. In 2006, when construction of compound wall to protect the acquired land started, tribal farmers who had continued to cultivate their land started agitating. In the ensuing police firing, 13 lives were lost. District Administration was concerned more about providing support to protect the land allotted to an industrial house, failing to even-handedly discharge its responsibilities towards R&R of innocent, illiterate, displaced tribal farmers who had lost their only asset which had given them a sense of security.

Curiously, another 3,000 acres had been acquired around Gopalpur Ganjam) in the name of a steel plant and port development for the same industrial house in mid-1990s for which compensation to farmers had been paid at ₹ 25,000 to ₹ 50,000 per acre, depending upon proximity of land from the main road and neighbouring towns. The provisions of land acquisition for 'public purposes' had been invoked which was in violation of law. Ten years later when land for Vedanta Group for their proposed University in Puri was acquired identically and was challenged in High Court, the procedure followed was found in violation of the law, and land acquisition was set aside. None had the courage to challenge this land acquisition, despite the influential promoter having declined to implement the steel plant project. I was told by Ganjam district administration and IDCO officials that money spent by the promoter for raising the compound wall to protect the acquired land was more than compensation paid out. Since the project did not see dawn, promises and expectations of employment for project-affected families remained nothing more than a pipe dream.

It was at this stage when resistance started gaining ground against displacements in Kalinga Nagar and Gopalpur. State Government belatedly realized its severity. It was forced to come out with a reasonable R&R Policy 2006, the first of its kind in the country, which was virtually duplicated by Central Government after sometime. It recognized not only the rights of those who lost their land, but for the first time covered landless families and marginalised communities who had been rendering various services to land-owners and thereby earning their livelihood. Hitherto, when land was acquired by the State in public interest, land losers got some compensation and homestead land elsewhere. No assistance was given to those who did not have land. R&R package now offered had a positive affect and promoters for whom land was acquired were made more accountable towards R&R of displaced families. One member of a displaced family now could opt for employment to be given by the promoter or an additional lumpsum in its lieu.

Due to delays in acquiring land, major linear road and rail projects were languishing. The situation was worrisome as these were lifelines for long-term development of the State, but were receiving least attention. Whenever political leadership pressed for higher investments by railways, their standard refrain had been that the State Government had not provided land for railway tracks. As a result, even the limited annual budget provisions could not be fully utilised. Expansion projects of National Highways were no different.

National Thermal Power Corporation and South Eastern Coalfield murmured similarly.

A positive outcome of R&R package offered by Central PSUs was that displaced families besides getting houses constructed for them with better infrastructure facilities at alternative sites and compensation, also got employment and annuity. Their package typically exceeded the provisions under new R&R Policy. In contrast, private corporates mostly generated high hopes at the time of land acquisition, but gave far less attention to implement R&R packages. Majority of displaced and project-affected families did not have a family member skilled enough to attract a decent job in the industry. This gap was exploited by private promoters, who promised employment to one member of each displaced family. Project proponents, despite being told to make provisions for vocational training for unskilled members of displaced families, simply cited lack of provision in R&R policy thus covering their own unwillingness. They preferred to provide one-time financial assistance in lieu of employment. I made it a point to review R&R aspects regularly, besides ensuring reviews by Collector and RDC. Continuous administrative pressure on them kept the hope of displaced families alive and Odisha did not face any major agitation on land acquisitions after serious attention was paid by Revenue Administration to proper R&R policy implementation.

It was atrocious that R&DM officials played to the gallery on land acquisition for PSUs, though that ultimately benefitted the State more. I pursued these projects with vigour, through online monitoring followed by regular meetings with district officials and video conferences, as any allegation of delay attributable to State Government leading to poor project progress, lower investment, or surrender of budgetary provisions was anathema to me. This pressure helped in transforming the situation in a short time. Railways were no longer able to claim that execution of Paradip-Haridaspur or Angul-Sukinda Railway lines could not be expedited due to delay in handing over land by State Government. I had cautioned Jajpur Collector that necessary administrative support must be made available to Railways to take possession of acquired land and during execution of projects. Temporary deployment of police to support the Railways was also to convey a stern message to anti-social elements to desist from indulging in extortion activities besides facilitating transfer of land.

It is not as if Railway personnel were always right. In a particular area on Paradip-Haridaspur line, they did not execute work even after paying compensation years back for acquired land. When farmers in the adjoining area were given higher amount of compensation later on, those having already received compensation for their land earlier, refused to vacate possession. Ex-gratia for additional amount had to be paid to these families totalling ₹ 15 crore simply because of delay in taking possession of land by Railways. None in Railways was held accountable, and sadly even after spending extra,

Railways did not show urgency to complete the work. Excuses for failing to implement projects in time were thus largely hollow. My constant advice to Railways was to take possession of government land alienated for their projects, get land records corrected, and fence it. Similar advice was given to Central PSUs. Land was acquired for Angul-Sukinda railway line in record time. The head of the project's Special Purpose Vehicle conveyed desperation to complete it by July 2017. But when per chance mid-2018, I had occasion to inquire about it, I was shocked to hear him saying that there was no question of Prime Minister Modi being allowed the satisfaction of inaugurating it before May 2019 even though funds and land were no longer constraints! This rail line passed through Odisha's mining belt and was reckoned to be commercially most profitable.

A large number of public functionaries in both Central and State Governments could be seen working as if reluctantly or only under compulsion on being threatened of action against them. They rarely considered the consequences of their inactions or wrong actions on the projects' future. At times, mischievous elements took full advantage of this situation as I saw in a village on Khordha-Nayagarh railway line near Begunia. In this case, possession over about three acres of government land had not been transferred to Railways for years. When Railways finally started work for laying the line, a dispute was raised by a person asserting that he had not been compensated for the land. He presented lease records and got his ownership confirmed through a favourable ruling of Settlement Commissioner. This had happened before my joining R&DM Department. The matter was brought to my notice as this piece of land was vital for the line. Railways had completed line-laying work from both sides and were ready to start train services Khordha to Begunia but for this small patch. Curiously, district administration was found supporting this individual's claims without verification. I called for the lease case records. None was found. My niggling doubts had been premised upon the fact that local Tahasildars did not have powers to grant lease of three acres. Enquiries revealed that no orders for such lease had been issued by State Government either; rather lease patta/ROR presented by claimant was fraudulently prepared. I instructed district administration to file a criminal case against the miscreant, who simply ran away from law after learning about it. The land was handed over to Railways within the next 24 hours, who luckily did not waste time and completed the missing link within a week. A train operated on the line within a month! Fake lease records and endorsement of claims over this land could not have taken place without the connivance of local Tahasil functionaries.

I found that requisitions for land acquisition for expansion of National Highways generally exceeded actual requirements. This happened in connivance with local revenue and highway officials. Since a large number of absentee land-owners had given their agricultural land to share-croppers, it was an opportunity for them to get compensation amounts which exceeded their economic returns from share-croppers. Even after receiving compensation, the extra land acquired for high ways still remained in their position. In Sundargarh, I discovered the same land being acquired twice. Indeed, farmers understood the real value of their land used for subsistence agriculture only after economic liberalisation since 1991 which emphasised development of public infrastructure and big private projects. Returns from land by way of compensation brought sums which probably had never been visualised by them earlier. Poor land-owners whose land was acquired for public and private projects, however, suffered differently. Touts of Chit Funds brainwashed them to deposit compensation money in these non-formal banking companies for better returns. Unable to handle huge compensation amounts, these erstwhile land-owners suffered when the touts vanished with the deposits.

Land Acquisition Act, 1894 was replaced by Right to Fair Compensation and Transparency in Land Acquisition, Rehabilitation & Resettlement Act, 2013 which came into force on 1January 2014. Provisions and procedures of the new law were so complicated that acquiring fresh land became virtually impossible. Both Central and State Governments held concurrent jurisdiction on the subject. Statutory Rules were required to lay detailed procedures for its implementation. I placed draft Rules before Chief Minister as soon as possible. Politics was playing its part and Chief Minister did not like to be seen either supporting or opposing the new law. Till I left R&DM Department, the draft Rules had not received approval of Government which indeed harmed Government's development agenda more than it did private sector projects. Non-approval of statutory rules had nothing to do with protecting the interest of farmers. Land acquisition is essential for development and is in the larger interest of the State. It is possible to ensure land acquisition with a humanitarian approach through proper implementation of R&R policy. State's political leadership rarely revealed its mind. On the one hand industrial houses were allowed to escape their social responsibilities which warranted spending a specified percentage from their profit towards periphery development in accordance with the Supreme Court's rulings. On the other, State leadership did not like to be seen to be acting against farmers whose land needed to be acquired even for critically important infrastructure projects in wider public interest. It was left to bureaucrats to take risks of land acquisition and remain ready to face consequences of any untoward situation. Many thus preferred to play safe considering the sensitivities and unpredictable behaviour of the polity.

Having been closely involved, I could say with conviction that land acquisition per se despite depriving farmers, especially illiterate subsistence farmers, of their source of livelihood was not the main cause of discontent and agitations that followed transfer of land. It was promoters' lack of commitment to fulfil their obligations under MOU signed with State Government. They were found more interested to acquire and hoard land well beyond use. The need of the hour was to curb this tendency. I got the Odisha Government Land Settlement Act amended to make it necessary to commence implementation of the project on acquired and leased land within a period of three years failing which this land could be resumed by State Government. If implemented fairly, the law could bring discipline and accountability. It would not grant promoters luxury of infinite time in not setting up industrial units after acquiring land. It is decades of delay, which tantamount to denial of their legitimate demand for proper compensation and rehabilitation that led to public unrest and death of innocent displaced persons. For R&R to be meaningful, displaced families need to be provided facilities and avenues for livelihood better than what they had before their land was acquired and in a timely manner.

Reformative Ransacking of Land Acquisition and R&R Rules

I had found my field visits and regular reviews in every assignment educative. A number of situations were invariably highlighted warranting changes in rules and procedures for land acquisition and R&R policy, including alienation of Government land to various departments, undertakings and private units which were in sync with changing times. I tried to affect the required reformative changes as speedily as possible despite considerable resistance from some colleagues who did not like to tinker with a system being followed for years. Some of these are recounted here.

R&R Policy, 2006 was a historic milestone which gave focused direction, underscoring its importance in light of rapid mineral-based industrialisation taking place in the State. This policy, however, suffered from bias against women. Corrective measures had been facing resistance in Government and from private industrial and mining entities. Persuasive efforts finally yielded the desired result when an amendment was agreed. A major unmarried daughter was included in the category of a separate family on par with a major unmarried son for the purpose of R&R of a displaced family. Hitherto, only a major unmarried or married son, and unmarried sisters and daughters above 30 years of age, were being counted as separate family for R&R benefits. The new amendment established gender parity.

To intensify R&R implementation and monitoring, in addition to review by Rehabilitation & Periphery Development Committee chaired by RDC, firm instructions were issued and strictly followed up for constitution of project-level R&R Committees headed by respective Collector for holding meetings at least once every month under intimation to Government in R&DM Department. Follow-up actions on decisions taken were monitored systematically. Every attempt was made to ensure that land acquisition and R&R went about in coordination. Perhaps, this was the reason for absence of any strong resistance movement in the State during my tenure despite large-scale land acquisition by Government for both public and private corporates. Revenue Division-wise reviews were also held by me regularly, and project proponents were continuously sensitised about their obligations along with consequences of neglecting R&R and periphery development. Allotment of homestead land for displaced families, adequate amenities in rehabilitation colonies, and secure employment with decent wages for a family member were given priority to ensure that socio-economic condition of displaced families did not deteriorate after they were relocated.

Delays and complicated procedures for land acquisition typically lead to cost escalation and postponement of government projects. Chief Secretary J.K. Mohapatra too felt it was unwise not to provide land for on-going social development projects like Primary or Community Health Centres, Anganwadis, Livestock Aid Centres, Rajiv Gandhi Seva Kendra, Village road, Gram Panchayat office building, and minor irrigation structures. These required only small pieces of land for those critically important projects. Executing agencies were found prone to making excuses of non-availability of land for their inability to execute their projects. I took Government orders with well-elaborated simplified procedures for direct purchase of private land for executing socially-important development projects. Purchase of private land not exceeding 10 hectares in a revenue village was permitted on payment of 175 percent of benchmark rate; the norm for acquiring private land under extant land acquisition law. Purchase of land could be done by the officer competent to file requisition for land acquisition. Funds provided in the budget for land acquisition could be utilised for its purchase. Exemption from stamp duty and registration charges were provided and land thus acquired could be mutated in favour of the department or PSU concerned instantly. Avenues for making excuses for delays and seeking cost escalation in smaller projects were thus plugged. However, even hereafter, tragically the executing agencies rarely took full advantage of the liberal land purchase policy.

I found that a simple matter of issuing clear-cut guidelines had the potential to address a land-related factor which had been delaying execution of large public sector projects and leading to encroachment of government land on highways. For land required for temporary use, such as storing construction material, plant and equipment used in construction or widening of roads, contractors/companies had to enter into long-term lease on payment of premium. No Government instructions or guidelines had been issued for this in the past. I saw that Rule 9 of Odisha Government Land Settlement Rules already enabled the Collector, with prior approval of RDC, to grant temporary lease of land whose immediate settlement cannot be foreseen. Taking the approval of Government, instructions were issued authorising Collectors to grant temporary lease on vacant government land for specific private purposes with prior permission of RDC. It was made clear that the temporary lease shall be a license only, which did not confer right, title, interest or exclusive possession over the land. User agency would pay license fee equivalent to one tenth of the market value of land, payable each year to State Government.

Permission to use it would be given or extended on year-to-year basis on payment of license fee in advance. User agency would be responsible and thus liable to pay compensation for any damages to the land as per determination made by District Collector. If during the subsistence of such permission, land was required to be leased out by Government for any particular purpose, user agency would have to vacate it without any compensation. This arrangement was a win-win situation for executing agencies and State Government, enabling expeditious implementation particularly of linear projects.

Implementation of major industrial projects, including thermal power plants, had been suffering in the absence of provisions for assigning government land for laying underground pipelines for water, gas, oil, and electricity and telecom cables, or for construction of pipelines/ channels for carrying industrial waste, etc. A number of representations lay unaddressed in R&DM Department. Formulation of an actionable uniform policy was essential. Despite resistance from conservative purists and status-quoists, policy guidelines were framed and issued to permit underground pipelines in tune with Petroleum and Minerals Pipelines (Acquisition of Right to User Inland) Act, 1962. Competent authorities were specified for granting permission for "right of way": (i) Collector, if the pipeline is laid within the territory of a district; (ii) RDC, if it passes through more than one district but remains within a revenue division; and (iii) Government in R&DM Department, if it passes through more than one revenue division. The entity now needed to simply file an application seeking permission for right-of-way from the competent authority along with land-use plan, project details and sketch map. Officers authorised by departments to file for requisition for alienation of Government land under law were declared as designated officers, whose views would be taken into account before orders were passed by competent authorities. Grant of right-to-way did not confer surface rights over land to the licensee and no buildings or structures would be constructed over the land. Pipelines could be laid below natural soil level at the minimum depth prescribed by engineering department. Excavated trenches for laying pipelines had to be filled up. Licensee could not claim exclusive right on right-of-way, was required to procure insurance from a reputed insurance company, and remove the pipelines after expiry of agreement. Plan and development of pipeline had to be compatible with proposed use and anticipated environmental impact. Necessary permission would have to be taken for forest lands and existing classification of land would remain unchanged. Licensee would pay 10 percent of market value/ benchmark value of land towards license fee. A standard form was prescribed for licence deed between licensee and competent authority. The policy was also a clear hint that project proponents could have agreements with similar terms and conditions for laying underground pipelines below private lands if the farmers concurred. This policy intervention helped many big industrial projects whose managers had been running from pillar to post for years.

Implementation of Forest Conservation Act as interpreted by Apex Court did not permit use of land classified as forest even if there was no tree cover for any other purpose without provisioning alternative afforestation on equal quantity of non-forest land elsewhere. State Government filed an affidavit in 1999 committing that no land that stood specified as forest in 1980 would be used in violation of this interpretation, while furnishing details of the State's forest land. Mining areas virtually overlapped with forests. Spurt in mining and mineral-based industries naturally put extra pressure on Government land which was also required for critically-important social sector projects such as distribution to landless families for agriculture and homestead purposes, community projects, etc. Land laws anyway did not permit land earmarked for purposes like community easement, cremation, grazing, etc. to be utilised for other purposes including compensatory afforestation. Many lessees of land for mining and mineral-based industries could not operate under these stipulations, and sent representations repeatedly seeking land to fulfil afforestation obligations.

After examination, Government orders were issued to Collectors clarifying that revenue land recorded as "forest" could be considered for purposes of afforestation. Alternatively, degraded forests twice in extent to the area being diverted for compensatory afforestation, where suitable non-forest land was not available for exchange, could be utilised for afforestation. This solution was in conformity with 2007 guidelines issued by Central Ministry of Environment & Forest. Government field functionaries appeared ignorant and heads of departments did not consider it appropriate to verify and clarify. The easiest option for them was to seek alienation of Government wasteland for compensatory afforestation. Due to scarcity of non-forest Government land, it was emphasised that project proponents requiring diversion of forest should go for private purchase of land or get it through land acquisition mode, if they did not want to take up afforestation on bald hills and revenue forest land was not available. It was clarified further that if available, surplus unobjectionable Government land might be offered on payment of premium for compensatory afforestation. I found some officials of State Forest & Environment Department, perhaps with ulterior motive and using their contacts in Central Environment Ministry, were at work to sabotage some mining and industrial projects in the guise of environment and forest protection.

A private power project was at the verge of critical stage, but project proponents were unable to commission it even after paying compensation towards acquired land. Local DFO held that acquired land stood classified as 'forest' in revenue records and he was not bound by 'no objection' given by his predecessor at the time of land acquisition years back. In a PIL filed in High Court against the project by an activist representing vested interests, DFO filed an affidavit in support of the position taken. Ironically, State Government was also not inclined to be seen opposing the PIL, despite having signed a MoU with the power company and having acquired land for it. The complex situation warranted clarity, and I decided to address it objectively regardless of consequences. After examining relevant land records, I found the objections raised by DFO unwarranted. Records revealed that land now being shown as 'forest with bushy growth' had been leased out for agriculture purposes to landless families in 1958-59. They had been cultivating it after clearing the bushes. During revisional settlement around 1980, it was duly recorded as 'agricultural land' in favour of lessees. This land had been acquired on payment of compensation following due process of law, and the then DFO had conveyed his no objection. The sudden objection raised by incoming DFO a couple of years later was strangely with the support of Principal Secretary of his department, who incidentally as my predecessor in R&DM Department had approved the land acquisition. I placed these facts before Chief Secretary explaining that misunderstanding could have arisen because original settlement records prepared prior to 1950 showed the land as 'bushy forest' and those records remained uncorrected after the land was leased out for 'agricultural purposes' to some landless families a decade later. Forest law of 1980 did not impose any restrictions on changing usage of such forest land retrospectively. Chief Secretary endorsed my position and advised Principal Secretary, Forest & Environment to file a revised affidavit in High Court clarifying the position as brought out by me. R&DM Department was asked for inputs on the land which were submitted instantly to Advocate General. As I was informed later, Forest Department remained reluctant to change its position in High Court. Finally, High Court rejected the PIL and also stand taken by DFO, while upholding the position based on land records which had been endorsed by me. Project proponents were relieved, despite delay and cost escalation due to a seemingly prompted PIL supported by State Forest Department without application of mind.

Similar problems were being faced in implementing Angul-Sukinda Railway line. Forest Department was not allowing laying of the line on private land acquired after compensation on the grounds that land stood classified as 'forest' in land records published before 1980. In consultation with State Law Department, I issued a circular clarifying that the status of land leased out by Government prior to the notification of Forest Act 1980 need not be questioned on the basis of interpretation of "forest" by Apex Court in 1996. I obtained opinions of two legal luminaries, K.K. Venugopal, a top Supreme Court lawyer who was appointed Attorney General after a couple of years, and Arijit Pasayat, a retired Supreme Court Judge who had headed the Green Bench for many years and given landmark judgments on forest and environmental issues. Both endorsed my position through detailed self-contained reasoned and sound advice. The tendency exemplified by the Hindi expression "*baal ki khaal nikalana*" and that of narrow departmentalism which satisfied, and perhaps quite sadistically so, only an individual's ego could neither be taken as a standard for upholding the majesty of law nor was it in public interest. State

Government thus suffered at times, and courts of India are overloaded, simply because the left hand of administration is not bothered to work in the knowledge of its right hand. Officers at the helm of affairs in associated departments are not necessarily in position due to their superior analytical capabilities and commitment to public service, but these commanding heights are clearly fodder to their ego.

Central Government supported opening of Central Schools and Navodaya Vidyalaya in remote districts to impart quality education free or at a highly subsidised cost. But Odisha's policy, which required premium to be paid for acquiring land for such schools, had stalled opening such institutions in about half-a-dozen in tribal and other backward districts. I found this insistence on payment of premium absurd. After convincing Finance Department that not establishing such quality educational institutions would only hurt the long-term public interest, I submitted a proposal and Government finally amended its policy. It now provided that lease of Government land could be sanctioned free of premium and incidental charges after payment of one rupee per annum in favour of Kendriya Vidyalaya Sangathan for school buildings, staff quarters, etc.up to 4 acres (8 acres in specified cases) in urban areas having population of more than 1 lakh, or up to 10 acres in those with population less than 1 lakh. For each residential Navodaya Vidyalaya, lease of land up to 30 acres could be given without premium and incidental charges. This single concession saw half-a-dozen Kendriya and Navodaya schools spring up in educationally-backward districts. I was happy to trigger the change.

With increase in production of rice, resulting in huge quantities of marketable surplus, farmers in Odisha of late had started feeling the pain of distress sales. State Marketing Agencies and FCI were unable to procure it mainly due to inadequate storage facilities. State Warehousing Corporation did not have funds to construct new storage godowns. Central Warehousing Corporation did not get Government land around the rice-growing centres at reasonable rates for creating 3 lakh MT additional storage space. State's Industrial Policy Resolution did not include subsidised land or Capital Investment Subsidy for warehousing. As Director, A&FP, I had experienced that without market intervention, including augmenting storage capacity, farmers would continue to suffer. Cabinet approved my proposal for making land available for construction of godowns by Central/State Warehousing Corporations for storage of food grains at subsidised rates. This initiative benefited farmers, besides generating wage employment albeit in a limited scale. Later on, I suggested inclusion of public sector storage facilities for receiving the same incentives as were to be granted to other industries when the State's new Industrial Policy Resolution was being formulated, but to no avail. Food Supply & Consumer Welfare Department was unconcerned!

OSHB, housing societies and development authorities were allotted Government land from time-to-time for construction and sale of houses to individuals. But, a clause in their lease deeds with State Government prohibited sub-lease of allotted land with these end users, which amounted to buyers being denied title over allotted property. Government orders were taken to remove the restrictive clause from lease deeds executed with housing bodies thereafter. It was notified that sub-lease could be executed by them with individual end-user beneficiary. It was also provided that housing bodies would specifically indicate this notification number in all their lease deeds executed with development authorities. This intervention addressed the long-standing demand of buyers of properties developed by Government agencies and societies, which despite being genuine had remained unaddressed for years.

Government's Poor R&R Track Record

The track record of State Government in R&R matters had been far from glorious. A large number of families displaced by Hirakud Multipurpose Project in 1950s, had been running from pillar to post for regularisation of homestead land allotted to them on land that stood recorded as 'forest' and for disbursement of compensation. Many of them suffered a second displacement for a similar project at Rengali in Angul district. Compensation amount was negligible, and that too had remained undisbursed to many. DC pattas (given by Deputy Commissioners temporarily) on village forest lands to these displaced families had not been regularised. In the year 2013, National Human Rights Commission took a serious view and sought an explanation from Chief Secretary, besides issuing a warning of adverse consequences for any further prolonging of State negligence. District/State administration had shown helplessness, citing provisions of Forest Conservation Act, 1980 as interpreted by Supreme Court that usage of any forest land for non-forestry purpose was not permitted without compensatory afforestation. The task of verification prior to disbursement of compensation to third generation of displaced families and regularisation of DC pattas had also become difficult after reorganisation of Sambalpur into four successor districts and Balangir into two where displaced families had been relocated more than 50-60 years back.

The families relocated for three generations on the forest land were demanding creation of separate revenue villages for them. I was convinced that their demands were genuine and did not mind taking risk of adverse judicial view in changing the classification of forest land on which DC pattas had been granted. I took the Collectors in confidence and drew a time-bound plan for completing this unfinished legacy work complicated by reorganisation of districts. Clear instructions were issued to Collectors to complete verification of legal heirs of displaced families using all possible means, including publications in newspapers, and to disburse any undisbursed amount of compensation as per the revised rates for which allocation were made. Government orders were conveyed for regularisation of DC pattas reasoning that classification of land had already changed for all practical purposes after decades of actual use as homestead. Proposals were required to be submitted to Director, Land Records & Settlement, for creation of new revenue villages. By following up the matter at every stage painstakingly, this inglorious legacy task of R&R of Hirakud project displaced families stood finally discharged in 2014. Apart from disbursement of compensation to legal heirs of displaced families, two revenue villages in Sambalpur and four in Jharsuguda were created and compliance was reported to National Human Rights Commission accordingly. The Damocles' Sword of fear of reclassification of 'forest' land waved about by Forest Department and Apex Green Court and of adverse consequences threatened by National Human Rights Commission did not spew any Government blood. I felt relieved simply because the shame the State Government had been living with, without taking note of the miserable situation suffered by three generations of displaced families, was now finally history.

In another matter, RSP faced frequent agitations from displaced families for not being provided with employment as promised. In 1993, district administration had prepared a list of 376 displaced families, out of a total of 1,098, still awaiting employment as per what was known as "TN Singh Formula" of 1967. Number of displaced families awaiting employment reported by RSP was 393. By now the company was facing a serious situation due to frequent blockades by displaced family members supported by local population. In my meeting with all concerned in December 2013 to discuss R&R issues, commercial stakes being high for the steel plant, RSP and SAIL agreed to a joint exercise with district administration to determine the correct number of families to be provided employment; sponsoring of applications by district administration would be completed by 31 March 2014; and RSP would ensure that candidates were provided training followed by employment within a definite time-frame not exceeding one year from receipt of recommendations from ADM Rourkela. Blockade ended after commitments were given byRSP and SAIL.

Another two sets of R&R of displaced families involving RSP are noteworthy. 16 families had been agitating for employment due to displacement for years after acquisition of their land for construction of a marshalling yard, which was transferred by RSP to South Eastern Railway. I succeeded in persuading RSP to agree to meet their demands, which were just and legitimate, not least since compensation provided was negligible. The second issue was equally serious, though ignored hitherto. Due to construction of Mandhira dam which supplied water to RSP, over 450 acres in adjoining villages had been affected by sand-cast and became unfit for agriculture. After initially agreeing to acquire this land for which initial notification under the Land Acquisition Act had been issued, RSP had withdrawn from their commitment. Affected farmers continued to agitate against their losses. The issue remains to be resolved.

Government land for HAL's manufacturing unit in Sunabeda (Koraput) was provided when Biju Patnaik was Chief Minister in early 1960s. Although HAL was willing to bear the cost of rehabilitation, 83 tribal families residing in HAL's compound were found to be still awaiting relocation. Encroachment and law and order problems were being faced at regular intervals, besides operational difficulties given this defence PSU's sensitive work. Chairman, HAL, sought my guidance for their early relocation elsewhere. HAL agreed to provide better living, and I initiated steps for relocation of families. HAL released ₹ 5 crore to Koraput district administration for development of a suitable site for construction of two-roomed houses with power and running water for each family not very far from that given to HAL earlier. HAL committed to adopt the relocated village and provide facilities for education and health in addition to unskilled employment to these families. Within a year, a new housing colony of 83 houses in Mohanpada village reached finishing stage. Towards the balance package agreed, it was planned to give an acre of developed agricultural land with irrigation facility, besides completing minor internal finishing works before proposed allottees occupied their newly-built houses within the next couple of months before onset of monsoon. In the meanwhile, I was transferred. Collector too was transferred. Her successor, despite being advised by me as Chief Administrator KBK districts, was indifferent to take the work to its logical end. I am told, the work remains as at that stage till date!

The sum and substance of these illustrations is that district/State administration and industrial entities need to give more attention to R&R for peaceful economic activities. Problems can be kept hidden for some time, but with the passage of time festering wounds can cause administrative havoc for successor administrators and industry managers. Although returns from agricultural land or value of crop yields are low, the land before it is acquired for industry keeps the entire family engaged round the year giving some economic security to successive generations. Compensation in monetary terms even in multiples of either value of land or annual yields earned cannot be acceptable as a viable trade off for the farmer. The poor landowner is neither a financial analyst nor a savvy business manager who can migrate to virgin areas and greener pastures for investment and better returns. R&R packages must include provisions for skill development followed by employment with the help of project proponents.

Abdication of Responsibility by Nodal Department/ Agency

Heavy industries including thermal power plants usually face problems even after land is acquired and handed over to them for their project. IDCO, under Industries Department, levied charges on project proponents for making land available along with requisite infrastructure in addition to facilitating clearances and providing other support services. In reality, IDCO did nothing more than handing over acquired land and its registration. I rarely found it to have gone beyond directing promoters to approach various departments for obtaining necessary clearances, including issuance of notifications for land acquisition. Thus, project proponents were found repeatedly visiting R&DM Department and district offices even though filing of requisitions citing public purpose for acquiring land was done by IDCO. R&DM officers could not be expected to know details of allotments of land for specific industrial or mining projects.

The task of assessing feasibility including requirement of land for industrial units lay with Industrial Promotion & Investment Corporation Ltd (IPICL). There was no satisfactory answer when I once asked it's MD why a larger piece of land had been proposed when a smaller one would suffice, especially when a significantly smaller one stood proposed for a bigger industrial project in the same sector. Norms appeared not to have been developed. The requirement of land projected by promoters was accepted by and large due to lack of expertise in project appraisal. This had potential to corrupt the system while granting clearances and at times led to an adversarial relationship between promoter and functionaries of departments. I did not believe in every promoter being viewed with suspicion, which has a negative overhang on R&R obligations, including periphery development works, critically important in the long-term interest of all stakeholders. Both IDCO and IPICL simply preferred to side-step their responsibilities and worked like post offices, casting full responsibility of the baby project on the promoter after signing the MoU and transferring acquired land to project proponents; a gala event with huge fanfare and publicity in the presence of Chief Minister. For these facilitating organisations, nay event managers, means are often the end.

Making Registration Offices Intrinsically 'Swatchh' and Modern

Unacknowledged and unstated, but known to every stakeholder was the dark side and messy affairs of 188 offices of District Sub-Registrars and Sub-Registrars in the State. Rarely were cases of registration of documents handled fairly and without involving intermediaries or brokers in towns and growth centres where value of land was appreciating fast. Terms for registration in Bhubaneswar were dictated by a bunch of rowdy advocates, though legal practitioners had no role to play under applicable law. R&DM Minister once narrated his own experience to me. Along with Inspector General (IG), Registration he had once visited the office of Sub-Registrar, Bhubaneswar. Brokers pretending to be lawyers not only misbehaved with him, but also asked him to pay a vehicle parking fee in the office compound where offices of Sub-Collector and Tahasildar were located. The main source of income of these advocates, in forceful possession of a couple of office rooms, was extortion in the name of facilitating registration of documents and providing copies of deeds executed earlier, besides parking fee.

There were three circle offices in the State Capital (Bhubaneswar, Chandrasekharpur and Khandgiri) for registration of documents. While Bhubaneswar Circle was headed by District Sub-Registrar, the remaining two were headed by Sub-Registrars independently. In practice, all three ran from the same crowded building in Bhubaneswar. After discussing the prevailing anarchy with Minister, Chief Secretary, and Collector, Khordha, it was decided that the other two circles should function from their prescribed headquarters for convenience of the public under their jurisdictions. Suitable buildings were identified in Chandrasekharpur and Khandgiri. Proposal for redeploying them was submitted to R&DM Minister. Bhubaneswar Bar Association got wind of it and started opposing the move. Some aggressive advocates threatened blockade of adjoining Puri main road and managed to convince two local MLAs, who then met R&DM Minister. On being redirected, they met me and when I did not yield to their pressure, one of them considered close to Chief Minister who after some time got inducted to the Cabinet, threatened that he would complain against me to Chief Minister! My submission that I was only implementing a Government decision to ensure delivery of services by decentralising administration incensed them. Minister, sensed the mood of MLAs and in a politically clever move, endorsed the proposal pending with him for approval of Chief Minister. After months of waiting, the file returned without approval. I felt helpless seeing my efforts to streamline administration of registration in Bhubaneswar being sabotaged. It was victory of vested interests over public interest to some extent.

I opted to move on to other important reforms of registration sector. Circle or benchmark rates of land, required to be reviewed annually, had not been revised for years in almost all districts in the face of protests and pressure tactics by vested interests mostly led by some lawyers. State Government's priority was to do nothing that could create law and order problems. Resultantly, actual revenues from stamp duty could not be realised by Government, while corrupt practices in registration offices generated black money. In this situation, Collectors stood restricted by rules to revise these rates up to 10 percent per annum. I was informed by many buyers who had spent their hard-earned money to purchase land and wanted to remain honest tax payers, that they could not register documents as per actual rate as they were not allowed to do so. According to a High Court ruling, registration officials could not ask for payment of stamp duty as per market rates of immovable properties. Market rates in many places in and around growth centres and district headquarters were more than 20 times higher than circle rates. For instance, while market rate in Sundarpada village near the State Capital was ₹ 5 crore per acre, its circle rate was a mere ₹ 5 lakh per acre.

I called for a time-bound exercise of 6-months for revision of circle/ benchmark rates in all districts. Loss of stamp duty and registration charges to State exchequer, as well as corrupt practices taking place under their nose, due to inaction on the part of Collectors and District Registrars was underscored. With vigorous pursuit, the objective could be achieved except for areas under Bhubaneswar and Sambalpur. A clutch of lawyers got a stay from High Court on revised circle rates on the technical grounds of wide-ranging consultations not being held and expert opinion not being taken before revision. In a few months though revision exercise was completed, revised circle/benchmark rates in Sambalpur and in the periphery of Bhubaneswar remained much lower than market rates. Thus, circle rate in Sundarpada (near Bhubaneswar) was revised to ₹ 50 lakh per acre from ₹ 5 lakh per acre, but actual market rate was around ₹ 5 crore per acre. Gap in Sambalpur town was similar. When Sambalpur District Sub-Registrar called for payment of stamp duty as per revised circle rates, he was brutally assaulted by some hooligans wearing the garb of lawyers who came to his office on the pretext of facilitating registration of documents. When District Collector rushed for his rescue, she too suffered verbal assault bordering on outraging her modesty from them. Despite SP and IGP being personally asked by me to intervene on receiving a telephonic call from District Collector, they declined to intervene without State Government giving orders in writing that no action would be taken against them for using force against the advocates on rampage. In vain I brought the matter in writing to the notice of DGP, Chief Secretary and Chief Minister' Office. Agitation by lawyers in Sambalpur continued. Out of fear, District Sub-Registrar did not file a FIR against those who had grievously injured him for discharging his responsibilities under law. RDC, whose office along with others including Senior Police officers and that of District Collector, was locked up from outside for six months by the agitating lawyers who held the keys to these locks. Ultimately, District Collector had to go through the ignominy of apologising and withdraw cases filed by her against the hooligans called advocates in order to avoid counter-cases being filed by them against her which were being registered by local police. Agitation was suspended after 6 months. State Government remained a silent spectator of this administrative paralysis.

For such anarchy, in many places some corrupt officials were also partly responsible. State Registration Service had been merged into ORS created in 2008. Some disgruntled officers legally challenged this merger even though promotion prospects in Registration Service were bleak as higher positions were held by officers of OAS or IAS. To my mind, two major incentives for resisting merger were extra income through unethical and illegal means working in Registrar offices and lesser scope for transfers. District Sub-Registrar of Puri, infamous for her doubtful integrity, had challenged merger of her service into ORS. She refused to relinquish charge, despite being transferred on grounds of major penalty proceedings pending against her. An enquiry substantiated that she had surreptitiously gone to Kolkata and Cuttack and registered documents of property holders who had died years back by faking their signatures and thumb impressions! She enjoyed the confidence of District

Collector, which added to the nervousness of District Registrar to relieve her from duty. On my instructions, she was relieved when she left the district without permission. Relieved in absentia, she filed a petition in SAT with her case curiously supported by Government Advocate. District Registrar presented the files containing her transfer and relief orders which showed that she stood relieved prior to her petition challenging her transfer had been filed in SAT. But he suffered humiliation in open court as the Tribunal presumed backdating of records by him. This I felt was too much. I sent a note to Law Department for removal of Government Advocate explaining his misconduct by supporting the delinquent officer rather than bringing out correct and relevant facts to the notice of SAT. The presiding Judge in SAT called me to say that Government Advocate should not be removed as he had done nothing wrong. I told him that a bullet once fired could not be returned to the barrel, and as such the orders passed by his Bench were unwarranted. District Sub-Registrar did not join her next place of posting. Charges framed against her inquired into by IG, Registration, stood substantiated fully. With the concurrence of Odisha Public Service Commission, she was removed from service. Unfortunately, Government many times supports officials with loose morals for reasons not difficult to visualise. About six months after my transfer from R&DM Department, she was reinstated in service by a Government which professed zero tolerance for corruption!

I felt that departmental actions taken against a few was hardly the solution for corrupt practices in Registration Offices. It was better to plug loop-holes in Registration and Stamp Acts especially after finding that some correctives attempted in the past through executive instructions had simply been set aside by High Court. The Court had reasoned that the right of registration could not be denied even if documents cited and presented for registration were defective and sellers did not have right, title and possession over the land under transaction. An Additional Secretary in State Government had once filed a representation before me stating that over 6 acres of his inherited land had been sold unknown, clandestinely. When the buyer started raising a compound wall, he objected but there was no legal provision for cancellation of registration. It was for this reason that land belonging to Government and public bodies, and also joint properties got easily sold by a shareholder beyond the knowledge of other co-owners. Power of attorney was often misused to avoid stamp duties, which helped in promoting corrupt practices in Registration offices. I even found my former boss of Industries Department making failed attempts to misuse the limited power of attorney given by a fellow retired IAS officer who had moved to Chennai to appropriate immovable property in Bhubaneswar after his death.

My proposal for amending the Registration Act was approved by Cabinet when it was explained how registration of land belonging to government, local bodies, religious endowments including of Lord Jagannath, Wakf Board,

Bhudan Yagna, etc. were taking place, apart from private properties where transferrers had no legitimate RoRs for satisfying the registering authority. A separate sub-section 22-A was inserted in the Act providing that the registering authority shall refuse to register any instrument relating to: (a) transfer, by way of sale, gift, mortgage, exchange of lease, of immovable properties of such religious endowments and public bodies unless a sanction in this regard issued by competent authority is produced before the registering officer; (b) cancellation of sale deed without the consent of person claiming land under this deed; and (c) transfer of immovable property, alienation or transfer of which is prohibited under any State or Central Act. It was also provided that Registering officer would not register any document presented to him unless transferrer produced RoRs which satisfied him that such person actually had right, title and interest over the transferred property.

With a sudden spurt in real estate sector in and around town centres in the last few years, it was vastly cheaper to develop and sell plots/apartments at high values after obtaining power of attorney from land owner thus circumventing taxes and duties. Many builders were found in nexus with landlords, making it necessary to amend the Stamp Act to check duty evasion. It was also necessary to protect the interests of aspirational buyers who bought properties from builders/developers by spending their hard-earned money for a toehold in towns. Many were getting cheated by those holding power of attorney who vanished after completing the transaction, leaving consumers helpless when original stakeholders raised objections and staked claim on it. Windfall profits were earned by an intermediary in the garb of builder/developer holding powers of attorney. The amended provisions in Schedule 1-A of Article 23 of the Act mandated payment of stamp duty on the basis of market value of the property on all instruments of agreement to sell it through any power of attorney holder or any authorised person other than father, mother, wife, husband, son, daughter, brother or sister which involved delivery of possession. Of course, stamp duty paid on such agreement to sell would be adjusted towards the total amount of duty chargeable on the conveyance at the time of actual execution of sale deed by this executant.

Another large loophole in the Stamp Act being exploited by big miners, which resulted in large losses of non-tax revenue to the State exchequer, was that even after expiry of mining lease, mines were operated without renewals. Thus, stamp duties were evaded by avoiding re-registration after every renewal of lease. Steel & Mines Department did not show interest in enforcing terms and conditions of a lease once a mine was sanctioned. This came out clearly during hearings of "Shah Commission" on a nationally publicised "Mining Scam" involving major mineral-bearing States. R&DM Department finally received inputs and proposal from this Department for inserting sub-section 3A(1) in the Act to arrest rampant leakage of revenue, which was promptly processed. After approval of Cabinet, the law was amended.

Computerisation of registration offices despite being funded by Central Government under NLRMP had hitherto not progressed. Vigorously pursuing the task, which facilitated online verification of RoRs before registering documents, optical fibre or broadband connectivity provided to the offices had been linked with the server that hosted RoRs for the State centrally in NIC. Documents registered from 1985 onwards were scanned and digitised in Bhubaneswar to make copies available online on payment of service charges. A system for receiving applications online for registration of documents was put in place, which reduced undue interference of agents/ advocates. Modernisation of Registration offices using process automation was achieved despite huge opposition from deed writers and stamp vendors. Although some progress was made in designing standard computerised drafts for registration of documents, the issue required more persuasive efforts. Formalising payment of stamp duties using a robust digital platform and e-Stamping remained to be just concluded when I left R&DM Department. Legal and administrative reforms arrested fraudulent registration to a large extent while computerisation contributed to improving the common man's experience in registration offices. Proof of a pudding is in its eating. As a result of changes in legal provisions and circle rates during 2013, non-tax revenues from registration charges, stamp duties and alienation of government land for Central Government projects registered a huge growth of 30 percent. Belying nay-sayers and those in State Finance Department who apprehended that reduction in number of documents registered by 30 percent might adversely impact revenue realisation, renewal and extension of mining leases alone generated over ₹ 100 crore, a sum otherwise being lost year-after-year due to loopholes in law and lack of adequate interest in enforcing conditions of mining lease.

No Political Traction for Dealing with Land Classification nor Share-Cropping

Appu Committee set up by Central Government in 1996 had suggested rationalisation of land classifications for agricultural land by proposing only four classes of agricultural land. Sanjib Hota Committee's report on 'Tax Reforms in Odisha' too had suggested recognizing only four classes of land in accordance with the provisions of Odisha Land Reform Act. These required amendment in Survey and Settlement Act/Rules which classified it differently in regions, and in more than a dozen categories. Usually, land classifications were determined based upon usage of land, during survey and settlement operations which used to be held earlier for mass updating of land records. In Odisha, land revenue had been abolished in mid-1970s. Updating of land records and change in classification also stopped receiving State Government's attention. Survey and settlement operations were discontinued. In the last decade, under pressure from rapid industrialisation and urbanisation, more than 1.50 lakh acres of agricultural land had either been acquired or were under acquisition for non-agricultural usage. Due to such large-scale changes in usage, I felt that State would gain by classifying land rationally in limited specified categories. It could happen seamlessly without requiring fresh revisional settlements by making suitable changes in Survey and Settlement Act. Annual rents could be collected from land which had been put to industrial, commercial, or institutional usage and State could benefit financially without reintroducing fresh rent on agricultural land.

R&DM Department got approval of Cabinet after explaining the issue logically for seamless changes in classification of land depending upon its usage and for specifying agricultural land across the State only in four classes in accordance with the provisions of Odisha Land Reform Act. The Bill introduced for amending Survey and Settlement Act was referred to a Select Committee to examine the proposed changes threadbare. The amendments were no ploy for levying fresh land revenue. Advantages of standardising agricultural land only in four classes lay in removing confusion and ambiguity; provisions of Land Reform and Survey and Settlement Acts would get harmonised; the new land classification would be similar to that in other progressive States; it would help in updating land records without specific survey and settlement operations, and compiling information from village to State level instantly which would help in robust planning for commercialisation of agriculture, including setting up agro-processing industries in high potential areas; in the event of non-agricultural use of land, the classification would change instantly; any revision in cess on agricultural land would take place only after amending Rules requiring Cabinet and Legislative approvals; and State would gain revenues as agricultural land converted for industrial and other commercial purpose would attract annual rent which would stand revised every 5 to 10 years depending upon circle rates across the State. Most members, including Chairman of Select Committee who was also the Speaker of Legislative Assembly besides coming from a farming background, supported the proposed legislation. One member who opposed the Bill was a retired OAS officer. Being Chief Whip of the ruling party, he prevailed upon all others. His argument was that people in villages knew the existing classifications and would misunderstand the proposed legal amendments even if aimed at providing uniformity in classes of land all over the State. This situation he said would go against the electoral interests of the ruling party. When the note containing approval of Chief Minister was brought to his notice, he questioned the ability of Chief Minister to understand the subject stating that bureaucrats around him had misled him for taking such orders. The Bill pending further discussion by Select Committee lapsed. I saw it as a major failure on my part in convincing the lone opposing member, but at the same time did not like to bring his resistance and insinuating remarks to the notice of Chief Minister which could have settled the matter instantly. Politics in any form was not what I ever thought of indulging in.

Another area crying for intervention but where I could not succeed was formalisation of share-cropping as contract farming. After a series of consultations with top officials, a Bill was drafted to provide necessary legislative recourse. Although share-cropping on lands, barring those of minors and disabled, is illegal *de jure*, I felt that its widespread existence *de facto* could not be allowed to continue endlessly since it places both owner and actual tiller of land at a disadvantage. A tiller, who does not own land, is rarely able to access institutional finance or any direct benefit transfers in the event of crop loss due to natural calamities. Fearing weakening of his legal claim to land itself, absentee landowners would not allow either of these to accrue to share-croppers. I felt that formalising share-cropping as contract farming would be a win-win situation for both. Absentee landlords could feel secure by executing legal contracts with cultivators even on long-term basis without land title rights accruing on cultivators. This could help in commercialisation of agriculture with the involvement of agro-processing industries interested in contract farming or buy-back arrangements. However, just as political will was found missing to implement land reforms even though the law had been enacted, I realised after doing considerable paperwork and consensus-building consultations that formalising sharecropping was also a "no go" area for political masters in the State.

Other Legislative and Administrative Reforms

In spite of many progressive laws in land administration, Odisha did not have a credible or rosy past in implementing them. Under Consolidation of Holding and Prevention of Fragmentation of Land Act, in some areas pattas/ RoRs were not distributed to tenants even after completing consolidation operations, either due to lack of interest of implementing authority or influence of vested interests. This created difficulties for every stakeholder in land transactions.

Problems being faced in villages surrounding Bhubaneswar where consolidation operations were completed and pattas distributed decades back were, however, of a different type. Despite agricultural land in villages receiving controlled irrigation in Kharif and Rabi, owners of farm land had lost interest in agriculture. Land was being sold in bulk to property developers and builders. Fragmentation of holding was not permissible under extant law. Builders and developers applied for change of classification of agricultural land into homestead to Tahasildar. Regardless, they sold the land either in smaller plots or constructed multi-storeyed apartments. With or without approval of rural local bodies, construction of apartments and development of colonies had taken place in peripheral areas of Bhubaneswar.

At this stage, in order to arrest unplanned growth in real estate sector, H&UD Department by a notification extended BDA's jurisdiction to 555 villages published under their master plan to make approval of housing plans mandatory. However, builders continued to buy land and construct apartments with impunity with the approval of rural local bodies on the strength of a High Court ruling. Law-abiding buyers suffered the most. R&DM Department received numerous representations from those who had purchased plots from developers and were not able to get approval to construct houses/ flats from BDA on purchased land. One representation was from Ramakant Rath, a former Chief Secretary, known for his thorough knowledge of revenue laws. He made a case explaining that law-abiding citizens could not construct dwelling units on land purchased by them from developers as the local Tahasildar, citing the law declined to change classification of land from agriculture to homestead.

Neither my predecessor nor Minister had been in favour of amending the law. H&UD Department having already issued a notification extending BDA's jurisdiction to 555 villages to facilitate planned urbanisation and regardless of classification of land as agricultural, its actual character having been substantially changed, the only option left was to effect necessary legal changes by accepting this reality. It was particularly alarming that small and marginal farmers were unable to take up agricultural activities as lands around their holdings had been sold and plotted into houses/ colonies. But, these farmers themselves were not being allowed to sell parts of their holdings to meet their urgent financial needs on the ground that holdings were not permitted to be fragmented under the extant law. Builders in connivance with some corrupt Tahasil officials took full advantage of this situation by persuading or forcing needy farmers to sell the entire holding instead at prices much lower than those the land could fetch if sold under plotted schemes. I was able to convince Government to amend the law. Sub-section (5) of Section 34 was inserted in the principal Act enabling transfers of any land for such public purpose, as may be specified, from time to time by notification by State Government. This amendment gave great relief to all the stakeholders.

Modernisation of Tahasils

It was inconceivable to ensure efficient delivery of services by R&DM Department without modernising Tahasils and securing transformative change in functioning of Tahasildars and RIs at the frontline of administration. About 20 lakh mutation cases were pending State-wide. Many Tahasil offices operated from old and dilapidated buildings. 141 new Tahasils had been created in 2008-09, but most of them were without buildings of their own even five years hence. Over one-third Tahasils ran without Tahasildars. Since Tahasils had been made coterminous with Blocks, over-burdened BDOs were kept in additional charge of new Tahasils which deteriorated the quality of Tahasil administration of revenue-related works. Office records of new Tahasils had not been segregated and lay in parent-Tahasil record rooms. RI circles remained to be reorganised. Though reorganisation of Tahasil administration had been packaged in the public interest just before the last general election, actions taken were diametrically opposite. Even ministerial manpower required to manage newly-created offices had not been sanctioned. Naturally, the outcome was worse than before despite achieving the desired electoral success. The problem stood compounded as recruitment of Group-C staff against vacancies had been centralised to State Subordinate Staff Commission which did not have requisite infrastructure to take up the recruitment.

I initiated steps to address all these critical issues simultaneously. There was no financial barrier for computerisation of land records (RoRs and case records) under NLRMP as Central Government happily provided additional funds. Besides Collectors had been sitting on huge caches of funds received earlier, while leaving actual work unattended. For each Tahasil a time-bound plan was drawn up in consultation with revenue functionaries to complete the work by involving private vendors selected at district level. Funds were also provided to Bharat Sanchar Nigam Ltd. for connecting Tahsils through optical fibre lines or broadband. Progress was reviewed fortnightly against prescribed milestones and timelines. Construction of new office buildings with modern record rooms and office-cum-residence for RIs was accorded top priority. Instead of surrendering budget provisions every year, I had succeeded in augmenting additional resources for new Tahsil offices and modern record rooms.

Prior to my taking charge of R&DM Department, State Government had passed the Service Delivery Act which called for delivery of specified services to public in a time-bound manner. Although enacted and publicised adequately, steps had not been taken to create infrastructure for implementation. I did not foresee any possibility of it being created in the near future, but tried to take full advantage of the legal intentions by issuing instructions that all field officials would be held accountable personally as in the case under Right to Information Act, if they failed in delivery of services within the specified timeframe. It worked. As already stated, promotional appointment of ORS officers had been taken up and within a few months and about 200 officers were in position as Additional Tahasildar. I also succeeded in securing one-time exemption from centralised recruitment of Group-C revenue staff in districts and down below. With effective monitoring and reviews, Collectors being appointing authority for clerical posts, recruitment process was completed within six months in most of the districts. Power granted to RDCs for reorganisation of RI circles was withdrawn when it was found that they had failed to execute the task wasting nearly two years, and re-assigned to Collectors. Since Collectors had already submitted proposals for approval to their respective RDCs, they could complete the task after being empowered almost immediately. As rightly said, administration was the art of possible.

A video conferencing facility was set up in R&DM Department and was used effectively to monitor progress of works in various locations. Monthly progress reports to be submitted by Chief Engineer (Rural Works) required visual details showing time and space with the latest status of each building. As I had expected, construction of buildings for all new Tahasil offices, except the two locked up in litigation due to local politics, and for R.I. offices/quarters were completed within six to ten months. 261 out of 317 Tahasils got connected either through optical fibre or broad-band for safe transmission of to-and-fro land records-related data. Computerisation of RoRs and important case records relating to leases, etc. from inception was completed in almost all Tahasil offices. Modern Record Rooms were in place in 279 Tahasils. Facilities for visitors seeking various services, online receipt of applications and delivery of services, computerisation and updating of RoRs, spic-and-span internal and external environment etc. resulted in making the working environment more conducive. Government allowed Tahasil offices to levy small charge for delivery of specified services and gave powers to utilise it for improving the service delivery systems further. The outcome witnessed by one-and-all was obvious.

Everyone concerned with land matters in rural or urban areas suffered due to abnormal delays in effecting mutations following division of inherited land in the family or after sale transactions. Procedurally, general and specific notices are envisaged in Mutation Manual, with 90 days' time before passing orders to effect changes. I found such a lengthy process contrarian after amending the Registration Act which required verification and certification by registering officers that transferrer had right, title, interest and possession over the land to be transacted. Mutation should thus take place within 24 hours after sale transaction suomotu without the necessity of buyer applying for it. Registration and Tahasil offices were interlinked and computerised. Instructions were issued to Sub-Registrar/District Sub-Registrars to forward information about registration of documents in a specified form to Tahasildar to start mutation proceedings instantly. Time period for notices to be issued by Tahasildars was reduced from 90 days to 15 days, with mandatory conclusion of uncontested mutation cases within 30 days. Mutation was notified as a service to be delivered under Service Delivery Act, despite initial resistance from some officials in my Department. I made it a point to regularly review disposal of pending mutation cases using video conferencing. Outcome became visible in the sense that annual disposal jumped from 3 lakhs to over 7 lakhs. State Lok Adalat, held once in six months, was also used to dispose mutation cases. High Court Justice P.K. Mohanty was impressed to find that 70 percent cases disposed of during Lok Adalat were on land matters by Tahasil officials. Odisha, hitherto low in national ranking in disposal of cases through Lok Adalats, suddenly rose up to be counted among the best-performing States.

Disposal of pendency improved by more than 200 percent due to reduced period of notice and continuous reviews. It was not enough. I wanted provisions for notice to be applied only in disputed and doubtful cases of mutation.

Mutation in practice was being done by RIs, while Tahasildars simply approved actions or corrections made by them. Only in contested cases, hearing had to be done by Tahasildar. Despite mutation being an administrative process, there were provisions for appeal before Sub-Collector. After Registration Act was amended, possibility of fraudulent cases of registration was virtually ruled out. I wanted mutations to be carried out immediately after registration of documents. Draft amendment in Odisha Survey & Settlement Rules, vetted by State Law Department and approved by Government, was published on 12 February 2015 in State's Extraordinary Gazette inviting views of general public within 30 days. No objections were received. The amended Rule was ready to be finally published or notified to form part of the Statue. In the meanwhile, my tenure ended. A few naysaying OAS officers suppressed and sabotaged bringing in reform for instant mutation in uncontested cases. The amended draft Rule is still displayed on the website of R&DM Department, but it has not been notified so far! Senior most officers remain unaware of what happens under their nose due to indifference or lack of interest.

Web-based mutation application software was developed involving NIC for seamless mutation after registration. It was customised by users' trial in Jatni Tahasil before its use by other Tahasils connected by optical fibre and virtual private network over broadband. NIC e-mail IDs were configured in e-Registration application for automatic transmission of form-3 to Tahasildar concerned immediately after completion of registration processes for instituting *suo moto* mutation. Once fully extended to all Tahasils and stabilised, Web-based mutation would reduce the time for mutation for updating RoRs seamlessly. The pilot stood carried out successfully. I could not have the satisfaction of extending it in other Tahasils which required just a few more days when I was transferred from R&DM Department.

In 2010, Union IT Department had sanctioned an e-District project which was part of e-Government mission-mode basket of projects for online delivery of services to citizens. Six out of thirty services pertained to R&DM Department at State level, such as caste certificates, miscellaneous certificates, registered sale deeds, and RoRs. Ganjam and Mayurbhanj were the pilot districts. More than ₹ 3 crore had been provided, giving costs of its various components, like software development, training, purchase of computers, and internet connection. State IT Department was nodal for implementing it, though covered services spanned other departments. I heard about this project accidentally during my familiarisation visit to a pilot district. When I tried to elicit details, nothing more than a letter issued to District Collectors to ensure its implementation from R&DM Department was presented before me. After obtaining the scheme's requirements from IT Department, a status report was sought from District Collectors. It was found that funds had been spent entirely on development of software, purchase of a few computers for district offices of line departments, and on administrative charges. Scope of the pilot project also had been inexplicably limited to one RI Circle of one Tahasil each in the two districts. The Bengaluru-based software company had withdrawn after developing the software when its demand for additional funds for extending the project to other Tahasils had not been agreed by State IT Department. In other words, the project stood buried and forgotten, which incidentally was the fate of many other useful IT projects in the State.

I found this project extremely useful if implemented sincerely after enactment of the service delivery law. During my visit to Ganjam and Mayurbhanj, I had received positive feedback about its potential on revenue services. I submitted a detailed note to Chief Secretary outlining its usefulness and drawing out deviations that had taken place. Software, though procured at a cost far beyond the ceiling prescribed by Central Government, was indeed a good product and could be utilised if service delivery charges leviable for online services were allowed to be utilised for purchase of laptops and data-cards for RIs/Tahasildars in addition to providing some more funds by State Government for procurement of other accessories. I did not waste time to call upon the two Collectors to fully cover both pilot districts instructing them to use existing IT infrastructure, and to bridge gaps in required equipment from savings under contingency funds of "Land acquisition rehabilitation and resettlement" wherever permissible. After some months, e-District project was extended beyond pilot districts. It was received very well by RIs, Tahasildars and public at large. But, field officers of other stakeholder departments remained oblivious and indifferent about the project despite receiving some free computers. It reminded me of another IT project called "Punarvas" for online monitoring of R&R and land administration on which ₹ 1.50 crore had been wasted. Thus, accountability was the last word to be given any consideration. The only outcome was expenditure of earmarked funds.

Plugging other Legal and Administrative Loopholes

Certified copies of orders reportedly passed by Tahasildars were being filed as secondary evidence by litigants in civil courts to claim title over government land in important locations. Tahasil office in Bhubaneswar usually claimed inability to produce original lease case records, citing misplacement or non-existence. Unscrupulous litigants took advantage of missing primary evidence and State Government lost properties worth crores. A few retired professors of a reputed Government engineering college filed a petition before me stating that Tahasildar, Bhubaneswar had discriminated in rejecting their mutation applications while permitting identical cases of some others who had constructed houses in Arya Palli colony, Chandrasekharpur. Land had been purchased by all society members from the same owner. Instant investigation into these allegations found that a large parcel of Government land sold on the basis of fraudulent RoR had been approved by BDA for building plans to construct houses without verifying original land records. All mutation applications of members of this society had been rejected rightly by

Tahasildar, Bhubaneswar. When case records were forwarded to Record Room, an additional Tahasildar who exercised the same power as Tahasildar connived with Record Keeper and Data Entry Operator to favour a few by creating new case records of identical number to replace the case records which contained rejection orders of Tahasildar, Bhubaneswar. Orders had been passed in fraudulent new case records allowing mutation, with simultaneous issuing of RoRs to the favoured applicants which were also uploaded on Bhulekh. Copies of these uploaded RoRs had been cited as evidence of discrimination by the complainants. Additional Tahasildar, who had retired in the meanwhile, was arrested after the original case records were found at his residence. I wanted the Record Keeper and Data Entry Operator to be treated similarly, but Collector transferred the former pending departmental proceedings and terminated the services of contractually-appointed Data Entry Operator, showing reluctance to implicate lower level functionaries in criminal cases.

Forum-shopping between two important laws with seemingly overlapping provisions was being indulged in by offenders to avoid or circumvent eviction proceedings. Tahasildar was the competent authority in OPLE Act for eviction of encroachments, while OPPE Act defined Estate Officer as notified by GA Department for district concerned as competent for eviction. Both laws dealt with eviction from government land. While scope of OPPE Act stood limited to specified areas, OPLE Act extended to the whole State. In consultation with Law Department, I got the matter examined and it was clarified that OPPE Act was a later and special law. Tahasildars were directed to transfer encroachment eviction proceedings in specified areas to Estate Officers. Field functionaries of Revenue Department would file cases for eviction under OPPE Act only where officers of no other department were authorized to do so. Ironically, GA Department had not notified Estate Officers for all specified areas. This lack of interest in implementing laws pervaded other departments too. Ignorance and confusion about legal provisions and lack of accountability to implement laws under their purview would continue to play against public interest if departments failed to work in conjunction with each other.

In 1994, Finance Department had issued a Resolution authorising District Collectors to issue guardianship certificate in case the pensioner was a minor or incapable of managing his own affairs. In the absence of specified procedure or standard format, Collectors had established their own varied procedures and formats. Uniformity was introduced by including guardianship certificate under "*Other Certificate of Miscellaneous Nature*" in Rule 3 of Odisha Miscellaneous Certificates Rules 1984. In addition to revising procedures, the amended Rules provided that guardianship certificate would be for limited purposes, such as receipt of pension/family pension and death/retirement, gratuity, etc. to the legal guardian of minor or person incapable of managing his own affairs, by Collector in the prescribed format. Collector would also be competent to revoke or modify its contents either on his own or on application by rightful aggrieved applicant after being satisfied on its merit. In another intervention to improve public service delivery system, affidavits whose requirement was forcing people to run from pillar to post besides incurring costs and delays were waived. For issuance of various miscellaneous certificates, the Rule was amended to provide for self-attestation in lieu of affidavit.

After introduction of e-Registration and digitisation of registered deeds executed after 1985, their scanned copies were uploaded and made available on State Government's portal by logging in for viewing without any charge, as was done for RoRs on Bhulekh. Provisions were made for online application to obtain authenticated digitally-signed copies of documents, issue of encumbrance certificate and other miscellaneous certificates on payment of specified service charges. More applications started flowing online for documents and certificates after old notifications and provisions of Record Manual were modified to provide for acceptance of digitally-signed documents and certificates by competent authorities State-wide as e-District project had been extended to all districts. Changes do not take place uniformly and laws and rules could not be sole instruments of change. Administrative systems need to understand that requisite infrastructure also needed to be created to facilitate implementation of legal changes. IT was deployed as a powerful tool to ensure timely delivery of certain services. Where requisite infrastructure existed, it was necessary that digitally-signed documents were accepted by competent authority like manually-signed copies prescribed conventionally. Ultimately, a time would come to go fully digital. R&DM Department remained proactive and on the forefront in applying IT for delivery of services in spite of facing initial resistance from those in charge of managing the system at its cutting edge and also in Government.

I had over four years left in government service when I joined R&DM Department and was in hurry to effect changes in laws, rules and procedures for land-related regulatory administration. I wanted to cut down time, costs and unnecessary processes which invariably delay delivery of services besides breeding corruption. For me, an uncertain tenure was like an opportunity of batting in slog overs or playing in T-20 cricket. Every player in my team, however, was not in tune with my thinking or functioning. Many found their Captain restless in a system where time and opportunities had little value. I was fortunate to have Ministers who rarely applied brakes or disapproved my initiatives. I enjoyed the confidence of Chief Minister too despite not being a compliant follower. I submitted files for reconsideration if orders passed in my perception were inconsistent or inappropriate. Political bosses were generous enough not to mis-understand me for that.

Settling Gramkanth Paromboke, Abadi, Khasmahal and Nazul Land

Odisha Government Land Settlement Rules, 1983 had been amended in 2010 for permanent settlement of Gramkanth Paramboke or Abadi land in possession of persons in exercise of their customary rights or usage, or having acquired it by way of transfer through registered deed of conveyance from persons in lawful possession of such land in exercise of customary rights and usage. It also covered those in possession of Khasmahal or Nazul land on the basis of lease granted by Government whether renewed or expired or registered sub-lease for homestead purposes. Though amended rules were aimed at benefitting lakhs of families in possession of such lands for generations, hardly any attention had been given to the actual implementation. I initiated a time-bound drive to implement these rules and within one year over 3 lakh families in Ganjam and Gajapati districts alone got their customary rights over homestead land regularised by receiving RoRs. The main problem of administration was that progressive provisions of laws, rules and schemes meant for the poor and general masses did not receive attention at appropriate level without a strong push and enforcement of accountability. These Rules were amended further in 2014, this time to provide for permanent settlement of such lands in possession of persons for purposes other than agriculture. A detailed procedure laid down along with application forms to be used for settlement of such land followed by vigorous monitoring, which resulted in benefitting more than 500,000 families.

Saga of Paradip Port

Paradip Port was taken over by Central Government in the early 1960s when Biju Patnaik was Chief Minister. State Government had agreed to transfer 6,000 acres of land for port development, but due to later-day differences this had not happened for three decades. After becoming Chief Minister again in 1990, Biju Patnaik wanted to settle the land issue and, in a meeting, held by him it was recorded that 6,000 acres in possession of Paradip Port would be alienated in favour of Central Government on payment of premium as per old rates. Central Government had paid premium, but port authorities went for litigation against State Government. Without enjoying right and title over it, port authority had been transferring some land by way of lease/sale to private persons. Further industrialisation or development of that area was difficult due to objections and disputes raised by port authority. Paradip Phosphate Ltd. after being privatised was not able expand due to one such land dispute. Similarly, State Government could not implement a Recycling Plant in Paradip for which World Bank had sanctioned loan.

I raised the issue with Chairman Paradip Port who agreed to joint verification of land and formal alienation of 6,000 acres. It was agreed that both sides would withdraw ongoing litigations in High Court and allow developmental activities after demarcating 6,000 acres for Paradip Port. But, Chairman Paradip Port suddenly did a volte face when joint verification was nearing completion. Luckily, a former colleague in Cabinet Secretariat was administrative head of Union Ministry of Shipping and his Joint Secretary was participating in these discussions. Based on feedback received from district administration, I brought to their notice irregularities being committed by Port authorities in transferring land to private persons including to a trade union leader for activities unrelated to port development. Incumbent Chairman, Paradip Port had an ignominious exit before completing his tenure. Land in possession of Paradip Port was demarcated to be alienated at long last, ending the dispute pending for more than 50 years. My satisfaction was that an old issue hurting all stakeholders came to an end.

Streamlining Administration and Other Interventions

Known as Revenue & Excise Department before Excise was carved out, R&DM Department was among the oldest and largest departments with about 45 sections. More than 40 percent of ministerial posts were vacant at the time of my joining it. The situation was bleak as recruitment had been held up for about ten years. Superannuating staff were being reemployed on contractual basis. State Government had extended the age of retirement from 58 to 60 years, instead of opening doors for recruitment at entry level. Absenteeism was more conspicuous than punctuality. Resultantly, untold damage took place which was reflected in deteriorating record keeping and day-to-day administration. It was difficult to lay hands on connected files for taking well-considered decisions on vital issues in a department which in the past took pride in quality of its records. Old files were jumbled up everywhere in sections with layers of dust over them. State Government had launched Odisha Secretariat Workflow Automation System (OSWAS) designed by Tata Consultancy Services in a bid to automate all Secretariat offices. Though officially in place since 2008, in the absence of requisite IT infrastructure and training none in the department used this useful tool. The prevailing anarchic and unhealthy atmosphere could create negativity in minds of even the sincerest workers.

I decided to replicate my past experiences, giving top priority to consignment of old records, disposal of unserviceable inventory, cleanliness and punctuality by indicating timelines fixed in consultation with officers and representatives of ministerial and Group-D staff. At the same time, Executive Engineer, Secretariat Maintenance Division and Secretary of Works Department were asked to undertake repairing of doors and windows, painting of walls, creating a separate washroom exclusively for women employees and installation of fixtures necessary for a modern office. GA Department approved necessary funds for internal fabrications. Heaps of old files and other records were identified and labelled for transfer to Record Room within a specified timeline. Truck-loads of old furniture including almirahs not found serviceable were disposed of and replaced. A fair amount of space became available. One big hall was converted into a Conference Room with video conferencing facilities. Within a period of six months, the department stood transformed and punctuality improved. Paucity of ministerial manpower, however, remained a constraint.

It was the right time to implement OSWAS single-mindedly. A programme providing 2-days' training to all officers and ministerial staff was executed. The vendor placed two personnel in the department exclusively for further hand-holding. Now staff resistance against OSWAS was replaced by genuine problems like slow speed of server, power failure and non-availability of adequate number of scanners, printers, etc. Ministerial staff continued to complain about increased workload, as in the event of system failure they had to work manually on physical files. I decided to procure required number of computers, scanners and printers for each section by utilising office contingency funds. A couple of scanners and printers were stolen from some sections, but that did not deter office automation. Contractual appointment of a few data entry operators and acquisition of computer literacy by all ministerial hands and officers improved functional efficiency of the department. None was now complaining about shortage of staff and misplacement of files after some time. It was easy to drag files pending with subordinate officials during exigencies or when the official was on leave.

When system failures were brought to the notice of Chief Secretary repeatedly, his intervention resulted in the problems being addressed. He also issued instructions to all departments that after a specified date, his office would stop receiving manual files without adequate justification. With his intervention, offices of Ministers and Chief Minister were made OSWAS-compliant. The chain got completed. R&DM became the champion department in implementing OSWAS. The summary prepared and circulated by IT Department regularly showed R&DM Department accounting for almost half of OSWAS work in the Secretariat for a long time. I felt rewarded when a lady Section Officer during her farewell speech at superannuation quite emotionally stated that she had initially disliked being forced to learn and adopt OSWAS at the fag-end of her service. But slowly she understood its usefulness, acquired working knowledge, and also started enjoying the work. She bought a personal computer with Internet connection and was able to engage her son and daughter in Bengaluru using Skype from her home! Record keeping quality in establishment matters improved considerably after office automation although my workload increased marginally.

A large department with sizable ministerial staff, massive field establishment and sensitive land-related legal and administrative issues to handle is expected to have its share of problems. Long-pending issues of personal entitlements and over 300 departmental proceedings at the time of my joining had demoralised OAS/ORS officers. With a systematic time-bound drive, it was possible to dispose of 90 percent of departmental proceedings. A couple of things I did not allow to be compromised in service were indiscipline and failure in achieving assigned goals for inaction or negligence. Perhaps, none having held the same posts could match me in initiating disciplinary proceedings against subordinates found lacking in discipline and showing negligence in discharge of duties and responsibilities. But I was equally quick in disposal of such proceedings which were a reformative tool rather than being a manifestation of my non-lenience or intolerance.

OAS cadre at entry level posts was controlled by R&DM Department. State Government had been following a policy of appeasement by bringing piecemeal promotional avenues from time to time to keep office bearers of OAS Association happy. Resulting imbalance and stagnation at various levels, and aberrations in cadre structure and management were brought to the notice of Government at the highest level. I had experience of rationalising OFS years back when I was Commercial Tax Commissioner. Since then, OAS officers had been citing the example of OFS cadre restructuring. After discussions with OAS Association and careful analysis, I was convinced that it needed to be restructured, after creation of ORS from where one third officers would get promoted to OAS in the course of time. Cadre restructuring plan prepared by me did not have any additional financial implication as the cadre strength was reduced by about 25 percent and number of promotional posts increased to make a robust pyramid. My views on restructuring did not go hand-in-hand with those of Chief Secretary, who appeared worried about triggering similar demands from other State Service Cadres. I was not involved in further deliberations. With no tangible arguments to reject what I had proposed; OAS cadre was finally restructured with a few changes on my proposal. With general election to be held in April-May 2014, political leadership believing in taking decisions that brought political gains found it expedient to broadly agree to OAS demands.

Except for OAS officers, provisions for training other State cadre services hardly existed. Inadequate training facilities for revenue functionaries had an adverse impact on quality of land administration. RIs were trained long back in regional RI Training Institutes, now defunct. In 2008, a new State cadre of ORS in Group-B had been created, the size of which was equal to that of OAS with provision for 50 percent direct recruitment and remaining 50 percent by way of promotion from field functionaries of revenue and other departments. But there was no facility to train them. I succeeded in ensuring promotional recruitment of about 200 ORS officers and also saw to it that State Public Service Commission recommended appointing an equal number of direct recruits. In order to meet their training needs, it was necessary to establish a dedicated training institute at State level. Hi-tech survey and settlement undertaken in nine districts also required special training of revenue functionaries.

Special Cell in R&DM Department had proactively recovered 606 acres of Government land in Gothapatna village adjoining Bhubaneswar. An area of 55 acres was set apart for constructing a new Revenue Officers' Training

Institute. I went ahead with its construction in advance of approvals. Secretary of Works Department as requested assigned one of his best Executive Engineers and ensured a good building plan at an estimated cost of about ₹ 25 crore. The complex included two hostels with capacity to host 210 officers, library, training rooms, conference hall, kitchen block, staff quarters, etc. Initially funds were utilised from overall departmental budget. By the next financial year when the institute complex had progressed sufficiently, I disclosed additional fund requirements to Finance Department. In 15 months, the complex was ready. On my request, Chief Secretary, Development Commissioner, and ACS Finance visited it at the finishing stage, and were surprised to find a beautiful training infrastructure shaped up so fast. I had no problems in getting required manpower for running it sanctioned along with recurring expenditure. Revenue Officers' Training Institute was formally inaugurated in October 2014 by Chief Minister. Even before inauguration, its premises were deployed for training Revenue Officers in hi-tech surveys and disaster management. Newly-promoted officers to ORS were trained using a bridge-training module specially designed for them. Concurrently, some young and experienced OAS officers were involved in designing other short and long-term training courses for ORS officers and newly-recruited RIs. Later, with financial support from the World Bank, a separate building for training in disaster management within the institute's compound was approved.

J.K. Mohapatra, then ACS Finance, when I joined this post had drawn attention to the need for improving the conditions of Circuit Houses, particularly in key locations like Bhubaneswar and Puri while promising financial support if required. Dilution in implementing rules governing Circuit Houses, which defined entitled dignitaries and maximum permissible period of accommodation over time, had badly-affected sanctity and environment of these prestigious symbols of State Government. Senior visiting dignitaries no more preferred Circuit House accommodation, though categorised as A-class, if other options were available. Even State Government officials preferred Guest Houses of Central PSUs or hotels during their tours. I got necessary renovations assessed in consultation with Collectors and officers of State Works Department and issued instructions indicating the time-frame for completing the task. With ACS Finance on my side, question of resource crunch did not arise. My experience with renovation of Bhubaneswar and Puri Circuit Houses was quite interesting and revealing.

When Puri district was reorganised on 1 April 1993, the successor Khordha district did not have infrastructure like Collectorate office building, residence for Collector, a separate Circuit House, etc. Khordha Collector opened a camp office in a couple of rooms in Bhubaneswar Circuit House. Another suite was earmarked for his accommodation. Yet another suite stood set apart for R&DM Minister. In the meanwhile, RDC Central Division had also staked claim in a suite for his camp office-cum-accommodation on permanent basis. Even after construction of a new Collectorate Office building, earmarking bungalow for accommodation, Khordha Collector continued to occupy the Circuit House rooms. While the ground floor of Circuit House thus remained fully taken, occupancy rate in remaining suites was less than 25 percent. As Khordha Collector mostly operated from Bhubaneswar and his so-called camp office drew crowds, the Circuit House became like any other poorly-managed public office. Naturally, senior officers visiting the State Capital preferred accommodation elsewhere. Incumbent Collector was not inclined to close down the camp office citing that she held her weekly grievance cell at Bhubaneswar as directed by Government at highest level. Nor did she like to use the office of Additional District Magistrate, Bhubaneswar for that purpose, what to speak of moving to her earmarked official residence at Khordha since the same had been converted into a new Circuit House.

I took R&DM Minister into confidence. He agreed to surrender his suite. I explained the rule position to Chief Secretary and took him on board for executing my plan to restore the Circuit House. Concerned engineers of Works Department had been assigned the task of renovation on war-footing. Khordha Collector was asked to move the camp office within 7 days to office of ADM, Bhubaneswar, but she tried to leverage her proximity with key officials in Chief Minister's Office. When Principal Secretary to Chief Minister conveyed what was described as the desire of Chief Minister against closure of so-called camp office on the ostensible ground of public getting aggrieved, I assured him that there was no question of my doing anything against public interest. I expedited the process of eviction and made it clear that henceforth no rooms would be earmarked for Collector, RDC or Minister in Circuit House either. I endorsed to GA Department that a residential house should be allotted to Collector, Khordha in Bhubaneswar considering her personal difficulties and official exigencies. Bhubaneswar Circuit House thus got a transformative face lift. It became spic and span, peaceful and a preferred place to stay. Instructions were issued to Collectors and RDCs to avoid availing hospitality elsewhere during their official visits. The improved environment resulted in over 90 percent occupancy. I did not allow interventions of senior officials from Chief Minister's Office in the affairs of Circuit House as I was sure that Chief Minister could have called and instructed Chief Secretary in case he had any reservation against restoration and rule-based use of Circuit House.

The case of Puri Circuit House was different. R&DM Department had released funds for adding another floor to the building. The amount got spent and work stopped in 1996 after casting of slab. Construction materials and debris remained scattered in mute witness, besides rendering it the ugliest site of the most beautiful place in Puri town facing Bay of Bengal. I was horrified to see the place. For years, successive Collectors of Puri and RDCs had paid no attention and Government in R&DM Department too remained a passive spectator. Chief Engineer, Works Department informed me that the construction was found by Principal Conservator of State Wildlife to be in violation of Coast Zone Regulations. On enquiry with the said officer, I found no such issue. When I warned Chief Engineer and Executive Engineer about misrepresenting facts, another explanation offered was that salinity had corroded the steel in the structure lying exposed for 15 years. Completion now would make the building unsafe. I asked Works Secretary to get the unsafe structure removed immediately along with debris and refund allocations spent in the name of adding a floor to the Circuit House in addition to charge-sheeting officers concerned. Within a week, Chief Engineer came and submitted that there would be no risk after chemical treatment and application of corrosion-resistant materials to the structure. He wanted six months' time to finish the work lying incomplete for more than 15 years, besides seeking some additional funds. Thus, the work got completed. After installing a lift and tastefully furnishing it, the new third floor of the prestigious Puri Circuit House on Sea that gave a beautiful view of Bay of Bengal at one end and Lord Jagannath Temple at the other became every VIP visitor's choice of stay.

The sum and substance of these narratives is that everything is doable in Government staying within the boundaries of rules and regulations if the officers concerned work with a sense of accountability and put their heart and mind into it. It is not difficult to implement a good decision within the specified time-frame, although a cynical view could be that bad decisions are implemented easily and quickly simply because the forces backing such decisions pursue it till the end for self-gain. Three other Circuit Houses in bad shape, at Rayagada, Nuapada and Koraput, were also transformed with additional floors constructed during my incumbency in R&DM Department. I disapproved and instructed to discontinue maintenance of Rayagada Circuit House by J.K. Paper Mills in the guise of CSR.

My experiences over time exposed me to the naked truth about difficulties and risks involved in eviction proceedings as no government wanted to be seen taking action against encroachers. I recall that despite receiving full compensation for their land, the erstwhile owners were not allowing construction of the four-lane approach road to the new sprawling complex of IIT Bhubaneswar. Well aware that it was not my duty to handle law and order situation being created by agents' provocateur whenever efforts for construction of road were made, Chief Secretary J.K. Mohapatra, in his last meeting before he left the State Government requested me to facilitate its construction. I accepted the responsibility albeit informally and proceeded to the site with Bhubaneswar Police Commissioner, Chief Engineer (Roads) and Khordha Collector. Under massive police protection, road works were resumed and continued round-the-clock despite incessant rains till completion, barring black-topping work. About 250 trees were removed within 24 hours under the supervision of DFO. Work pending for years could be completed in less than 10 days without allowing any law and order problem which had earlier been created by a ruling party leader and former member of Odisha Legislative Assembly from the area.

HIGH RISK BUT NO CHOICE: HEADING THE TASK FORCE ON QUOTAS

State Government at highest level had been facing flak for what was described as brazen misuse of powers showing favouritism in allotment of Government lands in and around Cuttack and Bhubaneswar. A couple of PILs had been filed in High Court by NGO-activists seeking CBI investigation. Regular protests had made the going tough despite the ruling party returning to power with a massive mandate in May 2014. When it was apprehended that High Court could pass orders for handing over the alleged charges of corruption to CBI, suddenly an order was passed by Chief Minister on 2 August 2014 for setting up a Task Force headed by me, with H&UD Commissioner-cum-Secretary and GA Special Secretary as members, to look into the alleged irregularities. Providing immediate relief to Government, High Court suspended its hearings on PILs. Protest movements against State Government also went into hibernation in anticipation of an unbiased report.

I was reluctant to take up the task. Prevarication, delay, and similar tools for dealing with difficult tasks were not in my DNA. Once assumed, it would be discharged with non-discrimination and purposefully. Having already created so many adversaries in the process of proactively pursuing cases against land mafia, I had neither time nor hunger for opening a veritable can of worms and losing more friends and creating more enemies. The public at large could say I did my job well, but I would be its sure victim despite doing no professional wrong. I was also undergoing a crisis in my personal life which had never been expected. I, thus, met both Chief Secretary and ACS to Chief Minister to convey my inability to take up the assignment. To my disappointment, I was told that it was impossible for them to advise Chief Minister to change his decision as they had not been consulted by him in taking it in the first place. My request for an appointment with Chief Minister was rejected by ACS to Chief Minister who I always counted among my dearest friends besides being a batchmate. I virtually cried before him while narrating the crisis on my personal front.

I made one last attempt through a written note to Chief Secretary stating that the order of 2 August 2014 issued by GA Department was vague as it did not specify the time period of alleged irregularities to be inquired into, besides which there was seemingly a conflict of interest as the two members assigned to the Task Force were from H&UD and GA Departments which were charged with alleged irregularities in allotment of land/houses/ flats. Chief Secretary requested not to embarrass the Chief Minister by pointing out faults in the order approved by him as he had reposed great confidence in me. He would not take my note on record either in case it got leaked to the media. He promised that the terms and reference would be made more specific shortly. But I was told that it was not for me to raise the issue of conflict of interest. Government would defend its decision, if the issue was raised by others at any point of time. I was also told that there would be no pressure to influence me as head the Task Force and I could go ahead with my findings objectively even if the other two members were not in agreement. Thus, on 11 August 2014, GA Department issued revised terms of reference by specifying the scope of probe and timeline to complete the enquiry. The modified mandate before me stated that (1) scope of review by Task Force would be the period from 01.01.1995 to 31.07.2014 in respect of (a) all cases of allotment of land/houses/flats out of discretionary quota, and (b) allotment of more than one unit of land/house/ flat to members of the same family; and that (2) the Task Force will submit its findings and recommendations to Government within a period of 4 months. Simultaneously, agencies concerned, namely, BDA, CDA, OSHB and GA Department were told to take action on the irregular allotments.

I had been holding substantive charge of Chief Administrator, KBK districts after my promotion to Apex Grade for a year now, while also working as ACS, R&DM Department and MD, OSDMA. These hardly gave me time for this added work as head of Task Force on a most controversial subject. Since escape from it was blocked, I decided to complete it within three months notwithstanding the allowed period of four months. State Government had a tendency of setting up Committees/Commissions to side-track pressing issues in order to present a fair face. Such bodies were allowed to function indefinitely knowing that public memory was short. Perhaps it was for this reason that the initial order issued by Government was vague, nor did it indicate any timeframe to complete the task. Being temperamentally impatient, Government decision on the Task Force definitely did not go hand-in-hand with my way of functioning.

I called meetings of the Task Force and also of senior officials of GA Department, BDA, CDA and OSHB instantly to underline the need for timely submission of relevant records to be examined. They were asked to notify nodal officers for presenting them. Both Task Force members authorised me to develop procedures for seeking records from the agencies. I clarified that delay or suppression of information would be treated adversely and report submitted to Government. I recorded the decisions taken in these meetings, including on working procedures and timelines for submission of inputs by all concerned. Since Government had not given any additional manpower, I utilised services of selected young officers of R&DM Department and OSDMA in addition to one officer each deputed by H&UD Department and OSHB. Records presented by BDA, CDA and OSHB were examined. Statements of those presenting them were recorded during closed door sessions. Data extracted was shared for their validation and correctness.

After almost non-stop exercises lasting about two months, I sought the isolation of Koraput Circuit House to draft and type the report with its detailed annexes of nearly 600 pages during Durga Puja vacation. On return, I shared the draft report with the two members of Task Force for their views. When one of them wanted to peruse the records underpinning the draft report, I sent to him all the volumes of shadow files furnished by BDA, CDA and OSHB weighing over 20 kg. I also sent a pen-drive containing names and details of about 16,000 persons who had benefited from allotments rightly or wrongly after 01.01.1995. The documents were returned back by him after 2 days. No views or suggestions were received from the two members. Having fine-tuned the draft in the meanwhile, I sent the revised copy to them in the last week of October 2014. The Task Force met to finally consider this draft on 30 October 2014. The draft report contained critical observations on the role of both H&UD and GA Departments. Both members, posted in these departments, were obviously not comfortable to endorse such remarks. I told them that they would be within their rights to record dissenting views and they would be respected for that. But as there was nothing in the report which was not based on verified facts, it would not be possible for me to change or dilute any portion of the report. Both members signed the report graciously and the meeting was over in about two hours. On 31 October 2014 at 10 a.m., I sent the report to Chief Secretary and felt greatly unburdened. The world outside did not know about it, but it was always my case whenever faced with multiple difficulties, I worked harder with complete anonymity.

The Task Force had kept in perspective generic policies, rules, regulations and public notifications laid out for the formulation and implementation of schemes and projects for allotment of lands/houses/flats in urban areas of Bhubaneswar and Cuttack during the review period by the four bodies under reference. Pertinent landmark judicial rulings especially of Supreme Court had guided the examination of records. Since the Task Force report is publicly available, I am limiting my narration herein to some common threads across schemes/ projects and resulting lapses in implementation which may be of interest.

Bhubaneswar Development Authority

From 01.01.1995 to 01.07.2014, BDA had brought out 21 new housing projects in addition to making allotment in 16 other ongoing projects. On examination, it was found that published Brochures outlined flexible and often contradictory, non-transparent provisions for allotments, such as "selection by means of lottery" or "as may be decided by the Authority". Discretionary power was literally handed out to the authority and used to enhance announced quota non-transparently. Provisions regarding 'late entry' were *ab initio* flawed after stating clearly that applications received after the last date would not be entertained. Scope of discretionary allotment had been surreptitiously enhanced along with provision for late entry in the scheme. Typically, formal announcements of even late entry closure dates were not made. Provisions had been made for collection of late entry fee at a prescribed rate, but in reality it had been waived thus giving financial advantage to late entrants. Provisions were made for preference to outright purchasers with a clear bias towards the rich, though the schemes were intended for those who could not afford to purchase land for houses at market rates. Decisions had been taken regarding allotment of all cancelled plots and houses at the discretion of Minister-cum-Chairman of BDA in violation of norms published in brochures and public notifications inviting applications. Additional allotments had been made in such cases without inviting fresh applications against cancelled allotments. Public in general was largely kept in dark in the matter of actual allotment procedure. In the absence of publicity measures at various stages of allotment, discretion virtually became the rule to favour well-connected ones. Large number of allotments shown as normal were discretionary as there were no criteria for determining eligibility to exercise power under discretionary quota and such allotments were taken as prerogatives of Minister-cum-Chairman BDA. This resulted in profiteering by persons who benefited multiple times and were allowed pre-position transfer of plots to others. Discretionary allotments invariably benefitted ineligible persons. Inconsistencies were in abundance in file notings, differently indicating number of applications in different phases and their consideration for allotment in addition to overwriting without justification. Where scheme-related main files had been lost, doubts were natural about office procedure and its implementation in BDA.

Cuttack Development Authority

Scrutiny of documents presented by CDA, which had implemented 7 projects after 01.01.1995, revealed more serious anomalies. Schemes floated by CDA had been diluted to such an extent that it was difficult to correlate provisions laid down in brochures with practices followed. For example, against a newspaper advertisement for allotment of developed plots in three sectors (6, 9 and 13), residential and commercial plots were allotted in eight sectors (1, 6, 7, 8, 9, 10, 11 and 13). Advertisements and brochures in CDA-floated schemes were general in nature, and silent about the number of plots available sector-wise. Essential conditions usually stated that applicant or any family member should not possess any plot, residential or commercial properties, or flat in Cuttack Municipal or CDA area, but no provision was made for action in case of suppression of facts by applicants. Resultantly, vested interests including close friends and relatives of a H&UD Minister got benefited the most as coordinates were not verified in a single case. The notified condition that allottee should construct building on allotted plot within 5 years and would not be allowed to transfer the land before making full payment and constructing building covering not less than 33.33 percent of allotted land was waived by CDA subsequently, which resulted in large-scale third-party transfers. Through CDA resolutions, discretionary power of its Chairman was enhanced by a 100 percent in violation of norms notified in scheme Brochure. Over nearly two decades, CDA was a tale of rules and procedure being followed as an exception.

Odisha State Housing Board

It was as clear as daylight that OSHB had hardly followed any consistent policy-driven objective norms for selection of beneficiaries. It had implemented 41 schemes after 01.01.1995, including old ongoing projects, most of which did not have brochures containing norms for selection. Schemes were open-ended and large-scale allotments were made on discretionary basis with occasional attempts to disguise them using expressions like "normal allotment" or "allotment by other methods". Reservation pattern followed varied from time to time, with hardly any correspondence between policy and eligibility norms on the one hand and implementation on the other. Notifications for many schemes had been published only on OSHB's Notice Board, while some schemes were floated exclusively for OSHB employees who did not take much time to encash the allotment by sale.

General Administration Department

GA Department effectively controlled the land in Bhubaneswar and peripheral villages for allotment under Section 3 of Government Grants Act 1895 on discretionary basis barring a few exceptions. This Act did not provide for any procedure for allotment of land nor had statutory rules been framed, a lacuna which invariably benefited a favourable few. GA Department had submitted in writing that no scheme or projects for allotment of land had been introduced during the period under review. Task Force had thus looked into extant policy framework and nature of both open-ended and close-ended schemes introduced thereunder albeit prior to the period of review which had guided GA Department in all allotment made in the stated period. Despite general allegations about irregularities in allotments, including in exchange of plots, the Task Force had no option but to remain silent in the absence of specifics and in light of the assertion in writing by GA Department that it had not made allotment of land to individuals other than to families of Kargil martyrs and award-winning sports personalities. As details of old allotments had not been submitted for verifying whether BDA and OSHB had allotted plots/ houses/ flats to such allottees or to their family members, the Task Force recommended separate verification for the sake of fairness.

Critical analysis and broad conclusions

It would not be far-fetched to say that the genesis for violation of norms lay in the path charted by GA Department when it had brought out schemes in 1973 for allotment of 1,000 plots and in 1989 for about 3,000 plots. Norms were loose and liberally violated in practice. These modalities and violations were followed on a much larger scale by the other instrumentalities of State, viz. BDA, CDA and OSHB. GA Department's 1989 scheme was meant for providing developed plots at reasonable rates to those having no land in specified areas in and around Bhubaneswar. But it was diluted to provide plots to family members of those already having land in the specified area. Schemes floated by BDA and OSHB followed suit and liberally allowed allotment of developed plots, houses and flats similarly despite notifications and scheme brochures not permitting such deviations. This resulted in hoarding of landed properties and third-party transfers even before taking possession of allotted plots. It was a case of profiteering without investment. No agencies bothered to invoke mandatory provisions announced through brochures for cancelling allotments if construction on developed plots did not take place within the notified period of 5 years.

Schemes launched by BDA, CDA and OSHB mostly provided for allotment by lottery or as decided by the Authority or Board's Regulations. Last dates for inviting applications were either not prescribed or ignored. Some schemes by BDA and OSHB were published only on their Notice Boards. CDA did not even publish its plotted development schemes for a number of sectors. Unallotted units were not notified again by inviting applications for allotment. No attempts were made to verify affidavits or undertakings nor addresses given in applications. In too many cases, spellings of names and addresses had been given differently by well-known prior beneficiaries of discretionary quota simply to hide themselves from being caught. It was impossible that such manipulative practices escaped the eyes of officials scrutinising applications. There was not a single case where allotment from discretionary quota had been made by mentioning grounds.

Sanction orders to lease out Government land to BDA, CDA and OSHB and terms and conditions of lease deeds clearly stated that lessee could not, without prior written consent of lessor, use or permit to use the land for any purpose other than that for which it was leased or transferred. But it was noticed that they had violated these conditions numerous times. In a large number of cases, permissions had been granted for transfer of allotted plots/houses to third parties without even having registered the property in the name of allottees! These bodies held properties as Trustees of the public and any alienation or allotment of properties without sanction of law amounted to breach of trust. These so-called Trustees had showered largesse to a few chosen beneficiaries according to their sweet will and whims throwing legal provisions to the winds. Ingredients for exercising power of discretionary quota had not been defined either by GA Department nor by BDA, CDA and OSHB. H&UD Minister exercised powers in a way which is not done even in relation to distributing personal wealth by individuals.

Section 3(5) of Odisha Development Authority Act 1982 read with sub-sections (5) and (8) provided for appointment of Chairperson to BDA and CDA. Although State Government had not appointed H&UD Minister as

Chairperson during the period from 1999 to 2004, he had been allowed to brazenly misuse powers for allotment of discretionary quota in complete disregard of the legal provisions.

There were cases disguised as normal allotment though made following dubious methods. Number of units transferred to third parties, including pre-position transfers during the period in reference, by BDA was 1,033, by CDA 2,332, and by OSHB 405. This was a clear indication of brokers having played a big role in connivance with key officials in the loot. Curiously, allotments had been made even before notifying housing schemes. Number of beneficiaries under discretionary quota, which had been doubled after notifying and launching schemes, was close 2,000 excluding disguised ones. Beneficiaries of multiple allotments were in hundreds. There was no limit to the method of madness in implementing housing projects by all three bodies which on paper at least were expected to uphold the public trust reposed on them. The Task Force suggested further audit of allotments made prior to 01.01.1995 to work out actual number of multiple allotments to ineligible recipients, their family members, and in respect of cases of dubious methods including displacement of main scheme files. However, it did not recommend enquiries by CBI, or State Vigilance, as at times these institutions were used selectively and to settle score with adversaries by Governments.

Submission of Report and its Expected Aftermath

Within a month of submission of the Task Force report, some noises were first heard in media reports. Civil society organisations involved in protests earlier became active again. PILs pending in High Court were revived by petitioners. High Court now passed orders that the report should be presented to it in a sealed cover. State Legislative Assembly was in session and voices on alleged irregularities were reverberating within its four walls too. Probably, it was 15 December 2014, when around 12:00 noon, while I was in a meeting with R&DM Minister fortuitously in Assembly premises, a call was received from Chief Minister's office that I was urgently required by him. I reached instantly to find that Chief Secretary, ACS to Chief Minister, the other two members of Task Force, and Private Secretary to Chief Minister were already present. It was not difficult to guess the agenda for discussion.

Chief Minister Naveen Patnaik never spoke extempore in any official meeting. He seemed comfortable reading out limited sentences drafted for him in the beginning of a meeting. There was no exception this time too. He read a prepared text which contained words of appreciation for the work done by the Task Force; specifically naming me for a great job done in a limited time and without any additional logistic support for it. He, however, desired that I should seek more time for submission of final report and wanted me to state in writing that the report submitted earlier was an interim one! I was told that additional resources and manpower, as required, would be made available for furnishing a more comprehensive report. It was clear that Chief Minister had been led to believe that the Task Force report did not cover all aspects. Besides, in the given situation it would be politically expedient to persuade the person heading the Task Force to say that the report submitted was an interim one. As it was not possible for me to accept the misleading impression generated by the senior-most officers in briefing Chief Minister, I requested them to enlighten me about what made the report incomplete meriting its treatment as an interim one. In response, Chief Secretary and ACS to Chief Minister variously said that the report did not cover critical observations made by C&AG in a recently released audit report, and that further investigations had been recommended which suggested that it was still incomplete. I was also told that the report needed to sanitise the office of Chief Minister clearly and categorically.

I asserted that it was against constitutional propriety for the Task Force to comment upon C&AG audit report as the only competent body to comment and take a view on it was the Public Accounts Committee of State Legislature. I had informally gone through C&AG audit report in relation to irregularities by CDA, and without referring to this audit report, the Task Force report had also brought out a number of irregularities which had escaped the notice of C&AG auditors. Thus, the Task Force report was far more specific and comprehensive in pinpointing many more irregularities covering a time span which was much longer than the period of audit by C&AG. I had not seen C&AG audit reports in relation to allotment of land by BDA and GA Department which were probably equally damaging. Interestingly, Accountant General who had submitted a series critical audit reports which were embarrassing State Government met me after a few months to say that he had been transferred to another State before completing his tenure in Odisha as the C&AG had been influenced to do so. I did not like his action when he informed me that copies of some of his critical audit reports were with a top activist lawyer of Supreme Court who could file a PIL to expose corruption of State Government. Ironically, this very officer took voluntary retirement from service after three years or so to join the very ruling party he had wanted to expose! he is an Honorable Rajya Sabha member now.

I further pointed out the position conveyed by Director Estate repeatedly in writing before the Task Force about GA Department not having made any discretionary allotments in the reference period. Special Secretary, GA Department, himself a member of Task Force had also held the same position. As regards recommendations for further investigation, it was necessary to verify allotment records for the period prior to 01.01.1995 to arrive at a definite conclusion as to whether individuals or family members who had received land/houses/flats from GA Department, BDA, CDA and OSHB after 01.01.1995 under discretionary quota or otherwise had not benefitted earlier. Multiple benefits given to an individual or family after 01.01.1995 was already covered. I further explained that despite repeated reminders, past details in relation to allotments had not been furnished by the agencies concerned stating on record that such records were not available. During scrutiny of records, it was also found that many cases of allotment had been shown as normal, though made by Ministers/ Heads of BDA, CDA and OSHB quietly on discretionary basis. The Task Force had, thus, recommended to engage retired auditors for making complete verification of all records since inception to find out additional irregularities and gauge the actual size of malaise. I finally submitted that if Government wanted to modify the terms of reference by enlarging the scope and period, the Task Force could accept the additional assignment and complete it provided agencies did not suppress relevant records. In relation to sanitising Chief Minister's office and his name, I stated that no documents stood presented to suggest any direct role of Chief Minister in the irregularities. At the end, I was blunt in stating that if the Task Force report was considered to be incomplete or containing loose-ends with reference to its terms and references, it must then be concluded that I was not equal to the task as the head of the Task Force.

Looking straight at Chief Minister, I had said that the only outcome of this painful exercise carried out over three months was that I would truly become "the odd man out", while nothing would happen to beneficiaries of irregular and illegal allotments who included MPs, MLAs, Ministers, senior IAS, IPS, OAS officers, top doctors, journalists, senior advocates and about a dozen sitting and former High Court Judges. The two Task Force members observed a stony silence. I closed my submission directly addressing Chief Minister that if I were in his place, I would accept this report and put it on Government's Web Portal before submitting it in a sealed cover to High Court. I added that Chief Minister had nothing to worry as mostly his former colleagues who had become political adversaries now stood exposed in the report as they were in charge of H&UD Department or headed BDA and CDA during the major part of the period of inquiry. The meeting ended without further discussion or remarks by Chief Minister.

Suddenly, a Cabinet meeting was called on 18 December 2014 to consider the Task Force report. Cabinet, after due perusal, accepted most of its recommendations. In relation to cancellation of allotments made during 1999 to 2004, which were *ab initio* void, as the Minister who had made the allotments did not have the authority to do so, not being appointed as chairperson of BDA and CDA, it was decided that the matter would be examined in consultation with Law Department and Advocate General of Odisha. I had already consulted Law Secretary before recommending cancellation of such allotments after citing relevant jurisprudence. Supreme Court judgment clearly laid down that "*an authority vested with powers to act under the statute alone should exercise its discretion following the procedure prescribed therein, and interference on the part of any authority to whom the statute does not confer any jurisdiction is wholly unwarranted in law. It violates the constitutional scheme.*" Apex Court had finally held that "*if an order in the initial stage is bad in law, then all further proceedings consequent thereto will be non-est, and have to be necessarily set aside*". It also surprised me that State Vigilance Organisation was called upon to enquire into those cases of multiple allotments to individuals/families, where such allotments had been made on the basis of false affidavits or misleading information in violation of specific schematic provisions, and initiate appropriate criminal action. This decision, I felt could be used selectively and unfairly. The procedure drawn subsequently in consultation with Law Department and Advocate General's office was a further dilution to facilitate escape routes to wise beneficiaries.

As I had predicted, I was going to be "the odd man out" and would suffer in many ways besides losing many friends and well-wishers. The PILs in High Court died down. After the Task Force report was placed in public domain, voices of so-called public-spirited activists also got drowned in the din that followed for few days. Only a handful of senior officials having received the benefit of discretionary quota or otherwise after 01.01.1995 suffered humiliation due to adverse publicity their names received selectively in print and electronic media, while darker fish got away. Grain and chaff were treated alike. As the one who had headed the Task Force and listed out beneficiaries, I had no plausible explanation for what had happened. I felt as if guilty to have named some of my illustrious seniors in the report.

HEIGHTENED PREPARATIONS: DISASTER MANAGEMENT

I was given additional charge of MD, OSDMA on 26 March 2013 about a month after my predecessor superannuated. Practically instantly, I found a note put up to me for approval of expenditure of ₹ 10 lakh, an amount earlier released for capacity building of disaster management personnel. But I could vividly recall that a similar proposal for conducting such training by this vendor requesting that it be recommended to OSDMA, had been rejected a few months back in R&DM Department. The vendor had met me more than once to pursue his proposal claiming, without substantiating it with detailed documents, that the Disaster Management Department of his university had been nationally recognized for studies and expertise in this field. Obviously, the vendor had received undue favour in OSDMA. Funds had been released for this so-called capacity building training from the corpus generated by interest money of allocations received under a World Bank-assisted scheme for execution of disaster-resistant infrastructure projects! According to extant rules, this interest money could not be diverted and had to be spent on projects only. This episode reconfirmed that this university owner enjoyed closeness with some key players in State Government, and was not used to take "no" for his proposals. Other wings of Government were also found to have released funds to his university in the name of training.

I sought details of places and personnel where OSDMA-funded training had been conducted along with components of expenditure and feedback from participants. In return, I was informed that a two-weeks' long training in mechanics had been organised for a few personnel of Odisha Disaster Rapid Action Force (ODRAF), which included skills in cutting trees, steel and reinforced cement concrete blocks and welding. While on a separate visit to review disaster preparedness, a mock drill of rescue operation by ODRAF personnel was presented to me at Chhatrapur, Ganjam. I was hardly surprised that ODRAF personnel, who had undergone training in mechanics conducted by that private university, could not perform simple welding to re-join two small steel pieces when asked to demonstrate their skill. Expenditure details furnished by recipient organisation had cited a major chunk spent on travel and allowances of so-called trainers besides boarding and lodging for participants. I was informed that funds had been released to the beneficiary on verbal instructions of a key government functionary. Regardless, I had no option but to reject the expenditure and order recovery. No refund, however, was made by the beneficiary till I left OSDMA.

Another proposal involving large expenditure concerned bills worth ₹ 1.0 crore raised under annual maintenance contract (AMC) for equipment purchased by OSDMA and supplied to user organisations including ODRAF, Fire Services and Multipurpose Cyclone Shelters (MCS). After Super Cyclone 1999, which had led to creation of OSDMA and five units of ODRAF, a large range of heavy mechanical devices and other equipment had been procured which included large diesel generator sets, imported power saws, safety equipment, and rubber boats for use in rescue and relief operations. GM, OSDMA, on deputation from WR Department for last four years, when asked to furnish details of inventory under AMC, offered the excuse that OSDMA had supplied all procurements to user agencies without maintaining an inventory. His excuse for granting AMC clearances without relevant details in earlier years was that he was following the usual practice. I gave him a format to prepare a statement containing details on equipment, dates on which equipment was put to test check/inspection by AMC holder, and certification by user agencies. The soft-spoken GM quietly managed reversion to his parent cadre instead! Finding his replacement quite deficient in every way, I pursued the preparation of inventory with user agencies. When information about functional status of tools started trickling in, it was found that many machines and equipment were not in serviceable condition though maintenance-related payments were made regularly. For example, about 30 percent of rubber boats had gone beyond repairs, but AMC bills made no mention of it. After some time, when reality started unfolding, ODRAF and Fire Service Department stated that there was no need for AMC any longer. They would take up repair and maintenance at their own workshops using operational grants/ contingency given by OSDMA and funds given by the administrative department.

It was disturbing to find funds squandered in the name of training and AMC charges without proper accounts being maintained in OSDMA. One option was to proceed against delinquents including some of my predecessors. I preferred to better spend my energies streamlining the system rather than in conducting a post-mortem, which probably would have remained an exercise in futility at the end of the day.

Vigorous Development: National Cyclone Risk Mitigation Project

The World Bank had provided funds under National Cyclone Risk Mitigation Project (NCRMP) for structural and non-structural mitigation efforts towards reducing risk and vulnerability to cyclone-related disasters of coastal Odisha and Andhra Pradesh as per agreement signed way back in January 2011. After detailed exercises by experts from IIT Kharagpur, 503 villages stood identified in 6 coastal districts (Balasore, Bhadrakh, Ganjam, Jagatsinghpur, Kendrapada, and Puri) for construction of (a) 12 massive Saline Embankments with a combined length of over 58.23 km (4 each in Kendrapara and Puri, 3 in Jagatsingpur, and one in Ganjam); (b) 154 MCS, including 5 large godowns in Jajpur and Khordha, all cyclone shelters within 10 km from high-tide line and maximum distance of 2 km from vulnerable villages; and (c) 218.50 km of approach roads linking MCSs to catchment villages.

Even after 2 years, there was no visible progress in project implementation. The World Bank officials finding that executing agencies lacked interest, had termed it a failure, while stinkers were also received from Central Government. Saline embankments had been abandoned due to land disputes and encroachments. About 50 MCSs stood awarded for construction, with hardly a dozen initiated. Though the easiest component, construction of approach roads providing connectivity to shelters had started but without being sure of the last village to be linked. In some, work had been abandoned due to encroachment of land or resistance from villagers who apprehended that existing natural drainage system would be adversely affected. State Government had committed availability of encumbrance-free land before the World Bank and there was no provision for any compensation. Considering adverse observations, a few meetings were held by Chief Minister in which timelines had been fixed to award contracts for all sanctioned MCSs and approach roads. In my capacity as Principal Secretary, R&DM Department, observing failure to report progress on decisions taken at highest level for retrieving the project, I had submitted a proposal to transfer MD, OSDMA. As usually happens in Government, merit and suitability are rarely taken as considerations in matters of transfers and postings. Incumbent MD despite being under departmental proceedings was elevated to a higher scale and also allowed to serve in OSDMA till his retirement. Perhaps he was rewarded for showering favours, which cost him nothing in person, such as releasing 'training' grants to a private institution owned by a person well-connected with those holding key posts.

After his superannuation, and when I took charge, I called the Chief Engineers of partner agencies, Rural Work and WR Departments, to draw up realistic action plans to expedite construction of all three project components.

It was not difficult to visualise the anarchy in the absence of proper assessment of glitches and rigorous monitoring in implementation of NCRMP. I visited the proposed sites of all 12 saline embankments along with senior engineers of WR Department, to reassess the difficulties. They had earlier justified abandoning this critically important component in the most-vulnerable coastal villages. In the course of discussions with villagers, I was impressed and got enthused by their eagerness for developing them albeit with some realignments in a few places. I felt these suggestions were genuine and would ensure better protection despite some cost escalation. Those allegedly opposing their development earlier, were now ready to spare some small fractions of their own land without compensation. It was clear that execution of saline embankments was being avoided earlier by OSDMA and WR Department without any solid reasons and simply to shirk responsibilities. I found substance too in assertions of Chief Engineers (Rural Works) regarding non-release of funds by OSDMA for preparation of DPRs, including soil testing for MCSs and approach roads. Contractors too complained about delays in clearing admissible dues.

In consultation with these senior engineers, funds were released for preparing DPRs and soil testing for all remaining projects; check-lists were prepared and approved for time-bound payment of dues of contractors; reporting system for NCRMP was revised; and monthly review meetings were scheduled on fixed dates to appraise physical and financial achievements in each project month-by-month based also on photographs of sites, with date and time. It was decided to award all remaining infrastructure projects including saline embankments through open tenders in next six months. Maximum time for completion of each project was shrunk from 24 to 15 months. Leaving my house at 6:00 a.m., I spent every public holiday inspecting projects and addressing problems on the spot. As administrative head of R&DM Department which controlled leases of minor minerals, I ensured that projects did not suffer due to non-availability of construction materials like sand, stone boulders, etc. Land disputes were addressed. District Collectors and Tahasildars were now taken on board and made responsible to hand over dispute-free sites in minimum possible time. With improvement in the quality of coordination, there was no reason for visible significant progress not taking place.

Terms of reference of respective contracts were now modified, which besides reducing overall period to 15 months, also established benchmarks as part of contractual obligations of contractors to be achieved within specified timelines for various stages of construction. Reports furnished by contractors were monitored electronically by making engineers use smart phones for taking photographs of projects' sites, which were uploaded on OSDMA's website.

Projects which lagged in progress were reviewed separately with contractors and engineers to resolve difficulties. I invariably inspected such projects within a week. As things started improving, contractors focussing on construction and timelines stopped making unnecessary rounds of OSDMA office. Complaints of delays in clearing dues became things of the past. But there were new problems, notably of extortions by village touts in some places. District administration was closely involved to redress all such problems.

Immediate steps were also taken to appoint required number of Junior/Assistant/Executive Engineers on contractual basis to supervise the work at the sites over next 15 months. Two retired Chief Engineers were appointed as Consultants to supplement the one in position. NCRMP allowed administrative charges within specified admissible limit for supervising projects. I engaged mostly retired experienced engineers while assigning all leg-work to fresh junior engineers. OSDMA being an autonomous body with Chief Secretary as Chairman of its Governing Body, I faced no problem in getting approval for engaging Consultants and other contractual technical staff. Consolidated remuneration of existing experts serving on contractual basis, which had not been revised since their appointment, was increased by about 60 percent considering their qualifications, loyalty to organisation, and commitment. Electronic payments to contractors were mandated, with no bill allowed to be kept pending in OSDMA beyond two working days and no unnecessary objections would be raised.

About a dozen shelters and approach roads were held up due to stay orders passed by High Court. Here it was ensured that counter affidavits were filed to get stays vacated by roping in Advocate General and pointing out ulterior motives and frivolousness of PILs filed by rival unsuccessful contractors. I also brought the matter informally to the notice of Chief Justice of Odisha, seeking his intervention when an opportunity came. A senior sitting Supreme Court Judge from Odisha, accompanied by Chief Justice of Odisha and another High Court Judge, had been holding meetings practically every month with Chief Secretary and other senior State Government officers calling for additional land and other administrative support for High Court and District Court, Bhubaneswar. I not only promptly addressed their land-related issues but used the opportunity to highlight difficulties faced by OSDMA due to these stay orders. I was advised by them to get the matters raised in the Court of Chief Justice. Thus, actions were taken which resulted in disposal of pending litigations and paving the way for implementing projects. Executing agencies and contractors could not find any new reasons for stalling them.

Soon after I had taken charge, in the first review meeting on World Bank projects attended by me in Delhi held by NDMA, I had felt embarrassed when NCRMP in Odisha was compared unfavourably seen as breathing its last against a successful similar World Bank-assisted project in Andhra Pradesh. By the next review meeting held about 6 months later, the tide had turned. In Odisha all projects stood awarded. A good number, hitherto languishing, had either been completed or were on the verge of completion. Both physical and financial achievements of Odisha appeared impressive and it was now Union Ministry of Finance which stood in the firing zone due to pendency of reimbursement claims. Odisha was marching ahead of Andhra Pradesh which attributed tardy progress to bifurcation of parent State.

Saline embankments constructed in the colonial era a century ago, had eroded completely. The proposed one would provide protection from cyclones and violent tidal waves, and arrest ingress of sea waters thereby protecting agricultural lands of coastal villages from salinity. But anti-social elements were now terrorising contractors for extortion in some areas in Kendrapada and Jagatsinghpur. Another issue was forest clearance as a couple of sites were within and around Bhitarkanika Sanctuary. Forest Department had raised mangrove plantations on lands which were shown in revenue records as old saline embankments. Super Cyclone 1999 had swept away many coastal villages of Jagatsinghpur due to non-maintenance of those embankments, besides adding to later-day vulnerability. Natural disasters can push millions into poverty and turn back the development clock by many years. I gave no choice to Collectors and other departments forcing them to leave no stones unturned in creating an environment conducive for executing saline embankments on war-footing. DPRs and project estimates had been modified by engineers of WR Department by agreeing to minor realignments requested by villagers in some places. Support received from DFO, Bhitarkanika Wildlife Sanctuary boosted the morale of engineers nervous of starting operations. All saline embankments, taken up immediately after monsoon, started progressing fast. The silver lining was the support of villagers, though a segment of one the projects was found held hostage by encroachers in Keutjung (Puri). Requirement of huge quantities of stone boulders and non-saline earth was facilitated by field functionaries of R&DM Department which controlled Sairat sources. Contractors were also asked to negotiate with farmers agreeable to sell earth unaffected by salinity for embankment formation. Transporting stones from quarries situated in neighbouring districts was facilitated.

Contractors were habituated to stall projects by undertaking some initial works as fast as possible and utilising advance funds released for mobilisation in a manner that left the line department with no option but to extend timelines and approve cost escalations. Upward cost revision is a part of contract agreement if delay is for reasons beyond the contractor's control to be certified by executive engineers concerned. To break this habit, I called for achieving monthly milestones within overall time-frame. I involved executants in monthly progress review meetings so that no fingers could be wrongfully cast for any delay. Regular visits to project sites gave me first hand understanding of real complications versus prompted or artificial difficulties as well as opportunities to redress the problems on the spot.

After preparation of DPRs strictly following the World Bank norms, all 12 saline embankments had been awarded through open transparent bids invited electronically leaving no scope for manual manipulation. By coincidence all 4 saline embankments in Rajnagar (Kendrapada), namely, Chasisava, Sasanpeta, and Rajnagar-Gopalpur (two separate units) were awarded in the first week of December 2013 to OCC under WR Department. OCC, belying its past track record, worked admirably and indeed set the tone for implementation for others too. Other saline embankments which progressed quite swiftly were Tandahara-Singarpala (in Astarang, Puri), Patua-Gadh Harishchandrapur and Bandar-Kathgardhi (A) (in Balikuda, Jagatsingpur); and Kharinala-Paliband (in Ganjam) which were awarded to different private contractors by mid-December 2013.

However, the biggest resource-rich contractor, who had been awarded Devi-Kathgadi (B) (in Balikuda, Jagatsingpur), besides Keutajanga, Nagar-Chhotipada and Badraul (in Astaranga, Puri), became difficult to handle after some time. Though execution of 3 embankments in Puri were taken up by him quickly after award, the largest and most difficult contract won by him was Bandar-Kathagadi (B) which was awarded early in January 2014. I came to know after closer scrutiny within a couple of months that progress at Bandar-Kathagadi (B) was least, despite initially registering better progress than others, because about fifty percent of construction had been reassigned by the contractor informally to a local gangster. The illegal sub-contractor in turn operated through his proxies and did not have capability to mobilise resources to implement it. The main contractor feared for his life as the gangster had once abducted his workers, besides blasting bombs on construction sites to bring him to heel, releasing them only after his demands were fulfilled. The gangster was evading arrest in a number of cases of dacoity and murder. I sought the intervention of IG Police and the gangster was arrested. His proxies vanished closing their camps on the work site instantly. I warned the contractor that he would face serious consequences, including criminal action, for subletting the work to local mafia. Bereft of any protection and further pretentions, the contractor could realize that I meant business. He pleaded for a single opportunity. True to his promise, work started with full gusto.

A genuine problem posed by this contractor related to a patch of 200 mts on which about 200 mangroves had been raised by forest officials after Super Cyclone-1999. I called DFO, Bhitarkanika Wildlife Sanctuary, and Collector, Jagatsinghpur to the site. Tahasildar presented land records which indicated that the old saline embankments had passed through this patch before vanishing. It was now decided to replant these young trees elsewhere without formally raising the matter. The work was carried out non-stop using JCBs and a large number of trucks and tractors. Within less than ten days, over 15 feet high and

36 feet wide compacted earthen base for the embankment was raised on this patch. Despite stealth and speed of work, a local newspaper featured it prominently highlighting the development. This was the only time when I got a bit scared of attracting the wrath of environmental activists supported by a shrill media. Luckily, the story was not picked up by others. None after visiting the site could have visualized what had happened. Villagers had fully supported the work. For some environmental activists, ever ready to publicise any aspect of administration appearing negative to serve unknown interests, there was nothing on the site for creating controversy.

Keutajanga saline embankment in Puri being constructed by this contractor was found being opposed by some farmers/ encroachers and fishermen. Seawater had already made deep ingress close to the village after the old embankment was swept away by Super Cyclone-1999. Fishermen had parked about a hundred boats there, while a section of farmers had since raised groundnut crops at the other end of this section of land. A serious law and order situation was brewing. The contractor was leveraging it as if to delay the project. I did not like to escalate the matter to the Government knowing that political leadership was risk averse. I opted instead to engage local community leaders and elected representatives to address the issue, along with local revenue functionaries. I heard the nay-sayers patiently and reminded them of the risk they faced if another Super Cyclone revisited the village without a saline embankment to resist the powerful tidal waves! At the end, majority of protesters agreed that the embankment would ensure their safety and security. Their suggested realignment which had a bearing on cost appeared reasonable enough to be accepted. Farmers who had raised groundnut crops on the site wanted that the work should start after 2 months when their crops would be harvested. That was not a viable option. In presence of contractor and villagers, I pronounced that as the land on which groundnut crops had been raised belonged to Government, local revenue functionaries would be held accountable if eviction of encroachers was not carried out. Work on 2 MCSs sanctioned for two villages at either ends of the saline embankment was also held up at plinth level in one place while it had not even been started on the other due to encroachment. When villagers demanded expeditious execution of both shelters, I instantly committed timelines for completing them in the light of spontaneous support from both villages. Neither engineers nor contractors now had any excuse for delay. Encroachments stood removed by the time I next visited the site after two weeks. I could hardly believe the progress achieved on the embankment and both cyclone shelters. After some time, groundnut cultivators withdrew their resistance and no other hindrance was raised.

Within three to ten months of my taking charge all pending projects had been awarded. The World Bank team visiting the State changed their narratives.

NCRMP of Odisha came to be termed a success story, with all three project components likely to be completed ahead of schedule. It was a win-win situation for all. 6 out of 12 saline embankments (4 in Kendrapada, one each in Puri and Ganjam) were completed except for grass-turfing by end of march 2015. The remaining six, whose completion date was June-July 2015, had registered substantial progress by March 2015. Some contractors, who had taken up MCS construction works in low-lying or other difficult areas without realising the enormity of their tasks, appeared financially weak. More efficient junior engineers were specially assigned to help them. By end of 2013-14, 140 out of 154 MCSs including godowns and most of the approach roads stood completed. It was the same administrative structure and manpower, yet the outcome was different.

Preparing the State Disaster Management Plan

National Disaster Management Act, 2005 called for preparation, coupled with annual review and updating of a disaster management plan by every State. Among States, Odisha suffered the most occurrences of natural calamities, especially cyclones and floods. Efforts to handle them were largely adhoc. Law vested responsibility of sectoral State Disaster Management Plans (SDMP) with respective departments, which were to be integrated by the State Disaster Management Authority (SDMA) whose existence was only on paper. Headed by Chief Minister, it was serviced by Special Relief Commissioner (SRC), who was found hardly interested to meet job requirements. No exercises had been undertaken by SDMA to prepare a consolidated plan. Indeed, NDMA had provided ₹ 10 lakh for its preparation to OSDMA by involving a consultancy organisation as if only to fulfil the legal requirement. The funds had been decided to be given to a private educational institution with no expertise in the field. One of my duties in Cabinet Secretariat earlier had been to coordinate with State Governments on disaster management-related issues. Naturally, I accorded priority to preparing a robust SDMP after I was appointed administrative head of R&DM Department responsible for managing natural calamity and relief operations.

OSDMA, in existence prior to constitution of SDMA, had a mandate to build capacity and develop disaster resistant infrastructure, particularly in flood and cyclone-prone coastal districts. My suggestion to merge SDMA and OSDMA was not found acceptable. I thus took steps to prepare a consolidated State-wide SDMP by OSDMA and called upon line departments to prepare their respective sectoral plans for preventing and managing possible disasters. The scope was enlarged to cover industrial disasters in view of increasing casualties seen occurring in steel and thermal power plants. I constituted a functional Committee in OSDMA chaired by me for evaluation of sectoral plans, which were then to be consolidated into SDMP. The Committee included a nodal officer from each department, experts, senior officials from UNDP,

UNICEF, State Red Cross, and John Ambulance (a reputed NGO) among others. No department could now escape its responsibility.

After rigorous and elaborate exercises, all completed within 5 months of taking charge, OSDMA developed a consolidated SDMP which defined possible natural and industrial disasters. It also prepared Standard Operating Procedures (SOPs) to tackle them at various levels of administration. Finalised after extensive stakeholder consultations, the document was published and circulated to all concerned with disaster management at the 3 tiers. ₹ 10 lakh was refunded to NDMA, no doubt disappointing a private educational institution.

Mock Drills to Test Preparedness: Leaving Nothing to Chance

Mock drills are vital to test the disaster management preparedness of first responders and agencies. Super Cyclone-1999 had taught bitter lessons, in the early aftermath of which State Government had invested in institutions like OSDMA and ODRAF, hard infrastructure and soft skills through OSDMA. A good number of flood and cyclone shelters had been constructed. Community members and organisations were trained to manage them as first responders whenever natural calamities hit their villages. Five units of ODRAF, each consisting of 50 trained State police force personnel deployed to strategically-located stations had been equipped with useful devices. MCS Management Maintenance Committees, with 50 percent representation of women, had been provided first-aid boxes, tool kits and loud-speakers to inform the people at large what to do when facing a calamity.

When I assumed charge, OSDMA's role was preparedness and rescue operations along with development of calamity-resilient community infrastructure focussing on the most vulnerable coastal villages. Having witnessed a reactive management of relief and rescue operations during Super Cyclone-1999, I did not wish to be caught napping whenever another disaster visited the State. I thus visited ODRAF units and vulnerable areas to witness mock drills involving community bodies and government agencies including NDRF. I personally participated by diving 30 to 40 feet deep in Mahanadi Barrage near Kundli, to be rescued in a mock drill by specialized ODRAF and NDRF personnel. My continuous refrain was that armed forces remain forever in battle-readiness by playing war games and upskilling themselves in new equipment and processes round the year. Likewise, regular mock drills were means to remain fully prepared to meet the challenges of unpredictable calamities. Mock drills could not be just rituals to be performed once a year. They required participation of all concerned. I thus attached great importance to such exercises.

Very Severe Cyclone Phailin Strikes, but Precious Lives Saved

As if vigorous development of infrastructure through NCRMP projects, preparation of SDMP, and mock drills were its harbingers, on 8 October 2013 a message was received from IMD about the formation of a depression over North Andaman Sea, which was moving westwards with a speed of 18 km/hour. Detected initially in Gulf of Thailand as a tropical depression on 4 October, it remained centred over North Andaman Sea about 1,350 km East/South-East of Paradip as reported at 11:30 hours IST. The system was predicted to intensify into a deep depression and further into a cyclonic storm by the next day and was to move West/North-Westwards towards North Andhra Pradesh and Odisha coast during the following 72 hours.

R&DM Department started monitoring the situation immediately, with round-the-clock tracking of the storm by GIS expert and technical staff in OSDMA. Once it intensified and became equivalent to Category-1 Hurricane on 10 October, its position and movement were intimated to District Collectors. Besides advertisements in local newspapers, it was broadcast through all possible channels. On 10 October, IMD further informed that it had intensified into a 'very severe' cyclonic storm named "Phailin" indicating threat to Odisha coast, providing also the track and system intensity. US Navy too reported that Phailin would become equivalent to a Category-4 Hurricane, reaching its peak intensity with wind speeds of 260 km/hour seen in a Category-5 Hurricane. Close monitoring of the cyclone with its clearly visible "eye" left no doubt about its direction. Soon, it could be pin-pointed that land-fall would be between Gopalpur (Ganjam) and Andhra Pradesh border. Phailin was now racing like a guided missile, menacingly as if throwing a challenge to State and district administration that they should now do whatsoever they could to save people, given the inevitability of large-scale physical devastation upon its land-fall and in its aftermath.

Collectors of 14 districts likely to be impacted were alerted regularly through fax, email and phone calls. Instructions were issued to convene meetings of District Disaster Management Authorities to review preparedness of departments including their field formations, and to alert NGOs, community bodies and public at large about the imminent disaster. Collectors were instructed to recall Government functionaries away on training or leave. Collectors of Ganjam and Puri were specifically asked to be ready with evacuation plan and to identify relief centres in safer locations which included MCSs that had either been completed or were nearly completed. Requisitions went to Central Government to deploy more NDRF units, defence forces, and helicopters. ODRAF units were redeployed and strategically placed.

It was a difficult situation as people were in festive mood with preparations to celebrate Durga Puja in high gear and Government functionaries in anticipation of puja holidays. Chief Secretary J.K. Mahapatra was on a tour to Rayagada, but returned instantly to Bhubaneswar considering the storm's intensity conveyed by weather forecasts. Storms had struck twice in 1999 within a fortnight of each other. He was the Secretary in Revenue Department at that time. Immediately, he took an emergency meeting with senior officers of all Government departments. All aspects were discussed, in particular, reliability and accuracy of IMD's prediction, ways and means to handle the developing situation including effective use of mass media for publicising warnings, institutional disaster management capabilities built up over past 10-12 years, robustness of communication infrastructure to withstand the critical hours, timely initiation of mass evacuation from high-risk zones, advanced deployment of ODRAF, NDRF, and Armed Forces, seamless coordination between State and Central agencies, monitoring of public response to alerts and advisories, rescue and relief operations with precision. The target would be to save every precious life. Chief Secretary suggested that a few senior Secretaries should volunteer for coordinating important operations in districts likely to be affected more and areas needing attention.

I volunteered to accept full responsibility to coordinate and monitor the situation in all districts centrally thereby avoiding gaps resulting from multiple communication or coordination centres. My submission implied that multiplicity usually meant diffusion of accountability. Besides, two emergency control rooms, one each in R&DM Department and OSDMA activated by me were monitoring, compiling and disseminating information both ways with District Collectors round-the-clock. Warnings about the calamity and instructions were being conveyed to all concerned without loss of time. Chief Secretary accepted my request to place services of a couple of young officers in OSDMA to assist me. Considering that luxury of puja holidays could not be afforded, orders of Chief Minister were sought to cancel the holidays of Government functionaries at all levels. As the situation was turning increasingly serious with every passing minute, I issued instructions at night on 10 October without awaiting Chief Minister's order for cancellation of leave and training and public holidays and for recalling officials on training. The office order issued by me also directed running round-the-clock Emergency Control Rooms in Block/Tehsil/Sub-Division/District. On the requests of district administration of districts likely to be affected, men and materials from neighbouring districts were provided to be diverted with immediate effect.

Despite being visited by cyclonic storms and sustaining heavy loss of life and properties at regular intervals, Odisha's approach and response to natural calamities remained reactive and not pro-active, a fact exemplified by a death toll of 183 in a relatively low intensity storm in Ganjam during 17-18 October 1999, and about 10,000 during a higher intensity cyclone 10 days later during 27-29 October 1999. Even after creating a number of flood and cyclone relief centres, with higher degree of training and community sensitisation thereafter, loss of life and property due to natural calamities, mostly floods, had more or less continued. I used to feel hurt when farcical presentations were made by senior officers attributing State's poverty and backwardness to natural calamities. After all, they made little effort to plug institutional weaknesses and leverage bountiful natural resources to achieve prosperity of its people.

Now, I bluntly told my team that it was an opportunity for us to show our capabilities and to reverse the negative impression by conveying helplessness and begging for mercy both during and after the natural calamity. The next 4 days after the 10th of October, I stayed in office in R&DM Department during the day and camped in OSDMA at night, all in the company of a couple of like-minded officers who had participated in relief operations during Super Cyclone 1999. Monitoring evacuations in vulnerable villages of Ganjam, Puri and three other coastal districts was high priority. During Super Cyclone-1999, relief materials from across India had flooded Bhubaneswar and fully-laden trucks stood stranded in the absence of proper arrangements to receive such materials centrally or direct the supplies to specific places for delivery. I did not like to repeat the ignominious past and, thus, drew up elaborate SOPs for receipt at State headquarters and movement of relief materials to affected areas. With logistics support from IDCO, a temporary office was opened at Kalinga Stadium where relief materials could be handled systematically. Specific duties were assigned to officers. As usually happens, more help comes when destruction coupled with mismanagement is higher. No relief materials were received this time as instead of adverse publicity, performance of the State in managing Phailin received national and international appreciation. The temporary office and facilities created in Kalinga Stadium remained unutilised!

After being alerted by R&DM Department, District Collectors and departments had already ensured prepositioning of men and materials. Special DG Police in charge of ODRAF, Additional DG (Fire Services), and NDRF Commandant had deployed their units as indicated by OSDMA in consultation with Collectors. Village level administrative units provided vital contact with villagers. MHA had diverted NDRF units to Odisha as per requirements. Coordination with key Central Government agencies was effectively managed. Perhaps for the first time in Odisha, columns of Army and units of Air Force and Navy had arrived before the natural calamity struck. A portion of old airport in Bhubaneswar was earmarked for Indian Air Force operations.

On 9 October, an inter-departmental co-ordination meeting was held by R&DM Minister to discuss issues at hand and take stock of preparatory works. Dissemination of cyclone alert and warning, arrangements to keep communication systems open, and persuasive contacts with fishing community not to go for fishing in turbulent waters; mock drills in places likely to be hit hard; constituting teams for search and rescue operations; requisitioning private boats; check-verification of equipment including power saws, rubber boats, diesel generator sets, loudspeakers, water pumps; stocking of tarpaulins and plastic sheets; evacuation plans; opening relief centres, preparing dry food packets and arranging other food and drinking water; storing kerosene, petroleum products and other essential commodities in shelters; deploying units of ODRAF, NDRF and Fire Services, etc., were taken up comprehensively.

Opening control rooms by departments; special care for evacuating children, and the old and infirm; stocking essential medicines, first aid kits; provisions for cattle feed; preparedness for restoring communication system and power supply; depleting excess water from reservoirs where necessary; supply of satellite phones to Collectors; awareness generation against use of unsafe buildings; closing educational institutions, Anganwadi centres; etc. were reiterated.

Another meeting followed on 10 October by Chief Minister to review the measures taken so far. Collectors participated through video conferencing and reported on their preparatory steps. Diverting materials including plastic sheets and tarpaulins from non-coastal to coastal districts was decided, besides deploying more manpower for preparing dry food packets in addition to procuring flattened rice and jaggery in larger quantities on war-footing from other States for distribution among calamity-affected people. Animal Husbandry Department was warned as progress reported by them in stocking fodder was found unsatisfactory. Recalling the past, they were apprehensive of witch-hunt for not following rules and procedures in its procurement. Since there was no time for inviting tenders, considering production constraints in the State they were told to invoke emergency provisions of Odisha's Relief Code to effect procurements from neighbouring States without losing any further time.

OSDMA separately held an emergency meeting with leading NGOs and UN organisations to tap their resources, prevent duplication of work, and concentration of operations in a few areas. Specific zones were allotted for their intervention in conjunction with local administration under intimation to Collectors. Despite limited capabilities, NGOs provide valuable support in niche areas. It was also important to involve them as an ignored or marginalised NGO fraternity could turn hostile and disruptive of State efforts. Office of SRC did a good job in keeping print and electronic media informed at regular intervals and thereby effectively managing them giving no scope to turn negative. Everything as planned was executed.

On 11 October, Collectors of coastal districts reported that mock drills had been held and video-recorded in many places. Shelters and other temporary relief centres were ready with utensils, food materials, etc. for three days. All shelter management committee members, volunteers and task force members were kept in readiness. Departments were again asked to intensify efforts for pre-positioning of materials, equipment and manpower required for restoring drinking water supply, road communication, power supply, telecom, and to address health-related issues. Satellite phones and police wireless systems of coastal districts were test-checked. As cyclonic winds were being felt increasingly, Collectors were told to implement evacuation plans, particularly from low-lying villages along the coast-line. It was as if the cyclonic storm, albeit traveling on the predicted path, was actually on a mission of vengeance.

The morning of 12 October dawned with news from coastal District Collectors to me that people likely to be affected were simply not ready to be evacuated. I had prescribed a format for submitting information by District Emergency Officers indicating names of villages and number of people evacuated and kept in identified relief centres numbering about 600. Progress in evacuation was negligible in spite of efforts and arrangements for food, drinking water, etc. made by district administration in safer locations. Ganjam district, likely to be bear the frontal blunt, was the most unsatisfactory. I shuddered visualising thousands of bodies, imagining a repeat of Super Cyclone-1999. Without seeking Government approval or consulting anyone, I issued strict directions orally and then in writing to Collectors to apply force, if necessary, for evacuation. Collectors of Ganjam and Puri in particular were warned that they would be accountable if despite sufficient time in hand, their failure in evacuation resulted in loss of life. I recalled to them provisions of NDM Act 2005 which empowered an authority to use force to evacuate people if they did not voluntarily move to safer locations. My threats and warnings had the desired effect. Ganjam Collector himself, with SP by his side, started moving with a loudspeaker in low-lying coastal villages. Other officers duly supported by police too moved around evacuating people similarly. Before the cyclonic storm's landfall at 9.30 p.m. on 12 October, despite rain and high-speed winds, more than 3.50 lakh people from low-lying vulnerable villages of Ganjam had been taken to relief centres in safer locations. More than a million people were evacuated from all coastal districts put together. Peak intensity of cyclone was at 223 km/hour in Puri and peak wind velocity recorded at Gopalpur was 214 km/hour.

The cyclonic storm triggered torrential rains across the State during 11-14 October. Precipitation was a high 241.10 mm in Ganjam. Heavy rains led to flash floods in Baitarini, Budhabalanga, Jalaka, Subarnarekha, and Rushikulya rivers, inundating large parts of downstream areas of Mayurbhanj, Balasore, Keonjhar, Bhadrak, Jajpur and Ganjam districts. About 1.33 crore people of 171 Blocks, 44 urban local bodies, 2,164 Gram Panchayats and 18,374 villages in 18 districts of the State got affected. Due to cyclone, toll on human lives was 21. Standing crops over 6.71 lakh hectares were destroyed. Every sector of economy suffered, with Ganjam and two adjoining Blocks of Puri district bearing the maximum brunt. Damage assessed after field verifications presented complete destruction of 7,174 pucca houses, 18,406 kutcha houses in addition to partial damage to 1,80,628 pucca and kutcha houses. Destruction of public infrastructure such as canal systems, roads, bridges, electrical installations, telecommunication infrastructure, public buildings including hospitals, educational institutions, drinking water supply projects, green cover, etc. was unprecedented.

Preparedness in managing the cyclone proved robust. All departments stood fully sensitised of the first-ever comprehensive SDMP which had laid down SOPs for various types of disasters. Weather forecasts by IMD were strikingly accurate. The path of cyclonic storm, with its threatening eye, moved exactly as predicted by IMD. I made the best use of my mobile phone to get updates on evacuation on hourly-basis through SMSs. Administration's hand was forced in using force to evacuate people many of whom would have suffered the fury of nature in its most extreme form. Round-the-clock monitoring of evacuation and other interventions notwithstanding, rescue teams saved many lives. Heavy rains preceding and succeeding the cyclone caused flash floods in various rivers.

In a case of rescue operation in Hinjili Block in Ganjam, 4 labourers of Balangir district working in a brick manufacturing unit got surrounded by rapidly rising flood waters of Rushikulya on 13 October. Rescue attempts by ODRAF, Fire Service, and NDRF failed despite the crisis occurring during day hours. I was informed by Collector in the evening that though the labourers were clinging precariously to their dear lives on a tree top, rescue teams had all but given up. I warned DIG Police who was supervising rescue operations that any withdrawal on the part of trained and well-equipped ODRAF and NDRF teams would be unacceptable if their lives were lost. Darkness was already setting in. The officer in charge of the police station had refused to join the rescue team; feared for his own life as he could not swim. In a meeting taken by Chief Minister at 7.00 p.m. when this matter was reported by me calling for action against this scared officer and other senior police officers in charge of rescue operations, none reacted as if the high possibility of loss of 4 lives had been accepted. After the meeting, I again called ODRAF and NDRF commandants, Fire Service head and DIG, Police and adjured them not to show timidity to evade rescue operations. They were asked to share efforts being made every half-hour, besides sending courageous joint teams of ODRAF and NDRF. I remained restless till I was informed after midnight that team efforts finally bore fruit and all 4 labourers were rescued. In the morning I heard that the tree had vanished without trace during the night.

Relief distribution and temporary restorations of power and telecom infrastructure, roads, and drinking water supply projects were undertaken in parallel on war-footing. Telecom towers in Ganjam stood fully or partially destroyed and satellite phones were being used in coordinating evacuation and rescue operations during critical junctures. Telephone service providers worked wonderfully to temporarily restore the network, barring in a few places of Ganjam and Puri districts. Mechanised power saws supplied to all MCSs and ODRAF units, were used extensively to cut and remove trees found blocking roads and other public places. NDRF and Armed Forces' units commendably supplemented local efforts to restore road communication up to Block level within 24 hours and up to Gram Panchayat level in 48 hours. It took some time to restore power supplies in all the towns and villages.

There was no scope for highlighting negative stories by media due to widespread power and telecom disruptions, which was perhaps the second-best part of successful evacuations and rescue operations. By the time networks were restored, massive relief operations had been mounted and monitored systematically. The situation was changing fast on the ground and people at large were satisfied with the care they got despite forced evacuations from low-lying villages. Media personnel who started visiting affected areas after 2-3 days, witnessed the mayhem caused by the fury of nature and, in the given adversity, commended the role of State/district administration, except in Mayurbhanj which was badly affected by flash floods immediately after the cyclone. RDC of Northern Division, formerly Collector of Mayurbhanj, was deputed to supervise the relief operations there. Despite complaints from public representatives about Collector's incompetence and negligence, I pleaded with Chief Secretary not to transfer him at that stage, which was agreed.

In the long history of natural calamities, a new benchmark was established by evacuating over a million people and in substantially achieving the objective of 'zero loss' of human life, though not literally. Death toll in Phailin-hit districts was limited to 21, of which 20 were on account of heart failure, collapse of house walls, falling of trees, snake-bites and diseases associated more with rains and floods which followed Phailin. The collective efforts by "Team Odisha" of which District Collectors were key players were universally applauded. The State appeared confident this time and did not seek charity. Some NGOs participate in relief works to find windows of opportunities to access donations within the country and abroad. But since Government agencies had taken them on board in managing the crisis effectively, in a way it deprived them of a role they usually played leveraging administrative incompetence and inactions. International media too praised the role of State administration. Despite my turning down the request of a reputed news agency 'Reuters' for an interview during the crisis, they came out with a positive story on 14 October 2013 under the title- "*How the Indian Bureaucrats got it right*". The story in brief contained narratives as follows:

> *"As the fiercest storm to hit India this century barrelled across the Bay of Bengal last week, a local mandarin frantically worked the phone from his hot and humid office, leading the charge in an operation to move nearly a million people to safety. We were telling people; 'look you have to choose between death and life', said Taradatt, who heads the Revenue and Disaster Management Department in the poverty-plagued eastern State of Orissa. "Those who were not willing (to be evacuated), I was telling the local officials to use force, because the rules permit that". When Cyclone Phailin slammed into Orissa and neighbouring Andhra Pradesh States with wind gusting at more than 200 KPH, India was braced for the worst. A Monster Storm that hit the very same region 14 years ago had killed 10,000 people. But this time, the death toll was astonishingly*

low, at the latest account just 21. It was rare moment of relief in this disaster-prone country, one that has already been hailed as a triumph of official heroism and defies the Indian bureaucracy's reputation for bungling and indecision. ...

Along with Taradatt, who just uses one name, junior officials also chipped in. As the storm closed in Odisha coastal district of Ganjam last Saturday, the senior most local Civil Servant Krishan Kumar was exhausted. For the past three nights, he had not slept, working without a break to set up hundreds of temporary shelters in schools and temples, and persuaded villagers to abandon ramshackle dwellings. "There was a lot of resistance to begin with" said 37-year old Kumar. The weather was very good, the sun was shining and to convince people was not an easy job. We had to move from village to village telling people what could happen". With a couple of hours to go before the storm made landfall, some 350,000 people living up to 10 km from shore line were safely sheltered for the night. Across the two eastern States, more than 1 million people were evacuated from their homes. ...

Back in the State Capital, Bhubaneswar, Disaster Management Chief Taradatt had also taken matters into his own hands as the cyclone approached. Original proposal to assign the task of evacuation to multiple civil servants was ditched after Taradatt volunteered to oversee it himself, an official who attended the early planning meeting told Reuters. The official said Taradatt worked day and night to liaise with district Chiefs like Kumar, and after the storm had blown over, he dived straight into the problems of an estimated quarter of a million people left stranded by the resulting floods. "I do not even have time for the calls of my family. My son called me from New Jersey to speak to me, but I told him sorry" Taradatt told Reuters from his government office, "right now, every moment is important, please excuse me".

Much of what went right in Odisha at the weekend can be traced to wake up call delivered by the 1999 cyclone, which thrashed the State...."

As it happens, every disaster is followed by visits of VIPs. Special Representative of UN Secretary General conveyed, through local UN officials, keenness to visit and commend the handling of Phailin and saving scores of lives. I requested postponing it till completion of restoration works. Similar advice was given to many others. Relief and restoration works had to proceed in parallel and be completed as fast as humanly possible. The biggest challenge was in restoration of power lines and replacement of totally destroyed transformers. In some places, people did not allow drawl of alternative high- and low-tension electric lines nor reconstruction and replacement of transformers at power stations apprehending further damage to their land and risks that followed in the event of similar natural calamity in future.

I distinctly remember that Secretary, Energy Department and MD, GRIDCO had gone to Jagannathpur (Ganjam) on 14 October after receiving a distress call that a group of about 250 villagers was opposing relocation of power station and transformers apprehending loss of their land. This power station was critical for restoring power to Berhampur and Chhatrapur towns. Police personnel had been outnumbered. Chief Minister was visiting the district that day. Although I was not directly concerned with it, MD GRIDCO and Energy Department sought my intervention. Local DIG and SP though busy with Chief Minister's visit agreed to my request to deploy enough force if efforts failed to dissuade the agitators after Chief Minister left the district. As District Collector, having handled flash floods which had wreaked havoc in Ganjam in 1991, it was not difficult to understand mob mentality and role played by local touts even during times of acute crisis. It was agreed that DIG would lead the police force, reach the site at 2:30 p.m. when protesters would have gone for lunch, and cordon off the whole area required for the new power station. Technical and other functionaries from the power company were told to remain ready with necessary materials and equipment to execute the work non-stop. It was a calculated risk and the State's political leadership would have never permitted it if consulted in advance. The strategy, however, worked. Protesters came back to the site finding themselves outnumbered. That evening Chief Minister took a meeting of senior officers involved in relief and restoration works. Secretary, Energy Department with a broad smile on his face recounted how my intervention had the desired effect. From my field experience, I feel that police force becomes more effective without being used ruthlessly, and people at large respect public servants who worked selflessly. Only a few touts needed to be isolated carefully from the mob to achieve the goal. As expected, the power station was reconstructed quickly, which immensely helped in restoring power supply in the district head quarters.

The fury of cyclone lasted for two days and its dust took a month to settle. Restorations of roads, power supply, drinking water supply, telecom networks etc. were completed, though temporarily. Enumeration of losses was also completed. It was now easier to host dignitaries, including from UN, UNICEF, UNDP, the World Bank, who were still keen to come. As I remained fully occupied in supervising assessment of damages, and disbursing relief and house-building assistance in accordance with Odisha Relief Code, I turned down requests from several IIMs and IITs to present the State's experiences in handling Phailin. IIM, Raipur wanted to felicitate OSDMA in an international conference and desired my presence. Since my interventions were required in ensuring completion of restoration works and a time-bound rehabilitation, I deputed other colleagues to present Phailin-related experiences.

On 23 December 2013, the Special Representative of UN General Secretary for Disaster Risk Reduction came to felicitate Chief Minister Naveen Patnaik by presenting a citation and inviting him to attend an international conference on risk reduction in Japan in 2014. UN Secretary General she said, highly appreciated the State's well-functioning disaster risk reduction system which included preparedness activities by families, communities, Government and NGOs. Odisha thus became the first State in South East Asia to be felicitated for disaster management. I had explained to her the sequence of events, and she was impressed. General elections for Lok Sabha and State Legislative Assembly were to take place in about 4 months' time. Large 'cut outs' showing Chief Minister being thus felicitated were advertised at hoardings at important places and in daily newspapers. The ruling party could not have got a better platform to showcase the State Government's performance in managing this Very Severe Cyclone contrasting with what happened during Super Cyclone-1999. Then, incumbent Chief Secretary had suddenly left for a longish private visit to USA when restoration and relief works warranted his leadership and guidance. In contrast, this time leave, public holidays and training had been denied to Government employees and incumbent Chief Secretary led from the front to run the show most admirably and consistently. Perhaps it was only expected that political leadership in the State appropriated the credit for handling Phailin and harvested electoral dividends. It was another matter that in none of his meetings, Chief Minister could be seen interested in any discussion beyond reading a brief text written for the consumption of general public through well-organised media coverage. I usually took advantage of his silence, indifference and lack of insights on issues discussed in meetings by taking his silence for approval.

National Cyclone Risk Mitigation Project-II

Vice Chairperson, NDMA, had conveyed a desire to visit the State. Management of Phailin had offered opportunities for reconstruction, rehabilitation and development of stronger infrastructure in coastal areas. I prepared a proposal for NCRMP-II for appraisal of Union Government, with NDMA's endorsement, and the World Bank with adequate justification. It was for developing cyclone-resistant infrastructure in villages devastated by Phailin within 5 km of high-tide lines. It was suggested to widen the scope and funding of ongoing World Bank-assisted NCRMP to provide for construction of MCSs in uncovered coastal villages along with approach roads and cyclone-resistant pucca houses for families who had lost their dwelling units. After all, use of unfinished shelters too had helped in saving scores of lives during Phailin. Time was short, only Chief Secretary was consulted. The meeting with Vice Chairman, NDMA yielded the desired result. The proposal was appreciated and endorsed instantly. Soon enough I had worked out the details for appraisal by Union Finance Ministry and the World Bank. Country Director of the World Bank, on visit to Ganjam, was impressed to find MCSs being run by community-based management committees. He readily conveyed that there was enough input to support my proposal to upscale NCRMP and widen its scope to include construction of cyclone-resistant houses in coastal villages. He shared with me how immediately after Phailin he was mobbed by media in Washington DC to answer as to how India could manage cyclone Phailin so effectively when resource-rich USA had failed to manage similar disasters!

After Super Cyclone-1999, State Government had taken steps and constructed 192 shelters in the most vulnerable villages of coastal districts within 10 km of the shoreline. These included 60 shelters constructed under Chief Minister's Relief Fund, 30 from Prime Minister's Relief Fund, 37 with the World Bank's assistance and 65 by Indian Red Cross Society. In the year 2007, IIT Kharagpur after a detailed scientific study had identified 503 locations in six coastal districts (Balasore, Bhadrak, Kendrapara, Jagatsinghpur, Puri and Ganjam) which were prone to cyclones and storm surges, and were within 10 km zone of shoreline. Thus, it was intended to ensure that every family within 10 km from shoreline had access to a safe shelter without having to run beyond 2.25 km and being obstructed by any natural barrier in the event of emergencies. IIT Kharagpur had also developed the structural design and drawing for the proposed structures which could withstand tremors up to 10 in Richter's scale. In addition to 192 shelters already in place in villages not necessarily identified by IIT Kharagpur, 149 approved under NCRMP, and 14 shelters under another World Bank-assisted Integrated Coast Zone Management Project were all under execution. There were 162 identified locations which did not have any provision for shelters. These were given top priority to address gaps along with good quality approach roads to link them with villages in the catchment area.

After door-to-door survey of houses in 5 coastal blocks of Ganjam (Chhatrapur, Chikiti, Ganjam, Khallikote, and Rangailunda), and in two adjoining blocks of Puri (Brahmagiri and Krushna Prasad), which had suffered the maximum devastation, it was proposed to construct 30,000 cyclone-resistant houses for the worst-affected families within 5 km from shoreline. Since Berhampur (Ganjam) had suffered equally, H&UD Department sought reconstruction of urban infrastructure to be included in the proposal. Prior to visit of the World Bank appraisal team, I had taken Government's approval on 24 December 2013 for policy guidelines which included a robust and time-bound grievance redressal mechanism at block and district levels. Beneficiaries would be approved by Gram Sabhas at village level in a transparent manner. The policy also provided that cyclone-resistant houses for affected families within 5 km from the high-tide line would be constructed only in villages which were situated on the left side of National Highway (in Ganjam) facing Bay of Bengal. Built at a cost of ₹ 3 lakh/unit, each house would have a minimum floor area of 294 square feet. Provision for site development, drinking water, electrification, household toilets and other community infrastructure was to be taken up under ongoing programmes and out of funds earmarked for implementation support and capacity building for disaster risk management.

After specifying the scope, the number of houses to be constructed came to about 22,500, which included 16,000 in 5 blocks of Ganjam, 300 in two blocks of Khordha around Chilika Lake, and 6,000 in two blocks of Puri district.

The project report approved by World Bank provided for clearance from Coast Zone Authority, compliance with coastal regulations and relocations without warranting land acquisition. There were no procedural complications or disputes regarding shelters and approach roads. But the conditions laid down for construction of houses which included involvement of an NGO for capacity building and community mobilisation were difficult to handle. I wanted to execute the project named "Odisha Disaster Recovery Project (ODRP)" quickly and made it clear that it would be possible for me to associate with it only if they accepted what I considered to be reasonable requirements. I had agreed to the condition to involving NGO Gram Vikas which was working in Odisha for about 30 years. But, the contractor-driven model proposed for construction of houses through open bids, called for preparation of DPRs and complicated time-taking formalities. It was impossible to involve contractors mandatorily to construct houses in a large number of villages spread over three districts. It was finally agreed that in case of lack of satisfactory response from contractors to tender bids, OSDMA could consider constructing houses through beneficiaries by ensuring that no house was left incomplete or unoccupied.

At an estimated cost of ₹ 1,312 crore with 30 percent cost-sharing by State Government, ODRP was finally approved by Government of India and the World Bank. Pending formal agreement, State Government was allowed to proceed with implementation with an assurance of expenditure being reimbursed later. State Government made budget provisions for 2014-15 accordingly. Against my insistence of a time-frame of 2 years, the World Bank suggested 5 years as per their standard practice. We settled at a 4-year period for execution of ODRP. I was determined to prove that execution of the project which mainly included cyclone-resistant houses, MCSs, approach roads, and restoration of Berhampur town's infrastructure could be completed in two years' period with effective monitoring and time-bound actions. I felt from experience that the World Bank's own unnecessary interventions through non-implementable conditions played no less role in delaying project implementation. Also, a shorter period would help in creating greater accountability in implementing agencies, besides reducing scope for repeated visits in the name of mid-terms appraisals, etc. by the World Bank.

DPRs for 162 additional cyclone shelters, 100 approach roads and 16,571 houses for 173 villages of Ganjam and Khordha districts in 141 relocation sites were quickly prepared. Construction of these 162 cyclone shelters progressed smoothly. There were no major problems in implementing approach roads either. After DPRs were prepared, open tenders were floated for cyclone-resistant houses. Each DPR was for 3,000 to 4,000 houses in order to make the housing project viable for execution by larger contractors, as per the first option given by the World Bank. Policy guidelines approved by Government had provided for setting up administrative structures headed by Collector at the district level and Tahasildar/BDO at Block/Tahasil level. OSDMA needed to submit proposals for clearance by Coast Zone Authority for construction of houses at relocation sites, as had been stipulated by the World Bank. Concurrently, RD Department was called upon to go ahead with implementing drinking water supply projects including sinking of tube wells to meet water needs during construction of housing colonies. Being administrative head of R&DM Department, it was not difficult for me to arrange land for houses at relocation sites despite occasional problems posed by some litigants and a few officials of Forest & Environment Department. I was keen to award all ODRP works and start construction before the onset of monsoon and succeeded in measurable part. The response from eligible contractors was inadequate and I was happy to have their bids rejected in order to follow the beneficiary or owner-driven construction model for houses.

However, owner-driven construction of houses was fraught with a variety of risks and problems. In coastal villages of Brahmagiri and Krishnaprasad blocks of Puri, Palli Sabhas were not allowed for approval of eligible beneficiaries by vested interests. Ironically, the local MLA who was a Minister in State Government came to my office suggesting not to implement ODRP in two Blocks under his assembly constituency so far as cyclone-resistant houses were concerned. According to him, there were serious law and order problems due to exclusion of ineligible families and in the given situation the only course of action was either to cover all families of affected villages or none. District administration also conveyed inability to hold Palli Sabhas for approving 6,000 eligible families identified jointly by Tahasil and Block field functionaries after door-to-door survey. Since it was not possible to wait indefinitely, I brought the impasse to the notice of Chief Minister and went ahead with work in Ganjam and Khordha.

OSDMA did not have independent administrative units at Block/Tahasil, Sub-Division or District levels. BDOs were already burdened with a large number of ongoing schemes. Sub-Collectors and Collectors were traditionally involved in coordinating relief operations at the time of calamities and did not have experience and confidence in implementing or supervising reconstruction works in such a large scale. I wanted them to be involved for construction of cyclone-resistant houses in a time-bound manner and ensured their participation in visiting sites and holding meetings with stakeholders. I did not like to issue guidelines for executing cyclone-resistant houses without taking officers at Block and district levels on board. The objective was to address anticipated problems collectively and ensure a feeling of belongingness in everyone's mind. Since additional manpower was required to exclusively supervise the works, Collectors and BDOs were told to hire services of retired engineers and accounting staff as necessary. I quickly approved their proposals in this regard. Finally, guidelines to be followed in executing houses were issued after being vetted by BDOs and Collectors. Provisions existed for outsourcing the required manpower under the head "project implementation support". Anticipating problems of sourcing materials for such a large number of houses in a limited number of Blocks, details of requirements of bricks, sand, steel, cement, etc. were worked out in consultation with engineers. Brick units in places around construction sites and elsewhere happily stepped up to ensure uninterrupted supply without raising approved rates to reap advantages from the situation. Tahasildars were instructed in writing not to levy charges against sand and stones used for construction of ODRP houses. Administrative costs as required were released to Collectors/BDOs in advance.

There was initial reluctance on the part of BDOs to operate funds directly. Their dilemma was solved by laying down a separate SOP and a transparent accounting system which envisaged opening of an account in the name of each beneficiary in the nearest Commercial or Regional Rural Bank branch and release of first instalment of ₹ 20,000 to the account after handing over patta over duly demarcated plot of Ac. 0.10 for construction of house. The time-frame indicated in works' orders to each beneficiary was one year from the date of receiving the first instalment. Junior Engineers including those specifically appointed contractually for a period of one year to supervise construction of houses were to be paid remuneration subject to achieving monthly yardsticks. In fact, a few of them left for not being equal to the task. NGO Gram Vikas not only organized training of masons, plumbers and carpenters on work sites in large numbers, but also provided a large contingent of manpower including engineering personnel available with them. Their architect designed the layouts by visiting each relocation site with remarkable efficiency and sense of commitment. The second instalment of ₹ 50,000 per beneficiary was paid after the house came up to plinth level, third instalment of ₹ 100,000 when the house was at roof level, fourth instalment of ₹ 50,000 after casting of roof, fifth instalment of ₹ 50,000 after removing centering materials and installation of fittings; and the last instalment of ₹ 30,000 after finishing the work.

No deviation from the standard plan in terms of quality and technical specifications was permissible except for additional floor area, and beneficiaries were in fact encouraged to do so by investing additional resources of their own. The procedure with fixed accountability worked effectively and there was healthy competition among beneficiaries in many places to construct bigger and better houses keeping in view their long-term requirements. There were a couple of allegations in relation to wrong selection of beneficiaries and undue demand by a lower-level functionary in a particular Block. I personally verified the allegations and found them without foundation except against a Block clerk. The Block functionary was placed under suspension by

District Collector instantly fixing his headquarters elsewhere. Thousands of houses in a number of new colonies were completed in less than a year as a result of dedicated services of field functionaries, effective monitoring and reviews regularly at district level. BDOs and Tahasildars made presentations in the review meetings showing the latest status of physical and financial progress with photographs of colonies that showed what had been achieved during the month under review. Simultaneously, progress in providing drinking water supply, electrification and community infrastructure including approach roads and MCSs were also reviewed. It was heartening to find some volunteers reach out from across India offering to build community infrastructure such as primary schools and Anganwadi Centres in these villages. The progress inspired all concerned.

Having handled an unprecedented flood which called for a massive rehabilitation plan involving relocation of large number of villages and construction of thousands of new houses as Collector in Ganjam district, I knew that what took years in other districts of Odisha, could be done in months in Ganjam considering the higher productivity and stronger determination of its people to achieve better economic gains. I had been able to motivate Government officials, but some problems being encountered had potential to derail the housing programme. These came from three quarters, namely, banks, field functionaries of Forest & Environment Department, and Finance Department. Despite release of funds in advance, some bank officials who appeared very supportive at the time of opening accounts were found returning the account holders empty handed even though the authorized officers had certified the progress and endorsed release of funds to beneficiaries. I had to bring such harassments to the notice of regional heads of banks who were warned that deposits would be transferred to cooperative banks if they treated the ODRP project as a means of deposit mobilization. Officials of Forest & Environment Department at the district level and at times at the State level too were found raising objections on proposals even when duly backed by GIS data for regulatory clearances. Lastly, due to delay in signing of loan agreement with the World Bank, the State Finance Department was unwilling to release further funds for construction of houses when the work was in full swing. Any break in construction work could break the rhythm of the project implementation. I had been allowed to utilize available NCRMP funds for additional MCSs. But similar window of facility was not being extended for construction of houses. State's share of 30 percent for the first year had been fully utilized. Eventually the problem was overcome after the tripartite agreement was signed and reimbursement claims were entertained. Luckily, the World Bank team which had been visiting the State regularly for appraisal, not only certified but also applauded the pace of work which helped to save me from the charge of creating liabilities due to my advance actions. My only objective was to ensure implementation of ODRP for rehabilitation of calamity-affected people before any force majeure occurred.

Although construction of a good number of houses had started in March-April 2014, the bulk were taken up in November 2014. By March 2015, more than 500 houses had been completed and occupied by beneficiaries. Chief Minister had inaugurated a couple of big colonies in the relocation sites. More than 10,000 houses were at finishing stage and remaining at advance stages of construction when I left OSDMA and R&DM Department on 21 April 2015. All 162 new MCSs, except 5, after being quickly awarded for execution had recorded good progress. My target was to get all 162 new MCSs under NCRMP-II and houses under ODRP completed by December 2015. Executing agencies had reported completion of 19 MCSs and substantial progress in case of all others. 11 approach roads under NCRMP-II out of 100 had been fully completed and remaining 89 were expected to be completed within the next 3-6 months.

One of the most satisfying part of my work in OSDMA was implementation of 12 saline embankments which had been written off as non-implementable. Completion of 6 of them excluding the minor finishing works, and substantial progress in respect of the remaining 6 now left little scope for these vital projects being buried unattended. Cumulative estimated cost of these 12 projects involving 52 sluices and 73 gates had to be revised from about ₹ 160 crore to about ₹ 190 crore due to some modifications in alignments made concurrently during execution. These structures gave a sense of protection to 249 most-vulnerable coastal villages with a combined population of more than 1.75 lakh besides saving 67,840.44 hectares of agricultural land from salinity. By the way, before these massive embankments could be completed, farmers having adjoining land had started economic activities for pisciculture including prawn culture using the robust upcoming structures for storing sweet water on the one side and saline on the other facing the Bay of Bengal.

ACS-cum-Development Commissioner who held additional charge of H&UD Department did not wish to involve OSDMA in implementing the urban infrastructure component of ODRP. He went for more methodical planning for systematic implementation, with appointment of a bevy of consultants and creation of a Project Management Unit. But ACS Finance did not agree to create additional posts for the Unit. After finding substantial progress in implementing other components, H&UD Department finally called OSDMA for help in implementing it. Paper packaging and office rituals did not necessarily translate into the desired outcome. The World Bank team had started commenting adversely on lack of progress in the urban reconstruction component of Berhampur while showering appreciation for swift and quality implementation of all other components by OSDMA. In the meanwhile, ACS-cum-Development Commissioner left on Central Deputation and the situation remained unchanged. From my long experience in Odisha, I am convinced that it is not difficult to implement projects in the State in a time-bound manner if those at the helm of affairs mean business and officers in charge of projects like to take some risks with some sense of accountability. In my view, the time-frame of two years was enough to wind up ODRP after completing all sanctioned projects.

ODRP also envisaged providing training infrastructure through a State Institute of Disaster Management. Chief Minister laid its foundation stone when he visited to inaugurate the Revenue Officers' Training Institute. Since formal financial concurrence and administrative approval from Finance Department and office of Chief Minister respectively were not received in spite of reminders, the work could not start during my tenure. I read a news item after more than two years that this Institute was finally accorded these approvals! Senior officers in key positions are substantially responsible for such delays. More often than not, those who need to ensure timely execution of project without cost escalation or loss of opportunity are indeed the ones responsible for its contrary outcome.

After the devastation caused by Phailin in the coastal districts, about ₹ 200 crore were received in Chief Minister's Relief Fund (CMRF), the bulk from Central PSUs having major stakes in Odisha. Usually funds from CMRF are used for populist schemes outside the State Budget. Chief Secretary quietly advised me to submit a proposal for utilising these moneys for creating additional calamity-resistant infrastructure before thoughts of channelizing them elsewhere could cross Chief Minister's mind with General Elections due a few months later. Thus, in the meeting of the body on administration of CMRF headed by Chief Secretary, it was decided to go for construction of 36 additional MCSs and 220 multipurpose flood shelters in cyclone and flood-prone areas, which were vulnerable but had not been covered under NCRMP-I or II and other schemes in the past. This additionality would help meet both demand by public representatives and requirements of all 30 districts for multipurpose flood shelters.

Collectors were asked to identify specific sites within the compound or adjoining government plots of Elementary Schools as the proposed structures like MCSs could also be put to use as additional class room facilities and for cultural events by village communities on payment of nominal charges. The task of constructing additional flood/ cyclone shelters from CMRF in coastal districts was assigned to OSDMA engineers whereas in non-coastal districts, it was assigned to Rural Works Department. Usually, by the time projects are awarded considerable cost escalation takes place due to delays in completion of pre-construction processes. I did not like to repeat mistakes of the past and saw to it that every project for which funds had been provided was taken to the logical end within a specified time-frame. Since allocations sanctioned from CMRF for 220 new multi-purpose flood shelters and 36 cyclone shelters were routed through OSDMA, construction work was started in all cases within 3 months. Executants were given 12 to 15 months time for completion. Most of the new shelters were nearing completion at the time of my departure from OSDMA. Total number of cyclone shelters in place when I joined OSDMA was about 200, which had increased to more than 400 when I left. Besides, 163 cyclone shelters were at various stages of construction. Similarly, 109 multipurpose flood shelters had been completed and 202 were at various stages of construction. With capacity building infrastructure in place and under creation, the State could handle the worst type of natural calamities requiring evacuation of entire population of the most-vulnerable villages in future.

Cyclone shelters constructed in the immediate aftermath of Super Cyclone-1999 had suffered multiple damage as they did not meet quality standards nor quality monitoring during construction. There were no provisions for repair and maintenance except in respect of 65 cyclone shelters constructed by the Indian Red Cross Society. This agency maintained these centres for many years before handing them over to the respective village committees with a corpus fund of ₹ 10 lakh each, the interest of which could be utilized for repairs. OSDMA had generated a huge amount of interest money from allocations received under various schemes over a period of time. I took approval of the Governing Body for special repairs and maintenance of old cyclone shelters at an average cost of ₹ 2 lakh each through engineers of Rural Works Department before these structures went beyond repairs and were declared unsafe. Besides ₹ 5 lakh was provided for each new MCS, the interest accrued of which could be used for special repairs and maintenance in future.

Although I could not see completion with my gross eyes of all the projects taken up during my tenure in OSDMA in spite of working at break-neck speed, the projects having gathered momentum had been brought to a stage in implementation from where slippages were most unlikely. My principal task in the departments and organisations I had worked was to contribute towards institution building in addition to recharging employees of my offices and attached bodies. It saddens me to witness the administration increasingly working in an ad hoc and fire-fighting mode as though that is a daily reality. Hardly any attention is given to document the experiences gained in the past for strengthening institutional memory and to get wiser in handling crisis situations and challenges arising in future. It was shocking to find that what to speak of documenting to learn from experience, even inventories of procurements made had not been prepared after Super Cyclone-1999. Bucking this trend, just as I had documented the Ganjam floods, I ensured documentation of preparatory steps taken to deal with the very severe cyclone Phailin by OSDMA, immediate rescue and relief operations, and reconstruction and rehabilitation development works necessary to get the socio-economic fabric re-stitched in order to better withstand any future calamity. These were published in the form of a book. I also saw to it that Odisha did not lose out on its experiences with capacity building over 14 years in the aftermath of Super Cyclone-1999. These were researched out, documented and published for the benefit of posterity.

Close to Settling Satbhaya

Rehabilitation of natural calamity-affected villages in a sustainable sense rarely receives priority of the State Government in spite of some occasional noises. It pains me immensely to recall that 5 out of a group of 7 villages (Satbhaya group of villages) in today's Kendrapara district had been swallowed by the Bay of Bengal. But the State Governments which from time to time had been announcing its noble intention to relocate and rehabilitate those still facing threats in the remaining 2 villages of Satbhaya and Kanhupur, has done nothing about it. The surrounding sea level was actually higher than that of these villages located inside Bhitarkanika Wildlife Sanctuary. A naturally formed sand-dune between the roaring Bay of Bengal and these two villages was the only protection cover which saved them. Anyone visiting these villages would get scared after hearing the warning sounds of the sea.

Having heard about the tragic and simultaneously scary plight faced for decades by 670 families still inhabiting these villages, I visited them with District Collector, DFO and other key administrative functionaries. During my three-hour long meeting with the villagers, they pleaded to be rescued and rehabilitated in the unsurveyed village called Bagpatia about 15 km away. This village had been identified in past for their resettlement. I visited the proposed site with the field officers. The low-lying unsurveyed area of Bagpatia village stood largely encroached including by some of those who had migrated from the 5 villages which had disappeared earlier. After my multiple meetings, one was held at the level of R&DM Minister when amongst others by ACS Forest & Environment, Principal Chief Conservator of Wildlife, Collector and Sub-Collector of Kendrapara, Tahasildar Rajnagar, etc, were present. It was decided to provide 0.10 acre of homestead land in Bagpatia to each eligible family of the 2 villages in addition to providing infrastructure like roads, drinking water facilities, power supply, school, Anganwadi Centre, community centre, MCS, etc. It was resolved to develop the site, the cost of which as estimated by Engineer-in-Chief of RD Department was about ₹ 3 crore. Steps were taken to complete the survey and settlement operations which had been discontinued at draft publication stage about a decade back, taking into account the allotment of house sites in favour of families to be relocated. In order to quell resistance from encroachers, it was agreed that they would be provided one acre land each if found eligible according to extant law. In the meeting held on 7 February 2014 at my level, Kendrapara Collector was desired to submit an action plan by end-May 2014 with estimates for developing the site including sand and earth filling of low-lying areas, approach road and other amenities which could not be provided under ongoing flagship programmes.

The rehabilitation plan prepared by district administration included commitment of Panchayat Raj Department to fund 670 houses under IAY, a drinking water supply project by RWSS Department involving sinking of deep bore well with provision for overhead tank, village electrification, etc. ₹ 3 crore was sanctioned from CMRF towards site development including an approach road inside Bagpatia village. OSDMA approved a new MCS and awarded the work quickly. School and Mass Education (S&ME) Department agreed to release funds for a new school building. Rajkanika BDO had already taken up construction of a community centre to meet the demand of neighbourhood villages and in anticipation of creation of a new colony.

The plan furnished by district administration was finally approved with some modifications in accordance with the wishes of local elected representatives to make the task of encroachment eviction easier. Soon after monsoon retreated, site development and plotted development works on the ground started. By end-March 2015, road formation and plotted development had progressed substantially. Land allottees were asked to go ahead with construction of houses for which financial assistance had been made available under IAY. It was planned to have a small pisciculture tank behind each house over an area of 4 decimal of land. Earth excavated for the tank could be used to raise the plinth of houses under construction. When work on raising the level of the approach road using funds from CMRF was in full swing, with about 100 tractors and other heavy mechanized devices engaged for development of site, formation of roads and other community infrastructure, I had to leave R&DM Department which shattered my mission of addressing this long-standing legacy issue by completing the rehabilitation of families of Satbhaya and Kanhupur villages in the new relocation site at Bagpatia by December 2015. I had a foreboding that in this case too the work would remain unattended in the years to come and history would continue to repeat itself.

The top leaderships in Government remain happy by providing and publicising one-time relief for accidents. Ex-gratia payment for loss of life due to disasters is now being demanded as an entitlement. None likes to delve into the root causes and address them in a sustained manner. Government work and accountability do not seem to be organically tied up. Public functionaries rather than being courageous leaders, are pliant followers. Officials at the cutting edge of administration are found spending their time in implementing entitlement-based relief by relegating their substantive original works to the background. Conventional revenue administration is no longer considered important. Tahasildars and RIs remain engaged in relief-related works since crop losses, etc. are assessed based on land-holding and RoRs. Many field officials having discounted their morality are found appropriating relief funds released for disbursement for crop losses in connivance with absentee landlords and otherwise.

* * * *

13

KBK Districts: Superior Endowments, Conspicuous Deficits

After my elevation to the Apex Scale along with other batch mates, I was posted as Chief Administrator, KBK Districts on 1 July 2013. Now designated as ACS, I continued to remain in additional charge of R&DM Department, and as MD, OSDMA. The new post has an interesting history.

The undivided districts of Kalahandi, Balangir and Koraput (KBK) had been suffering from wide and conspicuous development deficits. The region used to receive adverse publicity at national and global fora since the late 1980s. Serving as Prime Ministers Rajiv Gandhi and P.V. Narasimha Rao had paid visits to this region when a political agitation led by a young dalit leader of Kalahandi, Bhakta Charan Das, was aggressively highlighting its backwardness, alleged sale of children by families in distress, and incidents of malnutrition and so-called starvation deaths. Ironically, although political agitation was essentially against the ruling Congress Party in the State, the dalit leader who came from the principal opposition party at that time, himself migrated to the party he opposed, a few years later. This is symptomatic of how issues like poverty and malnutrition are leveraged for political gains by many. Nevertheless, some targeted programmes for mitigating development deficits of KBK Districts with Central Government interventions were started when the Congress Governments headed by Rajiv Gandhi and P.V. Narasimha Rao were in power at the Centre.

The first initiative for "Area Development and Poverty Termination" launched in select blocks of Kalahandi and Koraput in late 1980s, could not take off in a visible way due to financial and other constraints. The first resolution issued by Revenue and Excise Department on 16 April 1993 established a Steering Committee on Special Projects to develop and implement a basket of plans and programmes by Government agencies in 6 districts of Balangir, Kalahandi, Koraput, Malkangiri, Nabarangpur and Rayagada. It envisaged that the Special Project would be headed by a senior officer designated as Administrator, Special Project, with headquarters at Bhawanipatna (Kalahandi). The Administrator would coordinate the activities of various governmental agencies across agriculture, cooperation, irrigation, health and family welfare, revenue relief, school and mass education, tribal welfare and others. The Administrator had delegated powers to call for information, reports and returns from district level officers of line departments whenever considered necessary for effective supervision and monitoring of programmes. At this stage, GA Department created an ex-cadre post equivalent in status and responsibility to the post of RDC as provided in IAS cadre. Central funds were allocated for new schemes included in Long Term Action Plan (LTAP) for KBK Districts in addition to other flagship programmes. Later developments included addition of Sonepur and Nuapada districts which came into being with bifurcation of Balangir and Kalahandi. Headquarters of Administrator, Special Project were shifted to Sunabeda (Koraput) on 7 July 1994. State's Planning & Coordination Department now became nodal department for the Special Project. Sunabeda office of Administrator, Special Project was suddenly closed down on 4 May 1997. All records and assets were transferred to office of Collector, Koraput for no known reasons.

After a hiatus of three years, vide Resolution dated 14 March 2000, a Special Area Development Project was set up with a view to ensuring effective implementation of Revised Long-Term Action Plan (RLTAP) for all 8 KBK Districts, popularly known as "KBK Project". Headquarters of KBK Project were fixed at Koraput. It was now to be headed in proper hierarchy by an officer designated as Deputy Chief Administrator at Koraput as project head. Another post in the cadre schedule of IAS was created, designated as Chief Administrator, in Apex Grade with headquarters at Bhubaneswar. Supervisory powers delegated to the Chief Administrator were strengthened with other powers, which included recording remarks in confidential character rolls (CCRs) of officers up to the rank of heads of departments concerned with programmes of KBK Districts. He was also assigned responsibility for convening meetings of two State and Project Level Committees. The set up was further strengthened on 25 August 2000 by providing for a State Level Committee headed by Chief Minister with Chief Administrator, Special Area Development, and Special Chief Secretary to Government as its convener to review the implementation of RLTAP in KBK Districts.

Office of Chief Administrator, KBK Districts was made functional in Koraput with effect from 8 February 2001. As per a revised notification dated 19 July 2001, Chief Administrator was allowed to avail rent-free accommodation at Koraput for his residence. RDCs of Southern and Northern Divisions were designated as Deputy Chief Administrators for the districts under their jurisdiction from 27 February 2003 onwards. At substantive level too, Planning & Coordination Department through its Resolution dated 28 September 2006 called for increasing efforts to maintain the momentum gathered under RLTAP for upscaling public investments in KBK region. Each State department was mandated to allocate at least 30 percent of their Plan funds, including funds received by them under Central flagship programmes, to KBK Districts. Biju KBK Plan was added to the basket of schemes, which envisaged special allocation of ₹ 120 crore per year for implementing State and district sector programmes with provision of ₹ 1 crore per block for State sector schemes and ₹ 0.50 crore per block for district sector schemes annually. Guidelines were issued for integration of Biju KBK Plan with RLTAP. Apart from these three sources of funds, sizeable allocations were also received as flexi funds by Collectors under BRGF and Integrated Action Plan (IAP) to bridge the historical development deficit, and critical gaps in order to supplement the efforts for containing the deep inroads of insurgency of left-wing extremism. Improvements due to targeted schemes and additional allocations to KBK Districts became visible to some extent despite State Government not paying the desired attention to the required logistics, including posting of manpower, nor to compliances with resolutions passed for empowering the Chief Administrator, KBK Districts.

Although duties and responsibilities already cast on me as ACS, R&DM Department and MD, OSDMA were quite onerous, I thoroughly enjoyed this new assignment as it gave me unprecedented opportunities to contribute to securing improvements in these backward districts by passionately ensuring effective implementation of ongoing programmes of various line departments and specially targeted schemes. Bucking the practices of my predecessors who were wary of visiting these areas, I made it a point to spend at least 7 days on an average every month in KBK Districts. I designed and circulated formats for submission of monthly progress reports for every infrastructure project under implementation costing ₹ 10 lakh or above. Two Data Entry Operators sitting idle in KBK Project Office, duly helped by NIC's unit at Koraput which was conveniently located in the same building, assisted in designing and developing a simple software for monthly monitoring of physical targets and achievements supplemented by visual status reports. Planning Sections in offices of District Collectors in KBK Districts were made accountable for collecting the monthly progress reports from all line departments in the prescribed formats. There was thus no need to submit monthly progress reports in reams of papers. Electronic mode of transmission using internet connectivity was the only mode of communication needed to be followed mandatorily by line departments.

Collectors of KBK Districts, most of whom were direct recruit young officers, were happy to help me and I too enjoyed their company during field visits for spot decisions to resolve issues impeding planned progress. While I spent the day starting early morning at 6.00 a.m. up to about 3.00 p.m. in field visits, review meetings were held at district level at 4.00 p.m. which went up to 10.00 p.m. on most occasions. In review meetings, district heads of line departments made presentations on projects under implementation bringing out the difficulties and challenges faced in achieving monthly targets. Collective agreement on targets to be set for succeeding months as well as cumulatively across the project right till its conclusion. The presentations were placed on KBK website alongside my detailed review notes which I drafted personally, indicating milestones to be achieved during the next month. Extract of reviews along with my tour notes were transmitted to the heads of line Departments and Secretaries to the Government for interventions wherever required.

KBK Administration: A Curtain Raiser

In spite of being at the helm of district administration, Collectors were seldom found to be familiar with developmental plans and programmes of line departments other than that of Panchayat Raj, Women and Child Welfare and Food Supplies & Consumer Welfare, what to speak to presenting critical reviews and analyses for reform. Occasionally, they reviewed the RLTAP component which was implemented through Blocks. Senior officers heading the line Departments were also reactionary in their approach, and brought matters to notice only when they faced problems requiring intervention of district administration. Most of the time, Collectors were not even informed by district heads of line departments about their movements within or outside districts. Young and inexperienced officers holding posts of Collector after 4 years of service were also not able to assert themselves nor command the respect of departmental officers with experience of 25 to 30 years under their belt in their specialized field. Collectors mostly reviewed programme implementation through BDOs/ DRDAs.

My detailed reviews of plans and programmes, and inspection of ongoing projects in the presence of Collectors of KBK Districts was a 'win-win' situation for all concerned. Collectors became conversant with schemes implemented by line departments and started contributing to their implementation proactively in various ways. Thus, their support was no longer limited to law and order problems or dealing with occasional threats faced by district departmental heads responsible for infrastructure development. I issued instructions to departmental officers not to leave their districts without prior permission from District Collectors and informing me. The tendency among majority of officers in KBK Districts was to seek escape from their places of posting at slightest opportunities.

Officers of Works, Rural Works, Water Resources, Public Health Engineering, RWSS, etc., faced problems across the wide ambit of projects like construction of roads, bridges, buildings, irrigation, and providing drinking water on account of land disputes, forest clearances, issues of minor forest produce, difficulties in finding suitable sites for infrastructure projects, lack of police support when required, restrictions on blasting stones/rocks and sand-mining. Here, none other than District Collector could help them. Another problem was acute shortage of construction materials as contractors operating stone quarries on lease from R&DM Department showed a marked proclivity for offering their supplies to more profitable projects in neighbouring Andhra Pradesh and Chhattisgarh. This generally led to cost escalation and delays due to inadequate, untimely and costly supplies of such materials for implementation of infrastructure projects by local executing agencies in KBK Districts. When these were brought to my notice during project inspections and review meetings, Districts Collectors were usually caught unawares as they had never been taken into confidence as partners in these projects. Monthly participative reviews also helped settle difficulties faced by district heads of line departments in no time once these came to the notice of head of District Administration.

Stay in KBK Districts for work, and most certainly for residence, hardly offered adequate creature comforts to government functionaries. Their families could seldom support living away from the arc lights of bigger towns. These limitations, which were drawbacks to many, effectively discouraged them from accepting assignments here. In most of the districts, vacancies of doctors at any given point of time exceeded 50 percent. Situation in other departments responsible for implementation of important flagship schemes and land administration was equally bad. During my first visit to Malkangiri, I found that 3 out of 7 Blocks were without a regular BDO. Two of the four BDOs in position had vigilance cases and were facing major penalty proceedings. None of the PHCs had a medical officer and vacancies of doctors in Malkangiri were 70 percent of sanctioned posts. A doctor against whom local people were found protesting for negligence and incompetence had been continuing in district headquarters' hospital for nearly 25 years! An Executive Engineer of Rural Works Department was drawing his salary from the district while working in the office of Engineer-in-Chief at Bhubaneswar. All Junior Engineers of Works Department/Road & Building Department had been deployed to offices of Chief Engineers in Bhubaneswar, to the complete neglect of ongoing projects in the district. More than a hundred rural roads under PMGSY were either abandoned or had been reflected as incomplete for years. About 30-35 percent of estimated costs of these roads had been spent in earthwork in the name of road formations. During my inspection, I found no trace of any earthwork except some intermittent cross drainage structures using hume pipes.

The situation was more or less similar in other KBK Districts. Left Wing Extremism was the usual bogey cited for not completing all weather rural roads. In reality, contractors had vanished after being paid for labour-intensive earthwork and material-intensive components did not have enough margins to continue with these works. Departments responsible for development of infrastructure projects vital for overall development of KBK Districts seemed hardly bothered about the ultimate outcome. Many of them thought that posting by State Government to KBK Districts was punishment in itself and there could hardly be any other punishment or retribution for such apathy and negligence which could be meted out to them beyond! Secretaries or Heads of Department rarely toured these districts although State Government Circulars, reiterated periodically, provided for a head of department to tour districts for a total of at least 10 days every month. Mismatch between outlays and outcomes was difficult to miss during field visits. Real issues confronting KBK Districts hardly received serious attention of State Government and its implementing agencies.

There were structural problems which raised serious questions about the sincerity of State Government with regard to effectiveness of office of Chief Administrator, KBK Districts, from the very beginning. Musical chairs played out historically with location of office of Chief Administrator has been drawn out above. Relocation from Bhawanipatna without offering any rationale or serving any public purpose, seemed to have enabled the Administrator to admit his school-going kids in the Delhi Public School at Sunabeda, from where also it was finally closed down. There were many contradictions and mismatches in establishing offices of Special Area Development Project at Bhubaneswar as well as at Koraput. While State Government resolution dated 14 March 2000 stated in one paragraph that its headquarters would be at Koraput, in another it mentioned that Chief Administrator would have headquarters at Bhubaneswar. In the Order dated 19 July 2001, Chief Administrator was required to visit KBK Districts at least 7 days a month, but was allowed rent-free quarters at Koraput as though he was to station himself there. Except Dr. K.J.S. Chatrath, who stayed in Koraput for a few months, other KBK Chief Administrators had only sparingly visited KBK Districts. Three of my immediate predecessors had not visited KBK Districts even once.

Deputy Chief Administrator, head of Project Office at Koraput, was required to tour KBK Districts at least 10 days a month, had neither accommodation at Koraput nor exclusive transport to function effectively. Except one officer, whose presence was considered inconvenient at Bhubaneswar and was posted as Deputy Chief Administrator for about a year, none was posted there with independent charge. RDCs of Southern and Northern Divisions stood only notionally notified as Deputy Chief Administrators. Chief and Deputy Chief Administrators were required to submit their tour and review notes to Government, which happened rarely. Though I invariably submitted detailed tour notes within a few days of each tour, my recommendations for actions needed to be taken by departmental heads or Secretaries, unless specifically pursued by me, were perhaps even rarely read by recipients. State Level Committee, chaired by Chief Minister, never met to review RLTAP in KBK Districts. Provision for co-ordination through Project Level Committee chaired by Chief Secretary, had also remained on paper only.

The main office of Chief Administrator in State Capital had not been provided with bare essentials in terms office space and manpower. Probably due to the circumstances of KBK Chief Administrator holding additional charge of Member, Board of Revenue at some point, one room in his camp office at Bhubaneswar had been provided to function as office of KBK Chief Administrator. The room stood partitioned for sharing space with personal staff. Other than a Private Secretary and a Group-D employee, there was no administrative support in Bhubaneswar. My immediate predecessor had recalled the office vehicle along with driver and two Group-D employees from Project Office at Koraput, mainly for taking care of his residential needs at Bhubaneswar. Immediately after succeeding him, I restored the driver along with vehicle, and both Group-D staff to the Koraput office. In the KBK Project Office at Koraput, 7 out of 17 sanctioned posts including that of Deputy Chief Administrator were lying vacant. The local Tahasildar was officiating additionally as 'Drawing & Disbursing' authority.

Over nearly two decades of their notification, powers delegated to KBK Chief Administrator had never materialized. There was no evidence of re*cording remarks by any Chief Administrator in CCRs of officers up to the rank of Heads of Department. This also signalled that Departments had failed to establish a specificity of work allocation and chain of command which could have given a special focus to KBK projects in reality. Indeed, nothing existed on ground to suggest seriousness let alone consistency in planning, implementing and reviewing RLTAP in accordance with resolutions, notifications and orders issued by State Government from time to time. The post, however, did benefit some senior officers as the number of posts in Apex Grade in IAS cadre in Odisha had increased by one third after creating this post!

Notwithstanding such structural and logistics issues, I was of the view that implementation of plans and programmes could be improved substantially if implementing agencies were held accountable and essential support required by them was made available in time. Majority of government functionaries being habitual fence-sitters, there are just a few who either work hard temperamentally or indulge in corrupt practices whenever opportunity arrives. In my experience, effective supervision and a time-bound approach to implementing projects energizes the vast majority of fence-sitters and dedicated ones start emerging as leaders and role models. This process also marginalizes the corrupt ones and they have no option but to join and form part of the mainstream. It would not defy credibility to go so far as to say that indifference and inaction on the part of public servants in implementing projects can be worse than corrupt practices that may take place provided the projects are implemented vigorously to serve their objectives. It is not necessary for the supervisory officer to wield his supervisory power to write remarks in CCRs of those in charge of implementing projects. At least, I did not find the need to indulge in such petty feudalism in the field of development administration. Nor did my personal experiences in KBK Districts call for interventions by the so-called committees to carry out reviews for namesake or to bother a coordination mechanism from which nothing more might be expected other than fleetingly skimming the surface.

Critical Efforts: Intensity for Steady Transformation in KBK Districts

My first visit to KBK Project Office and Districts exposed me to the sclerosis of denial and delay that had set in. Widening of the road from Rayagada to Koraput and further from Koraput to Malkangiri under the "Ranchi-Vijayawada Corridor" had been approved way back in 2007 by Central Government and funds had been sanctioned in part for several stretches. After this State Highway was notified as National Highway, the State Works Department had stopped its maintenance. As a result, the normal road distance of 2 hours from Rayagada to Koraput took me more than 3 hours. The condition of road from Koraput to Malkangiri was much worse and the time it took me to reach Malkangiri was 5 hours. The actual travel time earlier used to be just over two hours. Successive floods and heavy rains had damaged the road that was not only the lifeline of Malkangiri district but was also vital for movement of Central Paramilitary Forces deployed there for anti-Naxal operations. Widening of road from Koraput to Jeypore had been abandoned after some initial activities due to a dispute with contractor. Public at large, transporters association and elected representatives had been making representations for years for interventions by State Government, but to no avail. On my first visit, I was mobbed by local gentry, traders, transporters and public representatives with their demand for repair of this most vital road majoring high on their list. I endorsed their demand, which was genuine and most legitimate, and requested for a few months' time to improve the condition. It was a rainy season and, thus, difficult to undertake major repairs even if resources were made available.

Another problem I noticed was that a contractor who had been assigned stretches for widening of this Corridor had stopped getting administrative and technical support from engineers of State Works Department. He had thus left portions of the road assigned to him incomplete. Perceived to be close to Pyari Mohan Mahapatra, who prior to May 2012, had virtually controlled State Administration by remote. Also considered not long ago to be a blue-eyed boy of Works Department, he had been assigned about 50 percent of major road works in southern division including a new bridge over river Bansadhara which connected the tribal districts of Rayagada, Koraput, Malkangiri and Nabarangpur with the rest of the State. Work on this major bridge had also stopped due to disputes between the Works Department and the contractor.

I called a meeting of senior engineers of Works Department including those in charge of National Highways in the State, and also contractors of major road projects. It was decided that contractors would repair portions of roads awarded to them, but special repairs and maintenance of remaining roads would be done by State Works Department. I invited Chief Engineer and Secretary Works Department to visit Malkangiri and Koraput in order to have a taste of negligence on their part by physically walking through the dilapidated roads, riddled with pot-holes as if thoroughly carpet-bombed. Disturbed by sheer administrative apathy that engulfed these poor districts, I could not prevent myself from issuing a stern warning to them that provisions of ST&SC (Prevention of Atrocities) Act could be invoked against senior officers and contractors if they continued to neglect their responsibilities. Works Department sought 4 months' time for carrying out special repairs of Koraput-Malkangiri road. The contractor promised to complete abandoned sections provided Forest & Environment Department allowed widening work and R&DM Department permitted extraction of construction materials. I assured contractors and Executive Engineers that problems in relation to construction materials would be addressed to their satisfaction by issuing enabling instructions to Tahasildars and Collectors within a week and desired that they too should indicate timelines and milestones in monthly progress reports accordingly. I issued instructions instantly to Collectors that on receipt of recommendations of Executive Engineers, contractors should be allowed to lift stones, sand and morrum on payment of standard rates till regular leases were granted so that execution of infrastructure projects did not suffer any longer on this count in KBK Districts.

In a separate meeting with DFOs, I asked them to suggest the ways and means to execute vital road projects visualizing as if they themselves were executants. I pointed out the fact that no new roads were being taken up and there was no question of deliberate felling of trees. I was happy to be informed by them that they too wanted expeditious widening of roads. They suggested that road widening works involving cutting of Ghats and blasting of rocks at several places should be done as fast as possible, and contractors should provide robust retaining walls to prevent landslides. It was vital to avoid controversies, which could be created by some activists alleging violations of environmental norms. I asked senior engineers and contractors to avail of this window of opportunity on war footing. Immediately after returning to Bhubaneswar, I obtained Government orders for relaxation with regard to auctioning of sairat sources in KBK Districts to facilitate lease of stone quarries, sand mining, etc. Abandoned works were resumed. Incomplete roads were completed as per mutually agreed programme. My first visit to KBK Project Office and adjoining districts became quite productive.

Special repairs of the road from Jeypore to Malkangiri, which had transformed itself beyond recognition at several places due to heavy damages by floods and incessant rains, were monitored by me personally on a fortnightly basis. Within less than six months, special repairs were completed. All concerned, including the Bus Owners Associations of Malkangiri and Koraput districts, conveyed special gratitude for the work. When it had taken me nearly five hours to reach Malkangiri from Koraput on my first visit, the time taken after five months was progressively reduced to a mere two-and-a-half hours.

Work on Koraput-Jeypore section of National Highway, which stood abandoned, was resumed and completed within six months, thereby reducing the travel time from more than one hour to less than 30 minutes! National Highway widening work from Jeypore to Nabarangpur had been neglected for years and included a new bridge between Boipariguda and Nabarangpur. It warranted a heavy hand to handle the contractor who was not amenable to persuasive words or warnings. On my advice, Nabarangpur District Collector who had ensured timely availability of construction materials by arresting their diversions to neighbouring States earlier, initiated action against him under preventive sections of Cr.P.C. for causing public nuisance resulting in a law and order situation. The contractor fell in line and work which was languishing for years got speeded up and completed quickly.

In Malkangiri district, Union Road Transport Ministry had sanctioned 9 road projects totalling about 300 km as part of a package to deal with Left Wing Extremism which stood awarded to three contractors based in Hyderabad and Pune. Although completion dates were about to expire, 4 roads had not even been started and the remaining 5 were unable to progress due to disputes between Executive Engineer and contractors, besides non-availability of construction materials. It was reported that Executive Engineer, National Highway had been continuously modifying the scope and specifications of projects and was not making available the designs for additional cross drainage structures suggested by him. This was found to be true after reality checks. Senior district police officials were also found denying permission for use of explosives for blasting to extract the construction materials. They apprehended that explosives might reach Naxal hands operating in the district and could be used for violent activities leading to casualties and demoralization of police and Central Paramilitary forces. Forest officials too were not granting permission for extraction of construction materials. These problems faced by the contractors were found to be genuine.

I had a closed-door meeting with District Collector, SP and DFO. It was agreed that contractors would be allowed to lift construction materials on payment of required fee on due certification by Executive Engineer with immediate effect and DFO would facilitate permission for stone quarries following the guidelines issued by Union Ministry of Environment & Forest. SP assured that no action would be taken against contractors for use of explosives on the strength of valid licenses. He also assured to dispose of applications pending in his office for grant of further explosive licenses by DM. The misunderstanding between Executive Engineer for National Highway and contractors on revised designs and specifications of structural works on roads having been sorted out, all three big contractors agreed to resume construction activities, including on 5 roads which had not even been started.

From Malkangiri, I proceeded to Kalahandi after a day long visit followed by another review meeting with district level officers in Nabarangpur. I was shocked to receive a message from Pune-based contractor that his 4 workers engaged in blasting in connection with road construction had been arrested by Malkangiri police and e xplosives seized! I suspected that Malkangiri SP had not duly passed on the decision to allow explosives fo r blasting onto lower level functionaries. My credibility as KBK Chief Administrator and resumed road construc tion were both at stake. I immediately spoke to DM and SP who were not aware of the arrests. I also spoke to Home Secretary and DG Police explaining that the contractor had only followed my instructions. Within 2 days , those arrested were released on bail and no further harassments was faced by contractor's workers therea fter. My quick intervention restored the confidence in KBK administration among other contractors too. It resulted in completion of all 4 incomplete roads in next six months at a speed rarely seen in public projects. I t was a matter of great satisfaction that 3 out of 5 remaining roads were also completed before I demitted office. While the road leading to Gurupriya Bridge was at an advanced stage of construction, the ninth one was faci ng stiff resistance from Naxal groups operating on Chhattisgarh side. About 25 km out of total 50 km of this road could only progress substantially.

Chief Secretary J.K. Mahapatra had personally ensured Government approval for construction of a bridge over Chitrakonda reservoir at Gurupriya for the third time, lucky as some would say. Efforts made twice in past had been aborted due to insurgency. It would not have been possible to transport heavy equipment without a robust road going right up to bridge construction site. A Kolkata-based firm had been awarded the contract for the bridge. But now, construction of road, which had not been started even two years after being awarded, helped the executant firm to mobilize its men and materials on the site of the bridge. Fortunately, a unit of BSF camped at the site to provide round-the-clock security support to this firm mitigated threats from Maoists. I reviewed the progress of work in terms of monthly milestones which had been mutually agreed. As always, the problems of delays and lags by Design Division of State Works Department in approving designs had to be addressed. Regular follow ups by me helped the firm for as long as I was in charge of KBK administration and the work progressed in accordance with prescribed time-schedule. I heaved a sigh of real relief when I saw a news item a few months back that Gurupriya bridge finally got completed even though it was more than two years after its due date. For sure, officers of the nodal Department would have been responsible for bulk of the delay and cost escalation. Work slowed down drastically after my departure from KBK Project in any case. Apathy and faint-hearted approach of State leadership also contributes to such delays. I was once conveyed instructions of Chief Minister by Chief Secretary on phone to cut short my visit when I was on a tour to Chitrakonda, which was considered to be a hotbed of Naxal groups. It was informed that intelligence agencies of the State and Central Governments had sent inputs about heightened risks in case I stayed in that area any longer or ventured beyond the area I was then in. Government at the highest level appeared more concerned about the impact of any adverse publicity and opted to convey a timid approach when the need of the hour was an aggressive and no holds barred pursuit of economic development and social welfare through rigorous implementation of the projects and schemes in Naxal-affected areas.

Construction of bridge over Bansadhara river at Ramnaguda (Rayagada) was a classic case of how a friendly relationship with a contractor turned hostile suddenly. Construction activities had stopped on this critically-important bridge without which road connectivity of Rayagada, Koraput, Nabarangpur and Malkangiri districts from divisional headquarters at Berhampur was impossible during rainy season. The bridge constructed on Bansadhara after 1981 flood washed away the old bridge, had again collapsed in less than 15 years of its construction. Ramnaguda which had developed as a vibrant trade and business centre in Rayagada district wore a deserted look after the bridge was washed away for the second time. The contractor, who was a favourite of Works Department at one time due to his perceived proximity with Pyari Mohan Mahapatra, could neither be removed nor taken on board to ensure completion of the bridge. Villagers suffering due to abnormal delays were on the war path and the contractor appeared mortally afraid of them. He avoided site visits and after executing about 25 percent work, discontinued the rest. The timeline for completion had long since expired.

I was thus hardly surprised to face a hostile crowd of hundreds of villagers who had assembled to ventilate their grievances against the contractor and Works Department's local officers when I first visited the site. By chance the contractor met me in the train when I was travelling to Koraput second time. He narrated his version, which was quite different from what had been conveyed by Secretary and Chief Engineer of Works Department in the review meetings held by Chief Minister. The contractor attributed the delay to faulty design of the bridge given to him in the beginning, besides land disputes on a portion of approach road. He asserted that when these problems were conveyed to Works Department, he had been asked to wait for the revised design. He promised that if revised design was supplied to him with necessary technical guidance and land for approach road was made available, the bridge could be completed within one year. After discussing it with Executive Engineer, Works Department at Rayagada, I found that the contractor's version was substantially correct. Chief Engineer and Secretary, Works Department thus came across as being more concerned about political fall-out of continuing with the contractor who had about a dozen of major road projects awarded to him in KBK Districts, all of which were thus in utterly avoidable limbo! I advised Chief Engineer and Works Secretary not to get constrained by extraneous considerations and having awarded the projects, it would be better to get them completed as early as possible. Local people who were agitating volunteered to provide their land for the approach road free of cost even without it being acquired. They had already suffered sufficiently. It was a pity that people in KBK Districts did not have a powerful voice, as did those in coastal districts who could make themselves heard loud in the corridors of power at Bhubaneswar.

It was easier to execute projects in KBK Districts than elsewhere in the State as construction materials and labour were easily available and incidents of extortion, barring by some active Naxal groups in hinterlands, were rare. The contractor had suffered when extremist groups destroyed one of his plants along with machines on Koraput-Rayagada road. He did not seek intervention by police or paramilitary forces, as according to him such interventions would prove costlier. He was confident of managing these groups through other means and only wanted administrative support for construction materials and timely technical supervision including supply of designs by Works Department. Ultimately, the design of Bansadhara Bridge and estimate were revised. Number of piles increased to 288 from 144; revised estimated cost came to ₹ 50 crore against original of about ₹ 25 crore. I had wanted contractor and local Executive Engineer, Works Department to remain present on site during my next visit to sort out land problems with villagers. No steps had been taken for land acquisition for the approach road so far. After initial agitation, villagers calmed down and agreed to donate their land if construction was resumed with seriousness. The executant agreed to engage heavier machines including more cranes with required manpower and requested for exclusive services of a competent engineer to guide and supervise construction work without interruption. On my request, Works Secretary posted one of his best Junior Engineers exclusively for this project. The work not only got resumed quickly but also progressed with pace. It gave me a great sense of satisfaction that the bridge had substantially progressed when I demitted charge of KBK administration. It got completed a few months later.

In my capacity as ACS, R&DM Department, I had taken Government orders to permit the departments to purchase private land up to 25 acres in any village for public projects and waived stamp duty and registration charges for such purchases. This helped shorten the time for procuring land by direct purchase in implementing linear projects requiring limited land. None of my predecessors Administrator had considered it worthwhile to give attention to infrastructure projects and other programmes of line departments. Those of them visiting KBK Districts occasionally remained confined to reviewing implementation of RLTAP for which the KBK Project had primarily been conceived. I looked at development of KBK Districts holistically and line departments at State level were pleased to find things moving due to my interventions. I did not require controlling powers over line departments to make things happen nor did I need to exercise the stick through adverse entries in CCRs of senior officers working in KBK Districts or at State level.

Execution of other Infrastructure Projects

Works Department was responsible for constructing office and residential buildings of departments in urban areas besides widening State and National Highways. Similar works in rural areas were executed by Rural Works Department. Progress in widening State and National Highways and PMGSY roads was expedited. In PMGSY alone, about 1,000 roads were completed during two years of my tenure as KBK Chief Administrator. The road from Bhawanipatna to Khariar which was in a terrible condition was widened speedily that halved travel time from 3-4 hours. The distance of about 90 km from Malkangiri to Motu, which took over 3 hours through insurgency-affected areas at the time of my first visit, could be negotiated in less than half that time when road widening and improvement work was completed about a year later.

It was indeed painful to find that more than 100 bridges which were crucial for all weather connectivity on major district roads and PMGSY roads had been lying incomplete for many years primarily due to sheer negligence of Rural Works Department. Works Department engineers were not lagging far behind in exhibiting similar negligence in constructing bridges on State Highways. Meticulous monitoring and reviews resulted in completion of all bridges except one in Nabarangpur over Indrawati, another in Balangir over Tel and the third in Kalahandi over Hathi. In all three cases, contractors were departmental high favourites from coastal districts but low on capabilities. Executing agencies pleaded for another six months to one year to complete these bridges. In one case, the contractor had to be changed.

Government Engineering College and its hostel buildings, Government Agriculture College, staff quarters and hostel building, ITI buildings, etc., in Bhawanipatna, headquarters of Kalahandi, designed to meet a critical institutional deficit had been left incomplete with poor quality construction although full funds had been made available for these signature projects, well packaged and publicised. Due dates of completion had expired years back. Concerns of teachers and students including girl students who thus suffered in multiple ways did not prick the conscience of engineers concerned. State Government had sanctioned a number of Industrial Training Institutes at Block level in KBK Districts and a few Training Centres for paramedics and nursing. Large sums of funds received for upgrading hospitals and doctors' quarters at district, sub-division and PHC/CHC levels under National Rural Health Mission had remained unutilised for years. There was no coordination among departments of technical education, H&FW, and Executive Engineers of Works and Rural Works. I succeeded in bringing all stakeholders under one roof to discuss and sort out inter-departmental missing links and drive a large number of neglected projects on the fast lane. Collectors of KBK Districts earlier unaware or neutral regarding infrastructure projects now became proactive and thus made a huge difference in facilitating quicker implementation. All these projects in terms of physical infrastructure were either completed or brought to finishing stage within two years of my tenure using the same official machinery.

A large number of works had not even been started citing that sites for construction had not been demarcated and handed over. Truly, the left and right hands of Government worked without co-ordination and control! Construction of new Collectorate buildings in Malkangiri, Sonepur, Nuapada and staff quarters in district headquarters did not receive desired attention of respective Collectors nor of Works Department. It was distressing to find that one of the Executive Engineers was not bothered even to speed up and complete construction of office building for his own Superintending Engineer. Collectors were unaware of allocations received by Executive Engineers who felt more comfortable exploiting their ignorance.

Purposefully, I started reviewing the works of line Departments in the presence of Collectors and district heads of these departments. The most effective tool to extract work from public functionaries is holding them accountable by catching out their inactions and negligence of duties in projects to be implemented by them. Reviews and field visits offered the best platform to also address inter-departmental issues including selection and handing over of sites in time. Confrontation or connivance between contractors and engineers of departments given lack of coordination with district administration was the main cause for communication infrastructure remaining unattended for a long time. Delay in implementing infrastructure projects by Works or Rural Works departments was naturally resented by public in many ways including by filing allegation petitions against some officials.

The overall socio-economic backwardness of KBK Districts could be attributed in large part to a very poor road communication network. Without proper roads and non-availability of rented accommodation in remote villages, public servants working in health, education, social welfare, drinking water supply, and other critical and welfare sectors fail in their effective delivery of public services. Resultantly, teachers, health workers, agriculture extension functionaries, and other public services delivery agents avoid visiting villages for implementing schemes. PDS, despite being highly subsidized, is seen to suffer hugely as actual charges for transportation and storage of essential commodities became way higher in KBK Districts than elsewhere. Shortage of technical manpower was definitely an issue but it was more worrisome that officers up to the level of Executive Engineer had been deputed elsewhere by their respective HODs or were enabled to remain absent from their duties in the assigned district. The larger tragedy was persistence of this lacunae-riddled public service despite plentiful funds available for construction of road networks, including bridges, and culverts, under PMGSY, additional SCA, RLTAP, BRGF, and IAP. Connectivity in rural areas remained a reprehensibly neglected field of work in KBK Districts.

The situation as I saw it was begging for transformation. I was ready and willing to systematically analyse and address factors cited for abnormal delays. I prescribed a simple format for seeking information showing the date of starting construction; name, address and phone numbers of the contractor; due date of completion; physical and financial progress; and name of Junior Engineer in charge of the project. As head of R&DM Department which decided the lease policy with auction of sairat sources like sand, murrum and stone quarries, I had no difficulty in ensuring availability of construction materials. Although the overall revenue collection in the State from the sairat sources had jumped up by more than 30 percent due to timely conclusion of lease processes, I was willing to use the wide headroom available to make adjustments in KBK Districts. In any event, for me the generation of revenue was incidental and timely execution of developmental works remained the primary objective.

I started inspecting roads, bridges and larger buildings under construction frequently and at random besides reviewing the progress in meetings with Collectolrs and Engineers, at times with contractors in attendance. Instead of conducting a post-mortem and fixing up responsibility for incurring expenditures in excess of the volume of work actually done, I was interested in getting the projects completed within the approved unit cost. I found limited truth in excuses that Naxal groups were threatening contractors engaged in execution of roads, bridges and buildings. The reality at times was also that some genuine contractors were not getting their claims released in time. Effective monitoring of projects led to a healthy competition among engineers as also among contractors when they started getting paid for work done by them regularly, barring a few exceptions in Malkangiri and Nabarangpur. Many contractors in these two districts had either passed away or simply vanished from the scene but suitable course correction had not been taken up. Roads, bridges and buildings left incomplete had to be retendered and awarded afresh. Executive Engineer of RD Department in Nabarangpur had a vigilance case against him in which he was finally convicted. The one in Malkangiri was rarely found present in the district and appeared to have the umbrella of protection of his Engineer-in-Chief. When both Executive Engineers were moved out, the situation started improving in both districts.

I received feedback from various quarters which helped in improving the situation. At times, administrators are found apprehensive of negative consequences on the basis of critical feedback including allegations which could emanate from vested interests too. Increasing tendency to avoid decisions also leads to critical representations and allegation petitions against decision-making and implementing officials. As I had experienced adversaries turning into admirers at the end of the day once decisions are taken transparently and projects are completed timely, I advised colleagues not to get distracted by momentary criticism while implementing projects. Efforts made without vested interest, plain negativity or angularity in implementation never go waste in the long run.

Handling implementation of infrastructure projects gave stressful moments occasionally. In Koraput, the pretentions of sincerity of an Executive Engineer of Rural Works Department in position for more than 10 years got exposed when his bluff was called that DFO was not allowing him to implement some of PMGSY roads for connecting villages bordering Chhattisgarh. He physically fainted in the review meeting, and had to be shifted to the hospital immediately. Much to my relief, he came back after full recovery four days later. A news item about the Executive Engineer having fainted in my review meeting had been published attributing it to a strong reprimand by "Terror Datt". After the incident, the officer sought my help for his transfer to a coastal district as he was unable to undertake frequent field visits being grossly overweight. I sent a proposal accordingly and pursued it as a result of which he was transferred to Jagatsinghpur. However, during my next visit to Koraput I found him in tears calling for his continuance in Koraput! I was informed by his Engineer-in-Chief that he had approached Chief Minister's office through his contacts which resulted in verbal instructions against moving him out of Koraput. After this incident, rather than interacting with this two-faced Executive Engineer, I opted to deal directly with his Assistant/Junior Engineers. My concern was to complete the task on hand.

RD Department accounted for the largest number of incomplete projects in KBK Districts funded under various State and Central Plan/ Non-Plan schemes. Other line departments concerned had also released budget provisions to RD Department for developing their institutional infrastructure including residential buildings. Funds for more than 1,000 sub-centres, primary and community health centres, etc. had been provided by H&FW Department in the last few years. S&ME Department had released allocations for construction of Model Higher Secondary School buildings in every Block under Rashtriya Madhyamik Shiksha Abhiyan in addition to a large number under SSA. R&DM Department too had released funds for construction of new Tahasil buildings and a large number of office-cum-residence buildings for RIs. I had obtained details of every single work before reviewing them, besides asking District Collectors to ensure suitable sites for their time-bound execution. Majority of buildings had not been started on the grounds of suitable sites not having been handed over. This task was easy in the case of Schools, Tahasil offices and Health Centres which already had extra Government land on which construction of additional buildings could be done without advancing excuses. Nevertheless, issues including selection of sites got sorted out in review meetings. It was clear that line departments simply worked like post offices and felt unburdened after release of allocations to their counterparts in RD Department. They were not interested in any follow through with Executive Engineers to its logical conclusion.

Departmentalism and large egos stand like high walls, constructed and nurtured with high maintenance over time, precluding interactions between executing agencies and funding Departments. Lack of interest in works manifested itself starkly when buildings got completed but line Departments avoided taking possession stating that it was not possible for them to put them into use due to non-availability of manpower. Inertia and reluctance to shift and occupy new premises compounded the problem! About 1,000 Sub-Centre buildings and a large number of quarters of doctors and paramedics for which H&FW Department had provided funds thus remained unoccupied due to such reluctance to operate from these new buildings situated in relatively remote locations. The situation was largely similar in respect of model higher secondary schools and ITI complexes as they could not be put to use in the absence of recruitment of required manpower. In sharp contrast, buildings for offices and residential quarters for functionaries of R&DM Department were fully occupied. Nothing in administration was impossible if there was appetite for work with some amount of accountability and risk-taking ability.

With persistent pursuit, Rural Works Department finally became the best performer among all departments in KBK Districts in respect of roads, bridges and buildings. The Department started receiving higher allocations under PMGSY from Central Government after completing more than 1,000 roads albeit long after the expiry of initial due dates. New road projects and bridges progressed in accordance with timelines. The usual excuses for delay on account of non-availability of construction materials, land disputes and objection by forest officials became history while I was heading KBK administration. Contractors became more responsive as they received timely payments and faced less problems. It has been my consistent experience through the decades that government functionaries are capable of delivering tasks assigned to them in time if discipline is enforced, functional freedom is provided and projects are effectively monitored. Faster and timely execution gave lesser scope for corrupt practices and created a 'win-win' situation for all stakeholders.

Capacity Building: Essential Nurturing, Mainstreaming Local Youth

One frequently-faced problem in KBK Districts was non-availability of local contractors. Like officers, most of the contractors were outsiders. This was also a reason for delays in implementing infrastructure projects. State Government had provided a 10 percent advantage to tribal contractors over others to promote local entrepreneurial skills in predominantly tribal areas, but to hardly any avail. While heading ST&SC Development Department between 2006-2008, and subsequently RD Department, I had got a 'Training Manual' prepared for "contract management" and issued instructions to Project Administrators of Integrated Tribal Development Agencies and to Collectors to organise training of educated tribal youth accordingly. The training scheme included 45 days initial training on beginning-to-end processes in implementing infrastructure projects followed by an attachment for four months with established contractors to observe, understand and participate in execution of projects. The final phase of 15 days' training was based on field experience of trainees. During attachment, a trainee youth would be paid wages by the contractor at the rate prescribed for a skilled worker. Expenditure in the first and final phases of training was to be borne by ITDAs and Blocks. Engineers and accounting personnel were the main resource persons and their stipend was provided from ongoing training schemes for self-employment. After my departure from the ST&SC and RD Departments, contract management training had been discontinued.

I now revived this training in KBK Districts. In predominantly tribal districts of Koraput, Malkangiri, Nabarangpur and Rayagada, where ITDAs functioned exclusively for tribal development, it was decided to select at least two tribal youth from each Gram Panchayat for the training. In addition, ITDAs and DRDAs were advised to mount large-scale training at Block level for masonry, carpentry, plumbing, etc., alongside contract management trainings, considering the huge requirement of skilled workers for emerging fields like rural housing, sanitation, and village electrification. During a field visit in Nabarangpur, I was pleased to find that trained youth of an entire batch in plumbing and masonry had found gainful employment in neighbouring district across the State border and were earning ₹ 300/- to ₹ 450/- each per day. I was informed by their family members that as trainees under a local master trainer, they had contributed in construction of a good number of houses under IAY.

Guidelines and training manual provided that trained tribal contractors would be upgraded with the passage of time depending upon their experience. Blocks, ITDAs and Rural Works Department had been told to assign projects costing ₹ 10 lakh each or below to trained tribal youths and extend hand-holding support in implementing such projects through them. This would not only empower them but would also help in greater participation of local communities. Dependence on outsiders in executing projects could also reduce apace with development of local entrepreneurial skills. ITDAs acted upon my advice with sincerity; Blocks acted to a lesser extent. However, engineers of Works and Rural Works Departments though involved in designing the Training Manual did not evince enough interest in involving trained tribal youths in execution of projects implemented by their departments.

Decentralization and Selection of Contractors on Nomination Basis

In Malkangiri and Rayagada, responses to bids invited for PMGSY roads were grossly slim. Union RD Ministry had relaxed PMGSY norms in respect of these districts. In the event of tenders remaining un-responsive, it had authorized a Committee headed by District Collector with SP, DFO and Rural Works Executive Engineer as members to select contractors on nomination basis and break road projects into smaller parts without deviating from quality standards. On a visit to Malkangiri, I found that more than 60 PMGSY roads projects were gathering dust due to non-responsive tenders. But State's RD Department was being inexplicably obdurate about not allowing District

Collector's Committee to exercise the alternative of selection of contractors on nomination basis. I discussed the issue with officers and local smaller contractors who could not compete with big contractors from outside the District. Fortunately, former Chief Secretary J.K. Mahapatra had joined as Secretary in Union RD Ministry. When I spoke to him, he readily agreed to issue instructions waiving the condition for the Committee to seek approval at State level for executing PMGSY roads through contractors selected in a few Naxal-affected districts by nomination and by splitting project estimates into smaller parts to involve more local eligible contractors without any compromise on quality and specifications. The proposal submitted by me while sitting in the office of Malkangiri Collector was approved and clarifications were issued within the week by Union RD Ministry.

Rather than appreciating the clarifications obtained, Engineer-in-Chief and Secretary in RD Department got angry with Executive Engineer for Rural Works and Malkangiri Collector for being thus bypassed. My intervention was viewed by them as unwarranted and beyond my brief. However, more than 25 PMGSY roads were awarded on nomination basis immediately after the clarificatory guidelines were received from Central Government and these works started progressing fast. The new Executive Engineer in Malkangiri was also more assertive and positive in comparison to his predecessor. PMGSY roads which had been left incomplete or stood abandoned for years altogether also started progressing well. I advised Collector and Rural Works Executive Engineer to involve tribal youths who had been trained in 'contract management' either individually or in groups for implementing smaller road projects with active hand-holding by respective Junior Engineers. In the long run, involvement of local contractors and participation of local communities was a more feasible and inclusive option for implementing Government-funded infrastructure projects in remote tribal districts.

Health and Family Welfare

In spite of adding up a sizeable physical infrastructure at district, sub-division, block and sub-centre levels, it was not possible to make any perceptible improvement in the actual delivery of health services. Major reasons were inadequate attention by State Government in posting doctors and other paramedical personnel to man the facilities, and even where some few had been posted, Health Department remained incapable of ensuring that they join for discharging their duties. I found contractually-appointed Ayurveda or Homeopathy doctors functioning under the administrative control of paramedical personnel in a number of Primary Health Centres! The pincer-grip hold of doctors practicing allopathy was such that they would themselves avoid working in PHCs but would not stomach practitioners of Ayurveda or Homeopathy taking charge of the Centres. Doctors were also not available at Community Health Centres as per the sanctioned strength as many of those posted there had been withdrawn and brought in to manage district hospitals.

Vacancies of doctors exceeded 70 percent in some KBK Districts. State Government frequently publicized a transfer policy that would provide for fixed tenure of 3 years and incentives for doctors to work in KBK Districts, but this deceptive propaganda was largely for public consumption.

Chief District Medical Officers and Additional Chief District Medical Officers pleaded helplessness when asked to ensure delivery of health services rigorously. From my interactions with officers in review meetings at district level, it was increasingly evident that the problems encountered in implementing health sector schemes were not insurmountable provided the State Government acted upon its own stated policy of a fixed tenure of 3 years for doctors in KBK Districts along with financial incentives. Just two caveats were needed, first, the subsequent posting should be in districts of their preference, and second, they should be allowed to retain quarters of their previous stations or in the State or divisional headquarters during their KBK tenure.

It was frequently found that primary and community health centres in Malkangiri, Nabarangpur, Koraput, Rayagada and Nuapada gave the appearance of being shelters for strays – human and animals. The high figure of about 80 percent institutional delivery by pregnant women being reported by the State Government was based on expenditures on incentives reported under Janani Suraksha Yojana on instutional deliveries. It included deliveries at sub-centres and belied the state of crumbling physical and human resources. During my visit to a sub-centre managed by a senior Auxiliary Nurse & Midwife about 40 km from the district headquarters in Kalahandi when I insisted to see the delivery infrastructure, I found a big poultry bird flying out as soon as the door of the so-called delivery room was opened reluctantly by her! Some district hospitals even did not have gynaecologists and anaesthetists in position. Although State Government had a scheme to provide free tools to all differently-abled persons, I found that in some districts ENT specialists and Orthopaedic surgeons were not in position for even certifying the physical disabilities. I could do nothing more than persistently informing H&FW Department about the state of affairs after every review meeting and accompanying field visits to KBK Districts.

The tragic and horrific tales involving deaths suffered by pregnant women, or of their new born, in roadside deliveries and their painful journeys in full-delivery state on foot or by crude hurriedly-cobbled up means of transport, such as in bedsheet-slings tied to poles supported on the shoulders of their menfolk, to distantly located health institutions and complaints from the local people about the absence of ambulance services in emergencies shook my soul to the extent that I found myself fearful of visiting remote villages at times. Naxal-infested villages never succeeded in checking my footsteps. But I would walk with a heavy heart to hear the plight of helpless poor in remote villages, which mass media rarely covered.

In a meeting held by Chief Minister when I explained the pathetic condition of Government hospitals in KBK Districts, he wanted to know how many IAS officers go to Government hospitals to consult doctors for treatment of their family members. I responded to his cynical counter-question perhaps needlessly, that personally I had seldom ever gone to a private hospital for my treatment or that of my family members and sincerely believed that Government doctors were more qualified and held far more varied experiences having managed humongous numbers of patients each day with hardly a fraction of equipment available to those in private hospitals. I added that the solution was effective management including utilization of services in places where no private health care system existed. It was now 7.00 p.m. when, as if on cue, a news item suddenly appeared on the television (kept on silent mode) in Chief Minister's office chamber highlighting the hopeless condition of Capital Hospital. It zoomed in on broken furniture and garbage which had crowded out the space meant for hospital beds! I could instantly urge Chief Minister to visualize how much worse the condition in health care institutions in KBK Districts was. While State-wide vacancies against sanctioned posts of doctors was about 30 percent, these rose up to 70 percent in KBK Districts. The fact remained that relatively more advanced coastal districts also had private health care facilities as an alternative, whereas in KBK Districts people were fully dependent on governmental health facilities and suffered more from their failures.

The Mess in Rural Water Supply and Sanitation (RWSS)

RWSS which was responsible for implementing schemes aimed at supply of safe drinking water and sanitation in rural areas was perhaps the worst performer among all State Government Departments in KBK Districts. Water supply in most villages for drinking purposes elsewhere in the State was augmented through tube wells. There were very few piped water supply projects, half of which remained defunct at any given point of time. KBK Districts received nothing but apathy and neglect from RWSS Department. Except during drought conditions, when small allocations were provided from Calamity Relief Fund or Chief Minister's Relief Fund for sinking of more tube wells in affected areas, desired priorities were not accorded by State Government to the schemes for drinking water supply by providing additional resources over what was allotted under Centrally Sponsored Schemes.

The main flaws in providing safe drinking water in KBK Districts arose from haphazard planning of drinking water projects and adhoc approach to implementing them. Every year a list of unserved villages was prepared and tube wells were sunk by the roadside nearest to the villages unconnected by road. Even if there were perennial streams near unserved villages, and piped water supply through gravity flow was possible, RWSS Department went for soft options of sinking tube wells through selected contractors. A tube well for drinking water needed to have an elevated platform, a small drain leading to a small soak-pit to avoid collecting unclean water which became a breeding ground for mosquitoes, besides contaminating the groundwater itself which got recycled through the same tube well if it was shallow. In reality, barring exceptions existing tube wells were found to contain nothing more than hand-held pumping devices. The methods of execution and expenditure were seldom known to the user public regardless of the fact that project guidelines mandated that details, such as cost, discharge and quality of water, and components of works, should be displayed on the tube well's platform.

Piped water supply projects, very few in number, were found to have a ridiculously short life becoming defunct within less than a year after their respective execution. Although, guidelines envisaged connections to individual households that agreed to pay monthly water usage charges, this was not done. Indeed, most of the piped water supply projects whether connected with rivers or deep bore wells did not provide for overhead tanks to ensure uninterrupted water supply. They were run for an hour in the morning and occasionally for a little while in the evening as if for demonstration purposes. Stand posts erected in villages at the tail end never received water as those in the beginning, not regulated effectively, remained open which only created unhealthy conditions due to continuous flow, stagnant and putrid water surrounding the base of stand posts. The expenditure incurred in implementing piped water supply projects was at best infructuous while consumers remained dependent on tube wells and other available natural water sources nearby. RWSS engineers washed off their hands stating that there were no provisions for maintenance of piped water supply projects and no community participation either. Procurements made centrally for supply of substandard materials with connivance of selected contractors, especially in drilling to get underground water, raised serious questions in relation to quality, quantity and costs.

To redress this grim situation, I repeatedly cautioned RWSS engineers at district level against any haphazard implementation of drinking water supply schemes, particularly piped water supply projects, besides bringing the matter to the notice of State Government. The element of accountability was missing completely. Gram Panchayats refused to take responsibility for maintaining carelessly-executed water supply projects and RWSS Department did not have resources and manpower to maintain them. Guidelines provided for organizing village committees for maintaining them, but no attention had been given to organize such committees. District Collectors were unable to do much even if they were aware of the ground reality. I came across an Executive Engineer in Malkangiri who had managed to get himself transferred elsewhere after he had misappropriated crores of rupees without actually implementing a single piped water supply project on the ground for villages and the town around Chitrakonda reservoir. I submitted a detailed report for action against that delinquent officer.

Nuapada district was a burning example of negligence at every level. About 50 percent of its villages acutely suffered from consumption of fluoride-contaminated drinking water so evident in terms of public sufferings with bodies of even children and youth showing deformities, stunting growth and other physical ailments. Piped water supply projects in the district required investments which in turn required specific and extra-budgetary provisions. Nuapada had a couple of major irrigation projects with huge water reservoirs. Even villagers displaced years back for these irrigation projects and relocated elsewhere, had been suffering due to fluorosis as groundwater in relocation sites stood contaminated. State Government had no problem in revising the cost of an irrigation project which was still incomplete despite cost escalation by about 10 times, but could not consider spending a fraction of the project cost for providing safe drinking water to villages situated at the periphery of these massive reservoirs. Visiting places badly affected by fluoride gave me the most painful feeling and yet I could do nothing more than making submissions to Government to address the problem by sanctioning vital funds.

Sanitation in rural areas despite being an important flagship scheme was suffering from similar neglect in KBK Districts, and probably elsewhere too. There was no justification for assigning implementation of sanitation programme requiring mass mobilization and participation to RWSS department, which did not have even junior engineers in all Blocks and had no existence below. Funds for sanitation programme largely came from MGNREGS handled by Panchayat Raj Department. RWSS implemented projects through contractors in a limited way and was no njnt in a position to executethe sanitation programme requiring construction of lakhs of individual household latrines in every district. Executive Engineers were unable to execute even a limited number of drinking water supply projects, what to speak of their handling sanitation schemes requiring mass mobilization and participation of the entire rural population.

In every review meeting, I impressed upon the district administration to involve grassroot organizations including Gram Panchayats in implementing sanitation programme, which was revamped as "Swachh Bharat" by the NDA Government at the Centre after some time. It was ironical that even houses constructed under IAY and Biju Awas Yojana with mandatory provisions for individual household latrines were executed without this component. I succeeded to some extent in liberating this programme from the clutches of RWSS in KBK Districts. Resultantly, districts showing construction of just a few hundred household latrines annually, suddenly jumped up to the bracket of five to ten thousand individual toilets annually. A large number of villages and Gram Panchayats in every district became open defecation free and a more conducive environment was created to achieve the goal of Swachh Bharat. In my assessment, sanitation remained the least prioritized scheme of State Government.

Elementary, Vocational and Higher Education in KBK Districts

Elementary education despite being critically important for qualitative development of human resource was another sector which suffered due to inadequate attention. Apart from rampant absenteeism of students as well as teachers in schools situated at remote locations of KBK Districts, allocations under the "Mid-Day Meal" scheme did not reach the ultimate stakeholders to the desired extent. In contrast, I recall well the glossy presentation of data by Secretary to the Department in review meetings held by Chief Minister or Chief Secretary at State level painting a rosy picture showing universal enrolment and regular functioning of schools. During my own field visits to schools undertaken at random and district-level reviews, I would frequently find the opposite of what was being presented at State level. Elementary education being close to my heart, I had done my best to promote tribal education in the past. Now many years later, as Chief Administrator, KBK Districts, I was getting frustrated to find deterioration in elementary education even in exclusive schools for tribal communities. Model School buildings under Rashtriya Madhyamik Shiksha Abhiyan remained unutilized even after the initially reluctant engineers of Rural Works Department completed those projects. My routine reviews and reminders on the matter sounded meaningless to those at the helm of affairs.

In order to respond to criticism of lack of infrastructure to universalize elementary education up to the secondary stage, State Government had upgraded all lower primary schools to upper primary level. Similarly, one upper primary school in each Gram Panchayat had been upgraded to High School. KBK Districts accounted for the largest number of such upgraded schools. But, Government order on such upgradation had not altered the ground reality as the posts of additional teachers required in the so-called upgraded schools had not been created even after years. Where posts existed in upgraded High Schools, appointments of headmasters and teachers for Science, Mathematics, and English, etc., had not been made. Large numbers of schools still remained with a single teacher, and many ran without teachers! In the given situation, it was impossible to visualize 100 per cent enrolment and retention in schools.

In my review reports, I cited these hard facts and pleaded for corrective steps. I was misunderstood for being critical and stating the reality. The International Fund for Agriculture Development (IFAD) report had highlighted the socio-economic conditions of tribal districts in Southern Odisha observing that the indices of development there were below those prevailing in sub-Saharan Africa. It underlined the falling standards of elementary education, pointing out that students in VII and VIII standards in these districts were unable to pass simple arithmetic tests. In the name of reforming the elementary education system by citing the provisions of Right to Education Act, the system of examination in schools up to secondary level had been waived and students promoted without holding tests in the lower classes. It was thus easy for S&ME Department to report a hundred per cent enrolment and above 90 percent retention in the absence of any effective system for monitoring enrolments and retention.

Direct recruitment of teachers in elementary schools had been stopped by the State Government. Contractually appointed Shiksha Sahayaks accounted for majority of teaching personnel in most elementary schools in KBK Districts. In fact, many trained graduate teachers were appointed under SSA as Shiksha Sahayaks contractually on a monthly remuneration of a mere ₹ 5,000/- each per month, which was 25 percent of the remuneration given to permanent Group D staff, and less than 50 percent of minimum wages for skilled labour under the law. With such meagre earnings, contractual staff could hardly be expected to stay motivated in teaching as a vocation. The result was misappropriation of mid-day meal funds and falling educational standards. Economically better-off families, including permanent teachers, could send their children to private schools including Saraswati Shishu Mandirs for quality education. Poor tribal families for whom education was the first-generation input had no such option. Having seen and undergone the disadvantages due to lack of access to elementary education in the formative phase of my own life, I felt as though time had negligently stood still. Apart from political leadership, bureaucracy of which I was a part, was equally responsible for this state of affairs and the legacy of productive lives lost due to lack of adequate physical and soft educational facilities.

As instructions issued by State Finance Department prohibited direct recruitment without its prior approval, the only method to fill up vacancies was through contractual appointment in primary schools of Shiksha Sahayaks holding B.Ed. degrees. This system also went against the interest of tribal areas, which lacked sufficient number of tribal candidates with the prescribed qualifications. The problem got compounded as S&ME Department had issued instructions to make contractual appointment of Shiksha Sahayaks by giving representations to ST&SC candidates in proportion to their population without relaxation of eligibility norms. Tribal districts in KBK region did not have enough teachers training facilities and the nodal department was unwilling to amend recruitment norms despite difficulties being explained repeatedly. In Rayagada alone, out of 1,451 primary schools, as many as 495 were with a single teacher and 97 without any teacher! The single-teacher schools rarely functioned effectively. Despite more than 400 upper primary schools being upgraded to High Schools years back, posts of headmasters and subject teachers had not even been created.

ST&SC Development Department in the recent past had thoughtlessly constructed buildings through the Integrated Tribal Development Agencies for opening of B.Ed. Colleges meant for tribal students in some KBK Districts. Neither had posts for teaching and non-teaching staff been created nor did the

Department have expertise to run such institutions. In fact, Rules of Business under the Constitution followed by Odisha did not permit ST&SC Development Department to venture into higher education which was the sole preserve of Education Department. Inclusive education not only helped in mainstreaming and assimilating students of marginalized communities but also prepared them better to face the competitive world with higher degree of confidence. I tried to discourage opening of higher educational institutions exclusively for STs&SCs and pleaded with State Government to sanction more hostels for ST&SC students in reputed educational institutions, post additional subject teachers, and provide scholarships to cover their educational expenses which was possible at lesser expenditure than was being incurred. I was of the view that hostels too should not be exclusive for ST&SC students at college and university level.

Luckily, Government agreed to transfer the infrastructure created for B.Ed. Colleges to S&ME Department and further upgrading of tribal High Schools was not pursued. Bureaucrats at the helm of affairs were substantially responsible for wrong advice to the political leadership or for failure in resisting populist political wishes which were not in consonance with the constitutional provision. Long back, a senior colleague of mine had told me that the role of a civil servant was comparable with that of a physician. If a diabetic patient wanted the physician to prescribe medicines for treatment which tasted sweet, he was not obliged to fulfil the patient's wishes. Similarly, bureaucrats are required to examine proposals on merit and put up the best options before the political leadership to take decisions. If their decision does not conform to legal and constitutional provisions, bureaucrats can convey inability to implement it. This golden rule for civil servants is increasingly being forgotten.

The condition of institutions set up for technical or vocational education in KBK Districts was equally deplorable. While building infrastructure for new Industrial Training Institutes (ITIs) at Block-level had been sanctioned and beautiful complexes were being brought up, more than 75 percent posts of teaching and other technical staff were lying vacant even in existing institutions. The State Finance Department was reluctant to sanction posts for freshly sanctioned ITIs and other vocational centres for which building complexes under RLTAP, BRGF, IAP, State Plan, etc. had either been completed or were nearing completion. When complaints from students who had been enrolled, highlighting the deficiencies in the existing technical institutions did not receive consideration, I saw many of them leaving these institutions. Although the State leadership never fell short in singing virtues of skilling the youth, such happenings never elicited a reality check. The nodal Department and State Finance Department individually and together were fully responsible for the paralysis in technical education in KBK Districts. Elected public representatives were either voiceless or of no consequence.

Bureaucratic apathy towards higher education in educationally-backward districts horrified me. Once prior to my appointment as KBK Chief

Administrator, in a meeting chaired by Chief Secretary I heard both Development Commissioner and Secretary, Higher Education Department, suggest that the State should not participate in implementing a new Centrally Sponsored Scheme introduced by Union HRD Ministry. This scheme provided Central financial support for opening new degree colleges in educationally-deficit districts if the State Government offered land free of cost and shared the operating costs. These two senior officers proposed that inability of State Government in implementing the Scheme should be conveyed, unless Central Government agreed to bear the full cost to run these higher educational institutions for all times to come! I felt that an opportunity to develop institutions was being lost. I was more convinced than ever that more than political leadership in the State, it was a short-sighted bureaucracy that was responsible for the pathetic status of education in KBK Districts. I actually felt ashamed as well as helpless. My disagreeing with these nay-saying senior officers was in vain. I could not convince them despite pointing out that we were holding positions in Government only due our good fortune of having access to higher education in the formative phase of our lives, and further that we have no ethical or professional right to deny it now to the vastly less fortunate ones.

Implementation of Priority Sector Programmes

State Government's attention through district administration was more towards implementing expenditure-driven poverty alleviation and employment generating schemes in rural areas. I spent less time in monitoring such schemes, though on various occasions in the course of field visits and reviews, I drew attention of Panchayat Raj Department to the visible anomalies, such as participating banks charging interest of 10 percent or more in rural livelihood projects against 2 percent after disbursement of 5 percent interest subvention, mismatch between muster rolls and job cards of those engaged in implementing MGNREGS, delays up to 6 months in payment of wages which discouraged able-bodied rural people from participating in government-supported employment guarantee programmes preferring wage employment elsewhere at even less than half of the wages paid instantly, etc.

Irrigation Projects in KBK Districts

KBK Districts lagged behind in generation of irrigation potential barring Kalahandi despite sizable investments through the years for construction of minor and medium irrigation projects and for exploitation of river and ground-water through community lift irrigation points and deep bore wells. Chief Minister held charge of WR Department since the year 2000 and as such availability of funds had never been a constraint. I tried to analyse as to what was ailing this sector which was vital for growth in agriculture. I was aghast when during my review of ongoing projects, it was realized that almost all the projects taken up after the year 2000 were either incomplete or abandoned even after incurring huge amounts of expenditure. Under AIBP and RIDF, Union Government and NABARD had released ₹ 137 crore for 89 minor irrigation projects to generate irrigation potential of over 11,353 hectares between 2008 and 2012 on the basis of DPRs backed by plans and estimates submitted by State Government. Although the period for completion of each minor irrigation project was one year from its date of award, not a single project had been completed despite full utilisation of allocations. No officer in WR Department had monitored these projects; most of the Executive Engineers who had spent the money stood transferred or promoted.

During field visits, I inspected some partly-constructed abandoned minor irrigation projects and advised officers to make every possible effort to complete them. Some of these had resulted in loss of land to farmers who had voluntarily donated it without seeking compensation in high hopes of getting benefits of irrigation for their remaining land. I also warned these functionaries of fixing accountability for wastage of funds. Some Executive Engineers pleaded helplessness and a few sought time for completing them. They had no plausible alibi for delays on account of land acquisition. In any case, R&DM Department had already permitted purchase of land up to 25 acres per village directly from farmers for implementing public projects. After a few months, not finding sufficient improvement in their status, the infructuous expenditure was brought to the notice of Chief Secretary and Development Commissioner through submission notes for information of Chief Minister. Some officers responsible for misappropriation of funds and wrong reporting including submission of false utilisation certificates had been promoted to higher ranks in the meanwhile. Probably they had taken advantage of Chief Minister himself being in charge of the department thinking that none would muster courage to scrutinize or question their works. Indeed, as my scrutiny intensified and persisted over time, I sensed increase in discomfort, even disapproval, amongst senior-most officials in receiving my reports highlighting lacunae and malfeasance in implementation of minor irrigation projects in KBK Districts. Going into that was not my remit.

There were two major and two medium irrigation projects in KBK Districts under implementation for more than 10 years. These projects held the potential to transform the agricultural economy in drought-prone districts if implemented with seriousness. The Ret medium irrigation project in Kalahandi had been approved at an estimated cost of ₹ 86.14 crore in the year 2003 to provide controlled irrigation over more than 9,000 hectares. Its actual commencement was in 2005. The canal system of this project had been completed years back and indeed become partly defunct. There was no indication as to when the head work including reservoir would be completed. The delay was being attributed to difficulties in finalizing the design of the head work. The cost of this project had been revised upwards by about 10 times.

Lower Indra major irrigation project was to create irrigation potential of about 12,000 hectares in Nuapada and about 18,000 hectares in neighbouring Balangir, both affected by chronic droughts leading to large-scale forced labour migration to other States. This project approved in the year 1999 at a cost of ₹ 211.70 crore, commenced in 2002. Project cost had since been revised to ₹ 1,600 crore, and a further upward revision was impending. Abnormal delay in completion of items of works, including digging main canals and installing spill-ways, was generally being attributed to Naxal threats, public agitation, and problems in land acquisition for construction of canal and fabrication of spill gates. I reviewed this project every two months and visited the so-called resistance sites in Nuapada and Balangir where the canal work had been held up due to alleged opposition by villagers. The fact of the matter was that people were unhappy due to abnormal delay and wanted the work to be completed even if they had to sacrifice some additional land without compensation. In Nuapada, a minor law and order problem had never been brought to the notice of District Administration and the moment it was reported during my review meeting, the District Collector addressed it to the satisfaction of the project authorities instantly. There was no Naxal problem or public resistance and these excuses had only been invented to hide departmental failure. Project engineers had constructed a massive Jagannath Temple in front of the dam; landscaped and beautified the area, without facing any public resistance or Naxal threats. On taking it up with Government, a Chief Engineer was posted who promised to complete installing spill gates within 6 months. Though substantial progress was made thereafter, the project had not been completed when I left charge of KBK administration.

The medium irrigation project in Titlagarh(Balangir) which was meant to provide irrigation over 2,000 hectares in addition to drinking water to the local area had been completed 5-6 years back barring a small portion of canal and its distributaries. OCC, assigned the task of completing the work, demanded extra funds over and above cost escalation of more than five times. It was also reported that the work involved controlled blasting of rocks and there was some opposition from a few families residing by the canal side. I visited the site with OCC and district administration functionaries. After making it abundantly clear that I would brook no delay beyond the time-line to be agreed for its completion, OCC finally agreed to resume and complete the work before June 2015. The incomplete canal was completed and there was no resistance from villagers against the needed controlled blasting. The project though completed did not provide irrigation in the ensuing Kharif season despite the officers concerned having made a commitment to that effect. The situation would surely have been different had the Department shown seriousness and fixed accountability against negligent officials.

The Lower Suktel Project in Balangir was the worst example of local vested interests operating in a corrupt alliance with some officers of WR

Department and thereby sabotaging a project approved in the year 1999 at an estimated cost of ₹ 217.013 crore. The land acquisition officer appointed by WR Department for this project had gone underground after allegedly committing misappropriation of around ₹ 50 crore. He had paid compensation to people in many villages whose land was not needed for the project and had not been notified for acquisition. Excessive amount had been paid without any verification as compensation for non-existent fruit bearing and big trees. The land acquisition officer was said to have been backed by the local influential Minister. This made his transfer from the place difficult even when his gross lapses started coming to the limelight. When ineligible people and those who had received huge amount of compensation unduly were told to refund after the land acquisition officer absconded, they started agitating against this major irrigation project which was to provide controlled irrigation over an area of more than 23,500 hectares. The project long yearned for by the people which could transform the agricultural economy of this drought prone district, suffered due to lack of effective monitoring and supervision. The estimated cost had increased by more than 10 times and none could predict its future.

Government of Odisha had introduced a heavily subsidized scheme for exploitation of groundwater for agriculture in the recent past. Implemented through Odisha Lift Irrigation Corporation, each deep bore well would cost ₹ 3.00 lakh on an average per farmer, and was subsidized to the extent of more than 90 percent including the cost of energization. Indeed, farmers were required to partly bear the cost of energization after their bore wells were declared successful by OLIC engineer-in-charge of the area. ST and SC farmers were required to deposit ₹ 10,000/- each towards bore well energization against ₹ 20,000/- each for other farmers. In KBK Districts, beneficiaries of bore wells were mandatorily getting sprinkler sets costing more than ₹ 35,000/- each, which was supplied free of cost by Horticulture Directorate in the name of promoting use of plastics in horticulture, a scheme funded by Union Agriculture Ministry with 70 percent subsidy. While ST and SC farmers were given additional subsidy of 30 percent from SCA which got routed through ITDAs and District Welfare Officers of KBK Districts, records were seen to have been manipulated for others showing 30 percent contribution by them voluntarily without involving financial institutions. In reality, the sprinklers sets supplied to such beneficiaries was worth only to the extent of 70 percent subsidy! In other words, subsidy for a bore well along with sprinkler set was more than 100 percent of unit cost! Curiously enough, there were no applications or documentations required for availing these benefits. During my field visits, I saw bigger and better off farmers with more than a bore well each on their land, by getting these in the name of two or more family members living off the same land. After getting a bore well energized, they were not interested to energize the other ones.

This supplier and contractor driven programme was being implemented casually in violation of standard norms which did not permit dovetailing of subsidy or disbursement of subsidy in cash/kind without bank loan. The unit cost of a sprinkler set had also been hiked in such a way that the so-called beneficiaries effectively did not have to pay his share of the cost and the supplier offered the sprinkler set at 70 percent of the unit cost. I could not find a single sprinkler set in operation anywhere even after inspecting hundreds of bore wells. What I found in some predominantly tribal villages was that some non-tribal beneficiaries had been presented as tribal farmers for availing further subsidy under SCA and thus attracting lesser contribution towards energisation. Usually, sprinkler system of irrigation is applied for pulses and oilseeds which do not require irrigation by way of flooding. The beneficiary farmers were mostly using bore wells for growing paddy or other commercial crops including vegetables for which sprinkler irrigation was irrelevant. They, however, used the plastic pipes of the sprinkler sets for taking water to their land parcels which were scattered. Many beneficiaries were found complaining that the discharge of water from their bore wells was inadequate and they could run the water lifting device for a limited period of half an hour or less, which on verification was found to be true. This probably was due to non-maintenance of a reasonable distance between two bore wells, inadequate depth of bore wells, and lesser availability of ground-water recharge. In most clusters, average distance between bore wells was 50 to 100 meters. Once bore wells were energized, there was no support towards maintenance services. This naturally displeased beneficiaries. I found many receiving good returns from agriculture including vegetable cultivation using groundwater, although there were complaints too on account of failures and lack of mechanism for addressing grievances.

My advice to OLIC officers was to involve field functionaries of Agriculture Department for suggesting suitable cropping, extension support services, including free soil-testing and plant protection measures, besides consulting Gram Sabhas for identification of eligible families. I called upon District Collectors to involve themselves in effective coordination with Energy Department to ensure timely energization of bore wells. The tendency among engineers of OLIC was not to inform line departments and avoid Collectors in implementing the bore well scheme. Corrupt practices and irregularities in execution were evident, which were brought to the notice of Secretary, WR Department, and Chief Secretary,. An Executive Engineer counted among the best performers was raided by Vigilance Department leading to recovery of huge amount of cash and other assets beyond his known source of income. I was happy that Chief Secretary, Development Commissioner and Secretary WR Department, based on my detailed notes issued revised guidelines disallowing dovetailing of subsidy and calling for proper documentation before hiring contractors for sinking bore wells on farm land of beneficiaries.

Although the bore well scheme was under implementation since 2010-11, only about 20 percent of total bore wells had been energized. After I started reviewing the programme vigorously, Collectors and officers of Agriculture Department of KBK Districts also started taking interest. Yet, at the end of my two years tenure as KBK Chief, 9,151 out of 18,899 bore wells in districts under my jurisdiction still remained to be energized. A large number of bore wells which had been sunk two-three years back remained to be energized due to lack of coordination between OLIC and Energy Department. It was ironical that in spite of publicizing the energisation programme, Odisha perhaps was the only major State where energy consumption in agriculture was less than one per cent. Officers of WR Department, particularly field functionaries, instead of taking advantage of the free hand and functional freedom given by Chief Minister, with hardly any financial constraints, misused the opportunities by implementing the programme haphazardly and dubiously as they thought none would review their works and question their credentials. The reality seemed never to have been reported to Chief Minister and detailed reports and actions of an officer now reviewing the scheme who did not belong to their Department was not appreciated. The inevitable was not difficult to guess in an administrative system devoid of morality, responsibility and accountability.

Closure of Innings as Chief Administrator, KBK Districts

Notwithstanding experiencing several bottlenecks, I was perhaps the only Chief Administrator in the history of KBK Project administration who enjoyed this work which did not come with the usual symbols or trappings of power. I tried to utilize every moment of my time, even in the final throes of my administrative career, for ensuring qualitative and quantitative improvement in schemes under implementation in KBK Districts. I was neither initially conscious nor concerned with the dawning realization that some of my proactive efforts, and participation in a couple of completely unrelated events, were going to be viewed adversely.

As MD, OSDMA, a post I held concurrently, Chief Secretary had assigned the task of preparing a SOPs for disaster management during Naba Kalebar Rath Yatra 2015. OSDMA prepared an exhaustive Disaster Management Plan with SOPs carefully embedded into it indicating the roles and responsibilities of all concerned and for facilitating on the spot decisions in the event of any unforeseen eventualities during the festivities. The preparation entailed several rounds of discussion with stakeholder Departments and leading civil society organizations who usually participated in the Rath Yatra. I got transferred from OSDMA when the document was in the final stage awaiting Government's approval. As I did not find any role for myself to contribute in the management of Rath Yatra, I opted to be of use elsewhere during the period and went to continue with my work in KBK Districts. When I was in Koraput KBK Project office, unexpectedly on 17 July 2015 a couple of members of the Koraput

Jagannath Temple Trust met me and requested to participate in the local Naba Kalebar Rath Yatra as Principal Servitor, a role conventionally performed by District Collector, by virtue of being head of the district administration. I was told that the District Collector was indisposed and had declined to perform the traditional rituals. The Naba Kalebar Rath Yatra was on 18 July 2015.

In the circumstances recounted to me, I accepted the invitation gracefully. I recalled attending the Rath Yatra at Puri for the first-time way back in 1984 soon after I joined the Odisha cadre of IAS. The year 2015 was going to be my last Rath Yatra before retirement. Despite not being a ritualistic man, I felt blessed to participate in the Naba Kalebar Rath Yatra of the main deity of "Shabara Tribe" who had graduated as Lord of the Universe with his main residential address now in Puri. I knew well through my stay in Odisha for three decades that Pyari Mohan Mahapatra was known to be the Chief Architect of this Jagannath Temple at Koraput. He was working initially as Deputy and later on as Chief Administrator of the Dandakaranya Project when the temple came into being. He had remained the mentor of Temple Trust since then. But, when I had given my consent on17 July 2015, I was ignorant about his presence in Koraput and also of his desire for me to participate in the Rath Yatra, a fact which was not revealed to me by two Trust members when I had accepted their invitation. In retrospect when regressive outcomes unfolded at my doorstep, I asked myself whether I would have accepted the invite had I known in advance about the desire of Pyari Babu for me to attend the function. In all likelihood, I would have found myself standing tall in the firm belief that the faith of Shabara Tribe and Lord Jagannath's attraction could not be undone by any negative association with the mentor of Temple Trust.

Pyari Mohan Mahapatra as a serving IAS officer had inspired me in the first few years of my service, but I hardly enjoyed his confidence when he joined politics and became the most powerful person in the ruling party. He was the last word in important administrative matters including in transfers and postings of senior officers till his political miscalculations backfired in May 2012. Perhaps I was among a handful of officers who were not found compliant by Pyari Babu when he was remote-controlling the State Government. It was equally well-known that his close coterie, and wider following in administration, switched sides instantly now that he had become persona non grata to the highest political dispensation and political pariah to all and sundry in Odisha's political space. Senior officers who used to wait in long queues to catch his eye and secure his blessings had started avoiding him. He was no longer the side on which the bread was buttered. I could gauge the real reason for the Koraput District Collector marking his absence at successive Rath Yatras from the year 2012 onwards. However, I did not anticipate the severity of retribution determined for me by the political Lord.

The second perhaps compounded development played out mischievously before the political leadership by those holding some antagonism towards me in State administration was an article I was persuaded to write by the associate editor of "The Indian Express" in lieu of an interview as a part of a programme dubbed by the newspaper as CSR. The newspaper had adopted four backward districts in Central India which included Nabarangpur, a KBK district, and wanted to make constructive contributions through a series of articles in the National Daily for the next one year on the changing face of these districts. When I declined to meet him to give an interview stating that I had never spoken to the media throughout my professional life and believed in anonymity as a civil servant, the associate editor who had been told to meet me by his contacts and had gone through volumes of my review reports on KBK Districts placed in the Web Portal of the Project, requested me to at least contribute an article on the issue of development in Nabarangpur district. I finally agreed to write it to focus on the issues which already stood detailed out in public domain on the condition that the article would not be specific to Nabarangpur or KBK Districts and would cover general issues concerning development of tribal districts.

Sitting in KBK Project office on a public holiday, I wrote the article which was published fully in the electronic edition of the Newspaper on 17 September 2015. The article was academic in nature and was based on my experience and understanding of the subject matter. Except one specific reference to Nabarangpur which indicated the manpower shortage with an example of Nabarangpur district which had nearly 70 percent vacancies of doctors, the article enumerated positive steps taken by State and Central Governments to reduce disparities between tribal and non-tribal areas across KBK Districts and focused on the way forward. The discordance of the title of the article, which was edited/ changed by the said Newspaper, with its subject matter is evident from a plain reading and is reproduced below:

"Why Development reached Nabarangpur late

Historically, the moniker "Excluded Areas" and "Partially Excluded Areas", applied by the colonial administration to the areas which got specified as "Scheduled Areas" under the new Constitution after independence set the tone for a policy of least intervention in all their developmental aspects. During the first three decades post-Independence, despite recognition that the Scheduled Areas usually have tribal communities in a majority and greatly suffered from the development deficits received barely any interventions by way of development of road communication, formal education, entrepreneurship promotion, etc due to a predominant perception that such interventions would lead to penetration of non-tribals to the tribal areas, which would result in destruction of tribal traditions and culture in addition to their exploitation. Interestingly, the least interventionist approach prompted and promoted by anthropologists lead by Elwin Verrier continued for a long time leading to the expression of arrogance in some quarters amounting to "History for us and Anthropology for you!". It is not surprising to find that the recommendations made by the Dhebar Commission (1960) and the Shilu Ao Committee (1967) for development interventions with simultaneous implementation of protective legislation did not receive the desired attention with any sense of urgency. Focus of policy planners and administrators remained on protective discrimination at the cost of assimilation through a balanced development.

A conceptual break from this practice was made through the introduction of the 'Tribal Sub Plan' (TSP) during the 5th Five Year Plan. It called for earmarking of budgetary provisions in proportion to the tribal population by concerned States and Central Ministries. But, in practice, it remained a half-hearted budgetary exercise on paper. It seemed as though the then Planning Commission did not have full clarity about formulating the 'TSP' and the strategy for development of 'Scheduled Areas'. The majority of the Central Ministries too did not earmark budgetary allocations of Plan Schemes/Programmes under their respective purview in proportion to the tribal population residing in the Scheduled Areas. Non-lapseability of budgetary allocations was an integral part of the TSP-based approach of Plans which could not be adhered to in practice. Similarly, non-divertability of such budgetary allocations, though provided for in rule, became a notional exercise of mere earmarking of allocations in practice, with diversions allowed frequently on vague grounds that the schemes were not feasible or the "catch-22" situation that the absorption capacity was limited. Most of the medium and major projects, involving huge budgetary provisions, for development of irrigation potential, industries, mining, etc. in the natural resources-rich Scheduled Areas exhibited ostensibly under the TSP heads, more often than not resulted in distress of tribal communities in terms of their displacement rather than benefiting them by way of providing employment, entrepreneurial development, irrigation facilities, etc.

Nevertheless, with the passage of time, the application of the TSP approach to various schemes/ projects did lead to higher investment in the tribal-majority areas from the 1980s and the result of specifically targeted schemes, including the flagship programmes, started making visible impact in improving the socio-economic conditions of tribal communities in particular, and the Scheduled Areas overall. It would be travesty of truth to say that nothing has improved over the years, though the large disparity between the tribal and non-tribal area in terms of development still exists due to a number of factors, which included but were not limited to a generalized normative approach in formulating and implementing the flagship programmes that formed part of what came to be known as "Bharat Nirman". Most of the flagship programmes adopted the population-criterion for selection of villages and projects, which failed to capture the reality of the thinly-populated tribal habitats, and therefore, could not benefit in equal measure these Scheduled Areas or make a dent in the development deficits suffered by them historically.

According to Article 244 of the Constitution, provisions of Vth Schedule to the Constitution shall apply to the administration and control of Scheduled Areas and Scheduled Tribes. The Vth Schedule provides that the Governor may by public notification direct as to whether any particular Act of Parliament or of the Legislature of the State shall apply or not to the Scheduled Areas or any part thereof. He may specify exceptions or modifications for implementing such laws in the Scheduled Areas. The Governor has powers to make Regulations for peace and good governance in Scheduled Areas of the State. In reality, Governors have not exercised powers and responsibilities conferred upon them under these provisions of the Constitution to the desired extent, and the enabling specificity and flexibility in the application of the Plan Schemes thus largely remained on paper. In addition, although various Expert Committees on administration of Scheduled Areas have recommended posting of competent and dedicated government functionaries to Scheduled Areas, again in reality it remains otherwise, with these areas being made sanctuaries for incompetent and delinquent officers, or the posts were at best left vacant. The extension of Panchayats to the Scheduled Areas (PESA) has further deteriorated the situation as the accountability of public servants got diffused and the law contained many unrealistic and un-implementable provisions.

The Desirable Course of Action

Implementation of protective legislation and social welfare measures needs to go hand in hand with vigorous implementation of flagship schemes and other developmental programmes in the Scheduled Areas. The geographical size of the Scheduled Areas and prevailing development deficits should be taken into account while allocating funds instead of earmarking budgetary allocations solely on the basis of proportion of tribal population. It may be noted that tribal communities constituting about 8 percent of the total population are in a majority in about 15 percent of the country's total geographical area, the major chunk of which is specified as Scheduled Area. In Odisha for instance, more than 45 percent of the State's geographical area has tribal communities in a majority, while Scheduled Areas constitute about 55 percent of the total geographical area of Jharkhand and 61 percent in Chhattisgarh. These areas are thinly populated with a large number of scattered villages. The tribal population of these States is about 23 percent, 32 percent, and 26 percent of the total population, respectively. Considering the fact that these large chunks of areas had been treated during the colonial era as

'Excluded' and 'Partially Excluded' and did not receive adequate attention for many decades even after Independence for development of communication network, education, health infrastructure, development of settled agriculture and allied sectors, etc., earmarking of funds solely in proportion to tribal population considering the whole State as a unit, particularly, for infrastructure development i.e. road communication, etc. becomes a case of 'too little and too late'. The existing practice of treating the State as a unit, and according greater priority to villages with higher population, for development of physical infrastructure (e.g. under PMGSY) invariably goes against the interests of thinly-populated Scheduled Area districts. It is a reality that the tribal areas are endowed with natural resources in abundance. Infrastructure development in these areas, particularly road communication and creation of irrigation potential, along with educational development and provision of public health facilities, will help the economy grow faster and reduce the inequity in developing the relatively poorer sections of the society.

Inadequate infrastructure for elementary education in Scheduled Areas:

The national norms for opening of schools, primary health centres (PHCs), sub-centres, etc. have been relaxed in favour of Scheduled Areas. However, the ground reality does not fully match with the stated policy. There are a large number of non-functional schools without teachers or partly functioning with a single teacher. The teachers themselves are often appointed on contractual basis with remuneration below the minimum wage rates. It is often forgotten that education is a first-generation input for tribal communities. Absence of conducive atmosphere at home and lack of awareness among parents place the tribal students at a disadvantage ab-initio. The deficit can be bridged by recruiting more teachers with proper remuneration and maintaining a healthy teacher-students ratio. Considering the poor communication facilities and non-availability of reasonable residential facilities in remote tribal villages around school premises, it is desirable to make provisions for accommodation of teachers, which is possible by adding two extra rooms for residential purposes to each of the existing school buildings. Sarva Shiksha Abhiyan guidelines which permit construction of additional class rooms can be modified to this effect.

Considering the low density of population in Scheduled Areas coupled with small and scattered villages, it may not be feasible to open schools within a distance of one km from the habitation everywhere, as the national policy envisages. The most viable option, therefore, is to open residential schools for the children of the smaller tribal habitations, which do not have primary schools within a distance of one km, which also cater to students from other poor tribal families, thereby provisioning for 100 percent enrolment. Although the Ministry of Tribal Affairs runs a scheme for opening of Ashram schools, clear stipulations need to be made to the effect that the first priority for admission in such schools will go to those tribal students from those habitats which do not have primary schools as per the prescribed national norms. In the absence of such priorities and stipulations, a few Ashram schools are opened casually and boarders of such schools do not necessarily include all the children in the school-going age group of villages which do not have primary schools within one km distance. Ministry of Tribal Affairs may, therefore, specify norms clearly stating that the first priority in admission would go to the students of villages which do not have accessible primary education.

It is often seen that the vacancies of teachers are justified on the ground of non-availability of eligible tribal candidates against the reserved posts. This situation is the result of inadequate attention towards tribal education in past. However, the minimum qualification prescribed for primary school teachers itself renders the tribal candidates ineligible. It is, therefore, necessary that the educational qualifications for primary schools in respect of tribal teachers are relaxed temporarily for a fixed period of time, of say, 10 years from the date of appointment. The appointment of less-qualified tribal candidates in primary schools can be made subject to their acquiring the required qualifications within 10 years of recruitment, wherever qualified tribal candidates for district cadre teacher's posts are not available. Simultaneously, development of educational training infrastructure must be taken up in each Scheduled Area district.

Flexible norms for implementation of flagship programmes:

Almost all the national flagship programmes have a clear bias in favour of bigger villages due to higher weightage for higher density of population. The population norms for selection of villages under the flagship programmes, whether it is for roads, electrification, drinking water or telecommunication, invariably go against the interest of thinly populated tribal villages in Scheduled Areas. The uniform approach followed in implementing flagship programmes, therefore, needs to be changed. It is also noticed that allocations are made for different components and flexibility for adjustments among various components is limited. There should be a mechanism to allow diversion of funds from one component to another or higher allocation of funds for the components which are considered more viable. For example, incentives are given under the National Rural Health Mission (NRHM) for institutional deliveries. In Scheduled Areas, the infrastructure for the institutional deliveries is grossly inadequate. To illustrate, in Odisha more than 50 to 70 percent of the posts of doctors remain vacant for years in some of the Scheduled Area districts, and equipment and other facilities hardly exist in PHCs. Road communication is far from satisfactory, thereby restricting approach to the district hospitals, in which too, only about 10 percent beds are earmarked as 'female wards'. It would doubtless be better if higher allocations under NRHM are earmarked for construction of PHCs, sub-centres and for providing incentives, including residential facilities, to the health functionaries posted at the Block and village levels. More posts for health workers need to be created in addition to special drives for filling up of the existing vacancies as there is no back-up from the private sector in these areas.

Administrative Infrastructure and Incentives:

The administrative infrastructure in the Scheduled Area districts is usually not strong enough to be effective for implementing most of the flagship schemes, which in reality at times tend to become expenditure-driven. Multiplicity of administration (ITDAs/ITDPs and DRDAs) which function in Scheduled Area districts with similar mandates and without any effective coordination between them has only added to the confusion among innocent tribals, besides diffusing accountability of the public functionaries. The extension of Panchayats to the Scheduled Areas has not succeeded in reconciling the dichotomy and administrative fragmentation by providing a single line of administration. The capacity and needs of line departments responsible for implementation of schemes need to go hand in hand with allocations that are received for various planned and non-planned programmes.

Moreover, since Scheduled Areas do not provide the essential infrastructure and facilities, government functionaries try to avoid postings in those areas. Functionaries of State cadres should, therefore, be provided with financial incentives and accommodation facilities for their families in the State or regional headquarters during their posting in the Scheduled Area districts. They could be given fixed tenure of one to two years to be followed by a choice posting as in Armed Forces.

Involvement of Tribal Communities in Implementing Programmes and their Empowerment:

One of the reasons cited for non-execution or delay in execution of development projects i.e. roads, bridges, minor irrigation projects, buildings etc. in tribal areas is unwillingness of contractors (who are mostly outsiders) to execute these works in remote locations and inadequate entrepreneurship among the local people. Steps have hardly been taken to train and build capacity and otherwise also encourage the local people to take up such vocations. Empanelment of contractors at the lowest level ('D' class) is usually done on the recommendation of bigger contractors who do not appear to be keen to involve the local/tribal people for executing projects. The local people, therefore, remain indifferent or uninvolved which ultimately leads to imbalance and conflicts. In any case, the process of development can not be sustained if it is merely superimposed from outside. It is therefore, necessary to identify the local tribal youth and train them to develop their entrepreneurial skills. Once the educated tribal youths are trained in the contract management, easily implementable and technically less complex projects can be awarded to them to start with, along with some hand-holding. Stipulations to this effect can be made in the flagship programmes. Over a period of time, trained tribal youth, with some experience in successfully implementing simpler projects, can graduate to higher levels to execute bigger and technically more complex projects. This would lead to actual empowerment in addition to breaking the dissonance between local communities and programme implementation.

Specially designed targeted projects:

Implementation of specially-designed and targeted schemes, with relatively small financial budgets, has nevertheless greatly contributed to the improvement of critical infrastructure of tribal districts. The Long-Term Action Plan (LTAP) introduced by the Central Government to address the development deficits of relatively backward and Left-Wing Extremism-affected KBK districts of Odisha helped in bridging many critical gaps. This scheme, rechristened the Revised Long-Term Action Plan (RLTAP), along with two other schemes, namely, the Backward Area Development Fund (BRGF) and Integrated Action Plan (IAP) gave impetus to decentralized planning and aimed at bridging those critical development deficits which remained unaddressed by other bigger central and centrally sponsored schemes. The district administrations leverage the flexi-funds available under these specially-designed and targeted schemes, which amounted to only about Rs. 60 crore per annum for each of the KBK districts of Odisha, but which hugely helped in dealing with the challenge of under-development. Unfortunately, these schemes which have been found to be effective have now been suddenly discontinued, and that too without even providing time and space for substitution and grounding of alternative viable schemes. This stoppage is bound to halt the growth impetus lately imparted to these Scheduled Areas, besides adversely impacting the vulnerable tribal communities. A more prudent approach would have been to allow continuance of such schemes on cost-sharing basis with States. Simultaneously, the States could have been encouraged to fully own up the specially-designed and targeted schemes without Central support.

In conclusion, it remains a truism in the case of Scheduled Areas as elsewhere that legal provisions in relation to entitlements and programmes alone cannot be the instruments of change in the absence of certain prerequisites and actions on ground".

State Planning and Coordination Department's notification of 10 September 2015, as reported in media stated that three senior officers including one from a batch below mine had been appointed for supervising developmental programmes in Malkangiri, Nabarangpur and Nuapada districts. I was informed by a senior officer in Planning & Coordination over phone that his Department had simply notified what Chief Minister desired. I was in Malkangiri at that time and felt it no longer desirable for me to continue with my tour. On return, I responded demi-officially on 14 September 2015 stating that the notification had a presumptive negative cast that either I was not equal to the task or that the post of KBK Chief Administrator was in actuality a parking place for an inconvenient officer. I conveyed my inability to visit these three districts, asserting that oversight by officials of same status amounted to duplication of work besides sending confusing signals to district administration.

As I had anticipated, I was informed over phone about my transfer at 3:30 p.m. on 24 September 2015 by Special Secretary, GA Department. He faxed me a copy of the transfer order and I instantly relinquished charge as Chief Administrator, KBK Districts. A couple of news items published in the newspapers "The Hindu" and "The Asian Age" were brought to my notice which attributed my transfer to my free and frank article in "The Indian Express", besides appreciating and acknowledging my work in KBK Districts. Neither of these events and reports held any meaning to me nor disturbed my peace of mind.

* * * *

14

The Past Gone, Seizing Today[1]: Closure of Innings

When the two additional charges of R&DM Department and OSDMA were withdrawn by the Government, while continuing as KBK Chief Administrator I was additionally given the post of Director General, Gopabandhu Academy of Administration (DG, GAA), the apex State Administrative Training Institute, with effect from 22 April 2015. This became my sole charge after 25 September 2015. My initial desire to lead the life of a teacher had remained unfulfilled. I was indeed happy to hold additional charge of DG, GAA, which offered me the possibility to take some lectures/ classes. I could also directly interact with administrative officers who came to the Academy for training in an array of mostly topical subjects. Having worked as Deputy Director General (DDG) in GAA for a brief period in the year 1999, I was also well aware of its functioning. Indeed, my first exposure to administration in Odisha was through GAA. Now, I was likely to conclude my innings and superannuate from it, which to me was a pleasant coincidence.

The Academy as I found after joining did not have the vibrancy I had seen in my earlier stint in spite of having improved infrastructure and other facilities in order to meet the training needs of State cadre services; its primary responsibility. After the 2006 batch of OAS, the main professional year-long training course for fresh recruits had stopped since recruitments were held up due to a number of litigations on reservations. Refresher training programmes for All India Service officers had also been discontinued as DoPT had stopped sponsoring such programmes, not being satisfied with the performance of this premier training institute. The regular faculty had shrunk in size, probably due to sparse training activities. It was also a bitter truth that State Government found GAA a place for parking senior officers perceived as inconvenient.

---

1. Robert Browning, *Rabbi Ben Ezra* "… Since life fleets, all is change; the past gone, seize today! …"

However, there was no dearth of funds to conduct short-term training courses. These training programmes were funded by Government of India, State Government and many other entities including UNDP, UNICEF, PSUs, etc. Fortunately, I was given additional charge of GAA in the beginning of the training calendar year and the training schedule for the year 2015-16 had not been finalized. That gave me scope to draw the training calendar for the whole year taking into account the backlog for which funds had been received in earlier years but trainings had not been conducted.

At the administrative end, although the Academy had a sprawling campus it needed attention for proper and sustained maintenance. Construction of a couple of training halls and a computer lab had not progressed despite expiry of timelines for completion. Strangely, furniture and computers had already been procured which had led to allegations of malpractices in procurements. Hostel rooms, except a few meant for IAS probationers, were not in habitable condition.Catering facility too was found to be drawing adverse feedback from participants of short-term training courses. The compound of the Academy had construction materials and debris scattered all over. Stocks of old and unserviceable furniture and garbage did not offer a healthy feeling and conducive atmosphere for training. The drainage system had become defunct due to lack of repairs and regular maintenance. It was not difficult to fix these problems by some amount of attention and decentralization with accountability. I called the engineers of Works and Public Health Engineering Departments and gave them tight timelines for completion of incomplete works including installation of a lift. The contractor was told to remove unwanted construction materials and store what was required properly in clearly designated places which were now drawn out. Special repairs of hostel rooms too were undertaken simultaneously.

Although the training academy had a good library, it needed to be organized and computerized. A time-bound programme was drawn up for cataloguing and computerization of books and records. Officers including regular faculty members were assigned specific supervisory tasks. Data entry operators were contracted as per the assessed requirement for computerization of the library.Progress of assigned work was reviewed on fortnightly basis.

Within the next 6 months, GAA campus got transformed with construction work completed, broken furniture disposed off, hostel rooms repaired and painted and catering services improved. The same manpower, hitherto unorganised, started managing the systems at GAA efficiently. I did not like to take up and fix up accountability for mismanagements, including on procurements, marred by allegations received prior to my joining here. Instead, I focused on streamlining the Academy's functioning. Indeed, the Accountant General who had wanted to audit its accounts was persuaded to wait for a few months. After things were set right, he lost interest in the audit he was desperate to conduct probably having received allegation petitions regarding malpractices in procurements suspected to have taken place.

The training environment improved which resulted in improvement in quality as well as quantity of the Academy's training output. The practice of providing course materials to trainees had been discontinued. Summaries of guest lectures held in the past which were being compiled, also stood abandoned. The same guest speakers were being invited for lectures in most of the courses regardless of poor feedback from trainee officers about many of them. These practices needed to be changed. I set up a small committee to prepare a directory of experts locally available who could be invited as guest speakers for different training courses and also to compile names of those involved in lecturing during the past 3 years along with their feedback scores. The task was completed quickly. It was now made mandatory for course coordinators to compile course materials for every training programme and present a copy to me in advance. UNDP and UNICEF were willing to extend training support which included evaluation of training modules and courses conducted in past. Considering the limited number of permanent faculty members in the Academy, I got three good consultants appointed whose services were also utilized for conducting training.

As a result of efforts made proactively, the usage of training infrastructure improved substantially including occupancy of hostels for participants. The total number of training courses conducted by GAA increased to 213 with participation of 6,959 officers in 2015-16 as against 151 courses conducted for 4,650 participants the previous year. DoPT took note of the improvements and made higher allocations for conducting a larger number of training courses during the year 2015-16. The number of training courses sponsored by them with participation of middle-level State Government officers increased from 74 courses attended by 2,350 officers during 2014-15to 114 courses with participation of 4,111 officers in 2015-16. DoPT in conjunction with UNDP also now selected GAA to hold a National Workshop for introducing innovative training techniques which had senior resource persons and training heads of neighbouring States in attendance. It was satisfying to find the State training academy regaining its prominence steadily. The library's automation was completed. The new training halls and computer laboratories became functional. Furniture and fixtures procured before construction of rooms had been completed and left lying scattered in corridors, were put to use effectively.

Preparation of 30 District Gazetteers: Unfinished Symphony?

What gave me greater satisfaction during my 14 months' tenure, which included additional charge of the Academy for the first five months and substantive charge thereafter till 30 June 2016, was preparation of 17 new and updating of 13 existing District Gazetteers, thus covering all 30 districts of the State. Historically, Imperial Gazetteers were prepared by colonial administrators for 6 districts of then Odisha: Angul, Balasore, Cuttack, Koraput, Puri and Sambalpur. After Independence, the scheme for compilation of District

Gazetteers had been transferred from Central Sector to State Sector in the year 1957. Within the State, the responsibility of developing them remained with Revenue Department for over 40 years before being transferred to GAA in the year 1999. Although 10 out of 13 districts had been reorganized into 27 in between 1992-94, and the total number of districts had increased from 13 to 30, this reality had not been captured by updating the existing 13 District Gazetteers, what to speak of compiling additional ones for recast 17 districts.

When I took charge at the helm of the Academy the full documentary of my three decades in administration covering every district played itself out before my eyes as though in a beautiful video-recall. I was mesmerized by the thought of capturing the evolution of 30 districts from their variously economic, sociological, political, and cultural captivating hues in individual compendia. I was sure that details documented, after authentication by State administration at district and other levels, would be useful to those who wanted to learn about the State. It was as though I was posted here towards the very end of my tenure to capture the State and its people in 30 administrative labours of love for them.

Without wasting any time and any further ado, I set about meticulously planning the execution of this mammoth self-task immediately after taking charge of the Academy with the highest sense of urgency. Having formed the draft template for the Gazetteer and drawn up the roadmap to their development, I took a series of time-bound initiatives from the first week of May 2015. The bedrock of these initiatives was the complete and continuous involvement of District Collectors and heads of line Departments at the district level responsible for coverage of issues and unearthing developments over time recorded authentically in their dusty files. The participation of scholars and experts, including some of the well-meaning, knowledgeable, serving and retired civil servants, was ensured to add the vital dose of completeness and coherence to the efforts of many in each district. A panel of 30 well-known such scholars and experts which included 6 retired top civil servants was prepared. They had needed no persuasion to add their might to collate, analyse and refine the draft of the District Gazetteer of their choice.

A standard synopsis for materials to be broadly included in each Gazetteer was prepared in the Academy in consultation with experts after wading through the old Gazetteers. This synopsis was sent to District Collectors to guide them for compilation of initial drafts. To further guide and facilitate the job of the Collector, a two-tiered structure at district level was put in place. A Committee headed by the Collector was specifically constituted for compiling the initial draft of each respective district. District Collectors were taken on board for determining the membership of their Committee. It would not only comprise of Heads of district-level line departments, but would include local experts to add useful facts and minutiae in the initial draft to be finalized at its level by the district concerned. At its second tier, to assist the Committee, Sub-

Committees were formed at the respective district level for drafting specific and thematic chapters within a specified time-frame. The District Collectors were told to submit their first-cut drafts prepared at district level for scrutiny and further interaction with the administration before the second-stage drafts were handed over to respective scholars and experts at State-level to provide their holistic consideration on the texts.

Simultaneously, I proposed the reconstitution of the State Advisory Committee and State Working Committee on Gazetteers to the Chief Secretary. These Committees had last been constituted in the year 1985 and none of their nominated members was around! DG, GAA was not even a member of these Committees.This was hardly surprising, as no thought or effort had been made to reconstitute these Committees after the Gazetteer Organization was transferred from Revenue Department to the Academy in the year 1999. The reconstituted Committees were notified quickly. The State Advisory Committee as reconstituted was now headed by Chief Secretary, in place of Chief Minister, and DG, GAA and eminent experts were included as its constituent members. DG, GAA was now the Chairperson of the State Working Committee, replacing the Member of Board of Revenue, and he was also notified as the Ex-officio Chief Editor of District Gazetteers, besides granting him full functional freedom to prepare and publish the latest editions.

As conceptualized, 30 eminent scholars/ experts were simultaneously appointed as Consulting Editors, one for each District Gazetteer, who voluntarily accepted the challenge of refining the second-stage draft to be prepared by the district level Committee in an iterative mode with GAA within a period of six months. Consulting Editors were given the option to visit their respective districts as and when felt necessary to interact with district level Committees at both the tiers and to interact with any local experts for clarity. District Collectors were asked to facilitate such visits, expenses of which were to be borne by GAA. I had got approval of the reconstituted State Advisory Committee at its first meeting on the requirement of funds along with the milestones and time-frame to complete the District Gazetteers. Consulting Editors were to furnish the final draft by end of April 2016 for final editorial task by the Chief Editor.

Since time was short, Government Press was taken on board and asked to go ahead with preparatory works for printing the District Gazetteers before 30 June 2016. Indeed, the State Advisory Committee in its second meeting held after the perusal of first rough drafts containing factual inputs and reference materials received from District Collectors had made substantive observations. It had also specified on indicative basis the size of the document, quality of paper to be used for printing it, number of copies, and normative cost, while authorizing the Chief Editor to work out the final details in consultation with Director of Odisha Government Press. The only formality remaining to be observed was that the final drafts of District Gazetteers needed to be placed before the State Advisory Committee at its third meeting for approval before being sent to Government Press for printing.

The time allotted for collection of materials for the initial draft by the District Collector was three months. GAA regularly monitored their progress and resolved glitches and nudged lagging Sub-Committees on any specific chapter or theme across districts. Accordingly, GAA started receiving the rough drafts from District Collectors beginning August 2015. After an in-house scrutiny of these drafts, comments and suggestions for addressing deficiencies and gaps were forwarded to the District Collectors concerned to enable them revise the drafts suitably with the help of experts at district level. A process of continuous monitoring and iterative development of the next stage of drafts was also followed.The second set of drafts were received by end-October 2015. These second-stage drafts were now placed for scrutiny at two levels, the first by the public at large by hosting them on the website of the Academy, and the second by the designated set of 30 Consulting Editors, one for each district.

Consulting Editors had already been provided with copies of old District Gazetteers of the mother districts along with draft synopsis of respective districts assigned to them to maintain some amount of uniformity. This advance action enabled them to study the old Gazetteers from the perspective of developing new ones besides carrying out the complex analysis of the evolutionary trends in the last many decades. Consulting Editors had full freedom to rearrange and add new chapters considering the uniqueness of their district and to cover any omitted or emerging field of importance by becoming creative and innovative. It had been made clear that the District Gazetteer being an authoritative document, it should reflect the history, geography, climate, natural phenomena, biodiversity, economic, political and administrative set-up to name a few, in all its hues and in a manner so as to highlight key developments over time. After all, these facets needed to be documented in ink to stand in testimony of the timelessness of the unique and prismatic local culture and ethos. The document could enable viewing the district way beyond the telescopic lens of mere geographical or political boundaries and administrative units.

A series of meetings were held with Consulting Editors to discuss the refinement of second-stage drafts prepared by the two-tiered Committees at district level to ensure accuracy, coherence, quality and content. Some Consulting Editors visited their respective districts repeatedly to interact with senior government officials, non-government organizations, local experts and persons concerned with the preparation of initial two drafts to seek further clarifications. The third-stage drafts, reviewed at the Academy with the Consulting Editors,were again forwarded torespective Collectors for authentication of content and further improvement, wherever felt necessary.

The final round of discussion on this fourth-stage draft Gazetteers with the respective Consulting Editors was held in April 2016. All the 30 documents were thus finalized after approval by the State Working Committee on Gazetteers.They were kept in readiness for printing by the Government Press. Necessary funds had been advanced to the Government Press for purchase of papers and to meet the other related requirements. Cover page, preface and other specifications had also been worked out simultaneously. The time in hand was limited and I was eager to see all the 30 District Gazetteers published within the timelines that had been set out for the task. Indeed, my sudden removal from the post of Chief Administrator, KBK Districts on 24 September 2015 was a blessing in disguise as that gave me an interrupted period of 9 months to singularly focus on the Gazetteer project.

The task of developing the updated Gazetteers for 30 districts was quite humongous requiring painstaking working on the successive 30 multi-stage drafts, as each evolved into District Gazetteer document of 400 to 500 pages. Even though the State Government had accepted the request of Union Ministry of Sports to spare my services in connection with South Asian Games, 2016 at Guwahati/ Shillong for over two and half months, I advanced the Gazetteer Project simultaneously apace with the prescribed timelines approved by the State Advisory Committee in its first meeting held on 21 August 2015 and reiterated in the second meeting held on 21 December 2015.

I had furnished a proposal to Chief Secretary on 10 March 2016 for the State Advisory Committee to take phase-wise consideration of District Gazetteers in April 2016 after they were reviewed, finalised and recommended by the State Working Committee on Gazetteers. I personally requested him in his capacity as Chairman of the State Advisory Committee to assign the dates for the proposed meetings any time after 6 April 2016 to enable the Gazetteers to benefit from the State Advisory Committee's guidance and approval considering the tight timelines for printing them by 30 June 2016. As desired by him, I sent four sample drafts of District Gazetteers in hard copies, which had been duly recommended by the State Working Committee in its meeting held on 11 April 2016, emphasizing that the documents of all 30 districts would be sent electronically to each member of the State Advisory Committee for their examination as part of the agenda papers as soon as dates for the State Advisory Committee meetings were indicated by him.

As providence seemed to have designed differently, the Chief Secretary in position since 30 November 2015 after the superannuation of the previous incumbent, prevaricated and stopped responding to my request. I had never thought that my frank discussions and issue-based disagreements with him on administrative matters including in meetings taken by Chief Minister when he had also served as his Additional Chief Secretary had been silently viewed with such adversity that he had not only become indifferent to my proposal but was refusing to take my calls. It became clear that my target to bring out District Gazetteers before calling it a day was now nearly impossible. Suddenly on 19 May 2016, I received a call from Office of Chief Minister conveying that Chief Minister desired to know when the District Gazetteers could be ready for formal release by him. I had never had occasion to discuss the project undertaken in GAA to develop/update District Gazetteers with Chief Minister or any senior officer in his office and was pleasantly surprised to find the enquiry being made on the matter from his office. I truthfully informed the senior official in Chief Minister's Office that the Gazetteers of all the 30 districts as approved by the State Working Committee were ready, but could not be formally released without approval of the State Advisory Committee, and I was not sure whether that was going to happen in the next few days. It was not possible for me to give any indication as to when the Gazetteers would be approved for printing by the State Advisory Committee. The alternative was that these could be released in electronic formats, as printing and binding required more time. This also could happen only after the State Advisory Committee endorsed the drafts as prepared. I informed the Chairman of State Advisory Committee-cum-Chief Secretary in writing about the enquiry made by Chief Minister's office and sent him duly bound hard copies of all the 30 District Gazetteers as approved by the State Working Committee, with copies to Chief Minister's office on 21 May 2016. There was no response; my calls again remained unanswered and my so-called ambition to conclude the Gazetteer project unfulfilled.

In spite of involving myself fully in the task assigned to me, I made conscious efforts to remain emotionally detached from my assignments by and large. The development of District Gazetteers was perhaps the only mission I got emotionally attached with at the concluding phase of my innings in administration. Perhaps it was a lesson and a message from providence not to develop attachment on any matter and to remain emotionally neutral in professional matters while making every possible effort to achieve the set-out goals. As my plan to stay within the timelines for completion of my dream project was going to remain unrealized, I requested Director NIC to allot more space for hosting all the 30 District Gazetteers, as finalized by the State Working Committee, on the website of GAA for facilitating any further deliberations on them and for any suitable use of stakeholders. This was done. However, I was informed by some officials associated with the Gazetteer project that after a few months of my retirement, orders were issued for removal of the newly developed Gazetteers from GAA's website. Having now been liberated from the bondage of administration for some months, I was happy to find that I had by now internalized the lesson in detachment from professional matters and I never ever found myself reflecting on what finally happened to my humongous efforts.

Interestingly, another batchmate who had taken charge as Additional Chief Secretary to Chief Minister told me just before my superannuation that a former Chief Secretary had cautioned both him and Chief Secretary against bringing out the District Gazetteers being worked on. He had tried to package his caution by casting an apprehension that the quality and contents of these documents which were being prepared in fourteen months would not be to the desired standards. According to him, updating a couple of District Gazetteers decades ago had taken a decade or more despite a very senior "retired" civil servant being given exclusive charge of the Gazetteer Organization duly supported by a number of research officers and other functionaries. This former Chief Secretary had enjoyed post-retirement employment for 5 years in a constitutional post and appeared to be angling for a decade-long assignment! I had enjoyed good relations with him, but I now realized that it was I who had failed to read his mind correctly when he had visited me some months earlier to compliment me for my initiatives to update and compile the District Gazetteers. He had conveyed his desire to contribute without remuneration if the Government wanted his services as Chief Editor of the District Gazetteers. I had then taken his complimentary words at face value, and had handed him a very rough initial draft of one District Gazetteer naively believing that he wished to contribute without any other angle or self-interest attached to it. A mere 10 days before my retirement I was told by a Deputy Director and a Senior Research Officer of the Gazetteer Section at GAA that the said retired Chief Secretary had also visited them once in my absence and warned against attempts to bring out the District Gazetteers in a hurry adding that he would personally lodge a protest before Chief Secretary and Chief Minister on this issue. It is futile to elaborate here that many contemporaries in other States and in Union Department of Personnel & Training evinced serious interest in the development of updated Odisha District Gazetteers.

Odisha, a State ranked amongst the highest in development potential given the abundance of its natural resources and endowed with highly productive and intelligent human resources, has not been able to find its rightful place in the comity of major States of the Indian Union. Probably, one of the reasons was the crab-mentality or jealous disposition coupled with lack of team spirit and self-serving pre-occupations of a few holding influential positions in the society and in the affairs of the State. This proclivity will have to change for better days to come.

Just a Bitter Taste at Closure of Administrative Innings

I became politically and administratively inconvenient on 16 December 2014 when I failed to bend and give the State Government an alibi it felt was desperately needed before the High Court. I had rejected outright the suggestion of the top brass, duly endorsed by his battery of top advisors, that I should state that the Report of the Task Force on allocation of houses/flats/land under Discretionary Quotas was an "interim" one, and thereby to seek more time for submission of a "final" Report. The Task Force Report, which was uniquely submitted in three months against the timeline of four months. It was unsparing, non-discriminatory, and without fear or favour named illegal beneficiaries most of whom were highly placed in their walks of life – legislature, executive, judiciary, fourth estate, and persons of eminence in private business and social strata. At a convenient moment when the heat and dust had settled a bit and sticky fingers could not be raised against them, I was quietly shifted out of R&DM Department on 20 April 2015. As compared to any other administrative head of that Department, I had arguably wreaked the maximum damage against vested interests who viewed Government land as freely available pure gold.

Reprisal was rather instant. On 28 July 2015, the Government in GA Department filed a Revision Case under the Odisha Estate Abolition (OEA) Act in the Court of Member Board of Revenue with regard to Ac.0.10 of land I had purchased in 1993 in Bhubaneswar under intimation to GA Department as per prescribed procedure. 22 years later, it was now alleged that illegality and fraud had been perpetrated, not by me I might add, but by those who existed no more – the original owner of that land, Tahasildar and Land Reform Commissioner. The piece of land in question stood recorded against the original owner, after many rounds of hearing, revisional hearings following the survey and settlement operations concluded in 1970s. The top official in GA Department, before deciding to file this case, seemed not to be bothered that Government was variously represented in the legal proceedings which had already concluded in 1977 after an elaborate order was passed by the highest land revenue authority and were seeking to question it 42 years after it was passed!Land Reforms Commissioner, enjoying the same legal powers as the Member, Board of Revenue, had passed the order well before I had even joined the IAS and been allotted Odisha cadre in 1983. That the OEA affected 51 other owners of the total piece of land in question, and that the original owner, his elder sons and the Revenue officers holding quasi-judicial powers at that time whose bona fides now being questioned were all long dead and gone and could not answer the questions was irrelevant for the servile minions of a political dispensation desperate for some straw to clutch on to.

When the fallacy in this governmental action was pointed out by me, retribution was again swift. Orders were passed on 10 September 2015 appointing "supervisory officers" for three out of eight KBK Districts handled by me. The simultaneous appointment of Chief Minister's ACS to oversee work in communally-sensitive Kandhamal (not a KBK district) was a mere distraction. Except one who was from a junior batch, all these supervisory officers held the same rank to mine. None of these officers while heading departments had taken the trouble nor time to tour KBK Districts regardless of mandatory requirement of such visits at regular intervals. The purpose of the said appointment appeared to be to seek to humiliate me. I politely and firmly questioned the propriety and far-reaching implications of overlaps and dichotomy in administration which would lead to diffusion of responsibility and lack of accountability through my letter dated 14 September 2015. Now that their 'retribution' had befallen me, it perhaps also hardly mattered as to how many days were actually spent supervising the three districts on field by the three Supervisors put together thereafter or indeed by my successors as KBK Chief Administrator after I had quit the charge. The only thing that mattered in essence was the accelerated development of KBK Districts. If the decision takers felt that it was best achieved by the responsibility being tossed around as if it was merely a game of musical chairs to be played out by its Chief Administrators or Supervisors whenever the music was switched on by the decision takers, so be it.

I think it was the veritable last straw on the back of the political camel when an article of mine committed to be written and sent to the Editor prior to the unfolding of the events from 10 September 2015, got published in the Indian Express on 17 September 2015. It hardly mattered that the whole article was positive. While laying out the status of KBK Districts and many progressive actions being taken by the State Government, it outlined the substantive way forward to bridge the development deficit of the region. Apparently, only a sentence in it could be considered hurtful: "*in reality it remains otherwise, with these areas being made sanctuaries for incompetent and delinquent officers, or the posts were at best left vacant.*" I suppose it came just too soon after the appointment of Supervisory Officers in three KBK Districts just a week prior. I was divested of my charge of Chief Administrator of KBK Districts on 24 September 2015.

The tragedy from my perspective was acute. Those who had selected me to head the Task Force, knew fully well about my unwavering commitment to the content and speed of execution of any assigned tasks. To suffer their revenge for denying to delay the submission of the Report was the worst to digest. Surely, having secured a reprieve for themselves from the activists because I had been chosen to head the Task Force, they should not have turned around to discredit me publicly. If they never intended that the Task Force should finish its tasks in the given time, they had an option to choose another who would have sought any amount of extension of time at their behest.

Temptation or Threat to Transfer and Organised Campaign

A member of the Task Force informed me once in the middle of December 2014 that after the submission of the Task Force Report when I had gone to LBSNAA at Mussoorie for delivering a Guest Lecture on disaster management, a proposal for my transfer was put up to the Chief Minister. This member, incidentally, had also worked as Private Secretary to Chief Minister years back and still remained close to his inner circle. But, Chief Minister rejected it outright and reprimanded his closest advisers who had mooted it. He had added that Chief Minister had great regard and liking for me. After a few days when Chief Minister wanted me to seek further time for preparing a "final" Report of the Task Force, I could fathom the truth. Obviously, the so-called high regard for me and rejection of my transfer proposal were not for nothing.

It was vexatious and troublesome that immediately after my departure from R&DM Department, there was nothing short of an organized campaign against me, with even attempts to discredit my work done while in service, which also appeared to being carried out in tandem with a section of print and electronic media. By a few possibly chosen ones, the multiple avenues to discredit me were publicized with alacrity. The Task Force Report had mentioned names of some of the top journalists and editors as illegal beneficiaries of discretionary quota. Since those named now stood to lose that largesse bestowed by State administration, they were more than willing to extend a large helping hand to my detractors, including the bureaucratic head of State Administration and lamentably some other top officials in Chief Minister's office whose request to treat the Task Force Report as an interim one so as to buy time for the beleaguered State Government, had been rejected by me in the presence of Chief Minister. After all, in my usual plainspeak, I had posed blunt questions on their understanding of the "terms and reference" of the mandate of the Task Force, statutory provisions, and propriety of their advice to Chief Minister.

The coterie of certain key officials was only interested in harassing me by engineering adverse publicity against me for my failure to toe their line on the saga of political largesse in discretionary quota allocations. They were also miffed with me for not favouring, even if it meant not being steadfast in government service, an encroacher of about 15 acres of valuable government land who appeared to be their fast friend. Perhaps with my proclivity towards straight-batting and persistence with cleaning out the Augean stables in every post I handled, I had wrong-footed and captured some other favourites of theirs. It was perhaps easy to use Member, Board of Revenue, as a tool against me in the whole exercise since his close relative was named in the list prepared by the Task Force of those who benefitted illegally from the State's largesse. Besides, he was perhaps still vulnerable, may be due to a bitter experience in the past; his name had unfairly figured in the list of corrupt officials on the website of CVC years back. Departmental proceedings against him had been concluded only a few months back. What else could explain why and how only my name was being singularly publicized out of 51 persons which actually included many senior government officers who had purchased land from the same owner of land. It would be laughable if only the intent had not been vicious. The revision case filed in the Court of Member, Board of Revenue, being devoid of merit was stayed by the High Court instantly on being challenged by me. GA Department was not interested in pursuing the litigation any more as the limited purpose of the engineered adverse publicity against me had been achieved. Those who filed the case had been admonished by the Court in the course of the hearing for suppressing vital facts and relevant legal provisions. The top officials also knew it well that the litigation would not withstand judicial scrutiny, but had been monitoring its proceeding closely hoping against odds of hearing something in their favour from the Court!

Anonymous Petition that was not Rightfully Consigned to Anonymity

The top functionary in GA Department, I found out was working on another plan simultaneously just to give him salacious moments and sadistic pleasure even if temporarily, which too ultimately could not be sustained on the factual test. An undated, anonymous allegation petition against me, which contained no name or address of the sender, received by Chief Secretary was forwarded to my successor one month after my departure from R&DM Department with directions to examine and put up quickly.

My successor, it seems did not choose to either apply her mind nor heed to the instructions to consign "anonymous complaints" to the veritable dust bin i.e. dismiss them *in limine*(at the very beginning), which stood issued and were applied against everyone similarly placed by both Central Government in Department of Personnel & Training and Central Vigilance Commission, as well as the State Government in GA Department. Anonymous complaints are defined as those which do not carry the name and address of the complainant. Similar treatment needed to be meted out to complaints which were pseudonymous and also those which were vague, trivial or frivolous. With approval of Chief Secretary swiftly granted the next day, the allegation petition was sent to the same vulnerable Member, Board of Revenue for carrying out the enquiry.

I came to know about this anonymous petition sometime in October 2015 when the Secretary in the office of Member, Board of Revenue met me on his own and confided that the anonymous petition had been handed over to him for enquiry. He had been directed by the Member to report directly in this matter to the Principal Secretary to Government in R&DM Department. Apparently, Member of Board of Revenue was not inclined to play ball fully this time. Secretary, Board of Revenue, gave me a copy of the allegation petition and the report he had already furnished to the Principal Secretary, R&DM Department, without my requesting him to do so.

Having done nothing for personal gain and discharged my responsibilities with public interest foremost in my mind, I had nothing to worry. As such, Secretary, Board of Revenue, in his report had already trashed the allegation petition and found nothing for anyone holding administrative powers to derive any satisfaction or leads to string me up with. The pre-judgement and prejudice of the top bosses of R&DM and GA Departments was thus borne out. Indeed, the report refuting the allegations outright could embarrass officers with any sense of self-respect holding these high posts in bureaucracy. In their desperate hurry, the heads of these bodies did not feel the need to go through the substance of the allegation petition to find it baseless and flawed and instead opted to forward it for enquiry to the officer who they thought could be manipulated.

In a curious and educative twist of situations, one of the anonymous petitions I had received when I was heading R&DM Department was against the very officer who had succeeded me and was now processing an anonymous, undated petition against me. She incidentally happened to be a trainee officer under me when I was Collector and District Magistrate. The anonymous petition against her had alleged her complicity with a real estate investor who had been arrested by the State Crime Branch for duping consumers. It was alleged that my successor too had purchased a piece of land from him. However, in the fitness of such matters, I had strictly gone by the prescribed procedure and guidelines in handling frivolous, anonymous complaints which otherwise had the potential to defame and demoralize well-meaning officers. That allegation petition had been consigned to anonymity by me. I had handled anonymous allegation petitions against ACS, Finance and other key officials similarly. I failed to understand whether the reason behind my successor's action was my failure in training her appropriately or inclusion of her husband's name in the list of beneficiaries of discretionary quota prepared by the Task Force headed by me. It was incidental that her husband happened to be my predecessor in R&DM Department, many of whose decisions I had reversed.

Another curious development that followed me after my departure from R&DM Department was a flood of hate emails, SMSs, and telephone calls from a person who used to flaunt his proximity with a top official in Chief Minister's office, Chief Secretary, Development Commissioner-cum-ACS, etc. A couple of District Collectors and a few Secretaries in Government had told me how he had mastered the art of getting his proposals recommended in order to access funds from some of the top PSUs in the guise of CSR and from various Government Departments in the guise of vocational trainings, etc. He was frustrated and at his wits end with me as I was making all-out efforts to recover about 15 acres of government land encroached by him while he was pulling all strings to retain it. When he did not desist despite my warnings to him that his hate mails would be reported to the police and Government, I had to send a note with copies of his threatening hate mails received by me to Chief Secretary and DG of Police with copy to Chief Minister's office. No action, however, was taken against him, although he stopped sending hate mails and threatening messages thereafter.

It is not as if I had not faced disturbing moments and difficult bosses in my professional life. I had faced CBI investigations twice, harassing situations in courts of law on a few occasions, and threats and intimidations many times without having committed any wrong deliberately or otherwise. I took these in my stride being symptomatic of professional hazards in public life. It was, however, painful and distressing for me to be subjected to baseless persecution and adverse publicity at the fag end of my professional career for no fault, and by a few of those in top posts now who had travelled the administrative road with me as friends and colleagues for more than 30 years. I had not expected to conclude my innings with any sense of bitterness. Indeed, what I have stated in this tale about them is not with a view to maligning them, but to recount events as these unfolded before my naked eyes demonstrating their eerie intent and uncanny behaviour. I had taken a few of them as my true personal friends for long and tried to unburden and exposed myself before them when felt in serious stress. It did deeply wound me, though without leaving permanent scars. Having lived an austere life, seen and acknowledged by one and all, some of my friends had misunderstood me and tried to present me in poor light towards end of my career. My family life, for long in stress, which suddenly scaled up to complete turmoil due to some misunderstandings, was also leveraged to discredit me by some of my former friends. But as I said the scars have largely faded, and I meet most of them these days with equanimity.

The philosophy of maximizing developmental and other socio-economic outcomes and accountability for my actions remained at the core of my service and career right till the end of my professional innings. I was among the fortunate few who not only got to be posted to various important positions and were allowed to function freely, but who also saw public satisfaction writ large on their faces as public service delivery improved noticeably. This was the sine qua non for as long as I held positions despite occasional bouts of confrontation with some of my bosses including Ministers in charge of the Department to which I stood assigned. I used to feel quite strongly that after most of these face-to-face interchanges, what I earned more was long-term respect from them than if I had opted for timidity and supplication. I thus also felt no bitterness on being transferred when some of my actions became unbearable to those in decision-making positions. It would, of course, be fair to say that I felt a twinge of disappointment that a couple of transfers happened when some key projects or areas of reforms undertaken by me were on the verge of conclusion and I could not tick them off as a job completed in the log-book of my mind. I remained convinced that posts considered to be insignificant or peripheral offered no less opportunities to contribute to the wider public good as do some others where long queues of hopeful officers-in-waiting are to be seen. Creature comforts which the so-called prized posts entailed never attracted me. Infinitely greater satisfaction lay in a job well done in each post.

Odisha: Paradoxes, Opportunities, Politics and Bureaucracy

Odisha State came into existence on 1 April 1936 with amalgamation of certain regions forming part of Bengal Presidency, Madras Presidency, Central Provinces and Bihar. It became part of the Indian Union after Independence. It was counted among socio-economically backward States with nearly 40 percent of its population being ST&SC taken together, with predominance of tribal population in about 50 percent of the State's geographical area which had remained largely inaccessible during colonial administration. A key reason for the State's continuing backwardness has been that for decades after Independence the backwardness of these tribal regions was romanticised in the name of diversity of culture. After creation of Odisha, administrative system of the State got aligned with Bihar. Odisha at higher level bureaucracy was administered by officers of Indian Civil Service (ICS) belonging to combined Bihar-Odisha cadre till Independence. This was why despite the influence of Bengal and Madras Presidencies and that of Central Provinces in adjoining areas, legal and administrative systems followed in Odisha were largely similar to those of Bihar.

Paradoxically, in spite of being one of the richest States of Indian Union in terms of natural resources, Odisha is still counted as one of its poorest even after more than 70 years of Independence. This dichotomy becomes manifest in some of the masterpieces of modern Odia literature. One of the most beautiful poetic expressions of Baikunthunath Patnaik in a devotional song which is often sung by his daughter Sundanda Patnaik, a doyen of Classical Hindustani music, conveys the richness of life in Odisha while acknowledging gratitude to the Almighty stating, "*You have enriched life in every possible way and, therefore, how can I complain that you have given me nothing*"! On the other hand, the contrast is manifest in the expressions of Radhanath Ray, another creative genius of the State when in his poetry while addressing the Goddess of Knowledge, he bluntly asks, "*why did you become so unkind to Odisha in spite of beauty and natural resources in abundance*"!

I found the human resources in the State highly intelligent and creative. Probably for this reason, the State was traditionally known as "Utkal Desh" (the land mass of creativity). It is also, however, true that the tribal areas had not witnessed socio-economic integration and infrastructure development to the desired extent even after Independence which resulted in regional imbalance and gave birth to left wing extremism. Indeed, even in areas in the State where considerable investments have taken place towards development of infrastructure in the recent past, the socio-economic situation has not changed in tangible ways as seen in other States, which indeed begs serious introspection and conducting of detailed independent studies. Odisha accounts for about 4 percent of the country's land mass and population, with more than 10 percent of water resources. Yet, the State continues to suffer due to drought, besides floods. The district which is affected the most due to drought and lack of irrigation potential is Balangir, paradoxically sandwiched between two of the largest rivers, the Mahanadi and the Tel. About half of the population of another drought-prone Nuapada district suffers from use of fluoride-contaminated ground-water in spite of having plenty of safe potable water which is wasted away in rivers and reservoirs. Productivity of agriculture continues to be far below the national average despite a very high level of soil fertility. Exploitation of ground-water despite the table being very high is negligible and consumption of energy in agriculture is a mere one percent. Reserves of major minerals, such as iron ore, chromite, bauxite, coal, etc. are simply incomparable with any other State. It is ironical that the areas with the largest reserves of major minerals, besides being home to a large number of perennial rivers and rivulets, are the poorest parts of the State!

There is no reason for this natural resources-rich State to suffer from poverty and backwardness with intelligent and creative human resources capital and liberal assimilative mindsets. In my assessment, the all-pervasive sense of complacency for long and absence of inspiring leadership in various fields in the recent times are the two main contributors which have denied Odisha its rightful place among developed Indian States. Perhaps, barring Biju Patnaik who is largely responsible for development of major infrastructure during his first two-and-a-half years tenure as Chief Minister in the early 1960s, and J.B. Patnaik's attempts to leave his foot-print by developing agriculture, the State's political leadership has not been inspirational and failed to motivate and drive it onto successively faster lanes of development. The increasing sense of complacency developed into a complaint-psychology finding fault with others in the neighbourhood or national leadership. Ascribing all the ills witnessed in the State to others cannot be taken as a healthy trend for a brighter future of an upwardly mobile society. Some of the populist schemes have only robbed the marginalized lot from a sense of self-pride, which indeed drives socio-economic development elsewhere. The amount of opportunities and scope for development Odisha offers to public servants, perhaps has no parallel elsewhere in the country. People in the State are largely law abiding, supportive and respectful towards high-performance administrative officers. There are no major distractions that prevent public servants from delivering their best. Yet, there is mismatch in terms of outcomes. The reasons need to be analysed.

In my assessment, the risk-taking capacity in administration is perceived to be declining over a period of time, particularly after the first term of Biju Patnaik as Chief Minister which was followed by adverse reports by CAG Audit and a Commission of Enquiry that looked into some of the daring decisions and actions of the most dynamic Chief Minister of the State. Political and administrative leadership in the State stopped being proactive and became more circumspect in taking and implementing decisions thereafter. This approach resulted in two potent and peculiarly unpleasant effects happening at once, a veritable double whammy of corruption and delays in implementation of critically-important developmental projects. The situation only deteriorated when the perception gained ground that the State vigilance machinery or CBI could be used as tools in the hands of Government to settle scores with administrators who did not fall in line and also with political adversaries. When half-a-dozen senior IAS officers are either placed under suspension or posted as 'officers without duty' in one stroke, departmental proceedings are kept pending for 10 to 15 years finally leading to acquittals or minor strictures, and criminal prosecutions against delinquents are not pursued by State's

Vigilance Department till the officers retired, the message conveyed becomes loud and clear. One could find instances of some of the best officers suffering due to decisions they took on merit, which were viewed as politically unrewarding, and on the other hand, pliant or compliant officers neither known for efficiency nor clean hands are seen to be rewarded with key assignments, barring exceptions.

Bureaucracy at the higher level, as I see it, has failed the State as much as the elected political executives. The tendency among a large number of officers of the elite service appears to be to live a cool and cosy material life even if that happens by being more biddable, yielding, and less courageous. There are very few civil servants holding that life without risk, scrutiny and appraisal is not worth living. Risks and hard work are no more seen leading to dignity, high regard and glory. A number of sincere civil servants are seen side-tracked or marginalized. Some of them start developing a side interest, such as pursuit of creative writing and make a concurrent career therein. Their positions in administration serve them well as springboards and suitably-placed stepping stones to reach out and establish themselves in the written, poetic, dramatic, artistic, and other literary worlds. Typically, it is difficult even for the best of writers in local vernacular language to earn a sustaining livelihood on the strength of their creative contributions, but these administrators have the cushion of an assured pay-packet and official residence and seldom have to worry and give up literary advancements for want of finances.

Perhaps the biggest strength of government servants, particularly in the elite services, is that those not caught and convicted in criminal cases enjoy virtually assured and timely promotions till retirement as if as a matter of right. In fact, getting in service appears to have become easier than getting out of service. There are a fortunate few like me, who lacked ability to jump into alternative disciplines concurrently to get established, and did not suffer in terms of being marginalized for not being compliant followers either. I was never a watchful careerist nor active in administrative socializing. Somehow I felt that it was unwarranted and entirely unnecessary for senior bureaucrats to succumb to their fear and convey helplessness when their actions taken in supplication under pressure were revealed. Indeed, by playing the developmental game correctly and with care there is hardly any risk of being out. The sense of fear and complacency directly correlates to lack of courage of conviction and will-power and unwillingness to apply one's mind to analyse the long-term outcome of inaction or rendering advice to only keep the bosses happy for momentary petty gains. It pained me to find some senior officers escalating simple or routine administrative decisions to the highest-level despite being empowered to take the call, only to avoid the associated responsibilities. The opportunity cost and losses in the event of delayed or wrong decisions in administration is no more a matter of concern. The vast majority of officers rarely take note of it in the increasingly competitive environment. The term accountability is also seldom found in administrative lexicon. Critically important major development projects are perpetually left incomplete as if to avoid accountability. For instance, major and medium irrigation projects which are critical to development of agriculture on which more than 50 percent of the population depended for subsistence livelihood remain partially implemented in spite of this sector getting the largest share of the State's planned budget. I was informed by a top administrator and expert in the field of irrigation that after the Hirakud major multipurpose project which was completed in mid-1950s, no major irrigation project in the State has been formally closed or completed despite expenditure being incurred in hundreds or thousands of multiples for much smaller similar projects than the Hirakud! I saw it with my eyes when I joined as Chief Administrator of KBK Districts.

I don't believe in romanticizing the past but could not escape sensing the spiralling deterioration in ethical standards of bureaucrats. Many of those holding key positions were seen deriving higher comfort in rendering political advice to their masters, thereby diluting their own administrative role. I was told by one of my colleagues who happened to have worked as Private Secretary to a senior Cabinet Minister in the State that during a general election, he was called to the residential office of Chief Minister by his Private Secretary and was given loads of high currency denominations for delivery to the Minister in his office vehicle to escape from being detected by the watchful eyes of election officials including poll observers. He had not expected this. I was also told by a senior most police officer that he was not only removed from his post when the ruling party returned to power after elections for his inability to assist the party in power by rendering services which were unacceptable to him. He was subjected to harassment in other forms. Criminal and departmental proceedings were drawn against him on the basis of audit paragraphs related to one of his old assignments to prevent him from being considered by the Central Government for the post of Director, CBI. It was his fair name and reputation that saved him when he challenged the vindictive actions of State Government in High Court even after the State Government filed an appeal against the High Court orders in the Supreme Court by hiring top legal luminaries. Luckily, he was allowed to go back on Central deputation from where he retired as head of the biggest central paramilitary force. When I asked him as to what stopped him from spending his post-retired life in Bhubaneswar being a native of Odisha, I was shocked to hear his apprehension that he could suffer again in the hand of a vindictive government if a pliable police functionary is persuaded to plant some narcotic substance and show recovery from his house by enacting a drama of search just to deny him freedom!

Identification with the parties in power, in particular, with the political leadership of the day by some members of the supposedly apolitical civil services is a signal to the vast majority of fence-sitters to either follow them to secure their meteoritic rise to so-called important positions or remain passive in the field of development administration. After all, operational risks might prove to be a barrier instead of smoothly leading them to more significant roles and responsibilities in future. Such perverse thinking on the part of the majority of fence sitters is not necessarily true. My personal experience guided me that some amount of risk taken in public interest might be misunderstood or exploited temporarily in the event of things not turning the intended way in terms of outcome expected for political gains of the political leadership. But it could give a high degree of satisfaction and sense of fulfilment in the long run. I did face CBI enquiries twice, but did not suffer in the long run for the risks I had taken in discharging my duties and responsibilities with pace and consistency. There were several instances when I conveyed my inability to do things which I felt were not in public interest or were against my conscience, but I did not have to suffer for that necessarily. In my opinion, temporary distractions and adverse publicity created by detractors and aggrieved vested interests should neither force nor constrain the capacity of a civil servant who is well protected by law as such things are inevitable professional hazards.

I did not like cultivating relationshipsnor sharing governmental actions with media and strongly believed in working in anonymity. This did lead to keeping occasional lapses hidden within bureaucratic file covers as these did not find their way into media reportage. A former MLA who had been welcomed to the ruling party after she deserted her original party suddenly lost favour of the State leadership when an enquiry conducted by RDC substantiated that she had been elected from a reserved constituency on the basis of a fraudulently-obtained ST certificate. The enquiry report had become public before it reached the office of Chief Minister. Paradoxically, I had submitted another report for removal of Chairperson of a Zila Parishad for fraudulently obtaining an ST certificate and appropriating a post reserved for ST in another district. This issue did not come into public light and so no action was taken against this ruling party functionary who had committed a similar fraud.

There were a few instances of All India Service officers not being allowed their entitlements despite Central Government bearing full expenses, in order to convey to the State and district service cadre employees who constituted the vast majority of government servants that the State leadership treated everyone equally. While the serving All India Services' officers quietly digested this, some of those who had retired, including a Chief Secretary, had to approach CAT to get their entitlements as arrears. This to my mind is also one of the factors that adversely affected the morals and motivation of officers to perform in Odisha. It is a truism that in a system where Constitutional provisions that give protection to public functionaries become a casualty, officers surrender their ability to perform and advise objectively and those still sticking to the Constitutional values get side-lined or suffer in multiple ways. Bureaucracy, in its history in the State, perhaps never stood as domesticated and subjugated, as in the last one and half decade, and the few exceptions that were seen only proved the rule.

Developmental Distortions

Diversity is a strength of Odisha. People in Northern Odisha and Ganjam are habitually hard-working and agriculturally quite advanced, while those from coastal Odisha are more creative in the fields of art and culture. Tribal communities at large are innocently simple and remain unexposed to development paradigms or societal compulsions. The common thread among all of them is that they are not overtly ambitious and remain easy going. Entitlement-based populist schemes attract the people instantly. In the event of natural or man-made calamities, they get satisfied and appear happy if ex-gratia relief and some amount of compensation are provided for the loss of life and property promptly. Not many like to go into causes of such disasters nor call for calamity-resistant measures by Government. Super Cyclone of 1999 resulted in about 10,000 human casualties. Jagatsinghpur which suffered the most received financial assistance for construction of pucca houses under Indira Awas Yojana. But the number of beneficiaries was more than the number of households in the district. Even after fifteen years of the disaster, it was not difficult for anyone to see that more than 50 percent houses in villages of Jagatsinghpur were still with mud walls and thatched roofs. This is precisely because relief and assistance were provided instantly, but State administration failed to maintain close watch over the redevelopment phase of construction of proper houses.Their vulnerability to another natural disaster befalling on at least 50 percent of the populace with devastating effect remains as before; this is a tragic example of temporary populism at its worst.

Unlike in progressive Southern States, beneficiaries of populist schemes in the State tend to lose their instinct for hard work which in turn silently and stealthily results in loss of pride and self-respect. This tendency also breeds corruption in an institutionalized and decentralized way. I proceeded against a Tahasildar departmentally and criminally who had misappropriated crores of rupees from the allocations made for distribution relief for crop loss which had been declared under political pressure. He had issued cheques in fake names of farmers which had been encashed in a neighbouring State. There was no complaint from individual farmers as they had not suffered any crop losses in reality. The misappropriation came to light when I ordered audit of Tahasil accounts. The reality one may find frequently in several parts of the State is that those owning farmland,but cultivated through share-croppers, get better returns by reporting crop losses due to natural calamities as they get relief from the Government both under calamity relief grant and crop insurance. Additionally, seeds are supplied by the Government in Agriculture Department at highly subsidized rates; lower than the support price for ordinary grains, and are mostly consumed as non-seeds. It is the share-cropper who suffers in multiple ways as he gets nothing; share-cropping being illegal in the State. A normal monsoon in some coastal districts is considered abnormal if those accustomed to receiving calamity relief grant fail to get their 'annual' entitlement! I have frequently heard social analysts attributing the unprecedented and continuing public support to Chief Minister Naveen Patnaik in the State to such distribution of freebies and populism.

Odisha suffered due to political instability between 1958 to 1980.Important laws relating to land reforms, including consolidation of holdings, did not receive the desired attention of administration and ruling parties. When political stability arrived, coincidentally there was broad-based opening of the Indian economy starting in the early 1990s creating potential to generate rapid economic growth nation-wide. But leadership in various fields in the State willy-nilly squandered these opportunities rather than grabbing them with both hands and outstretched arms. As if for public consumption, the State in the recent past went on signing MoUs for mineral-based industries involving captive mines to be given. Industrialist were invited from far and wide. Senior-most officers were sent to South Korea to invite the steel magnate POSCO. But after achieving one-time publicity, the foreign investor was shown the door as if to please a few who after taking compensation for encroached Government land started an agitation against the proposed industry. Yet selectively, even without signing MoUs, some preferred private companies were allowed lease for coal blocks. It was as if they wanted to gather windfall gains by selling out all the shares of the new company floated for getting coal blocks without the promised investment in the State. For inexplicable considerations, the proposal of a big company for investing ₹ 55,000 crore was not allowed to be cleared. It was, however, publicised as a great achievement after three years in a roadshow held by State Government in another State Capital to present Odisha as a preferred destination for industrialists! Prerequisites for balanced development of a State or society required transparency and sense of commitment besides absolute objectivity in applying statutory rules and procedures. Bad products can be marketed only temporarily even if they are packaged attractively.

What Ails Poverty Alleviation Programmes

It is not as if successive Governments after Independence have not given any attention to address the socio-economic disparities and backwardness. Indeed, poverty alleviation programmes including rural employment-generation schemes in the country have been implemented progressively in a big way, particularly after 1977. After attaining self-sufficiency in production of foodgrains to a great extent with the advent of Green Revolution, a new scheme for rural employment "Food for Work" was introduced in the year 1977 which, *inter alia*, provided for sharing the proceeds of the Green Revolution by making foodgrains available in the form of wages to families who did not have agricultural land to sustain livelihoods. This programme was expanded and renamed National Rural Employment Programme in 1980 under which wages were distributed partly in cash and partly in foodgrains at highly subsidized rates. It was further strengthened by introducing another scheme, RLEGP. A rural housing scheme for the poor SCs/STs families called IAY formed part of NREP and RLEGP. Jawahar Rozgar Yojana, and later on the Employment Assurance Scheme, subsumed the erstwhile employment-generating schemes of NREP and RLEGP in the late 1980s and early 1990s respectively, leading to NREGS which finally took the shape of MGNREGS through a Parliamentary enactment to provide for a minimum of 100 days wage employment on demand in rural areas. Perhaps India became the first major country in the world to have a law that defined entitlement of the poor for a guaranteed wage employment.

Antyodaya a family-oriented income-generating scheme for self-employment which was introduced in the year 1978 on a pilot basis by Rajasthan State Government was transformed into Integrated Rural Development Project in the year 1980 which was sponsored nationally by Central Government. Before its introduction, a Small and Marginal Farmers' Programme was being implemented through Small Farmers' Development Agencies at district level. TheseAgencies were converted into District Rural Development Agencies after the introduction of IRDP. A tool for improving the capacity of rural youth for self-employment was added to IRDP in the year 1983 with the moniker "Training of Youth for Self-Employment". Scheme on Development of Women and Children in Rural Areas was integrated in IRDP as another component to support groups of poor rural women for their income-generating activities and social development. Another targeted scheme was introduced for rehabilitation of released bonded labourers. Families below the poverty line eligible to be assisted under any of these poverty alleviation programmes were intended to be provided with subsidized loan for self-employment including training for skill upgradation of the rural youth to get self-employed. Besides these generalized anti-poverty programmes, Special Central Assistance was also provided by Central Government exclusively for ST&SC families with higher percentage of subsidy. Integrated Tribal Development Agencies in tribal districts functioned in parallel with DRDAs.

Conceptually, both sets of employment-generation as well as income-generating self-employment schemes appeared well designed. Perhaps with provision of just a bit of flexibility in their operating guidelines, these schemes could have been enabled to capture the diverse realities and needs of different regions and areas of the country. Even so, the real test of any programme lies in its implementation. Successful implementation of a beneficiary-oriented income-generating scheme requires involvement of banks as subsidized loan for viable ventures has to be given to the head of eligible household below the poverty line, who is selected by the village assembly. Even after establishing a network of Regional Rural Banks and branches of commercial banks in many rural areas, remote villages could not be brought effectively under the service areas of these financial institutions. The conflict between viability of income-generating schemes and choices of beneficiaries who were not fully aware of their repayment liabilities made implementation increasingly difficult. Inadquacy of required skills and backward and forwardlinkages, essential components of any beneficiary-oriented schemes, make delivery of intended benefits difficult. Unrealistic high annual targets leave little room for careful selection of beneficiaries, systematic appraisal of schemes involving line departments, sponsoring of applications to banks and disbursement within the specified time-frame in the absence of an enabling environment. Thus, it did not take much time for banks to register resistance or to become part of corrupt practices that started taking place in implementing the beneficiary-oriented income-generating schemes. Poor recovery of loans after expiry of gestation period limited the lending capacity of financial institutions. Self-employment schemes thus virtually degenerated into loan melas to be organised at the behest of important elected representatives. While addressing the beneficiaries, political leaders would openly tell them that they should not be worried about repayment as after sometime Government would waive the loan amount. This paved the way for cycle-after-cycle of misappropriation and embedded corrupt practices in the psyche of the politician, bureaucrat and beneficiary. The distortions that followed included misuse of loan by beneficiaries for consumption purposes, non-disbursement of subsequent instalments, disbursement of subsidy without loan, fake disbursements, decentralization of corruption involving banks and government officials and finally, increase in rural indebtedness as well as non-performing assets of the banking system.

The weak monitoring mechanism collapsed due to pressure to hurry up the reports on higher achievements. The party in power invariably tries to leverage beneficiary-oriented poverty alleviation schemes as its gift to the poor. Since there were a number of schemes under implementation through multitudes of agencies, multiplicities not only resulted in duplication and double-counting of beneficiaries and bred corrupt practices, but also shielded the corrupt through diffused accountability. The maximum coverage under income-generating schemes was in business and service sector schemes without the underlying bulwark of viability as disbursement of working capital and assets was easier in these sectors. Primary sector schemes where the chances of success were more received the least coverage. For example, dairy scheme did not receive adequate coverage in the absence of quality milch animals and backward-forward linkages. If a milch cow was somehow supplied as a first instalment, the beneficiary did not receive the second one on the grounds of poor maintenance of the first one, lack of animal healthcare infrastructure, etc. The second and third instalments for dug wells and water-lifting devices did not receive attention because the first instalment either had been misappropriated or the village was not electrified. On paper, in a large number of cases, units of loan were shown disbursed fully and subsidy adjusted to show better recovery performance for some time.

It is not as if beneficiary-oriented income-generating schemes did not have any horizontal impact. Some beneficiaries in villages around growth centres did improve their economic situation but their numbers are miniscule. Largely, limited assistance received by poor families has been used for consumption purposes and to survive at subsistence level. Every successive party in power uses poverty alleviation programmes to strengthen its hold over the poor and weaker sections of society before the degeneration in implementation gets fully exposed. Packaging of schemes as a contribution of leadership also by a supplicant bureaucracy contribute to deteriorating implementation, as it not only generates a perception within opposition parties that their followers are being discriminated, but also gives them the handle to generate a groundswell of adverse publicity against the schemes by highlighting corruption and painting loan recovery efforts as coercive actions against the poor. The valuable schemes thus lose their raison d'etre in the hullaballoo of trivia.

Rural employment-generating schemes performed relatively better and became more visible due to creation of community assets of durable nature, which were easily verifiable. However, here too the distortions started affecting them after some time. Allocations received needed to be distributed for projects to be implemented in villages under various Gram Panchayats proportionately. But the tendency to spend funds expeditiously in the name of labour-intensive works with lesser focus on creation of community assets has led to misuse and misappropriations. Block agencies do not have adequate engineering manpower for supervision and check-measurements of projects under implementation. Thus the quality of record-keeping has suffered tremendously. Misappropriation of foodgrains meant for workers towards wages in part finally led to full payment of wages in cash, which indeed made misappropriation easier and with lesser visibility. Although beneficiaries of houses under IAY were to be selected by village assemblies, in effect elected representatives of the ruling party have held sway in their selection as well as disbursement of assistance. The process rather than being guided by guidelines has got influenced by political considerations and corrupt practices in a decentralized manner. With morality of public functionaries available to any buyer at a huge discount, gaps between actual and intended benefits have increased exponentially as the allocations got upscaled over the passage of time. Very few beneficiaries have been lucky to receive full instalments against approved unit cost of houses. The gaps between houses taken up for construction and actually constructed also increased progressively in the absence of accountability and effective monitoring. In Odisha, State Government did not have resources to provide extra funds for development of rural areas or in relation to poverty alleviation schemes. Funds received under Central Sector

Schemes and Centrally Sponsored Programmes were distributed equally, albeit thinly, among scattered villages every year in proportion to the population which made creation of assets of durable nature even more difficult.

Like the family-oriented income-generating schemes, wage employment programmes including IAY were also packaged and presented by the parties in power as munificence from their leadership. This approach was bound to be opposed by political adversaries. Further, discrimination in allocation of funds in areas represented by opposition party leaders was bound to be protested. Distortions in implementing rural employment projects also became visible steadily. Schemes which were seen and used as tools to strengthen hold over rural population by the ruling dispensations became means for opposition parties and elements in media to expose the corruption in their implementation.

The ruling Congress lost its support base in Odisha after about 10 years of introducing the schemes which were used and perceived as inducements. Although results varied from area to area and everything could not and should not be seen negatively, dissonance between schematic objectives and outcomes, and mismatch between investments and returns were not difficult to lose sight of. My personal assessment is that despite being designed well theoretically, policy makers failed to take into account the available logistics and capacity of implementing agencies to handle the increasing number of populist schemes. Implementing agencies simply did not have requisite managerial skills and manpower.Yet they were saturated to the gills by multiple schemes and programmes of similar character and intent. Proliferation of schemes and implementing agencies made it difficult to fix accountability even in the event of wilful negligence or outright indulgence in corrupt practices. Political interference at the cutting edge of administration, packaging and publicity have impacted outcomes of implementation adversely. Results greatly depend on ability and sense of priorities of individual officials responsible for implementing self-employment and wage-employment programmes.

My Final Take

I feel that any National or State schemes projected for garnering public support in a political sense and association of political connotations, including naming of schemes after political leaders, *ab initio* erodes a huge chunk of its acceptability and credibility. It is, thus, desirable that schemes to be introduced are evolved maintaining political neutrality and by involving maximum consensus. National Development Council or similar bodies at National and State levels could perhaps discuss and approve National and State flagship schemes/ programmes in lesser numbers for better results by also embedding a sense of accountability. At the same time, capacity building including skilled manpower required for implementing plans and programmes must receive due attention along with track-and-trace type of detailed monitoring before following target-oriented and expenditure-driven approach in order to evaluate their results in terms of physical and financial achievements. Quality and quantity must go hand-in-hand.

Development interventions by the State may also not bring the intended results only through superimposed processes and enactments. The State becoming the sole proprietor of development is in fact neither viable nor desirable in a dynamic social set up, particularly when its agencies have limitations in matters of human welfare and development even with the best of intentions. There cannot be a "one stop shop" in a diverse country like India and a State like Odisha to bring about balanced development. Populist schemes for temporary political gains need to be evaluated seriously keeping in view durability of impacts. They need to be phased in or phased out accordingly. Programmes that have led to surrender of a sense of pride and self-respect of the populace through reliance on doles and handouts which have also resulted in complacency and psychological dependency are unlikely to travel long enough in facilitating much-needed socio-economic transformation.

Personally, I remain a die-hard optimist notwithstanding the aberrations of political leaders and other public functionaries or any widely prevailing cynicism about the deeply entrenched nexus between these two. Opportunities can be delayed but cannot be denied. What is more important is to somehow grab and utilise these opportunities when they arrive because these are widespread and available to one and all without systemic discrimination. A well-meaning public functionary will willy-nilly continue to play an important facilitating role like other instruments of society in a welfare State to find life meaningful. Failure on the part of those at the helm of affairs to quite easily ensure enduring and self-sustaining development in a State endowed richly with resources, however, reminds me of the famous saying of sage Veda Vyas in his book, the Shrimad Bhagwat Purana. Although stated in a spiritual context, it equally applies to the non-spiritual aspect of human development:

नृदेहमात्रं सुलभं सुदुर्लभं प्लवं सुकल्पं गुरुकर्णधारम्।
मयानुकूलेन नभस्वतेरिता पुमान्भवाब्धिं न तरेत्स आत्महा॥ (11/20/17).

(Even after being born a human which is the rarest of the rare, and in spite of a strongly built ship being steered by a competent crew in the right direction with strong tail-winds, one who fails to cross the worldly ocean indeed commits suicide.)

* * * *